20.00
Black Studies

BRITISH AND AMERICAN ABOLITIONISTS. AN EPISODE IN TRANSATLANTIC UNDERSTANDING

CLARE TAYLOR

Edinburgh University Press

Edinburgh University Press
22 George Square, Edinburgh

ISBN 0 85224 161 5

North America
Aldine Publishing Company
529 South Wabash Avenue
Chicago 60605

Library of Congress Catalog
Card Number 77-92287

Printed in Great Britain by
R & R Clark Ltd, Edinburgh

ACKNOWLEDGMENTS

I should like to thank the Boston Public Library for permission to publish extracts from the collection of anti-slavery manuscripts in their possession. Particular thanks are due to the staff of the Rare Books and Manuscripts Department of the Boston Public Library for their kindness and the help they gave me. I am most grateful to the Carnegie Trust for the Universities of Scotland for a Senior Studentship, and to the University of Edinburgh for a grant in aid of research and for the William Dickson Travel Prize. I am particularly indebted to my Supervisor, Professor George Shepperson of the University of Edinburgh, for his help and for his wide knowledge of the period. I should also like to thank Professor and Mrs David B. Davis for their kind hospitality, which made it possible for me to see the Samuel J. May Collection at Cornell; and to thank Miss Rhiannon Hughes, Mrs Gillian Glover and Mrs Carol O'Toole for their promptness and efficiency in typing the manuscripts.

Clare Taylor
Aberystwyth

CONTENTS

INTRODUCTION

The campaign against slavery, which was fought so actively in the nineteenth century, was among the most significant and characteristic movements of the age. It was one of the first social movements to operate on a truly international scale, for abolitionists were concerned not merely with slavery in the United States or the West Indies, but with conditions in Africa, the Near East, India, New Zealand and South America. "My country is the world and my countrymen are all mankind" was a favourite anti-slavery slogan, and abolitionists put this doctrine into practice by going to see for themselves the conditions they so deplored, encompassing the world by their missions to a degree which had never before been possible. But a new internationalism was not the only characteristic of the anti-slavery agitation, for the ethos behind the movement was one which was especially representative of nineteenth century thought as is seen by even a brief glance at some aspects of the abolitionists' principles. Not only was the brotherhood of man a cardinal tenet of the campaign, but the ideals of liberty and equality, which dominated contemporary political and philosphical beliefs, also found an obvious outlet in the abolitionists' cause. The anti-slavery advocate did not neglect contemporary religious beliefs, he fortified his views with the arguments offered by Evangelical Christianity, that slavery was a sin.

But international in scope though it was, the anti-slavery movement was largely in the hands of British and American abolitionists, who worked together so closely that it is impossible to discuss the organizations of one country without some reference to the societies of the other. This co-operation is significant, for it is indicative of the close intellectual and social ties which existed between the two countries at this period. The point has just been made that the anti-slavery movement was especially characteristic of the age, and we have seen that it embodied most of the ideas then dominant in European and American thought. What this meant in practice was that abolitionists in both countries could share a common intellectual heritage and form bonds of friendship which might transcend national rivalries and distinctions. This point may seem trivial, but it is significant, for the nineteenth century has more usually been noted for prejudice and hostility between the two countries.

In the nineteenth century abolitionists and politicians alike had to contend with the problem of slavery as a burning issue in international as well as national politics, and between 1800 and 1870 it entered into almost every aspect of Anglo-American relations, making them more complicated and difficult. It is well known that anti-slavery Britain enjoyed important and less competitive trading links with the cotton producing slave states of America than she had with the manufacturing North, who supported a tariff system, a policy quite counter to British free trade principles and economic interests. More important, however, the rivalry between the two countries, always a very real factor, reached points of extreme tension when the expansionist activities of the two countries conflicted. And since in the United States expansion involved the political debate whether territory should be slave-holding or not, the situation became exceedingly complex. It is only too clear that whenever British and American interests clashed in the years before 1870 – in Canada, Texas, Mexico, Central America and the Caribbean, the issue was always exacerbated by the slavery question. The United States could not annex Texas to the Union until the problem of whether it should be slave-holding or not was settled, even though British activity there was regarded as a direct threat to American prestige and security. Boundary disputes over Canada became entangled with the legal question of the return of fugitives from one country to the other – the Webster-Ashburton Treaty of 1842 nearly broke down over this. Indeed, slavery often seemed more apt to strain or break good feelings between the two countries than to ally them. There were, however, two counter-balancing factors: it was to the advantage of neither country to go to war with the other, a point realised by most clear-thinking people in Britain and America; and secondly the intervention of the abolitionists in these diplomatic affrays though it might at times enflame public opinion, especially in the United States, yet reminded influential sections that large pressure groups were working for peace between the two countries. Americans might accuse their abolitionists of being bought by "British gold" whenever they supported a British action; the British might taunt the Americans with their "peculiar institution" whenever they wished to forget political and social inequalities at home, but the reformers of both countries continued to strive for the overthrow of slavery, employing every means possible, jointly and separately, to accomplish this end. Thus the work of the abolitionists, especially in the years between 1830 and 1870, was far more than a pious social venture or even an experiment in international co-operation. It became a touchstone of Anglo-American friendship and an example of the close links between the two countries.

The anti-slavery campaign was an important factor in Anglo-American relations, but the British and American societies were by no means united and cohesive, but a schismatic, continually and bitterly divided collection of factions, agreed upon only one thing – that slavery was a sin and should be abolished. An understanding of these divisions is vital to a study of the anti-slavery connection if only for the fact that disputes followed their originators across the Atlantic. In America the anti-slavery crusade, except for a period during the 1830s when abolitionists managed to maintain a more or less unified front, was divided into various groups, an important section being represented by the American Anti-Slavery Society, led by William Lloyd Garrison and his Boston adherents, and supported to some extent by the Philadelphia circle; another wing by the American and Foreign Anti-Slavery Society, the rump of the original A.A.S.S., which drew its strength from the organizations built up in the 1830s by the Tappans, wealthy merchants of New York, and their helpers, James Gillespie Birney, Henry Stanton, and above all, Theodore Weld. This body had its centre in New York and drew support from the Middle West. Other groups, more sympathetic generally to the A.F.A.S.S., found an outlet in direct political agitation for emancipation – in lobbying Washington, or through political parties, first the Liberty Party, and later the Free Soil Party. The sectional alignments of the two major anti-slavery groups should not be stressed unduly, however, as the Garrison party had links with New York and the Mid West, and the Boston and Philadelphia connection was not always a cordial one. The Tappanite faction, on the other hand, never lost the support of a sizeable body of abolitionists in New England. The key, in fact, to the American divisions is not so much in the sectional differences, but in the personalities and beliefs of the leaders of the parties, especially those of William Lloyd Garrison.

In Britain a very similar division among anti-slavery sympathisers is to be found. The abolition societies were by no means disbanded after 1833 when emancipation had been won for slaves in British territories. Indeed, in the years leading up to the Civil War, the movement commanded probably a wider public support than it had originally, but it was, nonetheless, a divided force. The most powerful wing was certainly the British and Foreign Anti-Slavery Society founded by the Quaker, Joseph Sturge, with its headquarters in London, and supported by the older and influential generation of abolitionists, especially Thomas Clarkson, the Gurneys and other wealthy Quakers of the South of England. This party maintained the closest links with its namesake the American and Foreign Anti-Slavery Society. Less well known, however, are those provincial groups who gave their sympathies to Garrison and his party. Drawn mainly from the Edinburgh and Glasgow Societies, which were dominated by the two Quaker families of Wigham and Smeal; from the Irish societies, especially the Dublin party led by R. D. Webb; and from the West of England circles, supported by the Unitarian families of that area, these British Garrisonians formed a very important part of the British movement. One small section remains to be discussed: allied to the anti-slavery crusade but taking little active part in its organization were the Stafford House set of "fashionable philanthropists": the Duchess of Sutherland and her family, Lord Shaftesbury, Lady Byron and other well-to-do figures. Though small in number their influence was considerable – not least as an irritant to the general American public.

The Anglo-American anti-slavery connection has already received a fair degree of attention from historians, but they have almost entirely concentrated on the links between the British and the American and Foreign Anti-Slavery Societies. Yet the relations between the leaders of the "official" societies are by no means the whole history of this joint humanitarian action. The work of Garrison and his supporters contributed as much to the connection as did that of the Tappan-Sturge party; and had perhaps even more impact on British life and on the wider sphere of Anglo-American relations. We are here concerned with this faction, and it was with these purposes in view – at once to illustrate the links between British and American supporters of William Lloyd Garrison, and to attempt to show some of the importance of this connection that these selections from the Boston Anti-Slavery Papers have been made.

Various features characterise this connection from the outset. Perhaps one of the most important is that it shows so clearly what a monumental propaganda venture the whole anti-slavery movement was. A fact often ignored is that so many of the abolitionists in Britain and America were journalists – either editors of newspapers, writers of pamphlets or books; or, as printers and publishers, connected to the world of journalism. Many others less handy with the pen became speakers – winning great fame as itinerant lecturers for their societies. The abolitionists thus enjoyed the fullest possible means of disseminating their views on slavery. The Boston Papers plainly reveal the importance and predominance of journalism and public speaking within the movement, and in the later years especially, when friendships had been formed, the letters deal increasingly with the work of a small clique whose absorbing interest was in writing for and distributing their newspapers

– Garrison's *Liberator* and its New York counterpart, the *Anti-Slavery Standard*, as well as the British *Advocate*. Countless letters deal with the demands for articles or the more routine requirements of distribution and payment of subscriptions, for the abolitionists found that their most effective weapon was to vilify the institution of slavery, and to make Southern slaveholders in particular stand beyond the pale of social and religious fellowship. As a propaganda campaign theirs was unremitting, and served to keep feeling on the subject at an intense pitch. It little matters that the abolitionists had no concrete plan of campaign for emancipating the slave in the South, and that when the Civil War broke out slavery was not, technically, the issue over which it was fought. The public had been conditioned to think in terms of irreconcilable interests, and slavery had become an institution which could only be maintained at an impossible price.

But an interest in slavery was not the only factor binding the Garrison party together. A special feature of the Boston collection is the light it sheds on Irish-American relations at this period, for Irish abolitionists formed the backbone of Garrison's British supporters, and many letters discuss political events in Ireland and the attempt of reformers on both sides of the Atlantic to convert the Irish to anti-slavery principles, an almost completely hopeless venture. This attempt is all the more significant as it came at a time when the problem and position of the Irish immigrant, especially in Boston and Philadelphia, was one of the more important issues in American life, whilst the Irish question was certainly one of the gravest facing the British Government. Competing with Negro labour, it is scarcely surprising that the Irish immigrant in the United States had little sympathy or support for the anti-slavery movement, led as it was on both sides of the Atlantic by middle or upper class leaders, a group notoriously unsympathetic to the claims of the Irish worker. The connection of some of the Irish leaders, particularly O'Connell, with the abolition movement is interesting, though it is doubtful whether they were not merely seeking publicity for the cause of "slavery" in Ireland. However, from the letters it is clear that efforts in Dublin and Boston to win the Irish over to anti-slavery principles were unceasing, if productive of little.

The Garrisonian connection, too, is characterised by the leading role which women played in it. The link of the anti-slavery campaign to the movement for women's rights both in Britain and America, is well known, and it was very largely through the channels of the Garrison organization that the first personal contacts took place. But though many of the women engaged in anti-slavery activity sympathised with the demand for female emancipation, this was not universally so, and indeed the letters between the British and American women in the Boston collection show that their first loyalty was to the anti-slavery cause – and indefatigably they laboured on its behalf. Their main contribution was in helping to raise funds for the movement by collecting money personally and by holding Bazaars. It is around these Bazaars, especially the large Boston Bazaar, that the attention of the women abolitionists centred. British donations were prized, and the Boston correspondence is filled with letters dealing with the boxes sent annually to America. Important as a means of raising money, the Boston Bazaar served also as a focal point of co-operation, helping to bind together and keep alive for over twenty years the work of Anglo-American humanitarians.

Since Unitarians and Quakers in both countries had traditionally maintained very close links and interests, it is not surprising to find that many of the abolitionists belonged to these two groups. The Boston clique was dominated by the Unitarians, especially the wealthy members of Dr. Channing's church; while the Philadelphia group was mainly Quaker. In

Britain the Unitarians of London, Manchester and the West of England supported Garrison. Quaker sympathy was divided, however, the wealthy Quakers gave their allegiance to Joseph Sturge and the B.F.A.S.S., while less conservative groups in the North of England, and the Scottish and Irish Friends became Garrison's warmest supporters. Many Garrisonites, it is true, tended to break away from their faith or to adopt some of the more radical tenets of their sect, but though this led them all the more fiercely to denounce the "timid" Quakers or Unitarians who did not share their religious and humanitarian views, the countercharges of "heresy" and "non-respectability" were hard ones to bear, and ensured that free thought or unconventional religious beliefs did not spread unchecked among anti-slavery followers.

The political views of these British and American abolitionists are a no less interesting subject of study. As far as active politics are concerned, the Boston group tended to be Whig or deliberately to take no part in political action. Denouncing the Constitution and the government for their attitude to slavery, Garrison and his followers adopted a course of action which was not so much passive resistance as active withdrawal from every form of participation in political life. The politics of the British circle are less easy to define. As Nonconformists they generally supported the Whig- Liberal party, and as humanitarian reformers they were interested in and sympathetic to many other reform causes – including the more openly revolutionary ones, such as the Chartist or Irish repeal movements, or the Friends of Italy Society. But they were above all drawn mainly from a middle-class background, and their sympathy with any revolutionary form of activity was always tempered with caution. Nevertheless, once their conservative scruples were overcome, both in Britain and America abolitionists were keenly interested in and warmly sympathetic to the cause of freedom. They dabbled in the cause of freedom for English Nonconformists, Italian and Irish peasants, British workers and American slaves, but with the politics of freedom they usually had very little direct connection.

Of the individuals who played an important part in this coterie of abolitionists, undoubtedly the most striking was William Lloyd Garrison. The son of poor parents, he trained as a printer, and was introduced to the anti-slavery cause when he began work with Benjamin Lundy in the publication of Lundy's *Genius of Universal Emancipation*, one of the earliest abolition newspapers. He had settled permanently in Boston by 1830, and in the next year began publication of the *Liberator*, which even if its circulation was by no means large was yet the best known anti- slavery paper, notorious for its uncompromising attitude to slavery and to slaveowners. By 1833 he had founded the New England Anti-Slavery Society, and for the next seven years was active in anti-slavery organization, visiting Britain in 1833 to gain publicity and support for the American cause, and to counteract the influence of Elliott Cresson, the Secretary of the Colonization Society, who was advocating the repatriation of slaves to Africa. On his return to America Garrison helped to found the American Anti-Slavery Society, but he began to face increasing opposition not only in New England but also in New York, which was the headquarters of the new national Society. His high handed methods, his support for the active participation of women in anti-slavery work, and his unorthodox religious views, served to alienate him from many of his supporters, and a growing distaste for the civil disturbances which abolitionists' sentiments were provoking, caused a further reaction away from his extremist views. His New England Anti-Slavery Society divided, one wing becoming the Massachusetts Anti-Slavery Society, strongly conservative in religious and social views. By 1840 the American Anti-Slavery Society, too, was completely divided, a disruption in which Garrison played a leading role. He had never had the complete support of the Tappan brothers, and the breach widened considerably over Garrison's support for women as anti-slavery lecturers. Ironically, among the first to abandon Garrison on this matter were the Grimké sisters, whose work as anti-slavery lecturers Garrison had so warmly championed. With the marriage of Angelina Grimké to Theodore Weld, the Tappan's chief organiser, "Carolina's high-souled daughters" gave up their public appearances for more modest work among the Tappan circle. But Garrison continued to endorse "the woman question" at every opportunity, and at the Annual General Meeting of the American Anti-Slavery Society in May, 1840, by adroit and not over-scrupulous manoeuvering he was able to gain control of the Committee which then came out openly in support of women abolitionists.

The conflict at once spread to Britain, especially since many American abolitionists, including Garrison, came to London for the Great World Anti-Slavery Convention in June, 1840. Many British abolitionists were equally unhappy about the active participation of women in anti-slavery work, and the defeated rump of the American Anti-Slavery Society made common cause with conservative British abolitionists forming the American and Foreign Anti-Slavery Society which was to work in close harmony with its British counterpart. Garrison was not without his supporters in Britain, but in America his influence thereafter was mainly confined to Boston, to New York through the columns of the *Anti-Slavery Standard* when he could find an editor subservient to his views, and to a few friends in Philadelphia. His active work was by no means over, however. His influence in Britain was still considerable, and his visit to that country in 1846 was the signal for another wave of anti-slavery agitation. He continued to write and speak against American slavery throughout the 1850s denouncing the actions of the federal government which seemed to support at every turn the most extreme claims of the slaveholders. He warmly supported Lincoln and the North during the Civil War, but at its conclusion ended his connection with formal anti-slavery work. His later years were devoted to various journalistic tasks, though he maintained a keen interest in most of the reform movements, not least in the cause of civil rights for the negro.

Much has been written of Garrison, and his contribution to the abolition campaign is still being assessed. His first biographers regarded him as the champion and liberator of the slave, but his reputation has latterly been attacked, and his importance to the anti-slavery movement questioned; only recently has there been a swing again in his favour. The most common charge brought against Garrison, however, is still the old one made by his pro-slavery enemies, that he was a fanatic bordering on madness, but that this description of him is dangerously exaggerated is clear from even a brief study of his life and work. It cannot be denied that Garrison's opinions were unconventional, that he held them tenaciously and dogmatically, though sincerely, and that he was prepared to fight for all his heresies, even at the cost of wrecking anti-slavery groups, as time and again was the case. His influence, indeed, upon the actual organization of the abolition movement both in Britain and America was largely a destructive one. But he was at the same time an excellent journalist; his style may at times be exaggerated (as was that of his pro-slavery opponents), yet it is always clear, forceful, and colourful – and he knew perfectly the value of publicity. A hypochondriac, an opportunist often in need of money, which he was none too scrupulous about obtaining, he nonetheless inspired his friends with a loyalty and friendship which was only matched by the hatred he fostered among his enemies. His views, the cause of so much internal dissension among abolitionists, deserve closer attention.

Often framed to fit the circumstances, not always logically consistent, nor possibly even his own, they were frequently unacceptable, incomprehensible and even repugnant to many people in Britain and America, – they reflected the views of a section of the intellectual world of nineteenth century Boston. That slavery was a sin and should be abolished at once, was one of his earliest conclusions, developed largely by British precepts, which reached him through Benjamin Lundy. He early showed a complete intolerance of any other attitude to slavery, whether it was the views of the Colonization Society, the temporising actions of the Federal Government, or the outright defence of the slave system by the South, and this absolute and vigorous intolerance of any form of opposition to his views remained one of his chief characteristics. His support for the Grimké sisters when they came to lecture in New England first led him to champion the rights of women to take part in anti-slavery affairs, and when this aroused scandalised opposition from the New England clergy, he was led on to attack certain of the church's teachings – notably the sanctity of the Sabbath. There is nothing extreme in Garrison's religious views: they were basically those of Evangelical Protestantism, and though he ostentatiously denied that any church had a superior merit, in doctrine he rejected only the most extreme claims of fundamentalism, particularly the view that the Sabbath was divinely ordained and that every word of the Scriptures was sacred. But he attacked his clerical foes in the most immoderate terms, and their countercharges made his religious views appear wildly heretical, tainting him for all time as "unrespectable". It was this charge of heresy which was largely responsible for so much contemporary criticism, suspicion and distrust of Garrison.

Belief in the perfectibility of man and in the imperfectibility of his institutions is in fact the basis of Garrison's thought. The church was an imperfect instrument of God's will, and was moreover unsympathetic to Garrison's activities, and he therefore condemned it strongly. His attitude to the Federal government and to the Constitution is very similar. Since the federal government was unable to take any action with regard to slavery, and as the Constitution as it then existed could be used actively to defend slavery, he became an advocate of "no-human government", an argument based on the doctrine that ideally man should not need to be governed, as the champions of Utopian communities were at that point proclaiming. By 1842 Garrison had come out for a repeal of the Union (and it is interesting that he had recently been in contact with Daniel O'Connell and was familiar with the arguments for the repeal of the British Act of Union with Ireland). In the following year he made his famous denunciation of the Constitution as "a covenant with death and an agreement with hell" – and later advised abolitionists to have "no union with slaveholders" – to take no active part in political life to the extent even of refusing to pay any taxes, and passively to resist all actions of the pro-slavery government. Far from shaping or even prophesying the course which the North should take with regard to slavery, Garrison was in part advocating the path which the South was to take in the winter and spring of 1860 to 1861.

But however unoriginal or even temperate his views may seem to us today, they were forcefully stated and firmly held. There was never any tinge of hypocrisy about Garrison; he championed any cause which sought to free human kind from oppressive or tyrannical restraints on liberty. Less bound by middle-class shibboleths than most of his fellow workers, his views led him to defend reforms which ranged from the rights of the African slaves, through free thought in religion, Chartist demands, Irish wrongs, Italian aspirations, to temperance and world peace. That he was an opportunist and did not scruple to make use of people or events is clear. He probably did more than any other reformer to divide the anti-slavery societies, but he yet remains one of the most noted figures in the anti-slavery world. Without the stimulus of his views and his personality the abolition movement both in Britain and America would have been very different. That his views transcend, in however limited a form, the anti-slavery field is no real discredit to him. Indeed, to consider Garrison purely as an anti-slavery agitator is to do him scant justice. His real place is among the leading figures of nineteenth century American journalism.

Three other figures appear on the correspondence as being close allies and disciples of Garrison. John Anderson Collins, who made a stormy tour of Britain from 1840 to 1841 to collect funds for the American Anti-Slavery Society, held all Garrison's views, but lacked much of his ability. Collins' connection with the abolition movement was fairly brief and by the mid 40's he had deserted the cause and moved West. Henry Clarke Wright, on the other hand, was closely attached to Garrison throughout the entire campaign, and it is possible that some of Garrison's views, especially his religious beliefs, were first propounded by Wright. Even more prone to stir up controversy than Garrison, one of his most active spells of work during the years 1843 to 1846 when he visited Britain and inflamed Scottish opinion against the collection of money from the South by the Free Church of Scotland. Parker Pillsbury, the third of these adherents to find a prominent place in the papers, was an even more contentious figure than Collins or Wright. He worked in Britain during the 1850s when he revealed himself as a man not only quick to take offence, but only too ready to see offence meant when none was intended. Like Garrison, all three were from relatively humble New England origins, and earned their livelihood by writing and speaking for the anti-slavery cause.

Allied to Garrison but almost totally unlike him in temperament was the well-to-do and cultured Bostonian, Wendell Phillips. Sacrificing considerable social position Phillips was first drawn to abolition after the murder of Elijah Lovejoy who died defending his anti-slavery press from a mob in 1837; and later he earned a reputation as one of the most eloquent and militant speakers on the anti-slavery platform. His unexceptionable attitude to matters outside the slavery question, his easy and charming social manners and his high intelligence, made him a much more welcome visiting lecturer than Garrison, Wright or Pillsbury in Britain, and placed him finally in a position of rivalry to Garrison for leadership of the New England abolitionists. A very much more likeable figure than Garrison, and a very honourable and sincere man, he gave to the Boston group both leadership and cohesion, and to the cause of the slave a selfless and lifelong devotion.

Though Garrison and Phillips are undoubtedly the leading figures in the Boston anti-slavery world, less well known but dominating the Boston correspondence are three other reformers who were probably more responsible for maintaining the Anglo-American connection than any of the other American abolitionists. The first of these, Samuel May Jr., was a gentle, kindly Unitarian clergyman from Leicester, Massachusetts, who is too often confused with his more active cousin, Samuel J. May. It was Samuel May of Leicester, however, who was responsible for bringing many of the British Unitarians into the anti-slavery field during his visit to Britain in 1843. He maintained a constant correspondence with British friends, especially R. D. Webb and J. B. Estlin; and it was May who handled much of the organization of the Boston Bazaar.

Edmund Quincy also maintained a very interesting correspondence with Webb. Belonging to a prominent New England family, Quincy, too, turned his back on social position and a successful career to work for abolition, and became one of the most active writers for the cause. The mainstay of several abolition newspapers, his gossipy letters to Webb are invaluable for the sidelights they shed on the "Boston clique".

In her own way, though, Maria Weston Chapman was probably the most influential New England abolitionist after Garrison and Phillips. Belonging to another well-to-do New England family, she was brought up by her uncle, Joshua Bates, a financier who had close links with London banking circles. Educated partly in London, his niece had, therefore, already formed connections in British circles, which partly account for her later understanding of British affairs and her close friendship with Harriet Martineau. During the early years of her marriage to Henry Chapman, a wealthy Boston merchant, Maria Weston Chapman took an extremely active part in Boston abolitionist circles. She was prominent in the Boston Female Anti-Slavery Society, and was chiefly responsible for the formation and work of the annual Bazaar, which for most of its existence was organized by her sisters. Something of a snob, Maria Weston Chapman was a very worldly and practical woman, and though she spent several years in Paris seeing to the education of her children, she yet kept herself fully informed of anti-slavery affairs at home, and carried the battle for Garrisonian abolition to England when she made extended visits there. A strong-minded, supremely capable, confident woman, she both wrote for and aided the organizational work of the anti-slavery societies and having determined to support Garrison she gave money and energy unstintingly to the cause. Warmly admired by the women, though somewhat resented by the men for her high-handed methods, she nonetheless helped to maintain public interest in abolitionism, not only in Boston but even more so in Britain, where admiration for Mrs. Chapman and her sisters was largely responsible for the continuing work for the Boston Bazaar. Interestingly, although her conduct was praised by supporters of woman's rights, she herself apparently took little part in this campaign, and clung to every prerogative which respectability and social position afforded her. Her sisters, the Westons, and the two Philadelphia Quakeresses, Lucretia Mott and Sarah Pugh, also corresponded regularly with British women, with whom they maintained the closest friendship.

One final word on the American abolitionists must be given to the Negro reformers who toured Britain or sought refuge there. Frederick Douglass, who became the foremost Negro abolitionist and editor of the *North Star*, is undoubtedly the best known of them, but there were others who were among the most distinguished American Negroes of their day, leading figures in their churches and gifted writers. Unfortunately, they too often had insufficient money or influence to become speakers in their own right, and tended to be used by anti-slavery societies for party ends. Especially after the passing of the Fugitive Slave Law, when many escaped slaves came to Britain, and when the success of *Uncle Tom's Cabin* was at its height, the presence of a Negro abolitionist on the anti-slavery platform was almost a popular necessity.

Of the British abolitionists, certainly the closest counterpart to Garrison was George Thompson. Like Garrison he came of a poor family, and first made his name as a paid lecturer of the Agency Committee, which had been formed by James Cropper in the last years of the fight against West Indian slavery. Meeting Garrison on his visit to Britain in 1833, Thompson at once struck up a friendship with him, but, by accepting his invitation to tour America in 1834-35, caused some of the most violent civil disturbances in that country which the 1830s produced. Continually faced by a shortage of money, Thompson's career as an anti-slavery orator was broken by his excursions into other fields, which resulted in charges of being time-serving from abolition friends. On his return from America he was for a while a lecturer for the British India Society and made a visit to India early in the 1840s. From this interest in British India he found other causes to champion.

He accepted the charge to plead the case of the Rajah of Sattara, who had been deposed by the East India Company, and agreed to act as the Agent of the Emperor of Delhi. But he was also anxious to take part in politics; while in India he had spoken on various social topics (chiefly on education) – none very controversial, and was given the title of "the Father of political education in India" by an admiring disciple. On his return from India he became a lecturer for the Anti-Corn-Law League – the British India Society having merged with the Free Traders and by 1849 had been elected Member of Parliament for the Tower Hamlets. Thompson was incapable of channelling his energies, however. From 1850 to 1851 he paid another visit to the United States where he was received with almost as much hostility by American audiences as in 1835, but his long absence alienated his constituents at home and he lost his seat in the election of 1852. Thereafter Thompson's career became a desperate attempt to recapture past glories. He made another visit to India, but fell so gravely ill that he was sent home and was for a time completely paralysed. His financial affairs at this point became so desperate that abolitionists were forced to take up a collection for him. The Civil War offered him a further opportunity to exercise his talents as an anti-slavery speaker, and although his influence had clearly declined his reputation remained. On a visit to America in the 1860s he was honoured by Lincoln, and, with the rise of popular admiration for Garrison, Thompson's last days were spent in some degree of public respect and reflected glory.

A gifted orator, but too beset by financial problems and possibly too unstable ever to have a permanent influence on the anti-slavery movement, Thompson owed a great deal to his son-in-law, Frederick William Chesson, who by the 1850s had begun to work for the cause. A journalist, Chesson's attempts to form a national society for the British Garrisonians were unceasing, and it was he who was largely responsible for organizing anti-slavery activity in Britain during the Civil War.

But undoubtedly the figure who emerges most prominently from the correspondence is Richard Davis Webb. A Dublin printer and, originally, a Quaker, he was an ardent supporter of Garrison and one of the most active anti-slavery workers. First interested in American slavery after reading Harriet Martineau's *Martyr Age*, he printed many of the books and pamphlets which appeared in Britain on American slavery; wrote for American abolitionist newspapers; edited and published the British *Anti- Slavery Advocate;* and was responsible for most of the details of collecting and shipping the donations to the Boston Bazaar. Diffident, but a clear and interesting writer, he contributed more to keeping together the Anglo-American connection than any other British abolitionist. Moreover he was at the same time a shrewd and detached commentator on contemporary events, and his letters are invaluable for the light they shed on affairs, especially in Ireland.

Almost as important as Webb to the British Garrison party was John Bishop Estlin. A Bristol Unitarian, and famous as an ophthalmic surgeon, he became interested in the anti-slavery campaign, after meeting Samuel May of Leicester, and gave generously both of time and money to furthering the cause. More conservative in outlook than many of the British friends of Garrison, he was for a while regarded by them as a somewhat doubtfull ally. But Estlin's practical outlook led him to realize that some form of central organization in Britain was vital to the Garrison party if it were to become more than a sewing circle or newspaper fraternity. His daughter, Mary Estlin, identified herself wholeheartedly with her father's work, and maintained close friendships with most of the British and American women abolitionists with whom she corresponded until her death. It was largely due to the unfailing generosity and hospitality of Mary Estlin and her father that the Garrison party was able to gain such a hold in the West of England, and indeed the work of the Estlins contributed in no small measure to the eventual success of the party throughout the country.

Important as Mary Estlin was, the most influential woman in British anti-slavery circles was undoubtedly Elizabeth Pease Nichol. Disowned for marrying outside the Society of Friends, she belonged to that group of Quaker women who considered it their duty to labour actively for the improvement of social conditions. Working always within the circle of her home, the sympathies of Elizabeth Pease Nichol were nonetheless broad enough to embrace the more radical tenets of Chartism, the cause of Italian unification, and the rights of women, as well as the most extreme claims of Garrison-led abolitionism. A charming, gentle woman, with a delightful sense of humour, she was drawn into anti-slavery work through the interests of her father, Joseph Pease, who devoted himself to the problem of slavery in British India; but long after her father's death she continued to exercise her unflinching and enthusiastic efforts for the cause.

Taking a less prominent place in the Boston papers, but as important to the movement as Webb or Estlin, were the Scottish groups of abolitionists. Of these the most important were John Murray and William Smeal of Glasgow, and the Wigham family of Edinburgh. The Smeals and Wighams were Quakers who remained faithful to Garrison in spite of considerable opposition from their abolitionist friends to Garrison's religious views. Eliza Wigham, the most active correspondent and author of a book on the American anti-slavery movement, is revealed as another of the gentle but steadfast Friends who drew into anti-slavery activity many of her relations in the North of England and in Ireland. Her work for the cause was unceasing, and extended far beyond the bounds of support for the Boston Bazaar.

One other group forms an extremely interesting part of the British correspondence: a coterie of radical thinking social reformers, sympathetic to American ideas and attracted to the beliefs of the Garrison party. People such as William and Mary Howitt, the Quaker writers and social reformers; William Ashurst, the radical lawyer; Joseph Barker, the free-thought preacher; the Chartist leaders, Henry Vincent and William Lovett; the Irish leader, Daniel O'Connell – all had an interest in anti-slavery agitation mainly for ideological reasons, though they were not above using it as a sounding board for their other ideas. The conservative leadership of the B.F.A.S.S., being so little sympathetic to them, they were drawn increasingly to a connection with the Garrison group who were prepared to tolerate fairly radical social and political reforms.

The letters in the collection for the 1830s are relatively few in number, but from them a clear picture of the anti-slavery connection nonetheless emerges. In spite of the fact that British Emancipation was achieved in 1833, the British movement became in many ways more active and more closely linked with the newly emerging American societies in the years following the 1833 victory. Moreover there is a certain similarity in the history of the two movements at this time: the mushroom growth of abolition parties in America is matched in Britain by the rise of provincial as well as national societies with the aim of ending conditions of near slavery in other British territories. The importance of the British movement to the American reformers is very great. The Americans were not only stimulated by the British achievement but by other and more tangible factors. British methods of organization, especially sending out itinerant lecturers; the British creed of "immediate emancipation" modified for American purposes to "immediate emancipation gradually accomplished"; the British example of petitioning the central government were all adopted in American circles. For many years the anniversary of British West Indian Emancipation was celebrated by

Massachusetts abolitionists at picnics and more formal gatherings. At the same time the British were constantly aware of events in the United States, and slowly the issue of American slavery began to absorb the energies of their societies. Abolitionists from both countries maintained the liveliest interest in each other's work, and by exchange of letters, newspapers, pamphlets and lecturers maintained a high standard of co-operation.

Garrison's visit to Britain in 1834 was an important one, for he not only reinforced his links with British friends, but actively enlisted the support of British abolitionists in his campaign against the American Colonization Society, whose aim of repatriating slaves seemed to him to be shirking the real issue: immediate emancipation. His visit was returned by George Thompson who made a memorable tour of the United States from the summer of 1834 to the autumn of 1835. The American abolitionists had been facing strong opposition to their work not only in the South but in the North, where their meetings had been mobbed, and damage done to their property. Thompson's visit was the signal for fresh violence, ending in the famous "Boston mob", by no means the worst of these outbreaks, but so publicised by the Bostonians, conscious of their heritage as the "cradle of freedom", that the Boston mob has assumed an undue prominence in anti-slavery history. Thompson was not the last of these British visitors, however, in spite of the hostile reception he received and the very real anti-British prejudice his work occasioned. Letters mention especially the tour of John Scoble, another old member of the British Agency Committee, and that of Harriet Martineau. But after 1835 the letters are more and more concerned with the internal difficulties which the Bostonians were having to face. The first indication of these problems came from opposition to the increasingly active part women were playing in the movement. When Prudence Crandall attempted to take coloured pupils at her school in Canterbury, Connecticut, she had met with such opposition that her plans had to be abandoned, though her actions had received the support and sympathy of British as well as American abolitionists. But it was not until Sarah and Angelina Grimké, sisters from a prominent slaveholding South Carolina family, who had broken with their home and later joined the anti-slavery campaign, had begun to make their contribution by public speaking that opposition, which had already been growing towards Garrison, found a head. The attack on him by the clergy in the Clerical Appeal widened into a quarrel in which the issue of women taking part in public life, Garrison's religious views and the compromising attitude of the American churches to Southern slavery were all involved. British abolitionists took a very real interest in these debates and divisions, but they were at the same time preoccupied with their own activities – and for Garrison's friends this centred especially round the cause of slavery in British India. Led by Joseph Pease and supported by George Thompson, the British India Society had been drawn into the Manchester-led free trade movement, and after the death of Joseph Pease, ceased to function as a separate party. American abolitionists expressed the closest interest in this society, but in doing so they were faced by a very real and partly acknowledged dilemma. Patriotic as well as humanitarian instincts might lead them to support the British India movement for, while slavery existed in India, Britain could not adopt a "holier than thou" attitude to the United States, but only the most extreme abolitionist could welcome what was in effect an attack on his country's trade on the grounds that it was also an economic blow to American slavery. This is brought out most clearly in the letters between Edward Davis and Elizabeth Pease.

The letters of the 1830s are dominated by the work of Garrison and

Thompson; by the societies they founded; the controversies they aroused and the workers they called into action, especially the women, who early entered into correspondence with one another. There is very little mention of contemporary events in letters apart from one or two gloomy forebodings on affairs in Texas and Mexico. In both countries abolitionists found full scope for positive action in the fight against slavery; internal divisions existed but had not yet reached a final breaking point.The Anglo-American anti-slavery connection in these years was both harmonious and mutually sympathetic.

With the first months of 1840, however, the situation altered rapidly. In America resentment of Garrison's leadership, dislike of his views, and the increasing impossibility of maintaining a national society all found a head in the May meeting of the American Anti-Slavery Society. There Garrison's foes, from New England and New York, having failed to check him in his determination to place women in executive positions on the society broke away from the old organization to form a new society of their own. Feelings were given no chance to subside with the holding of a world's Anti-Slavery Conference in London in the following month, to which most of the leading American abolitionists had been invited. The disease of dissension was thus carried to London at a time when passions were still at their height. In London Garrison and his friends suffered a defeat by the refusal to allow women to sit as delegates to the convention. Other issues were involved, however: the convention was largely sponsored and run by Joseph Sturge and many of the older and more conservative Quakers; on the other hand the leading American woman delegate, Lucretia Mott, was a Quaker who supported the Hicksite group, then out of fellowship with the main body of British and American Friends. These factors, combined with the rumours of Garrison's "infidelity" and the issue of the "woman question" were too much for the majority of the abolitionists present who drew the line at associating with heretics and the supporters of women's rights. In the months after the convention teams of American abolitionists toured Britain explaining their side of the question, rather than pleading the cause of the slave. London and the B.F.A.S.S. were lost to Garrison; Edinburgh and Glasgow remained faithful, though not without some disagreements; whilst Dublin, under Webb, who had met Garrison at the Convention, committed itself wholeheartedly to his cause.

After the Convention, therefore, the anti-slavery movement was completely divided. Sturge and Scoble of the B.F.A.S.S., with the Tappans, Leavitt, Birney and Stanton became villains, little better than slaveholders, to the Garrison supporters. After these divisions, too, the outlook of the Boston abolitionists changed, and a feeling grew that little positive good could be achieved at home, with a corresponding emphasis on securing sympathy both for the slave and their own society in Britain. John A. Collins' tour was especially designed to this end, as was that of Henry Clarke Wright, who, aided first by Frederick Douglass and later by Garrison himself, roused intense public feeling in Scotland against the Free Church of Scotland for accepting money from churches in the Southern states of America. They carried this campaign to London, where the Americans inveighed against the Evangelical Alliance, an international convention of Protestant clergy then being held. This attack was merely an extension of the old fight against the American churches for their hostility to Garrison and his fellow abolitionists; that their efforts had interesting repercussions in Scotland where the cry of "send back the money" was also taken up by the enemies of the newly formed Free Church of Scotland, is clear; but that they did little more than confine support of Garrison to a minority group is also apparent. The failure of Garrison's attempt to form and keep in operation an Anti-Slavery League which would win influential support for his party was a problem which faced the group over the next decade.

The efforts of the Garrison party in Britain to form a central organization continued throughout the 1850s. They were aided in this by further visits of American abolitionists, especially by Parker Pillsbury and Sarah Pugh, and by an ever increasing number of Negro lecturers. But the internal quarrels of the abolitionists reveal only how impotent they were rapidly becoming. Groups in Edinburgh and Glasgow, never entirely happy with Garrison's religious views, broke away to form new associations; while Harriet Beecher Stowe, whose book, *Uncle Tom's Cabin*, enjoyed an unprecedented popular success, captured the public imagination and support. Attempts at a rapprochement with the B.F.A.S.S. failed, and it was only the founding of a newspaper, the *British Advocate*, by Estlin, and in 1859 a new attempt by Chesson to re-establish the old Anti-Slavery League, which marked any new and positive advance toward strengthening the connection.

But it is not the bickerings of anti-slavery groups which are really important in the 1850s. In the earlier years abolitionists in both countries had been concerned with Irish politics and Chartist disturbances; now all attention was focussed on American affairs. The political compromise of 1850 over slavery in Congress; the Fugitive Slave Law, which had such dramatic repercussions in Boston; the Kansas question and the John Brown raid all dominate the scene. In neither country did the abolitionists take any positive action to guide the course of events. Even the John Brown raid, with which they warmly sympathised, was carried out without the complicity or foreknowledge of Garrison and his friends. But their letters are revealing and important as the record of a pressure group, informed and strongly biased, and not without some local influence and standing.

With the coming of the Civil War, however, every aspect of the anti-slavery connection was called into force. A first consequence of the war was the immediate and bitter breakdown of friendly relations between the two Governments. The hostility of all Americans to the British Proclamation of Neutrality, the British bewilderment at, and unwillingness to support, a war fought not for slavery but to preserve the Union – seen in the furore over the Trent affair and the building of ships for the Confederate cause – are reflected in the abolitionists' letters. Indeed, anti-British feeling among the Boston abolitionists never abated entirely, and was still high at the time of the Governor Eyre incident in 1865, for almost without exception American abolitionists placed loyalty to their country above anti-slavery friendships.

But anti-slavery friendships were not to be dismissed so lightly. The attempts of the British Garrison party, now led by F. W. Chesson, to form a central organization which would attract influential support, suddenly met with brilliant success as the Civil War brought the issue of slavery so prominently before men's minds, and for the first time anti-slavery activity in Britain was led by Garrison's supporters and not by Sturge or the Stafford House set. The forming of the Emancipation Society, an outgrowth of Chesson's earlier London Emancipation Society, gave a focal point to all who supported not merely the cause of slavery but who championed America and American democracy. The part played by the Anglo-American anti-slavery connection during the Civil War is very difficult if not impossible to assess, but it cannot be discarded as negligible. It is very probable that the great mass meetings to rally British support for the North, held early in 1863, did little in fact to influence the British government who had already by that date determined finally on a course of strict neutrality. But Lincoln on the other hand, was well aware that war with Britain, and even France, was a possibility, and he took every step available to him to win anti-slavery support abroad. George Thompson on a visit to America was invited to speak before Congress, a notable step since he had scarcely thirty years previously been denounced by Congress as a foreign incendiary. A Treaty with effectual provisions to put down the slave trade was concluded with Britain; the President personally sent a reply to the Manchester working men who had petitioned him to abolish slavery; and an Emancipation Proclamation was put forward – a Proclamation which if it did not effectively abolish slavery in the United States, yet gave colour to the view that the Civil War was a moral crusade. By stressing this view in Britain the Emancipation Society ensured that a Northern victory must have the support of a majority of the British people.

But the success of the British Garrison party had other repercussions. On one level it firmly established Garrison's reputation as the champion of the slave. Since it was Garrison's adherents who were taking the lead in stirring up anti-slavery feeling in Britain, Garrison became the hero of the cause by the end of the Civil War, and in the tributes paid him at the breakfast given in his honour in London in 1867 we see that the old image of him as a heretic and incendiary had gone, and a new one, the Emancipator and father of the cause of freedom, had taken its place. Not unfittingly, the British Garrisonians who had contributed so materially to keeping alive Garrison's party in the States also helped to create his reputation for posterity.

The importance of the Garrison connection does not end here, however. Particularly in Britain it had always served to attract various interests: Irish repealers, Chartists, Italian patriots, champions of women's rights and of social reform of every description; though not until the Civil War offered the opportunity did the Garrison party finally win the support of a group of any influence – intellectuals, prominent Nonconformist leaders and radical politicians of some standing. They were attracted to Garrison and his supporters rather than the more conservative B.F.A.S.S. or the Stafford House set, and thus it was on the platform of the radical wing of the anti-slavery movement that these extraneous groups met and aired their views. These men were not simply interested in the cause of Negro slavery, they used the anti-slavery movement as a stalking horse for wider interests, which centred on a belief in a more egalitarian form of democracy and ended in a demand for the extension of the franchise. In the 1860s the Emancipation Societies were not of course the only or the most important channel through which the Parliamentary reform movement flowed, but they were an important one, for they brought together various sections who were interested not only in Negro slavery but in political reforms and at the same time sympathetic to American democratic ideas, which had emerged so triumphantly at the close of the Civil War.

The Anglo-American abolitionists might directly wield little influence and engage chiefly in internal squabbles of little interest save to themselves, but they did forge bonds of friendship between the two countries which might crack even if they did not break completely under the strain of the Civil War. Moreover, being simply what they were: "a venomous but influential group" as a diplomatist once described them – they formed a section of the community whose feelings neither the American nor the British government could entirely ignore. To what extent they were responsible for keeping Britain and America at peace is not clear; to what degree they helped bring about a greater degree of Anglo-American understanding may never be fully determined. But the strength of their connection remains undoubted. Made up of quarrels and petty rivalries as well as common ideals and beliefs, the connection serves as a reminder that Britain and America were at no time totally independent of each other; that close friendships, co-operation and understanding existed side by side with hostility and prejudice. That peace prevailed was by no means entirely due to the abolitionists, but the co-operation of forty years may not be set aside lightly, and is in itself a testimony to the existence and value of this North Atlantic community.

The selections made from the Boston Papers stop at 1870 with a brief mention of the Alabama Arbitration – possibly an unwilling though nonetheless ungrudging and peaceful settlement of Anglo-American differences. But the Collection does not end there. To the end of their days the British and American abolitionists continued to correspond, though their letters at this point deal increasingly with personal matters only. The entire collection, which includes not only the Garrison Papers, but also the May, Estlin, Thompson, Weston and Chapman Papers, is in itself largely the result of Anglo-American co-operation, for many of the British abolitionists, among them the Webb family, Elizabeth Pease Nichol and the Carpenters, sent their letters to Garrison's sons when they began to write their father's biography. It is these bequests which give a special interest and unity to the Boston Papers and must serve as justification for excluding from the present study letters which are to be found in other collections. To print all the existing letters written by Garrison and his friends is unpractical; the best solution seemed to be to select from the collection which they themselves had made. It was impossible to include all the letters in the Boston Collection, which runs to many thousand items, but the theme for such a selection is readily obvious: the Boston Papers are an important source of information regarding the American anti-slavery campaign, but their greatest value is the light they shed on the work of British and American abolitionists in this field of humanitarian endeavour.

But though the Boston Papers are a major anti-slavery collection, there are already in existence several edited texts of anti-slavery material. The most important of these are the works by A. H. Abel & F. J. Klingberg, *A Sidelight on Anglo-American Relations* (Lancaster, Penn., 1927); G. H. Barnes and Dwight L. Dumond, *Letters of Theodore Dwight Weld, Angelina Grimké Weld and Sarah Grimké*, 2 vols., (New York, 1934), and Dwight L. Dumond, *Letters of James Gillespie Birney*, (New York, 1938). This present work, it is hoped, will supplement these earlier volumes, and extend to some extent the views they advance. When making the selection two principles were observed; for a letter to be included it had to deal with some topic of general Anglo-American interest (e.g. Irish affairs) or it had to illustrate the close links existing between the British and American abolitionists, and some of the importance of this association. The second requirement was more difficult to fulfil, and many letters were excluded on the grounds that they simply contained personal gossip, or repeated information which other letters described more fully. As to the method of transcription, all the letters are as faithful a copy as possible, and no attempt has been made to alter the spelling or punctuation of the original writer. Annotation of the letters has been kept to a minimum, and confined to biographical details, which have been expanded in some instances to help elucidate obscure passages, a general knowledge of the period being assumed on the part of the reader.

Many volumes would be needed to do full justice to the Garrisonian collection. The abolitionists who formed it were magnificent correspondents, commenting with vigour and intelligence on the world around them. One of the greatest tributes to their work is the letters which they exchanged with each other, the main body of which is in the Boston Public Library. As a record of the social history of the two countries in the middle years of the nineteenth century the collection is remarkable; as a testimony to forty years of international co-operation it is possibly unique.

THE LETTERS

MS.A.1.2. vol. 2 1832 Anti-Slavery Letters to Garrison [1]
No. 21 Joseph Phillips[1] *to William Lloyd Garrison*

Anti-Slavery Office, 18 Aldermanbury London
June 6. 1832.

Wm. Lloyd Garrison

Dear Sir

About 12 months since I sent you from this office with a sett of Anti Slavery Reporters with some other publications, that I thought would be valuable to you requesting in return your newspaper and any information you could give me respecting that disgracefull conspiracy against the rights and liberties of free sub[jects] in America, called the Colonization Society. I have in conjunction with my kind friend Capt. Charles Stuart[2] done everything that lays in my power to neutralize Mr. Elliot Cresson's[3] sophistry and as I occasionally travel as an agent of the Anti Slavery Society in various parts of England I have invariably succeeded (except in a few solitary instances) in removing the baneful effect he produced – but I am much in want of documentary evidence from America to meet him especially all laws made against the free black and collour[d] population of America. State laws & by long rep – you would particularly oblige me by sending your papers, as I never receive any answer to my letter from you. Mr. William Biddle the bearer of this is a Gentleman of Respectability who can give you every information respecting the Anti Slavery cause here, and any service you can confer upon him and family will particularly oblige. he will give you a 4th Volume of Reporters should it not be agreable to have a mutual correspondence. please to favor me with a few lines acknowledging this.

Your most sincere well wisher & friend

Josh Phillips

---

1. Joseph Phillips worked actively for the British anti-slavery movement in the years before the 1833 Emancipation Act, though little is known of him personally today. He was the author of various abolitionist pamphlets, including *The West India question, the outline of a plan for the total....abolition of slavery throughout the British colonies*, London, 1833.
2. Captain Charles Stuart (1783-1865) was born in Jamaica and served with the British Army in India. A deeply religious man, he devoted his later life to the anti-slavery movement, working for the cause in Britain, America and the West Indies. Though a poor speaker and a somewhat eccentric figure, he nonetheless had wide influence in anti-slavery circles, especially on his friend and pupil, Theodore Weld. Travelling frequently between Britain and America, he was instrumental in bringing the British and American Movements into very close alliance. He wrote several tracts in defence of the anti-slavery cause.
3. Elliot Cresson (1796-1854), a wealthy Quaker merchant and philanthropist, was the Secretary of the American Colonization Society, whose aim was to repatriate the Negroes by organising their return to Africa and resettlement there. The Society came in for attack from American anti-slavery circles who felt that Colonization was evading the real issue – abolition. Cresson came to Britain in 1831, and spent two years there touring the country seeking funds and support for his cause. As a result of intervention by American abolitionists, his mission and the Colonization question became hotly debated in Britain.

MS.A.1.2. vol. 2 Anti-Slavery Letters to Garrison [2]
No. 35 Arnold Buffum[1] to William Lloyd Garrison

Boston 10 mo 18 1832

My dear Garrison,

We have had considerable conversation here relative to sending an Agent to England to collect subscriptions for our proposed school for colored youth and as far as I can learn there seems to be but one opinion on the subject and that is that if the means of defraying the expenses can be obtained it will be best that thou should go immediately to England for that purpose. It really appears to me that it is a most important measure to be immediately adopted I can entertain no doubt but thou would there meet the most cordial reception and receive liberal contributions toward this most desirable object I have consulted several of the most wealthy men in Providence on the subject they highly approve the measure and will contribute toward its accomplishment please get on thy way to Boston a few hundred if possible toward the expenses of a voyage to Europe and come up and sail from New York the first of next month that is my most decided opinion. If the money for the expenses cannot be got elsewhere I will go to New Bedford and beg hard and I believe I can get it there at any rate I will try as soon as I know thou hast decided to go. A Colored man now here from Petersburg Virginia states that they have there had a missionary society and that they have been obliged to give it up in consequence of the new laws which prohibit them from meeting and that they have a fund of $200 which they want to give where it will be used for the benefit of the colored people he thinks they will give it to us.

Please to write me immediately in reply address to me at Lowell and oblige thy assured friend

Arnold Buffum.

Garrison in England will do the cause more good in 3 months than in 12 in America in the reception he will there meet and by his communications through the columns of the liberator &c &c excuse the great h[aste?] which almost precludes thought.

MS.A.1.1. vol. 1 Anti-Slavery Letters from Garrison [3]
No. 20 William Lloyd Garrison to Samuel J. May[1]

Boston, Dec. 4, 1832.

Beloved Brother:

At the time of our annual meeting, there will be in this city at least

---

1. Arnold Buffum (1782-1859), a Quaker abolitionist, had travelled extensively abroad, and had close friends in British anti-slavery circles. He became the first President of the New England Anti-Slavery Society, and lectured as its agent for some years.

1. Samuel Joseph May (1797-1871), a Unitarian minister and cousin of Samuel May Jr. of Leicester, helped Garrison in the organization of the N.E.A.S.S. He was active in the anti-slavery cause, especially in Connecticut, where he championed Prudence Crandall (see below), and later in New York State. His *Recollections of the Anti-Slavery Conflict*, Boston, 1868, is a useful, if partisan, account of the abolitionists' campaign.

six hundred members of the Legislature, a large portion of whom we shall probably secure as auditors: hence it is highly important that we should make a demonstration of strength and talent on that occasion.

Our cause goes on prosperously. Indeed, when I consider the brevity of the period in which we have been engaged, and the nature and number of the obstacles which towered in our path, I am surprised to observe the impression we have made upon the nation.

Our coadjutators in England are fighting most manfully, with spiritual weapons against sin and cruelty. I have just received from them a large bundle of anti-slavery pamphlets, tracts, circulars, &c. &c. the perusal of which is almost too much for my poor nerves. The British abolitionists waste no ammunition – every shot tells – *they write in earnest* – they call, as did old John Knox, a fig a fig, and a spade a spade. When I see what they are doing, and read what they write, I blush to think of my own past apathy and mourn in view of my poverty of thought and language.

By all means come at our annual meeting, if possible.

This letter, I trust, will find you and your lady, as it leaves me, in the enjoyment of good health.

Your steadfast friend,

Wm. Lloyd Garrison

MS.A.1.2. vol. 1 Anti-Slavery Letters to Garrison [4]
No. 21 Nathan Winslow[1] *to William Lloyd Garrison*

Portland, 3 mo. 10 1833.

My dear Friend,

I notice by the last Liberator thou art making arrangements to embark for England, and will just inform thee, that a few days since, I gave Jonathan Backhouse[2], an English Friend, a letter of introduction to thee. I hope thou wilt see him before embarking on thy mission.

He is an orthodox minister, a strong abolitionist, an influential man in England, and intimately acquainted with Clarkson[3], and Cropper[4]. I think

1. Nathan Winslow (1785-1861) was a Quaker merchant of Portland, Maine, and a supporter of the *Liberator.*

2. Jonathan Backhouse (1779-1842) of Polam Hill, Darlington, was a banker and minister in the Society of Friends. He had close ties with American Quakers, for with his wife, Hannah, (1787-1850) the daughter of Joseph Gurney and aunt of Elizabeth Pease, he toured North America from 1830 to 1835, where both were active in combating the influence of the American Hicksites. See *Extracts from the Journal and Letters of Hannah Chapman Backhouse,* London, 1858.

3. Thomas Clarkson (1760-1846) was one of the foremost British abolitionists, and was active in the campaign for abolition of the slave trade and West Indian emancipation.

4. James Cropper (1773-1840), a wealthy Quaker merchant, was active in the campaign for West Indian emancipation and to achieve this end helped to organize a more radical wing of the British anti-slavery movement, the Agency Committee. He took a keen interest in the American abolition movement, and had considerable influence in anti-slavery circles in both countries.

thou wilt be gratified with his acquaintance. I understand his wife was in Boston, while he was with us. She is also a minister, and a very intelligent woman. They are probably now in Salem or Lynn.

A bundle of the Annual Report of the Anti-Slavery Society was received this morning. I think the material good, and well arranged.

I hope Miss Crandall's[5] school will succeed in defiance of its dastardly opposers.

What have you in prospect for the Manual Labor School? I feel a great interest in its location and prosperity.

The seeds of anti-slavery are sown in this place, and I trust that the cause of truth, righteousness, and freedom, will ultimately prevail over error, deception, and hypocrisy.

I hope to receive a letter from thee before thy departure, and shall be very desirous to hear from thee frequently by letters during thy absence. My family join me in wishing thee a pleasant and prosperous voyage.

Thine affectionately,

N. Winslow

By L.E.W.

MS.A.1.1. vol. 1 Anti-Slavery Letters from Garrison [5]
No. 24 Extract from a letter from William Lloyd Garrison to Miss Harriet Minot of Haverhill, Mass.

Boston, March 19, 1833.

... In the course of a few weeks, I expect to leave my native land on an important mission to England, on behalf of the great and glorious cause of African emancipation. This mission will occupy six months – perhaps a year. What my reception will be in that country, – should I be wafted safely across the deep, – I cannot doubt. There, I shall breathe freely – there, my sentiments and language on the subject of slavery will receive the acclamations of the people – there, my spirit will be elevated and strengthened in the presence of Clarkson, and Wilberforce,[1] and Brougham,[2] and Buxton,[3]

---

5. Prudence Crandall (1803-1889), a Quaker educator and reformer, attempted to admit coloured girls to her school in Canterbury, Connecticut, but met with violent opposition from the townspeople and had to abandon the project. Her cause was warmly championed by Garrison and other New England abolitionists, and roused much British sympathy.

1. William Wilberforce (1759-1833), philanthropist and reformer, was a leader of the anti-slavery movement in Britain. He formed the Sierra Leone Company for liberated slaves, and was active in the Parliamentary campaign for the extinction of the slave trade, and later for West Indian Emancipation.
2. Henry Peter, Baron Brougham & Vaux (1786-1868), the famous radical politician and at this time Lord Chancellor, was a consistent champion of anti-slavery policies in Parliament.
3. Sir Thomas Fowell Buxton (1786-1845) was also a leading British abolitionist, and connected by marriage to two of the leading Quaker families, the Gurneys and the

and O'Connell,[4] and their noble coadjutors – there, I can tell the story of the black man's wrongs, in this land of liberty and light, to hearts that will melt with pity, and devise liberally for his rescue, – there, I shall doubtless be permitted to address those of your own sex who are animated with zeal for the overthrow of slavery which many waters cannot quench. Delightful anticipation!

MS.A.1.2. vol. 3 Anti-Slavery Letters to Garrison [6]
No. 28 Arthur Tappan[1] to William Lloyd Garrison

N. York March 22 1833

Dear Sir

I recd. yours of the 16th. In your previous letter you did not propose to give me security for a letter of credit in England other than the responsibility of the Anti Slavery Socy. Now you know as well as myself that the responsibility of a society is not a tangible sort of thing and I feared that when I had to pay the money it would not be forthcoming. I am willing however to *advance the money* on a note of hand (that will be punctually paid) payable at a bank in Boston in three months if this will accomodate the society.[2]

If you go to England, I hope you will collect a large quantity of pamphlets tracts &c which are no longer of use there, & send them over here for distribution. You may get them I suppose at little or no expense – In haste

Yr friend

A Tappan.

Frys. He succeeded Wilberforce as the leader of the anti-slavery cause in Parliament. He was responsible for founding the Aborigines Protection Society and the Society for the Extinction of the Slave Trade and the Civilization of Africa. The outgrowth of this last society was the ill-fated Niger expedition, which though it failed to open up the Niger delta to cultivation, helped later to create an interest in the development of central Africa.

4. Daniel O'Connell (1775-1847), the Irish political agitator and reformer, took up the cause of anti-slavery and did not hesitate to draw the parallel between "slavery" in Ireland and in other parts of the world.

1. Arthur Tappan (1786-1865), a wealthy New York silk merchant, was the leader of New York philanthropic circles. With his brother, Lewis, (1788-1873) he dominated and financed much of the early American anti-slavery movement, and helped to form the American Anti-Slavery Society in 1833. After the financial crisis of 1837 Arthur Tappan withdrew from the movement; but Lewis continued to take an active part in anti-slavery affairs, and was the leader of the more conservative wing of the American movement following the divisions of 1840, maintaining also a long correspondence with his British supporters. See A.H. Abel & F.J. Klingberg, *A Side-Light on Anglo-American Relations, 1839-1858*, Lancaster, Pennsylvania, 1927.

2. There was considerable difficulty over the repayment of this sum. Garrison was also advanced money for his return from Britain by the Rev. Nathaniel Paul, (see below) a friend of the Tappans, but failed to account for this sum satisfactorily, thus placing Paul in a very difficult financial position.

17 Store Street
Bedford Square
7 mo 5 1833

Esteemed Friend

I did not receive thy letter untill about 3 O Clock I went at once to Z. Macaulay[1] but he was not in he called upon me in the evening & we had a good deal of conversation – He thought we might justly give offence in America if we were to hold a meeting where the assured & leading object was the Abolition of slavery in the United States and [there]fore our object should be to oppose the tendency of the American Colonization Society to which the people of this County had been called upon to contribute, it would also be well to have the points of discussion and course of proceedings more fully defined before any meeting was fixed – Z M thought Lord Suffield[2] might be willing to take the chair if applied to, but he doubted whether he was so fully acquainted with the subject as to make it desirable – Jos Sturge[3] was with us & will give thee any further information – I am to be in the neighbourhood of Aldermanbury at 6 o clock this evening if we could meet there at 5 oclock we might have farther conversation perhaps thou will see Jos Sturge Cap Stuart &c & get them to attend me. I hope I may see J Sturge at breakfast this morning & we may have further talk & if anything is fixed different he will tell thee but I did not like [to? submit?] saying what had past in time for the first delivery

I am with much regard

Thy sincere friend

James Cropper.

---

1. Zachary Macaulay (1768-1838), philanthropist and reformer, was one of the founders of the British Anti-Slavery Society. He was for a time Governor of the Sierra Leone Company and later editor of several anti-slavery journals.
2. Edward Assheton, 3rd Lord Suffield, (1781-1835) took an interest in abolition and signed the protest against the Colonization Society.
3. Joseph Sturge (1793-1859), one of the most famous of the Victorian Quaker philanthropists and reformers, was active in many reform movements. The son-in-law of James Cropper, he soon became a leading British abolitionist, but as the founder and leader of the B.F.A.S.S. he was attacked by many of Garrison's supporters after the divisions in the anti-slavery movement. He nonetheless retained close links with American abolitionists, especially the Tappans and their circle. Apart from his work with the B.F.A.S.S., he made a tour of the West Indies in 1837, and as a result was instrumental in having the apprenticeship system ended. He was also sympathetic to the Chartists and to other working class movements.

MS.A.1.2. vol. 3 Anti-Slavery Letters to Garrison [8]
No. 65 Joseph Phillips to William Lloyd Garrison

18 Aldermanbury London Augt 30/33

Dear and Valuable Friend and Brother

I duly received from Portsmouth your letter of 25th inst. and am surprised you had not received one from me with 3 Patriots.

Our mutual friend Capt Stuart left London for Bath on the 23rd and expected to leave England in 3 weeks from that date if he did change his mind I trust his friends will not induce him to deviate from this noble path of duty in my humble opinion prepared for him by divine appointment his experience, and decision of character, and uncompromising hostility to slavyare valuable acquisitions in forming your fundamentals in your anticipated National Anti-Slavy Society.

Your two communications has been received and are now in my possession in consequence of the Editor of the Patriot refusing to publish them. I was not satisfied with his reasons – such as – your letters was too long – nobody would read them – the subject was nearly exhausted – they must admit the reply of E Cresson and his friends which would promote a long and unprofitable discussion these were the principle objections. I then stipulated that they would not admit any remarks of Elliott Cressons upon yr last reply to only a part of his, unless they would publish your last, then I conceived their columns only would be open to him subject to an answer from yr friends, this was agreed to and a promise to publish extracts from the "Liberator" which I shall send. They kindly lent me a letter they received for publication but refused – the writer I understand is a banker of considerable wealth &c &c I took the liberty of making a copy of it for your perusal – it will show you to what shifts E.C. is compeld to adopt to get tools to expose their folly in writing such nonsense. I have made up a parcel of books for him, but without his knowledge where from as I trust his mind will open to conviction to receive the truth.

I shall keep a watchful eye over E.C. and anything that may be published with the aid of friends in London. Cresson called at the office to see Pringle to make some complaint. Mr. Hill who was foremost kindly committed the particulars to paper at my request and [it] is now enclosed. I have just heard that Cresson is gone to Brighton – I anticipated this movement a month since and sent some tracts there but if I find my information correct I shall make up a parcel and send it to Sir R Bloomfield and request his active opposition to his scheme. I have written O'Connell but received no answer he had left town before I received your letter. I now send a copy obtained from Johnstone & paid him one guinea at your request.

Mr. Paul[1] is still with me Mrs. P my wife & children [?] their kind

---

1. Rev. Nathaniel Paul (d. 1839) was an American Negro minister and a protégé of Arthur Tappan. He had been for some time in Britain collecting money for a school for coloured pupils, but worked with Garrison during his visit, advancing him money for his return passage. He married an English wife who later found her position in America one of great difficulty in spite of help from the Boston abolitionists.

remembrances to you. We feel very much your absence and Captn Stuart but we are thankful for the time we were permitted to enjoy it. May it prove a blessing to all of us in time and in Eternity.

Since you left my mind has been like a troubled ocean from the uncertainty of the future, anxious to avoid however profitable an [?] which will deprive me of opportunities of benefitting my fellow creatures – by the Grace of God I am determined to leave all in his hands and again to renew my covenant to be his and entirely devoted to his service to do with me as best pleases him, at the same time using all lawful means of enquiry, without anxious cares and misgivings.

I shall be very anxious to hear from you and receive your Liberator regular[ly] in your absence that will be the best substitute – to select matter for publication as I fear Cresson will not leave England so long as he can get money. I have no doubt he anticipates the reception he will meet on his return to the U.S. and he would rather bask in the sun-shine of his hole and corner popularity here than merit it – I have not heard from G. Thompson since you left or from R^{d} Ball[2] –

Although unknown give my sincerest respects and regards to that good and great man Arthur Tappan. May the God of Love fill his heart with all peace.

Farewell my dear Brother in Christ and remember in your prayers your humble coadjutor & sincere friend

Josh Phillips

To Mr Wm. Lloyd Garrison

P.S. My best respects to A Buffum – Mr. Knapp[3] & Rev^{d} Mr Williams.

MS.A.1.2. vol. 3 Anti-Slavery Letters to Garrison [9]
No. 66 Nathaniel Paul to William Lloyd Garrison

London August 31 1833

My Dear friend Garrison

... Your letter arrived from Portsmouth & I was much grieved to think that the papers were not to be found that friend Phillips took it upon himself to see that they were sent but there seems to be some mistake some where. However I hope that the pressent parcel will reach you in a few days after your arrival. You will see that the Patriot & the Advocate both contain your communications but the Editor of [the] Patriot of this week has not followed it up as I expected The reason I understand that he assigns is that he thinks best not to continue the controversy I am not anctious about his publishing more unless Cresson should attempt to answer & if he does there are enough ready to

---

2. Richard Ball (? – 1862) was another British Quaker active in the Anti-Slavery Movement. He later became a leading member of the B.F.A.S.S.
3. Isaac Knapp (1804-1843) was one of the founder members of the N.E.A.S.S. and worked with Garrison on the *Liberator.* A devoted reformer, he was a poor businessman, and his partnership with Garrison had to be dissolved.

meet him – Cresson has been to the Anti-Slavery Office & is quite disturbed at your last publication & thinks hard that he should be called an imposter &c and inquire of Pringle why you should date your letters from 10 Aldermanbury (you may see his reasons for this) Pringle gave him no satisfaction but told him that he believed that he Cresson has said quite a hard thing about Garrison which[?] I do not know what he means to do now nor is it possible to find our One day he is pretending that he is going to return immediately to the United States the next we hear of him in another mention trying to get up meetings. Mr. [Burt?] said that Cresson told a friend of his that Garrison had ruined his cause in this country & he must now leave for America he is a most deceiving hypocrite but depend upon it he will be watched. I have had five hundred copys of your letter published I expect to engage Scoble for a time to travel with me in trying to promote my object. Capt. Stuart left the Saturday after you did for Bath where he is expected to remain for a time & then proceed to Belfast & from thence to America. Mrs. Paul's health is still poor but some better than when you left I expect to leave London for good in the course of a week travel through the North of England vissit Scotland & return to America but I very much fear that I shall not be able to return before Spring Phillips has received since you left 4 numbers of the Liberator together with some other Pamphlets for Thompson which I have had the pleasure of perusing I find that Miss Crandall has bene prosecuted & committed to prison (so much the better) I have scribled a letter for Judson[1] which I send you & if you think proper you will publish & if not please send it & throw it into the Post Office There is nothing of importance that has occured to my knowledge since you left the friends. We hold you in kind remembrance & your vissit will I think prove a blessing to the cause of Emancipation. And now my dear brother adieu may God still strengthen your hands to the work in which you are engaged & may it please him to spare my life to meet you in Boston. Please to remember me to all my relation[s] & inquiring friends & believe me very truly yours in the bonds of the gospel

Nathl. Paul

W L Garrison Esqr

MS.A.1.2. vol. 4 1834 Anti-Slavery Letters to Garrison [10]
No. 24 George Thompson to William Lloyd Garrison

18 Aldermanbury – London
March 27, 1834.

My very dear friend & Brother,

Pardon if you can the silence of your friend – You have doubtless often censured my silence and perhaps attributed it to a forgetfulness of the cause. I admit, the inference is natural but [by?] to assure you from my inmost heart that you have been ever with me in your labours, trials, persecutions, zeal

1. Possibly Andrew T. Judson (1784-1853), who was an agent of the Colonization Society, the Town Clerk of Canterbury, Connecticut and one of the leading figures in the attack upon Miss Crandall.

and devotion; and, although I have been so mysteriously silent, yet have I been doing all I could to promote the great cause to which you have consecrated all your energies. The only reasons I can assign at present for my protracted silence are 1st I have always desired to send you a very full account of all my proceedings and have therefore waited for a suitable opportunity. 2nd my time and strength have been so entirely monopolized by my home engagements that I have had no opportunity for furnishing you with the details I desired to send. I trust however that we shall soon meet, and I will then explain at large. I had hoped to have been by this time on the eve of starting for the United States but find it necessary to remain in Gt. Britain a few weeks longer in order that I may form some auxiliaries in aid of the society which has recently been formed in London, the prospectus of which I send you herewith.

I was greatly delighted with the proceedings in Philadelphia in Dec^{r} – last[1] – In such a spirit, with such views, principles, and plans, you must overcome all obstacles. You have laid hold upon *omnipotence*. Believe and all things are possible.

I hope to start for New York by the latter end of May at the farthest. On my arrival I shall consult with your society and act as you may deem best for the advancement of the cause –

Scotland did nobly. I shall be able to visit your country principally through the liberality of the friends in Edinburgh and Glasgow – You were much wanted in both Cities. Should you live to visit our country again you will do well to shew yourself amongst your many warm, though unknown friends in Scotland. Captain Stuart will bring out with him a splendid present for Miss Crandall, obtained by me for her during my stay in *Edinburgh*. When I come I shall bring with me a piece of plate from *Glasgow* sent by the ladies there to Miss Crandall. A report has been spread in London that Miss C. has fled to Canada. Is it true? I hope not.

I send you a memorial prepared by G. Stephen[2] which we have some thoughts of getting signed as a national document and forwarded to the U[nited] States. I do not send to any one beside yourself deeming you the best judge of whether it should meet the public eye. *I* should say no! Since it may be forwarded and in such a case ought to be *new*.

I have a relative who is about to sail for New York and proceed from thence to Baltimore to which place he is invited as a minister. By him I shall forward a parcel for you which I trust will contain more information than this.

I trust our dear friend Captn Stuart will arrive in safety. May he be made an abundant blessing. I long to be with you – Nothing but the belief that I am imperatively needed here could keep me another fortnight in England.

---

1. The inaugural meeting of the American Anti-Slavery Society.
2. Sir George Stephen (1794-1879) had been active in British anti-slavery circles since 1826, when he collected evidence for Buxton that slavery existed in Mauritius. He worked also for prison reform and other humanitariun activities. His *Anti-Slavery Recollections*, London, 1854, is useful for an account of the early years of the movement.

That Heaven may bless you in mind & body and crown your devoted labours with a speedy and happy triumph, prays your Atlantic friend.

G. Thompson.

MS.A.1.2. vol. 4 Anti-Slavery Letters to Garrison [11]
No. 39 James Cropper to William Lloyd Garrison

Liverpool, 5th Mo. 17th, 1834.

William Lloyd Garrison:

Dear Friend–

I have just received the Liberator bound for 1833, for which thou will please to accept my cordial thanks. I had ordered through my friend Jos Sturge the Liberator to be sent to me regularly but I know he has ordered some others at the same time & I hope to see him next week when I shall know if any have been received & if not the order must have miscarried & he should write again.

The friends of Negro emancipation were greatly rejoiced to see your manly Declaration against Slavery:[1] it was right to attack it in unflinching language, founded upon the unchanging basis of truth. These enormous evils should thus be denounced as they deserve. But every one must see, that the question on one side in the United States is beset with difficulties, which may seem to be almost insurmountable; for if you could succeed in convincing the people in the free states & if the General Government were sincerely disposed to abolish slavery they have not, by the Constitution, the power to do it. And as to the Slave States, it would have been as reasonable to expect emancipation to originate in the Assembly of Jamaica. If many of the individual slave holders were fully convinced of the sin of holding their fellow men in slavery, & were satisfied to make the sacrifices, still the laws of the state would prevent them from carrying their [?] wishes into effect – There is, however, a more cheering view of the subject, & its holders are quite as likely as other men to be worked upon by their own interest. If it can be made clear to them, that they will be pecuniary gainers by changing the condition of the Slaves (to emancipate them not being in their power) they may say to them that if they will produce to them as many bags of Cotton Tierces of Rice or Hogsheads of Tobacco as they have done as slaves, they will no longer interfer with them, but let them occupy the land and work it in their own way, at their own times, and feed & clothe themselves as they like: they will exercise no other mastership over them but such as is required for their protection – I believe all parties would soon have reason to be satisfied – In America there are numerous instances of Slavery & free Labour being seen in operation side by side where the advantages of the latter are most obvious, in this respect you have great advantages as compared with our Colonies – Any one slave holder may begin the experiment but must not expect to be freed from care; his slaves (as they will still legally be) will expect the kind directions &

---

1. The Declaration of Sentiments drawn up at the inaugural meeting of the A.A.S.S. in Philadelphia.

instructions of a Father; they will need his help & must have it or the chance of success will be very small – if no other Slaveholders will try the experiment and our Society (that is) the Yearly Meeting of North Carolina have for many years been compelled to hold slaves because they could not safely emancipate them, because they might be enduced to try the plan if the subject was brought before them, but it would be of no use to try it except under the care of some zealous active man who would go into it with the industry and attention which a mans own interest generally secures; indeed it would be better if it were undertaken by some man for his own profit; for then if successful the example would be complete & it would be certain to be followed – Surely this much however can be effected & if succeeds a very great step will be made – This Yearly Meeting could easily manage their slaves. – They would need no other punishment for the idle and refractory than to hold out the threat of sending them to Liberia, and if they would not submit to that, they would have no other resource than giving them their freedom, an act good in itself, but as in its consequences it would be a severe punishment should only be resorted to in case of necessity. – The existence of these people in a state of slavery proves the difficulty that individual slave holders would feel who wished to give freedom to their slaves –

Such are my views of one mode at least to which your aims should be subjected, never however forgetting to open the eyes of the people to the enormities of slavery for if the people of the Slave States had no hopes whatever of assistance from the free states in putting down an insurrection their fears would induce them to look more seriously at the whole subject & at every practical remedy. – It is of vast importance to continue the exposure of the Colonization Society. I am grieved to find that some people (well disposed to our cause) seem to be disposed to look at the opinions of good men rather than take the trouble to investigate the nature of the thing for themselves.

I am just about to try an experiment which if it succeeds would be of vast importance to the Coloured people in your country whether children or grown up, I send the[e] a copy of my plan if some individual or society in America would take it up it would be most desirable –

I shall be glad to hear from thee as to the progress of our cause & am with great regard

Thy sincere friend

James Cropper

I hope our good friend Stuart will be safely arrived in America before this time.

I have taken no active part in promoting [?] America, I did however contribute to a fund which is placed at Stuart's disposal. – I am a little afraid of our stepping out of our proper place in paying Agents to travel in the United States but I am satisfied there is a degree of apathy from which it is needful the people in your country should by some means be aroused.

J.C.

No. 31 William Lloyd Garrison to Robert Purvis[1]

Boston, May 20, 1834.

My Dear Purvis:

Since my return, I have been so disturbed and distracted by conflicting engagements & duties, as to be unable to send you half as many letters to my dear friends in England, as I contemplated when I saw you. You will be disappointed, and I am sorry; but I dare not delay any longer. Should you fail to go immediately, (and I know not how you can be spared from this country,) I wish you would put the accompanying letters in the Liverpool and London mail bags, erasing the line at the bottom referring to yourself.

The persons whom I meant to introduce you to by letter, are – James Ryley[2] & Dr. Hancock,[3] Liverpool; Joseph Sturge, Birmingham; Arthur West, Bath; Elizabeth & Mary Dudley,[4] Peckham, nr. London; Wm. Allen,[5] Richard Barrett,[6] Joseph Phillips, Danl. O'Connell, Dr. Lushington,[7] George Stephen, Joseph & Emmanuel Cooper,[8] John Scoble[9] &c &c. I hope you will become acquainted with all these.

You will be able to communicate many interesting facts to our English brethren. Be sure to take out with you our latest anti-slavery publications. Mr. Bell will give you copies of the Liberator.

If practicable, let me hear from you on your arrival in England....

Remember me in a very special manner to my dear friend, the Rev. Nath[l]. Paul, and also to his estimable lady.

1. Robert Purvis (1810-98) was a leader of the coloured citizens of Philadelphia – the group from which the *Liberator* drew its chief support. Purvis was later to become one of the most energetic workers for the Underground Railroad in Pennsylvania.
2. James Ryley (1768-1845) had married Margaret Cropper, James Cropper's sister.
3. Dr. Thomas Hancock (1783-1849) was a famous Quaker doctor and writer.
4. Elizabeth (1799-1849) and Mary Dudley were Ministers in the Society of Friends.
5. William Allen (1770-1843) was a leading English Quaker, the friend of Wilberforce and Clarkson, and had worked for the anti-slavery movement since the days of the agitation for the abolition of the slave trade. A scientist and philanthropist he worked also for education and other social reforms, though his strong religious views led him into disagreement with more radical thinkers such as James Mill and also with Robert Owen, with whom he cooperated for a time over the model factory at New Lanark. Allen travelled extensively on the Continent examining social conditions there and interviewing statesmen and rulers.
6. Richard Barrett (1784-1855) was another Minister in the Society of Friends.
7. Dr. Stephen Lushington (1782-1873) had worked closely with Sir Thomas Fowell Buxton in the campaign for British emancipation. He was also active in Parliamentary reform circles.
8. Joseph (1800-1881) and Emmanuel Cooper were Quakers, active in anti-slavery circles, and later members of the British and Foreign Anti-Slavery Society.
9. John Scoble was one of the agents appointed by the Agency Committee to lecture on anti-slavery in 1831. From 1837 to 1839 he visited the West Indies and the United States, and later became Secretary of the B.F.A.S.S., and from then on a target of attack by the Garrisonites. He left Britain in 1852, and until about 1865 worked in the United States and in Canada.

I write and conclude in very great haste but am ever
Your affectionate friend,
Wm. Lloyd Garrison.

N.B. I have written to Mr. Thompson, because I think it highly probable you will arrive in London before his departure for this country.

MS.A.1.2. vol. 4 Anti-Slavery Letters to Garrison [13]
No. 46 Louis O. Cowan to William Lloyd Garrison

Augusta, June 21, 1834

Mr. William Lloyd Garrison

Sir,

... I perceive by your paper that Geo. Thompson Esq. of England is coming among us. The unparalleled success of his labors in his own country is a powerful recommendation of his talents and devotion to the cause of human liberty. I presume there will be many who will raise the cry of foreigner interfering in our domestic concerns. But is philanthropy confined by the boundaries of countries, or must it exert itself only within the limited sphere of neighbourhood limits. As you truly say that 'our country is the world and our countrymen all mankind' and the person who would raise such objections cannot be friends of human liberty!...

I am, Sir, very Respecty

Your Obt. Servt.

Louis O. Cowan.

MS.A.9.2. vol. 7 The Weston Papers [14]
No. 32 George Thompson to Robert Purvis

39 Mount Pleasant
Liverpool, August 9, 1834.

My dear friend

... I have seen the New York papers up to the 17. ultimo. The riots[1] prove nothing but the dispositions of a few thieves and ruffians to make the question of abolition a pretext for disorder that they may with impunity plunder of their property a few citizens and at the same time gratify their malicious prejudice against the colored population. All these things will work together for good. I hope & pray that the abolitionists may remain firm. These ebullitions will have their day – they will soon subside and all traces of these riots will be lost save in the infamy which will rest upon the heads of the unfortunates....

Your friend & brother

Geo. Thompson.

---

1. Many anti-slavery meetings at this time were broken up by mobs, the most serious riots being in Boston (see below), and in Philadelphia, when Pennsylvania Hall was burnt to the ground.

MS.A.1.2. vol. 4 1834 Anti-Slavery Letters to Garrison [15]
No. 59 George Thompson to William Lloyd Garrison

130 Nassau Street
New York – Sept. 24/34

My dear friend & brother–

I arrived upon your shores on Saturday last bringing with me Mrs. Thompson, and our dear children and our servant. I was warmly greeted by the abolitionists of this city, but somewhat anxiously received by the other dwellers in this the commercial metropolis of the *freest* empire under the sun. The particulars you shall have when we meet. They will bring another blush for your country upon your cheek – I long to see you and as soon as I can get through my business here intend to travel northward taking Boston in my way. Let me hear from you, if possible by return of post and give me your advice as to the best plan for the settlement of my family.

We had a pleasant voyage of 34 days and are all much improved in health. I have been delighted with all I have yet witnessed in this country save the conduct and disposition of its rational & accountable inhabitants. I feel that I could love this land and its people with all my heart were but oppression banished, and the language of all hearts this "The liberty we love we will bestow".

I find you are now a married man. May heaven help your union! Present my best respects to Mrs. Garrison whom I hope to see soon – I have been busy today at the Customs where all my anti-slavery luggage has been overhauled – a silver salver presented by the ladies of Glasgow to Miss Crandall attracted special attention.

In haste

Your affectionate friend
& devoted fellow Labourer

Geo: Thompson.

MS.A.1.2. vol. 4 Anti-Slavery Letters to Garrison [16]
No. 62 Thomas Fowell Buxton to William Lloyd Garrison

Cromer Sepr 30, 1834.

My dear friend:

I was very much obliged by your letter, introducing Mr. *Robert Purvis.* I much regretted that I did not see him on his first arrival, but I found that he almost immediately quitted London. I was there for two days last week & was so fortunate as to see him for a few moments – I think he told me that he sailed on the 4th of Oct.^{r} & as he offered to convey a letter to you – I must not lose todays post.

With respect to the protest against the Colonization Society, you tell me that the partizans of that cause have circulated the story, "that Wilberforce signed it when in the last stages of dissolution, unconscious of what he did." There is not, I assure you, one word of the truth in the report. He was apparently in good health at the time – in full possession of his faculties – & neither he nor his friends expected that his invaluable life was so near its close. He wrote me a letter enclosing the protest. I have sent it with a multitude of others, to his son, who is writing his life. If it were here, I would forward it to you, as the best of all proofs that the vigour of his understanding was not impaired. You are at liberty to make any use you please of this contradiction. We are now daily expecting intelligence from Jamaica, as to the way in which the first of August passed. You know that I had little confidence, or rather no confidence at all in the apprenticeship system. I trust it will speedily be supplanted by the simpler – the wiser – the more natural plan of labour for wages. In the interim, I fervently pray that there may be no convulsion in the colonies.

I have neither time nor room to tell you how anxiously, & with what deep feelings of interest we turn our eyes to the subject of slavery in America. I have long been intending to commit some observations on that great subject to paper for the purpose of circulation in America. Much business, & a variety of duties, public & private, have hitherto interfered; but I hope soon to begin that task. I know I must write so as not to [give] offence to your Countrymen; but between ourselves it is not easy to speak of the existence of slavery in your free states with moderation. It is, in fact, the most marvellous inconsistency that ever the world saw. My daughter was married on the first of August. My wife desires to be kindly remembered to you, for I assure you, I entertain a *very high* sense of your zeal & fidelity in our good cause.

Yrs. very truly, my dear friend,

T. Fowell Buxton.

MS.A.1.2. vol. 4 Anti-Slavery Letters to Garrison [17]
No. 71 George Thompson to George William Benson[1]

Mrs. Tappan's Boarding House
Roxbury, Near Boston, Nov. 1, 1834.

My dear Sir,

I wrote you on the 8th ultimo, stating my intention to be present at your anti Slavery meeting in Providence on the 14th inst. Since then, I have been earnestly requested to attend an anti slavery Convention for the State of New Hampshire, to be holden at Concord on the 11th. The friends here deem it very important that I should render all the assistance I can at the Convention, and have suggested the propriety of writing you, to enquire if your meeting could be *postponed for a week*, in which case not only could *I* be with you, but several able friends, who otherwise would be prevented. Will you consult the friends in your State, and make up your minds by Saturday next, on which day I shall pass through Providence on my way here from New York, and shall endeavour to stay a few hours with you?

---

1. George William Benson (1808-1879), a wool merchant of Providence, Rhode Island, was Garrison's brother-in-law, and an active anti-slavery worker.

Since my last, I have been eighteen days absent in the State of Maine: attending the State A.S. Convention in Augusta, and holding Meetings at Hallowell, Waterville, Brunswick, & Portland. I delivered about 10 lectures, besides many shorter addresses – The meetings are all numerously and respectably attended. Not the slightest approach to confusion was exhibited at any one of them. Many of them were distinguished by peculiar solemnity and deep feeling. I have been much delighted with this town and abundantly encouraged to go on with the work which I have entered.

"The best of all is, God is with us."
Yours very truly
Geo: Thompson.

Mr. Geo. Wm. Benson
Providence.

MS.A.9.2. vol. 7 The Weston Papers [18]
Nos. 40-41 George Thompson to Robert Purvis

Mrs. Tappan's Boarding House,
Roxbury near Boston,
Nov. 10, 1834.

My dear friend

...When we met in New York, we were both so hurried, that although there were many things to talk about, and some of them of much importance, we had no opportunity. I regret this, but trust that ere long, we shall meet again, & then enter fully into the present state of anti-slavery affairs. Our prospects are encouraging, but we have arrived at a juncture requiring special wisdom, zeal, & devotion. Every man must be at his post. None can be spared. No strength must be mis-directed or suffered to lie unemployed. *The coloured people claim our special attention.* They can greatly help *us* and help *themselves.* All then must fall into the ranks; become disciplined abolitionists & go forth to battle in consolidated array. Shame! upon any soldier, who, during the campaign, shall seek for ease, or ask for leave of absence. Disgrace and infamy rest on any who desert, however hot the strife, – however forlorn the expedition! We want *recruiting officers.* We want *Directing minds.* We want captains of *hundreds,* and captains of *fifties,* and captains of *tens. You* my friend must buckle on your armour – uplift your banner rally your forces, and onwards to the field. The *how* and the *where* we must discuss when we meet. – Before that pleasure arrives, however, there is one topic, which I must recommend to your prompt, kindly & anxious consideration. It is *the present state & prospects of the Liberator.* I have recently had a good deal of conversation with Mr. Garrison, and have been inexpressibly grieved to find that he seriously contemplates *giving up* that paper, in consequence of his inability to make it pay its expenses. He has a large number of subscribers but a very great many of them are in long arrears. There are upwards of $2000 outstanding subscriptions, which he knows not how to obtain, and for want of which, the paper is in danger of destruction. There are few things which would pain me so much as the *downfall of the*

Liberator. I am willing to strain every nerve & make every possible sacrifice to sustain it. I have just taken about 1,500 copies of various past dates, from the beginning of the present year, & have agreed to take 125 copies weekly from the first of January 1834. I have also got orders for 100 copies weekly in New York. There are *many powerful reasons why* the Liberator should be sustained, and sustained *efficiently*.

1. It is conducted with talent & zeal; & is guided by *thorough-going* abolition *principles*.

2. It is the *only* paper which unsparingly denounces *hypocrisy*, *meanness*, & expediency; & without respect of persons, exposes the naked deformities of the system at the South; & the wickedness & guilt of the *saintly prejudices* of the North.

3. It is highly probable that most of the apparent boldness of some other journals is attributed to the unflinching honesty, & retributive severity of the *Liberator* &, that if it were suffered to expire, they would fall below the mark of "*immediate abolition.*"

4. It is, as you well know, a paper that stands very high in G^{t} Britain; and if it were to sink, I know not what the friends there would think, nor what I should be able to say.

5. Lastly; it was the *first* paper which in *this country* blew the blast of immediate emancipation without expatriation, and called into life, & then valued, organised, and cheered onwards, the true friends of the coloured people, *enslaved & free*. And shall it *now sink?* Sink! Surrounded by thousands, who owe their first right views, & warm feelings, to its luminous reasonings; its glowing & irresistible appeals? Sink! when the principles it was the first manfully to enunciate & defend – & that too with the certain prospect of persecution, & poverty & contempt – have become widely recognised & made the bases of action?

Sink! while publications which started into being long after it had boldly braved the battle & the breeze, are living & flourishing by the advocacy of opinion copied from its pages?

Sink! at a period when we especially need it, as a beacon light to guard & guide our precious cause amidst the shallows, & whirlpools that surround it!

Sink! – No. It *must not* – it *shall not* sink. Forbid it, every feeling of gratitude, justice, & magnanimity in the breasts of true hearted American abolitionists. It must be rescued from danger, established & supported....

Come then my dear brother & fellow labourer join with me in holding up the hands of Wm. L. Garrison. Let us determine to relieve him from a weight of care & apprehension which like an incubus oppresses & paralyses him. Will you do what you can? Consult your friends. Get the paper as widely into circulation as possible. Get persons to become responsible for a certain number of copies [& etc.?]. Garrison is now attempting to make some arrangements with the New England Anti-Slavery Socy. upon the subject. He wants to get rid of the book-keeping, money-getting part of the business: & I think the sooner he does so, the better. Write him an encouraging letter

& say what it is likely may be done in Pennsylvania after the expiration of the present year.

It is likely I shall be in the City of New York in the first or second week in December for the purpose of delivering an address and doing other business. Could you meet me there for the purpose of going more fully into this & other matters? It is likely also that I shall be passing through Philadelphia at the end of December on my way to Washington to attend the meeting of the Colonisation Society. If so I shall expect the pleasure of an introduction through you to Mrs Purvis, Mr. Foster[1] & many other friends. In the meantime give my respects to all...

On Tuesday I attend a Convention at Concord N.H. On Saturday & Sunday I expect to be at Haverhill, Masss. On Wednesday the 19th I am to be at Providence. R.I. After that at Salem, & Lowell, Mass.

I feel happy in my work. I have already had abundant proofs that I have not laboured in vain. I am willing to spend and be spent in the hallowed undertaking. I thank God that I live in a day when the cause of humanity is finding friends & winning triumphs.

You will learn that many noble spirits have entered the field since you left. A Birney[2] & a Weld[3] are already engaged as agents in the cause & will go forth unfettered & inflamed to spend the holy fire that shall consume the scourges of oppression.

Write me immediately according to the address at the head of this. – Don't be offended at this long scrawl. I have written you out of the fulness of my heart, with all possible freedom because I esteem and love you, & because I believe *Your heart is as mine.*

May every blessing be yours! –
So prays your fellow labourer & affectionate friend

Geo. Thompson.

---

1. Stephen Symonds Foster (1809-1881) worked for several years as an anti-slavery agent and lecturer. He was a close friend of Garrison and shared all his radical views. After his marriage to Abby Kelly (see below) he settled on a farm near Worcester, Massachusetts, and though both continued to work for abolition, they were also active in promoting other reforms.

2. James Gillespie Birney (1792-1857) had been a well known Southern lawyer. Sympathetic to anti-slavery principles, he had first been an agent of the Colonization Society before being converted by Theodore Weld to immediate abolition. He worked with Weld in the 1830s as a lecturer, travelling through the Mid-West and New England, and allying himself with the American Anti-Slavery Society. In 1840 and 1844 he stood for office as the Presidential Candidate of the Liberty Party. He became an invalid in 1845 and spent the last years of his life in retirement. For an appreciation of his work see Dwight L. Dumond (ed.) *Letters of James Gillespie Birney, 1831-1857*, 2 vols. New York, 1938.

3. Theodore Dwight Weld (1803-1895) was one of the most influential of the Mid-West group of abolitionists. He toured the country in the 1830s as head of a band of lecturers, but his excessive modesty made him refuse any office in abolition circles. After 1840 he was particularly influential in guiding the work of the Washington Lobby, a political section of the anti-slavery movement. See G.H. Barnes, *The Anti-Slavery Impulse 1830-1844*, New York, 1933; and G.H. Barnes and D.L. Dumond (eds.), *Weld-Grimké Letters*, 2 vols. New York, 1934.

MS.A.1.2. vol. 5 Anti-Slavery Letters to Garrison [19]
No. 11 William Oakes to Samuel E. Sewall[1]

Ipswich Jany 30, 1835

Dear Sir,

...Mr. Thompson was sick & in poor condition when I heard of him at Salem. His personal appearance is very much against him as an orator, which proves the high character of his eloquence. He is no doubt a man of great & ready talents & possesses many & almost opposite qualifications of a public speaker – I doubt whether there is any person in the country better qualified to address a common audience. He will do us I think immense good. I fear that too much exercise & the climate, may at some time seriously injure his health....

Yours truly

Wm. Oakes

MS.A.1.2. vol. 5 Anti-Slavery Letters to Garrison [20]
No. 21 Henry E. Benson[1] *to George Benson*

New York City.
March 27th 1835

My dear Brother,

Agreably to my promise in a letter sent you yesterday, I set me down to give you a short description of my jaunt to the city of Philadelphia. We left here on Tuesday morn 17th inst by the steam boat and landed about 10 o'clock at Amboy – here we took the cars & travelled as far as Bordentown & again embarked upon a steam boat on the Delaware & sailed down the River. Landed at Philadelphia between 3 & 4 in the aft. Our party consisted of Garrison, Thompson, Ibbotson,[2] Cambell, and Dr. Cox.[3] We had a very warm discussion going down the Delaware. Slaveholders and colonizationists, the genuine negro haters, opposed us. It resulted as it begun, by both parties being satisfied with their own opinions.

Thompson went to the house of Abraham L Pennock a wealthy orthodox friend, Garrison to friend Motts & I took up my abode with Mr. Purvis. During our stay we all experienced the utmost kindness at the hands of our many friends. On the

---

1. Samuel Edmund Sewall (1799-1888), a prominent Boston Lawyer, had been one of the founders of the N.E.A.S.S., and was a close friend of Garrison until 1840 when he joined the Liberty Party. He later appeared in several fugitive slave cases, as the advocate of the runaways.

1. Henry Egbert Benson (1814-1837) was the brother of George Benson, and the close friend and brother-in-law of Garrison. He too was active in the cause.
2. Probably Henry Ibbotson, a merchant of Sheffield, England, a friend of Thompson and who was at this time living in New York City.
3. Dr. Samuel Hanson Cox (1793-1881), a Presbyterian minister in New York City, had joined the A.A.S.S. after a visit to Britain in 1832, and was for a time one of the most notable clerical opponents of slavery. He soon withdrew his support from the movement, however, and devoted himself to theological studies, serving on the faculties of Auburn Theological Seminary and Union Theological Seminary.

same evening we all met at the house of Mr. James Forten.[4] I was much pleased with his family. They inquired after you (as did many of your friends) and wanted to know if you *arrived at Boston in time to get married!* – You will recollect your hasty departure at the time of the convention. Here a large number of our friends has assembled.

I saw while there the widow of the lamented Evan Lewis[5] – Mrs. *More*[6] a real driver in the Anti Slavery cause. Mrs. Lucretia Mott a lovely woman & her husband[7] – the meek & kindhearted Lydia White.[8] The walking antiquity – Joshua Coffin[9] – the index of the past, the present & to come. Dr. Atlee, a timid but amiable man – Thos Shipley the signer of the Declaration.[10] Mr. Sutcliffe another signer of the instrument from Ohio. Arnold Buffum, who has lately invented a wheel for a steam engine on the rotary motion which he says will work well – and for which he says he shall obtain a patent and be enabled to give the anti slavery cause five thousand pounds! He is sure of success & has employed Trip formerly of Providence to manufacture a small engine promising if he succeeds to give him five thousand Dollars. Both are looking out for an immense fortune!! I also saw Miss Grimké[11] a sister of the late Thos. S. of South Carolina. She is a stiff orthodox quaker about 35 years old, but gave Garrison 50 dollars for the cause. I saw two of the sisters of Dr. Cox, who are fine women, & Hicksite preachers. I mention the above concluding you are aquainted with most of them.

---

4. James Forten (1766-1842) was a wealthy and influential coloured businessman of Philadelphia. His daughter married Robert Purvis.

5. Evan Lewis (1782-1834) was a Pennsylvania Quaker who had played a leading part in the organization of the A.A.S.S.

6. Possibly Esther Moore (c.1774-1854) a Philadelphia Quaker.

7. James Mott (1788-1868) was a Quaker Philanthropist, and, with his wife, Lucretia Coffin Mott (1793-1880), a leader of the Philadelphia anti-slavery circle. Lucretia Mott was famous as a Hicksite preacher in Quaker meetings and took also a deep interest in women's rights – her views on this subject influencing many important leaders of the feminist movement, especially Elizabeth Cady Stanton. Both the Motts visited Britain in 1840 to attend the 1840 Anti-Slavery Convention; James Mott subsequently publishing his account: *Three Months in Great Britain*, Philadelphia, 1841; while Lucretia's diary of the event has recently been edited and published; *Slavery and the Woman Question* (ed. Frederick B. Tolles, Supplement no. 23 of the *Journal of the Friends Historical Society*).

8. Lydia White was another of the Philadelphia Quaker circle. She was active in the Free Produce Association.

9. Joshua Coffin (1792-1864), the historian of Newbury, Massachusetts, was an active member of the N.E.A.S.S.

10. Dr. Edwin P. Atlee (c.1799-1836) and Thomas Shipley (1787-1836) were active in Philadelphia anti-slavery circles, and in the formation of the American Anti-Slavery Society, Shipley signing the Declaration of Sentiments in which the society set forth its principles.

11. Sarah Moore Grimké (1792-1873) came from a prominent South Carolina family, but with her sister Angelina (1805-1879) left the South, adopted the Quaker faith, and became a staunch abolitionist. The conversion of "Carolina's high souled daughters" was much heralded in anti-slavery circles; Garrison became their friend, and under his guidance they began to lecture publicly on anti-slavery among the first women to take this step. This action roused great controversy, particularly in New England where they undertook their work; but shortly after Angelina's marriage to Theodore Weld in 1838 both sisters abandoned their public career.

Wednesday Eve – Thompson lectured in the Cherry Street Presbyterian meeting house. A large audience present who cheered him *not withstanding* the expressed wish of the Quakers to the contrary. The cause must come out of their hands – save a dozen, not one of the Quakers there will ever do any good to the cause, but but rather retard it. They are altogether too *pharasaical* – one cannot attend our meetings, because they *applaud* – another because Thompson makes too long prayers – and a third because he uses *warlike* figures in expressing his ideas.

Thursday Eve. Present at friend Buffums, a very large & interesting assemblage of the friends of our cause.

Friday Eve. Thompson commenced a lecture on St. Domingo in the same place as on the former evening. When the address was half through there was a simultaneous rush from under the galleries towards the centre of the house. Some cried fire – others that a mob had come – One went through the window – sash & all was followed by a man and woman – Everything in confusion – Some fainted – some shouted – others were drunk with fear – I sat on the pulpit stairs where I could witness it all. As soon as order was restored & about half the audience had returned, it was stated that the gall[er]ies owing to the immense pressure upon them had settled some inches, the noise of which caused the rush above mentioned. None were hurt. It is well the people in the galleries kept quiet – they were not aware of the cause. Had they rushed towards the door, they must inevitably have fallen & those below crushed to death. The meeting then quietly adjourned.

Saturday aft he addressed the ladies in a school room 60 were added to the Society.

Sunday evening he delivered an admirable address to the colored people in the Bethel Church. About three thousand were present – all colored. It was a very interesting meeting.

On Monday evening the friends assembled at Dr. Parishes & on Tuesday evening at Thomas Shipleys. These meetings were highly interesting. On neither of the two last named evenings could a place be obtained for a public meeting. Returned on Wednesday & took up our abode at the house of Mr. John Rankin[12] a kind & generous friend of our cause. Garrison is in Brooklyn and Thompson left here for there this aft by way of Norwich. He expects to be here by Tuesday night, and before if possible. Dr. Cox & Leavitt[13] you knew were appointed delegates to England. The former cannot get released from an engagement at the Auburn Seminary – where he is to go as professor, so neither will go.

---

12. John Rankin (1793-1886) was active in anti-slavery circles in New York City.
13. Rev. Joshua Leavitt (1794-1873) lectured on various reforms including women's rights and free trade, but was especially active in the anti-slavery field. A member of the Tappan circle, he edited the New York *Evangelist*, the *Emancipator*, and later the *Independent*. He supported political action as a means of achieving emancipation; helped to form the Liberty Party, and was a member of the Washington Lobby.

Judge Jay's admirable book[14] is for sale, hope you will have them in Providence soon. Do say where Mary Pearson's lives when you write again.

The friends of the cause in Philadelphia gave upwards of $500 towards paying off the old debts of the Liberator. I expect Brother Garrison will soon stand on a good foundation as regards pecuniary affairs....

I have not written home of late but have sent them two living Epistles in the shape of Thompson & Garrison. Farewell – Burn this hasty scrawl & write soon to your affectionate brother.

Henry E. Benson

Geo. W. Benson.

MS.A.4.1. The Child Papers [21]
No. 43 ? to David Lee Child[1]

Canaan N. H. Oct. 8 1835

Dear Sir,

X Will slaveholding be given up in Texas without a bloody contest to retain it? I think not, and will not Santa Anna have to contend with fearful odds for its suppression? Texas is becoming daily more & more important as it respects American slavery. Its continuance there in my humble opinion settles its continuance in the United States. See the interest that begins to be manifested in its concerns in the Southern & South-western newspapers, the one in the New Orleans The American of the 15th ult calling on the Lynchmen, particularly of the Western States, to assist *their brethren & fellow citizens*, the Texanians, in case of a war with Santa Anna. The security & perpetuity of American slavery depend upon the possession of Texas by slaveholders. That country free & capable of self defence, would *indeed* be an asylum of oppressed humanity. The house of bondage would be a little too near the land of freedom, for the easy retention of its inmates. A smart likely young male negro would hardly be worth twelve or fourteen hundred dollars in [Redrium ?] valley, if a land almost in sight would convert him from a chattel – a brute – to a man. Why the fearful odds? Such is the rage among the slave-holders of the South & the dough faces of the north for slavery, that if Texas can not be obtained by purchase our Govt. will pick a quarrel about a boundary or something else with the Mexican govt., pounce upon it, take & claim it by conquest. Why sir it is as plain as the nose in your face, that nothing but a

---

14. *An Inquiry into the Character and Tendency of the American Colonization and American Anti-Slavery Societies*, New York, 1835. William Jay (1789-1858) the author of this and other works on anti-slavery, was a judge and social reformer who ruined a career in law by his championship of the anti-slavery cause. He was a member of the Tappan circle and active in the reform movements of the day.

1. David Lee Child (1794-1874) was one of the earliest members of the New England Anti-Slavery Society, though he was never wholly sympathetic to Garrison. With his wife, Lydia Maria Child (1802-1880), he engaged in anti-slavery journalism, and was for a short time editor of the *Anti-Slavery Standard.*

continual extention of territory can secure the continuance of slavery. Texas obtained & incorporated into this govt. in half a century at farthest, Mexico herself will be swallowed up by the rapacious monster – American slavery – far distant then will be the day when slavery will find the limit of profitable employment & work its own destruction by a superabundance of slaves. Why was Louisiana purchased & then the Floridas, and why must Texas now be faught or conquered? Clearly for the benefit of slavery for a [?] No other motive operates for the purchase of Louisiana & the Floridas, & none other now operates for the acquisition of Texas. What would slaves be worth in Virginia & the old slave states, if they could not sell or send them out of their limits? Nothing – aye worse than that – they would be a burden – an intolerable tax – Hence the slave states would sooner consent to the entire, immediate, & unconditional emancipation of their slaves, than to the suppression of the domestic slave trade. Southern statesmen never gave the true reason for the purchases named, & northern honesty & stupidity could never discover it. Abolition has brought to light the cunning craftiness of the south. But too late. There is not virtue enough remaining at the North to be benefitted by the discovery. What then is to prevent the interminableness of American slavery? The possession of Texas by Great Britain. It would be a splendid dependency – of more importance to her by far than any other of her transatlantic possessions – a source of revenue, instead of a bill of expense, as most of her colonies are. It would open a most inviting field for the surplus population of her West Indian Islands – two hundred thousand no doubt these now beyond the point of profitable employment – & an extensive & brilliant market for her manufactures. But after all I am too much of an American to wish that Great Britain should become the [possessor ?] of it. As an enemy she has too many points of annoyance now about us to allow the indulgence of such a wish, perhaps – if she were I do not know that she could hold it. Southern cupidity would call the nations to arms against the possession, & northern fear would respond to the call lest a non-compliance should disolve the Union. It would be a retreat for runaway slaves & hence an alleged legitimate cause of war. If Bermuda were within gun-shot, would she not have to take it, for her temerity in touching Southern chivalry in so tender a point as she did? Thank you for your Sept 29th & for the interest you take in my affairs. You will probably see Mr. [Scoble ?] & receive a letter by him from me before this reaches you. Hope to hear from you soon. Tell Mrs. Child that when I am rich enough I will give her a handsome salary to be my neighbour

Very truly

?

Look at a map again & see its extent of boundary upon slaveholding.

MS.A.4.1. The Child Papers [22]
No. 44 David Lee Child to E.S. Abdy[1]

New York Oct. 22d. 1835.

My dear Friend,

Since I wrote you on the 5th ult, the Texas drama has opened in good earnest, and act first scene 2d is proceeding. The first scene was the lately address and protestation of the settlers to Santa Anna that their intentions were perfectly loyal & pacific. I knew better, and that this was only a *ruse* de guerre to stay the preparations against them. Santa Anna I am informed on the highest authority was not deluded but went steadily forward. Then the masks disguise was thrown aside & the second scene now commences with a convention or congress of Delegates from all parts of Texas, the object of which is stated to declare the territory *independent* of Mexico. This is in itself nothing, but there is that behind the scenes which is serious. They will have help from the U.S. to any extent required for resisting destroying the Mexican forces. Already a New Orleans paper has sounded summons to the Lynchmen of the whole South West to come to the rescue of their *brethren*, the Texians. This I think will be the form in which assistance will in the first instance be given & voluntary squadrons with secret countenance & assurances from the President of [the] U.S. But for this the late convention in Texas (Oct. 15) would not have been held. To facilitate the [fatal?] usurpation contemplated, it appears that Jackson did some time ago obtain a cession from certain Indians, of a portion of their territory *within the limits of the State of Texas.* Thus while Jackson is denying to the Indian tribes within the limits of any state of U.S. all right not only to sovreignity but also to the soil, is expelling them (& here I am humbled to say it) from their heretage, & their [improved?] homes of their childhood, he is affecting to treat with Mexican tribes as perfectly independent nations & purchasing of them the rights both of sovreignty and soil. Can any one fail to see for what object this color of a title has been obtained?

That object is now to be arrived at more directly by patronizing the intruding, law breaking & voracious, treacherous rebels of Texas. And the war, my excellent friend, will be a war of color. It is first to preserve unlawful negro slaves now in Texas; *secondly* to send lawfully [?] negro slaves there; & thirdly to wrest territory from a nation despised by Anglo-Americans partly on account of the approximation of their complexion to the negro & their contempt of distinction founded on complexion but above all their sympathy at the same time with the colored races. How shocking & how shallow. I feel disposed to quarrel with old England for not bringing us up better....

---

1. Edward Strutt Abdy (1791-1846) was a fellow of Jesus College, Cambridge. He visited America from 1833 to 1834 and published his *Journal of a Residence and Tour in the United States of North America from April, 1833 to October 1834,* 3 vols. London, 1838. His visit was coloured by his strong anti-slavery feelings, which were strengthened by a meeting with Garrison, just before the latter sailed for England on his first visit to that country.

To other motives which strongly impel the South to this enterprise is that of preventing Texas from becoming a refuge of runaway slaves. Many have escaped from Louisiana, and found safety not in Texas, because I believe they pursue and take them without ceremony where the population is principally American, but in the adjoining state of [Tomenclipas?]. I lately heard from a gentleman who is lately come from that state the following incident. Fifteen slave [?] a Parish or county of Louisiana, determined to fly from bondage. They provided themselves with arms and rations, and in the night mounted their masters horses and set off. The next morning their flight was discovered and [a] strong party of planters & overseers started in pursuit. After riding far into Texas they came in sight of the fugitives and animated at the sight, they spurred their horses forward with redoubled speed. The negroes kept a good lookout, and then instead of flying faster faced about and stood firm with arms in hand. At this the pursuing party slackened their pace and soon halted. Those fellows are going to fight [??] I know him well who commands them & if they are all like him we shall have a hard time of it. At this time the slaves began to move slowly and in good order toward their [?] masters, and they turned to retreat, whereupon the late fugitives now the pursuers, accelerated their pace. The runaways did so too, and directly both parties were in full race. After the whites had disappeared, the negroes turned and pursued their way. They arrived at Matamoras on the river del Norte are now settled, & flourishing in that neighbourhood. To illustrate further the power of this fear of losing slaves by elopement I would remind you of the applications, which have been made by our government to yours to stop the escape of slaves to Canada, by surrendering up the fugitives to their masters. When the Treaty for the purchase of Florida (a treaty originating on previous invasions by Gen. Jackson, & in the fear on the part of Spain of a renewal of them), it was stated in a secret session of the House of Representatives, that this province must be had, otherwise the [Georgians?] would take it, for that the President had recd. one hundred and fifty letters from the inhabitants of that state, declaring that so many of their slaves ran away and found refuge there, and were protected & formed into soldiers by the Spaniards that [they?] were resolved to endure it no longer.

These materials will enable you to judge how necessary it is that the English abolitionists should not sleep at this crisis. I think some important events will fall out before this reaches you. My reliance is on British philanthropists and their government which is fortunately under the administration of the US. abolitionists.

I will add to my own views an extract from a letter just received from a gentleman who has paid much attention to this question.

I dissent entirely from my friends to the policy of making Texas a British possession. It would disturb the peace of both our continents besides being a Utopian concept in itself. Magnanimous Britain must protect Mexico, if necessary and make no conquest but that of the devout gratitude of that nation and of all good men. This will be better aye, and more profitable also than the possession of Texas. Her manufacturers and her emigrants would find a reception there as well and more widely without than with the ownership of the province. When I write again I shall speak more of private matter – Meantime I will observe that our departure for Eng[land] is postponed until January for the cause which I mentioned in my short letter of August 16th. Ever your affect^{e} friend

D.L. Child

(To E^{d} S. Abdy Esq.)

MS.A.9.2. vol. 7 The Weston Papers [23]
No. 70 Deborah Weston[1] *to Mary Weston*[1]

Thursday noon (October 22, 1835).

Dear Aunt Mary,

Oh such an afternoon as we passed yesterday! the morning was bad enough, but the hour between 5 & 6 was the most distressing & exciting & [sic] I ever passed in my life! Then was the time that we heard that Garrison was in the hands of the mob with his clothes all torn off and a rope around his neck. I staid at home & kept school, with not the least feeling in my hands & feet. Not one of the girls having the slightest suspicion of what was going on; I was very much on my guard & trust there was no apparent difference in my manner. I called at Maria's[1] at noon, & found Maria very calm & composed but very *resolved.* Henry[1] was wonderfully supported & did manfully, except that he was considerably frightened for his wife's personal safety. He insisted upon going to the meeting. Warren[1] came home to tea with the news that Garrison was safe in jail, rescued as it was reported by an enormous truckman of the name of Aaron Cooley, who took him up in his arms & lifted him as high as he could & trampled through the crowd with all fury. Sarah Ann has just called with her story to tell. I should think by her that Mr. Bailey was the one that saved Garrison, at any rate he stood by him all the time & helped dress him when they got him into the city hall, broke a man's arm with his umbrella in his defence & was one of the men who brought round the carriage.

Caroline[1] will give you a full account of the meeting. I never saw Anne so over-whelmed in my life, the whole society had borne it admirably, the most quiet & perfect composure of demeanour was maintained by them all. Mary Parker's[2] voice was as clear & as firm as ever when she made the opening prayer & what was done was done "decently & in order." As soon as tea was over Warren went off to see what was going on, things seemed to be quieting down in town so he came back to Maria's, thinking if there was anything going on it would be done there, Henry went down to Chauncey Place to comfort them & Maria & Warren were left alone. Henry had hardly gone when there was a ring & two gentlemen wished to see Mr. Chapman. Maria invited them both in to wait for Mr. C. & they introduced them-

---

1. See Weston-Chapman family tree, Appendix I.
2. Mary Parker (1802-41) was the President of the Boston Female Anti-Slavery Society.

selves as Daniel Parkman & Edward Prescott. They came thinking that Thompson was there to advise his instant removal. I speak says Prescott as a *man* just from a mob. And I listen says Maria as a *woman* just from a mob. They had a long talk & took their departure with many protestations of friendship. There had been a cry of "to West Street" a good many times among the mob, they had hardly gone when 4 men came who proved to be Homer of the Commercial, Henry Williams, a Mr. Davenport & one other man. Maria says the Lord delivered them into her hand. They staid till ½ past 11. She giving it to them all the time. Warren was in such a state of exaltation when we got home that we concluded he must have had a lovely mob. Maria called this morning & said that she had never had such a delightful time in her life. She had said everything she wanted to. Melania[3] called this morning & said that they expected that Maria's house was going all last night; for that David their man told them that the cry was repeatedly raised among the mob "to West Street, Chapman's opposite Homer's stable." Thompson's picture & little Lizzy & Henry were sent off. Homer was rather startled when he found that they had sent off their children. We have no doubt that they came from the mob to see if Thompson were there. Caroline & Anne will both write, so I have written at random anything I could think of first. Henry bears this manfully. Caroline says she cannot finish her letter in time for she has just begun to write it. It will come by mail tomorrow morning. It is near 4 so I must close.

Yours in love

Debora Weston

Caroline will tell you about the meeting, they adjourned to Maria's Anne is now at Mr. Bailey's.

MS.A.1.2. vol. 5 1835 Anti-Slavery Letters to Garrison [24]
No. 60 George Thompson to William Lloyd Garrison

Marblehead beach – Thursday afternoon,
Oct. 22, 1835.

My beloved brother Garrison:

The news has reached me of yesterday's proceedings in Boston. I rejoice that you have escaped the jaws of the lion, and are yet among the living – the living to praise God. To Him let us render our humble acknowledgements. May you be sustained under your present afflictions, & survive to behold the triumph of those principles which you can have for some years lived only to advocate! I sympathise with you, & every sufferer in our holy cause, and could almost envy you the honour of having been assailed by a blood-thirsty multitude. Put your trust in that Being who smiles at the wrath of men, & will

3. Melania Ammidon was another leading member of the Boston Female Anti-Slavery Society.

cause it to advance his glory. After all, what have our enemies done? What have their tar & feathers, their demolitions, their lacerations, scourgings & hangings effected? Have they extinguished *the truth?* No. Have they shaken our *principles?* No. Have they proved *wrong* to be *right; falsehood, truth; cruelty, kindness;* or *slavery, liberty?* No.... Our *principles live*, & are triumphing in every direction. The God of the American slave sits high on his throne, counting the sighs & groans of his people, and will come down to deliver. Abolitionists live, and multiply, & daily wax stronger & stronger in the work of mercy they have laid hold upon, nor can any scourges our enemies can plait, nor any gibbets they can erect, be aught but the emblems of their own insinuation and madness.

I think I can see the end of these outbreakings. The opposers of this cause have themselves a bitter lesson to learn. They will rouse a spirit which will speedily turn to rend them, when it is too late to prevent it. Let them make mob-law paramount to all other law, and those respectable instigators will at no distant day be destroyed by the recoil of their own weapons.

Our cause advances rapidly, majestically, & gloriously – Who can stay its course?

I have not time to write more. My heart is with you. As the soul of Jonathan was knit to the soul of David, so is my soul to your soul. Your joys, sorrows, perils, persecutions, friends & foes are mine. May God direct us in this crisis, & enable us with meekness & wisdom to do his perfect will, & cheerfully suffer everything which awaits us.

Your unalterably attached friend & brother,

Geo. Thompson.

MS.A.9.2. vol. 7 1798-1835 The Weston Papers [25]
No. 71 Anne Warren Weston[1] *to Mary Weston*

Oct. 27. 1835.
Tuesday morning.

Dear Aunt Mary,

I had a very pleasant & short ride into town for Mr. K. took the shortest & most direct road. I found them all in as good a state as could be expected. I enclose a note which would have come to me Saturday night if Polly had come. Also I send the Liberator which did not get out till Monday; as they were warned directly out of the building, and had to move not having any lease. Where the Liberator press is we cant tell, but it is somewhere or other printing away. I think it is a very good Liberator indeed except Burleigh's account of the mob. He has not made it half bad enough, but Garrison will put that all right when he comes back. When that will be I do not know, but hope soon. Saturday afternoon Maria went down to see

1. See Weston-Chapman family tree, Appendix I.

Thompson with Brethren Fuller[2] Southwick,[3] & Tillson.[4] He has been obliged tc leave Lynn, so great is the uproar there, and he & family have moved to a place near Salem, called Northfields or North Shields, to the house of one Spencer, a devoted friend of the cause. Spencer has sent to Boston & changed his own horse & chaise so that it may not be known, & has it hid away in his barn; in order to flee with Thomson in case of alarm. Different clothes are prepared also for him to slip on in a minute. You see by this that he is looked upon as in great danger. Maria saw him but a short time, but said that he never appeared in better spirits. He mourned someone, Garrison, but thought it would be all for the best. We said that when he should relate things to the crowded audiences of England they would be all in tears at the recital. Maris said Mrs T. never appeared so well; she was very glad to see her, kissed her & really appeared quite interesting. Keep this fact as to Thompson's retreat all to yourself, for it is private even among the brethren. Maria hopes that things will be so that he can come to Weymouth. At any rate, you go on stirring up the Emancipation Society & we will see what we can do. It is reported & believed in Boston that he has sailed for England, that he was last Thursday in Newport in the *disguise of a woman* & what else I know not. There is not yet that state of feeling in Boston that I had hoped. *There is great fear among the brethren* and all the resisters are gone. Amasa Walker[5] *has flinched* altogether. It is said he will not have an abolition paper in his house, but that I hope is false. At any rate, keep it all to yourself. Conceal the conduct of the brethren as much as possible. There was no monthly concert last night as there was no place to hold it but 46, & they were afraid to risk that as it is the only place now left for a.s. folks to meet together in. I think this was very wrong in them, for I would have removed the most valuable of the books & run the risque But Deacon Gulliver *omitted* to give notice at the Free Church, *not daring* to do so. The Deacon is I think a perfect coward, not daring to peep these times. Debora went to the Free Church part of the day, but was so provoked she could scarcely stay. No notice was taken of the events of the week or any sound abolition preached. To say the truth I know not where I shall go to church, for *there* I will not go unless they amend. Brother Wright at the Mission House preached the only suitable sermon that was preached in town....

(Unsigned – A.W.W.)

---

2. Probably John E. Fuller who had helped to found the N.E.A.S.S., but later broke with Garrison and joined the conservative Massachusetts Abolition Society.

3. Joseph Southwick (c.1781-1866) was a Massachusetts Quaker. He had attended the first meeting of the A.A.S.S. at Philadelphia and signed the Declaration of Sentiments. He took an active part in the N.E.A.S.S.

4. Joseph Tillson was another member of the N.E.A.S.S. who later broke with Garrison and joined the Massachusetts Abolition Society.

5. Amasa Walker (1799-1876) was originally a businessman, but his interest in anti-slavery led him to become Professor of Political Economy at Oberlin in 1842. He later worked for the Free Soil Party, was active in politics, and was a voluminous writer.

MS.A.1.2. vol. 5 Anti-Slavery Letters to Garrison [26]
No. 71 George Thompson to Henry Clarke Wright[1]

Boston, Thursday, Nov. 5. 1835

My dear friend & brother/

...You have so often heard me speak out my sentiments in reference to the slavery of this country that I need not in this communication attempt any exposition. The *end* I seek; the *principles* upon which I proceed; – the high, catholic, & missionary ground upon which I justify my country to America – the *measures* I recommend – the course I have pursued; my views of expediency, consequently the amount of deference to be paid to what is called *public opinion*, &c, are all known together – would they were known to all! You know that all my views, principles, plans & purposes as far as they have been revealed (and it would be impossible to pursue a more *open* course) have been founded on the *word of God*, and like that word, consistent with the peace, safety, and salvation alike, of the oppressor and oppressed.

You do me but justice in believing that I am the friend of the land over which you are weeping. I do believe myself to be the friend of America. I could fearlessly drag forth from the deepest recessof my soul the worst wish I cherish for this people, and submit it, in the light of heaven and eternity, to the judgement of the most jealous patriot that ever yearned over the interests of this republic. I look with inexpressible grief upon the doings of those who boast their attachment to "the Union," "the Constitution," the good and glory of the nation &c. I see them violating every wholesome law – trampling down every heaven-born, fire-side right, and leading a hoodwinked multitude to commit a suicidal act upon their own liberties.

I would fain have awakened the citizens of America to a just apprehension of what makes for the honor, happiness, & safety of the Union – the welfare of *all* Columbia's sons – nay the continuance of a free government upon this Continent, but alas, alas! the truth has proved too bitter – he who in Christian kindness bore it to these shores and braves every danger to proclaim it, has been branded as a felon and a foe, and is driven back to the country from which he came, to tell the sad story that, the arms of America are open to all foreigners *but* those who bring *the truth*, and in the spirit of the Gospel cry aloud against the sinking sins of the people.

Think not however I despond in reference to the onward progress of the cause. No – I never cherished a brighter hope of the redemption of the land than *now.* The country is awake ... America can *sleep no more* – the Church already bows before the Lord arrayed in the garments of repentance. I see a bow in the clouds and my heart exults in the ultimate triumph

---

1. Henry Clarke Wright (1797-1839) was one of the most unorthodox of the Garrison abolitionists, and possibly influenced Garrison in some of his more extreme views. Throughout his career as an anti-slavery lecturer, his championship of "no-human government," "non-resistance" and Anti-Sabbath doctrines created extreme public opposition and division in the anti-slavery ranks. He made a visit to Britain from 1843 to 1846 when he was chiefly responsible for raising public opinion against the acceptance of money by the Free Church of Scotland from Presbyterians in the Southern States of America.

which the friends of the slave are ordained to achieve in the truly sublime contest upon which in the strength of Jehovah they have entered. I see the negro exalted high above the heads of the people, the object of universal attention, and I feel a conviction that the gaze of the nation can never be withdrawn, nor the tongue of his advocate be silenced, till his fetters are riven, and the sighing of the prisoner, and the stern accents of insulted justice, are changed for the song of triumphant mercy, and the swelling anthem of a *free people!* Haste Glorious day! amen ....

Believe me when I say, that wherever I may be; I shall ever be the friend of America. Though I speak of her sins, it will be in love

> Nay, shrink not, for it must be told,
> Columbia's sons are *bought & sold!*

Europe must be made acquainted with the inconsistencies & sins of the country, the one loud lasting peal of remonstrance may break upon the ear of the oppressor, and what cannot be effected by an appeal to humanity, be obtained by the operations of wounded pride.

With high esteem
& grateful affection

Your friend & brother

Geo: Thompson.

MS.A.1.1. vol. 1 Anti-Slavery Letters from Garrison [27]
No. 80 William Lloyd Garrison to his wife

Boston, Nov. 9, 1835.

My dear Wife:

Yesterday (Sabbath) forenoon, I concluded not to go to church, because, to confess the truth, I had not replaced my torn pantaloons, and as the weather was too warm to justify the wearing of a cloak. About eleven o'clock, one of Mrs. Southwick's daughters came down to our house, and gave me the startling information that my dear friend Thompson would leave the country in the course of an hour – that he was going to sail in a packet for St. John – and that he wished to see me immediately. Of course, I went in all haste and with much trepidation; for the idea of separating from him – perhaps till the close of life – filled my soul with anguish. I found his wife in tears; she could not go with him, and no doubt felt somewhat unhappy. She is to visit her sister at Baltimore, and will then sail for England. My heart swells with sorrow, my cheeks burn with indignation, when I think of the treatment which Thompson has received at the hands of the people of this country. If he were a murderer, or a parricide, he could not be treated more shamefully than he has been. To think of his being in danger of assassination, even in broad daylight – nay, even in the streets of Boston! Shame – infamy upon the city! But I have no time to moralise – but you will feel deeply, without the aid of my comments. Suffice it to say, Mr. Chapman took Mr. T. down to the wharf in a carriage, saw him safely on board the packet, and the vessel move down the harbor. So we trust he is now on his way to a place of safety and rest. From

St. John he will sail for England. Mr. Knapp will probably go down to him, to convey his baggage safely.

Our election, today, has passed off quietly. Several votes have been cast for me, but how many is not yet known. We have not been disturbed at the house, and I walk through the city without receiving any insult.

I have no lamp – and it is so dark (I am writing at the office) that I cannot see to write more. I am in very good health and spirits, and hope you and the rest of the household are in a similar condition.

Adieu! ever yours,

W.L. Garrison.

MS.A.1.2. vol. 5 Anti-Slavery Letters to Garrison [28]
No. 73 George Thompson to William Lloyd Garrison

St. John, New Brunswick,
November 25. 1835.

My dear brother,

The time fixed for my departure from this place, and this Continent is three o'clk this afternoon, and I must therefore be very brief in my communication having yet many dear friends to write to.

I cannot as yet reply to your truly valuable communications as they deserve. You must permit me to delay until I reach my native shores – then I trust to be able to find time to discuss at large the important topics adverted to in your several favours. For the present, let me say, *that your views are precisely mine.* I have generally endeavoured to put the most favourable construction upon the *letter* of the Constitution, although I ever deemed it *a bartering away in perpetuity the rights* – the heaven originated rights of the home-born sons and daughters of Columbia. Soon after I arrived, (at Augusta, Maine) I went fully into the discussion of the spirit, character, and consequences of "*the compact*". and developed your views almost precisely, but some friends, to whose judgment I felt bound to defer, thought it would be sound policy to leave to *native Citizens of America* the duty of holding up "*the instrument*" in its true light. I rejoice you have laid hold upon the subject Let me exhort you to keep there. I like division of labor – be it *your work* to display the essential wickedness of a document brought forward in the revolutionary struggle to form the basis upon which every national institution should be reared, which violated every principle maintained in that struggle, and left without law, without liberty, without protection, without compassion, one sixth portion of the immortal population of the land to herd, propagate, labor & die amongst the beasts of the field, the human cattle – the rational non-entities of free, equal, enlightened, independent, Christian America!!

A little while and I shall be upon the billows – less turbulent & cruel in their most angry form, than the gentlemen of property and standing in the U.S. from the knife of whose hired myrmidons I go to find shelter and a field for unobstructed labor in the cause of God & bleeding humanity. In leaving America

I consulted *usefulness* – not *safety*. Understand me. I believe my life was sought. I believe many were prepared to take it – many were prepared to rejoice over the deed: and I left your country under the conviction that I could not go abroad without the almost certain prospect of death – but still, had there been reason to believe, that by staying, & falling on your soil, I should thereby have done the will of God, and the best thing to advance the cause, I trust I should not have hesitated to remain & be offered up. The finger of Providence seemed to point to Great Britain as a scene of labor not to be neglected for the problematical good which a longer continuance in the U.S. might effect – *There* was a field wide, open, secure, rich, waving already, white unto the harvest – the public in the fittest possible state to receive the information I had collected, & the appeals I was qualified to found upon that evidence. After viewing the matter deliberately, and I trust prayerfully, I came to the decision that the path of duty lay across the waters, and then, through the length & breadth of the kingdom, publishing everywhere the wrongs of the American Slave, and calling upon man, woman, & child, to join in one united and overwhelming remonstrace against the unmatched wickedness of American slavery.

Let me hear from you often when I reach England. Give your letters to Mr. Benson to direct them to John Scoble Esq. 18 Aldermanbury, London.

My thanks for the Whigs – they will do good service – can you not collect and send me some more?

I will write you soon

Yours very affectionately

Geo: Thompson.

MS.A.1.2. vol. 6 1836-1837 Anti-Slavery Letters to Garrison [29]
No. 29 Thomas Price[1] *to William Lloyd Garrison*

London Sepr 19. 1836.

My dear Sir,

Though my personal acquaintance with you during your visit to England was very limited, I have never failed to regard your [?] with the deepest interest; & to commend you & your noble associates to the protection & guidance of the father of the spirits of all flesh. In order to make known your principles & proceedings, your sufferings & their noble endurance to the [?] people of this country I have commenced a small periodical the first three numbers of which I now send you. A deep & thrilling [?] of interest is felt throughout Britain in your movements. In their intrepidity, amplitude, & [?] integrity we recognize the proofs of a divine impulse & for that success we daily bless the God of our Salvation. May you still be helped from above with all wisdom, patience & fidelity, that under God you may become

1. Rev. Thomas Price, editor of the *Eclectic Review* and a Baptist minister, had met Garrison on his visit to Britain in 1833. Price wrote various articles chiefly on West Indian slavery.

the instruments of rescuing your country from the deepest guilt, & our holy religion from the foul blot which slave holding & slavery sanctioning professors have imprinted on her lovely face.

If you deem the accompanying publication [??] calculated to promote your object you will not perhaps shrink from the trouble of supplying me with information which you may deemed suitable. Anything of this kind may be forwarded to my friend Mr. Scoble directed to me, & it will not fail of reaching its destination. In the mean time believe me my dear Sir to remain with unfeigned respect & attachment

Yours very truly

Thomas Price

MS.A.4.1. The Child Papers 1808-1838 [30]
No. 49 David Lee Child to George Thompson

2 Queen St. Place Cheapside
Nov 30 – 1836

My dear friend,

I recd your kind letter of the 27th with great pleasure, and glad I am to be still in England to reply to it. I thank you sincerely for your tempting proposal to become my companion and guide in visiting some parts of your lovely and glorious land, but much I fear that I shall be obliged to decline it altogether. I am determined to see you on my way home and that is all that I can promise myself. I shall not be able to attend any public meeting. Nothing would be more agreeable to me, but I am in Europe upon a mission with which any engagement of that nature would be incompatible. I hope to pass thro England in April or sooner if I can sooner accomplish the objects of the voyage. I will advise you from Paris of the time. Address me if you please to *the care of Welles & Co. Paris.*

I have marked in the newspaper you was so good to send me a few errors of no great consequence, except as they might furnish a handle to the enemy, who will be glad to divert attention from the main question. It is desirable I think to hold to the British public in this discussion the fact that the US never had Texas, nor the color of a claim to it; and that it has always been an integral part of Mexico. John Quincy Adams disposes of this topic very decisively in his speech. A claim has not been pretended, except by ruffian writers for newspapers who surrounded Andrew Machiavel Jackson, and are ever ready to execute his corrupt and tyrannical behests especially when they tend to enlarge and perpetuate slave-holding power. The American *people* never entertained a serious thought that way. There will be a tremendous set to betwixt north & south in Congress at the approaching session which is to commence on Monday next.

I have not had time since the rect of your letter to commit anything to paper touching the affair of Texas. I rejoice that you are going to print, and I pray that your appeal to this great nation may arouse them to a full sense of the peril in which the abolition question in *all* its aspects and British political and pecuniary interests are placed in that distant quarter. I have not been idle in private since I came here.

I send you some pamphlets. That on the war in Texas is by Benjamin Lundy,[1] a most competent and honest witness. You will find a fund of valuable and fresh matter there. I throw into my parcel for you an old letter written at New York but not sent because it was written so badly. It will give you my views and those of other abolitionists in the U States on Breckenridges[2] exhibition of himself. He was a living argument on your side — a mind scaithed and a heart hardened by the curse of slavery. Dr. Wardlaw's[3] admirable speech at the subsequent meeting was refreshing and delightful to us all in America. How I wish I could see you and talk over a thousand things, which I cannot write. Mr. Birney, whom I heard on Sunday, had a capital allusion to American slavery and American prejudice.

When you rejoin Mrs. Thompson remember me affectionately to her. Farewell my dear friend. That the blessing of God may rest upon you is the earnest prayer of

Yr Friend & Fellow Servant

D.L. Child.

MS.A.1.2. vol. 41 1818-1900 Anti-Slavery Letters to Garrison [31]
No. 19 Jane Smeal[1] to Elizabeth Pease[2]

Glasgow 21st of 12th Month 1836.

Dear friend

... The effect produced by George Thompson's addresses at Darlington is

---

1. Benjamin Lundy (1789-1839) had been engaged in anti-slavery activity in various parts of America since 1815, and had close ties with British abolitionists. He founded and edited the *Genius of Universal Emancipation* — the paper whose principles had so influenced Garrison when he first began work for it as a young man. Lundy was responsible also for founding the *Pennsylvania Freeman.*
2. Rev. Robert J. Breckinridge (1800-1871) was a prominent member of the Colonization Society. He was at this time on a visit to Britain, and had been engaged in a much publicised debate with George Thompson in Glasgow.
3. Rev. Ralph Wardlaw (1779-1853), a Glasgow Congregational minister, was a very popular preacher, and had been given an honorary D.D. from an American College for his theological writings. He took an active interest in the anti-slavery cause, and frequently lent his chapel to visiting lecturers. As a result of the divisions of 1840, he broke with the Glasgow Emancipation Society because of its sympathy for Garrison, and devoted his energies thereafter to forming an anti-slavery group in Glasgow, which would be hostile to any of Garrison's "heresies."

1. Jane Smeal, the sister of William Smeal of Glasgow, married John Wigham of Edinburgh and was active in Edinburgh anti-slavery circles. See Appendix II.
2. Elizabeth Pease (1807-1897), the daughter of Joseph Pease, a noted Quaker liberal and abolitionist (see below), was extremely active in anti-slavery circles, and throughout her life remained a close friend of Garrison and of members of the Boston clique. Interested in a number of liberal causes, she was one of the most remarkable Quakers of her generation. She married Professor John Nichol of the University of Glasgow, and, moving to Scotland, continued her philanthropic work there.

such as might naturally be expected to follow wherever his noble sentiments and touching appeals and electrifying eloquence are heard — but it is astonishing that among the many thousands who listen, and approve, and applaud, so few comparatively feel themselves compelled to offer a portion of their means, their energy, and time to the promotion of such a Holy Cause.

Your Resolutions and Addresses are most excellent and appropriate — they are inserted in this days Chronicle a copy of which I shall send in course. —

The females in this city who have much leisure for Philanthropic objects are I believe very numerous — but unhappily that is not the class who take an active part in this cause here — neither the Noble, the rich, nor the learned are to be found advocating or countenancing our object, our Subscribers and most efficient members are all in the middling and working classes but they evince great zeal and labour very harmoniously together — Our Rules are exceedingly simple. We are an auxiliary to the Glasgow Emancipation Society having for its object the extinction of Slavery and the Slave trade throughout the world; and all friendly to this object who contribute 2/6 and upwards a year to the funds are members — these funds go to assist in defraying the expenses of the Parent Society in procuring, printing and circulating intelligence — and in support of their agent George Thompson while publicly advocating the right of America's millions of slaves! — The Editor of the Glasgow Chronicle has long advocated the antislavery cause — and always cheerfully affords room for any communication the Committee wish to make public; in return for which kindness they frequently purchase a number of papers on these occasions sometimes 2 & 300 and send them far and near — from which they have known great good to result — and after an article has appeared in the papers we can get a quantity thrown off the same types very cheap for local circulation — I send here with copies of a few things that have been got done in that way from time to time, also a few pamphlets some of which may not be new to thee but thou wilt know in that case how to dispose of them — I hope the Address to Ministers of Religion &c will please thee it was published last Spring and has been widely circulated both in Scotland and England.

We have written to several societies and individuals in America during the present year, but have received no communications of a later date than those brought over by G. Thompson. We learn however that the cause is making an amazing progress. We are anxiously and daily expecting to hear of the arrival of Dr. Beman and G. Smith. I trust their visit will do much for the cause of Universal Emancipation. We should like to have them G.T. and D.L. Child at our next anniversary which is held in the 2nd or 3rd month — as my time for writing is expired I must stop — and am only sorry that I have had nothing more interesting to write. My brother had a letter from G.T. since he got home — his wife had been unwell but was better. He had not decided on his next movements but we hope he will take some rest. I am thy obliged and sincere Friend.

Jane Smeal Jr.

MS.A.4.1. The Child Papers [32]
No. 50 Thomas Sturge[1] *to David Lee Child*

New Kent Road 27.4. mo. 1837

To D Lee Child

In reply to thy question I think permission may be granted to admit thee freely to a Sugar house & I am quite willing to promote thy wishes in that respect. I consider it quite as important to understand the process of refining as making sugar but I think thou art mistaken in thinking it (refining) will be useful as affording a succession of employment in the Summer. There have been many patents taken out for improvements in sugar refining the whole of which may be known by consulting the patents themselves which can be done here, by those who wish to do so.

I am pleased to hear of thy wife's welfare & hope thy journey to France will have answered thy purpose. I quite expect there must have been some strong excitement in America on the subject of slavery to cause the President to express himself so strongly on its favour, but the present pecuniary distress so greatly pressing on America will I hope produce a good result to the slaves. I entertain a strong opinion that the present distress in America mainly arises from a great extension of slave cultivation & that the land speculations have chiefly been caused by the prospect of getting great prices from planters, who wanting capital & being quite reckless were willing to get land & slaves at any cost, regardless whether they could ever pay or not.

Thy friend resp^{y}.

Thos. Sturge.

MS.A.1.2. vol. 41 Anti-Slavery Letters to Garrison [33]
No. 21 Jane Smeal to Elizabeth Pease

Glasgow 6th month 3rd – 1837.

My dear Friend

...We have had two letters this week from George Thompson but the first very short mentioning his having been detained longer than he expected in Sussex – his having embraced Joseph Sturge – the select committee being re-opened – J.S. to be examined first – he having an inconveivable mass of evidence of the most overwhelming nature – his uncertainty of the length of time he may be detained London – and what is of most importance his health being *very good* – &c &c – That received yesterday contains very varied intelligence – some of it highly pleasing and portion of it very painful – He says he has "been much engaged with Mr. Sturge and Dr. Palmer".[1] In the

1. Thomas Sturge, a Quaker businessman, was a cousin of Joseph Sturge. Unlike his cousin, however, he was a Garrison supporter, and with his sister, Esther, contributed liberally to the funds of "Old Organization."

1. Dr. Palmer was one of the stipendiary magistrates appointed to visit Jamaica to see that the apprenticeship system was being fairly carried out.

course of the week will be published a thrilling narrative from the lips of the black boy brought over by Mr. Sturge. I will not anticipate his history of the horrors of the Apprenticeship but will send it as soon as it is out. I was at Devonshire House on Monday evening when it was resolved to raise some money for the purpose of agitating the Country.

Mr. Sturge gave an affecting account of his Mission. About 1500 friends were present. It is probable £2000 will be contributed. Josiah Forster,[2] Geo. Stacey,[3] & R. Barrett are to manage the fund. Tonight the 31st I lecture in Dr. Price's Chapel. Mr. Cheevor[4] a Clergyman from Salem, Mass, is here and I have given some time to him. He will accompany me to Scotland and assist at our anniversary Meeting in Edinburgh. We shall probably proceed to Birmingham on Monday, attend a public meeting to be given to Mr. Sturge on Tuesday morning – on Wednesday proceed to Liverpool and from thence to Glasgow, where of course we shall see the friends of our cause before I leave for Edinburgh"... We must now buckle on the armour for the extinction of the Apprenticeship. Sturge is for *whole measures.* I want to learn the plan of action and then to work with all the strength I have. I perhaps ought to say that Cheevor is one of the earliest friends of the cause in America & a man of much talent. Mr. Sturge is now before the Committee. This is the first day of its sitting. They take Sturge first Lord Sligo[5] second and Dr. Palmer third. I have just been informed that Tappan's House has failed in consequence of the commercial panic in the United States." –

Thou wilt probably have heard more than is contained in the above extract, but I have had great pleasure in copying it. Tappan's failure is a serious Calamity. G.T. makes no remark on it, perhaps he doubted its truth, but it is now in the newspapers and I fear but too true....

I am thy sincere friend

Jane Smeal Jr.

---

2. Josiah Forster (1782-1870) came from a Quaker family which was actively interested in the affairs of American Quakers. He was a loyal member of the B.F.A.S.S. and visited the United States in 1845. His brother, William Forster, had married the sister of Sir Thomas Fowell Buxton, and their son, William Edward Forster, was also active in the anti-slavery cause.

3. George Stacey (1786-1857) was an influential British Quaker who was later to oppose the admission of women to the 1840 Convention.

4. Rev. George B. Cheever (1807-1890) was a Congregational minister and uncompromising reformer with a genius for provoking controversy. Cheever at this date was at the beginning of his career. Later, a pastor of churches in New England and New York City he advocated many social reforms. He came out militantly in support of abolition in the late 1850s, and as a result nearly lost his post as minister of the Church of the Puritans in New York City. To gain money for his cause he visited Britain from 1860 to 1861.

5. Howe Peter Browne (1788-1845), 2nd Marquis of Sligo, had been Governor of Jamaica.

MS.A.13.1. The Thompson Papers [34]
No. 3 George Thompson to Edward Baldwin[1] *of 28 Upper Sackville St. Dublin*

118 Princes Street,
Edinburgh; July 26. 1837.

My dear friend,

Yours, dated Dublin, July 17, did not reach me till last evening, when I returned from a visit to Aberdeen. I hasten to assure you that I shall have much pleasure in visiting Ireland, and co-operation to the utmost of my ability with the "Friends of the Negro" in the just and necessary work of putting an end to the odious and oppressive scheme of West India Apprenticeship. I need not give you any information respecting my anti-slavery views & principles. I trust your exposition of them will be acceptable to your Hibernian Friends. I am really delighted with the prospect of embracing you upon the soil you love, and which I love, and love specially for the wrongs of its people. My hands are more than full with work here, & in England, but I will make my other engagements yield.

I am thus circumstanced. I have to visit Perth and Dundee & Montrose *next week*, and give a lecture in each place. Early in the following week, say of August 2nd or 3rd I could start for Dublin. Write me if possible by return and say by what route I had better reach you. Say also if I may leave all preliminaries to you and your friends in Dublin. I suppose I had better take them to Belfast via Glasgow.

We shall have much to talk about when we meet. Mrs. Thompson would much like to see Ireland, but is not in circumstances to travel. She desires to be very kindly remembered.

Believe me,

Very truly yours

Geo. Thompson.

MS.A.13.1. The Thompson Papers [35]
No. 7 George Thompson to Edward Baldwin

Leeds, September 14. 1837.

My dear Baldwin,

I send you the Emancipator. I put it into my pocket that I might look it over on my way to Kingstown, and omitted to give it [to] you at our parting. I trust you will not be materially inconvenienced by the delay.

The Kidnapping of Apprentices. On this subject my information is derived from

---

1. Edward Baldwin was Secretary of the Hibernian Anti-Slavery Society. In 1838, together with James Webb and Richard Allen, he presented to Queen Victoria the Irish women's petition for the abolition of the apprenticeship system in the West Indies.

Mrs Child, the well known authoress, and Mr. Van Ranseall er[1] a respectable colored man in the city of New York. I have not their letters with me, but distinctly recollect the facts they stated: viz, that the Vigilance Committee of New York* had obtained a knowledge of three cases of persons (W.In. Negro apprentices) brought them to New York to be sold to the slave traders from the South. One, they had succeeded in rescuing. The other had been sold into perpetual bondage. You are at liberty to mention the names of my informants. They both deemed the subject worthy the serious attention of the British people. I believe [?] Buxton was made aware of the circumstance.

I have spoken four times this week. Three of my speeches (though delivered on Missionary platforms) have been upon the subject of the apprenticeship. Resolutions have been given me denouncing the vile system as a fraud upon the negro and his friends, and a serious obstruction to the success of the missionary. Thus you see I am bringing the question before large meetings tonight & tomorrow night – next week will be occupied in a similar way...

Like yourself my hands are very full. I am glad to hear of the b:kfast meeting & its fruits – onwards!

Yours most truly

G. Thompson

I will send the Leeds Mercury of Saturday [?]

* A committee of abolitionists for protecting the rights of the free colored people. Looking after kidnappers, defending fugitive slaves &c.

MS.A.1.2. vol. 6 1836-1837 Anti-Slavery Letters to Garrison [36]
No. 72 John Scoble to William Lloyd Garrison

London, 1st Oct. 1837

My dear Garrison,

...Whilst I feel cheered by the rapid extension of anti-slavery principles in the United States, I feel depressed at the state of the anti-slavery cause here. India, with her millions of slaves, is imploring assistance. Africa, degraded and depopulated by an atrocious Slave Trade, is calling for help. Our own Colonies, burthened by a cruel system of apprenticeship, demands our aid; and we find ourselves without a Leader in the House of Commons, or a single Peer in the House of Lords, to represent our principles or to urge our prayers! The country is, I believe, sound to the heart's core; but our statesmen (prob pudor!) like your own, are mere party men. Everything is sacrificed to party. Tories, Whigs, Radicals, all will sacrifice the noblest principles of justice, and the dearest rights of humanity, to political expediency. But the people, the people, will soon be thundering again at the doors of the legislature. We are preparing for the campaign; and with a good cause, and the blessing of God, I trust, we shall ultimately triumph. The English Female Address, on behalf

---

1. Thomas Van Rensalaer, a prominent Negro of New York City, was active in anti-slavery affairs there, and later edited the *Ram's Horn* with Frederick Douglass.

of the Apprenticed Labourers & the British colonies, to our youthful Queen has, in a very short space of time, received 430,000 signatures! The women of Scotland are actively engaged in procuring signatures to their address; and the daughters of Erin are behind neither, in the zeal with which they have undertaken the cause of the oppressed. Let me beg of you, my dear Friend, to order that a copy of the Liberator newspaper be regularly forwarded to 18 Aldermanbury. We have not received a copy of your paper for two years!

The question about the Texas is beginning to be better understood here than formerly; and I trust that our Government will express itself, fully and unequivocally, upon the subject, during the ensuing session of Parliament. As a merely political question, however, I care little about it. With me, it derives its paramount importance from the influence it has on the question of general liberty and the ultimate happiness of the human race. It is impossible to regard without shuddering the annexation of the Texas to your Union! What evil passions has not the bare mention of it called into play? What murder, robbery and spoilation, has it not already perpetuated and what merciless cruelties and horrors will follow its train, should its abettors accomplish their unholy object?

Yours affectionately,
tho' in haste,

Jno. Scoble

MS.A.13.1. The Thompson Papers [37]
No. 6 George Thompson to Edward Baldwin

118 Princes Street,
Edinburgh Oct. 26
1837

My dear friend,

I obtained your kind letter in course of post this morning, and as we have just had a committee meeting on the subject of a delegation to London. I sit down to give you the result. After much deliberation concerning the priority of demanding the immediate *extinction* of the Apprenticeship rather than the redress of abuses it was resolved that one be sent to cooperate *most cordially* with those who shall meet in London on the 13th proximo. When the election for a delegate took place the appointment fell upon me. If therefore, I am able to leave Mrs. Thompson I shall go to London, and listen to the proposals of the friends there. There is one circumstance which reconciles me to this appointment, it is that I shall be disposed most fully to concur in *thoroughgoing measures*, for although we have many uncompromising men amongst us in this city, it is possible we might have had one representing the body here who would have been inclined to listen to the (so-called) dictates of prudence and expediency, and so have retarded rather than helped the cause.

I was delighted to see Captain Stuart. He did our committee here good by his noble adherence to principle, and his fearless denunciation of timid measures. He leaves in the evening for Newcastle – thence to Darlington, Leeds, Sheffield, Manchester & Liverpool to Birmingham. I trust his visit will be of much service to the cause.

Mrs. Thompson has been much worse since I saw you, having had another attack of inflammation. She is now a little better. Is there any probability of your being in London at the meeting to be held? I shall be truly delighted to see you there. Pray let me hear from you soon. I [?] intend to visit Belfast and give some lectures there. As soon as I can determine the time, I will communicate with the proper parties. Oblige me by giving my kindest regards to Mr. & Mrs. Russell – the Webbs – Bewleys – Harveys Orpens &c &c &c. Dont forget me to Mrs. Almar – nor to Mrs. Jacob –

Ever most truly yours

Geo. Thompson.

MS.A.1.1. vol. 2 1836-1837 Anti-Slavery Letters from Garrison [38]
No. 69 William Lloyd Garrison to Elizabeth Pease
(Garrison's first letter to Elizabeth Pease)

Boston, Nov. 6th, 1837.

Esteemed Friend,

There are many of my countrymen who regard me as a rash disturber of the peace of society, scarcely fit to be tolerated upon my native soil; and though they have not said of me what was charged against my Master, namely, that "he hath a devil," yet they do not scruple to give me the apostolic character of being "a seditious and pestilent fellow." How does it happen, then, that you, a stranger to me personally, a "foreigner" on the other side of the Atlantic, are disposed to cherish a good opinion of me, to approbate my labours, & even to aid me in my "incendiary" and "fanatical" purposes by a generous donation? Ought not my own countrymen to know me better than a resident in England? Their testimony is very strong against me; it is unequivocal; it goes to impeach my sanity, if not to injure my moral character. Ah! they are not disinterested witnesses. I have not only accused them of being hostile to the rights of man, and in ranking immortal souls among cattle and creeping things, of having exalted themselves above all that is called God, but I have sustained the dreadful accusation by plenary evidence: hence their hatred of me. The act of violence is in their hand and they know it; their feet run to evil, and they make haste to shed innocent blood; and whosoever among them that departeth from evil, maketh himself a prey; for truth hath fallen in the street, and equity cannot enter....

My beloved and invaluable coadjutor, Angelina E. Grimké has promptly conveyed to me the five guineas which you were pleased to transmit in the letter she has recently received from you. I receive the gift as a token of your sympathy for the suffering and the dumb in this recreant land, whose cause it is my happiness to advocate, and for whose deliverance from bondage all that I have and am is pledged, without any reservation whatsoever. My heart is grateful in view of your kindness, and especially to know that I possess your esteem; but you shall not be burdened with mere words in return. Deep and genuine emotion has no "set phrase of speech."

With regard to the present state of the anti-slavery question in this country, you will be pleased to learn that the friends of the slave are daily multiplying in all parts of the non-slaveholding states; that there are now not less than twelve hundred anti-slavery societies in existence; that the spirit of lawless violence is in great measure subdued, not by the arm of the law, but by the power of truth and the victorious endurance of suffering innocence; that, in New England, all organized opposition to our cause has vanished; that our efforts are unceasing to gain a complete mastery over the public sentiment of the nation; and that in Massachusetts, where, only two years since *abolition* was a mere football among all political parties to show their contempt and dexterity in kicking it, these same parties are now "bowing and scraping" to us, with cap in hand, at every new election, knowing as they do that we hold the balance of power in our hands, and can award victory or defeat according to their espousal of the cause of liberty.

Upon the slave holding states, we make no perceptible impression. No opponent of slavery can tread upon their soil, as an abolitionist, without the risk of martyrdom. I have relinquished the expectation, that they will ever, by mere moral suasion, consent to emancipate their victims. I believe that nothing but the exterminating judgments of heaven can shatter the chain of the slave, and destroy the power of his oppressor. The wildest animals may be tamed in the course of time; but tyrants, as all history shows, must be destroyed. I am clear, moreover, in the conviction, that, although astonishing changes have taken place in favor of emancipation among the people of the nominally free states within the last five years, the fate of this nation is, nevertheless, sealed. Repentance, if it come at all, will come too late. Our sins have gone up over our heads, and our iniquities into the clouds, and a just God means to dash us in pieces as a potter's vessel is broken....

As in England, so in this country – the women have done and are doing more for the extirpation of slavery than the other sex. In their petitions to Congress, they outnumber us at least three, perhaps five to one. At the recent session of that body, a million of names were sent in, in the course of a month, remonstrating against the annexation of Texas to the United States. Of that immense number, a very large proportion were females. Our gifted friends, the Grimkés, are exerting an almost angelic influence wherever they go. Their public lectures are thronged by both sexes, and their triumph over prejudice and error has been most signal.

It is now more than eight years since I entered upon this mighty work. The more I labor, the less weary I grow. Rely upon it, American Abolitionists will never give up the conflict through fatigue, pusillanimity or apathy. Come what may, they can no more be divorced from the cause, than they can give up their allegiance to God. Some of them may – nay, some of them have in a trying hour, turned recreant; but the great body fear God and will keep his commandments.

The many dear friends in England, with whom it was my privilege to become acquainted, are none of them forgotten by me. My heart swells and my eyes moisten as I think of their kindness. It is not probable that we shall ever meet again on earth – may – we all meet in Heaven to be parted no more!

Your grateful & admiring friend,

Wm. Lloyd Garrison.

MS.A.1.2. vol. 41 Anti-Slavery Letters to Garrison [39]
No. 27 Maria Weston Chapman to Elizabeth Pease

Boston Dec 30th 1837.

Elizabeth Pease

Dear friend,

Though in the greatest haste I *cannot* let this opportunity pass without thanking you for the beautiful articles for our fair which we receive through Angelina E. Grimké. They were the means of bringing throngs to purchase, who would otherwise [have] passed by on the other side; nothing could have been more opportune than their arrival. Please to express to those to whom, with yourself we are so deeply indebted, our warmest thanks on behalf of the slave. The Address from the Ladies of Darlington, signed by yourself & Miss Wemyss, has been published in all the Anti-Slavery periodicals, & has been the means of encouraging the hearts of thousands.

You will doubtless have seen the accounts of the murder of our devoted brother in the cause, E.P. Lovejoy,[1] at Alton, in the state – the *free* state – of Illinois, for the crime of being an abolitionist, & maintaining free discussion; but you can hardly realize the feelings of the abolitionists.– We feel that there is no law for us. Such an enormity occasioned a public meeting to be called here in Boston, but though the requisition was signed first by the Rev. Dr. Channing,[2] than whom no man among us has been more unpleasant, the meeting was boisterous & divided. It was distinctly stated by him that slavery would not be discussed in the meeting; – but simply resolutions against mob-violence. Yet the meeting had very nearly itself been a mob. But free discussion of the *subject of free discussion* prevailed, & we went home with a feeling of security for life & property, *for the present.* But I fear when I see the strength of slavery *here*, & how the institutions of the South are interwoven with our own free ones – not openly indeed, but like the roots of giant trees, *beneath the soil.* – I fear that abolition will be resisted by the south, to her own destruction, & by

---

1. Elijah P. Lovejoy (1802-1837) was a militant abolitionist in Illinois, and editor of the *Alton Observer.* His press had been twice destroyed by mobs, and Lovejoy lost his life in defending his paper in a third attack; his "martyrdom" becoming one of the great issues in anti-slavery history.
2. William Ellery Channing (1789-1842), famous New England Unitarian minister, theologian and liberal, was no friend of slavery, but declined to link himself with any of the anti-slavery societies. He condemned Lovejoy's death, and was one of the moving spirits behind the protest meeting in Faneuil Hall; but at the same time he made it plain that the purpose of the meeting was to defend the principles of free speech, and not the party ends of the abolitionists. His unwillingness to accede to some of the demands of the abolitionists not unnaturally drew strong protests from militants like Maria Weston Chapman.

the North till the last possible day of grace. May God strengthen us to endure!

Yours gratefully

Maria W. Chapman

MS.A.1.1. vol. 3 1838-1843 Anti-Slavery Letters from Garrison [40]
No. 13 William Lloyd Garrison to Francis Jackson[1]

Brooklyn, June 18, 1838.

My dear friend:

...My views of the Sabbath accord with those which were entertained by Calvin, Belsham, Priestly, Penn, Fox, and Barclay, and which chiefly distinguish the Society of Friends from other religious sects. As a Christian, I hold the sanctification of seven days in a week, instead of one day in seven, as under the Jewish institution. I discard all human creeds, and all ecclesiastical combinations, and all observances of times and seasons, and all rites, ceremonies, forms and ordinances, as constituting no part of Christianity, and as being contrary to that liberty wherewith Christ makes his people free. I deny that there is, now, any wordly santuary or ordinance of divine service, or any priestly office, except that which is exclusively occupied by him "who is set on the right hand of the throne of the Majesty in the heavens." I believe that the worship of God is not a thing of time or place – is neither a spasmodical nor formal observance – appertains to no particular locality or select building – but is simple, unbroken, perpetual obedience of the heart, and entire consecration of body and soul, mind and strength, reputation and property, to the service of God, "which is our reasonable service." I believe that prayer is the breath of the soul, not to be repeated at set times, or resorted to as a papist counts over his beads, but that all prayer is comprehended in a single sentence – "*Thy* will be done *on earth*, as it is done *in heaven.*" I am not a Trinitarian, Unitarian, Baptist, Methodist, Swedenborgian, Friend, Perfectionist, or member of any other sect, but simply, in profession, determined like Paul to know nothing but "Christ, and him crucified." I believe from passing from death into life – in being born of God – in becoming a new creature in Christ Jesus – in being crucified to the world – in present, perfect, and perpetual deliverance from sin – unswerving allegiance to the one great Law-giver of heaven and earth, whose glorious name is Love....

Your much obliged friend,

Wm. Lloyd Garrison.

---

1. Francis Jackson (1789-1861), a wealthy merchant and a prominent Boston Unitarian, was for many years President of the Massachusetts Anti-Slavery Society. He supported the Boston Female Anti-Slavery Society and gave liberally to the *Liberator.*

No. 42 Anne Knight[1] *to William Lloyd Garrison*

Paris Rue du Faubourg du Roule 24
7 mo 14 1838

My dear friend & brother

Receive my best thanks for thy animated letter & the lively animated bearer of it who truly cheered me in the accounts which he gave confirming thy surprising history of your acceleration, of your *progressing* to use a favourite Americanism & my predictions that your march to emancipation will not be a very *lengthy* one. Thy statements are really wonderful & almost incredible they are however fully confirmed by my friend Edward Davis[2] surely the horn of liberty is not far distant what a day will it be for America how will true Christians rejoice at *that* sun rising & more solid real joy than that for which our poor western islanders were in devout prostration on their mountain tops watching eagerly the rising of that sun whose fevered rays were going to augment the bitter sufferings of their new-fangled bondage I hope the hideous enthralment is coming to an end for every vessel brings to our ports tidings of other planters coming to emancipation from motives of self interest! They only wanted to see if & how much more they could plunder from an outraged people in the form of compensation we have all reasons to hope that for the Africans liberty may be obtained – and then– then – the Hill Coolies! That frightful shame in which the villainous Gladstone has succeeded entrap our little queen by the connivance of Lord Glenelg & his party, & supported by that recreant bedauber of the Russel name they will make this fair vestal crowned in the west a slave monarch as well as her predecessor poor England! the ghost of venal statesmen, its brave people enlightened warmed *moved* to march to fight against the citadel & – fall into ambush! There's our lot & all that has been done for the poor slave appears to enhance their misery the slave trade nominally suppressed but really doubled with added horrors of the middle passage & other nations bribed into increased perfidy to what then is all our stir? it may be this full many a flower is born to blush unseen & waste its sweetness on the desert air – no longer desert air but among hosts of their countrymen developed into double sweetness yes if developed it calls forth into energetic action whose powers which other wise would have lain hid perhaps or very sentimentalized in half action half thought half feeling see the difference this is a heart labour calling forth sympathisers of youthful bosoms no longer confined to reading a tender heart breaking story of fiction & weeping as they read they learn of real woe & lash themselves to its redress your countrymen would not have known the rich treasures in its bosom but for this & now what do you see? for dry bones, an exceeding great army! This is the Lord's doing and marvellous in our eyes...how glorious are the tidings we receive! let us press forward in spite

---

1. Anne Knight (1792-1862), a Quakeress from Chelmsford, worked hard for the anti-slavery cause in its early years, together with her sister and brother-in-law, John Chandler. Later she turned her energies to the woman suffrage movement; was instrumental in forming the Sheffield Female Political Association; and wrote one of the earliest tracts on women's rights.
2. Edward Morris Davis (1811-1887), a son-in-law of James and Lucretia Mott, was active in Philadelphia anti-slavery circles.

of discouragement I hope Texas will not be added to the slaveries of your republican aristocracy I long to see your glorious country freed from its vile chains & flourishing over its head a *legitimate* star spangled banner oh what mill stones are war & slavery round the neck of my fair island preventing its advancing through the earth according to the merits of its industry & science & with her son Jonathan holding up glorious & brilliant gas-light to the world...I hope you will [?] your intercourse with Europe on these affairs & remain with cordial best wishes thy sincere & obliged friend

Anne Knight

MS.A.1.2. vol. 41 Anti-Slavery Letters to Garrison [42]
No. 30 Maria Weston Chapman to Elizabeth Pease

Boston Aug 30 1838

Dear friend,

...The progress of the cause here is still onward. The greatest obstacles that it meets are thrown in its way by the bigotry of Religionists, who as little comprehend its broad & radiant principles as the bat & noonday sun. "We could forgive you anything" they say to the abolitionists, "but your injurious attempts to identify your principles with religion!" Meanwhile the practical movements throughout the country are all influenced by this subject. The politicians have hitherto been somewhat puzzled to find differences enough in their respective creeds for the creation of two parties – It will not long be so "Freedom" & "Slavery" will soon be the rallying forces – not "Clay" & "Van Buren". I have so short a notion of this opportunity that I cannot even stop to pick up such pamphlets &c as might prove interesting to you. I merely send such as chance to lie on my table. I ought renewedly to thank you for the beautiful additions to our fair, which we receive through Angelina Grimké...A night or two after [the wedding of Angelina Grimké] the city of Philadelphia was like a city about to be sacked & pillaged. Then areas of Southerners were seen spurring on a furious mob to raze the houses of the abolitionists. Fortunately the sacrifices of the Friends of old were yet of power to stay the hand of devastation. The mob respected the dwellings of Quakers, to which body the Abolitionists, especially the prominent ones of Philadelphia belong, & nothing was destroyed but the beautiful & spacious hall which had been just built.

I thank you most warmly for the little book "Wrongs of Africa" with the Address bound with it. The sympathy & prayers of England are most precious to us. The inhabitants of Massachusetts are of pure English descent & whatever may betide no example or exhortion can ever be so powerful with them, for ages yet to come, as that of England.

In spite of all the efforts of travellers & reviewers of both countries, each to recommend his own at the [expense?] of the other, New Englanders will always cherish the thought that they share with you of [Old?] England, a common ancestor & language; that in their veins as in yours flows the "sangre azul" – "the azure Gothic blood." God grant your example in the

West Indian colonies may be speedily efficacious. (I send you Whittiers[1] poems which I ought to apologise for sending)...

I am affectionately yours for universal rights

Maria W. Chapman

MS.A.1.2. vol. 8 1839 Anti-Slavery Letters to Garrison [43]
No. 3 George Thompson to William Lloyd Garrison

8 Duncan Street, Newington.
Edinburgh, January 5, 1839

My dear Friend:

... Do not think, because I do not write to America, that I do not think of America. I devour with eagerness everything in the shape of information respecting your anti-slavery movement. I am disposed to think that I am as familiar with the details of the question, as it is possible to be on this side of the Atlantic. The *education* I obtained, during my short residence in the United States, enables me to understand pretty well the bearing and comparative importance of the events recorded in your anti-slavery periodical, and by constant and regular reading, I keep up with you in your glorious career, and complete from time to time my historical knowledge. You express a wish to have me by your side. O, with what [?] and fulness of desire I could exclaim, "Amen, with all my heart!" To keep on this side the water is an art of daily self-denial. I am only reconciled to my painful separation by the consideration that the little I can do for the cause of universal freedom is, for the present, better done here than it could be with you. I cherish, nevertheless, a strong and confident hope that I shall see you again, and be allowed to do and suffer something more in the field of warfare, which is endeared to me not less by the insults and injuries I received, than by the kindness and proofs of affection so abundantly furnished me by my fellow-soldiers.

Since the abolition of the apprenticeship in the West Indies, I have been engaged, as my health allowed me, in bringing before the public the claims of the London Aborigines Protection Society, a most praiseworthy and valuable institution, founded by Mr. Buxton and other philanthropic individuals, with a view to the improvement of the condition of the native inhabitants of our Colonies and the world at large. I have sent you several newspapers containing a pretty full exposition of the principles and plans of this new Society. While advocating its claims to public support, I am by no means precluded from pleading the cause of the slave. On the contrary, the Slavery of India, the Slave Trade of Africa, and the freedom and welfare of the Negro wherever found, are matters of special and legitimate

---

1. John Greenleaf Whittier (1807-1892), the New England Quaker poet, was first recognised by Garrison, who published some of his early verse; but Whittier, though active in anti-slavery work, was never wholly in sympathy with Garrison, and worked mainly with Stanton and Weld. Shy and a poor speaker, his most important work was probably in organising the petition campaign, which after 1835 so flooded Congress that the notorious gag rules were adopted on the plea that the business of Congress would otherwise be impeded.

interest. It is likely, however, that the present state of British India will be that part of the great subject which we still feel it our duty to press upon the immediate attention of the people and parliament. In consequence, my recent public addresses have had a particular reference to the oppressions practiced by British rulers upon one hundred million of our fellow subjects in our Eastern Empire. [We?] hope by a vigorous effort to effect an early alter[ation] in the administration of public affairs in India – such an alteration as will relieve the bulk of the natives (the cultivators of the soil) from the existing evils of the revenue system, and lead to the abolition of slavery throughout the country. This will be another glorious achievement....

Believe me with growing affection,

Your [?] friend,

Geo. Thompson.

MS.A.1.2. vol. 8 1839 Anti-Slavery Letters to Garrison [44]
No. 4 George Thompson to Richard Davis Webb

Darlington, January 26, 1839.

My dear friend/

...On looking over your letter I find your list (of writings on American anti-slavery) contains most of the works adapted for the English reader. *Weld* has prepared an interesting work on the *Bible question*, but I know not of anything besides. Some years ago he published an admirable report on Manual Labour Schools.

I have the Westminster with Miss Harriet's article[1] here by my elbow. It is a glorious production. I should like to see it reprinted and widely scattered. Pray my dear fd go on in the good work of diffusing American publications. They cannot but do great good.

Let me have a line from you again to this place. It will be duly forwarded to me.

Ever with kindest regards to Mrs. Webb.

Yours most truly

Geo Thompson

---

1. Harriet Martineau's article eulogising the American abolitionists, "The Martyr Age of the United States", published in the *Westminster Review* for December, 1838. Harriet Martineau (1802-1876), author, journalist, economist and traveller, was one of the most widely known figures of her time. Coming from a prominent Unitarian family, she visited America from 1834 to 1836, and her views on anti-slavery were greatly strengthened by her meetings and friendships with the Boston Unitarians and abolitionists. It was during this visit that she met her lifelong friend, Maria Weston Chapman. In addition to *The Martyr Age*, Harriet Martineau wrote also *Society in America*, London, 1837, and *Retrospect of Western Travel*, London, 1838 – also drawn from her experiences of American life.

MS.A.1.2. vol. 8 1839 Anti-Slavery Letters to Garrison [45]
No. 6 George Thompson to R.D. Webb

Darlington, Feb. 15, 1839.

My dear friend/

... I thank you for your kindness in regard of the books. Pray send everything you deem interesting. By all means urge the reprinting of Harriet's [Martineau] most interesting article. It must be printed & widely circulated on both sides of the pond. Could the writings of our noble souled fds. in America be got into the hands and hearts of the philanthropists of Britain, much good wd be done. They would be baptized more deeply than ever into the spirit of universal benevolence.

I am now working for the Hindoo. I have just lectured at Newcastle, North & South Shields, Kendal, Carlisle and Darlington. On Monday I go to Sheffield & thence to London. The summer must not be permitted to pass without an effort to rouse the Emeralders. Alas, alas! except on party questions you are as sluggish as your own Liffey. When will the time come when Ireland, no longer distracted by political & polemical contests, will have her heart affected and sanctified by the contemplation of the sorrows and slavery of others, and engaged in a glorious effort to make the world as free from tyrants and oppressors as she is herself from the venomous reptiles of the Earth? My address in "the great metropolis" will be 4 Bloomfield Street Finsbury. Love to Mrs. Webb & all the Webbs & Allens.

Yours affecy.

Geo. Thompson.

MS.A.9.2. vol. 11 1839 (1) The Weston Papers [46]
No. 73 Mary Wigham[1] to Maria Weston Chapman

5 Gray Street, Edinburgh, 4th Month 1st '39.

My dear friend,

Having recently been appointed Secretary to our Emancipation Society, I have felt extremely desirous of reopening the correspondence with yours, which has been discontinued since the resignation of Mrs. Erskine; knowing as I do, what a stimulus it is to the zeal of the friends of the great cause here, to receive from time to time accounts of your unwearied and indefatigable labours on behalf of the oppressed; and being informed by my friends Elizabeth Pease & Jane Smeal that it is equally grateful to your feelings to be assured of the continued sympathy felt with you by your fellow labourers on this side of the wide atlantic – It is truly gratifying to receive such encouraging accounts of the progress your work is making, and although for the present, owing to the resolutions lately passed by Congress, it may not appear to be quite so prosperous, still there is no doubt that a cause so righteous will ultimately triumph, and we have held up to us the soul sustaining promise that in due time we "shall reap if we faint not" and "grow not weary in well doing" – The annals of past events afford us

---

1. See Wigham family tree. Appendix II.

abundant proof that persecution and opposition always tend to promote inquiry, and to further that object which they would fain discourage.

I have much grieved to hear of the shameful part which the members of the Society of Friends have been, and are I fear, still acting towards their coloured brethren, particularly in Philadelphia – It is indeed strangely inconsistent with the principles which they profess to hold, but I do hope that Christian expostulation will open their eyes to the sinfulness of despising a fellow immortal, endowed with all the faculties which they possess, because "he has a skin not coloured as their own" – The accounts we receive from the West Indies of the behaviour of the Negroes are truly satisfactory, they fully confirm all the expectations we entertained respecting them, and more than silence the tongues of those who alledged so confidently that *they were not fit for freedom* – A most affecting proof of their being grateful for kindness shewn to them has been given, by their having subscribed, all of their own accord, a sufficient sum of money to purchase a very handsome Testimonial to the Marquis of Sligo which was lately presented to him by Joseph Sturge & a few other philanthropic gentlemen who had been appointed by the negros themselves their delegates for this purpose. Although there seems little for us to do in this sphere of action at present yet it is needful that we do not relax in our vigilance, as it is not to be supposed that a change of system has changed the *hearts* of the planters, for they appear to be doing all they can to oppress and injure the race, now so happily released from their bondage –

The state of the aborigines of the British dependencies, more especially of those of British India, has lately claimed our serious attention, and we have resolved to unite their claims to the objects of the Emancipation Society – It is a very wide field of labour thus opened before our view, rendered more so by the great ignorance of the nation at large upon the subject; our valued friend George Thompson is at present engaged in endeavouring, by his powerful eloquence, to enlighten the minds of the people, and to rouse them to the consideration of the awful responsibility we are under to do all in our power to ameliorate the condition of 100 millions of our fellow-subjects, who are groaning under the accumulated wrongs inflicted upon them by *British* rule.

Hoping that thou will kindly write before long giving us an account of your exertions, believe me to be

Thine very sincerely

Mary Wigham.

MS.A.1.2. vol. 8 Anti-Slavery Letters to Garrison [47]
No. 28 Sarah M. Grimké to Elizabeth Pease

Fort Lee 5/14/39

My dear Friend

I wrote thee about a month since a *very* long letter in reply to the last I received from thee requesting some information relative to prejudice as it is manifested in the Society of Friends – In that letter I mentioned the course so far as I knew anything about it that has been pursued by J.J.G.[1] since he has been in this country – a pamphlet has recently appeared entitled "Free & Friendly remarks" &c &c in the famous speech of Henry Clay in support of Southern slavery. I hope my brother will be able to procure it & send it with a package of books & pamphlets by the friends who will present this letter.

I write now chiefly to introduce to thyself & thy father [2] two abolitionists[3] who have gone on a mission to England to obtain funds for an institution in the State of Ohio where colored youths of both sexes are received & enjoy all the literary & social advantages which the white students enjoy. I need not say anything respecting Oberlin Seminary as all I could say is embodied in a document which they take with them & to which the name of many of our most valuable men & women are appended. I am aware dear Elizabeth that the philanthropists of Great Britain have great claims & high responsibilities resting on them in their own country, but I also know that their hearts are enlarged towards the colored population of America & I believe they will rejoice to aid in the development of that wealth of intellect which is to be found in that class of oppressed Americans which only needs the hand of culture to render it a blessing to themselves & to the world. In the U.S. prejudice closes almost every avenue of knowledge & where the professors of an Institution are willing to throw open the portals of science to all without respect to color, the same cruel prejudice condemns that Institution to drag on without the aid of such funds as are necessary to carry on its operations. I appeal to your sympathy & benevolence with entire confidence & ask for the dear brethren who have undertaken this mission of love whatever the Lord may prompt you to do. Receive them in the name of the Lord Jesus Christ & whatever ye do for them & their mission place it to his account.

Thine for the oppressed

Sarah M. Grimké

P.S. One of the copies of "Slavery as it is"[4] is intended for Jonathan & Hannah C. Backhouse please hand it to them with my love –

I have omitted one important fact viz that Oberlin is the only seminary in the U.S. where colored girls can obtain a liberal education.

---

1. Joseph John Gurney (1788-1847), famous Quaker philanthropist, religious writer and banker, was at this date on a visit to North America and the West Indies, where he travelled from 1837 to 1840. He wrote *A Winter in the West Indies, Described in Familiar Letters to Henry Clay of Kentucky*, London, 1841. His third wife was the American Quakeress, Eliza P. Kirkbridge, who had been a companion of Hannah Backhouse during her stay in America.
2. Joseph Pease (1772-1846) was a Quaker manufacturer and philanthropist. He took an active interest in anti-slavery affairs, and was mainly instrumental in founding the British India Society and in promoting work for the abolition of slavery in India.
3. John Keep (1781-1870) and William Dawes (1799-1888) undertook a mission to England to collect money for Oberlin College. Keep was a Congregational minister and President of the Board of Trustees of Oberlin College. In this position he had cast the deciding vote for the admission of Negro students.
4. Theodore Dwight Weld, *American Slavery as it is. Testimony of a Thousand Witnesses*, 1839. One of the important books on anti-slavery, it was from this work that Harriet Beecher Stowe was later to draw for details for her *Uncle Tom's Cabin*.

London, 7 mo. 11th, 1839.

My dear friend,

I feel that I have a great weight of obligation to discharge for the two interesting letters which I have recently been favoured with from thee. Yet at present I fear I can do little more than thank thee with the assurance that every line you write & every pamphlet or paper sent to us from your Land is animating & strengthening to our hearts.

My dear father [along] with a few other Individuals has recently witnessed the commencement of a great – a mighty work – one which he had had much at heart for the last twelve month – the Establishment of a society for bettering the condition of our hundred millions of fellow subjects in British India. Of the preliminary steps to this important result thou hast doubtless heard thro' Geo. Thompson & the public papers. The Society was ushered into existence at a large public meeting on the 6th inst. at which Lord Brougham presided & at which Daniel O'Connell pleaded the cause with eloquence & power. It is delightful to behold such a head & heart & tongue enlisted on the side of the dumb. Our poor fellow beings in India are steeped in poverty & wretchedness, ground down to the very Earth beneath a pressure of Taxation which inflicts unutterable misery upon *them* – nourishes & perpetuates the system of Slavery throughout the world & consequently gives vitality to the Slave Trade with its ten thousand horrors. This *must* become speedily obvious to all who will be at the pains of investigating the matter. *You* will see, & many of you do already perhaps, perceive, that the efforts for India, if [brot.] to a practical result, *are* doing your work for you & aim at the very object you are seeking to accomplish – viz. to bring free labour into competition with Slave – Labour is but 2d a day in *our own* India, from whence we might be under a wise & humane policy, have all the articles which we now obtain from the sinews of the Slave in Foreign Countries. How can the [one] stand against the other?

The bearings which this great question has on the Anti-Slavery subject renders it tenfold dear to my heart. When you have read & thought respecting it I feel assured that the Abolitionists in America *must* see it in this light. If you do, I know you will rejoice to lend a hand of help & you may render this infant cause *most essential* service, by embodying your sentiments & giving a written expression of them to the "British India Society" here – pray think about this – & send a welcome, *official* or *individual* or *both* from your Land as early as possible. It will cheer the spirits of *all* who have entered on the work – & will tend to enlist the Anti-Slavery party here, too many of whom fear that the present movement is distracting public attention from that cause & who have not investigated the matter sufficiently to see that the *British India* is in fact an "Anti-Slavery Society." Anything addressed to me I shall always forward with pleasure. I have requested that a copy of the publications of the Society – which are yet but few in number – may be put up & I hope G.T. has written thee as well. He has just been in and tells me I must conclude as the parcel is going. I have no time to buy a new copy but send thee one of my own of T.F.

Buxton's work[1] – The "English in India" contains Wm. Howitt's Chapters on the subject,[2] which I have had reprinted from his larger work, with an appendix containing a few extracts illustrative of the present state of the people there. More of these shall be sent with the [?] & a few other articles which we are gradually mustering together for your fair. There is very little anti-slavery [?] to be had here now – all that seems worth sending, shall be forward[d]. Be assured it is a great pleasure to be able to do *anything* for you however trifling. I have no time to enter into the subject of thy last....

I grieve that differences of opinion should arise among the friends of the cause I have not had any communications from the opposite party. It wd. be useful & safe for us to know the names of all those who are *recreant* – whom we have been accustomed to regard as sound. Neither have I time to do more than touch on the deputation on behalf of the Oberlin Institute. They are welcome to our shores & have much interested us in the object of their mission. Geo. Thompson is now in London – his health is I hope rather better than it was some time ago. But his energetic [mind?] wears his delicate frame...

Be kind enough to present the little volume to W.L.Garrison with my Christian regards. I sent a few things & a hasty scrawl to him last winter but I believe the box had not been received....

Believe me truly & affecly. thy friend

Eliz. Pease.

MS.A.1.2. vol. 8 1839 Anti-Slavery Letters to Garrison [49]
No. 45[1] *Wendell Phillips*[2] *to George Thompson*

London, July 29, 1839.

My dear Thompson,

I am very sorry to say *No* to your pressing request, but I cannot come to Glasgow. Duty takes me elsewhere; my heart will be with you though on the 1st of August; and I need not say how much pleasure it would give me to meet on that day especially the men to whom my country owes so much, and on the spot dear to every American abolitionist, as the scene of your

---

1. T. F. Buxton, *The African Slave Trade*, London, 1839.
2. Probably Howitt's *Colonization and Christianity: A History of Natives by Europeans*, London, 1838. William Howitt (1792-1879), Quaker journalist and author of many works of a moralistic nature, with his wife, Mary Howitt (1799-1888), entertained many of the visiting American abolitionists and were responsible for introducing Garrison to some of the leaders of the British anti-slavery movement.

1. J. H. Bell, *British Folk and British India*, London, 1891, p.70, mentions that this letter was written specially to be read at the 5th Annual meeting of the Glasgow Emancipation Society.
2. Wendell Phillips (1811-1884) came from a prominent Boston family. He first became active in anti-slavery circles in 1837, after the death of Lovejoy, and thereafter was one of the most noted anti-slavery speakers. He was greatly admired by British abolitionists, though he retained his ultra radical views on abolition and other reforms, breaking even with Garrison in 1864 over the renomination of Lincoln, a political action which Phillips in no degree supported.

triumphant refutation and stern rebuke of Breckenridge. I do not think any of you can conceive the feelings with which an American treads such scenes. You cannot realize the debt of gratitude he feels to be due and is eager to pay to, those who have spoken in behalf of humanity, and whose voices have come to him across the water. The vale of Leven[3], Exeter Hall, Glasgow and Birmingham are consecrated spots, – the land of Scoble and Sturge, of Wardlaw & Buxton, of Clarkson & O'Connell, is Holy Land to us. Would I could be with you to thank the English abolitionists, in the Slaves' name, for the great experiment they have tried in behalf of humanity – for providing in the face of the world, the safety and expediency of immediate emancipation – for writing out the demonstration of the problem as if with letters of light in the blue vault of heaven:- to thank thee too for the fidelity with which they have rebuked the apathy and denounced the guilt of the American Church in standing aloof from this great struggle for freedom in modern times. The appeals and exhortations which have from time to time, gone out from among you, may seem to have fallen to the ground in vain; but far from it: they have awakened, in some degree at least, a slumbering church to a great national sin, and they have strengthened greatly hands which were almost ready to faint in the struggle with a giant evil. We need them still – spare us not a moment from your Christian rebukes –give us line upon line, and precept upon precept. Our enterprise is eminently a religious one, dependent for success entirely on the religious sentiment of the people. It is in hearts that wait not for the results of West India experiments – that look to duty, and not to consequences – that disdain to make the *fears* of one class of men the *measures* of the rights of another – that dread no evil in the doing of God's commands – tis on such that the weight of our cause mainly rests, and on the conversion of those, whose characters will make them such, that its future progress must depend. It is upon *just such minds* that your appeals have most affect. I hardly exaggerate when I say that the sympathy and brotherly appeals of British Christians are the sheet anchor of our cause. Did they realise that slavery is most frequently defended now in America from the Bible, that when abolitionists rebuke the Church for upholding it, they are charged with hostility to Christianity itself, they would feel this. If we construe a text in favour of liberty, it is set down to partiality and prejudice. A *European* construction is decisive. *Our* rebukes lose much of force, when they are represented, though falsely, to spring from personal hostility – from a zeal which undue attention to a single subject has made to outrun discretion. *Your* appeals sink deep – they can neither be avoided nor blunted by any such pretence, and their first result must be conviction. Distance lends them something of the awful weight of the verdict of posterity. May they never cease. Let the light of your example shine constantly upon us, till our Church, beneath its rays, like Egypt's statue, shall break forth into the music of consistent action. England too is the fountain-head of our literature. The slightest censure, every argument, every rebuke on the page of your Reviews strikes on the ear of the remotest dweller in our country. Thank God that, in this, the sceptre has not yet departed from Judah – that it

3. The vale of Leven was a district around the Clydeside which had sent an anti-slavery petition to the United States in 1836 from the women of this area. This petition was later "unfurled over the heads of thousands" at an anti-slavery anniversary in New York.

dwells still in the land of Vane & Milton, of Pym and Hampden, of Sharp, Cowper & Wilberforce.... You have influence, where we are not even heard. The prejudice which treads underfoot and vulgar abolitionists – dares not proscribe the literature of the world. In the name of the slave, I beseech you let that literature speak out in deep, stern, indignant tones....
I am rejoiced to hear of your new movement in regard to India. It seals the fate of the slave system in America.The industry of the pagan shall yet wring from Christian hands the prey they would not yield to the demands of conscience, or the claims of religion. Hasten the day! for it lies with you, when the prophecy of of our Randolph, himself a slaveholder, shall be fulfilled – that the time would come when masters would fly their slaves, instead of slaves their masters, so valueless would be a slave's labour in comparison with his support. To you – to the sunny plains of Hindostan we shall owe it – if our beautiful prairies are unpolluted by the footsteps of a slaveholder – that the march of civilization westward will be changed from the progress of the manacled slave coffle, at the bidding of the lash, to the quiet step of families carrying peace, intelligence and religion, as their household goods. Mr. Clay has cooly calculated the value of sinews and muscles – of the bodies and souls of men – and then asked us whether we could reasonably expect the South to surrender 1,200,000,000 of dollars at the bidding abstract principles? Be just to India, – waken that industry along her coast, which oppression has kept landlocked and idle – break the spell which binds the genius of her fertile plains, and we shall see this property in man become like the gold in India's fairy tales – dust in the slaveholder's grasp. You cannot imagine, my dear brother, the impulse this new development in England's power will give the anti-slavery cause in America. It is just what we need to touch a class of men who seem almost out of the pale of religious influence. Much as our efforts have been blessed; – much as they have accomplished, – though truth has often floated further on the shouts of a mob, than our feeble voices could have carried it, – still our progress has served but to show us more clearly the Alps which lie beyond. The evil is so deep rooted, the weight of interest and prejudice enlisted on its side so vast – ambition clinging to political power, wealth to the means of further gain – that we have sometimes feared they would be able to put off emancipation till the charter of the slave's freedom would be sealed with blood – that our day of freedom would be Egypt's, when "God came forth from his place, His right hand clothed in thunder," & the jubilee of Isreal was echoed by Egypt's wailing for her first-born.

It is not the thoughtful, the sober minded, the conscientious, for whom we fear. With them truth will finally prevail. It is not that we want eloquence or christian zeal enough to sustain the conflict with such – and with your aid to come off conquerors. We know, as your Whately[4] says of Gaileo, that if Garrison could have been answered, he had never been mobbed – that May's Christian firmness – Smith's[5] world-wide philanthropy – Chapman's daring energy – and Weld's

---

4. Archbishop Richard Whately (1781-1863), noted theologian and Archbishop of Dublin, was a founder of the Broad Church movement. His study of economics, his liberal view in politics, and his theological opinions, made him a somewhat controversial but still a leading figure in his day. He took an active but not uncritical view of the abolition movement.

5. Gerrit Smith (1797-1874), philanthropic millionaire of western New York, was an active member of the Tappan circle. His niece, Elizabeth Cady, married Henry B. Stanton.

soul of fire – can never be quelled, and will finally kindle a public feeling, before which opposition must melt away. But how hard to reach the callous heart of selfishness – the blinded conscience, over which a corrupt church has thrown its shield, lest any ray of truth pierces its dark chambers! How shall we address that large class of men with whom dollars are always a weightier consideration than duties – prices current stronger arguments than proof of holy writ? But India can speak in tones which will command a hearing.... But from India, a voice comes clothed with the omnipotence of self-interest, and the wisdom which might have been slighted from the pulpit, will be to such men, oracular from the market place. Gladly will we make a pilgrimage, and bow with eastern devotion on the banks of the Ganges, if his holy waters shall be able to wear away the fetters of the slave.

God speed the progress of your society! May it soon find in its ranks the whole phalanx of sacred and veteran abolitionists! No single, divided effort, but a united one to grapple with the wealth, influence, and power, embattled against you. Is it not Schiller who says:– "Divide the thunder into single notes, and it becomes a lullaby for children – but pour it forth into one quick peal, and the royal sound shall shake the heavens;" so may it be with you – & God grant, that without waiting for the "United States to be consistent" – before our ears are dust, the jubilee of emancipated millions may reach us from Mexico to the Potomac, & from the Atlantic to the Rocky mountains!

Yours truly, and most affy. Wendell Phillips.

MS.A.9.2. vol. 12 1839 (2) The Weston Papers [50]
No. 6 Ann and Wendell Phillips[1] *to Maria Weston Chapman*

London July 30th 1839 No. 3.

Cousin Mary's last was "a conclusion in which nothing was concluded," so I number this 3 as a sort of continuation of hers, & to you dear Maria, as it will contain business of yours.

We are in London & have seen Thompson! Wendell intends writing Garrison, so he will then more than supply my deficiencies, but a letter from me by way of a relish. I first saw the 'Great Panjandrum' in a momentary call at our lodgings, & he employed his time in urging us to go to Glasgow with him to speak on the first of August. It would have detained us from France ten days or a fortnight, the climate is also cold & damp here, we feared if we waited he might not reach Italy by the last of September or October or I might fall sick as I did last year. So, much as our hearts were moved thitherward, we had to say no. Caroline, you will feel for me when I knew I *must* decline such earnest entreaties as these, "you *will* go with us, & I will make you as merry as I can & you shall go by a beautiful route to Lochs Lomand & Katrine, now, will you go? Is there no hope for me?"

But disappointment as it was we felt it would not be right for us to be

1. Ann Terry Greene Phillips (1813-1886) was the wife of Wendell Phillips, and a connection of the Westons. She was an invalid for most of her married life, a factor which many abolitionists felt acted as a check on her husband's activities, though in fact she encouraged Phillips in his most extreme radical views.

going *North* when we should be going *South.* It is *sad* for *me* to think of, but I am trying hard to get health & then I shall not be such a stumbling block in dear Wendell's path. It is no light trial I assure you. I asked Thompson if there was no way of W's speaking in London, but he said not; they do *not* get up *spontaneous* meetings as we do, only at particular times. I find there is no such thing as his speaking unless we go so far as Glasgow. I regret it much, for next year it will be nothing, comparatively, there will be so many Americans here. Wendell has written Thompson a letter to read at the meeting, it will be published & sent to some of you. That was, you know *well*, as he could not speak. My second & last sight of Thompson (for I was out when he last called) was at his lodgings Finsbury Square. There I saw *Mrs.* T. also Elizabeth Pease. For yr. particular edification I will begin with the room. About the size of yr. *small* parlor, Maria, sofa, centre table, books on shelves, & tables, beautiful portfolios for papers, lovely inkstand &c quite study fashion. I looked round, a la Yankee, books seemed to be nearly all upon India, directly or indirectly, India in every form – Ah says I, "how many would be glad to be here" & "what *would*, what would I give to see them, Maria Chapman, *all*, *all must* come come next year, men and women too, do they not mean to?" Elizabeth Pease too is very anxious, those of you who can possibly come, should, she longs to see you all, hopes you will come, Maria. Miss Pease I like much. Thompson told us she was his right hand man, his amanuensis, his counsellor everything. Thompson appears very much absorbed in this India question, conversed very little when I saw him, evidently *much* on his mind. Thompson jumps up & says "now you should see the little articles we have purchased for the Fair, if they will answer. *His hands* unfold the papers, think of that Caroline, & he says then that blue basket is my taste, that green pincushion with the white fringe is my choice, this little Scotch thistle also –" Think, you will see & touch the things *he* has handled.

I thanked them over & over for their things, told them they could not imagine how delighted you would be, thanked Elizabeth Pease over & over for the Darlington things two years ago, how well they sold &c. I did all I could in way of thanks & *broad hints for the future*, I *fought manfully* I assure you. They showed me one or two specimins of china they are going to send you which I *know* you will like. They are going to send a good many pamphlets, & some pretty little books, "the Wrongs of Africa," which I think will sell well. Thompson said something about picking up a few things in Glasgow & sending some engravings of himself which are to be struck off, all of which offers I warmly seconded. I *hope* he *will*, but I fear in the press of business these last *may* fall through. There is no prospect of Thompson's going to America, & now I know some little of this India question, I think he will do most good here. Should the experiment succeed, (you will have a full account by the pamphlets) it will give slavery its deathblow. They calculate that England can be *fully supplied* with cotton from her East India possessions. Thousands of starving men are ready to live for a penny a day. The soil is favourable as there is already abundance of Indigenous cotton there. Time & energy are only requisite, the thing is done. The slave must be then almost a deadweight upon his holder's hands; for other countries will also supply themselves from India, & *interest* will at last compel them to let the oppressed go free. It is a most distressing question. Yes, Elizabeth Pease is a very intelligent & interesting woman. She says Thompson has told her so much of America & all the abolitionists she longs to see them. You, Maria, she particularly spoke of. She asked me if you were not *educated a "friend."* She appears quite like *one of us.* She asked all kind of questions about the Grimkés. Saturday last, Thompson went to Glasgow. Yesterday Miss P. & myself went to a Bazaar. When I tell you, dear Maria, that I stayed there *three hours* looking at things, that ever since we left home I have been saying to W. "look around, see if you see any new fashion for M.W.C." you will take the will for the deed & forgive any little articles if they are not exactly what you would have liked. *I have done my best.* I looked at hosts of children's dresses but could see nothing particularly new or pretty. The fashions as far as I can see are the same as with us for women's & children's dresses. The women wear mantillas in some form or other. Small French merino shawls lined with different colours are the rage....

Yrs. A.T.G.P.

MS.A.1.2. vol. 8 1839 Anti-Slavery Letters to Garrison [51]
No. 49 Angelina Grimké Weld to Elizabeth Pease

8th month 14th 1839
Fort Lee N. Jersey.

My dear friend,

...The Box thou hast mentioned in several of thy letters as having been sent by Jane Smeal, I believe, has never been received; it is the same, I presume, which Julia Tappan told me, some time since, that she has been expecting for months, but could hear nothing of. Dost thou know in what vessel it was shipped, in what month and from what part? We have never seen Howitt's work on Colonization, except so much of it as was published in 'The English in India'. This we received in two packages by Edward Davis. What dreadful developments it contains! What a curse have civilised nations invariably been to the barbarians among whom they have settled, what a hissing and a by word must we be among the heathen! Look not only at India, but at the World. Have we not always robbed the ignorant and the defenceless of whatever we wanted? In Africa we wanted men, so we organized a regular system of war, kidnapping and plunder in order to get what we wanted. In South America we wanted *gold* and *silver* and precious *stones;* here too we resorted to violence and blood. In No[rth] America we wanted land, and here we have had recourse to extermination, fraud, persecution, force and fear – rooting up the Aborigines from the land of their fathers and casting them headlong into their graves, or driving them beyond the Rocky Mountains in the midst of cold and hunger, nakedness and disease, and death. In Asia we wanted *revenue;* there heavy taxation was resorted to, and who can paint the horrors which have followed the conq[u]erors car, *whenever* civilised man has set his foot upon the soil of the Savage and planted the standard of his Christian sovreign.

There is no document of modern times which I have read with deeper interest than the Prospectus of the Periodical Publication which the British India Society designed to issue; it was a noble specimen of enlargedness of heart and grandness of design. As an American I rejoiced to see that England's philanthropists remembered they had determined "the cause that they know not, to search out." May the Lord's blessing rest abundantly upon their labors of love, and surely it will, for who does not know that just in proportion as we obey the command "thou shalt love thy neighbour as thyself," and suffer our hearts to go forth in sympathy and prayer for the poor and the oppressed, we received into our bosoms the sweet rewards of peace and joy and love, so that even were our labours useless in relieving them, we can say "Lord it is enough". Let me assure thee that thou art greatly mistaken if thou supposest that the contents of the letters are not as deeply interesting to us, as thou sayest our's are to thee. The India society has claimed a large share of our sympathy and we do most heartily bid you Godspeed. We have no fears of its organization *at this juncture* affecting unfavourably the cause of Emancipation in the West Indies, for altho' we know that the slaveholders *in heart* there will need to be watched, lest the chain of slavery be refastened on the limbs of the new born free men, and that the lifting up of these from ignorance and degradation will require great expenditures of funds and labor (and *this* elevation, be it remembered, is the only safeguard against their reenslavement) yet I can see no antagonistic principles between the two enterprises, and believe they may be carried on simultaneously and harmoniously. We were very glad to see that the subject of *free products* was again agitated in England, for, for several years Theodore & ourselves have felt its importance & believed ourselves morally bound to use no other – and have been grieved that our brother Wm. L. Garrison should have so completely abandoned the noble position he once occupied on this subject, because the weight of his example & influence are very extensive. The fact is, in this country it is in some cases impossible to be *wholly* clear – in country towns & remote places it is often impracticable to obtain free cotton, & until Emancipation was effected in the West Indies, to get free groceries, without a great deal of trouble & some additional expense – & these great difficulties have operated most unfavourably in blinding the consciences even of high professors & faithful laborers in the Anti Slavery cause. We accordingly find, that just in proportion as the facilities increase for the procurment of free articles, that people's eyes are opened to the duty of abstaining from the use of those raised by slave-labour. Only let Great Britain refuse to purchase American cotton, & let her manufacturers assure us of the pureness of their fabrics, & I am confident that 10s of thousands in the northern states would rejoice to purchase them in preference to our home manufactures made out of slave grown cotton. And surely if the East Indies can supply her with cotton, is she not solemnly bound to purchase it there, in preference to ours, (leaving the freeness of the article out of the question) because by so doing she would be promoting internal improvements, encouraging industry & stimulating to enterprize those very people whom she has, by her misguided policy & oppressive taxation, reduced to penury & scourged with the scorpion whips of famine, pestilence & death How

I should rejoice to hear of England's adopting laws in favor of the importation of East India cotton, even if she is not yet prepared to say to the slave-holder of N & S America when they come to her market with their stolen goods – go home & pay your laborers, & then will we trade with you; for we dare not any longer be the receivers of stolen goods & the "companions of thieves."

I often feel, like thyself, ready to despair of my Country, ready to believe that, notwithstanding all the moral effort which has been put forth in behalf of the slave-holder's of the South, they WILL NOT repent, and that deliverance to the captive will at last come in terrible judgment, I say this, because I see not any witnesses raised up in the *midst of themselves*, who are ready to go to prison and to death, if need be, in testifying against the monarch sin; and I see not any Abolitionists from the North commissioned to go down and preach with all boldness against this mother of abominations. Now when I look at the Lord's dealing with those natives whom he designed to save, I see that he either raised up prophets in the midst of them, delivered from among them, or he sent his servants to cry aloud in their streets and call them to repentance. I can see the iron hearted opposition of the north gradually yielding to the heavy strokes of the hammer of truth. I can see the fruits of labor here, therefore I believe we shall be saved; but at the South a sullen, death like silence prevails, save when the bursts of unholy indignation at "Northern interference" are heard to issue from the mouths of slaveholding divines and southern [de]magogues. Everything that is done there in favour of the slave is done in a corner and spoken in the ear; the reign of terror is not over and perhaps never will be until the huge bastile tumbles into ruin, and its very foundations are plowed up. We are anxious to hear what the South will say to "Slavery as it is". The testimonies to her cruelty are so overwhelming and appear to be so incontrovertible, that we cannot imagine how she will defend herself against such bloody accusations; and yet, if she coes not, her silencce will only sink the brand of infamy still deeper in her brazen forehead.

We have lately seen two very interesting letters from gentlemen in Tennessee and Western Virginia. Some large landholders in that vicinity have pledged themselves never to sell their land to anyone who will cultivate it by slave-labor, and they are very desirous of inducing Abolitionists to purchase small tracts, go down and settle them and then exert their influence to organize the new state. We have not yet heard of anyone acceding to their proposal, and cannot yet tell how it will work, tho' we heartily wish prosperity to any scheme which may tend to overthrow the unholy alliance between the slave states.

Sister and myself did not attend the Convention of Women in Philadelphia last Spring. We had fully intended to do so but my indisposition prevented, for I found that if I went, I should not be able to attend the sittings, and therefore tho't it best to stay at home.

I rejoice in the prospect of the World's Convention to be held in England next Spring. What a deeply interesting and important meeting it will be! What a privilege to be there, and in all probability thou wilt enjoy it. Oh how *blessed* thou art in seeing they beloved father so devoted in the cause of the poor, and being a co-worker with him, in travelling with him and participating in the rich feast he is continually partaking of in prosecuting his work of faith and labor galore. In they parents heart thou findest every noble feeling of benevolence vibrating in sweet unison with thy own – how blessed thou art! The Lord is his wisdom, denied this to our departed Mother that we thought and acted as we have done on the subject of slavery – a grief to all our brothers and sisters; but it is a solace to our hearts to *know* that *she* always felt and acknowledged that whatever we did in the Anti Slavery cause, we did from a deep and solemn sense of duty. She never in all her letters asked us to cease our efforts on behalf of the slave, but said she prayed God to bless them if our views were right and her's were wrong. O! if she had not died a slaveholder! but we are dumb – we lay our mouths in the dust.

We have been expecting Charles Stuart in this country for nearly two months and have now abandoned the hope of seeing him, for we suppose that not being able to procure a passage from the W.I. to the United States, he has sailed for England. As the best beloved friend of my Theodore, and as a truly Christian philanthropist, I have greatly desired to see him under our roof, and to know him, for as yet I have had a very slight acquaintance with him; but he is doing a great work and I desire not that he should come down from it. I am willing to wait the Lord's time. I have not yet seen John Scoble but we expect him in the boat this evening. His lectures, we understand, are doing great good wherever he goes and we joy in his success and pray that his labours may be abundantly blessed. If his business admitted of it, we could wish he could stay with us a year or two. We are now prepared to listen to a "foreign emissary", and bringing such facts as he does fresh from the W.I. he can speak with a power and authority on immediate Emancipation, which none who have not been near and eye witness can do.

22nd. I intend to have added more to this already long letter, but feel too unwell today to make the exertion; have just risen from the bed to assure thee of my sincere wishes for they perseverance and success in the work thou has begun.

and to subscribe myself Thy Friend

A. G. Weld –

Shouldst thou see G[eorge] T[hompson] please say to him that I have received his letter and hope soon to answer it.

MS.A.1.2. vol. 8 1839 Anti-Slavery Letters to Garrison [52]
No. 50 Maria Weston Chapman to Elizabeth Pease

Boston Aug. 20th 1839

Elizabeth Pease

Dear Friend,

Before I touch on any other subject, let me congratulate you – ourselves – the *world*, on the formation of the British India Society; for surely there is no part of the world to which it will not communicate a happy & powerful impulse. I see at a glance what its effect must be on American slavery, & cast my whole spirit across the Atlantic, towards you in England who have devised, & are carrying it forward, in joyful cooperation & hope....

Mr. Scoble, by whom this letter will reach you, has been lecturing on the W.I. Emancipation to vast audiences; – 3000 persons, it is estimated heard his last address in Boston. Is it not grievous to reflect, that just as Freedom was beginning to obtain a general hearing among us, the love of some should have waxed so cold, that they are labouring to extinguish the religious opinions of their brethren on other subjects, instead of cooperating with them against our common enemy? but so it is – & we have already lost the *keen edge* of our suffering on account of their conduct. The whole affair seems like a perfect riddle to the friends of the cause at a distance from Boston. When the mystery was at its heighth, I was requested to deliver an address at Lynn before the Abolitionists there, in the course of which, I adverted to the "difficulty"

I found the minds of the friends much relieved by such information as my personal knowledge enabled me to give; & their wishes for a report of what I had said, for publication induced me to think that a history of the affair, (which is, at the bottom, only a struggle of the sectarian with the Universal, induced by the terrors of some, lest strong sympathy in principle should efface the lines between "Congregationalists" & "Friend" – "Calvinist" & "Unitarian,") might do good to those who saw "A quarrel but nothing wherefore," & who were made the dupes of intolerance & intrigue disguised as abolition. Pray accept the Book – "Right and Wrong in Massachusetts"[1] Perhaps it will be hardly intelligible to you, as I could take much local information for granted in the minds of readers here, for whom the book was written....

You can hardly imagine with what satisfaction I received your letters, or how widely the intelligence they give, diffuses pleasure & hope.

With grateful & affectionate regard,

I am your friend

Maria Weston Chapman.

MS.A.1.2. vol. 8 Anti-Slavery Letters to Garrison [53]
No. 51 Maria Weston Chapman to Elizabeth Pease

Boston August 20th 1839

Elizabeth Pease,

Dear friend,

I open my little parcel to ask a favour of you. We are preparing a little book to be called the Liberty Bell for our fair in October – an annual it will be if it takes [place] this year. To make it attractive we want

---

1. Maria Weston Chapman's articles on the divisions in the Massachusetts anti-slavery movement, collected and published in Boston in 1840.

pieces (either grave or gay – lively or severe as their muse dictates) from those whose names are dear to the abolitionists. You will not refuse us yours? Ever so short an article (indeed our limits will not admit of long ones) will be a *very* great favour. May we expect it by the next Packet? I dare hardly hope that George Thompson's engagement will permit him to give us such an article, yet I could wish you to second such a request to him. What can we do here to further any plans of yours? Our hearts are with you & you may depend on us to fulfil your wishes upon your signifying them, to the extent of our power.

With a heart filled with grateful regard I am yours for the cause of Universal humanity.

Maria Weston Chapman

MS.A.1.2. vol. 8 Anti-Slavery Letters to Garrison [54]
No. 59 Sarah M. Grimké to Elizabeth Pease

Fort Lee 8/25/39

My dear Friend

I wrote thee a few days since by our beloved brother John Scoble of whom we may say as the apostle did of Titus "God who comforteth those that are cast down comforted us by the coming of Titus". It seemed indeed a special favor that his steps were directed to the United States for the testimony of an Englishman would probably have more weight than that of American abolitionists. He spent about a day with us & delighted & instructed us with the interesting accounts he gave of some of our colored brethren in the W.I. while at the same time he unfolded a state of feeling & an assumption of power on the part of the slaveholders which plainly evinces that the spirit of despotism still reigns in their hearts & that oppression has not ceased out of the land. Shall we not then praise the Lord for his goodness that he hath sent out his servants to search into the cause of the suffering & the dumb, & to expose the abominations which still exist. This mission of our dear brethren to the British possessions on this side the Atlantic is a most soul satisfying assurance that Jehova is fulfilling his gracious promise "For the sighing of the poor, for the crying of the needy now will I arise with the Lord."....

affectionately thine

Sarah M Grimké

We feel some anxiety about our dear brother Charles Stuart whom we have been expecting for nearly two months as his last letter mentions he expected to be in Jamaica about the 23rd of 6th month & sail thence very soon for New York – we conclude that if his life & health have been preserved he would not obtain a passage to the U.S. & has therefore returned to England without coming to America – this has been no small disappointment, but we rejoice that the good man's steps are ordered of the Lord & doubt not that whatever events have occurred to him are in mercy & that all things are working together for his good....

MS.A.9.2. vol. 12 (2) 1839 The Weston Papers [55]
No. 40 Elizabeth Pease to Maria Weston Chapman

28th of 9 mo.

My dear Friend,

Tho' uncertain *when* this may reach thee, as a private opportunity presents I feel unwilling to let it pass without enclosing a document which has within the last two days been issued by the committee of the B.I. Society. I think its contents will still further elucidate the subject which we all have so much at heart. Please to give on to W.L. Garrison with my very kind regards – & be kind enough to distribute the remainder as thou thinks best.

Having but a few moments to put my parcel, I can do no more at present than offer thee my heartfelt thanks for thy welcome letters by J. Scoble. The encouragement they contained for our enterprize has cheered the spirits of the *few* who are at present labouring in it. "Right & Wrong" I have perused with deep interest. How it will delight us all if permitted to be at the Convention next year to welcome *thee*, W.L.G. & any other of our A.S. Friends. I hope you will send a large deputation from your land. Excuse these hasty lines & believe me, thy affec^{e} & obliged friend.

E. Pease.

MS.A.9.2. vol. 12 (2) 1839 The Weston Papers [56]
No. 62 Elizabeth Pease to Maria Weston Chapman

7 South St., Finsbury, London
26 of 10. mo. 1839.

My dear Friend,

I take advantage of the return of Charles Bossom & the permission he kindly gives of *loading* him with our pamphlets to send thee the little matters which have been lately issued from our British India Press. To thank thee too for thy most acceptable & cheering communications of Augt last, & for the copy of "Right & Wrong" which I have perused with deep interest yet at the same time, with sorrow that there should at this critical & important juncture, exist anything like a division in the ranks of the abolitionists. Still I trust all are *in heart* true to the slave, how ever much of human frailty may have crept in to impede the usefulness of some, who were were once regarded as pillars in carrying forward your noble enterprise. Let us then pray that the breach may be quickly healed & that all may yet work together for good to the great cause of human freedom...

With regard to thy request to have a few lines from my poor pen for your little periodical,[1] I can only say that so far as sincerity of desire for the success of your abolition movement is concerned, & interest in the cause, I should be sorry to yield to *any* in the wish to comply, but *power* I have

1. Probably the "Liberty Bell", the annual paper of the Boston Female Anti-Slavery Society.

not. The will must therefore, be in this case accepted for the deed. I fear that the request did not reach G. Thompson in time, which added to his arduous & pressing engagements must plead his apology. Thou wilt however I suppose hear from himself, if time permits him to write by C.B. He was here for two days early in the week, but has returned to complete a course of lectures at Manchester – which have cost him great labour & fatigue – but have excited a wonderful sensation – considering that when he went there, the most entire ignorance & apathy prevailed regarding India.

The expression of your sentiments respecting the India movement conveys both comfort & encouragement to the few who are labouring in the cause. You can help it *greatly* by expressing your approbation of & interest in it, in your abolition papers which are read in this country. Nothing I believe will tend more surely to direct the attention of our anti-slavery friends here to the question, than to find that you regard it as a powerful auxiliary to the success of your cause. At present but few have entered into it sufficiently to see the importance of its bearings in this light. John Scoble either mislaid or forgot the letter from the Mass Society until a week ago, so that it has not yet been read to the committee – I am sure they will feel greatly indebted for so encouraging & valuable a communication, and it will of course receive an official acknowledgement when reference is made in any of your papers to the B.I. Society, I should feel particularly obliged by having a copy forwarded to me. I sh^{d} also much like to have the "Liberator" regularly; except when thou hast kindly enclosed at various times, in a parcel, it never reaches me. To me it is far the most interesting of the A.S. papers.

What a treat is in store for the friends of the Slave, when the gatherings from all parts takes place in June.[2] If nothing unforseen occur to prevent it, it is our full intention to be here at the time, when I trust we shall have the pleasure of becoming acquainted with many, who tho' *personally* unknown are far from feeling to be strangers to us. – *Thyself* I ardently hope amongst the number here....

Thy very sincere friend,

Eliz Pease.

MS.A.9.2. vol. 12 (2) The Weston Papers [57]
No. 73 Anne Knight to Maria Weston Chapman

Anti Slavery Office,
27 New Broad Street.
30/10. 39.

My dear friend,

Hearing at the office from Mr. Keep that Bossom is going by the

2. The World's Anti-Slavery Convention, held in London in June, 1840. The suggestion for it probably came from Joshua Leavitt, the editor of the Emancipator, and was eagerly taken up by Joseph Sturge and other British abolitionists.

British Queen after tomorrow I must avail myself of the opportunity to send thee my warm acknowledgments for thy great kindness in sending me so large a bounty. In Paris I have left thy letter with a dear friend Madame Vardel an Irish lady residing there of great influence & taste & integrity She engaged to procure all the articles of taste to thy request & we have arranged that she shall speak with thy cousin on his way from Italy & I hope the result will be entirely to thy satisfaction Many thanks for thy kind gift of papers I feel your women to be far above us in the attitude of Christian action & endurance but I fear my beloved friend for those women who have withdrawn from the ranks of justice I fear that they have not enough kept in view the total nothingness of human effort without reliance & faith in the only source of all good the Divine Saviour of men they have not enough acknowledged "Him their greater" & so they have been permitted to fall may they repent & seek forgiveness of this their turpitude pray send me at thy leisure again of your proceedings they interest me much; I have pleasing information for thee my sister Maria & her husband John Candler[1] are gone this week to Jamaica to see how we as *friends* can best help the cause of the negroes in the West Indies they will be at Kingston Jamaica pray write to them & send what information thou canst about American affairs & try to help them, I am sure they will be ready to reciprocate in any way to thy kindness.

I am in great haste & only time to assure thee of the gratitude & best wishes of thy truly affectionate friend

Anne Knight

MS.A.9.2. vol. 12 (2) 1839 The Weston Papers [58]
No. 76 William Adam[1] to Maria Weston Chapman

Cambridge [Mass.] Nov. 5, 1839.

Dear Madam,

I return Mr. Thompson's letter with thanks. It is characteristic of his ardent & enthusiastic mind. Without fully sharing his sanguine expectations of the effect on American slavery to arise from the extension of cotton cultivation in India, I am sure that it would produce the happiest consequences, in combination with other causes, to the starving & degraded population of India itself; and its *collateral* effect might be more powerful than I anticipate.

As a member of the committee of the British India Society I am prepared to stand before the American public as its advocate to the full extent of its

1. John Candler (1787-1869) was a minister in the Society of Friends. Extracts from his journal, kept during his visit to the West Indies, were later published.

1. William Adam had been in India for twenty years as a missionary and Commissioner of Vernacular Education during the administration of Lord William Bentinck. He returned to Britain in 1838 and in the following year was appointed Professor of Oriental Languages at Harvard. He wrote *Reports on Vernacular Education in Bengal and Behar*, 1838; and *The Law and Custom of Slavery in British India*, London, 1840.

object. With that view six weeks ago I began to prepare a course of lectures on India, proposing to announce them for delivery on or about the 1st of February when my college duties will leave me more at leisure. Mr. Thompson's letter and the publications I have lately received from him, strongly confirm me in this purpose and I shall be happy to receive any suggestions which you or others may offer,

I am, dear madam,
with much respect
yours very faithfully

W. Adam.

MS.A.1.2. vol. 8 1839 Anti-Slavery Letters to Garrison [59]
No. 89 E.M. Davis to Elizabeth Pease

Philada. 12th mo. 11th 1839

My dear friend

...If the moral influences of Great Britain can root out the principle that man can rightfully hold property in man – as I believe it can; crush the system of slavery in our country as well as others; compel Texas to abolish slavery before her independence can be recognised by England, and better the condition of one hundred millions in the East – how great, how awful is her responsibility, if she does not exert this moral power without delay....

I have read O'Connell's appeal to the anti-slavery people of your country. Can it be possible that anyone, who reads and ponders on it, will consent to remain idle. Your wealthy men should pour out their money in deep & broad streams, that information should be spread before your people on this subject. I send thee several copies of a work relating to the admissions of Texas to our "Union". It was written by our lamented friend B. Lundy and has exerted an unexpected and successful influence upon our thinking population. This "valley of rascals" and harbour of runaway rogues,* pretends to be opposed to the *foreign* slave trade, says so in the constitution and yet admits them from the United States which in a legal point of view is as foreign as Cuba. This wonderful inconsistency is accounted for in the fact that the populations of this country is really made up of native Americans, who have not lived in their adopted one long enough to forget old associations. But even with Cuba the slave trade is carried on to a very great extent, the authorities do not object to it, & who, knowing them, could expect them to?

I suppose thee is aware that the authorities of Trinidad are offering inducements to the descendants of Africans to emigrate to that island. The ship Archer left this port on the 4th with 180 of our coloured citizens. I blush to look at the

* It is a proverb *throughout our country* when a person has wronged another by cheating or murdering him that he has "gone to Texas", and every one is so well acquainted with this fact that editors in noticing such runaways, economise room by putting the initials G.T.T. after their names.

main reason for their leaving *Just before starting, a slave catcher from the city of Baltimore entered and examined this ship, to see if any one was aboard, who had taken the liberty to claim his own person.* Some Bibles were procured for them, and as far as I know, they left in comparatively good spirits, some with great joy....

with great sincerity
thy friend

Edward M. Davis.

MS.A.1.2. vol. 8 1839 Anti-Slavery Letters to Garrison [60]
No. 93 Edward M. Davis to Elizabeth Pease

Philada. 12th mo 28th. 1839

Respected Friend

...Some time since I wrote to G. Thompson in reference to the influence of T F Buxton in this country & the use that the colonizationists are making of his views. We are all on tip-toe to know whether he disagrees with the opinion he with others expressed in 1833 in the famous Protest....

East India reform seems to me to be not merely practicable, but of easy accomplishment. It is obviously connected with the commercial prosperity of Great Britain, and the pecuniary interest of almost every Englishman, & it is wholly dependent on the will of the British Parliament. Whenever East India cotton shall either drive the slave cotton from the European market, or greatly reduce its price, American Slavery will have recd. its death blow; and since its wasteful tendency can only be supported under extravagant profits; and because the execrable wickedness of the system will be felt and acknowledged the moment it ceases to be lucrative.

The friends of East India reform may be assured of the sympathy of every real Philanthropist, and especially of every American abolitionist.... Our anti-slavery cause is steadily advancing, and its influence has been great enough to keep Henry Clay from being nominated to the next Presidency which is a great thing, not so much a victory as a sign of our strength. For these men who have the power of nominating would as soon bow to the dark spirit of slavery for aid as they would to the pure & powerful angel of abolitionism. They were from all parts of the Union & selected for the express purpose of nominating some popular man for President. They rejected Clay because of his slavocracy (a new word) knowing that with him defeat was certain. They all hate abolitionism but are compelled to ask of it aid. I have heard it compared to a drunkard as reeling along the streets at night, when his whole person comes in contact with a lamp post, it impedes his progress & bruises his body, but supports him from falling.... thine as ever

Edw. M. Davis

No. 20 Maria Weston Chapman to Elizabeth Pease

Boston March 16th 1840

My dear friend,

Your letter & newspapers, with those of George Thompson were received with great satisfaction pr Great Western. How many thanks do I owe both of you for keeping me informed of the movements on this B.I. question. One so interesting from its very vastness alone that one would think every human soul, as stamped with the infinite *must* be drawn irresistibly to its support. I see you are occasionally encountering the hostile feeling that grows out of want of conviction that "our country is the world – our country-men all mankind" – as in the feelings excited in the minds of the Chartists. If a feeling be raised in the midst of a people that is striving for its own benefit which shall induce that people to labour for *others*, the moral foundation is laid on which the superstructure of their own claims can be erected. But while self is the dominant idea, there can be no self-sacrifice, & without self-sacrifice no salvation. Therefore I lament that those who are striving for the right of suffrage in England would not rejoice to see wrong abolished in India, or should think that their own case would not be improved by efforts to ameliorate suffering in any part of the globe....

We are in hot conflict with the political demon. It cries out that we torment it not by calling our cause a religious question, & I grieve to say that some are deceived, I hope only temporarily, by its suggestions. The facts are that the movement for distinct a.s. nominations in Western New York, (where their idea is strongest) was suggested & urged by the Democratic party there, to weaken the forces of the Whigs, & put them in the minority. Some of the abolitionists were deceived, & instead of maintaining a position from whence they could influence the politicians, suffered the politicians to make use of them.

The Garrison-haters in Massachusetts joyfully seized the idea as one which would prolong their existence by giving them a more plausible pretext for opposition to the Massachusetts Anti Slavery Society. It is wise I think, that the treachery which it is important to the cause to expose *here*, should not be noticed in England otherwise than by that natural coldness which involuntarily comes over us when we meet one whom we know has betrayed principles & persons....

You suggest to me the preparation of some thing which may aid your cause – the cause of British India. I will not promise, but it shall be nothing but dissatisfaction with the effort after I have made it that shall prevent my complying. I will submit my best exertions to be decision of my best judgment; & the *latter approving*, you shall have the result. But I fear my will may be greater than my power. With most affectionate regard I am your friend,

Maria Weston Chapman.

MS.A.9.2. vol. 13 pt. 1 1840 The Weston Papers [62]
No. 44 Henrietta Sargent[1] *to David Lee Child*

March 24 1840

Dear Friend,

As you have volunteered to bring before the Masstts A.S. Board the subject of sending Mr William Adam as their delegate to the World's Convention; I wish you to state to the Board that Mr. Adam has resided twenty one years in Bengal as a Missionary an[d] Editor – and the Company's servant to visit all the provinces and report on the schools; which last duty occupied him for five years, and introduced him to the character, the wants, and the cruel oppression of the natives. As a *philanthropist*, a scholar and a Christian, no one is better qualified in G. Britain or in America to stand shoulder to shoulder with George Thompson, and before the world, plead the cause of the poor slave in British India. The abolitionists of this country owe a debt to the friends of humanity in Gt. Britain for sending to us George Thompson, that they may in no way so well discharge, as by aiding Mr. Adam to attend this Convention, prompted as he is by no selfish view, but by the desire of informing the British people that when they boast that every British subject is a free man, their congratulations are premature, that their work is only half done, and that the East India Company's government has perpetuated and sometimes aggravated slavery....

Yours ever

Henrietta Sargent.

MS.A.1.2. vol. 9 (1) 1840 Anti-Slavery Letters to Garrison [63]
No. 23 E.M. Davis to Elizabeth Pease

Philad[a] 3 mo. 30th 1840

My dear friend

Within the last two weeks we have had a number of arrivals from Europe some of the ships having [taken] over 80 days others less than 23!! By several of these I have received English papers containing speeches of that untiring friend of the oppressed in all lands, Geo Thompson, on the subject of British India & the opium trade. Also two letters from thee, one written on the sheet containing the report of the Darlington Anti S & B I. Societies.... Each and all of these are full of interest and serve to impart new vigor to the spirit already engendered by the former publications we have had. The subject of B.I. & the expected war with China are much talked of.[1] The enemies of England love to write about these alarming and sorrowful subjects. They reflet [sic] no credit but on the other hand dishonor upon Great Britain. Our political men say there is a great danger of a war between G. Britain & the

---

1. Henrietta Sargent (1785-1871) was a member of the Boston Female Anti-Slavery Society.

1. This was the Opium War between Britain and China.

United States.[2] It is shuddering to think of the misery that would result from such a contact. I am not convinced that our funds could be as well spent in England by B I S as here by the A S Society. *You* force slavery from its present location by appealing to the avaricious feelings of the slave holder. *We* exterminate it by appealing to his conscience and understanding. Suppose you are successful in supplying England with free cotton from the East Indies to the exclusion of ours, would this prove to our planters that slavery is sinful? No! only that his business is unprofitable. The result might & I doubt not would be, to do away with our slave holding Laws but not our slave holding spirit.

I was much astonished to find that the *rich* with you, are not anti-slavery. But it is just so here, the wealthy are either too busy in securing what they have or making more to pay any attention to the moral reforms of the day. There are some noble exceptions....

I remain thy obliged friend E. M. Davis

MS.A.1.1. vol. 3 1838-1843 Anti-Slavery Letters from Garrison [64]
No. 51 William Lloyd Garrison to Helen Garrison

London, June 29, 1840.

My dear Helen:

...The first thing which you and the household, and all our anti-slavery friends, will wish to hear about, is the Convention. On the score of respectability, talent, and numbers, it deserves much consideration; but it was sadly deficient in freedom of thought, speech and action, having been under the exclusive management of the London Committee, whose dominion was recognised as absolute. At the opening of the Convention, Wendell Phillips moved that the female delegates from the U.S. be admitted to seats therein; which motion he sustained in a spirited manner, and was followed by Bradburn[1] and Prof. Adam, and one or two others, on the same side. It was rejected, however, by a very large majority, on the ground of custom and usage. George Thompson deprecated its introduction, and urged Wendell to withdraw it! All this was some days before our arrival. As soon as we learnt the result, — and, especially, that the London Committee assumed to take the management of affairs into their own hands, — we (i.e. Rogers,[2] Redmond,[3] Wm. Adams of Pawtucket,[4] and myself,) refused to take a seat in the Convention, or to enrol

---

2. This was at the time of the negotiations between Britain and the United States in Washington which resulted in the Webster-Ashburton Treaty, when Canadian boundary disputes, the Texas question and the Creole Case all served to create extremely tense relations between the two countries.

1. Rev. George Bradburn (1806-1880) was a friend and supporter of Garrison. He attended the 1840 Convention as a delegate from Massachusetts.
2. Rev. Nathaniel Paul Rogers (1794-1846) was another Garrison supporter. He edited the *Herald of Freedom* for the New Hampshire Anti-Slavery Society until 1844. He was very radical in his views.
3. Charles Lennox Remond (1810-1873), a free born Negro from Salem, Mass., was for many years an agent of the Mass. Anti-Slavery Society. He toured Britain after the 1840 Convention, lecturing on behalf of the Garrison party.
4. William Adams was another New England delegate and Garrison supporter.

our names on the list of delegates. This created much uneasiness on the part of that body, and no pains were spared to seduce us from our position; but we remained unflexible to the end – looking on, as silent spectators, from the galleries, from day to day. I am quite certain, from all that has transpired, that, had we arrived few days before the opening of the Convention, we would have carried our point triumphantly. As it is, we have not visited this country in vain. The "woman question" has been fairly started, and will be canvassed from the Lands End to John O' Groats' house. Already, many excellent and noble minds are highly displeased at the decision of the Convention, and denounce it strongly. The new organizers have done what they could to injure us, and have succeeded in creating some prejudice against us, especially on the part of the clergy; but the effect will be temporary. We have all been treated with the utmost respect and hospitality, and invitations to go here and there are pouring in from all quarters. An excellent Protest against the exclusion of women was drawn up by Prof. Adam, and signed by himself, Phillips, Bradburn, Mott, Col. Miller,[5] &c, and presented to the Convention, which, on the motion of Colver[6] seconded by Scoble, was laid on the table, and refused a place among the printed proceedings! We, who refused to connect ourselves with the Convention, shall have a separate Protest of our own, which we shall publish in some one of the London newspapers. Rely upon it, we have acted most wisely in this matter; but I cannot now go into particulars. For the proceedings of the convention, I refer you to the papers accompanying this. It was in session only ten days, but disposed of a considerable amount of business. On Wednesday, a public meeting was held in Exeter Hall, and went off with great eclat. The assembly was immense, and the various speakers were received in the most enthusiastic manner. When O'Connell made his appearance, the applause was absolutely deafening. He made a speech of great power, and denounced American slaveholders in blistering language – at the same time paying the highest compliments to American abolitionists. No invitation was given to Thompson, Phillips, or myself, to speak; but Birney was assigned a part, and so was Stanton.[7] Remond stepped forward of his own accord, and was repeatedly cheered by the audience. He took them by surprise, and acquitted himself very creditably. Prejudice against color is unknown here.

Rogers and I have boarded at the same house with Stanton and his wife, Colver,

---

5. Colonel Jonathan P. Miller (c.1797-1847), a delegate from Vermont, was a veteran of the War of 1812, and of the Greek War of Independence.

6. Rev. Nathaniel Colver (1794-1870) was a Baptist minister and among the group of Massachusetts conservatives who rejected Garrison's leadership, and broke away to form the Massachusetts Abolition Society. He later became the minister of churches in Cincinatti and Chicago, and gave up some of his anti-slavery work.

7. Henry Brewster Stanton (1805-1887) was one of the most active of the agents of the American Anti-Slavery Society in the 1830's, after his conversion by Charles Grandison Finney, the noted Evangelist. In the 1840's he took up law and settled in Boston where he continued to take an interest in the political work of the anti-slavery movement. His wife, Elizabeth Cady Stanton (1815-1902), was the niece of Gerrit Smith. She was very active in later years in the cause of woman's rights, an interest which had been greatly stimulated by her meeting with the American women delegates to the 1840 Convention, especially Lucretia Mott.

Grosvenor,[8] James and Lucretia Mott, Isaac Winslow and daughter,[9] Abby Southwick, (who are all well,) and several other delegates. Mrs. Stanton is a fearless woman, and goes for woman's rights with all her soul. Stanton voted right in Convention on the [woman] question. We have been to see Westminster Abbey, the Museum, the Tunnel, The Tower, St. Paul's, etc.etc. The talk now is, that we shall leave for Scotland in the course of a week, under the care and guidance of George Thompson. I feel considerable curiosity to see Glasgow and Edinburgh, and the Scottish highlands; yet can I truly say, "there's no place like home." Some of the Irish delegates insist upon it that I shall take a trip to Ireland. Perhaps we may conclude to visit Dublin. I have shaken hands with O'Connell repeatedly....

I have been introduced to Lady Byron,[10] the Countess of Brunswick,[11] Mrs Opie,[12] Mary and William Howitt, Elizabeth Fry,[13] Anna Braithwaite,[14] and other noted women. A splendid soiree has been given to the foreign delegates, at which I spoke. Several elegant entertainments have also been made for us. I let out all my heresies, in my intercourse with those who invite us together, and have made no little stir in consequence. Slavery out of the question, our country is a century in advance of England on the score of reform, and of general intelligence and morality. We, in New England, scarcely dream of the privileges we enjoy, and the enviable conditions in which we are placed as contrasted with the state of things here.

Dear Thompson has not been strengthened to do battle for us, as I had confidently hoped he would be. He is placed in a difficult position, and seems disposed to take the ground of non-commital, publicly respecting the controversy which is going on in the United States. Yet I trust he will soon see his way clear to speak out in our behalf....

I am waiting with all a husband's and parent's anxiety, to hear from you. May the intelligence prove pleasurable to my soul! Dearest I am
your loving husband,

Wm. Lloyd Garrison..

---

8. Cyrus P. Grosvenor, a New England Baptist minister, was active in Anti-Slavery work, and later took a prominent part in the Liberty Party.
9. Isaac Winslow (1787-1867), a Quaker merchant of Portland, Maine, and his daughter Emily (b.1822), were delegates to the Convention, as was Abby Southwick.
10. Lady Byron (1792-1860) was the widow of the poet. She was active in reform and charitable causes, and was later to be a friend of Harriet Beecher Stowe.
11. The Countess of Brunswick was, like Lady Byron, one of the Stafford House set of "fashionable philanthropists."
12. Mrs. Amelia Opie (1769-1853) was a novelist and poet, and also devoted much of her interests to social reforms. She attended the 1840 Convention as a delegate from Norwich.
13. Elizabeth Fry (1780-1845) was one of the most active Quaker philanthropists and reformers. She is chiefly remembered for her work for prison reform.
14. Anna Braithwaite (1788-1859), an English Quakeress and the wife of Isaac Braithwaite, was a minister in the Society of Friends and made three visits to America in the 1820's.

Accounts of the Irish delegation to the 1840 Convention, copied by Alfred Webb from papers in the possession of Sarah Poole. Extracts from this MS. give "singular proof of the light and life the abolitionist movement brought into a quiet Quaker circle in Ireland."

"The principle persons referred to in the circle are
My father & mother, Richard & Hannah Webb, then aged 35 and 31.
Thomas (or Tom) his brother and Mary Webb, then aged 34 and 30.
(Their father, my grandfather, is occasionally referred to)
Maria Waring, my mother's sister, then aged 22.
My father's beloved cousins
Sarah & Lizzy Poole then aged 26 and 22
their mother (Aunt Mary) & little brother Jacob are occasionally mentioned.
Richard Allen's[1] name will be well remembered
Charles Corkran, a Unitarian minister, an old & close friend
James Haughton,[2] true to the last....

From the Conventants

6th month 1840

Richard Allen. – Here we are all in London. We sailed on Fourth-day evening, and spent yesterday seeing sundry grand sights. We met Birney, etc. etc., and Richard then introduced himself to him, and we had some talk with him. Last night we got among the American delegates, and heard Lucretia Mott make a speech. There are besides five or six *Lady* American delegates – a blooming company – none of them look much more than twenty.

James H. Webb

We this day saw the man best worth seeing in England – Thomas Clarkson. He came into the meeting about half-past ten, leaning on Joseph Sturge and William Allen, and followed by his daughter-in-law and grandson. A short time before he entered it was proposed that there should be no noisy demonstration, but that the best demonstration would be to receive him standing, which was cordially responded to. He was introduced by Joseph Sturge in a feeling and most appropriate manner after which T.C. spoke, and a more interesting scene could not be; – and literally there was hardly a dry eye in the meeting whilst Clarkson was speaking. O'Connell came in, and they were commencing to clap when there was a general hush; but in order to prevent him from thinking there was any disrespect to him, J. Sturge explained the reason to him promptly and agreably. He also was well received.

---

1. Richard Allen (1803-1886), a Dublin Quaker and corn merchant, was the Secretary of the Hibernian Anti-Slavery Society and the Hibernian British India Society.
2. James Haughton (1795-1873), a Dublin corn merchant also, was active in philanthropic and reform circles. Born a Quaker, he became a Unitarian later in life. He was liberal in his political views, supported free trade, and was an admirer of Daniel O'Connell.

We went to the Freemason's Hall at ten o'clock; there we saw Charles Stewart, George Thompson, Edward Baldwin, James Birney, James Haughton, Billy Martin,[3] R.R. Moore,[4] Lucretia Mott, and a great many others that we had not known before. They stood or sat apart for a long time, talking to and recognising each other. After some time it was announced that Clarkson was coming in, and they were requested not to clap, but to stand up instead. It was extremely beautiful and refined to receive him in this manner. While he was there, there were several attempts at clapping, to express approbation at what was said, but they were always hushed down. He came in leaning on Joseph Sturge and they all rose up. He sat in the chair. Then we all sat down and there was a perfect stillness of a minute or two. Joseph Sturge, at Clarkson's left hand, stood up then spoke nicely about Clarkson, and how he had been after suffering extreme illness. He said he was sure they would not object to the exception that had been made to the rule against admitting any one not a delegate; and he produced little Thomas Clarkson, grandson to the abolitionist, a little boy, nine years old today. His mother was sitting at the right hand of his grandfather. Joseph Sturge did it very nicely. He laid his hands on the child's head, and implored that a double portion of the spirit that had rested on his grandfather might rest on him. It was a beautiful sight. An American – Drew – addressed Clarkson and presented him with a book from the American abolitionists, about the Pennsylvania Hall. Afterwards an emancipated West Indian came and shook hands with him, and spoke well. "Look at me and go on," he said over and over: and it was grand. O'Connell – it was delightful to see and listen to him – He put his arms across, and put on such a droll, happy, comical pose. The glory of going there – to the Convention – this meeting! It was almost too great a privilege; but there is no use in trying to express it. It was glorious and grand beyond all expression – "The World's Convention" I suppose thou heard that there were women delegates over. They were women, mind, not ladies; it is a fine thing to be a woman, not a lady – a woman has a dignity. There was such a rout about them today – those silly men didn't choose to receive them. They were sitting among the other women that came to see and hear. There were seven of them. Their men stood up grandly and valiantly for them, not for their private's sake's, of course; but for the principle. And they were a fine principle of the strong, firm, American abolitionists. But it went against them in the end. I believe the discussion of it lasted for hours. Birney was against them. One of them, Wendell Phillips, is coming here to breakfast in the morning. It was well Clarkson went away before it began. Joseph Sturge looked grieved. Part of the time it was quite impossible to know what was said. Cries of "order, order," "Divide, divide," "No, no, no, no, no," "Vote, vote, vote," "Chair, chair" were dinging in our ears.

---

3. 'Billy' Martin was a Quaker and Irish temperance reformer. It was he who persuaded Father Mathew to begin his work for temperance.

4. Robert Ross Rowan Moore, (1811-1864), a political economist, was a member of the Irish anti-slavery society, and in 1841 succeeded in opposing a scene for deporting apprentices to the West Indies. He was introduced to John Bright by George Thompson, and became a member of the Anti-Corn Law League, taking an active part thereafter in the movement for free trade.

It was extremely interesting. It was just like a House of Commons uproar. Thompson told me there was no use in calling out to him, for it would only keep him the longer; and a delightful looking young American man that Hannah and I had taken a great fancy to, stood there like a rock, and told them he was well used to tumultuous assemblies. It ended against the women, and it was miserable to see, the friendly way they were after the meeting – smiling and pleasant.

From Richard

I went to meet Thompson yesterday (First day) morning, and found him in the street coming to breakfast with us. We had a pleasant time. My father and Tom went to one of the country meetings – the rest of us to Westminster meeting – a very neat little house where nobody minded us. Then home, where where we found Thompson, snug on some chairs. He had been greatly exhausted with the weeks labours, and was glad of the quiet haven of rest After Dinner, Hannah and I went to St. Paul's, and took a walk through one of the queer little back streets; and afterwards we all went, excepting Thompson, who remained at home, to Hyde Park, to see the Queen and the fashionable evening promenade of the nobility etc. On Seventh-day I was a good while sitting by Lady Byron, and we had a speech from the Poet Campbell.[5] We also had Birney to tea. Those American abolitionists are noble people – men and women. Some [of] them are rather haughty and scornful of our poor little anti-slavery spirit; but others, and the greatest amongst them, are as meek and humble as martyrs. Their company is quite refreshing, strengthening, and delightful. Garrison is somewhat impetuous, like a moral torrent. His flow of language is wonderful; – not what is commonly called eloquent, but fluent from the heart. The women are intelligent pleasant, unassuming, and one of them, Lucretia Mott – as plain a Friend as my mother and a Hicksite preacher – is considered a person of great ability. Garrison calls her "that almost peerless woman." There is a split amongst the abolitionists here and in America. One party, who have peculiar government principles and [are] in favour of the right of women to participate in their discussions are the disciples of Garrison. The others, who oppose such views, are generally united with by such of the Clergy as are abolitionists. Birney belongs to this party. Both are firms to the great cause; but I could have the most dependence upon the old or Garrison party. Birney, however, is a noble and admirable man. We have had the fragrant presence in our meetings of O'Connell Dr. Bowring,[6] a celebrated linguist, the promoter of education and political economy, Dr. Madden;[7] Amelia Opie attends regularly; Isambert,[8] a

5. Thomas Campbell, (1777-1844) Scottish poet and writer, helped to found the University of London.

6. Dr. John Bowring (1792-1872), famous as a linguist and traveller, for a time edited the *Westminster Review.* He was for many years a Member of Parliament, and helped in the formation of the Anti-Corn Law League.

7. Dr. R. R. Madden (1798-1886) was an Irish doctor and traveller, who did much work to put down the slave trade. He was in the United States at the time of the Amistad case, and gave evidence on behalf of the Negroes.

8. François-André Isambert (1792-1857) was a famous French jurist and advocate.

celebrated French philanthropist; William Allen, and loads of stars higher than these. Garrison is exceedingly free and courteous, very communicative and full of his subject. In some respects he is awful; but I could hardly make this clear in a moment. We have members here who who have suffered greatly in the cause – men of great ability, great endurance, wonderful loftiness of mind. We felt but as pigmies beside them. "Vale, oh vale, he replied."

From Hannah.

Many a time we have been thinking of you since we came. Yesterday I was thinking most of Lizzy, when we had so much of Thompson, in that lazy, quiet, enjoyable way – when he was lying back in the easy chair, and talking over old recollections – some belonging to your Wicklow trip, and James' short browsers. He compared him to a young fawn tripping lightly over the brook – and he had old remembrances of an expedition to Richmond Hill fourteen or fifteen years ago, with his sister and a young lady who jilted him afterwards – "for I began to fall in love very soon after I was qualified." And Sarah was much in my mind last 7th day, when there was a most interesting discussion about the propriety of giving up the use of all slave-grown produce, "as far as practicable." It was introduced by Captain Stewart. Finally, after many had spoken for and against, it was decided that it was not a practicable thing, as even the metal of our common pieces of money was obtained from the mine by slave labour; and so it was left. Yet the best speeches (as to principle) were on the abstinence side. The others mostly went on the principle of expedience, and in a lower tone.

It is most delightful to be listening to them – it shows that the rights of women (of which we have heard so much here) are making some way, since we are allowed the privilege of sitting there at all. Garrison is a fine fellow – so pure and unselfish – straight to the point of what he deems rights, no matter what lies between. All the Americans are heroes, though not all seeing with the same eye – the women too.

From Maria

I have not much of Thompson to tell thee. I care most for Garrison, and Bradburn, and Hockings, than for him. He breakfasted here one morning – that was all; his speeches when he make them, are eloquent and fascinating, and he has a kind of bewitching gracefulness about him.

Long life to these American abolitionists. They are a glorious crew. William Lloyd Garrison is one of God's nobility. I dont think I ever saw such an angelic, holy looking face. He is just like a holy pure thing set up high, that was not to be touched; not that he is unapproachable. I have not been speaking to him, but Richard has a good deal. He was here one evening. He was said to be very like the picture, but his face is not pale as I fancied. But he will not sit as a delegate or take any part in the business. He sits in the gallery which is open for visitors. He disapproves of the manner they are transacting the business in. He was not here in the beginning or perhaps it might have been constructed differently. He stays out on principle. He is high, and holy, and pure looking; – I dont mean by high, aristocratic, but angelic.

George Bradburn is the one that has bewitched me. He is deaf. Wendell Phillips is delightful too; – they are strong and fine, and firm – they are American abolitionists, a new race of being. How easy it is for them to speak when one walks with them in the street, for that was the only time I attempted it. Bradburn with his deafness even is more *comeatable* to me than Thompson. He, and Phillips and Garrison are women's rights' men, and one feels themselves more in their presence on that account. Thompson has just said something about Bradburn (Thompson was at the lodgings when M. was writing) – He's a clumsy fellow you know; he hits hard." But there is no use in trying to describe them – they are some of the moral aristocracy." They regard women not as dolls, but as human beings.

Stuart is delightful; – he was here yesterday morning. He is full of love, it even overflows and seems to pour into one, and makes one almost feel as if they were full of love too. He is very amusing. He screeches out in the meetings and says "Dear brother," and "Dear sister" out of the meetings. He wears a leathern pouch suspended to a strap, which is fastened round his shoulder. Hannah asked him was it necessary – "not necessary but useful; this is not necessary on this dear sisters' head", (putting his finger on the band round my head), "and this is not necessary" (putting his hand to Hannah's cap). Then he emptied it out to show what it contained. I think Sarah would be delighted with him.

From Richard to Lizzy

James Haughton arrived yesterday (from London). He was here today to see us, and brought the very unwelcome news that Garrison (who promised if he came to Dublin to lodge with us) had given up the notion of travelling, and had resolved to return to America by some vessel which was to sail from Liverpool yesterday. I hope this is not the case and that we shall see his face once more. My admiration of his is by no means lessened by what I have seen and heard of him. His complexion [is] exactly like Theodore [Juliot's] – his teeth white – head bald – gold spectacles – remaining hair black as a raven's – face red – look determined – smile sweet. He is a noble fellow. It was well worth going to London to see him. Where is his match? His nonfollowers adore him. He is an apostle with all the mildness, energy, fearlessness, and determination of Peter or Paul...I was much disappointed that Whittier was not there; but this could not be helped, and we saw fine old Clarkson, I believe in one of the most striking situations of his whole life – receiving the silent tribute of respect and veneration of one of the most remarkable convocations that ever assembled.

Hannah to Sarah

Richard is sending you "golden stores" from the mines of North America. He is writing, so I suppose he will tell you of our many letters, the last being from the Motts. It is *fine* (as Maria says) to be getting letters from such people, of such wide philanthropy and such noble spirit. We need grace to remember that these noble views and principles apply as truly to the small everyday matters of life, as to the more high and stirring warfare in which some of these veterans are engaged.

Richard to Sarah and Lizzy

Dearly beloved, I send you the "Nonresistant" for last year, and seven papers – "Liberators" and "Anti-Slavery Standards" – dashing papers, which are now almost my only reading. Hannah says that they make other writing seem *quite small*, and so they do – to me at least – there is such freedom of soul – such noble independence of spirit – such unshackled energy of intellect about them – their aim is so noble – so disinterested. They are so fearless of opposition that it is like breathing on the free mountain top, to revel in their treasures.

Richard to Sarah.

Dublin, 3rd of 8th month, 1840

My dear Sarah,

About a week ago I wrote to Lizzy telling her that Garrison and his friend N.P. Rogers of New Hampshire, editor of an abolition paper, "The Herald of Freedom", would be with us on fourth day morning, and inviting us to come and have his company. Thou wert not specially invited because I thought Lizzy most likely to come, and thou wert not without knowing that thou would be heartily welcome whether L. could come or not. Well, this day week I wrote in great haste to tell Aunt Mary* that the Robinson's would be going on 4th day to Falmouth and that Jacob† should be sent immediately. On third-day evening I went to the Wexford coach, fully expecting to see Lizzy and Jacob; but there was no sign of her there, nor has there been ever since; and Garrison came, and Garrison went away, and we know nothing at all about you. I asked Hannah this morning (while trying to account for so complete a silence at such a time) whether she thought it possible that Lizzie could be offended with me for not pressing her very hard. I thought nothing more was necessary than to give her the wind of the world. But it cant be helped now. He is to sail in the "Acadia" steamer for Boston from Liverpool in the 4th. He arrived on Fourth-day morning about the very hour that the Robinson's, James White, and his son James, went on their way to Falmouth. I went down to the river and met the steamer they were coming in from Glasgow, just entering the river. They dined with us that day without company. We had a large party to meet them in the evening, and in the course of the day Charles Corkran and I walked into the Liberty and through the poorest and grandest parts of the city with Garrison, Rogers being unwell after the voyage. Next morning R. & A. Allen, Maria, James Haughton, Garrison, Rogers, & myself went out to Thomas Webb's lodgings near Killiney Hill, and just opposite Dalkney Island. We had a delightful morning, and between rambling on the Hill, talking and admiring, we did not get into town till half past two. Then they rested awhile, and went out to Greenmount to dinner and tea, and met another large party. On 6th day morning we breakfasted at 8 and did not leave it till half past 11. Visited Petrie's Antiquarian Museum and the Custom House shops, where Mathew gave the pledge. Then home. I called to tell O'Connell that Garrison wanted to see him; he told

* Sarah & Lizzy's mother.

† Their brother who was going to school. A.W.

me he would call at our house. He came in about half an hour after, and was very friendly and pleasant, stopped for about twenty minutes & gave his autograph to Maria, who is in glory. We dined at Richard Allens, and had a very large company to tea. At 9½ came home. Packed up, and at 10½ Richard Allen, Thomas, Mary and I accompanied them to the steamer at Kingstown which sailed at half past 11. Tom and Mary left them at the ship, and we waited till they sailed. We then went on to Toms, lodged there, and came in next morning. Tom knows that my opinions of Garrison before I saw him were pretty high. Well! I liked him better than I hoped, and having more constant and familiar intercourse with him there, my admiration and veneration were raised to, I think as high a pitch as they could be towards any man. The purity of his mind, the sublimity of his views, for the happiness of regeneration of mankind, his personal mildness, the simplicity of his manner, and the absence of pretence, his far-seeing mental vision, the rapidity with which he holds them, are, (as far as my opportunity of observing men has extended) not only extraordinary but enexampled. It is no longer surprising that his influence should be so powerful, or that tens of thousands of the most enlightened, most pious and most devoted of the American abolitionists should stand faithfully by him, as their head, in their illustrious and holy enterprise unawed by sectarian clamour, or the fears of the timid or the insinuations of envy, or by the boldness and originality of his own views – which whilst they breathe nothing but glory to God in the highest, peace, and on earth good will to men, are in their working utterly hostile to the passions, the prejudices, the ambitions, the pride, and the wickedness of the world. Hannah wrote some few lines about him in a little book of Maria's which I may as well copy, as they give somewhat striking though succinct synopsis of his opinions.

"William Lloyd Garrison, who is he?
Not an innovator, but a noble, fearless reformer. He brings no new gospel, but would revive and enforce the gospel, and would have men to throw away all the sectarian glasses through which they have so long studied it, where those glasses magnify, diminish, distort or discolour the truth.

What would he have?
He would have us to become obedient children, to enter on our birthright of holiness and happiness, to follow the holy example set before us by Jesus, walking in his spirit 'overcoming evil with good.'

What results would he look for?
A world in which there would be no slaves, no kings, no beggers, no lawyers, no doctors, no soldiers, no palaces, no prisons, no creeds, no clergy, no sects, no war, no grinding labour, no luxurious idleness, no peculiar Sabbath or Temple, but every day and every place 'holiness unto the Lord', no restraints but mutual restraints, no constraining power but love. Shall we judge such a man because he may go a little further than we are prepared to follow? Let us first consult our conscience and our Testament"

The variety of people whom we had to meet him at our house and elsewhere was very great. But all, without a single exception appeared astonished and delighted with him and many declared what they might truly say – that he was by odds the most interesting man they had ever known. Rogers is a noble fellow, too – a self sacrificing, highminded abolitionist, who has given up his prospects in life as a lawyer for the sake of the cause. We all become greatly attached to him, and got a profile of him done while he was here, which he told me was the first likeness of him ever taken. Maria goes tomorrow; Garrisonized and abolitionized to the backbone.

Yours affectionately

Richard D. Webb.

(Continuation of the preceding letter in Hannah Webb's writing [sic])
...And now it is second day evening and Richard is gone off to Liverpool to see off Garrison and Rogers. (They sail for America tomorrow) and have a few minutes more of their company. No accounting for Webbs; but I am Webb enough to encourage him, as much as I could, to go; – for when will he see such a man again. He has written nothing about money, but I think he has made an arrangement about it with James. Debby is not now expected till early next month, Anne meanwhile goes to pay her last visit to her old home. How long do you stay among the rocks and waves? Has it been of use to thee? This is glorious weather for all of us. Love to little Alf. Has he courage for the third dip? When will you send us Jacob? In haste, from yours

Hannah.

MS.A.9.2. vol. 13 pt. 1 1840 The Weston Papers [66]
No. 104 Elizabeth Pease to ?

London July 17 1840

My dear Friend

...I feel self condemned in not having sent one line to thee or to any of my Transatlantic correspondents since the commencement of the Convention – the fact is, I have felt it to be a difficult subject to write about, and & knowing how many abler pens were likely to be employed in thy service I reconciled myself to silence. And now that I have taken my pen I seem so lost in the multiplicity of topics I wish to touch on – that, but for appearance sake I fain would leave our most excellent & – how do I rejoice to say, *mutual* friend Garrison, to speak all for me; – he knows my mind & heart, we have canvassed everything together, & inexpressible has been the treat & the privilege of doing so with me, whom to know must be to love, admire & appreciate. Thanks to some who have hardly taken him by the hand, abstaining from all intercourse with him, who have sat in judgment, censured & condemned alike both him & many of his opinions. Thanks to such as these I have been privileged with a much larger share of his company than I ever dared to anticipate wd. fall to my lot – & I feel that the fault is my own if I have not been benefitted & instructed by it. There are many other dear & honoured ones, on whom I should like to dwell, but I need only say that American Abolitionists have realised most fully the anticipations – & these were no mean ones – which I had formed of them. There was one choice spirit, N.P. Rogers, ever by the side of Garrison, who is always associated & identified with him – they are twin brothers in worth & excellence &

true abolitionism. The Phillips's have been our near neighbours & feel like old & dear personal friends...
W.L.G. & N.P. Rogers have accompanied Geo. Thompson to Scotland, where I doubt not they will breathe a more *free* & genial atmosphere than they did here, where the murky mists of prejudice obscure the discernment ever, of what is *due* to men who have sacrificed so much & come so far to advocate the cause of the slave. Such also was the spirit of exclusion manifested towards those noble women who had left family & home on this mission of Love & Mercy – Every obstacle was thrown in the way & no public opportunity was ever afforded them for a free interchange of sentiment with their English sisters. I regretted it deeply & several of us mourned over our utter inability to help it – had we been at our homes, we might have exerted an influence, but here we felt ourselves to be powerless.

Notwithstanding, however, that there were many things to be regretted, & human frailty in some measure marred its lustre, great, very great good will I have no doubt result from the recent Convention. Such an assemblage must give an impulse to the cause of Freedom, the world over – the principles it upheld, the sentiments it has sent forth, the information it has elicited cannot but beneficially affect the condition of the slaves everywhere. Yet as was admitted by all, or all save one, who addressed us from your land it must be to British India that we must look for influencing the slave-holders upon whose *conscience* you have no hold & who can be moved only by appeals to self interest. We rejoice indeed, that we have had the good fortune to engage the services of Professor Adam. I look upon this, as the most auspicious Event that could have occurred for the British India Society – he is in every way qualified to render it essential service – his knowledge of India, & stability of purpose & of principle eminently fit him for the office he had undertaken. The health of Geo[rge] Thompson too, is improving, so that I hope there is a prospect of prosecuting the British India cause, with far more energy & effect, than it has yet been. Symptoms of good from the formation of the society already begin to appear – the E.I. Company are directing their attention to the cultivation of cotton in India – many of them, we are told a *majority* of the directors, are in favour of abolishing the opium monopoly & are thinking also of very greatly reducing the tax on salt – these are cheering indications & bid the labourers go on, nothing doubting but that justice & Truth & Humanity will triumph in the end...

Believe me as ever, sincerely & affectionately thine, in behalf of oppressed humanity

Eliz. Pease.

MS.A.1.2. vol 9 (1) 1840 Anti-Slavery Letters to Garrison [67]
No. 75 Elizabeth Pease to William Lloyd Garrison

2 Christopher St. Finsbury
London 18 inst.

My dear Friend

...I trust soon to hear that you have had a pleasant journey & are now enjoying the free & genial atmosphere of Scotland, after the murky mists of prejudice, by which you were surrounded here & which obscured the discernment of what was ever *due* to men, aye & to women too, who have sacrificed so much & come so far to advocate the cause of the slave. Well, all will yet work together for good I have no doubt, – tho' every day tells of friends gone over to "New Organisation" (& such is in truth the case here) do thou preserve, for if Truth & the God of Truth be on our side, what signifies it who may be against us And if, at any time, I can lift a straw, in this country, to help any of those great enterprises, in which thou art labouring, & regarding which my own judgment may be convinced, the effort shall not be wanting; of this, at least rest assured, that thou wilt ever have the best wishes of thy sincere & affec[e] friend.

Eliz[th] Pease....

Since writing the foregoing my father has shewn me a letter which he rec.[d] a few days ago, from Thos. Clarkson in which he says "I wish to know whether the colonization socy. *still exists* & its present state, whether it increases or is stationary – whether Liberia is flourishing, & whether it keeps to its word or contract to put down slavery in Africa; (I am told that it does) but above all I wish to know, in what respects the Colonization Soc[y] *has injured the cause of abolition in America.* Unless I have an answer to this last question, I cannot write my Letter. If therefore, Mr. Garrison cannot come down to Playford, he may write to me & give me the particulars."

This morning's post brought a few lines from T.C. in reply to the note written at thy request, & enclosing the "Freeman" – in it, he says "It will be 5 or 6 days before I can get my American Letter begun & finished." I suppose, therefore, he has found the information he required & is not now waiting to hear from thee.

MS.A.9.2. vol 13 pt. 1 1840 The Weston Papers [68]
No. 112 Lucretia Mott to Maria Weston Chapman

Dublin 7 mo. 29th 1840

Dear Maria,

I remember how many and kind and long have been they messages of this sort to me, and now that our dear Wm. L.G. & N.P. Rogers are about to leave us setting their faces homeward, I feel that somewhat is due from me to thee. But how to accomplish it I find not, for we are from day to day so in the midst of bustle & commotion & excitment, pleasurable & otherwise, that to write seems quite out of the question. Our friends too can tell you so much better than I can narrate here, the story of our coming across the Atlantic to attend a 'World's Convention' – simple souls! and on our arrival the grave information awaited us, that it was no more than a conference of the British & Foreign A.S. Society, to be composed of such numbers as their com. of arrangement should choose to select – that the name of 'the World's Convention" was merely a "poetical license" – (alias a rhetorical flourish) – and that the "com." in their wisdom has seen meet to ordain and enact, that women should not compose part of their august body. That they further, *as wise men should*, had a resolution prepared for this said 'conference' as one of its first measures. That all the arrangements of said committee be sanctioned & approved by the conference. Of course we would not "thrust ourselves forward" into *such* a meeting, but having come so far to see what could be done for the slave, & being thus prevented doing anything ourselves, we were willing to be mere lookers on & listeners from without, as by so doing we should be the means of many more women having an invitation to sit as spectators – which we found was accounted a very high privilege in this land – by their women who had hitherto most submissively gone forth into all the streets, lanes, highways & byepaths to get signers to petitions, & had been lauded – long & loud for this drudgery, but who had not been *permitted* even to *sit* with their brethren, nor indeed much by themselves in public meetings – having transacted their business, as we were informed, by committees.

In vain we endeavoured to have a public meeting called for women – although a few Anne Knight, Elizh Pease &c – did all they could to promote it. At length we gave up in despair & left London satisfied – that "when for the time they ought to be teachers, they have need that one teach them which be the first principles" of Human Freedom.... We had many opportunities with members of the "new organization", & with the com. & with individuals, to present them their injustice to us to the cause of the slave as well as their own inconsistency. These we improved & had many a battle wherein we came off as we think victorious. But a "World's Convention" has yet to be held. That the feelings of the British public would not have been as outraged as we were given to understand, by our admission, is abundantly evinced in the readiness with which I have meeting at the Town Hall was as heartily cheered as if I had been worth hearing. And an invitation sent to the chair to me to appoint a special meeting....

Since we came to Dublin I have accepted an invitation to speak in a Temperance Mg. – not the least manifestation of dissafisfaction – altho' unexpected to most present – but on the contrary " cheers long & loud " – & not merited either – but such is the custom in this land – and I mention it as proof that the objections to our admission were all hollow....

Wm. L.G. will tell you what glorious meetings they have had in Scotland. – We rejoice that we have stayed here to see them once more....

ever thine

L. Mott.

No. 91 William Smeal[1] *to William Lloyd Garrison*

Glasgow, 8 month 1/40

My dear *frd.*

I take the opp[y] of transmitting the enclos'd, to apprize thee, by desire of our frd., Wm. Adam, who has his information thro' C.L Remond, the latter having received a letter from America yesterday – that *R.R. Gurley,*[2] & a Coloured female, named Ela, have just arrived in Liverpool. Now Wm. Adam thinks thou *ought to know this* & not only so, but that it would be well for thee to *Challenge R.R.G.* on the Colonization question. W.A. thinks it probable he will be *very quiet* till thou art away – & *then* he will come out. Think of this, if thou can *possibly* stay longer.

Now *entre nous*, I suspected there wd. be some misgivings about our *Female* friends in certain quarters; and my suspicion is confirmed. For a note from Dr. Wardlaw is just to hand, putting to me the question, – "Is it intended that the *female American Delegates*, to whom so repeated & pointed allusion was made on Monday evening last, *take any part in the proceedings* of our Annual Meeting – or that *they appear on the platform in their capacity of Delegates.*" I have an apprehension that this is preparatory to opposition not only on Dr. W's part, but it may be, on that of others in the Committee. I have, however, taken care, not in any way to commit myself. For, in the Advt., Bills, &c I have, after naming *Keep & Dawes* in connexion with *their* Institution, it is added "others of the American Delegates, it is expected, will be present" – If the Women are *refused* the platform, & *interdicted* speaking, it shall be known to whom belongs the *odium*. Assured I am, it will not be *the people*, in pub: meeting assembled. In replying to the Doctor, I have told him I really was unable to answer his question, either as to one point or the other – all I know was, that James Mott & his wife had arrived, & that others were expected, & that I hoped *the Anti Slavery Public* would have the pleasure of seeing them. I intend urging G.T. to return here from Edin[r] as, *in the event* of a Committee Meeting to determine the matter *pro* or *con*, G.T. will be of service in helping the *right* settlement of the question –

In great, haste, & with dear love to N.P.R. & thyself, I am truly thy frd.

Wm. Smeal

---

1. William Smeal (1793-1877), a Glasgow tea merchant and Quaker, was a Secretary of the Glasgow Emancipation Society, and for many years a friend and supporter of Garrison.
2. Rev. Ralph Randolph Gurley (1797-1872) was a Secretary of the American Colonization Society. Like Cresson, he visited Britain to try to promote the aims of the Society.

No. 89 John Murray[1] *to William Lloyd Garrison*

Bowling Bay 1st Augt 1840

My Dear Friend
Wm Lloyd Garrison

Be it known to you and to all other zealous Anti-Slavery and Anti-Colonization Advocates such as you that R. R. Gurley Secretary and unceasing advocate of that most unprincipled and oppressive of all professing Philanthropic schemes – or perhaps the only professedly philanthropic scheme which practically degenerates to the antipode of its profession – is arrived in London – as Mr. Remond is informed by the letter from his friend in London W.L. Jeffers and will doubtless be about to congratulate himself and Sir Thomas F. Buxton privately if not publicly on the *entire* congeniality of their views on the "*Colonization*" scheme.

I write this therefore that you and G Thompson and friend Rogers & the other friends of the cause may know the fact, and consult together whether it might not be desirable even yet, if the passage could be transferred to another vessel of the same company – for you to [re]main a week or two and challenge the Lion to a discussion in London – which doubtless Sir T.F. Buxton would be desirous he would do so as distinctly to clear him from the contagious infection even by implication of such an inhuman Monster.

I need not dilate on his Gurley's influence or attempt to produce an influence in London & elsewhere in this country – doubtless he has assurance enough for anything – nor need I portray to you the necessity of some vigorous effort being made & that *immediately* by you or somebody else to drag him & his schemes before the Public; even although he should prefer to work in private, and to shew him & it up to the People of England *in their proper character.* You have by this the fact before you – if this reaches you which I trust it will – of his being *there* & you may be assured, *not for no purpose* and I leave it with wiser heads than mine to say what should be done to neutralize his poisonous action....

At this moment – enter Mr. Keep from Oberlin last from London & Bristol and after a few words conversation he is *quite of opinion* that W.L. Garrison if we could only intercept him on his return to America is the *very best person to meet Gurley.* But I shall allow W L G to have an opinion in the matter....

Since reading the above to Mr. Keep, he desires me to add – that he regards it as of *immense importance to the cause,* that Gurley should be so effectually met here as to be deprived of the possiblility of making *even the smallest impression here – but* that he should be most completely blown up – at least his sentiments & his diabolical scheme [of] Colonization – altho' you should spend a year in it, and that you are *really the fittest person,* for the work – Hoping this may reach you and friend Rogers well & that you

---

1. **John Murray (d.1849) was a Secretary of the Glasgow Emancipation Society and a friend of the Garrison party.**

may both be spared to arrive at your homes in safety and find your respective families well is the prayer of [?] Dear friend

yours sincerely
John Murray

MS.A.1.1. vol. 3 1838-1843 Anti-Slavery Letters from Garrison [71]
No. 55 William Lloyd Garrison to Joseph Pease

Liverpool, August 3, 1840.

Esteemed Friend,

At your request, I sit down to give you my opinion as to the prospect prospect of the speedy and peaceable overthrow of slavery in the United States. Let me say then –

1. That Christianity sanctions the use of nothing but moral and religious means and measures for the suppression of any sin, or the overthrow of any system of iniquity – in other words, it forbids the doing of evil that good may come, however vast the good to be achieved, or small the evil to be resorted to for its accomplishment. To bring the products of free labor into competition with those of slave labor, and thus secure the abolition of slavery and the slave trade throughout the world, is a peaceable, legitimate and Christian measure, which commends itself to the approval of all good men.

2. That there is not any instance recorded, either in sacred or profane history, in which the oppressors and enslavers of mankind, except in individual cases, have been induced, by mere moral suasion, to surrender their despotic power, and let the oppressedgo free; but, in nearly every instance, from the time that Pharaoh and his hosts were drowned in the Red Sea, down to the present day, they have persisted in their evil course until sudden destruction came upon them, or they were compelled to surrender their illgotten power in some other manner.

3. That the emancipation of the eight hundred thousand bondmen in the British West Indian Colonies forms no exception to this lamentable truth – as it was effected by the collosal power of the mother country, and in opposition to the feelings and wishes of the West India planters. That power, it is true, was stirred up by the moral and religious action of the people of England; but, had the liberation of the West India slaves depended upon the triumph of moral suasion *in the colonies* over the depravity of the planters there is not the slightest probability that it would have taken place. Indeed, it is certain that the planters would never have allowed any anti-slavery agitation among them. The mere suspicion, a few years since, that the Weslyan and Baptist missionaries sympathised with the slave population, and were hostile to slavery, raised such a tempest of fury against them, that their chapels were ruthlessly destroyed, and they were either cast into prison, or compelled to flee for their lives. The slaveholding power, wherever it holds absolute sway, will never tolerate any movement for its overthrow. There is, therefore, no liberty of speech or of the press in the slave States of America, and

consequently, no chance for the exercise of moral influence against slavery in that section of the country.

4. That, of all oppressors and tyrants who have cursed and afflictted mankind, none have ever equalled the enslavers of the coloured race – *especially American republican slaveholders*, – in ferociousness of spirit, moral turpitude of character, and desperate depravity of heart. I regard their conversion, as a body, to the side of bleeding humanity, by appeals to their understanding, consciences, and hearts, about as hopeless as any attempt to transform wolves and hyenas into lambs and doves, by the same process. Their understandings have become brutish, their consciences seared as with a hot iron, and their hearts harder than adamant.

5. That nothing will induce them to manumit themselves but an utter inability to compete with the labor of free men, in raising those productions which now give life and sustenance to the slave system; in connection with a rectified public sentiment, that shall everywhere regard them as the deadliest enemies of the human race.

6. That it is by the cultivation of cotton alone, and the purchase of that article by British manufacturers, that American slavery puts at defiance the opinions of the civilised world, baffles the efforts of the abolitionists of England and America for its speedy overthrow, and raises an impenetrable wall of defence against the attacks of its enemies.

7. That if England would supply herself with free cotton from some other part of the world, to the exculsion of all slave grown cotton, it is quite certain that, within seven years, American slavery would be peaceably abolished, from absolute necessity, as well as from the moral change which will by that time have been wrought in the free states of America, in opposition to that hideous system of plunder and outrage.

8. That it now seems to be placed beyond all doubt, that cotton can be grown by free labor at a much less expense, and in far greater abundance, in British India, than it is now done by slave labor in the United States: hence, that England, as a matter of self-interest, as well as on the score of humanity, should without delay redress the wrongs of India, give protection and encouragement to its oppressed and suffering population, and thus obtain a cheap, permanent and abundant supply of free cotton from her own vast and fertile possessions in the East.

I am sure that your British India movement will fill the hearts of American Slaveholders with dismay. May speedy and complete success attend it! – I see no reason why it should not receive the zealous and hearty support of the friends of humanity in Great Britain, especially of all genuine abolitionists on both sides of the Atlantic. For all that you are doing to promote it, (and no man can be doing more,) and for all your previous efforts in the cause of West India emancipation, I honor and praise you. Be not weary in well-doing, and you cannot fail of success. The case is one of great urgency. Let no time be lost, therefore, in laying all the fact respecting India before the people. Those facts can never be listened to with indifference by them, but will cause their hearts to burn like fire. They will rally *en masse* under the broad banner of universal emancipation, and their motto will be – "Justice for India!"

Freedom for the American slave! Prosperity to England! Good will to all mankind!...

I remain, dear sir, with the highest respect,
your faithful friend and coadjutor,

Wm. Lloyd Garrison.

Joseph Pease.

MS.A.1.2. vol. 9 (1) 1840 Anti-Slavery Letters to Garrison [72]
No. 92 George Thompson to R.D. Webb

Edinburgh
Aug 9. 1840.

My dear Richard/

I am glad that you and I are among the few in this country who are able & willing to see admire & love the excellencies of the truly great & noble men about whom you have favoured me with so interesting a letter. You did right in being with them at the last. Heaven speed their passage to the desired haven and crown their labours with success and them with glory honour & immortality! Tomorrow (I write this on Sunday) I go to Glasgow, and will take with me the "Nonresistant" & the [?] which shall be left at Smeal's to abide your order. I can only send you one of each. We held the annual meeting of the Glasgow Society on Friday night at which Dawes, Keep and Remond were the American speakers – we adjourned the discussion till Monday when we are to be favoured (?) with the presence and co-operation of Messrs. Birney Stanton & Scoble! You shall have a full account of what is done in due time.

I received Garrison's farewell letter thro' Miss Pease who seems quite in love with W.L.G. & to find in his name and virtues an exhaustless theme for her prolific pen. She seems to mourn his departure with a deep & unaffected sorrow. The Motts with Miss Pugh & Miss Kimber are in Glasgow. L.M.holds a meeting tonight in the Unitarian Chapel in that city . Hannah Backhouse is also there and speaking today so that Smeal may say "The *bane & antidote* are both before me.

Your letters are ever welcomed. As you are all Irish & I am half Scotch – we may feel some pride in looking back upon the pleasant times our beloved friends now on the ocean were permitted to spend in the green isles & among the hills of Scotland. I know you feel this.

Love to all. I mean to see Ireland before the year expires. Remond is much better.

Yours affecy

Geo. Thompson.

Brooklyn, August 1840

My dear bro. Wright,

... How much I desire to see you! I will not attempt to give you even a synopsis of the events which transpired during my brief sojourn in England, Scotland and Ireland – not, at least, until we shall be permitted to see each other, face to face. Let me assure you that I regard my mission as one of the most important movements of my li fe; that everything looks well for our side of the question across the great waters; that the rejection of the American female delegation by the London Convention, and the refusal of Rogers, Remond, Adams, and myself, to become members of the same, have done more to bring up for the consideration of Europe the rights of women, than could have been accomplished in any other manner; that, wherever we travelled, not withstanding our contumacious (!) behaviour towards the Convention, we were hailed as the benefactors of our race; that we "sifted into" the minds of those with whom we came in contact, all sorts of "heresies" and "extraneous topics", in relation to Temperance, Non-Resistance, Moral Reform, Human Rights, Holiness, &c, &c; that we have secured the personal acquaintance and friendship of some of the noblest spirits of the age, who will co-operate with us in all our efforts to subvert the empire of Satan; and that, in due season, the fruits of our millions will be made manifest to all eyes. On the subject of non-resistance, I had very much to say in England, Scotland and the Emerald Isle; especially in view of the monuments and statues erected in honor of moral and military warriors, and of the numerous castles, and forts, and arsenals, and armed troops, which were everywhere to be seen. I carried out with me six bound volumes of the Non-Resistant, six copies of the engraved Declaration of Sentiments, and a bundle of non-resistant tracts, all which I distributed in the most judicious manner, and to great acceptance. Some converts were made before our departure, and many minds are laboring with the great question. As the temperance cause is somewhat unpopular in England, and the great mass of the abolitionists there are in the daily habit of using wine, porter, and other intoxicating liquors. I said much privately and publicly in favour of total abstinence, and rebuked them faithfully for their criminal indulgence. In short, I did what I could for the redemption of the human race.

Dear Rogers was my companion on all occasions, and assisted me in my labors very materially. He was exceedingly well received, and has won for himself a good reputation. It is somewhat doubtful whether he will go to New York; but I think he will not be able to resist our importunities. Indeed, *he must go* – and greatly will our new organization antagonists tremble on seeing him actually in the editorial chair of the "Standard" – and so will all, who are endeavouring to stop the march of reform through this country and the world.

As to George Thompson, I can say, that he is with us, through evil report and through good report – for better, for worse, – on the woman question – on the side of non-resistance, old organisation, etc. His speech at the London Convention was unfortunate and incoherent, which he now ridicules, and of which he is ashamed, but which was extorted under peculiar circumstances and without reflection. "Richard himself again," and nobly will he do battle for us....

Your faithfull coadjutor,

Wm. Lloyd Garrison.

MS.A.9.2. vol. 14 pt. 2 1840 The Weston Papers [74]
No. 13 Elizabeth Pease to Maria Weston Chapman

n.d.

My dear Friend

Our dear Friends W. & A. Phillips in a letter which I recd from thee a short time ago, remind me of thy desire to have a few of D O'Connell's autographs for your fair. Truly gratified do I feel in being able to fulfill it, to some small extent – It was my good fortune to be in his company more than once last week – & he kindly wrote me thirteen cards, ten of which I enclose to thee – he is the most good natured, kind-hearted person you can coneive – & I hope I may at some future time be able again to avail myself of his kindness, for your benefit. O'Connell most generously left his urgent engagements in Ireland last week to attend a meeting here on behalf of British India. – "the most important question," as he styles it in his speech, which he has ever advocated, & he promised to come again before Parlt. meets to give the cause another help. The meeting was highly interesting & encouraging – but it is needless for me to enlarge upon it, as thou wilt receive a paper herewith, & our friend Charles Remond is giving a detailed account of it to W.L.G. Charles contributed to its interest in no small degree – indeed he has been a great attraction at all the meetings which he has attended altho' he has cut himself off *very much* from the sympathies of a large class of "abolitionists" by his noble refusal to ally himself with "new organization"....

I grieve that the Anti-Slavery public of Great Britain shd. be so indisposed to you. In all honesty & sincerity, I strive to give them the *Truth*, as it appears to me wherever I possess any little influence, but this was always *small*, very *small*, & is everyday becoming less , in consequence of taking the unpopular side – So it will be for a while, but Right will triumph in the end...

I trust we shall be able to send you a better rept. of our meeting soon in a pamphlet form. The papers do none of the speeches justice. Both G.T.'s & O'Connell's were splendid. Ever with highest regard

Thine truly,

E. Pease.

Boston, Sept. 1, 1840

Esteemed Friend:

... I hope that, ere this, you have had your contemplated meetings in Manchester in reference to the British India question; that the great advocate of the human race, the fearless and eloquent O'Connell, and that no less eminent and faithful friend of all mankind, George Thompson, were present on the occasion, to lift up their inspiring voices in behalf of the poor natives of India; that a mighty impetus was given to your movement, which nothing shall be able to resist, and that it is the determination of the Committee of the British India Society to take bold and decisive measures, both in relation to the people and government of Great Britain, that justice may not be delayed and that the grand remedy for slavery and the slave trade may be speedily applied. Why should there be any hesitancy in the matter? Is not India groaning under the weight of British oppression? Are not millions of her inhabitants systematically plundered not only of their most sacred rights, but even of the food which is necessary to sustain life? In the midst of fertility and abundance are they not visited by the most frightful famines, in a manner unexampled in the history of a downtrodden people? And are not the people and government of England responsible for it all? And is it not clear that, by relieving India, and giving full scope to the cultivation of cotton by the remunerated labor of her population, the prospects of England will be greatly advanced, her character redeemed in the eyes of all mankind, and India saved from starvation and ruin? Is it not equally clear, that if Great Britain will but supply herself with free grown to the exclusion from her market of our slave grown cotton, a blow will be struck at the American slave system, from which it can never recover? It seems very strange, nay, quite incomprehensible to me, that the abolitionists of England do not espouse the British India movement *en masse.* Already, there is much consternation on this side of the Atlantic, among the planters and their northern adherents, in relation to that movement. My eye at this moment rests upon a copy of the New York Herald (a violent proslavery journal), in which a tocsin of alarm is sounded in the ear of the slave-holding States. The editor cried out lustily against " the villainous designs of the Abolitionists to destroy the interests of the Southern planter," and adds, "Much as we detest the conduct and principles of the insurgent and scandalous Abolitionists, we feel bound to give them (i.e. the facts in relation to your British India movement) in order to put our Southern friend on their guard against the infamous designs of these crazy scoundrels." This is a high panegyric upon your proceedings, and should mightily encourage you to go forward in your great work of human redemption....

My mind constantly returns to England, and I often think of the pleasant interviews we enjoyed together. It is possible, perhaps probable, that we may never meet again on earth; but I will cherish the hope that it may be otherwise.

We are now in the midst of a hot political excitement in this country, in relation to the Presidency. The whole nation is politically insane, and reason will not be restored, (if then,) until the question be settled, whether Martin Van Buren or William Henry Harrison be the successfull candidate. Both of them are mortally hostile to the anti-slavery cause, and deserve to be covered with infamy, rather than with laurels. O, the inconsistency of my countrymen!

Wishing to be cordially remembered to your wife, Elizabeth, and son, I remain, gratefully,

Your friend and coadjutor,

Wm. Lloyd Garrison.

MS.A.1.2. vol. 9 (1) 1840 Anti-Slavery Letters to Garrison [76]
No. 109 R.D. Webb to William Lloyd Garrison

Dublin, 2nd of 9th month 1840

My dear Friend:

George Bradburn has been with us for the last ten days and we have enjoyed him exceedingly. He is a free minded man full of drollery & humour, and is not afraid to say what he thinks. He is almost the last of the abolitionists that we are likely to see for some time. Birney & Stanton will be here, but we wont be so much at our ease with them nor will we feel the same sympathy with them that we have with you. You would make honester men of us if we had more of your company. I seem to breathe a freer air when you are with me. I never longed so much to see any one as thyself – and it is much to say that I am not disappointed. But I like you all – and Rogers is a noble fellow. We are longing to see some of your papers containing your own remarks on what happened here. I have had a deal of talk with George Bradburn about Edmund Quincy,[1] whom I wishes to know more of from what I heard from thee....

Thy views as explained by thyself, attracted very great attention when thou wert here, even from individuals who are not generally willing to give in to a new idea. But thy hostility to creeds has drawn forth a threat from a young clergyman, whom thou met at James Haughton's, that in the next world thou would probably find good reason to repent such sentiments in this!...

Now "to conclude & come to an end" as some of our Irish ballads say, although thou wilt often forget us we can never forget thee & we are determined not to leave thee long unaware of our existence. Anything thou may write to me will be valued & will be sure to go the rounds of our little circle and something farther. And if Edmund Quincy or any of thy fellow labourers in your glorious efforts should come to Dublin thy sign manual will assure him bed & board and a most hearty welcome at my house and all sorts of pleasant faces amongst thy attached friends here.... I am thine very affectionately

Rich[d] D. Webb

---

1. **Edmund Quincy (1808-1877) was one of the leaders of the Boston clique. Quincy sacrificed his high social position to work for the anti-slavery cause, which he championed through his writings. He was for many years one of the editors of the *Anti-Slavery Standard*, and wrote also for other anti-slavery journals.**

Boston, Sept. 6, 1840

My Dear bro. May:

Your kind "Welcome home again!" comes joyously to my ears, among the thousand congratulations that have been given to me on my safe return from the old world. During my absence, I saw much that was magnificent, wonderful, curious, strange, pleasant, afflicting; but my mind is too much confused, by the multitudinous array of objects and incidents, to allow me to state anything accurately. All that the Tower, Westminster Abbey, St. Paul's, the British Museum, and many other famous places contain, I have seen, and gazed upon, till my eyes were weary of sight-seeing. England, in beauty, order and cultivation of soil, is indisputably the Eden of the world; but alas! the old serpent is in it, and as full of false-hood and mischief as ever. Oppression, degradation, vice, starvation are there, side by side with monarchy, royalty, aristocracy, monopoly. England is on a volcano which, if it explode, will cover her with desolation. Should Victoria suddenly expire, in all probability there would be a revolution that would scatter to the four winds her present form of government, and establish a republican one in its place. But the people need more light as well as more bread, and they are determined to have both, or perish in the attempt. I could not enjoy the beautiful landscape of England, because of the suffering and want staring me in the face, on the one hand, and the opulence and splendour dazzling my vision, on the other. O, to think that God – our kind, merciful, loving Creator – has filled this earth with abundance for all, and yet that nine-tenths of mankind are living in squalid poverty and abject servitude in order to sustain in idleness and profligacy the one-tenth!

I was much pleased with Scotland – better pleased than with England. Her scenery, indeed, is not so beautiful, but it is far more grand and sublime; and she has enough of beauty to atone for what is wild and rude in her formation. I like her people better than I do the people of England: they are more like New Englanders in their appearance and manners. I was exceedingly pleased with the Irish friends I saw in Dublin, and received from them a welcome most cordial and ardent. But I must wait until I see you, and then you shall hear all about the "gipseying" of bro. Rogers and myself. I must contrive to come down and see you on some Saturday, and remain with you till Monday, lecturing on Sabbath evening, if agreeable. This I will try to do in the course of two or three weeks....

Ever lovingly yours,

Wm. Lloyd Garrison.

No. 121 William Bassett[1] *to Elizabeth Pease*

Lynn. 9 mo. 23. 1840.

My dear friend

I take pleasure in commending to thy attention our beloved brother John A. Collins,[2] Genl Agent of the Mass. Anti-Slavery Society, and one of the most devoted and indefatigable friends of the slave. Nothing more need be said to induce thee to afford him such assistance as may be in thy power in forwarding the objects of his mission, which he will make known to thee.

He is fully in the confidence of the "Old Organization" Abolitionists of Massachusetts and the whole country, and is abundantly qualified to represent them among our friends in Great Britain. We hope he may do much to promote a more perfect understanding of the true nature of the difficulties subsisting here among the professed friends of Emancipation.

Owing to the unparalleled commercial embarrassment under which we have suffered for the past years the absorbtion of energies of many of our friends in the present political contest, and the necessities imposed upon us by the "new organization" movement, we find ourselves in a state of almost unprecedented pecuniary suffering. Any aid which our transatlantic friends may furnish will be peculiarly grateful, and we feel more encouraged to appeal to the true friends of freedom there, from the fact that they are likely to be *misrepresented* by the committee of [the] British & Foreign A.S. Society, and consequently will be less inclined to sustain *them.* We are now passing through a crisis which calls upon every friend of our cause to make sacrifices in its behalf.

Anyattention which thou may show to our brother will be gratefully acknowledged by

Thy sincere friend

Wm. Bassett.

Elizth Pease.

---

1. William Bassett (1803-1871) was a Quaker shoemaker who was expelled from the Society of Friends for his radical anti-slavery views, after the publication of his *Letter to a Member of the Society of Friends, in Reply to Objections against joining Anti-Slavery Societies,* Boston, 1837. He conducted a lengthy correspondence with Elizabeth Pease, who wrote her article on *The Society of Friends in the United States and their Views on the Slavery Question,* 1840 from information supplied by Bassett.
2. John Anderson Collins (1810-1899) became the General Agent of the Massachusetts Anti-Slavery Society in 1839. His tour of Britain in 1840-41 to collect money for the American Anti-Slavery Society was conducted amid bitter partisan warfare. In spite of this he succeeded in raising a fair sum. He soon abandoned anti-slavery work, however, and migrated west where he established a community on the Fourieristic principle.

Boston, Sept. 30, 1840.

My dear friend,

Thomas Clarkson's letter, repudiating the Colonization Society, is of great value, and will make a salutary impression upon the public mind. I am overjoyed to think that the dear old man has publicly abandoned that wicked combination, and left it to perish in infamy. It would have been most afflicting to all the genuine friends of bleeding humanity, if he had gone down to the grave even ostensibly as a supporter of that Society. I am surprised, nevertheless, that, in stating his objections to it, he does not say a word about its impious doctrines and pro-slavery principles. He really seems to be wholly ignorant of them!

Little did I think, my dear friend, that you would so soon see among you another of our anti-slavery band in Massachusetts; but I am as happy to introduce to you, (as I doubt not you will be to see him,) my esteemed friend and coadjutor, John A. Collins, the General Agent of the Massachusetts Anti-Slavery Society, and a member of our Board of Managers. He is a free spirit, a lover of universal reform, most zealous and efficient as an advocate of emancipation, one who has made large sacrifices for our cause, is thoroughly conversant will all the schisms that have taken place in our ranks, and is generally successful in whatever he undertakes. The object of his mission he will lay before you and the other choice spirits in England, so that I need not go into any details in this letter. Sufficient to say, that, in consequence of the political excitement now raging like a whirlwind in this country – the embarassed state of the times – and, especially, the blow which our third party abolitionists and the new organizationists have given to the anti-slavery enterprise – we are really in a more critical situation than we have ever been before, and, unless we can get some aid from abroad, I am apprehensive that the American Anti-Slavery Society, with the National Standard, Rogers and all, must sink. We have, you may rest assured, strained every nerve to sustain ourselves; and it is with the greatest reluctance that we send our bro. Collins on his mission. It is a dernier resort, "for better, for worse." We are well aware how many are the calls made upon our British friends, to promote objects of charity, mercy and religion; but we know, too, that they have realized the truth of the Savior's declaration, that "it is more blessed to give than to receive." In attempting to put away the evil that is in the world, we must forget all national distinctions and geographical boundaries, and remember that we are indeed members of one family, to whom there is nothing foreign, nothing remote. I have told my friend Collins of the difficulties that will lie in his path, especially in consequence of the introduction of the new organized spirit among you in England. He goes out, therefore, with very moderate expectations; for even a little assistance will amount to a great deal at this juncture. We trust, for ourselves, that his mission will be short, for we cannot spare him long abroad. I rely very much upon your judgment, and also that of Geo. Thompson, in this emergency. Do counsel my friend Collins, for he will need need to be wise as a serpent, and harmless as a dove. He goes out in behalf of the American Society, the Executive Committee of which, I presume, will send an address by him to the anti-slavery friends in England. Our Board, also, will furnish him with some credentials....

You must let me hear from you as often as convenient. I will *try* to be punctual in giving letter for letter. My time here is very much absorbed in the anti-slavery and non-resistance enterprises; and I cannot write so frequently as I should otherwise be glad to do. I have not, as yet, said much about the state of things in England in the Liberator; but intend to as soon as our State meetings shall have been concluded.

As soon as a correct report of your grand meetings inManchester, in behalf of British India, shall reach me, I will commence the publication of proceedings I still look to that movement with the deepest interest, and shall aid it to the utmost of my poor ability....

I wish I was in Darlington today, provided I could return home to-morrow – or, rather, provided the Atlantic did not roll between. All I can do is, to desire to be affectionately remembered to your father, mother, brother, and all your enquiring friends. In haste,

Yours, in every good work,

Wm. Lloyd Garrison

MS.A.1.2. vol. 10 (2) 1840 Anti-Slavery Letters to Garrison [80]
No. 7 Maria Weston Chapman to Elizabeth Pease

Boston Sept 30th 1840

Elizabeth Pease
Dear Friend

...Let me occupy the remainder of this letter in introducing to you our dear friend, *John A. Collins*, a member of the board of officers of the Massachusetts Anti Slavery Society, and delegated from the American Anti Slavery Society also, to endeavour to relieve a temporary difficulty for money that we labour under through the baseness of the last year's committee in sacrificing our means, & taking the "Emancipator", our weekly national paper, out of our hands. I felt deeply pained that we were obliged to resort to this means at first: but a moment's thought tells me I was wrong to feel so. Is not the cause of Righteousness & of God the same the world over? Is not the Christian's country this world & his countrymen all mankind? As to the feeling that at first rose in my mind, that England with her thousands of artisans – England with vast responsibilities in Ireland & to British India, should not be applied to, I find it will not bear examination. For should we receive enough from her to supply our present temporary necessity, we should not have taken it from the suffering dying Englishman, but from some one till then, perhaps indifferent to all suffering, whose heart might be enlarged by the gift....

If, dear friend, you could give our friend Collins a list of names such as he could apply to with most hope of finding sympathy & aid, (I suppose those in England who have borne more of the pecuniary burdens of the A.S. cause are so new-organized or prejudiced by Birney & Stanton & Scoble that they would be a hopeless case,) it would be of the greatest service. I have written to Harriet Martineau who is my friend of many years, & trust she will be able to set influences in motion – which may aid him. Do you know her? If not, how much do I wish you might have that pleasure) for her the similar one of knowing you....

Ever faithfully & devotedly yours for
Freedom & humanity

Maria W. Chapman.

MS.A.1.2. vol. 10 (1) 1840 Anti-Slavery Letters to Garrison [81]
No. 28 George Thompson to R.D. Webb

8 Duncan Street,
Newington, Edinbro'.
Nov. 2. 1840

My dear friend

Mr. Collins, a delegate from the American Anti Slavery Society, is now under my roof. He comes here to solicit funds to keep afloat the ark of Abolition in the United States, whose existence is now threatened, but the combined operation of *the money pressure* (of three year's duration) *The Presidential Election*, and the *spirit of New Organization.* He says, unless the people of this country extend pecuniary aid sufficient to sustain the Am. Soc. for a few months it must sink. He has at present seen only Miss Pease and a few of our British India Society in London, who are friends to Garrison and the Old Organization. We have talked much respecting the course he ought to take, and I am disposed to think he cannot do better than commence a tour with *Charles Remond* – hold meetings – present the great question of American slavery – keep clear of controverted topics & make his appeal for help as though no prejudice existed. In private he must be prepared to answer questions, meet objections and if he is publicly attacked he can defend himself and his friends. Tell me if you could take him & Remond in Ireland for a week or two while the way is opened for them at a few places in England. Here our friends have I fear been surfeited with meetings & I dare scarcely mention another or ask for any aid as Dawes & Keep have recently reaped the field and scarcely left a solitary ear for any one else. See R. Allen and let me hear from you as soon as possible. I believe our friend Collins with Remond (who proceeds admirably in his public addresses) w^d make a deep impression. Where in Ireland besides Dublin w^d they be likely to find a few warm fds. who w^d make arrangements for them?

I write in haste. I w^d send a letter to Mr. Allen also but in writing to you I know I send to him also.

I shall leave home for Lancashire the latter end of the week.

Yrs affec^y. – Geo. Thompson.

No. 32 R.D. Webb to Elizabeth Pease

Dublin 11th month 4 1840

My Dear Friend

As we have had our visit from the London Committees deputation think thou wilt like to know that I thought of them in their corporate & individual capacity. We had our meeting in a small theatre which being held in the evening was well attended by the poorer and much the best and most public spirited class of the community – the teetotal tradesmen & operators of Dublin, who I hope are the materials from which a free, enlightened, & intelligent Christian people will at no distant day appear. They listened to the address of Birney & Stanton with deep interest and to that of Scoble with great and natural delight. For the happy condition of the liberated slaves shadows for the future state of Ireland when she reaps the full fruit of her escape from the Drunken House of Bondage. The next meeting was held by day in the Rotunda & was attended by a respectable audience who listened with great attention but I would much prefer the ragamuffins for they have kind hearts which swell with generous emotions – and they will make sacrifices to promote the liberation of the slave which those who call themselves their brothers have no notion of. I hope before very long there will be thousands upon thousands of the people of Dublin full of zeal in the anti-slavery cause.

James Haughton & myself with some of our friends who attend Temperance meetings and address the people have lattery lost no opportunity of lugging in anti-slavery on the Temperance "platform" in a way which would shock and horrify a new organizationist – we "overlay" the Temperance cause, as Scoble would say, most shamelessly & shamefully & perseveringly with abolition. Stanton thinks it is a political [?] of the great importance to send over such of our emigrants as intend to settle in the United States fully embued with anti-slavery sentiments. I hope but little from the political efforts which are being made by the *third party* – nonetheless it is of consequence that all means should be taken to change the miserably corrupt state of Dublin sentiment in America.

I had little opportunity of knowing Stanton – he does not appear to me to be easy of access. I had no familiar conversation with him. Birney I greatly admire – There is dignity, candour, truthfulness – a quiet cheerfulness about him, an assurance that he would not stoop to any mean action, which form you to respect him – Then his great & noble sacrifices for the cause & the knowledge that but for his adherence to principle he might now be a rich & prosperous man in the common acceptance of the terms. I did not hear him volunteer a syllable in deprecation of Garrison or anybody else. He evidently thinks the Nonresistants one of the many sects which swarm in America who are brought into existence by the prevalent freedom of opinion & who go into the most outrageous extremes of profession and practice. He instanced the conduct of some Perfectionists and others whose acts were absolutely revolting – but they were not nonresistants – and it will never do to judge one body of men by the conduct of another or the principles of any society by the shortcoming of any or all of its members... He spoke to me high term of Garrison's abilities but says that he thinks himself destined to reform the world & that Luther was nothing to him. May be he does think so — and what if he be a great reformer? Surely, if the Nonresistant principles be correct — if they are the real essence of Christianity — & if the present effort to promulgate them be successful, Luthers reformation will be considered as nothing in comparison with Garrison's reformation. Never let us flinch from the truth, though others sneer at our confidence. Garrison is a far more original — a far more extraordinary man than ninety nine out of one hundred of those that the world wonders at. Birney has nothing of that fearlessness and expansiveness of mind which so eminently distinguishes Garrison but I greatly honour his devotion to the slave and his clear and convincing way of pleading the cause of the oppressed.

Mrs. Stanton is one in ten thousand — I have met with very few women I consider equal to her — such eloquence, such simplicity of manner — such naivete, a clearsightedness, candor, openness, such love for all that is great and good, so much of the spirit of old organization, and a hearty well grounded horror of Scoble which I imagine will gratify thee as much as I fear it did myself. His unsleeping hostility, his watchful malignity against the old organizationists in general & Garrison in particular are odious beyond measure.... The impressions he left after him was that of a self-willed, tyranically minded, narrow souled, clever bigot.... Our rich people care little for the cause here — and most of the very few who are interested for its success have very little superfluity of this world's wealth. Although I would rejoice to see Remond & Collins here, I could not encourage them to come with any hope of reaping much advantage in the way of funds. I do not know of more than half a dozen who would be likely to give — there may be more, but I dont know them. Then I fear that Scoble has poisoned the way for them in wealthy England & that they would meet but a cold reception from most of the known friends of the antislavery cause in your country. I greatly desire to know thy opinion about Collins and Remond's prospects, & what thou thinks they ought to do.

In the Liberator for the 16th of October there is a resolution *passed unanimously* after a debate in which Garrison Rogers & others took part, in which it is declared that "of all proslavery hostilities that which wears the guise of new organization is *the most dangerous & malignant*" — Now I confess I cannot swallow this. Surely Birney, Arthur Tappan, Gerrit Smith, Jay & Whittier are not proslavery men although their views on all subjects may not be so far darting as those of our old organization friends. Perhaps if we had Garrison to explain what he meant the matter might not be so obscure — but as it is, I do not like such an intolerant declaration. I wish thou could give me thy interpretation. I am the more desirous, because my excellent friend James Haughton is a good deal annoyed by it. He thinks that if the charge be true Tappan & Birney & their friends are not men to be trusted or kindly received — if it be false then are the Old Organizationists very much in the wrong in condemning such men in such a manner. Do read me this riddle & thou will oblige me very much. It must be a fine quiet pleasant sort of thing to be a Catholic with your conscience out of your way, snug & warm in the priest's pocket — you then have no further trouble with it — you are saved the bother of thinking & balancing and hesitating between two or five hundred opinions. I am often so puzzled that I dont know what to think....

Thine very truly
Rich D. Webb.

MS.A.1.2. vol. 10 Anti-Slavery Letters to Garrison [83]
No. 34 J.A. Collins to Charles Stuart

8 Duncan St. Newington, Nov. 6th 1840

Dear Brother Stewart,

You are probably aware that the committee of the Edinburgh Emancipation Society, are to meet on Monday "to hear statements from yourself & me respecting the cause of the Division existing among the Abolitionists of the United States." I have no doubt but that you have a desire to bring the truth before the abolitionists of this city & [to] do this it is important that some definite proposition should be before them touching the cause of division & that each of us speak alternately 15, 20 or 30 minutes until the discussion may close.

You will, no doubt, see the importance of this arrangement as without it each of us may talk for three or four hours without enlightening the committee on the subject which convened. Understanding as you do the rise and progress of the anti-slavery cause in America, it occurs to me that the following proposition, embodying the professed cause of division, would be the proper one for discussion:–

That these abolitionists in the United States, technically called new organizationists, were justified in seceding from the Mass. & Am. A.S. Society, from the oft repeated & successful attempts of the majority to bring in & make those societies responsible for the doctrines of nonresistance, woman's rights &c &c If this proposition does not suit you (which I am confident [it] will) will you have the goodness to draft one to suit yourselves & forward it to me forthwith & believe me your sincerely in the cause of truth and freedom

(John A. Collins)

MS.A.1.2. vol. 10 Anti-Slavery Letters to Garrison [84]
No. 36 Charles Stuart to J.A. Collins

Meadowside.

Dear Collins

I do not agree with you in the views which you kindly state to me, in your letter of 6th.

The proper course, in my opinion, will be, for you to complete your address & then for me to answer it; each uninterrupted by & each using his own discretion, as far as the feelings & time of the Committee, may admit.

If however you would prefer it, I am quite willing to proceed at once without any reply, together with such other matter as may occur to me, & then, when I have done to leave you to proceed, without interruptions; but I should prefer the former

Yours sincerely,

C. Stuart.

7th Novr.

No. 38 John Bowring to William Lloyd Garrison

London 9 Nov 1840

My dear Sir

I was most happy to receive intelligence of our transatlantic friends through Mr. Collins who brought me your favour of the 30 September. We have discussed with him the course of his proceedings – & I anticipated the pleasure of hearing of him from Darlington whither he went from Town, – but he has not written. He arrives at an unfavourable moment – so many appeals have lately been made to the public for objects, connected directly or indirectly with the slavery question that we fear the response will not be be what under other cicumstances might have been hoped for. At this moment too the land is in so uneasy state from the "rumours of wars" wars which are rolling around us – & which I am afraid to own how alarming I deem them to be. For I know not where this unwarrantable meddling is to end – & think we have complicated affairs enough of our own to settle without embroiling ourselves with the settlement of Turkish disputes[1]. Again I fear the woman's question – to me of singular interest – will be a stumbling block on the way of Mr. Collins. How often have I regretted that this subject was launched with so little [combination ?] – so little preparation – so little knowledge of the manner in which it had been entangled by the fears of some and the follies of others. But bear up ! In the coming of these women will form an era in the future history of philanthropic daring. They made a deep, if not a wide impression – & have created apostles if as yet they have not multitudes of followers. The experiment was well worth making. It honored America – it will instruct England – If in some matters of high civilization you are *behind* – in this matter of courageous benevolence how far are you *before* us !

My grateful affections are with them and you.
Ever faithfully yours

John Bowring

---

1. Egypt under Mehemet Ali and his son Ibrahim had successfully attacked their overlord, Turkey, an action which at once drew the attention of the great powers of Europe. France secretly favoured Egypt; Russia hoped to get concessions from Turkey, whilst Britain aimed at a settlement which would favour neither of these two European powers. Under the guidance of Palmerston a Convention was signed in London in July, 1840, limiting the gains of the Khedive of Egypt. France, however, had been excluded from the Convention, and in the months following tension in Britain was high, as the Royal Navy had to take action to force Mehemet Ali to agree to the Convention's terms, whilst France was openly hostile to Britain over the whole affair.

Tynemouth.
Nov$^{br.}$ 9th

My dear Sir,

I have no hesitation in writing to you without loss of time . Would I c^{d} give you help & comfort in doing so! I never think of your errant here, & its causes, without deep concern; for I see no way in which I can help you. I never saw the Duchess of Sutherland, & have no knowledge, except from others, of her dispositions about the cause; & therefore it wd., I feel, be an impertinence in me to take any step in regard to her Surely our friend Garrison, whom she made an effort to meet & converse with, is the proper person to make an application to her. Upon enquiry & reflection I find that my friends have responded so nobly to my calls upon them in behalf of the Oberlin, that I ought not to apply to them again. It is understood that the effort they & I (upon them have made is, if not a final one, meant to last a long while, – amidst the insatiable calls of our poor population' & I am certain that it wd. most materially & permanently injure your cause if the present case were urged upon them. It is no easy matter, engaged as such people are, with a thousand affairs at home, to keep them at all informed about the great question over the water. Such an appeal as this, following upon their later liberal charity, would, I am confident, alienate them entirely from a cause wh they regard already as degraded by quarrels, while I sh^{d} not be able to raise a pound.

I do not, however, (deeply as I sympathise in your grief & annoyances) despair of the cause because your object may fail. Nothing will ever persuade me that, after the hearts of thousands have been for years devoted to the cause, through every species of suffering it will now perish for want of the setting up of a single newspaper. Truth cannot be so put down; rely upon it, it will find its own mode of expression. I shd. have been glad if your misson cd. have succeeded. I shall not be disheartened if it fails; – nor will you, I am sure.

I shall never cease to watch & work for the cause where I can. May God prosper it and bless you, & the brave hearts that beat only for the truth, & to aid the oppressed!

I hope to write very soon to Mrs. Loring, on the subject of your mission. Miss Smith sends you her regards with mine.

Believe me,
dear Sir,
very truly yours
Harriet Martineau.

No. 92 C.C. Burleigh[1] to Maria Weston Chapman

n.d.

My dear friend,

I have but a moment to spare, & must plunge in without preface even to tell why I am in haste. When Collins was here I could not talk much with him, for it was my busy time. I felt "*no unity*" with the English mission there, but was less unfavourable to it than I have become on reflection & the information from our friends just arrived. If it be not too late, I do wish it might be abandoned. J. & L. Mott think it exceedingly injudicious, & that Collins will hardly get enough to pay his expenses. Going from our side he will be discountenanced by the great body of British Abolitionists, & the few who will welcome him are not able to give much, but *will* give what they can, without his going, so that the mission will absorb that little, which might otherwise go to sustain our general operations. In a word they think it will not do good adequate to its cost, & may do harm. I have spoken to almost nobody here about it, for Collins so wished, but so far as I know, the step will find no favor here. McKim[2] fully agrees with the Motts – He thinks too that so important a step ought not to have been taken by our Ex Com without more deliberation & consultation with friends in various parts, than can have preceded this sudden resolution, especially considering that we have objected to the old Com. for having at times taken too much upon themselves. In aiming to secure the confidence of British Abolitionists we ought not to risk too much the weakening of that of our friends at home. As to this movement, I do not think an abolitionist here who would cordially approve it, whilst most if not all would *dis*approve it decidedly.

As to what Pa. will do for the Am. Soc I cannot speak with confidence. We are somewhat in debt, & just now our expenses are outrunning our receipts. The principal part of the burden has fallen on the city. Our country friends are slow in sending in their contributions – though considering the "hard times", the political fever &c &c, it is not wonderful. But my time is up, & I must close abruptly. Kind remembrance to your husband & sisters & all the true hearts. Tell [W.M.C. ?] I would write to him but have not time now.

In great haste, yours truly, C.C. Burleigh.

---

1. Charles Calistus Burleigh (1810-1878), a somewhat eccentric journalist and lecturer, remained faithful to Garrison and his party throughout the anti-slavery campaign, serving for a time as editor of the *Pennsylvania Freeman*, an anti-slavery paper, largely the organ of the Philadelphia group. After 1859 he acted as corresponding Secretary of the A.A.S.S.
2. James Miller McKim (1810-1874) was one of the most active of the Pennsylvania abolitionists. He worked as an anti-slavery lecturer, and was also for years editor of the *Pennsylvania Freeman*, and an active participant in the Underground Railroad.

MS.A.1.2. vol. 10 Anti-Slavery Letters to Garrison [88]
No. 55 Abby Kimber[1] to George Thompson

Kimberton 11/26 – 1840.

My dear Friend

An opportunity presenting across "the Ferry", as the New Yorkers call the broad Atlantic, I cannot resist the temptation of congratulating you upon the advancement "Women's Rights" have made in Scotland since we were at Glasgow, we were only a few months before the age it seems, and can not set up for such *notable innovations*, as you would have persuaded us, we were. I suppose the Lady Chartists of Glasgow made the programme for themselves, as they seem to have flourished most – Our American Ladies, have not been behind their sisters of Scotland, in this *reform!* All over our country they have been embroidering Harrison Banners, and have presented them before thousands – with all the "pomp and circumstance" of political meetings, nay they have been in some instances sung political songs with their brethren "in arms" – and more, the very children are glowing with party ambition....

I see you have had your Edinburgh meeting for Birney, Stanton & Scoble and a Temperance Meeting – where thou didst insinuate a *pun* publicly, on our friend Brewster's[2] name – I was ready on reading it to cry, Oh! oh! – order order! Chair chair! – none but Philadelphians, "go unpunished for a pun" – and *they* have lived down the prejudice against them....

I have written in such violent haste that I cannot think of half I wanted to say – as I had not intended favoring thee by this opportunity – but it "[?] me great" to see how the women of Scotland were acting in defiance of public opinion – as I cannot seal with a *coronet I do not fear* that my letter will be embalmed with those of the "Mother of the Gracchi" –

With love to Ann and the bairns –
Thy sincere friend

A. Kimber

MS.A.1.2. vol. 10 Anti-Slavery Letters to Garrison [89]
No. 58 J.A. Collins to Elizabeth Pease

Nov. 27 [1840]

Dr. Friend,

...I have suggested to Mr. Adam the propriety of sending an agent

---

1. Abby Kimber (1804-1871), an active Philadelphia Quaker and abolitionist, was one of the delegates appointed by the Philadelphia Female Anti-Slavery Society to the 1840 Convention.
2. Rev. Patrick Brewster (1788-1859), Scottish Chartist and Presbyterian minister, was famous for his speeches and writing on behalf of the poor of Paisley and Glasgow. Although he staunchly defended the position of the Moral Force Chartists and working class rights, he remained within the Established Church of Scotland at the time of the Disruption.

to America to raise funds for B. India. In another, I will expose a few reasons. No doubt large amounts might be raised from those who do nothing for us. In fact, it would be a fine thing to interest them to act for our cause....

Have you seen a few of the last numbers of the *Times* newspaper? It has come out in defending the ministry in recognising the independence of the Texian government. I like the arguments no more than the deed itself, yet if England is a slaveholding nation, as can be easily proved, I cannot for my life see the propriety of her refusing to recognise Texas, merely because she is guilty of slaveholding. But, if, as is the general impression, this Government considers slaveholding a crime – at war with the dearest rights of man & incompatible with civilization, then I cannot understand by what course of reasoning she is recognised.

This morning's Times has four columns devoted to a review of Sir Geo. Stephens letter on the Niger expedition, & most unmercifully dissecting, exposing & ridiculing Sir Fowells scheme of African Civilization.[1] I wish you to let me know whether you receive the Times & if not, I will forward them to you or such of them as contains important matter. Attacks have been made upon the Colonization Society through the columns of the Times but I regret to learn that its Secretary, R.R. Gurley has not been permitted a defence through the same channel. I am for full free & candid & open discussion. I have not the least doubt that the scheme would find many strong advocates among Englishmen & for such to espouse the cause, would increase the zeal & efficiency of abolitionists. God would [overrule ?] it for great good.

I have just had some very interesting letters from some Scotch friends. Would that circumstances would permit me to visit this country from one end to the other, to correct false impressions with respect to certain great principles.

Please convey my warm & affectionate regards to your dear family & say to your father, that I have been for some time writing him a letter. From my conversation with him on British India I have been led to examine the subject more fully & have become vastly more interested in it than when I was in Darlington though I was greatly interested in it then. It embraces ⅛ of the population of the globe. How I should like to engage in a cause giving the whole human family their rights. But enough – affectionately yours J.A. Collins.

MS.A.9.2. vol. 14 The Weston Papers [90]
No. 69-70 J.A. Collins to Maria Weston Chapman

London, Dec. 3d, 1840. 6 Queen St Place, Southwark Bridge

My dear Friend,

Yours of the 30th of Oct. was received the 24th Ultimo, for which

---

1. In 1839 Sir Thomas Fowell Buxton formed the Society for the Extinction of the Slave Trade and the Civilization of Africa and with Government aid set up an expedition to explore the Niger and if possible enter into commercial treaties with the natives. It was an ill-fated expedition, many of the members dying of fever, and by 1843 the Society was dissolved. But it had opened up British interest and influence in this region which was to develop steadily throughout the century.

you have my grateful acknowledgements. Would that I could be placed within the doors of 11 West St this evening, & listen to all the marvellous things that have transpired since I left. Could I spend one hour with some score or two of those faithful, true & tried friends whom I might name, one or two months more of banishment might be made tolerable. I never knew before what it was to be homesick. Had I visited England under any other auspices than Garrison abolitionism, with but one exception, & that is [slay ?] I should have been more cordially received. Even R. R. Gurley, of colonization memory, can gain a hearing among abolitionists, who treat me comparatively with contempt. Nine tenths of anti-slav[er]y in this country would be rank proslav[er]y with us. Genuine abolitionism, in this country is situated as Isaiah, the prophet describes the daughter of Zion to be in, "desolate as a cottage in a vineyard, as a lodge in a garden of cucumbers, as a besieged city. Except the lord of hosts has lifted us a very small remnant, we should have been as Sodom & we should have been like unto Gomorrah." Though the whole horizon is beclouded, with the exception of one clear spot, no bigger than a man's hand, yet that will ultimately scatter, devour & annihilate the whole fig & *smoke*, consequent upon the influence of crafty priests & politicians & bigoted & honest people.

I have put off writing hoping from day to day to get something to write, but as yet, I have met with discouragement from almost every quarter, & there are but very few indeed, who feel and care but very little about our American trials. Those firmly to our measures, on account of the great opposition they occasion, do not feel prepared to take sides openly, while those unfriendly, spake neither money , time nor pains to combat them in every form and shape and as a general principle either by means foul or fair. I will make no apologies, however, for not writing, but will give you such information as I can upon this sheet, more or less....

I... delivered my introductions to Dr. John Bowring & Mr. W. Ashurst, [1] solicitor, i.e. a lawyer of the third rank. I found Bowring to be a gentleman, whose time was greatly occupied in governmental affairs, but exceedingly interested & gave me a most cordial welcome, but as he is a political man, the circle in which he moves are so much interested in Whig reform that they think and care but very little about negro emancipation in the U.S. But Ashurst I found to be a cold, selfish mortal & very indifferent withal, who, after about three minutes conversation insinuated that his time was money, upon which, failing to interest him, bid him good morning & was off in a tangent. I called upon Prof. Adam, & though very limited in his influence, from his short residence and limited acquaintance, rendered me every possible assistance in his power. He is one of the most bold, zealous, unflinching & uncompromising abolitionists I have met with in all my intercourse with British Philanthropists. For his assistance, though ineffectual, the Am. Abolitionists are under great obligations to Mr. Adams. After spending better than a week in London, laboring with indefatigable zeal, in endeavouring to

---

1. William Henry Ashurst (1792-1855), a London minister, writer and free thinker, was active in many radical reform movements "including Parliamentary reform, abolition of Church rates, postal reform and women's rights". He greatly admired American institutes, and visited America in the early 1850's. He was a close friend of Garrison and Lucretia Mott, and contributed regularly to the *Liberator*.

interest some leading characters, so as to be able to have a social meeting for advice &c & succeeded in getting four together. Such jealousies exist between Whigs and tories & Churchmen & dissenters, and it was thought inexpedient for either of the gentlemen compasing my most *august assemblage*, to introduce me to Buxton, Gurney et al of that stamp, but advised me to visit Geo. Thompson, to whom I had previously forwarded my letters &c. On my road to Edinburgh I visited the Peases of Darlington I found in Elizabeth, a host of herself. To meet such a spirit in England, was like to me, the parched Arabian of the burning desert lighting upon an oasis. In strength of intellect, freedom & enlargement of soul, liberality & in firmness of purpose, she is inferior to but few, if any of Freedom's daughters in the United States. She gave me fifty pounds. Her father is literally a man of one idea. British India is his hob[b]y. It is with him, the universal panacea for all the ails flesh is heir to.

I next visited Harriet Martineau, as I proceeded to Edinburgh I found her quite infirm though nothing so feeble as I had expected to find her. She remarked, in the commencement of our conversation that she could not do anything for me directly or indirectly as she had exhausted all her resources, both pecuniary & influential upon Keep & Dawes for the Oberlin. In fact I could not interest her in the subject. She would not be made to believe that salvation of our Society or the cause could be dependent upon a few thousand pounds. I have a letter from her, for which you can judge for yourself.

Geo Thompson received me most cordially, and profered me every assistance in his power to enable me to succeed & was almost the only being who gave me the least encouragement. Yet, poor fellow, had he been acquainted with the feeling then existing, in his own adopted city to cripple his influence, he would have talked very differently. Stanton, Birney & Scoble too were in Edinburgh, but the presence of Thompson & Remond greatly embarrassed them in their movements & so they resorted to stratagems to rid themselves of these two, whose influence they greatly feared. A committee meeting was called at which Thompson was invited but Birney took it into his head to go out into the country to visit some Scottish scenery. So he pounced upon Thompson & Remond to attend him & meetStanton & Scoble at Glasgow. They not discovering the trick, assented, when the remaining two had full scope. They succeeded, effectually, in poisoning their minds. When Thompson introduced me among his friends as a delegate from the American Anti Slavery Society, the question of Garrisonism was instantly raised, & when inquiries were made as to when & where they had received the information, Thompson discovered the trick. He then succeeded in getting a committee meeting, of the men's society called, to have me give the other side of the story, but a day previous to the meeting, who should present himself, but that ignorant tool of Joseph Sturge, Chas. Stuart, who is travelling the kingdom, ostensibly to wake up the women, but really to sift in New Organization & get the societies to become auxiliary to the B & F Society. Stuart remarked that he made it his duty to enlighten the people, the first thing, on the subject of new and old organization. I think him the greatest ignoramus, on this matter, I ever met with. He knows just as much about the Am. controversy, as *it* knows about him. I found that it had been industriously circulated that Garrison was a socinian & in that place nothing that could be said of him, could have murdered hisinfluence more than this.

The day of the meeting came & I resolved to say nothing of the difficulties until forced to by Stuart of some of his friends. I talked for something like an hour on the great change wrought, within a few years, in public sentiment, with respect to the subject of slavery, the great interests to our country, to the cause & to the world, dependent &c upon the existence of our society & winding up with an appeal &c when one of the disorganisers wished to know how much the women's right questions & no government theory contributed to depress us – This opened an opportunity for me to go into the subject. Thompson by some remarks gave the com. to understand where they might find him & Remond made some very good remarks. Stuart said, notwithstanding the mud and sophistry which had been introduced, the subject really had but one side – that the society which I represent was entirely unworthy their confidence and support, – that it was anything but an abolition society, & that the Am & F.A.S.S. was *the Am. Society* – That the colored people almost to a man were the Tappan etc. etc. & begged the com. to have another meeting to hear us continue our statements, which was granted. The com. with but one or two exceptions sympathising with him. The next day the female com. convened to hear statements from me, when Stuart thrust himself & reiterated the old stereotyped objections. The subject being thus opened, Stuart, Thompson Remond & myself continued the discussion for better than three hours. Thompson acquitted himself at this meeting most manfully. He talked like an old organized abolitionist. Some of the women, who could hear Garrison & his coadjutors traduced by Stuart, were exceedingly horrified when I exposed the duplicity and treachery of the new organisers, & would beg me to desist, as it was so painful to have such good men as she was confident some of the new organizers were, implicated. With but few exceptions we found that the women, having left their father's house & cleaved to their husbands, were one with their lords, in this sense at least. Thompson was poorly prepared to see matters turn thus, especially in Edinburgh when his influence has been, previously almost omnipotent & from a class too, who had apparently drank deep at Freedom's fountain, and who hailed his return with such rapturous joy, from America & his twin brother Garrison, & pledged themselves to be one with them in principle, action, hope, fear, victory or defeat, till their heads were mingled with the earth or the slave ushered into freedom. Instead of being armed with additional strength, sufficient for the occasion, he appeared disheartened, & gladly availed himself of an invitation to visit Manchester, to learn the place before the next committee meeting. The engagement was previously made but he might have spent 12 hours in the place longer than he did & have reached Manchester in season when four hours delay would have permitted him to have attended through the entire meeting. Though Thompson's heart soul and sympathy is entirely with us, yet he sighs for his influence. He lacks faith in God. Though bold, free and enlarged in his mind, he is not the man I once considered him. Situated as he is in this country, I think his speech on Mrs. Mott's admission to the World's!!!! convention is what should have been expected from him. He is in my estimation, emphatically a *creature* of circumstances. With the bold and daring, in a cause his conscience approves, Geo. Thompson would be bold & daring. If there should in this country, arise a party advancing the cause of religious liberty, Thompson would associate with them & be one of their fearless champions. In the U.S. he would be bold, if he should happen to get under the right influence. He is not prepared or qualified to lead a cause through the assaults of its enemies & the treachery of its friends. He would be a most valuable auxiliary to us. His eloquence is captivating. He would be glad to remove could he be cleared from the British India Society, but he is so intimately connected with that society that I think it doubtful whether he can dissolve his connection with it before a year or two without great loss to that society. He says that Rogers had no warrant from him to state that he thought of coming to the U.S. He wishes nothing may be said in our journals with respect to his visiting our country, as proposed by him as it might lessen the confidence of the com. in him. He wishes me, when I write home, to remember him kindly to yourself, husband, & [?] of sisters and all who might enquire for him.

One word with respect to the committee meeting. I had previously, to the meeting written Stuart requesting him to discuss the merits of new organization on the alleged ground of division by its friends & as laid down in its official documents – each to speak alternately, for 20 or 30 minutes until the subject should be used up. This he refused to do but wanted me to close my speech & then let him have the entire field. The day arrived, & I laid before the com. our correspondence & remarked to [him?] that such and such were the charges brought vs. our society &represented as the grounds of decision that if Stuart could sustain those charges, the Am. Society would stand guilty [but ?] for them, but if not, it would stand acquitted. They finally over-ruled that I asked too much, but as a compromise, they gave Stuart ¾ of an hour to make his speech, whereupon he pulled from his bosom a small book from which he read for about 35 minutes, a most indifferent & prosy essay, reiterating the same things previously stated, such as that the Am. Socty. was a woman's rights intrusion society, that Garrison was an apostate – that Gerrit Smith & Beriah Greene[2] had done as much as Garrison to put down Colonization, insinuating at the same time a compliment to Chas Stuart. That Garrison entertained sentiments which his soul abhorred &c &c You of course can anticipate my arguments & the class of facts I should introduce. The com. being entirely composed of evangelicals & mostly of the evangelical order, their prejudices were strong against me & did not mean to be convinced. However, after this meeting I found a change. Invitations began to flock in, to breakfast here, dine there & sup somewhere else, and I was resolved not to leave the place until I had broken down that prejudice & to a considerable extent I flatter myself a good state of feeling was produced. I verily believe that soon after Stanton had visited that place, those who received Garrison with such enthusiasm would not have treated him with common civility. Stuart left the place greatly disheartened, but took his influence along with him as a goodly number of those who gave him at first a most cordial greeting, became my warmest friends.

There is one lady in Edinburgh who would be a very valuable woman with whom to correspond. In personal appearance she reminds me of Mrs. Child. In variety of talent executive tact, powers of endurance she reminds me of Mrs. Chapman. She is also a woman of a superior mind, very liberal in her views, though

---

2. Beriah Green (1795-1874), a minister and for a time the President of Oneida Institute, had been elected the President of the A.A.S.S. at its initial meeting. He later conducted a Manual Labour School in Whitesborough, New York.

connected with a most bigoted baptist society. My labors were so great that I became completely exhausted – she took me to her house, nursed me up and performed most of my labor herself. Her addrs. is "Mrs Harriet Gairdner, 16 Morrison Crescent, Edinburgh." She is the wife of one Dr. Gairdner who has not much interest in the cause. I raised only about 50 pounds in this place.

Remond & myself next proceeded to this city, where we have been for some time negociating with Buxton the Dutchess of Sutherland[3] and others of that school. I have but little hopes of succeeding with Buxton as the committee of the Br & F.S. are using all their power to crush him – & more recently the London Times has come out against his scheme threatening to devour it. It grows out of some personal considerations of the part of the Times & on the part of the A.S. committee from a jealousy that their influence will be made to suffer somewhat. I perceive from the last Am. & F. Reporter, that they disclaim all sympathy with Buxton's scheme. I mean by *this*, the new organized committee. I look upon Af. Civilization as a subject of great moment. If I can succeed in getting a start from a few of the influentials, I shall [ride?] into the country & endeavour to hold meetings but without such an influence it is impossible to get up a meeting. In this country, every thing goes by the influence of great names. I think I shall succeed in raising something if my health permits me to labor, but I am almost disabled by the London fogs, which are so dense as will almost permit one to rest by leaning upon them. I am reduced almost to a skeleton. My cough has increased to a fearful degree. I am advised by the medicals to quit the country for Rome as soon as possible, which I should certainly do were it possible. But this crisis my purse forbids, & I will be satisfied to let the issue be what it may. It is well I visited this country provided I do not raise a farthing. New organization flourishes in the dark & it cannot succeed only by jesuitical, false & treacherous means, which I have succeeded in dispensing & hope to do more....

Were I free to visit the country without making an appeal for funds, on my own responsibility, I could get up meetings without difficulty & produce an amount of influence which I cannot now do, as an appeal for funds, in this, as in all other countries, predisposes the mind to take the opposite side of the question to satisfy their consciences for not contributing. Any individual in this country, from America, that would adopt such a cause would be sustained by private contributions....

J.A. Collins

The present ministry have recognized the independence of the Texian government. It does not create much disturbance. The British people are rejoicing on account of the birth of a princess. Buxton has written R. R. Gurley a very excellent letter & I will forward it but Birney took me home with him and I presume it is published before this. Buxton has dealt nobly with him.

---

3. Harriet Elizabeth Leveson-Gower, Duchess of Sutherland (1806-1868), after her marriage made Stafford House, her London home, a centre of society and philanthropic circles. She was especially interested in the American anti-slavery movement.

No. 31 J.A. Collins to the Committee of the B.F.A.S.S.

[Printed Circular] 6, Queen Street Place, Southwark Bridge, London
December 10th 1840

To the Committee of the British and Foreign Anti-Slavery Society

Gentlemen,

I am deputed by the American Anti-Slavery Society to solicit pecuniary aid in this country, to enable it to continue its exertions for the abolitions of slavery in America.

It is with great reuctance that the Committee of the American Anti-Slavery Society feel compelled to call upon their friends in Great Britain for pecuniary assistance, as they would have rejoiced to have been able to sustain their operations for the oppressed Slave, without being compelled so to do.

The recent monetary difficulties through which North America has been struggling for the last three years, have been so oppressive, and the sacrifices which the friends of the Negro have been called upon to make, have been so great, that they, however willing, are no longer able, without some aid, to sustain the Anti-Slavery cause.

The late contest, for the election of a President, has likewise been detrimental to the cause of abolition, in as much as political opinions, by dividing men for a time, during a period of excitement, and attracting attention to another subject, begets for a while an estrangement between those who were heretofore united in the attainment of one grand object, and causes a diversion of funds to political objects, which had probably otherwise, been devoted to emancipate those in bonds.[1]

We trust, however, that if the Society can obtain the sum of 2000 Pounds, it will enable it to retain its ground, until circumstances shall be so altered that the friends of abolition in America may again be able to carry on the work of the Society without further assistance.

I therefore address myself to the Committee of the British and Foreign Anti-Slavery Society for a grant of such a sum of money as it may be in their power to contribute, in aid of the American Anti-Slavery Society; but should the Committee be unable from want of funds, to make any grant, then it only remains for me earnestly to solicit from them an expression of their cordial desire for the success of the American Anti-Slavery Society.

To you, as the acknowledged Society for the Abolition of Slavery, both in this country and all over the world, I enclose my credentials, signed by Charles

---

1. The divisions in the American anti-slavery movement in 1840 were further deepened by the recent formation of the Liberty Party, the Anti-Slavery political party which had contested the Presidential election in November, and which had now drawn off a certain amount of support to create an anti-slavery lobby in Washington.

Marriott,[2] Secretary, and James S. Gibbons,[3] Chairman of the Executive Committee of the American Anti-Slavery Society, dated New York, Sept. 25th 1840, and trust that the appeal thus made may meet with your cordial approval.

A reply is respectfully solicited as early as the convenience of the Committee will permit.

With fraternal feelings, and a desire for your prosperity and faithful continuance in every good word and work, I subscribe myself,

Yours, very respectfully for the cause,

J. A. Collins.
Representative of the American Anti-Slavery Society.

To J. H. Tredgold, Esq.,
Secretary to the British & Foreign Anti-Slavery Society.

MS.A.1.2. vol. 10 Anti-Slavery Letters to Garrison [92]
No. 111 J.A. Collins to William Lloyd Garrison

6 Queen St. Place, Southwark Bridge, Dec. 27/40

My Beloved Garrison,

... In our country, too much, vastly too much has been made of English anti-slavery feeling & sympathy. They can talk against slavery because they have never been corrupted by its presence upon their own soil. The English can never condemn our prejudice against color, our negro seats & negro cars, while they are exercising the same prejudice against poverty, that we do against color. It is unphilosophical to think that the British people as a nation should be in favor of genuine freedom, for upon an analysis of the principles of the British government, as developed by its system of legislation &c it will be found to be a vast and complicated system of slavery. It is a dangerous species of slavery, as it is subtle and intangible. It gives to the poor subject the ostensible appearance of freedom the more successfully to grind him to powder. In this country, as in the Southern States, the law making power is in the hands of the few, who, like the Southern oppressors have counted it to their own advantage. Look at the nobility & gentry of this country, & trace back their ancestry & you will find that they have done nothing but consume & yet have got in their possession, all the buildings, ship, manufacturies, & fabrics of every kind, which the working classes and their ancestry have brought into existence. Now one of the first principles of human rights, is, that the laborer is entitled to the fruit of his own labor. But we find the poorer & laboring classes in this country, in this respect, precisely in the same condition with the slaves of our country,

2. Charles Marriott was a Quaker living in Athens, New York, who was disowned by Hicksite Friends for his anti-slavery activities.

3. James Sloan Gibbons (1810-1892), a Quaker businessman living in New York, was the only member of the old A.A.S.S. not to go over with the Tappans to the A.F.A.S.S. in 1840, but to remain a firm friend of the Garrison party. He was one of the main supporters of the *Anti-Slavery Standard.*

and the fruits of the one, are similar to the fruits of the other, viz. degradation licentiousness, & crime, though less of physical cruelty & more of mental suffering. This being a correct view of the case, how, I ask, how is it possible for the British people sustaining such a system, to be in favour of abolition as we understand it; – which will place the slave upon a national & political equality with his master? Those American abolitionists who visit this country, & do not bear openly their testimony against British oppression, are in my opinion as unworthy [of] the name of abolitionists of those Englishmen visiting America, who carry their anti-slavery in their pockets or leave it behind.

I have found but a very few devoted friends of liberty in this country. Wm. Adam is the most fearless, upright man I have met with in the kingdom. His soul is free and enlarged, with a large amount of sympathy & intellect. Dr. John Bowring is another noble & generous spirit. His kindness to me has been very great. He speaks of you with a great deal of warmth and affection. Ashurst was quite scaly in his appearance & treatment. He did not treat me with hardly the civilities of common politeness. Geo. Thompson, a most amiable and affectionate spirit, though in his nature timid & compromising. His approbativeness is quite too large for his self-esteem. It is hard for him to go against the will of his friends. I have not had the pleasure of hearing him speak publicly, as yet. But the most noble of all the English spirits I have met with is Elizabeth Pease. What an enlarged & free mind! How faithful & uncompromising! How liberal & self-denying! How social and amiable. She possesses qualifications sufficient to constitute her *emphatically, a noble woman.*

I have not yet seen Murray, Smeal, Webb or Haughton, though I have become acquainted by letter with most of them.

You say I must return as soon as possible, if I do not succeed in raising money. Though I must confess I found everything about as you describe it yet I thank the Lord for directing me to this country. New organization is & has been making sad work with the English abolitionists. The Broad St. Committee never devised a more crafty & subtle plan for taking revenge upon yourself than by securing Birney, Stanton & Stuart to travel the country ostensibly to create an anti-slavery feeling, but really to sow discord & retail falsehood & calumny. Whenever I have fallen in their wake I find the people possessing the most distorted views respecting yourself and the genuine Am. abolition. They appear to feel that Weld organisation, of the Garrison school, is the climax of absurdities. That you are a Unitarian, which is sufficient reason for casting both yourself and old organization beyond the pale of union or sympathy. They really believe, & consider their position indisputable, that the Am. As. S. Society is but another name for a *Woman's rights* & no human government Society, & that it was from the continual thrusting in of these extraneous topics that such noble! spirits as Stanton, Birney, Tappan et. al. were compelled for the sake of peace and the poor slave to, peaceably, withdraws and form another antislavery association. But when the subject is presented to them in its true light they are confounded, yet they passed this country, deaf to everything like British oppression, and not in the least exciting English prejudices, and also under the auspices of the Broad St. Committee, that it is very hard to persuade the English, that such kind, pretty & peaceable men as B & S advocate a false principle, or be actuate by any other motive than that [of] pure love to the slave. The contrast between yourself and them was so great that my argument loses half its force, as they have seen you both &c &c Yet I am happy to say that my mission to this country has not been without some service to the cause. I have got things in such a train that it will be almost impossible for me to leave before the first of February. What I have been doing was preparatory, and now I am nearly prepared to storm the castle. The B & F Com have done infinite evil to our cause by holding the appearance, to the abolitionists of this country, of neutrality. To make them show their colors, I have addressed them a note with my credentials requesting their aid and countenance. In doing this, I had another object, and that was to get before the Committee, and if I can get an audience to an explanation of the real position of our society & of all the facts connected with it I am sure it will be divided, & then old organization will soon assume a tangible appearance. The com. are to meet the first of Jany., and no doubt they will refuse me both their money & their countenance, when I shall demand the reasons & when they are given shall beg the privilege of showing them that the charges have no existence in fact. All the quakers upon the committee, that I have been favoured with an interview are anxious to have me meet the com. but the Revds. are opposed to being disturbed upon the question, as a matter of course.

I regret that I have no more to show for my labors, but I can assure you I never wrote so many letters in the same time, & performed so much real hard labor in my life. The English are a slow moving people & this will somewhat account for it.

I had an interview with Sir T. F. Buxton, but his mind is so completely absorbed in his civilization scheme, which is suffering somewhat from the jealousies of the Br[oad] St. Com. and an attack made upon it by "*The Times*" arising as I understand, from some personal affair between one of the proprietors of that paper & Sir Geo. Stephens, that he could not give me much of his time, & so great were the demands upon his purse that giving money was out of the question. I wrote him several letters & the following note will exhibit his feelings towards yourself and our society: "If I were to show you the amount of drain which has taken place upon my purse in the last few months, for matters solely connected with the negroes, I am sure you would not apply to me. But feeling *sincerely* desirous of showing that I am not deaf to an appeal from a Society to which my friend Garrison belongs, I send you the enclosed trifle" (ten pounds) "I cannot however authorize you to make applications as under my sanction or by my direction, for the truth is, the A.S. people of this country have already been pressed too hard." &c &c Saml. Gurney & Thos Sturge each have given fifty pounds, & with the various influences I have secured I shall be able to hold public meetings in spite of the com. when I have no doubt we shall get some money & fully expose the selfishness & deception of new organization. I think I am now prepared to do more good for the cause the the next month than for the two past months, yet if it is the decision of our Bd that I must return immediately I shall be most obedient to their commands. It is the decided opinion of our friends that I must not leave till the middle of May, though their view does not have great influence with me as I understand our position....

That spirit of faith & meekness & of love, in one word, the spirit of our Divine

Master may be upon you & guide you into all truth and love is the prayer of your loving friend J. A. Collins.

MS.A.1.2. vol. 11 (1) 1841 Anti-Slavery Letters to Garrison [93]
No. 4 George Bradburn to R.D. Webb

Boston, January 1st, 1841.

My dear Webb:

... I have received several papers from Ireland, since my return, some, I suppose, from yourself, some from friend Allen, some from friend Haughton, and some from Mr. Standfield of Belfast; the contents of all of which were not so much read as devoured by me, especially as they, in some instances, contained articles from the pens of all or several of these friends. It rejoices my heart, to witness the interest you all continue to manifest in the cause of humanity, whether it be manifested in the form of sympathy for the enslaved, or for the intemperate. I should be glad to hear that you were all to become "Repealers", also. But what will the author of the Repeal Movement say to the rascally conduct of his British ministry in recognising the national independence of Texas, that "nest of plundering pirates", as I once heard him call it? It makes the heart of philanthropy sick, to think of this recreant conduct, and especially to read the laudations of it which have appeared in some of the English papers. The ministry enjoyed an enviable opportunity of bearing testimony against the infernal system of slavery, but it seems they were willing to forego it, to strike hands with men-stealers, robbers, and murderers, for the sake of putting a few shillings into John Bull's long purse. I have heard of nothing so deeply damnable for a long while....

My affectionate regards to your wife, and believe me very affectionately yours &c.

Geo. Bradburn.

MS.A.1.2. vol. 11 (1) 1841 Anti-Slavery Letters to Garrison [94]
No. 7 J.A. Collins to William Lloyd Garrison

Ipswich Jany 1st. 1841.

My dear Brother Garrison,

... Unless we succeed better than we have as yet done, you may expect to see me on the 15th of February. Would that I could leave earlier than the 1st proximo, but I have not as yet heard one word from the Broad St. Com. I am daily expecting a summons to appear before them. By the way, the Sabbath Convention has entirely changed the issue. Woman's rights & nongovernmentism are quite respectable, when compared to your religious views.... The Unitarians in this country are by far the most liberal & enlarged class of Christians, but, they are generally very wordly minded & do not take interest in anything but the accumulation of worldly honours & emoluments, with now and then, a peace offering to the cause of education. But few are what you would term, genuine reformers. I have fallen in with a few, however, who are in practice what they profess to be in theory. When I arrive at home I shall have a long story to relate to you. Your influence, in this country, is damned, by the sly & false & wicked thrust made at your religious views. Owenism in Gt. Btn. is considered double distilled infidelity. Your views are being considered of the Owen School. You are the *Great Lyon* which stands in my way. Yet if I had nothing to do but enlighten the public minds on this subject we should get along very well, but when we show up the division, as we have to, from the opposition we meet with, and after setting forth our position, it is hard to raise money, I can assure you. It is next to impossible to carry both together & actually impossible to get a farthing without combatting the opposition constantly crossing my path. I feel the importance of having some able man in this country to keep the subject before the public. It should not be allowed to die away. As soon as I am off the new organization click will not give sleep to their eyes or slumber to their eyelids until every mind is brought to embrace their views. A good man, faithful to his principles, from our country, acquainted with all the facts in the case, would galvanise the country on this subject....

In the greatest haste, from your affectionate friend & brother 'till death

John A Collins

MS.A.1.2. vol. 11 (1) 1841 Anti-Slavery Letters to Garrison [95]
No. 5 B.F.A.S.S. to J.A. Collins

British & Foreign Anti Slavery Society for the Abolition of Slavery & the Slave Trade Throughout the World

27, New Broad Street, London.
January 2nd 1841.

Mr. J. A. Collins –

Sir

Your letter to the Committee of the British & Foreign Anti Slavery Society was laid before them at their meeting yesterday and was taken by them into full consideration. It appears that the Committee are to regard you as an authorized representative of the American Anti Slavery Society, on whose behalf you are deputed to raise funds in Great Britain and that you apply to them, either for "a grant of a sum of money" or for "an expression of their cordial desire for the success" of the Society you represent.

With respect to the former part of the alternative, the Committee have to observe, that, whatever the amount of these funds might be – they could not consider themselves entitled to dispose of them in the way you desire, so that they feel it their duty to decline altogether the consideration of a money grant. And easy as the adoption of the latter part of the alternative might appear, and painful as it is to find any ground for hesitation in this respect, the committee are nevertheless constrained to say that the course recently pursued by the American Anti Slavery Society has alienated their confidence –

According to your request the Committee forward this reply at the earliest moment. They have heard something indirectly of your wishing an interview with them, but they wait, before saying anything on this point, until they shall understand from yourself that this is your desire.

I am sir,
Yours respectfully
J. H. Tredgold
Secretary

Mr. J. A. Collins.

MS.A.9.2. vol. 15 (1) 1841 The Weston Papers [96]
No. 6 J.A. Collins to Henry Grafton Chapman

Norwich, Jany 2, 1841

My Dear Friend,

I had expected, till this morning to have remitted three hundred pounds to you, by the steamer, which sails from Liverpool the 4th inst., but I find no letters or bill as we had previously suggested. I regret this very much, as I am confident you must be suffering greatly. I do not know as I can promise another farthing. I would as soon go among the Southern slaveholders to solicit aid, as among the abolitionists of Great Britain. So much has been done, by Prest. Birney, Stanton, & *Van Buren* John Scoble, as they, in the capacity of philanthropic gentlemen, travelled all over the kingdom, to prejudice the mind of the leading abolitionists of the country, that we are shunned by them as we should have been by the rankest pro slav[er]y men of our country. And if, by a special act of grace, on their part, some one, more magnanimous than the rest, condescends to give us audience, we had as many objections to answer & remove, urged against us by an English abolitionist as by an Am apologist. So strong is the anti-slay current against us, that but few, when they are convinced, have moral courage sufficient to face the opposition.

I have received, this moment, through the post, from the hands of E. Pease, the following extracts, written either to the Broad St. Committee or to a prominent abolitionist.

"Boston, Nov. 30. 1840"

"Extract of a letter of Rev. Nathl. Colver." "Garrison has just headed an infidel convention, gathered from different states to call in question the validity of the Sabbath, the Church and the ministry. It was quite a gathering, & I went in, with two or three other ministers, & discussed it with them for days."

"Wm. L. Garrison's influence is on the wane – he so identifies himself with every infidel fanaticism, which floats, as to have lost his *hold* on the *good.* He has recently headed a convention to inveigh against the Sabbath, the Church, & the ministry. It was affecting to see what a company he had identified himself with – the mildest of the no-marriage perfectionists – Transcendentalists & Cape Cod – all the harmonious effort against the Bible as our Standard of faith, and especially, in denouncing the ministry &c I think the a.s. cause will ultimately shake itself from that which has been a source of great *reproach*, & embarrassment – it has really been a cause of great trouble.

J. A. Collins, has in a few weeks since left for England, under suspicious circumstances. What are his objects we know not, but we fear to practice some imposition upon British sympathy for our cause. I hope you will beware of him – *he is not entitled to your confidence.* Friends here feel deeply on the subject, will you, if possible, ascertain what are his objects, & give us early notice."

Thus much for these letters, punctuated & underscored as per copy. I draw off in great haste, that you have it by the Caledonian which is to sail the fourth.

I find that the opposition is increasing in consequence of these letters to an inconceivable length. I shall have my hands more than full to warn off those more than murderous thrusts. Let Colver read these extracts in the Liberator. Send over some letters to prominent abolitionists upon this subject. Let the Board of the Am. Mass. N H & Penn Societies come out at once.

I have just this moment received a letter from Thomas Sturge saying that I must appear in London forthwith. I can assure you that I will do the best I can. But being unknown, cannot have great influence.

If a real steam can be raised, I may be able to raise some money, but I am inclined to believe that it is completely a case with us. Things have now assumed such an appearance, that I cannot leave until the storm subsides or increases to such a height as to blow me away.

Let a mustering of our Board be called forthwith & some documents be prepared not only for the American but also the Mass and other Societies, which will set forth in a clear, full & explicit manner the real cause of this division. Let is be made to appear that this is but the taking of the old pro slay. arg[ument] of '33 '34 & '35. Don't fail to have it done immediately.

Chas & myself start for London this 4 P.M. We have had but one hours sleep & now we shall be under the necessity of riding all night.

In the greatest haste, I am your sincere friend. Love to all my friends

J.A. Collins

P.S. The poor man's heart (I mean Charles') is almost broken. He had hardly been able to endure the opposition, & now he is but poorly prepared for the crisis.

I think it would be well to write E. Pease, Thompson; & Thos. Sturge by all means. Sir T. F. Buxton & the B. & F.A.S. Society. Write to Danl. O'Connell & to Dr. John Bowring. If Dr. Channing was only true a letter from him would be of infinite service as he is venerated in this country universally. But I presume he is as much frightened as the rest at the Sabbath & other questions.

Darlington Feby 27. 184[1]

My dear Friend

...Thy two letters, of Decr 30 & Jany 31 came together by the "Acadia", all their contents, both of a public and private nature are deeply interesting – in all your trials & difficulties you have my heartfelt sympathy – at *present*, they are many & great – but I do rejoice in the belief they portend the dawn of brighter days & that you & your cause, will at no distant period, appear to the world with an aspect of brightness & purity, such as have never before adorned it. Surely, "New Organization" must be at a very low ebb, or men claiming the character of *Gentlemen*, leaving wholly out of the question, that of the *Christian*, could never condescend to the paltry means, to which they have resorted, I lament to say, on both sides the Atlantic, in order to effect the downfall of the true, liberal, antisectarian & [?] Association. When the weapons of individual malice, & the lowest & most disgusting personal slander, have to be called into service, it is a sure & most satisfactory indication, that all other resources have failed, & that no substantial ground of objection can be alleged. That these weapons will prove alike powerless, is as certain as that they are unchristian, ungentlemanly & degrading. I could not have believed twelve months ago, that the members of the London committee wd have stopped to second such efforts; but alas! experience teaches us many painful lessons – the language which they *seem* to hold out, to the victims of sectarian bigotry, & the perpetrators of these dark acts of malice & revenge, with you, is – "send us over all the scandal you can gather together, & we will see to its circulation in this country." Scarcely had we received the accounts of the castigation which were so justly recd, than we discover that the extracts from the Massts Abolitionist[1] for Jany, containing the base attack upon J. A. Collins, were in circulation thro' the country – accompanied by the document issued by the Abolition Socy, on the 1st of Feby, corroborating the assertions of Colver & declaring that the statements in his letters to Jos. Sturge were entitled to entire confidence – also the preamble & resolution adopted at the board of Managers of the Massts ASS – of a contrary import.... Such conduct on the part of men associated (professedly) for the advancement of the cause of Justice & Mercy, must be revolting to every honourable mind – but it is all, we feel persuaded, working together for good – they have overshot their aim – disgust is awakened in the minds of many, in various parts of the country – & it has also prompted JAC to unfold the whole affair, and to speak unreservedly of the Broad St. Comtees in the Appx to the pamphlet which he is preparing.[2]

---

1. The newspaper started by the anti-Garrison Massachusetts abolitionists.
2. J. A. Collins, *Right and Wrong Among the Abolitionists of the United States.* Glasgow, 1841.

We have felt much sympathy for our friend JAC. His position has been one of peculiar difficulty, embarrasment & trial – but I feel assured his mission will greatly help the cause of *true* abolition amongst us. You will no doubt, receive letters from him by this packet, I need not, therefore, enter into detail, respecting his recent movements....

Believe me to be most truly thy affectionate friend

Eliz^th Pease

MS.A.1.1. vol 3 Anti-Slavery Letters from Garrison [98]
No. 76 William Lloyd Garrison to Elizabeth Pease

Boston, March 1, 1841.

Dear Friend.

...I am very much obliged to you for your letter by the Brittania, and do not regret, on the whole, that bro. Collins has concluded to remain until the selling of the steamer of the 4th inst.; though I trust he will not miss coming at that time, for his presence here now is indisputable. In whatever he has been called to encounter, on your side of the Atlantic, by the evil spirit that reigns there, as well as here, in the Anti-Slavery ranks, I deeply sympathize with him. The attempt of Nathaniel Colver to injure his character is exciting among all the true-hearted friends of our cause among us an intense feeling of indignation and abhorrence; and in the sequel it will be sure to recoil upon the head of that unhappy man. Equally abortive will be the effort of N.C. to affect my religious character by his absurd and monstrous statement to Joseph Sturge, that I have headed an infidel convention. Even supposing the charge were true, I should like to know by what authority British *abolitionists*, as such, undertake to judge me, for this cause, *on the anti-slavery platform.* I need not say to you, that the charge is both groundless and malicious; that my religious views are of the most elevated, the most spiritual character; that I esteem the holy scriptures above all the books in the universe, and always appeal to "the law and the testimony" to prove all my peculiar doctrines; that, in regard to my religious sentiments, they are almost identical with those of Barclay, Penn, and Fox; that, respecting the Sabbath, the Church, and the ministry, Joseph Sturge and I (if he be a genuine Friend) harmonize in opinion; that I believe in an indwelling Christ, and in his righteousness alone; that I glory in nothing here below, save in Christ and his crucified; that I believe that all the works of the devil are to be destroyed, and our Lord is to reign from sea to sea, even to the ends of the earth; and that I profess to have passed from death unto life, and know by happy experience that there is no condemnation to them who are in Christ Jesus, who walk not after the flesh, but after the spirit. The truth is, N. Colver has a mortal antipathy to all the distinctive views of Friends, and he regards them all as infidel: yet he writes to Joseph Sturge as though he fully agreed with him as to the nature of the Sabbath, and as though I held to purely infidel views on this subject!! Why does not Joseph Sturge, as an honest man and a sincere friend to the anti-slavery cause, (I will not refer to his former professions of personal friendship for me,) inform me by letter of what he has received from N. Colver and others, touching my religious character? Why does he not express a wish to hear what I can say in self-defence? I confess, I am grieved and astonished at his conduct, and am forced to regard him less highly than I once did. By the next packet I hope to be able to address a letter to him on this subject.

I am sorry, very sorry, (and very much surprised, too,) that bro. Collins should have applied to the London Committee for aid or approbation. It was an error of judgment, simply, but, after what we, who sent him out, have said of [the ?] Committee, it looks upon the face of it like an [imposition?]. We suppose he would make his appeal to the abolitionists at large, and take his chance accordingly. I fear, also, that he may not have been so guarded at all times in his language as could have been desirable, respecting the transfer of the Emancipator – a transfer that was certainly very dishonourable, and wholly unworthy of the character of those who participate in it. Yet I doubt not that the mission of J.A.C. will do much for our persecuted enterprise.

For what you have done to aid him, we all feel under the deepest obligations. May heaven reward you a hundred fold! Fear not that truth shall not triumph over falsehood , right over wrong, and freedom over slavery....

The fate of the Amistad captives[1] will soon be determined. J. Q. Adams is now pleading their case in the most powerful manner. It is impossible to predict the result. My best regards to your father and mother. – There is no one in the world that I have a stronger desire to see again than yourself.

Yours gratefully,

Wm. Lloyd Garrison

MS.A.1.2. vol. 11 (1) Anti-Slavery Letters to Garrison [99]
No. 138 (J.A. Collins ?) to ?

Glasgow. April 3d 4 p.m. 1841

My Beloved Brother,

...The Glasgow Com. are all in a hubbub. Wardlaw & Hugh[1] have resigned. The other night five more tendered their resignation, after the com. had two to one, voted to give me a most beautiful letter, which was an eloquent appeal to the abolitionists of Gt. Btn showing at the same time as clear as words could make it, precisely where they stood. These priests & their tools offered their resignation not on the main question, but on account of haste & the Com. after passing the letter through two to one voted to let it lay

1. In 1839 slaves destined for Cuba aboard the *Amistad*, a Spanish slaver, mutinied, but the crew managed to steer the ship into an American port where the ship and its cargo were promptly seized by American officials. The case roused much debate in American political circles, and it was not expected that the government would free the slaves as they did in fact, after a much publicised trial at Hartford, Connecticut.

1. Rev. Dr. Hugh Heugh (1782-1846), a leader of the Secession church in Scotland, and minister of a fashionable Glasgow Church, was active in the religious life of the day. He was made a D.D. of Pittsburgh, Pennsylvania in 1831.

over for another fortnight and give them an opportunity of packing the meeting & voting the com out of the com. as there are about 60 members and only about 7 or 8 active ones. Since I have been in this vicinity the Com. have had nearly half a dozen meetings & 19 are the most that was ever out, since its establishment. All the A. S. of this place is with us. I am anxious to get the public expression of Ireland & Scotland for us or else when I am gone the divided state of feeling will be lost in indifference. Get them publically committed & they have a character to sustain. The Unitarians sympathise with us quite strongly.

I am getting up, or am likely to, an old organization journal. By this means our principles can be brought before the public & the calumnies of the seceders refuted. I think I shall succeed in this. But I am not certain....

(MS. incomplete)

MS.A.9.2. vol. 15 The Weston Papers [100]
No. 34 Thomas Sturge to the Chapmans

New Kent Road 5th of 4th mo. 1841

Esteemed Friends

Henry G & Maria Weston Chapman

In reply to your letter dated Cape Haytien 22nd Feby 1841 in which you ask to be informed "as to the state of the cause of freedom universally in England; particularly whether it has ever been made a test of fitness to co-operate with the friends of the cause there, that the persons proposing to do so should be under the protection & government of some large religious sect", my answer is first, – that in England there exists universal liberty & a degree of freedom which I believe it is very difficult for persons in other countries to form a just conception – 2nd that it is not required as a test of fitness to co-operate in the cause (of seeking the freedom of the slave or any benevolent object) that those who wish to do so should be under the protection & government of some large religious sect or members of any particular religious body.

To obtain any righteous object, it is common to seek the assistance of all, whatever their religious sentiments may be or whatever private opinions they may entertain; while however this is the case, great care is usually taken that those who may be selected as a committee to conduct any benevolent undertaking should be persons of unimpeachable character who are likely to work well together lest the cause should be hurt. It sometimes happens that in a committee a few of the members may be so illiberal as to object to a man because he may be a Roman Catholic or a Unitarian (by which latter term is understood one who denies the divinity of Christ) when this occurs it causes unpleasantness & the committee commonly endeavour to steer that course which they think most likely to accomplish the object which they have in view, by the withdrawal of the objections, sometimes it is of the party objected to. This however does not prevent such persons from assisting by pecuniary means or of their being members of the association, it is merely local, – for instance

– a committee might be formed in London & not act with a particular Roman Catholic or a Unitarian or Methodist while at Liverpool or Birmingham a man of either of those religious professions might be so generally esteemed & able, that his assistance would be eagerly sought, By this you will understand there is no rule of exclusion for any & should it happen that different auxiliary associations were to depute such an one to meet a general meeting of the whole body in conference, he would be there admitted & take his place & whatever he might advise would be attended to according as it should be judged wise & good. In general very great care is taken in such meetings to prevent any one from introducing any particular religious opinions & speakers who thus go out of their way are generally called to order.

If your question "as to the state of freedom generally in England" means the state of the public feeling in favour of the slave I should say there is only one universal feeling in his favour & a detestation of slavery wherever it exists together with a general willingness that the produce of free labour come whence it may should be admitted on more favourable terms than the produce of slavery – there had long existed on the part of our Cotton Manufacturers a wish that this country might obtain a supply of cotton raised by free labour & that they may not be dependant on America. Great efforts have been quietly made with the East India Company to induce them to encourage the growth of a superior quality in India. The directors have responded to the call & several persons experienced in the growth of Cotton in America have long been sent out with a good selection of seed & the requisite machinery. Of late the quality has been improved in India & it comes in better condition. As soon as those sent out can introduce better seed great hope is entertained not only that the quality will be greatly improved, but that it will be produced more abundantly. In like manner the importation of Sugar from India is about five times greater than it was four years ago with a prospect that there will be made by free labour in India alone in a short time a quantity sufficient for the consumption of Europe at so low a cost that slave produce will not be able to compete with it. Here I would observe that while Professor Adams has shown, there exists a species of slavery in India more akin to the system of villianage which formerly prevailed over Europe & exists to some extent still – yet this state of things in India is not in any degree to be compared to that forced labour which prevailed in our West India Colonies & in America, nevertheless so objectionable is slavery in any form that I doubt not the British public as soon as they are fully convinced of its existence in India, will be clamorous that full liberty shall be extended to the people there.

I view every step the Government there have taken in the last few years, as tending to improve the civil condition of the people & that ere long villianage or slavery will cease in India.

In this country we may be considered as having two bodies seeking the welfare of the Negro but following different roads both however doing great good. I should be glad if I could report that both had always acted harmoniously & without interfering with the other: I can however say with pleasure that although the association for the civilization of Africa was assailed through the medium of the paper & by some of the members of the British & Foreign Anti-Slavery Society, yet the association were not provoked to any angry reply –

conscious of the justice of its course it could well bear with some invidious aspersions even altho' they were made by men whom they well know to be friends to the slave. They were quite unwilling to enter into a controversy, but instead of entering into a quarrel, individuals attended the committee of the British & Foreign Anti-Slavery Society & remonstrated with it. On that occasion an attendance of several members whose names are of great value, but who usually do not attend was obtained, since which time things have gone on well. Joseph John Gurney wrote a letter of strong remonstrance & sent it (I believe to every member of the Committee) & afterwards attended with some other & thus this good result was obtained. It is very difficult to raise a controversy in England about the way in which a benevolent society thinks fit to attain its end. The English public do not interest themselves about the disputes between persons so as to become partizans – they often judge wisely when they say there are faults on both sides & that it is foolish to waste strength in disputing, when they ought to be working. The public says that if such a body are dissatisfied let them do better if they can, but not occupy themselves with finding fault with others while they do nothing. You probably are aware that the association for the civilization of Africa has the perfect good wishes of government. T.F. Buxton is the founder of this society, almost all the old abolitionists are members of the Committee except a few of our friends (quakers) belonging to the British Anti-Slavery Committee, who perhaps from not fully understanding the course to be followed, might fear a compromise of their principles. Our base is wide enough – we have on our Committee Lords & Members of Parliament – that strenuous strickler for all the rights of the Church of England, Sir Robert Inglis[1], by many dissenters called a bigot, but be called what he may, I think him a very kind & benevolent & good-tempered man, acting cordially with Methodists Quakers (of whom we muster three on the Committee) together with many other persons without once making any difficulty about their religious opinions. I cannot enter fully into the plane of this association, sufficient to say its object is to civilize Africa using only Christian means, such as I, a friend & lover of Peace can cordially unite with. When sufficient information respecting the interior of Africa is obtained, & Government shall have succeeded in making such treaties with the kings & rulers of the interior of Africa, as are judged needful for the protecting of Merchants & the cultivation of the soil while prosecuting their peaceful labours – it is expected that an agricultural society will be formed whose object it will be to aid the natives by encouraging them to raise cotton to supersede slave-grown cotton of America (of this we are sanguine) & other produce, & that establishments will be formed at different places where they may always find a market for their goods & purchase English manufactures.

By the expedition now about sailing authority is given to form one or more farming establishments to be managed by people of colour of blackmen, to affect which a sum of about $4000 was put down by about 8 individuals as a contribution, & they have sent out a variety of cotton seed of the best quality & a cotton gin – It is a well established fact cotton is indigenous in Africa, that it is both spun & woven & dyed there & for native use, & cotton cloth a

---

1. Sir Robert Harvy Inglis (1786-1855) was a Tory Politician and a leader of the Conservative forces in Parliament. He was for many years a director of the East India Company.

few years since (as it may still do) formed an article of export to the Brazils. One condition of the treaties to be made with native princes is that the slave trade shall be abandoned & that all slaves coming within British protection shall be free & not be reclaimed. It is the object of Government to annihilate slavery. England does not propose to herself exclusive advantage by her treaties, but American, French & other nations will equally participate in free trade.

It is not needful that I should say much about your esteemed friend J.A. Collins. I think he arrived in this country at what may be termed an unhappy period when many of the members of the British & Foreign Anti-Slavery Society by being misinformed of the state of things in America, had committed themselves by uniting in the views of the American & Foreign Anti-Slavery Society not at the time being aware that they by so acting might obstruct the usefulness of women. I believe such persons to have been deceived. In this country there is no clear perception of the motives that induces the body in America to endeavour to put women down. – There being only one Anti-Slavery Society viz. the British & Foreign, it was another untoward circumstance that J. A. Collins did not bring credentials numerously signed addressed to that Society, for had he done so no room would have been left for some of the members of the Anti-Slavery Society to have circulated the surmises & reports to his disadvantage which were sent from America. This is not said by way of excusing their conduct which must be condemned as unjust & wholly unwarrantable in Christian professors. It is at the same time an instance of how easy it is for men to fall into error who wish to do rightly, and we may use it [as] a lesson reflected back on ourselves that we may not judge those too severely who are not yet enlightened enough to perceive that the practice of slavery is a sin. I mention this particularly because I think the Christian bodies who refuse to partake of the sacrament with other Christian professors, who are not yet convinced of the Sin of Slavery, properly & are not likely to win them over to a righteous course – & that their so refusing is an exercise of church dominion likely to injure those who practice it, by making them think themselves more righteous than others. All labour with slave-holders to convince them of their error should be adorned by the patience & forbearance of Christian love. The situation of JA Collins was a distressing one, in as much as being in poor health when he arrived, he met with a very unkind & uncalled for opposition from a violent man, a Captain Stewart . I do not however doubt that Captn Stewart is a most sincere & zealous abolitionist, capable of a great pleasantness of manner & patience & persuasive power – but from some weakness capable of a degree of inveteracy more befitting those bereft of reason than a peaceable Christian. I have heard his conduct condemned but this did not prevent your friend Collins being greatly hurt by it, & I do not wonder that this, and the improper conduct of the British & Foreign Anti-Slavery Committee made him almost despair of obtaining justice from the latter body. Had he been in that state of good health in which a man is able to bear all unkindness with perfect calmness, I think he would not only have received justice at their hands, but that that body would have discovered the error they were betrayed into, by the American & Foreign Anti Slavery body. When a Society send on such a mission as that which brought J A Collins to this country, do they not commit a great error in sending one person alone, & would they not do much better by sending two in company. Man is the same as ever he was – the disciples endued with all needful power were sent out in companies of two & two and John Bunyan illustrates the advantage of two in his account of Faithful & Hopeful. Man wants a companion to consult with & assist in bearing the burden two can carry more easily than one.

After saying so much on the wish of the English manufacturers to obtain cotton by free labour, I wish distinctly to be understood that I approve of the encouragement that is thus given to obtain cotton from other & fresh sources, because I view it as one of the most powerful means of abolishing slavery. The effect of it I expect will be that cotton will cease to be produced in America by slave labour.

The Growers under the present system will naturally feel alarmed & angry at first, but when necessity shall compel them to set their sl[aves] free, they will discover that cotton can be produced so much mo[re] cheaply by free labour that they will not under these altered circumstances fear competition with any part of the world. The slaveholder must abandon the love of power & command over his slave, a motive which is perhaps one of the most powerful in making them cling to the system. He need not fear any loss of property by the change from slavery to freedom, for no sooner shall that change take place, than the value of his plantations will be found to increase, & they then alone will be quite equal to the present value of the land & slaves, This has been found to be the case in the West Indies, the planter could not believe it at first, but it was quickly discovered by land owners, & I well remember that as soon as slavery was ended in Antigua, that a gentleman in London was waited on by a planter & offered £1000 a year as a rent for his estate in that island which for many years yielded no return whatever, he accepted the offer, but in about one hour afterwards another person called on him & offered £1500 a year for the same estate. In pursuing your exertions in America for the abolition of Slavery, I am not aware whether or not you have endevoured to demonstrate to the Planters that they would be gainers by changing the system, – if you have not yet done so, is it not important to shew them such would be the result. It will not require any great efort to demonstrate the profit which will arise to them even setting out by merging the value of the slaves into land – the land at present isof small value because an estate of 1000 acres may require 100 slaves at a cost of 500 Dollars each to cultivate it, & it only can pay a profit after the interest of the cost of the land together with 50000 Dollars, the outlay for the slaves is reimbursed with interest in a certain number of years – but sink the 5000 Dollars the cost of the slave & add the "present value of the land" to it & the 5000 Dollars instead of disappearing with the lives of the slaves, as it now does, becomes the permanent value of the land because tilled by the labour of free men – out of this better state arises those solid advantages to commerce which ever attends that greatly increased demand for the necessities & comforts of life that man in a state of freedom requires. This is again proved by the increase in quantity & quality of our exports to the West Indies – the free Slave will not purchase those inferior & almost worthless goods which he was accustomed to in slavery but the merchant is obliged to supply good & superior articles, & he finds his account in doing so – and doubtless your manufacturers & traders would benefit in the same way.

This country is not quite free from bigots, nor can we expect it to be, for bigotry is like a rank weed whatever pains we may take to eradicate it from one individual it will spring up afresh in others. As an antidote, it might be well for us all to study the 13th chapter of 1st Corinthians. 1.6. mo. I delayed this letter in order to give you the result of the Debate on the proposals of ministers to reduce the duties on Slave grown sugar – This proposal was strongly supported by the manufacturing interest in this country & by Merchants concerned in the Brazilian trade & with the island of Cuba after a debate of several nights it was not carried – but although the measure was lost the fact that many who are strenuous in their exertions to do away slavery, were by any causes or circumstances induced to range themselves with those who wished the duty to be reduced on slave grown sugar, is to be truly lamented. But so it is, and such is the nature of man, that no sooner is the advantage held up to his sight than he wishes for it and begins to consider whether there is anything wrong in reaching out his hand to take it – and to reconcile the wrong act to himself he persuades himself that others in distress will be relieved & so deludes himself into the belief it cannot be wrong, especially as he is quite sure his motive is good. With sincere desire that your cause may go on & be blessed – your friend respectfully

Thomas Sturge

MS.A.1.2. vol. 12 (1) Anti-Slavery Letters to Garrison [101]
No. 3 Elizabeth Pease to J.A. Collins

Darlington 28th Inst.
[April 1841]

My dear Friend

I have read with much interest thy own & Wm. Smeal's accounts of your meeting as well as that given in the "Argus", which W.S. says, certainly appears to be "shamefully onesided." Such a report going through the country is a "bon bouche" for the enemy & I sadly fear will do great harm. You have, however, I shd. hope circulated the impartial acct. in the "Post". It is laughable to witness the tumult in which we poor women, throw these reverend clericals – it comports badly with our alleged weakness & inferiority – why be so scared at a being who has not the power of doing harm. I am anxious to hear how the meeting last eveg went off & what is to be the future course of the committee it grieves me to think of that once united & efficient body being torn by dissensions. Charles L. Remond has given three Lectures here, the concluding one last eveg. – his audiences have been very good & evinced great interest – but among a few, strong prejudice exists against him, on acct. of his known predelection for Garrison & co. Had I been aware how thoroughly staunch an old organizer he was, I shd. never have deemed a caution or word of advice needful – he met the Ladies Comtee one day, & has visited several of our friends privately. His future plans are not yet fixed. Thou wd. find that his silence respecting thy Letter of Invitation to Glasgow did not proceed from any bitterness of spirits but because he was out of Town when it arrived. I never saw anyone further from evincing anything like bitterness or the least unpleasant disposition — & as regards thyself, whenever a word is uttered, against thee or thy cause relative to the divisions Charles is the first to explain & defend it. Poor fellow, he has a great deal to bear himself — as soon as it is found that he is staying long enough in a place to make friends — winning people over (by his honest answers when applied to for information — he never introduces the divisions of himself to old organ, the satellites of the seceders are out upon him. G.T. really has more on his hands & upon his mind than he can get thro' consistently with his health — he is greatly to be felt for — & I am quite sure, his inability to join in [?] of his old friends, is a great trial to him. Mrs. Mawson said she had requested him to give the £2 for her — probably he has forgotten it....

In haste, believe me sincerely thy friend

Eliz Pease.

MS.A.1.2. vol. 12 (1) Anti-Slavery Letters to Garrison [102]
No. 146 Elizabeth Pease to J.A. Collins

London
Saturday

My dear Friend

...I have this morning rec^{d} a letter from Wm. Smeal, it is quite delightful to see how these two men — W.S. & J.M. stand in the foreground of the battle without flinching.

GT. has been up for a few days — he & my father & another B.I. man, are off today to Manchester — to see the Anti Corn Law folks — & endeavour to arrange matters for carrying on the two noble objects in unison — they are become so much indentified, in Free Trade principles that I hope the measure may be advantageous for both — they will not let us have G T to ourselves, *peaceably*. Another "World's Convention" in 1842!!!! The new organized are entering warmly into the Anti Corn Law Struggle — See Torrey's Letter[1] — Leavitt has memorialized Congress something about it — & the Emancipator writes columns about it. — give Garrison, Bradburn & co a *hint* to *give us* a word on the subject, in its A.S. aspect, that *we* may flourish off the old organizers in the Advocate & Anti Bread Tax circular — it wd help *you* & *us* ....

Believe me, sincerely — thy friend

E.P.

---

1. Rev. Charles Turner Torrey (1813-1846) was a minister, leader of the anti-Garrison Conservatives in New England and writer on anti-slavery matters. He was arrested as an abolitionist in 1842 while reporting a convention of slaveholders in Annapolis, but was defended by friends, and ordered to pay $500 to keep the peace. He was arrested again in Baltimore, and sentenced to six years for assisting slaves to escape. He died in prison — an anti-slavery 'martyr'.

No. 8 [J.A. Collins ?] to William Lloyd Garrison

33 Duke St, Glasgow, May 2d 1841

My dear Garrison,

I improve a few minutes before the mail starts for Liverpool to explain the reasons why I am not on my way to America. I am greatly distressed in consequence of my long absence from home, yet I am confident that if you could see the precise position in which I am placed, and all the circumstances connected with our cause in this country, you would unanimously say "stay another month."... Glasgow was never in a greater fever. The clergy who rule by the general consent on infidel and christian and hence hold the press, pulpit and popular opinion in their own possession, are in great consternation. Rev. Drs. Wardlaw Hugh & King[1] & many others exercise all the cunning of politicians, all the bitterness of slaveholders & all the cant on the question of slavery as our blackhearted new organization whiners. They are frightened. They are mad. They have none to defend new organization & they dare not openly make any direct attack on us or our society... Probably you have seen an account of our public meetings – the course pursued by the Glasgow Emancipation Committee &c. The meeting in Rev. Mr. Nesbitt's chapel was the largest anti-Slavery meeting ever before held in this city – 2500 present... our meeting inthe Bazaar was a splendid affair – not far from 5000 present. Some say more, some less – the Papers say 4000. The papers have made it appear as low as they dare. It was got up by the most respectable citizens of Glasgow... The cause of old organization has taken a deep and lasting hold of the true friends of this country. I would say in Glasgow and vicinity, and the country at large where the question is understood. The clergy here, as in America, are digging their own graves. For me to leave just now... would be to lose a good portion of my labor & also would greatly offend and discourage the good friends who have gathered around me. I must, therefore, stay till the 4th of June when I shall positively come home.

By plotting & packaging on the part of the clergy & [sleepy?] & most foolish credulity on the part of my friends, the Glasgow Em. Com. became new organized. I then told them that I would leave unless they would put themselves under my direction and do according to my commandments, which if they would, I would again restore the com. to them. They agreed to it. The com. had refused to call a meeting at the request of 600 members & friends of the society. A meeting of the members & fds. of the Society was called in the first place, at which the secretaries were instructed to call a public meeting of the society, which should be considered an official meeting of society – Strong resolutions were passed. A large number added to the com. which throws the balance back into the hands of Smeal & Murray. They call it Yankeeism. Smeal says they may call it what they please. They have got the society back into their own hands, where they do not again foolishly mean to lose it....

---

1. Rev. Dr. David King (c.1808-?), United Presbyterian clergyman and author of several works of theology, was for many years rector of Greyfriars Church, Glasgow. He was an LL.D. of Glasgow University.

MS.A.1.2. vol. 12 (1) Anti-Slavery Letters to Garrison [104]
No. 9 Elizabeth Pease to William Lloyd Garrison

Darlington, May 2, 1841.

My dear Friend,

...We do heartily rejoice with you, in the victory achieved by the release of the Amistad captives. It is a glorious triumph, calculated to strike terror into the heart of the oppressor. The barriers raised up by the unholy prejudice against colour seem rapidly giving way before the light of Truth & Love. And here we have much to encourage [us] regarding our British India Movement. The interest in its behalf is fast increasing in this country, & the accounts from India, of the increased cultivation of sugar & other articles of tropical produce, are very cheering. The recent act of Parlt. equalizing the duties on rum has now placed the sugar of the East Indies on an equal footing with that of the West. When similar encouragement is given to the cultivation of cotton, by relieving the lands fit for its growth, from their present heavy taxation, we may hope to see our markets filled with the free grown cotton of our own India instead of that of slaveholding America....

Eliz. Pease.

MS.A.1.2. vol. 12 (1) Anti-Slavery Letters to Garrison [105]
No. 13 Elizabeth Pease to J.A. Collins

Darlington May 12.

My dear friend

I was much pleased to receive the reports of the proceedings at your meeting, as I had been wishing for a few copies of the admirable speech of Dr. Ritchie – I have no acquaintance with him, that it would only be a piece of impertinence on my part were I to offer him my congratulations on the position which he occupies – tho' I *could* do it from my heart. I feel anxious, however, that whilst you refuse to make any concessions of principle to the clergy – you may avoid a similar error regarding the Chartists & what had the resolution about universal suffrage to do with the object of the meeting if they will not permit you to be *abolitionists* on your own ground, without subscribing to their views as well, I wd have no more to do with *them*, than I wd. with those among the clergy who require submission to *their* domination My whole hearted sympathies go with the Chartists in their grievance & in their principles (as far as I understand them) tho' I do not approve of all their measures – but I wd. not sacrifice my independence to them, or to anyone else, perhaps my fears are groundless, but I was half afraid that a kind of *compromise* had been made with them....

Sincerely thy friend

Elizth Pease....

MS.A.1.2. vol. 12 (1) 1841 Anti-Slavery Letters to Garrison [106]
No. 35 R.D. Webb to William Lloyd Garrison

Dublin, 30th of Fifth Month 1841.

My dear Garrison

J A Collins left us two days since on his return to Glasgow after spending about a week here, very much to our satisfaction, though not to any great pecuniary profit. The greater part of the time he was with us, he was visiting about — we wanted to make him feel at home first, and to get people to look at him without being frightened — and we are not without hope of some success in this laudable endeavour. He has already gone the round of our circle and has seen several who are not of us but who may be disposed favourably to the object of his mission. He is gone to Glasgow again in order to take some further part in the Battle Royal which his presence has called forth in the midst of Glasgow anti—slavery. Roger's estimate of British abolition *in the mass* is the right one — and therefore none need wonder that it cannot withstand the power of the clergy or burst through the trammels of sect. I heard many rumours of Collins being rash and intemperate, before I saw him. Since I have conversed with him, he appears to me to be honest and straightforward. His mode of procedure may not be the best for the collection of *golden* opinions, or for the lightening of purses — but is it not better for the eventual success of your cause & the progress of truth that the true principles of liberty and moral independence should be accepted by a few who are willing to receive them, than that you should receive temporary assistance from rich men who would reject you with scorn & hatred if they were conscious of the soul exalting tendency of your large hearted philanthropy ?...

Believe me thine faithfully,

Rich[d] D Webb

MS.A.1.1. vol. 3 Anti-Slavery Letters to Garrison [107]
No. 77 William Lloyd Garrison to Elizabeth Pease

Boston, June 1, 1841.

Beloved Friend:

...It is a most extraordinary thing, that I am put on trial for my religious opinions among the abolitionists of England! Pray, what have they to do with those opinions, *as abolitionists?* Who are they, but persons belonging to every religious sect, every political party, every shade of religious belief? Standing with them on the anti-slavery platform, what right have I to rebuke, censure or denounce them for making an attack upon me, in this behalf? I am willing to give them the right hand of fellowship in an anti-slavery capacity. Why cannot they exhibit as catholic a spirit toward myself?

It is equally extraordinary, that my bitterest opponents in England are found in the Society of Friends — seeing that I am persecuted here for the crime of cherishing their peculiar sentiments, substantially, in regard to the Sabbath, the church, and the ministry — and seeing, too, that those who have raised a hue-and-cry against me are "hireling priests"! The head and front of my offending consists in my being a Quaker indeed! How shall it be accounted for, that such men as Joseph Sturge and Josiah Forster are disposed to believe all that may emanate from the lips of those sturdy upholders of priestcraft, Nathaniel Colver and Amos A. Phelps[1] ? I am an "infidel", forsooth, because I do *not* believe in the inherent holiness of the first day of the week; in a regular priesthood; in a mere flesh-and-blood corporation as constituting the true Church of Christ; in temple worship as a part of the new dispensation; in being baptized with water, and observing the "ordinance" of the supper – &c. &c. &c. I am an infidel because I *do* believe in consecrating all time, and body and soul, unto God; in "a royal priesthood, a chosen generation;" in a spiritual church, built up of lively stones, the head of which is Christ; in worshiping God in spirit and in truth, without regard to time or place; in being baptized with the Holy Spirit, and enjoying spiritual communion with the Father – &c. &c. If this be infidelity, then is Quakerism infidelity....

Yours admiring friend,

Wm. Lloyd Garrison.

MS.A.1.2. vol. 12 (1) Anti-Slavery Letters to Garrison [108]
No. 44 Harriet Gairdner to J.A. Collins

19th June, [1841]
North Ferry.

My dear Friend

... What a state of excitement the whole country is in about the elections[1] , a couple of months ago I felt as if the present minority were incapable of exciting the least interest, but now tho' tardily & unwillingly, they propose to give us repeal of these odious Corn Laws & sugar duties, earnest of free trade in other branches & of a better system I feel myself getting quite keen in their cause & am ready to trust them a little longer especially as the aristocratic spirit is too strong yet to be openly defied, O'Connell's directions to the Irish electors are capital, how do we need such a leader in this island, the corn & other monopolising taxes would have been repealed ere this if he had been leader of the English as he is of the Irish people & able to turn his splendid power to the monstrous misdeeds of the India government, by the way the India question is gaining ground tho' [Howitt?] & our friend G. Thompson need not despair but I hope some of the commercial towns will

---

1. Rev. Amos Augustus Phelps, (1804-1847) the minister of the Pine St. Congregational Church of Boston, was the Agent of the Massachusetts Anti-Slavery Society. He later led the revolt of the New England conservatives and helped to form the Massachusetts Abolition Society as a protest against Garrison's religious views and his championship of women's rights.

1. This was the General Election of 1841 which began on June 28 and ended on July 17, resulting in a decisive victory for Sir Robert Peel and the Tories. The Whigs had fallen over the question of the repeal of the Sugar Duties, and it was expected that Peel and his party would usher in a new age of free trade.

send some members to the next parliament who have sound views on that subject.

My mother desires to be kindly remembered & believe me ever faithfully yours

H. Gairdner

MS.A.9.2. vol. 15 pt. 1 1841 The Weston Papers [109]
No. 50 Elizabeth Pease to Anne Warren Weston

London June 24, 1841.

My dear Friend

... Geo Thompson is, I am glad to say, looking remarkably well – the British India Socy have consented, at the urgent request of the Anti-Corn Law League, to allow him to devote his energies to their cause during their present struggle against the unjust monopoly of the staff of life – & they agree in return, afterwards to throw the weight of their influence into our cause – thus we hope, mutual advantage will result from a temporary union of these kindred objects. G.T. is truly to be felt for in the turn which affairs have taken in Glasgow, the late a.s. comtee there comprising as it did some of his earliest & best friends –still I believe he will not allow truth to suffer from a regard to any friendships, however dear or long cherished. He disappointed you at the Convention & I can truly say, my heart sunk within me when I heard some portions of his speech on that occasion – but, I fully believe, that even then he wd. have taken a far bolder & firmer stand, had he been made more fully aware of the importance of the question, & its various bearings on the welfare of the a.s. cause. J.A. Collins can tell thee that he acted *nobly* in the presence of the Edinburgh Comtee – & yet, remembering the Convention, I am not surprised, at a fear arising whether the present trying crisis may prove too much for his stability – but, I honestly believe, that he will stand firm...

With regard to my *political* tendencies, about which thou enquires – I return an answer which my friends here wd. term very *ungenteel* – for they are *ultra radical;* to sympathise with the poor oppressed Chartists is considered *vulgar* – but I *do most sincerely* – condemning of course *in them* as I wd. in any, an appeal to physical force – but their transgressions in this way have been wonderfully few – considering the oppression they are enduring, & their deprivation of rights as human beings, I am often filled with astonishment at their patience & forbearance. I know I am not capable of taking a comprehensive view of what wd be the effect of their principles, were they carried out in action – but it appears to me that they ask nothing more than what accords with the grand principle of the natural equality of man – a principal alas! almost buried, in this land, beneath the rubbish of an hereditary aristocracy & the farce of a state religion – the natural consequences of which are the love of patronage & power in the *great* – the domination of the few over the many, & the destruction of the rights of the great mass of the people. The five points of the Charter, are these, Universal Suffrage, vote by ballot, annual parliaments, no money qualification for members, & a salary for members of parliament. It is thought most unaccountable for a *gentleman* to say he sees nothing wrong in these – but for a lady to do so is almost outrageous – I have nevertheless frequently done so, & am generally answered – that the people are not *ready* for all this – now this appears to me, nothing but a slaveholder's argument – the slave was not prepared for liberty – & the people are not prepared for their rights. How, I shd. like to know, are they to become prepared for them, if they continue to be withheld?....

thy truly affec^{e} friend

Elizth Pease.

MS.A.1.2. vol. 12 (1) Anti-Slavery Letters to Garrison [110]
No. 72 J.A. Collins to Elizabeth Pease

Liverpool, July 4/41.

My Dear Friend,

...I leave the country with increased rather than diminished admiration for the good people of Great Britain. I have received more kindness than I could possibly have expected under similar circumstances. Here, as in America, each party sympathise with those of their own click & pretty generally oppose those who are of different opinions.

The people of this country are liberal minded. They should be instructed. They should have their liberty for they are slaves. Slaves, though not absolute, yet to all intents and purposes, slaves. It has all, in my humble estimation, grown out of the system of exchange, by which one class of men can secure the fruits of the poor labourer without returning him an equivalent. You know my views on views on this subject, therefore I would not, had I time, annoy you by dwelling on them. Slay. is a great evil, war is a great evil – Intemperance is a great evil, but the greatest of all the evils – in fact the father of these evils is the money catching system.

How I should be pleased to see you become interested in this question also. I entreat you to let not your own position prevent your giving this subject a free, full and candid investigation. I have not commenced practicing upon my views, but I am resolved to make myself a liar rather than make the Great God & father of us all the author of our misery. I hope before I die to carry out these views most fully.

But I will not say more at this time upon this question. Slay. & nonresistance occupy your mind. Let me say nothing that may discourage you from a work so glorious. Through you, our cause had a name in England. And by you, God willing I trust, it will increase until it shall cover the whole land. I do not like to say farewell, yet I must. Farewell to yourself, to your father to Ed. Oxley. I meant to have written him.

My regards to Mrs Pease

In the greatest confusion
I remain your obliged friend

J. A. Collins.

MS.A.9.2. vol. 15 pt. 1 1841 The Weston Papers [111]
No. 93 Charles Lenox Remond to Maria Weston Chapman

15 Lever Street. Manchester England
Tuesday November 16th, 1841.

Esteemed Friend Mrs. Chapman

...For the past three months I have been much occupied in lecturing under most flattering auspices in Ireland and am pleased to say as my belief that I have been instrumental in awakening much interest for the furtherance of the good cause, and the next year will prove the test of its permanence. I was less shackled & crippled by the unwarrantable apprehensions & fears, defamation & slander in [sic] which follows in the wake of New Organization than at any time since my travels in Great Britain and thereby gave me a freedom of dealing & treating of the subject I have long desired & thank God for, especially as I was determined to remain until I could do so, and I rejoice in the prospect of departing the country uncompromised in my old organization principles & independant of N. Organization influence & this will prove the kenest cut of all to the *devotees* of "*27 New Broad Street, London*", and to the worthiest of Englands Anti Slavery worthies, Geo. Thompson & Elizabeth Pease are to the poor slaves, O'organization & myself more than to any others am am I indebted & grateful. This however is in confidence until it is my happiness to meet the faithful ones "in propria persona."

Your sincere & obliged Friend

C. Lenox Remond.

MS.A.1.2. vol. 12 (1) Anti-Slavery Letters to Garrison [112]
No. 129 R.D. Webb to Maria Weston Chapman

Dublin 20th of 11th month 1841

Irish jottings for Maria W. Chapman.

In thy admirable Eighth Report of the Massachusetts Ladies A.S. Society the Glasgow Ladies in particular are highly commended for their address to the women of Great Britain.

I think George Bradburn said that the cloud of bigotry is so thick in Glasgow, you could cut it.

C.L. Remond told me that when he was in Glasgow he could find no trace of the ladies society formed by John Collins nor of Mary Welsh, who signed the address above alluded to.

When J.A. Collins was here he was extremely anxious that we should promote the formation of a ladies A.S. Committee. We refused, knowing that we had no materials. He thought us greatly mistaken. Even now, I know of no women in Dublin likely to *act* as a Committee, except three, Wilhelmina Downes, Anne Allen and my wife, all of whom are known to nearly all the Americans who were over here, after the Convention....

I believe the people here are no better than your people as to Anti Slavery or anything else, except that they have never been placed in the same circumstances. The proslavery feeling only wants to be aroused and it would soon wake up in full activity. Touch *church* or touch *party* in your antislavery efforts, and all their zeal for the Slaves would be scattered in the twinkling of an eye.

The clergy, of course, are no better. We have only one zealous Anti Slavery clergyman of any kind in Ireland – that I know of.

Religious bigotry is almost universal. The Catholics and their priests are unutterably bigoted. It is *their duty* to be so. The Protestants are almost all the same in this respect. They hate and fear the Catholics. The Catholics hate them, and hope to tread them down....

What can be expected amongst such people. I am sick of the praise the English receive from Abolitionists in America. They dont deserve it – nor the Irish – nor the Scotch. See how the glory of Glasgow anti-slavery melted away at the breath of their priests and New Organization. Was ever known such potent calumny as John Scoble's and H.B. Stanton's, when they travelled together under the auspices of the B & F A S Committee? It is a perpetual marvel to me how they did so much in so short a space of time. Does it not speak volumes for their ability, & for the ingorance of the people. I suppose they whispered "Infidel! Unitarian! Women becoming lords of the creation – Non-resistance – bloodshed and anarchy." They need have said no more when presto! all their hearers grew pale, and banished the American Society from their purses and their prayers forever....

Is not the address we are getting up from the People of Ireland to their countrymen & country women in America, a farce? How few among the tens of thousands who have already signed understand what they put their names to!

Is it moral to use such machinery?

There are a few women in Limerick – a few in Cork – a few in Waterford – a few in Wexford, with you, heart and soul. They read the Liberator and the Standard & your names are household words among them. As to the men, they are very few – but so are the women....

I feel greatly interested in the success of your next Bazaar and of our share in particular – because I think it desirable that a good effort should be produced upon *you*, in order that it may come back to encourage *us*....

Thy allusion to New organization in England is only just. The London Committee could not help being what they were. They had no idea of your liberty or your light. They love titles and titled people – they are no nonresistants and their vision is clouded by wealth and wordly importance – though there are many kindhearted and munificient men among them....

Thine respectfully

Richd D. Webb.

No. 104 Jane Jennings & Ladies of the Cork-Slavery Society to Maria Weston Chapman

Cork Dec. 1st 1841

Dear Mrs Chapman

A few members of the Cork Ladies' Anti-Slavery Society feeling anxious to express their interest in the efforts of the old Organized Abolitionists, take this opportunity of doing it. We know in part the trials, persecutions, and calumnies to which you have been exposed, our indignation is strong against the originators of the seceding Society. We hope the principles of the tried and faithful friends of humanity will not be much longer misunderstood by those to whom they were so cruelly misrepresented, and happy are we that our powerful and warmhearted advocate George Thompson has espoused the cause of the true Society.

...The lectures of our friend Charles L. Remond have been productive of much good no one could listen unmoved to his appeals on behalf of the suffering and oppressed – if such as he had come long since amongst us the clouds of ignorance with which we are surrounded would have been dispelled and our sympathy would not have been so long withheld.

Many of our Society are ignorant of the late divisions in America, we think it better not to press the subject on them until a permanent [?] shall be established, at present it is the broad principle of Anti-Slavery which has appealed to their hearts.

We desire also to express our interest in you personally, and our sorrow and sympathy for the cause which drew you from the scene of your labours and usefulness – of Mr. Garrison too we cannot speak in terms sufficiently expressive of our admiration and respect – others also too numerous to mention are enshrined in our hearts as the worthy coadjutors of, and fellow labourers with you and him in the high and holy cause in which you are engaged.

With feelings of affection and the highest esteem we remain dear Mrs. Chapman

Your very sincere friends

Jane Jennings
Hannah E. White
Alicia Hughes
Helen Jennings
Charlotte Jennings
Jane White
Isabel Jennings Sec.

MS.A.9.2. vol. 15 pt. 1 1841 The Weston Papers [114]
No. 122 Elizabeth Pease to Anne Warren Weston

Darlington Decr 30. 1841

...Your cause is assuming an aspect increasingly interesting & encouraging – the numerous withdrawals from proslavery churches must strike dismay into the hearts of the apologists for slavery, & of time serving, cowardly professors of religion, who are striving to please both parties. Glad too, I am, to see that the cotton interest are taking the alarm at our British India movement – it is a sure indication that the friends of India have not based their sanguine expectations with respect to its anti-slavery tendency, on falacious grounds, for self interest makes people keen sighted in the perception of what ever effects it. I was pleased to see that the integrity of John A. Collins had been so triumphantly vindicated, after all the wicked aspersions of his enemies. I never doubted it, yet it is satisfactory to have the *proof*, to put into the hands of those who do. We hear little now of Old & New Organization – ... the London committee are very peaceably pursuing their own objects in their own way – but what they are doing, I do not know, except, that the "Reporter" tells us from time to time, of deputations to this & that great man & visits at foreign courts, & addresses to crowned heads &c &c they seem fond of spreading themselves far & wide, & letting their existence be known to all the world, but whether any great amount of *fruit* will be seen, I somewhat doubt. I am glad, however, that they have taken up the question of slavery in the East Indies – the more it is agitated the better Geo. Thompson is dividing his labours between India & the Corn Laws – & is, I fear, greatly overworking himself. The Anti Bread Tax agitation is going forward with an energy, which, I hope, is the precursor of success – Lecturers are hard at work, enlightening the country – the women are getting up a national bazaar,in a scale far exceeding anything of the kind ever seen in this country, & are preparing a memorial for presentation to the Queen. Every human person must rejoice at the probable downfall of this branch on monopoly – yet, its delay is doing immense good; it is teaching the middle classes their powerlessness to resist the Aristocracy & Landocracy & shewing them that the political liberty & equality of the people, whose rights they have too long treated with neglect or disdain, is necessary to *their own* independence. We have been accustomed to cry out against the oppressive domination of the artistocracy – *& most justly* – but are not those who raise the outcry, actuated by the self same spirit, when they deny to "the poor, but honest & industrious labourer, a voice in the Legislation – have we any business to complain that our rights are trampled upon, when we thus unscrupulously trample on the rights of others. We treat the working classes as aliens, as foreigners, as interests, except when we want to carry some measure of self-interest – then we appeal to them as rational & intelligent beings, capable of reasoning & deciding on questions of Justice & Injustice – so long as they are called on to judge on the extension of some privilege to ourselves – but, if they dare to exercise this judgment in favour of *their own* privileges, or *rights* even, then, forsooth they are ignorant, misled by passion & incapable of coming to a just conclusion. Ah, my dear Friend, the Slaveocrat spirit is not confined to the Southern States of America – unregenerate man delights to trample on his fellow man – the world over – I was, for a moment, surprised to read Buckingham's account[1] of the Tory feeling prevailing in [Re?] publican America, & which is confirmed by thee – but, why shd. we wonder at it – Toryism is the embodyment of pride, the love of power, the desire for domination & these are feelings natural to the heart of Man – the longer I live, &

---

1. James Silk Buckingham's *America, Historical, Statistics, and Descriptive*, 1841. Buckingham (1786-1855) was a noted traveller and social reformer. He made extensive visits to India and to the United States.

the more I reflect, the more convinced am I, that to carry out into practice, the grand republican doctrine, of the equality of man – consequently of the equal rights of all – you must be under the influence of the spirit & precepts of the Gospel – which is a religion of *love*, which teaches the universal brotherhood of Man & strikes at the corrupt [?] of selfishness.

The condition of the labouring classes in our manufacturing districts is deplorable in the extreme – thousands & tens of thousands know not where to get food to sustain life; to sustain it in health & strength is out of the question – They have pawned nearly every article of bed & of body clothing & in many instances literally have nothing to sit down upon & only shavings to lie on. That they keep quiet – that they do not rise up & use the power that they possess – seize upon that which their oppressors have plundered them of – steep the nation in bloodshed & rebellion, is to my mind, little short of miraculous. To endure such misery with the forbearance which they do, seeing at the same time their lordly tyrants living in splendour, luxury, & idleness, unmindful of their wrongs, denying their wretchedness – must be the effect of a higher power than that which any degree of mere human fortitude could bestow. Oh! my heart is sad when I reflect on the miseries of my countrymen, my brethren, my equals – & on the wickedness of the perpetrators of such cruelty...'Think too of our atrocities in heathen Lands, wherever the English have colonised – & now behold them carrying devastation & war into China, because, they have the morality to refuse our poison. Was such iniquity ever heard of before, yet we call ourselves a Xtian nation! But my paper warns me to stop. I was going, however, to tell thee, in proof of the state of our poor that in Paisley there are upwards of *13,000*, who are supported solely from a charitable fund which has been raised for the purpose, on a pittance of d1¼ to d1½ per day & this even, it is feared must be discontinued, thro' lack of means....

Believe me very affecly thine

Elizth Pease.

MS.A.1.2. vol. 12 (2) Anti-Slavery Letters to Garrison [115]
No. 1 J.A. Collins to R.D. Webb

Boston Jany 1, 1842.

My dear Webb,

...Old organization is being again restored to public confidence. That jealousy, alienation and even opposition has, to a very great extent, subsided, and has given place to confidence, sympathy and in hundreds of instances to hearty and efficient co-operation. Your co-operation tells mightily in our cause. Irish, Scotch and English interference is to slavery, what Spanish flies is to a fever. Give more and more of your interference. Your remonstrance has reached us with 58000 names – How soon will the other 42000 reach us? Loring,[1] Phillips, Jackson, Garrison and myself were appointed a committee,

---

1. Ellis Gray Loring (1803-1858), a prominent Boston Unitarian, was one of the earliest members of the N.E.A.S.S. In spite of the fact that his support of the anti-slavery movement cost him many clients in his legal practice, he remained firm in his championship of the slave.

by our Board to get up an Irish meeting and have this address presented them. I called yesterday on the Editor of the Pilot, a Catholic & Irish paper . He was opposed to slavery. It would not do, however, for them to take hold of the question of abolition. O'Connell had done them much mischief by this contempt frequently expressed of slaveholders. The Irish were suffering much in consequence of his course – Said he should be willing to insert an advertisement announcing the meeting etc. Well, now he is the thermometer of the Irish feeling in this country – We shall have it published in all the Irish or Catholic papers. This we shall have to pay for yet it is as good an investment as we can make of our money. By the next Boat you may expect to hear much about your address.

A most interesting case has recently occurred which cannot fail to attract much attention on both sides of the Atlantic. You have no doubt ere this been made acquainted with all the facts in the case. I refer to the Creole vessel[2] which with 147 Am. slaves, runs into one of your W. I. islands & their gained their liberty by virtue of British law – Thanks to the authorities of New Providence for their humanity. Yet for my life I cannot see by what principle of English law the authorities of N.P. imprisoned those who were accused of murder. England does not recognise slavery to be right. Slavery cannot exist within the pale of her influence – Now supposing this vessel had been an Algerine vessel & the few white men on board had been Algerienes and the 147 Negroes had been American gentlemen & these American Gents had murdered some of these Algerienes & had run the vessel into N.B.? Think you the British authorities would have imprisoned them for such patriotism? I tell you nay – Then British influence is somewhat in favor of slavery or at least it caters somewhat to the slaveholding prejudices of the 19th century. It is however a great victory that so many should be left to go free – I wish your Society would correspond with the proper English authorities on this point of the question, which imprisoned those patriots – It is a new Armistad [sic] case, & no doubt grew out of it. It shows that such intelligence gets among our [thugs ?] and moves them to a aspire for freedom. It is producing a tremendous excitement among our menstealing statesmen at Washington. Such things work wonders for our cause. The debates in Congress will be this year unusually interesting, in as much as the slave question is beginning to come up in almost every question. Negro emancipation in itself will soon be the most popular question among us – It will only be the application of the anti-slavery principles in the various departments of society that will render it unpopular. This will necessarily prevent our organizations from ever becoming popular.

You have no doubt seen something of the breeze of Johnny Q Adams made in Congress of the gag question.[3] The old man has got a face of brass. He does

---

2. The *Creole* was a vessel engaged in the coastal slave trade. While travelling from Hampton Roads to New Orleans in November, 1841, the slaves aboard her mutinied, killing one of the crew; and then put in to Nassau in the Bahamas. British officials hanged the murderers, but held that the remaining slaves were free. This action roused much controversy in the United States and helped to complicate the Webster-Ashburton negotiations. Although the slaves were never returned, the case was submitted to the Anglo-American mixed claims commission under the convention of 1853, and the United States was awarded $110,330.

3. John Quincy Adams, as a Member of the House of Representatives, undertook

not fear the very devil. The Tariff question will produce much squirming and agitation as the question bears strongly on the use of slave [?] of free grown produce.... I fear there is a secret movement with our manstealing president – the Patriachs of the South – our Northern land speculators & the renegades in Texas to admit that filthy rotten and murderous Republic!! into the union with a slavery constitution the most damnable. Mexico has fitted out under Gen. St. Anna a strong expedition against Texas and are sanguine of success. I want to say I hope they will be successful but you know I'm a nonresistant....

Hastily yours with Great Respect

J.A. Collins.

MS.A.1.2. vol. 12 (2) Anti-Slavery Letters to Garrison [116]
No. 25 Sarah M. Grimké to Elizabeth Pease

Belleville (N.J.) 2/11/42

Dear friend,

...Our beloved Theodore has been in Washington for the last six weeks. He was urgently requested to go there by the abolition members of Congress, that he might be ready when the subject of slavery was introduced to aid them with his researches and advice. Perhaps no man in the anti-slavery ranks possesses so much information on all points connected with this subject as Theodore, no one has by patient research and close investigation and deep thinking possessed themselves of so many facts, and such a knowledge of the philosophy of slavery. Thou hast no doubt seen enough of what has been going on in Congress to know the position in which J.Q. Adams has been placed. In speaking of the case T. remarks – "The effect on the slaveholders has been perfectly confounding. They have resorted to every artifice and device to put him down, threats and fury, questions of order, motions to lay on the table, refusals to adjourn in order to tire him out, starting out with explanations and under pretext of explaining going into harangues, invectives and accusations against him, etc., but all in vain. The old Nestor has cast all their counsels headlong, turned all their guns against themselves, smiting the whole host with dismay and discomfiture. The slave holder feels that their end draweth nigh. The almost universal bankruptcy that now whelms the South, the low price of their only great staple cotton, and the European markets from immense regions open to the culture of the east – added to this the necessity of resorting to direct taxation for the support of the national government, the existing difficulties with G.B. portending war at no great distance, and the certainty that in such a case the first demonstration would be made upon the southern coast, and the standard of freedom to the slave unfurled everywhere; all these things and divers others

---

to present anti-slavery petitions to the House. He himself held no very strong abolitionist principles – but the right of petition had been secured in the First Amendment of the Bill of Rights, and Adams felt it his duty to preserve this liberty of the citizens. But when anti-slavery petitions began to flood Congress, Southern members demanded that these be laid on the table without receiving notice. Adams felt that these "gag rules" were striking at liberty, and constitutional rights and devoted the remainder of his career to fighting for freedom of speech in Congress – a struggle in which he had the wholehearted support of the abolitionists.

brough by God's providence in point blank range, the combustible train all laid into the very centre of the magazine and the blazing brand waving over them, fills them with rage and consternation." At the close of this letter he says, "Mr. Adams case has just been disposed of by laying the whole subject on the table forever. Thus the resolutions of Gilmer of Va.[1] and Marshall of Ky[2] to inflict censure upon Mr. Adams is complete. This is the first victory over the slaveholders *in a body* ever yet achieved since the foundation of the government, and from this time their downfall takes its date, it will be as certain as that Haman." It is impossible to look at the southern portion of our country without deep anguish of heart. They seem to be filling up the measures of their iniquities and thus preparing themselves for the signal judgments of God, when he will arise to make inquisition for blood. If Texas is annexed to the Union as is contemplated by some of the southern statesmen, it will cap the climax of our natural transgressions.

The Creole case has struck terror into the slaveholders, and if England sustains her free institutions and refuses to regard human beings as property, this circumstance will do much towards furthering emancipation.

If I understand Charles Stuart's mission to England, it was to establish female anti-slavery societies, but I forget whether especially in reference to slavery in America. How does he succeed and how is the anti-slavery cause in America now regarded? I trust the energy and interest of English philanthropists will not cease until every claim is broken.

With regard to the rights of women, I am persuaded that the more thou examinest this important subject the more thou wilt find in it to interest thee, and the more thou wilt see that our rights are the same as men's, altho' circumstances may render our status different. It is plainly the right of all human beings to cultivate the powers which God has given us; it is plainly the duty of woman to nurse her offspring; it cannot be the duty of man because God has not furnished him with the nourishment necessary for the infant. That the London Ctte. had no right to reject the female delegates is perfectly clear. I think it was an unwarrantable assumption of power, and when they better understand the rights of women as human beings, they will see that they are co-equal with their own.

I cannot see my dear friend that the public expression of my opinion on the subject of the rights of women, would at all tend to set at rest the strife and animosity of the parties in the anti-slavery cause. I am persuaded that before this question came up the seeds of discord were already sown, the clergy and their adherents were looking with a jealous eye at the antisectarian spirit, which rose up under the fostering care of humanity, and overlooking the mere differences of opinion kept its eye fixed on the great principles of liberty. When the woman question came up it only caused the seed to send forth shoots; and if this had not been brought up, something else would doubtless have produced the same effect. But even allowing that the woman question had originated the dispute, what demonstration can we give that our opinions have not changed, which

---

1. Thomas W. Gilmer (1802-1844) was a member of the House of Representatives (1841-1844); Governor of Virginia (1840-1841); and Secretary of the Navy (1844).
2. Thomas F. Marshall (1801-1861) also served in the House of Representatives.

would be likely to satisfy those who insist upon public action as the only satisfactory evidence, while we believe that God calls now to other duties, to the living out of our anti slavery principles in every day life, to assert our unchanged opinions as to the equality of the sexes at the family altar, around the social board and on all the occasions which may and do arise in domestic life? Had those who have been engaged in the controversy, professedly on the woman question, been contending only for the great principles which lie at the bottom of the question, they would have manifested a different spirit from that which has been manifested, they could not have descended to the low abuse and recrimination and endeavors to prove that true men were false, which has characterized their writings and speeches and conversation even more than those of their opponents. They seem to me to have identified self with the principles they were defending and hence there has been so much pride of opinion and such bitterness against those who differed from them. Whenever any occasion comes up on which we can express our sentiments, or act them out, we do it as Angelina did lately in a letter in reply to an invitation to attend the annual Mtg. of the Penn. a.s.so. As I did last summer at a temperance meeting. When the lecturer closed his remarks, I rose and stated that I wished to add some corroborative testimony. No objection was raised and I made the statement I wished. Believe me dear Elizabeth it is not so much a want of knowledge as a want of a right state of heart which induced the contention existing in the A.s. ranks. Oh how unworthy abolitionists have shown themselves of being used by God to overthrow the blood-stained temple of slavery. But blessed be God it will be overthrown. Charles Stuart took much pains to ascertain the real cause of the dissension in our ranks. I know not what conclusion he arrived at but perhaps he might help thee to form a correct judgment. If thou seest him tell him Theodore is still in Washington and is in excellent health....

The letters of our dear friend Joseph Sturge did not appear to be calculated to influence the Society of Friends; they are stagnant as the dead sea, and it will require some terrible explosion to move them, settled down in theie the firm conviction that they are right. There is no way of getting at them; their thoughts are bounded by the narrow circle of their own society; that is their idol and this incapacitates them from looking over the theatre of the world and seeing the horrible tragedies which are exhibited. They have lost the realizing sense of that solemn truth that to tell a starving brother to be warmed and filled, without furnishing the means, is a mockery of his woes and an insult to God. Hence in their annual epistles they express sympathy for the slave, but do not lift their fingers to break his chains. The very constitution and doctrine of the society on the subject of infallibility in elders, ministers, etc., crushes the freedom of the mind, and almost inevitably leads to a surrender of the conscience into the keeping of those to whom we are taught to look as the vice regents of God; this is the state of the society in this country, this was the effect produced on my own mind by membership and contact with Friends. I have been told by some of the most spiritual and valuable members, that I might *think* differently from the society but never *give utterance* to my convictions. There are a few who are not enslaved but they are rare exceptions.

I entirely agree with thee respecting William Bassett.

There are some things about non-resistance which seem to me so utterly inconsistent with the character of God as an unchangeable being that I cannot receive them; one is the rejection of the old testament as a rule of faith and practice; they insist that Christ was disannuling the moral law of the old testament in his sermon on the mount, instead of which he was drawing a comparison between the traditions of the scribes, etc., and what was in reality the essence and spirit of the law which God had given the Jews. See a chapter in Caroline Fry's "Example of Christ" on this subject.

Many thanks for thy details about E[ast] I[ndian] affairs and the condition of the people of England; does it not seem as tho' some signal judgment would ere long be poured out on Eu[rope] and Am.? Farewell – please offer our respects to thy father –

Affy. Thine

Sarah M. Grimké.

MS.A.1.2. vol. 12 (2) Anti-Slavery Letters to Garrison [117]
No. 27 John Curtis to R.D. Webb

London Feb. 14th 1842.

Dear Friend

...Sir Robert's Corn Law propositions has been received in England with a perfect howl – The Anti Corn Law Conference here held all last week and went off with great *Eclat* – speaking enough to carry a windmill – London however is by no means moved – The suffrage question is exciting great attention among the reformers. Great hopes are entertained of an union of the middle & working classes. "*Peaceful resistance*" is becoming quite a popular doctrine.[1]

Through the influence of Joseph Sturge I got the New Broad Street Committee together a day or two since in order to see if I could interest them with the antislavery aspects of the Anti Corn law question. Little prospect I fear of their doing anything which the present ministry may consider too political....

Yours most truly

John Curtis.

---

1. On February 9th Peel had introduced a Bill which would substitute a sliding scale of duties on cereals in place of the fixed duties then obtaining – an attempt to reach a compromise between the Free Traders and the Protectionists. The immediate effect of this Bill was to provoke a series of demonstrations against the Government by Free Traders in London, and to give impetus to the movement, led by Joseph Sturge, for complete suffrage. Sturge, however, was to find little support for his political programme among his Quaker colleagues of the B.F.A.S.S. – "the New Broad Street Committee."

MS.B.1.6. vol. 1 The May Papers [118]
No. 25 J.A. Collins to Samuel May[1] Jr.

Boston, February 28th 1842

My Dear Friend May

....Have you read that infamous letter of instructions to Ed. Everett,[2] our English minister, touching the Creole case, from that pliant dough faced sycophant, and tool of Southern slaveholding, Daniel Webster, our truckling Secretary of State? He fairly out Calhoun's Calhoun himself. If his Richmond electioneering speech has not already damned him in the minds of honourable and highminded men, this last effort of his, will, I think, in the language of his southern task masters, completely "*use him up.*"

What a golden opportunity Ed. Everett has now to immortalize his name by refusing to obey these barbarous and inhuman restrictions. But Everett is not the man for such a crisis. My kind regards to Mrs. May.

Hastily yours affectionately

J.A. Collins.

MS.A.1.2. vol. 12 (2) Anti-Slavery Letters to Garrison [119]
No. 28 E.M. Davis to Elizabeth Pease

Philad[a] 2nd mo. 15th 1842

My dear friend

... By our faithful papers the Standard & Liberator thee will get much of the anti slavery news, but they will not convey to thee an idea of half the anti slavery feeling that has been aroused and developed within the last 3 months & no one event has contributed so much, as the systematised effort in the House of R. at Washington on the part of the Southern delegation to trample, through J. Q. Adams, on the rights of northern citizens. I have been completely astonished to find the community so well served in Anti Slavery and to find so many alive to their rights. I had feared that the abolition of Slavery must be brought about by *blood* but a ray of hope for its peaceful overthrow has beamed upon us. Everywhere in the north have the papers come out boldly for the right of Petition & unless they are again magnetised by the threats of the South, we may soon expect that right regained, and it is so identified with our movements, that it will be counted our victory, as it should be. The Policy of

---

1. Rev. Samuel May Jr. of Leicester, Massachusetts, (1810-1899) was a Unitarian clergyman, cousin of Samuel J. May and friend and supporter of Garrison. On his visit to Britain in 1843 he introduced many British Unitarians to the question of American slavery.

2. Edward Everett (1794-1865) Unitarian clergyman, teacher and statesman, was the American minister to the Court of St. James from 1841 to 1845. He represented the conservative northern interests and was very sympathetic to Southern views on slaveholding. For a copy of the letter and some contemporary comments on it see *The Creole Case, and Mr. Webster's Despatch; with the comments of the N.Y. American*, New York, 1842.

Wickedness is always bad, & seldom is it more clearly verified than in the coupling, by the South, the right regained, and it is so identified with our movements, that it will be counted our victory, as it should be. The Policy of Wickedness is always bad, & seldom is it more clearly verified than in the coupling, by the South, the right of petition & the abolition of Slavery. Their answer was "if their petitions are received, their prayers may be granted. We will nip this fanaticism in the bud." Now they have *nipped it indeed,* our impolicy not abolition, for *it* prospers continually....

3rd mo 4th I was compelled to lay away my sheet until this time. T.D. Weld on his way from Washington is with us today & says that our cause is prospering there, that the slave holding members are overwhelmed with consternation. The people generally seem to feel that some important development was about to be made. I do not doubt but that some compromise will be effected, but wo[e] betide the northern men who do such a tratuous [sic] act to the cause of liberty as to compromise with the slave tyrants of the South. Public opinion at the North has changed within a few years & her representatives dare not tamper with her as they once could. The subject of British India is taking root in this country particularly that [?] which naturally interest the south, viz. the growing of cotton in India, the publications thee has sent to me at various periods have done much good but will do more. I have now an application through my brother from the *chairman of the com^{e} on manufactures in the Senate of the U.S. for information on this subject.* Of course I am collecting all I can get. By some means or other a part of my British India Advocate never came to hand, nos. 5.6.7.8. & 11 and if thee could send them to me it would be favouring the cause of human rights. These papers are very good but would be better if they contained more statistical information on the cotton subject. I send thee one of our *one cent* papers published today that has a very favorable article in on the subject of B.I. cotton. It would be well to publish it. This paper has a daily circulation of nearly 30,000 copies & is the best one in our city. The Irish address my dear friend is making a great noise with us, but public & private it is pronounced *a base fabrication* & the honour of abolitionists is at stake in the community for its truthfulness. We must have proof of its authenticity & when they send it, those who do, let them send another address containing more arguments. More than a million of copies of this address will be circulated I handed a copy to an Irish man the other day, but when he saw what it was he threw it away & would not pick it up. I did though.... Why does O'Connel not send *his* address in his own burning & enspiriting words to his countrymen here. Is he like other statesmen ever ready to promise, but slow to perform. I hope not. He knows not his influence in this country, how much those who hate him even, would give to know what he has to say. He owes it to the slave to use the influence he has or withdraw his promise, that defered hope may go back....

Why are not the abolitionists of G. Britain, Chartists Repealers & ultra Democrats? If hatred of oppression has taken root in the *soul* not in the *fancy*, will not those who cherish it, favour political as well as personal and I may ask religious liberty? There is no beauty in that love of liberty which sympathises with the American Slave and forgets the oppressed at home. But my paper is full and after asking when may we hope to see thee in America? I have but room to add that I am thy friend as ever Edward M. Davis

Dublin 22nd of 2nd mo. 1842.

More jottings for Maria W. Chapman.

... Nineteen out of twenty English Quakers are decided Radicals or at least whigs. Nineteen out of twenty Irish Quakers are rank tories and bigoted enemies to the Catholics – political enemies, I mean. They are professedly orthodox, on both sides of the Irish sea – but in England there is a strong tendency to high evangelical views – to *Gurneyism.* In Ireland, they are mostly Hicksites, without knowing it or suspecting it. They abhor Hicksites and Unitarianism. Nonresistance is looked on as no better than Hicksism and what Hicksism is they don't clearly know. My belief is that neither division of the Quaker body in America, nor yet the body as it exists unbroken here, is the same, even in doctrine, with the early Quakers of George Fox's time. The Hicksites are nearer to it – but they have none of the reformatory spirit of the old time. They are parrots – they speak but they neither understand nor feel what they say. The horrow of nonresistance is absolutely ludicrous – since many of the minutes in their "Statute Law" are to the fullest extent Nonresistant – as much so as H.C. Wright could desire. The Irish friends think the English too political – & possibly they are so – but they themselves substitute nothing better nor as good. They are thoroughly *in the quiet.* They prefer peace principles but they do nothing for the general promoting of peace: This damnable Chinese war doesn't move them. They are opposed to Capital Punishment – yet a man was hanged in Dublin lately, and the friends, as *friends,* would not even protest against the legal murder. They hate Garrison more than the Duke of Wellington. They are sluggish and bigoted beyond measure. In one point they exceed all other bodies that I know of. They are more munificient for the promotion of good objects. It was by their purses the antislavery struggle has been maintained...

Remond carried more money out of Ireland for himself than Collins got for the American Anti Slavery Society. This was, first, because he was a coloured man; then because he was eloquent – then because he has good manners – then because he is young, handsome, and interesting. He has great tact and discretion. Collins has neither the one nor the other. He often told me I was *New organized,* which if I had been disposed to mind him, would have affronted me exceedingly. Collins used to lug in by the neck and heels his thoughts on Exchange, into Anti Slavery gatherings, where no one (not even himself) could comprehend his crotchets. He is full of wildness and originality. He used to worry us with his bewildering speculations, though I am not readily tired in this way when there is any tolerable show of reason in a man's madness...

O'Connell in his pamphlet says the Irish people (that is, the Catholic people of Ireland, seven eighths of the whole) wish for a repeal of the Union, preserving fealty to the British crown. This I don't believe. They wish for a repeal, for they hate England – but they certainly dont wish for that refinement in British connexion implied in the bond created by the same crown. Popery ever acts on the ground of expediency – not of principle. His pamphlet shows O'Connell to be a true son of the Church. It says great things and consents to little things. I think him sincere on great questions of civil & religious liberty – but I would wonder at nothing mean paltry or roundabout in the mode of his carrying out his details. He is a politician – and how a politician can be upright and consistent is more than I can understand. His versatility & inexhaustible energy are amazing. I may seem like an American blaspheming Washington. But the truth is not to be put aside for either Washington or O'Connell.

There is a class of highly educated, deeply read, young men of great ability and enthusiasm, full of Irish nationality, hatred of England, strong for repeal. They are banded together by mutual sentiment and literary tastes. They are directing all their power to turn the natural intelligent opinion of Ireland in their own direction. Since 1798 when such as them were hanged, banished, or imprisoned, until now, there has been no such class. They are abundantly bloody minded, and would laugh nonresistance & H.C. Wright to scorn with all his Scripture quotations...

... Joseph Sturge is looked on with great disapprobation by Friends in Ireland. They as I have said are Tories, he is not only a liberal but a Reformer. He is a Radical. He opposes the Corn Laws, tooth and nail. And yet he is , compared with you, a staunch conservative and looks I suppose with holy horror on the Editor of the Nonresistant....

MS.A.1.1. vol. 3 Anti-Slavery Letters from Garrison [121]
No. 85 William Lloyd Garrison to R.D. Webb

Feb. 27. 1842.

Dear Richard D. Webb:

...Our meeting in Faneuil Hall, to unrol the Irish Address, with its sixty thousand signatures, was indescribably enthusiastic, and has produced a great impression on the public mind. I am sorry to add, and you will be not less ashamed to hear, that the two Irish papers in Boston sneer at the Address, and denounce it and the abolitionists in true pro-slavery style. I fear they will keep the great mass of your countrymen here from uniting with us ....

I am with all my heart your friend,

Wm Lloyd Garrison.

MS.A.9.2. vol. 17 The Weston Papers [122]
No. 36 Elizabeth Pease to ?

2 mo. 28. 1842

[no salutation]

... Our dear friend, G.T. has been & still is labouring indefatigably in the Anti Corn Law question – his advocacy is invaluable – he has diffused light & knowledge on the subject, far & wide – he has conciliated the Chartists & in many instances convinced the agriculturists of their true interests. The other night, he addressed a meeting in the open air, of upwards of 10,000.

Govt. sent down officers to watch proceedings & persons – all was peace & union between the middle & labouring classes. The cruel & insane policy of Sir Robt. Peel has done more than anything to bring about this most desirable consummation – the only one under providence, waiting to put a speedy end to aristocratic oppression. The cause of the people is advancing rapidly – tho' one dreads the ordeal thro' which the country have to pass, ere they obtain their just & reasonable demands – such is the blind & wicked determination of their lordly tyrants to retain their power to plunder & oppress. The forebearance & patience of the poor starving operatives can never be sufficiently commended – yet there is a point beyond which human endurance cannot go, & one could not wonder at hearing, any day, of an outbreak – tho' I am thankful to say, no symptoms of such a catastrophe appear at present....

thy affec[e] friend

Eliz[th] Pease.

MS.A.1.1. vol. 3/Anti-Slavery Letters from Garrison [123]
No. 87 William Lloyd Garrison to George Benson

Boston, March 22, 1842

Dear George:

...If all be well, (and, so mutable are all things here below, we can promise nothing as to the future without prefixing an *if*,) I shall go to Albany about the 21st of April, in company with C.L. Remond, to attend an anti-slavery convention which our friends intend to get up in that city, with special reference to the Irish Address. We shall carry that Address along with us. There is a pretty large Irish population in Albany, and an Irish Repeal Association; but the Argus has had the effrontery and folly to deny the authenticity of the Address, and, of course, a meeting called with especial reference to it will be pretty sure to be well attended, and to create a wholesome excitement....

... For my own part, I avow myself to be both an Irish Repealer and an American Repealer. I go for the repeal of the Union between England and Ireland, and for the repeal of the union between the North and the South. We must dissolve all connexion with these murderers of fathers, and murderers of mothers, and murderers of liberty, and traffickers in human flesh, and blasphemers against the Almighty, at the South. What have we in common with them? What have we gained, what have we not lost, by our alliance with them? Are not their principles, their pursuits, their policies, their interests, their designs, their feelings, utterly diverse from ours. Why, then, be subject to their dominion? Why not have the Union dissolved in form, as it is in fact – especially if the form gives ample protection to the slave system, by securing for it all the physical force of the North? It is not then treason against the cause of liberty to cry, "Down with every slaveholding Union!" Therefore I raise that cry! And, O, that I had a voice louder than a thousand thunders, that it might shake the land, and electrify the dead – the dead in sin, I mean – those slain by the hand of slavery.

How marvellously Providence works! The Irish Address, I trust, is to be the means of breaking up a stupendous conspiracy, which I believe is going on between the leading Irish demagogues, the leading pseudo-democrats, and the Southern Slaveholders. Mark three things. First – The Irish population among us is nearly all "democratic". Secondly – the cry in favour of Irish Repeal is now raised extensively throughout the South, and sustained by the leading democratic journals, – and why? To secure the aid of the Irish voters on the side of slavery, and to bring them united strength to bear against the anti-slavery enterprise! Also if possible, by sending over donations to Ireland, to stop O'Connells mouth on the subject of slavery, and to prevent any more "interference" , on that point, from that side of the Atlantic! Hence, I observe, at the Repeal Meetings, in various parts of the country, resolutions and declarations, which amount to sacred pledges, that these "repealers" will stand by southern institutions, at all hazards! Now, by the Address, which will cause every toad to start up into a devil as soon as he is touched, we shall be able to prove this matter to the bottom. If O'Connell and our friends in Ireland remain true to us, and renew their spirited attacks upon American slavery, and cry out against this unholy and frightful league between southern slave-drivers and his countrymen in America, then it will put down at the South this pretended sympathy for Ireland, and be the means of advancing our movement still more rapidly.

In this week's Liberator, I shall publish copious extracts from O'Connell's speeches, for the last ten years, against American slavery. They will seethe like lightning, and smite like thunderbolts. No man, in the wide world, has spoken so strongly against the soul-drivers of this land as O'Connell.

Is it not heart cheering to know that the British government will not give up the Creole?....

For a few days past, I have been somewhat feverish, and do not feel in a very good condition now.

Remember me with a brother's affection to Anne and Catherine, and give my friendly remembrances to Wm. Adam, D.L. Child, &c.

Yours, faithfully, Wm. Lloyd Garrison.

MS.A.1.2. vol. 12 (2) Anti-Slavery Letters to Garrison [124]
No. 39 Wendell Phillips to Richard Allen

Boston March 30 1842

My dear Friend

...You see by the papers the manner in which certain prints (the Pilot & others) have received your address with its long catalogue of signatures. Those papers are the organs & influential controllers of the Irish & Catholic population here. What will you do? They deny its authority? Say O'Connell signed it without knowing or caring about the abolitionists here, but the real ground of objection is this. The Repeal Agitation in this country extends through all the States & has received some strong aid in the South. You have seen the speech of Wm. M. Johnson true in itself absurd as coming from one in his circumstances, a slave holder. Well the repealers are afraid if they exhibit even individually any sympathy with the abolitionists, they shall lose their union with all the Repealers at the South — of course we cannot ask the Repeal *Association as such* to take ground on the question. I have heard this motive in a Repeal Meeting appealed to though not in so many words avowed. Now between you & me ... the Irish here are usually an illiterate mass in general and entirely and mostly under the control of those few among them who have education or those who act as their lawyers or the few who court office by begging their votes. For my idea — the Repeal agitation in this country is hearty and sincere in the talk of the Irish, but with those who *conduct* the movement & keep up the system, it is only a scheme intended to operate on this side the water & secure offices for hungry demagogues. But don't quote me to this for though *I* have all confidence in my own views, yet my means of observation have been slight & I do not wish to express them publicly. Still I think the Repeal associations are tools in the hands of second rate politicians here to make themselves *first rate.* Now what we want you & O'Connell to think it your duty to do is to send us a startling scorching bitter unsparing,pointed rebuke (& publish it in your own papers as well as send it to us) telling the Repealers here that you dont want the money or voices of slaveholders or their friends — that you repudiate all connection with a Repeal society which holds its peace on negro slavery in order to cozen favor with those who[se] hands are bloody with its guilt. Laugh, hoot, scorn, hiss, spit at the recreant Irishman who holds off from his sympathy the abolitionist & clasps the slaveholder's toady to his bosom: reject all aid from such with scorn: Tell them theypollute the cause they wish others to think they want to help — make them feel small — They say you don't know the abolitionist, he is a bloody fanatic — O'Connell would scorn & detest him — speak on this point — They stultify old Danl. in trying to make their readers believe he don't know [what] he is about but has been humbugged by Remond!!

There can't be any fear Danl will speak out & speak right on this matter — He & you will never get a cent or but little from the South — all the contributions North & South are not worth one of his words. And to permit the Repealers with their present position to claim his countenance in taking the brightest jewel from his crown — that consistency, which all the world can see the flashing of as it sits so regally on his brow: I long to get sight of the lightning flash, the [?] bolt with which you will annihilate these mock pretenders to liberty. I spoke here once at a repeal meeting. Never shall I do it again — O'Connell never could have breathed there unless his electricity had been able to purify the air — Low mean politics — demagogical Earthly [?] — pah the mouth tasted bad for days after. Webb & you & Haughton would have fainted — so unlike abolition meeting. Yet the poor people who flung up their hats & shouted — are true metal. In right hands — fit for great things but we cannot get between them & their leaders — can't get their ear I am afraid — the Protestants though are some of them with us & in time we can do much. ...

Kindest regards to [yourself?] Yours truly

W. Phillips.

MS.A.9.2. vol. 17 1842 The Weston Papers [125]
No. 37 Mary Welsh to Maria Weston Chapman

Glasgow March 1st 1842

Mrs. Chapman

Very Dear Friend

Your welcome letter announcing the safe arrival of the box reached us duly, it gave us the greatest pleasure imaginable to know that you were so much pleased with its contents, your second addressed to our committee has also been received for which accept our thanks, the information it contains relating to the sale of the articles shall be so very useful to us if enabled to furnish anything for next year which I sincerely hope we will, it should be inserted in our annual report so that all into whose hands it may fall shall know what is most suited for the fair at that season of the year. I know them who are beginning to do a little for it already, we shall now work with more certainty as regards the kind of articles to be done, on the former occasion it was more guess work than anything else ....

With regard to the clerical party & those influenced by them who opposed our worthy friend Mr. Collins when here we have only to say that as far as our observation goes they are doing nothing & saying as little the clergy have lost their Anti-Slavery influence in Glasgow (indeed their influence is giving way in more ways than one) I believe they are feeling it and not a little humbled at it yet not sufficiently so as to lead them to acknowledge it, the delay they pled for has never been explained neither will it we believe, however we cheerfully hazard that the truth it will make its own way into men's hearts whether they end it or not.

I remain yours for our committee

in the cause of freedom. Mary Welsh

MS.A.1.2. vol. 12 (2) Anti-Slavery Letters to Garrison [126]
No. 41 J.A. Collins to R.D. Webb

Boston April 2 1842.

My dear Friend,

... One thing after another is constantly happening to keep our land in a state of perfect fermentation in relation to slavery. If we need the maturing of all the plans, for the bringing about of the great object we have in view, we could project nothing better adopted to promote it, than those, which Providence produces in the right time and place. The Amistad with her 40 human victims landing upon the shores of the free – rather of the slave states, – the attempt of Texas to gain admission to the union in 1838, the shunning of our petitions on the floor of Congress. John Quincy Adams' valorous defence of the right of petition – the base attempt of the south to ensnare him – the case of the Creole – the decision of the Supreme Court of the United States annuling state laws granting jury trial to the panting fugitive – the entire bankruptcy of the South – the general prostration of business of the North – the censure of Giddings[1] a member of Congress from Ohio, by the House of Representatives in Congress, for presenting his thoughts to that body in relation to the Creole, the possibility, nay the probability of a war with England not for liberty – but to defend "*the peculiar institutions of the South,*" the hostilities between Texas and Mexico – and the desire of our Southern despots to have the matter defeated – *these* and hundreds of other circumstances, have awakened a Northern feeling which can never slumber nor sleep while there is one manacled victim in our land. This being accomplished, our country like Great Britain, proud of this act of philanthropy, will unite with her, in waging a war of extermination against slavery throughout the habitable globe; – and what man can resist the moral influence of these two nations when devoted to acts of virtue and benevolence, instead of selfishness and blood....

But my object in writing you at this time is to speak of the effects of the Irish Address upon our community, and the importance of your taking *immediate*, *positive* and *efficient* action thereupon. Now is the time for Daniel O'Connell to speak to the American papers with a trumpet tongue. The roarings of his voice should strike the rocky mountains and echo back upon the plains and valleys of the whole United States. You have seen probably by the papers the position [?] national Irish Association has taken on the question of slavery, and have read no doubt – the sentiments expressed by Bishop Hughes[2] of New York – the Boston Pilot and other Irish papers. This position taken by those associations, journals, and individuals which to a very great extent moulds and governs the sentiments of the Irish emigrants unfortunate for us – nearly all the Irish are associated with the large democratic party which is no more nor less than a conspiracy against the principles of true democracy. There are however just enough of the Irish connected with the Whig party to make that party as mute as a corpse in relation to the advantage the democratic journals and orators are now taking of the present position of the Irish of this country, in relation to the "Address". Every possible effort is now made by the leaders of the democratic party, and also of the Irish, to deceive the great mass of the Irishmen of this country in relation to the design of the Irish Address & the designs and objects of the abolitionists. Nine tenths of the Irish, are at heart, thorough going abolitionists. Yet it is very easy for these orators and editors who are capable of making "the worse appear the better case", to make them believe that patriotism, religion and philanthropy demands their non-interference with slavery. Now if O'Connell will write the Address to the Irish of this country which he agreed to at the "World's Convention" and to me, when Haughton

---

1. Joshua Reed Giddings (1795-1864), an anti-slavery Whig from Ohio, was one of the leading members of the Washington Anti-Slavery lobby. After presenting his resolutions on the Creole case, and being censured by the House of Representatives, he resigned and was re-elected by his constitutents, a signal victory for the anti-slavery lobbyists.

2. Archbishop John Hughes (1797-1868), born in Ireland, was a leader of the Roman Catholic Church and of the Irish in America. He worked actively to strengthen the American Catholic Church, and helped to found the American College in Rome. He did not support slavery, but at the same time opposed the Irish Manifesto. During the Civil War he defended the Union cause in Europe.

and myself called on him at his house in Dublin we will publish it with the Irish address with extracts from his speeches and scatter them in the form of a pamphlet broad cast among the Irish of this country. Of course we shall add the names to the address of Father Matthew[3] – Bishops Priests – Dr. Madden and other influential abolitionists of Ireland. We want the Irish papers to speak out boldly on this question also. This is important. *They must do it.* The repealers of Ireland must not be afraid that it will diminish their friends at all from this country, as everybody knows that O'Connell and all the Irish of Ireland are abolitionists and will be honoured by all for their fidelity to the cause of human freedom, but will be most throughly disposed of they are made to succumb for a few paltry dollars. I have no fear of O'Connell backing out. I know something of the trying position he occupies at home among his own friends as he denounces American slavery while he needs the money of the Irish of this country to sustain his repeal operations. This exhibits on his part – a fineness of principle – a decision of character worthy of the man, His word is almost law – with ninetenths of the Irish in this country – and that of Father Matthew is nearly as great. Hence the efforts of those interested to make the Irish Address with the signatures of O'Connell and Father Matthew *a forgery....*

Affectionately yours – Hastily   J.A. Collins.

MS.A.1.2. vol. 12 (2) Anti-Slavery Letters to Garrison [127]
No. 59 Elizabeth Neall[1] to Elizabeth Pease

Philada 6 mo. 18. 42.

My dear friend

...The Liberty Party are going on valiantly. Leavitt at Washington, who doubtless considers himself the high priest of abolitionism, because he wields his mighty pen from our slave holding capital, from the midst of "the assembled wisdom of the nation." Perhaps he thinks that the delivrance of the slave depends upon his watching the petty drama which is every year enacted upon the stage of our House of Representatives, and by the occasional glimpses wh. he may get behind the scenes, at the wires and strings of party machinery and management. Alas! for the slave if his only hope rests with these men, upon that Representative Body. Why will not our Leavitts & Birneys and Whittiers and Smiths learn that there is a power mightier than that of Church or State, broader and higher and deeper, controlling and moving these – the *Moral* power of the Nation.

The winter at Washington has been quite exciting and interesting. At the time of the attack upon J.Q. Adams[2] I went down there to hear his defence;

---

3. Father Mathew (1790-1856) was a famous Irish temperance reformer.

1. Elizabeth J. Neall (1819-?) became the wife of Sydney Howard Gay, the editor of the *Anti-Slavery Standard*. A Quakeress from Philadelphia, she was another of the delegation appointed to the 1840 Convention by the Philadelphia Female Anti-Slavery Society.

2. John Quincy Adams had determined to take up the question of slavery even

and if my veneration were more easily moved towards "the great men" who figure upon our political boards than it is, I might have been even more affected with the sight than I was, but it was a touching picture. Gray haired virtue defending itself against imprudent envy and malignant hate. Of course the old man was victorious: and to be there to witness the discomfiture of the southern soul-drivers was quite refreshing. That and the Giddings affair hast done much towards calling out the Press – Hast read Giddings speech on the Florida war delivered some two years since. He displayed his abilities and excellence of character in that able and eloquent paper. I was happy to find Lord Morpeth[3] so much interested during Adams' Trial: He sat by him daily and listened with fixed attention to his every word: He expressed himself with much feeling about it; and I am sure must have left our Legislative Halls impressed with no very favorable opinion of the principle or the Sagacity of our statesmen. But when brought to the true test, those of your own country stand no higher than ours. Enlightened and Christian England! who can read of her starving millions – and of her wars abroad – the revelations of Geo. Thompson in relation to the Afghanistan war – & the accounts of the Chinese war, and not feel humbled and grieved and indignant, that in these days of Christian civilization atrocities so awful are committed, set on foot and supported by the Religion and the Government of the most renowned and enlightened Christian nation on the Globe. How much I regret that Mr. Macauley[4] has opposed the granting of the Chartist Petition. I have so admired and respected him for his high and generous impulses and for his gigantic intellectual gifts – that my spirit is hurt to discover that I have set up another "idol but to find him clay." I could not have imagined Mr. Macauley, judging from his writings, opposed to granting the enjoyment of the largest liberty of the people. He may think, as he says, that the right of universal suffrage is allowed the people now, might create anarchy and bloodshed, but how short-sighted must he be. I remember in one of his articles, in wh. he defends Democratic institutions, he says, that "a man who forms an abstract idea of a constitution, without reference to the people who are to be governed by it, is as absurd as a Tailor who measures the clothes of all his customers by the stature of the Belvedere Apollo." He

---

more vigorously, and using a Southern petition praying that he be removed from the Senate Foreign Relations Committee as a pretext, he claimed the right to speak in his own defence, but made instead a long speech attacking Southern slavery. Angry with him for upsetting the political equilibrium, the Whigs used another petition, which Adams presented shortly after, demanding the dissolution of the Union – as grounds for a motion of censure on Adams. His trial was a dramatic one, but so strong was Northern opinion on his side that it became clear to the Whigs that their attempt to discipline Adams would have such grave political repercussions, that the charges were dropped.

3. George William Frederick Howard, Lord Morpeth, afterwards 7th Earl of Carlisle, (1802-1864), was noted for his liberal views during the 1830's when he served as Chief Secretary for Ireland, and M.P. for the West Riding. He later held various political posts, and in 1855 was appointed Lord Lieutenant for Ireland, a post which he held for several years. He took a very real interest in social reforms, including the Anti-Slavery movement. His sister was the Duchess of Sutherland, who dabbled so energetically in anti-slavery affairs.

4. Thomas Babington Macaulay (1800-1859) was the son of Zachary Macaulay, the abolitionist, and was famous as a writer, historian, and one of the chief spokesmen for the liberal principles of the day. His works were widely read in America, and his essays in particular won high approval there.

may think the Chartists as absurd as the Tailor: but what arrogance for him to decide upon the matter. Doesn't every man know how he wishes to be governed. Mr. M. has been my darling and I had hoped that he would someday stand foremost in advocating the Rights of the many against the usurpations of the few. The Dissolution Question is creating quite a stir among us. Garrison is accused of inconsistency in upholding it because it is a Political Question. Is it so very political for him to declare a repeal of the Union between Liberty & Slavery, between Right and Wrong? Must one use political measures in declaring that the Union between Freedom and Oppression must & shall cease – It seems to me that the Abolitionists dissolved their connection with the South and its hateful institution, when they formed the Am. Anti Slavery Soc. & pledged themselves not to relinquish their efforts to repeal the Union between Liberty & Slavery, until the shout of Emancipation should ring through all our vallies and along our hillsides and mountain tops –

New England abolitionism differs so from ours here in Penn. that I often wish for a little of the fiery spirit that lives and thrives among the rocky fastness and rough bleak hill of our Yankee Caledonia. The quiet "waiting" Quaker abolitionists here can ill bear the impetuous driving of the New England people who go to the tune (pardon me) of "devil take the hindmost." They cannot see that these fanatical measures will do ought for the cause and so we sit quietly and allow the Yankees to do nearly all the planning & the cutting & fitting, esteeming ourselves quite courageous if we sew up a few seems in the governments wh. have been prepared by the energies and labors of our furious and fanatical Yankees brethren – And everything good takes root and grows in that sterile soil. Whether from our quiet temperament or from our near vicinity to the south, and its influences wh. always paralyse whatever comes within their reach that is good, or true, that we are so far wanting in action, I cannot tell, but certainly we are far in the rear....

Believe me most truly thy affec. friend E.J. Neall

MS.A.4.6. A vol. 1 The Chapman Papers [128]
No. 3 Margaret New to M.W. Chapman

13 Grays Inn Terrace, London
7 September/41

Madam

In a letter addressed by you some years since, to the Dutchesse de Broglie,[1] you say that *any* expression of friendly interest would be a gratification to you. I therefore venture to address you feeling assured you will not disregard the expression of heartfelt interest and sympathy of a female of the *Mother Country.*

---

1. Probably Albertine, the wife of Leonce-Victor, duc de Broglie, Minister of Louis Philippe. She was the illegitimate daughter of Madame De Staël and Benjamin Constant, and so moved in the most noted French liberal reform circles. This correspondence is an interesting example of Maria Weston Chapman's acquaintance with such groups – an acquaintance which she assiduously cultivated.

Would I could give more than sympathy of the high and noble cause you have so nobly come forward to advocate: how must the poor slaves bless your name and existence, and look forward to you as the one who is determined to accomplish their emancipation for emancipated they will be and principally through your noble conduct. How refreshing it is to find, that there are women, who will in spite of the opposition of the envious and the *interested* stand boldly forth both with voice and pen and steadily advocate the cause of the oppressed.

I was first made acquainted with your admirable conduct by an article in the London & Westminster Review written by my talented country woman, Harriet Martineau, in which the sufferings you have undergone, are vividly depicted. How indignant did I feel, when I read of the persecutions you have been compelled to undergo and principally from those *calling* themselves *Gentlemen,* they are a disgrace to that name, and the country and age in which they live.

I have not for some time had any information regarding your proceedings, but I should like to learn how you are progressing, *well,* I sincerely hope – If you can now and then spare a few minutes of your valuable time, and will write to *me*, how proud and happy I shall be .... It is a selfish wish, but it is mine, that you would use all your energies towards bettering the condition both political and social of the women of this country, we are in such a fearful state of bondage tis dreadful to contemplate, and we have so feww women of moral courage sufficient to attempt a change. My friend Mrs. Toll is one of the few she is a woman following in your own footsteps. Thrice blessed are the women who *do* advance some steps from the old beaten path and do not heed the sneers of the world, but go right onward in their right doing....

I remain Madam
with the utmost admiration and respect
yours sincerely

Margaret New.

MS.A.9.2. vol. 17 1843 The Weston Papers
No. 93 R.R. Madden to Maria Weston Chapman [129]

London
40 Sloane Square
Chelsea
27 Augt 1842

My dear Madam

... When I reflect how our cause is served in this country, I could wish that you & your enlightened country-women Mrs. Child and Mrs. Sigourney would come to England on a mission devoted to the task of inspiring our fair ladies with a higher sense of their duties to humanity, and an idea that God sent them into this world for other purposes, besides perfection in those accomplishments to which all their time in early life is devoted and on which all their energies are so lamentable wasted.

I am inclined to think that an American lady like Mrs. Chapman who would come to this country on such a mission, and who would deliver a course of lectures on the subject of the obligations of women to society, and especially to the cause of humanity wherever its interests are outraged, would do much good and a great deal to advance the question of women's rights. I beg you to remember me most kindly to Mrs. Child, to Mr. Garrison, Dr. Channing and all my anti-slavery friends at Boston and believe me

My dear Madam

Very truly yours

R.R. Madden.

MS.A.1.2. vol. 12 (2) Anti-Slavery Letters to Garrison [130]
No. 77 Wendell Phillips to Elizabeth Pease

Lynn Aug 12th 1842.

(no salutation)

... I want you (when you get, as a German told me he did by drinking of the spa, "*too strong*") to write me a letter, telling the names of leading men, members of Parlia., & speakers among the Chartists – how many votes they can count on in [the] H.C. – any statistics about them. Which article they shall find the *best*, if there are indeed any, in the Quarterly Review about them. &c. I have by C.L.R.'s kindness the Charter & your pamphlets & our newspapers throw much light on their movements. The reviews, which we have, of course tell something – but I intend to write a lecture for the Lyceum here about Chartism & want to make a show by sketching men & speakers which no publication will give me, but perhaps a few lines of what is commonplace knowledge in the snug sanctum of Feethams would be novelty here & make a glowworm of me for many nights....What a fearful crisis you seem to be in. I feel for you. I never understood the (unjust) tiger like strength of your *Government* till now. Here light does not follow the day quicker than our Govemt. changes at the peoples bidding. But when discontent, with starvation for her ally, stands with guns shotted to their lips ever against your aristocracy, the little junto in the scale with desperate millions, itself blindly, madly confident will not, like Pharaoh of old, "let my people go"...

Yrs truly

Wendell P.

MS.A.1.2. vol. 12 (2) Anti-Slavery Letters to Garrison [131]
No. 79 Elizabeth Pease to Wendell and Ann Phillips

Darlington Augst 16 1842

Dearest Wendell & Ann

...The packet which conveys this will carry out woeful tidings of the state of this country – disturbances – delayed till *all* hope of relief was over – have at length commenced,& they wd. form one of the principal topics of my letter but for the difficulty of obtaining accurate information – at such times there are always so many rumours afloat, that 'tis hard to distinguish between true & false Certain however it is that we have arrived at an awful period in our country's history – that multitudes are marching thro' the manufacturing districts of Lancashire & Yorkshire – compelling the mills to stop work – that when the masters refuse to do so, the people extinguish the fires & when resistance is offered, commence to break the windows & commit other acts of violence – always, so far as we know, carefully avoiding the endangering of human life. Tis said they have taken up the railways in some parts – compelled the people employed in them to give up work – & that in Leeds the public omnibuses had been smashed in pieces. It was also rumoured yesterday that the military – large bodies of whom have been sent down from London – had fired in Manchester & killed 35. I hope 'tis not true – such an act wd. be the signal for bloodshed on the part of the mob, & who can say, where it wd. end. The whole appears to be regularly organized & thoroughly digested plan. – & so secret are they that little is know with regard to their ultimate designs – one would suppose their aim must be to stop all commerce & traffic & thereby compel the Govt. to yield to their reasonable demands. They have reached Leeds & we expect soon to be visited by a deputation, to stop the mills & other large works in this Town & in all probability the colleries in the neighbourhood, which supply the London market. The people must live by plunder, so far as one can see, so that we shall probably all be more or less of sufferers – indeed, security of property seems at an end – in Manchester the multitude go from door to door (almost) demanding provisions or money – the shops have been shut for several days & the streets filled with the military. One's whole sympathies go with the disorganisers – driven as they are almost to desperation, by insult & injury heaped upon them by those who, if actions be right interpreters of feelings, consider they are but chattels made to minister to their luxury & add to their wealth. The little security which human laws or human power ever seemed to give, is now at an end – for 'tis most evident that the power is now, or will very shortly be, in the hands of the people whom, as a whole, I believe there is little reason to fear, but, the few wicked & reckless, who will mix themselves with the rest, may do serious damage & endanger life as well as property. Yet there is a power above them & on this divine arm, is the only safe & secure resting place – the only stay & consolation to the mind when all that is usually termed human protection, does but add to the danger & insecurity. My fears wd. be less, were the soldiers & military all to be disbanded, instead, of being in use, I believe they do but drive the populace to greater desperation & deeds of violence. Sir Robert Peel & several of his colleagues were intending to visit the Marquis of Londonderry, whose seat is in this neighbourhood, but they are compelled to remain in Town & keep the privy Council in session, to receive reports from the disturbed districts. We are all on the alert for tidings – since I sat down to scrawl this sheet I have heard that the people are demanding specie payment, wh. must hamper the banks & the country at large sadly – large bodies of troops have again been despatched from London – while passing through the streets the people assembled in a large multitude, groaned, hissed & shouting "Be men, & dont kill your poor starving countrymen" – on reaching Euston Square the throng had filled the Square in order to prevent their taking the railway – the police were assembled & dispersed them. But I forgot that you will have the full & circumstantial account in the papers & up to a later date than I can give – so I need not fill my space with any more of my scraps of intelligence – but, truly, one cannot banish the subject from one's mind, for we know not what a day may bring forth. The head of the Chartists in this Town has recd. instructions to commence operations here – stopping the factories &c so we shall be like our neighbours soon probably. *I* shall expect to be treated with favour, for he & I have exchanged our paper & I've helped to distribute their Chartist documents!! so I've a right to expect protection – have I not?!!! No, 'tis too serious a subject to joke on – human protection is little to [be] counted on at such a time....

The "Sun" contains a speech eight hours long of G.T.'s at the India House – what a triumphant defence of the Rajah & humiliating expose for the E.I. Company.[1] There was a grand entertainment at the Mansion house, that same day, to which the Directors were specially invited & sadly against their will partaking of the feast. G.T. & the other liberal Candidate lost their Election at Southampton through the gross bribery of the Tories – the last time I heard, they were intending to petition against the return. I could not but rather regard that G.T. yielded to the solicitations to stand. In my opinion he is better *out* of parlt. than *in* it....

Never say another word about bad writing – or I shall conclude a gentle rebuke for me is implied – *this* is really too *bad.* But it will assure you, I trust, of the sincere & unabated affection of your sister Elizabeth....

MS.A.1.2. vol. 12 (2) Anti-Slavery Letters to Garrison [132]
No. 91 Sarah Pugh[1] to Elizabeth Pease

Philad^{a} 9/20th – 42

My dear Friend

...With what interest do I read your papers in reference to the Corn Law, independently of the principle involved are they not associated with those in whom I am so much interested? With George Thompson...with thyself and all in Britain for whom we care. Is it not strange that Blackwoods can "deny a national distress". Professor Wilson[2] must have had a *chill* on his heart when he wrote of the present sufferings as being "no more than one of chills or alternating states of depression, which belongs to commerce by its general nature"...A large portion of your population must be unconscious of the misery existing in their very midst – as are our northern people of the horrors of Southern Slavery. They read only papers that are interested in

---

1. In 1839 the Rajah of Satara was deposed on a charge of misgovernment by the East India Company, and his place was given to his brother. He protested against this action and brought a suit against the Court of Directors of the East India Company – a long drawn out and unsuccessful case which was mainly conducted for him by George Thompson.

1. Sarah Pugh (1800-1884), a Philadelphia Quakeress and another delegate to the 1840 Convention, remained on the closest terms with many of the British women abolitionists and until her death maintained a correspondence with Mary Estlin.
2. John Wilson (1785-1854), a Professor of Moral Philosophy at the University of Edinburgh, was a long standing contributor to *Blackwood's Magazine* on a wide ranging number of topics. He is best known as the creator of "Christopher North."

covering up the evil – at least feel it impolitic to expose it. The Anti-Slavery & Chartist papers are left for the vulgar....

The Magnolia a Southern Monthly has just been handed to me to read an article on Indian & American Cotton – written to prove that the South has nothing to fear from India. It is attempted to be proved that the cotton of India must cost in England two cents a pound more than American. – The East India Company is charged with all the Abolition efforts that have been made from the time of Wilberforce and Clarkson – The Company produced the insurrection in San Domingo "Ogē was taken by Clarkson to London and furnished with military supplies and equipments" – it is undoubted fact that the notorious Thompson was employed and paid by the *Honorable* East India Company. "We would wager our right to the freedom of speech that could his credentials have been examined they would have been found bearing [?] at the India House" – "These slick & slippered corporators have been sitting with dignified severity in World's Conventions." "The wisdom of sages never invented a better economical system for a pauper population than our much abused Domestic [features?] The system of *associated labor* in the Southern States.Is this not a precious article? Associated labor!! So gentle. With kind remembrances to thy parents dear George Thompson & family – fondly & truly thy friend

Sarah Pugh.

MS.A.1.2. vol. 12 (2) Anti-Slavery Letters to Garrison [133]
No. 93 J.S. Gibbons to Elizabeth Pease

New York 9 mo. 25. 1842

My dear friend

... I am glad to see that recent demonstrations of popular violence among your manufacturers, subside, & that quiet again reigns. Now may God bless this period of restored peace to you, by a serious and availing effort on the part of your rulers to ameliorate the condition from which that disaffection & violence springs. These are times for great progress in social good – times for the development of great principles. Common misery binds the suffering labourers of Europe & America in sympathy with each other. The width of the Atlantic will not prevent them from shaking hands with each other. Thus, the sense of humanity spreads, and manhood grows. Its reasonable demands for amelioration must be satisfied...

with most affectionate friendly regards & interest –

J.S. Gibbons.

MS.A.1.2. vol. 12 (2) Anti-Slavery Letters to Garrison [134]
No. 94 Elizabeth Pease to Wendell and Ann Phillips

Feethams 9 mo. 29, 1842

... My pen must stop its vagaries & come to the sober topic of this letter – which is to return my honest thanks for the questions Wendell put to me on Chartism – they taught me how little I *really knew* on the subject notwithstanding that I reckon myself one of their body – so off I sent them to our friend Ashurst for replies – telling him all the information I cd obtain wd be spread before the Lyceum at Boston – *he*, most kindly copied them for three of the leading Chartists to answer – & thus, I have the promise of a store of knowledge which it will delight me to send, as it has to gain. I hope I may have a letter from Ashurst in time to enclose in this, tho' if not, it shall go without – notwithstanding that it will be like sending a nut without its kernel. Mr. Lovett[1], a great man among *my people*, has written a few particulars which will be embodied in Ashurst's letter & has sent a number of pamphlets, which have not yet come to my hand, but, I hope the next packet will convey the whole budget... We had a visit from Jos. Sturge & his friend Arthur Allbright[2] a few days since – they were two nights & a day with us – & being on a suffrage mission, we heard a deal on the subject. It appears to me, to lie at the very foundation of the prosperity – almost of the existence – of this country. Surely it is to class Legislation that nearly all the evils which affect Gt. Britain & render her a curse, instead of a blessing, to other nations – is to be attributed and so long as this hydra-headed monster is suffered to remain, it is vain to strike off one of its heads – in the shape of the Corn Laws, Monopoly, union of church & state or aught else; – till it is *destroyed* utterly – blood, bones & sinews – like the fabled monster of old, *two* heads will spring up to fill the place of one. Tis expecting too much of poor human nature, to anticipate that those who have the power will legislate against their own interests – tho they *might* have been a *little* more modest, than to rob the people of £50,000,000 a year, which it is calculated they do, to put into their own pockets, by food taxes, & monopolies of one sort or another. My opinion is that Jos. Sturge & his friends wd. have done better had they retained the name of Chartists – tis only in name they differ from the *Moral Force* Chartists (there are *very few* indeed who now advocate physical force) & why succumb to the prejudices of the middle classes by rejecting an appellation which tells you their principles at once. Jos. Sturge is acting a bold & independent part on this subject – we must honour him for it....The Tory papers abuse him with great violence – which is a good sign – & he has been advised by several 'Friends' to resign his membership in our Society – tho' we have very few Tories in our sect in England (in Ireland the case is the reverse) yet but few will go with J.S. He was saying that "Friends" here were worse than in America, they wd. open their meeting houses, in some places, to abolition – but, he did not know one in this country, which wd. be open to his present mission. He places the two questions side by side of each other on the same basis of principle...

10 mo. 2... I believe I made a strange omission in my last, & never told thee how greatly Patrick Brewster (of Paisley) was delighted with the "Slave of Poverty" I sent him a copy, & he wrote me back that the

---

1. William Lovett (1799-1877), a Moderate Force Chartist on close terms with British and American abolitionists, was one of the most notable of the Chartist leaders, and was especially active in seeking a rapprochement with middle class liberals. Both he and Henry Vincent (see below) joined the Anti-Slavery League. His later years were devoted to work for popular education.
2. Arthur Albright (1811-1900) was connected by marriage to Joseph Sturge. He later became a very successful businessman in his own right.

sentiments were precisely those for which he had been brought under ecclesiastical censure & that he was anxious to know whether he could procure the succeeding nos. of the "N.Y. Quarly. Pamphleteer" in this country. I sent one to Ashurst, & he wished for some to give to some of the leading Chartists, but I have not heard his opinion.... *I believe,* the Chartists generally hold the doctrine of the equality of women's rights – but I am not sure whether they do not consider that when she *marries,* she merges her political right in those of her husband – *one* of them, writing on the subject, advocates all unmarried females having a vote but not the married, and I rather suppose Jos. Sturge holds this opinion – at least he said something about giving to women under some circumstances, a vote – he was just going out at the time – & his visit was so short that I forgot to enquire afterwards about it. Buckingham does not, I think restrict the right to unmarried women.

George Thompson intends to take his departure for India on the 1st prox. England has lately been visited by a native merchant of immense wealth – Dwarkanath Tagore – he appears to feel greatly for the poor classes in his country – to be aware of the grievances under which they labour & anxious to relieve them. During his stay he has been much with G.T. & made a friend & confident of him – & he, it is who promotes this step – he pays G.T.'s expenses & allows his wife & family a maintenance during his absence, which they say, will be 8 months. I shd. think it probable that it wd. be much longer – at any rate, shd his mission be safely accomplished he will obtain a large amount of valuable information & as he hopes, establish a more efficient cooperation at Calcutta & Bombay than can be effected in any other way. Yet it is a formidable undertaking & I cannot help fears for his health. He intends to go by sea to Malta, there meet Dwarkanath who goes thro' France, & thence they will take the overland route – to Bombay, I suppose....

Believe me, dear W & A with a sister's love

to be your own

Elizabeth.

MS.A.4.6.A vol. 1 The Chapman Papers [135]
No. 32 Mary Welsh to Maria Weston Chapman

Glasgow Novr 15th 1842 33 Duke St.

Very Dear Friend

I am afraid ere this you will be concluding that your Glasgow friends have grown cold in the cause of the slave, owing to their long silence, glad I am to assure you this is not the case, we intended to have dispatched a box of articles for your coming Bazaar with the vessel which sails the 18th of Decr. We trust nothing will prevent it leaving them and hope sincerely it will reach you in full time for the fair, the reason of this detention was in consequence of our annual meeting not taking place until the 24th of last month, (no doubt you have seen from the newspapers the particulars of it so that it is unnecessary for me to say anything about it here) from the time it should have taken place until then we were occasionally corresponding with Geo. Thompson about it, we felt it was convenient for him to be present, this delay preventing the publication of our report and also the public intimation of our box. For the sake of those friends who might not have heard of it till they were at the meeting we all announced that we would not close it until the 20th of this month, we were much afraid that it would prove a failure this year as it was long before friends would begin to work yet our prospects were a little better than there were. The great depression in trade and the starving thousands with which we are surrounded is a grand excuse for many to do nothing for their suffering brethren at a distance, yet the result of our experience and observation goes to prove that those who aid benevolent societies at all generally have something for everyone and those who love only themselves take advantage of such times as the present to excuse doing altogether. Many times are we told when pleading the cause of the American slave that really so many at home need assistance there can be no wisdom in going so far to seek objects of benevolence. However in the midst of all these difficulties we have mustered a few things which we hope you will receive as the free will offerings of your much attached friends, interested indeed we are in the cause and anxious to do much more than we have ever done were it in our power but the commercial distress of our country meets us at every step, we live in the midst of a people borne down with oppression what will be the end of it is hard to say but the rod of the oppressor in this land as well as in yours *must be broken....*

Believe me to remain your faithful Friend for our common cause

Mary Welsh.

MS.A.1.2. vol. 13 1843 Anti-Slavery Letters to Garrison [136]
No. 6 Elizabeth Pease to Wendell Phillips

Darlington 1 mo. 31. 1843.

Dear Wendell

... The perusal of thy Chartist Lecture has given me both pleasure & instruction – & I've no doubt but Mr. Ashurst wd be delighted to see what a noble figure his materials cut, wrought up by such able hands. I sent him a "Tribune" but have heard nothing since. I also lent them both to one of the principal Chartists in this town – & he writes me he is very glad to see the question is at last obtaining interest in America.

I'm sorry for Jos. Sturge, in reference to the Birmingham Conference[1] which he took such pains to get up. I scarcely know in what light he regards it, but it seems, I believe, generally feared, that it has retarded instead of advancing the cause of true reform, and still, there is another point of view, in which one is ready to hope, the divisions may be useful – the timid & hesitating may perhaps be brought more readily into the views & to unite with a respectable body of the middle classes, when cleared of the "unwashed". It's a wrong feeling – but we know it's one that prevails among many – yet after all the point to be desired is a cordial cooperation

---

1. Joseph Sturge attempted at Birmingham to form a Complete Suffrage Union, which would give middle class backing to the more moderate of the Chartists' demands. This was denounced by the physical force Chartists, and the attempt was a failure.

between the middle & labouring classes. Neither class can, separately, carry anything against our selfish aristocracy. "Entre nous" – *we* are jealous – there's something of the spirit of "27" displayed by J.S. & a few of his favourite colleagues – else why so positive in insisting on no bill being discussed except their own pet bantling – of 5½ hours length – besides, Mr. Lovett, a good man & true, reasonable, rational & enlightened as acknowledged by all – & a member too of the Council – never saw nor I think heard of J.S.'s bill, till he saw it in print. We ought not to grudge without knowing *all* particulars but you & I can *believe* such doings, from knowledge of the past. However, be it as it may, I'm sorry for J.S. for he has certainly acted a generous part in his warm espousal of the poor man's rights....

Ever your affec^{e} sister

E.P.

MS.A.1.2. vol. 13 1843 Anti-Slavery Letters to Garrison [137]
No.7 R.D. Webb to Maria Weston Chapman

Dublin, 2nd of second month 1843

Dear Friend

Maria W. Chapman

...Oblige me by thanking Wendell Phillips in my name for his lecture on Chartism and for the paper "Watchman! What of the Night?" I read Right & Wrong in Britain long ago and had forgotten I ever saw that article. I have sold & given away so many Anti-Slavery books in order to spread the knowledge they contain that my own library is very small compared with what it might be. As to the Chartists, W.P. speaks boldly and beautifully – but I dont know what to say. I have *small hope* and so whatever little I have, is barely enough for Nonresistance – for the good *it* may do, by working upon individual conviction. Elizabeth Pease thinks that the materials are fast multiplying for a noble army of disciples of H.C. Wright's peaceful (though they be) wild & fanatical doctrines. I have great ultimate faith in truth & justice though I cannot help seeing that the obstacles which lie in their way are tremendous. I look upon Joseph Sturge as decidedly one of the most honest Chartists in England – one of those who would sacrifice the most for the poor, and would stand up most boldly for their rights. If he be, thou will say, what shall we say of the rest? I think him bigotted and somewhat narrow minded of course – but that his aspirations & efforts are for the right I have no doubt. But when we consider the power, the wealth, the station, the consideration and the influence which the aristocracy enjoy – how the people are ready to bow down before them in their presence however they may revile them in their absence how church and state and crown and government are mixed up with aristocratic influence and associations – when we look at all these things – I don't know what to say of Chartism or to hope from the people from its influence, however we may like it in popular gathering or in an American lecturer. The present government may do as they please with Chartism. They are powerful – they have the confidence of the clergy and the aristocracy – and the middle classes crouch before the mighty confederation – however they may crow in the newspapers....

Thine ever respectfully

Rich[d] D. Webb.

MS.A.9.2. vol. 18 pt. 1 1843 The Weston Papers [138]
No. 12 Sarah and Lizzy Poole to Maria Weston Chapman

Growton, Feb. 25th 1843.

My dear friend,

...We owe your noble band much, indeed! We live in the agitation you create, for in our own land is the stillness of death; such a stillness as always reigns where a sceptered monarch treads, where time worn institutions remain in all their power though the ages that called for them have passed. I love agitation, for *life* never exists *motionless.* Our struggle for free trade is a glorious struggle; and we may yet *hope*, should commercial liberty be gained. But I am writing like a patriot; and a patriot, in the common sense of the term, I do not profess to be. Even a philanthropist has plenty of room in England – in *England*, if anywhere, & so H.C. Wright seems to think, for he has a sleepless time of it amongst us....My brother has just this moment received a note from him, in which he says (It is dated from Manchester) "I have lectured at the rate of once a day for the last twelve days, and meetings are appointed for about every day for fifteen to come, so I am desperately pushed – driving hither and thither. I wouldn't mind if I could *sleep*, but I am doomed to almost perpetual wakefulness; I spent two nights recently with John Bright. He is a glorious fellow! Gone to London, now, to agitate there. Cobden has been giving it to *Peel* – and Peel has made a fool of himself. There is great excitement about the Corn Laws and the League. The Anti-Leaguers are pushing the League up to come out on the doctrine of absolute Free Trade – No restriction. They taunt, and say they dare not – But Bright does – Moore does – Thompson does. The two last nights I lectured in Bolton – was with Henry Ashworth. Friends Meeting houses were open for me in Rochdale and Bolton. "&c – H.C. Wright attacks the roots of the corrupt tree, he seeks an entrance into the inner temple of the heart. Our dear friend is much beloved by many in Ireland. Ireland has not greatly aided your Bazaar this year. You can scarcely expect a barren soil to yield rich produce. Remond's presence and eloquent appeals did much to arouse a transient zeal on behalf of "the Cause"; but that quickly vanished. The Irish, you know, are a mercurial race. We must only hope that as information spreads, *hearts* will be gained – and *hearts* can never desert it, until its triumph shall be complete. Kind remembrance to C.L. Remond – could he not sometimes afford an hour to his Irish friends? – A parcel of Liberators arrived a few days past, & we have, since their arrival, been living *in your midst* – hanging on your words. But I must "cease," as my half sheet is filled.

With much regard – I remain yours, very truly.

Sarah Poole.

Dear Friend

... Henry C. Wright has won his way to all our hearts – he wrote several letters to us from Manchester, one of them gives a most vivid description of Anti Corn Law meetings – of O'Connell, Moore, Buckingham &c, &c – I ought not to forget Colonel T.P. Thompson[1] ; whom H.C.W. greatly liked – ...England and Scotland are boldly struggling for the nation's life – Ireland is indifferent to the Free Trade Movement – the landowners are almost universally opposed to any alteration – and the farmers fear that they should be dreadfully rack-rented if "protection" were removed, – that rents would not be lowered to suit altered circumstances – To those who fully understand the subject the Corn Laws must appear suicidal. –

Please excuse this hasty production, and believe me

Your grateful friend

Lizzy Poole.

MS.A.1.1. vol. 3 Anti-Slavery Letters from Garrison [139]
No. 101 William Lloyd Garrison to Elizabeth Pease

Boston, Feb. 28, 1843

My dear friend Elizabeth:

...The present condition of England strikes me not only as extremely melancholy, but as absolutely frightful. What a spectacle, in a country famous for its industry and its fertility, to see vast multitudes of the people famishing for bread! What is to be the end of all this? Of all your reform parties, not one goes far enough, not one is based on the broad immovable foundation of human rights – not one raises the standard of Christian revolt against the powers of darkness. The repeal of the Corn Laws may do something for the relief of the people – the extension of the right of suffrage may ultimately do more; but these measures are not radical, but only palliative. Palliation, it may be said, is better than unmitigated suffering, and so it is, *pro tempore;* but there is nothing so good as a blow aimed at the right source. The people are crushed beneath an overgrown monarchy and a bloated aristocracy, and are made the victims of an atrocious alliance between Church and State. Why not then boldly aim for the destruction of these? I confess it excites my [derision?], and awakens indignant feelings in my bosom when I read the proceedings of your Anti-Corn Law men, your Free Suffrage declaimers, your roaring Chartists, at their Soirees and on other social or convivial occasions, and see that Queen Victoria, and Prince Albert, and the rest of the royal brood, are complimented on "sentiments", and cheered as if they were the benefactors of old England! The watchword should be, – at the risk of martyrdom, or execution for high treason, – Down with the throne! Down with the aristocracy! Down with the accursed union between Church and State! The rights of God and man should be defended at all hazards. Of course, I desire the shedding of no blood, but only the utterance of great and terrible truths, and the use of those weapons which are mighty, through

---

1. Colonel Thomas Perronet Thompson (1783-1869), soldier and politician, was active in radical politics.

God, to the pulling down of strongholds. None but nonresistants, indeed and in truth, in spirit and in life, are qualified to carry on such a warfare. Some of them would probably die as martyrs; but this is far better than that a whole people should perish. Without a miracle, if things continue long in their present state, it seems to me England cannot escape a bloody revolution....

So! there is to be another General Anti-Slavery Convention held in London, in June next – and the whole world of women have been duly notified that none but "gentlemen" will be admitted as members! Of course, the American Anti-Slavery Society and its auxiliaries will not consent to be represented on the occasion, even by "gentlemen"....

Farewell, beloved friend:

Wm. Lloyd Garrison.

MS.A.1.2. vol. 13 1843 Anti-Slavery Letters to Garrison [140]
No. 13 John Murray to Elizabeth Pease

Bowling Bay
near Glasgow 12th March, 1843

Dear Friend

I was agreably surprised this Morning by the receipt of a letter from you – & you may be as much surprised to know that your name is on a Memorandum on my writing desk as one among some other whom I was to write to in a few days – Therefore before I reply to yours I may as well say something on the subject of which I was to write you. – You would have received some weeks ago a Colonial Gazette forwarded at my request by W. Smeal – and I presume you would be at no loss to discover whether he indicated it or not – the object for which it was sent viz to draw your attention to the very important subject of [a] scheme of Emigration from Africa to the West Indies which is intended to be the means of abolishing Slavery & the Slave Trade. I can form no idea what your opinion on that subject may be, but am aware of the indoctrinating system which the B & F Anti-Slavery Society have been pursuing in the A.S. Reporter in reference to that subject to shew as they hold the dangerous quarter from which it has originated and the pernicious effects it may be expected to produce – It has originated say they from the West Indians – but they tell us that Lord Stanley with the assistance of two Parliamentary Commits. have also had a hand in it. [While?] Sir Geo. Stephen also claims its paternity & they tell us to place no confidence in Govt. for it will undoubtedly become a species of Slave Trade – that if you can believe it a Govt. which has expended such large sums of money for the Abolition of Slavery & the Slave Trade will now countenance a system of sending out vessels to Africa for Free Emigrants & after getting them on board will sell them to the Planters in the W.I. as Slaves or in their colonies where slavery is as much abolished as in England they will allow them to be made slaves – that the Men & Women whipping system will be renewed & Slave Marts re-established –

Can you believe all this? And as to Foreign Colonies they conclude it certain that we are setting them a very bad example of humanity by employing Free Labour – for they will assuredly profess to imitate us & also carry away free Emigrants – only to Enslave them. – There is no pleasing such prophets – "We have piped unto them & they have not danced." If the British use Free Emigrants as Labourers it will be a bad example to Foreign Powers & sure am I if they use slave labour it will be no better. But I wish you and your Friends would examine without prejudice the argument of the B & F but with caution & circumspection and see what they are really worth and examine also equally judiciously the proposed scheme – & let me recommend to you for your information the Colonial Gazette in which are many excellent articles by McGregor & Laird....

I am yours sincerely

John Murray.

MS.A.1.2. vol. 13 1843 Anti-Slavery Letters to Garrison [141]
No. 22 Maria Weston Chapman to Elizabeth Pease

Boston March 31st 1843

My dear Friend,

I rejoice that you are in England at this important crisis of her history. One faithful hearted man's labours may do much towards [clothing?] her with "the preparation of the gospel of peace" without which, so little can be done in the way of Reform. I am deeply interested for the common people of England; no less so than for our own slaves – the corresponding class in this country. No wonder the British & Foreign Committee have publicly announced that they have no sympathy with the Am. A.S. Soc. If the Chartists were all in their enterprise pledged to peaceful measures only, they would be the corresponding class to the abolitionists. But I fear from what I can gather from the English papers, that the true Chartists are not peace-men & the hereditary peace-men not the Chartists. Pray let me know if this be so in reality. It seems to me as if the quakers were impressed with the idea that nothing could be done in England but by & through the nobility, which is as much as if we should assume that here [in?] the United States, we must depend for reform solely on the slave holders....

Yours

M.W.Chapman.

MS.A.9.2. vol. 18 pt. 1 1843 The Weston Papers [142]
No. 28 Isabel Jennings to Maria Weston Chapman

Cork April 12, 1843

Dear Mrs. Chapman

...We looked with great anxiety for an account of Garrison's recovery

– he suffered very much – will you tell him he has friends in Cork who often think of him with delight and admiration....America was never a 'new world' to us until we knew of Garrison and Mrs. Chapman and N.P. Rogers and Mrs. Child and Wendell Phillips and Henry C. Wright – and Mr. Remond who first (after Miss Martineau's book[1]) introduced them to us personally and interested us in them – we do feel very, very grateful to him for the knowledge and when we think, instead of condemning us for our culpable ignorance how kindly he treated us and told us everything we do admire him for it. It is very hard for me to think that 'tis far short of two years since we first felt that Americans were our bretheren – and not the inhabitants of a world with which we had no feelings in common – for tho' Miss M.'s book was *read* it was not *felt* until after C.L. Remond's visit Besides anti-slavery non-resistance is now added – before Henry C. Wright's visit Hannah E. White and I were of one mind on the subject – but when talking with him we felt still more that love and that alone can cast out fear and that fear is torment – whether it be fear of God or fear of men....

Yours gratefully

Jane Jennings.

MS.A.4.1. The Child Papers [143]
No. 69 David Lee Child to ?

Washington Ap. 21, 1843

My dearFriend,

I should not have dunned anti Slavery with her great heart and her small means, if I had not staid here so long as to get quite out at the elbows. How I have been occupied you will partly see by the accompaniment to this. I have felt for some time as if it would refresh my spirit to have a letter, or a conversation with you. It is evident to my mind that the great crisis in the affairs of slavery and of this union is rapidly advancing. Neck or nothing is I think the maxim now with the slave-holders and their government for it is *wholly* theirs. I think the next Congress will be the most dangerous to the cause of freedom and justice that has ever asembled yet. Upshur a bold bad slave breeder from the old Eastern Shore, rabid for the annexation of Texas, is going to take Webster's place, Cushing Upshur's. To be sure no man could act much worse than Webster has much of his time, but the father of lies could not be worse than Upshur. What an agent to manage our foreign affairs and to get up a war, as they mean to do!. Oh how I want to confer with the sage and penetrating spirits at Boston. I am tired to death of this disolute city, disolute in every sense, but it is good in one. It represents aptly that desolation of moral principles on which the government was founded, and which characterises it. Nobody in the nation takes any interest in it, any more than a man does in a slaughterhouse, where he goes for his meat. They are trying to get up a national Institute in imitation of the French, but it is generally conceeded that it is to be a failure. There is nothing in the government as now, and in fact always administered – nor,

---

1. Harriet Martineau's *The Martyr Age in the United States.*

nor at the seat of it, around which affection can cling. Upshur has declared repeatedly of late that we ought to have Texas, and we will have it. A friend of mine was in his office a short time ago, and Upshur introduced this subject. My friend, who is a member & still here, told him the North never would consent "God d-n it said he, I will spend the last drop of my blood before I will yield to that d-d spirit that is rising at the North. We *ought* to have Texas and you *ought* to consent". Since that he added in another conversation "We will have it". Thus also said a member of Congress to a Mass member. There is great activity now in the Cabinet on the subject, for this proposition of Sta Anna has alarmed them. A new Charge was started off a few days ago because the one they had was not able and energetic enough. They are also alarmed at the meeting of South American Plenipotentaries at Lima. When Webster was told of it about a month ago, he *started.* It seemed that the affair has been so conducted that our Govt. was not only not invited, but not informed. That Congress of Nations will undoubtedly settle this matter of search for slave trading pirates, and settle it in accordance with Great Britain. Thus the iron shroud closes upon slavery. I do not believe anything will come of Santa Anna's propositions to the Texans. His object is to resuscitate in Texas a party which has always been in favor of peace but has been overawed by Brigands.

Very affect[ionatel]y yr. friend & Fellow Servant

D. L. Child

MS.960 Webb-Quincy Correspondence 1843-1872 [144]
pp. 2-4 R. D. Webb to Edmund Quincy

Dublin, 16th of Eight month 1843

My dear Quincy

...Thou art desirous to know what we mean to do *when* we repeal the Union. I do not know – nor do I believe does anybody else. I have a hearty contempt for politics and politicians. I don't believe in the possibility of their strict adherence to principle. I don't believe that Irish Repealers are a bit wiser or more consistent or more virtuous than English or Irish Anti Repealers. I believe that the idea of O'Connell consists in complete legislative indifference to England, with allegiance to the queen or king of England, a more extended suffrage, and a similarly constituted Legislature of king, lords & commons. His chief argument, or at least his most seductive one with the people consists in that of fixity of tenure, which I believe means some law by which the land should be secured in *perpetuity*, in some way that I don't understand, to the present tenants, instead of holding it for a term of years from their landlords, as they do now. This would be in effect a transference by law of the land from its present acknowledged owners to a great greater number of people, who now only hold it by leave for a certain annual rent. The claims of the present landlord would be in some way acknowledged and compensated by this measure – but his perpetual right, as I understand it, would be transferred to his new tenant. This is a short and decisive way of consulting the greatest happiness of the greatest number – but whether it is just I leave for them to determine.

Ireland has now been confiscated and subdivided among new owners, over and over, and this it seems to me would be a new confiscation and subdivision. The popular idea of repeal consists [in?] I believe in the prospect of a general saturnalia for servants and labourers, Catholic ascendancy, the restoration of old churches and the accession of new ones to the *true faith* – the expulsion of protestants by hook or by crook – and a very natural hope that as the Protestants have had their turn, it is time for the Catholics to have a chance now. When we consider how poor and oppressed Ireland has been – how heart rending and enflaming her history – how her people have suffered – what a hideous policy has been pursued against her until within the last 20 years – it is no matter that the mass of the Catholics (who are three fourths of the people) should think all these things. And the mob (?), as they are – at least nine tenths of them, amongst the most bigoted in Europe, firmly attached to their priests, *who are all raised from the ranks,* and full of religious enthusiasm. It is not so strange that things are as I represent. It would be wonderful, arguing from the ordinary springs of human action, if it were otherwise. If Ireland were really and entirely independent of England, as most repealers, in spite of their loyal professions, would I am sure wish it to be, I dont see how she could stand for any length of time alone, without an army or navy, and with one fourth of her population (and that fourth by far the most wealthy and intelligent) devoted to English connexions, unless the Protestants were expelled & their property confiscated. There is not in the world a more discordant population than that of Ireland. The suspicion & distrust, not to say cherished & hoarded animosity, (the legacy of ages) they entertain towards one another are I think irreconcilable – or at least invincible for my purpose of mutual cooperation and self government – This is lamentable but it is true. Another cherished idea of Repealers in towns would be the exclusion by law of all foreign manufacturers for the encouragement of the home artist and operative. In other words they would establish a cordon militaire all round Ireland to prevent the people of Ireland from smuggling in any better or cheaper ware of any kind than would be manufactured in Ireland by Irishmen I believe that ninetenths of the Irish Catholics are repealers – and no wonder – but I also think that the remaining tenth consists of the most wealthy and intelligent portion of the whole. As to political purity, and distinct ideas of civil and religious liberty I believe the Irish Repealers are not a whit in advance of the rest of the people of the British Islands. They are *repealers* and that is all. Their moral position is much vaunted as sublime, all conquering & so forth – but it is *not* moral power – it is physical force. When 100,000 people meet, and threaten, & bluster of what they could do, and will do, unless – it is ridiculous to speak of moral power. The people don't know what this means – except that it is not fighting. O'Connell knows that fighting wont do – and he is right – but he nevertheless hopes to overawe the government by their reiterated exhibitions of the moral powers of an ignorant, bigotted, & excitable people caught to the very verge of insurrection – well disposed to try what they can effect with pike and gun. Civil war is a terrible thing. We had a terrible but very limited insurrection in 1798. [Five?] weeks in two or three counties gave samples of almost all kinds of cruel & bloody deeds of civil rapine and religious

[?]. If there be another it will be more general and more terrible — for the people are more numerous, more intelligent, more powerful, more excited, and to the full as fanatical. Inglis[1], an English traveller, and one of the most liberal and the best that has written about Ireland, remarks at the end of his two volumes that there is no country in Europe more ripe for the Inquisition than Ireland, and I believe there is not one. Look at Popery in the page of history, and ask thyself if it is to be wondered at that she should be looked for. It is the most natural thing in the world. O'Connell himself is either a great bigot or a rank hypocrit. I believe him to be the former. In his *last* abolition speech in which he clinches his former one, he meanly throws sop to Cerberus by denouncing Garrison as "a Mr. Lloyd Garrison with whom he could have no intercourse" on account of his religious or rather irreligious opinions." His speech was good, but this damned it. He is as strong against slavery as ever — he wont retract a word he has said against it — but he has nothing to do with the abolitionists — or any other party in America. Look at the Irish address — and thou wilt see his name signed — and *deliberately* signed — to a piece of advice to the Irish in America "to join *the abolitionists.*" James Haughton, who is a great worshipper of O'Connells — for he can swallow any amount of inconsistency committed by those he loves — wrote him a note the day after this speech, defending Garrison in the warmest and most hearty manner and reminding him how much W.L.G. had done & suffered for the slave & how he (Daniel himself) had treated him with such respect & had called upon him (an unwonted honour) in the Royal Exchange & then & there I brought up the subject of O'Connells derogatory remarks upon Garrison & before a crowded assembly of "Dan's Own" I defended and glorified him at great length and to such purpose that the ragamuffins — (for to tell the truth, our audiences are mostly ragged) cheered repeatedly the picture I drew for them of Garrisons noble devotedness amongst you. O'Connell has not handled a penny less than £500,000 of the hard earned money of the Irish people. Is Garrison rich? In point of moral qualities there is no shadow of comparison between the two men — whatever there may be in intellect. Only look at any of Dan's *demonstrative* speeches at Baltinglass, Tuan, Tara or elsewhere, and you will see how little of moral power there is in them — how much of [?] excitement, inflammatory eloquence, and mere swagger they contain. He is admitted by all to be a man of stupendous talents, amazing quickness, readiness, power of application, energy, & industry — but he is one on whose word I would have no dependency, on whose principle I would have no reliance. I think him a bigoted man but not a consistent man. As respects his Anti Slavery career, bear in mind that this is a popular subject in this country — it is a good subject for claptrap speeches & for the early establishment of a reputation. Nevertheless I dont believe O'Connell would show a whit more consistency as a lover of universal liberty were he in America than Webster does. The feeling throughout Ireland amongst the Anti Repealers (who consist of nearly all Protestants and most wealthy Catholics who have anything to lose) is that an insurrection will be attempted if the people lose all hope of repeal on any

1. Henry David Inglis (1795-1835) was a traveller and author of several works including *Ireland in 1834.*

other terms. And what chance there is of it by legal means I cannot imagine. All the English & Scotch M.P.s are opposed to it, & not more than 50 out of the 100 Irish members of Parliament are in favour of the measure. Almost all places of strength in Ireland are very fortified, manned, & supplied with coal & provisions to stand a seige. You read of magistrates throwing up their commissions on account of the Government suspending any who have taken part in Repeal movements – but you must bear in mind that many of them have done so not because they are themselves in favour of Repeal but because they think the government have unfairly interfered with the liberty of the subject. The Catholic priesthood are the only influential class who favour this measure – it is true their influence is immense – and it must be remembered that they have everything to gain & nothing to lose by a struggle. If there be a repeal by fair means or foul they become the lords of the ascendant. If the effort fail, protected by their *sacred* character they are as [worse] off as they were before. I rely for the credit thou will give to what I tell thee not upon my being one who [sic] has so much identity of opinion on many points with thyself, but upon the apparent truthfulness and reasonableness of what I say. For it is extremely difficult to ascertain the truth in party questions as on any question but one of pure mathematics. Where people can differ in *opinion*, they will differ ad infinitum. Take ten Irishmen equally intelligent & trustworthy and it is most likely if they belong to different shades of political bias, reside some in town – some in the country – some in Ulster – others in Leinster – some Catholics – some churchmen – some dissenters – that thou will get a different testimony from each of the ten. They will all tell the truth – but each a different truth – and the only way of reconciling the discordant mass of evidence will be by selecting that portion of it to form thy conclusions from, which seems to thee most likely *under the circumstances* to be true. This again will depend upon thy turn of mind. There is as great a thirst now for Catholic ascendancy as ever there was for Protestant ascendancy. No wonder. It would be more wonderful if there were not. Dont heed the disclaimer. If the Catholic who speaks, is a man & a politician, he must be a liar, unless he have an uncommon endowment of self denial. As matters really stand, Ireland is much less lightly taxed than England – indeed we have no taxation except that of the excise or such as we pay indirectly by the consumption of tea, coffee, sugar, tobacco & other imports. Then we have the poor rate, and taxes for local purposes, of which the only one which is fairly objectionable (I dont speak as a *nonresistant*, but as a common Christian) is the [?] *money* in towns and the tithe in the country. The Catholics & Protestants are on equal terms. The only ascendancy is that which can be obtained by numerical superiority by outvoting – and except in some parts of Ulster, the Catholics generally have the upper hand here. In England the taxes are tremendously heavy. England returns for 12 millions 500 M.P.s – Ireland for 8 millions only 105. In other words 1 English voter has as much political power as 3½ Irishmen. And the decision of such questions depends in Parliament far more upon the good will of English than of Irish members. The good will of England towards Ireland (apart from the influence of the clergy and some old lingering prejudices) I believe to be warm and sincere. The best place would be I think that which has been proposed to have sort of local, colonial parliaments like the Canadians for the regulation of home matters in Ireland, leaving the government of the Empire as at present in the hands of the Imperial Assembly. But any moderate plan of this kind would come far short of the aspirations of the people who in the country parts talk openly of a new subdivision of property and of the *ould* owners coming by their own again. Now I have talked a terrible deal about repeal. I have written by request to Thomas Davis & N.P. Rogers – and its a tiresome & hopeless subject – at least to a man who abhors discord & blood, and the ferocious passions which this agitation has roused up (not created) in the bosoms of my passionate and hot blooded countrymen. Catch a raw emigrant from Ireland and ask him what he thinks of Repeal. Treat him cautiously & dont laugh at him or rouse his suspicions – Thou will soon find from him whether what I say is like the truth. I am not a rich man – I am no landholder – I live in Dublin & have as little to lose by such a *row* as most men – and I dont think my fears have prompted what I say. I saw some very foolish high-go-mad remarks of Y in the Liberator about the cruelty and tyranny of England &c &c &c connected with the Repeal question see how the pro-slavery Irish drop it now that Dan pinches their toes about the darling *institution* of their adopted country....

Goodby to you all – I wish I could go with this letter myself. My love to the Boston clique unless there be some it wd not do to love & give them my respects

thine affectionately

Richd D Webb

MS.A.1.2. vol. 13 1843 Anti-Slavery Letters to Garrison [145]
No. 49 Elizabeth Reid[1] *to Wendell and Ann Phillips*

Augst 26th
1843
21 York Terrace
Regents Park.

My dear Mr. & Mrs. Phillips

...Do you not view our Irish affairs with great interest? What a liberal aid have you given to the Repeal Rent! O'Connell & the Irish ought to have the prayers of America. But such an independence as your states achieved nobody, I hope, wishes for; they say not. We are too close neighbours for that. A federal government they desire & will have, under one monarch. Till England & Scotland are wise enough to copy your govt. – a waste of time....

Your very affectionate friend

Elizth J. Reid

---

1. Mrs. Elizabeth J. Reid (1789-1866), described as "an opulent Unitarian lady," was active in social work in London, and founded Bedford College for women. She was a close friend of Harriet Martineau.

MS.B.1.6. vol. 1 1837-1845 The May Papers [146]
No. 32 George Armstrong[1] *to Samuel May*

Clifton. Bristol
Sept. 14, 1843.

Rev. S. May

My dear Sir,

Thank you for your truly valuable letter to Mr. James, which he has permitted me to see.

Most earnestly I wish you may be able to attend the meeting at Manchester. Your information would be more valuable to them and through them to others. It is information absolutely necessary for our English Unitarians.

I wish extremely that you could prepare a statement of the facts and names you mention, – for insertion in the Christian Reformer at the earliest possible period.

I fear you would not transmit it in time for the forthcoming number of the 1st of October. But at the latest, do be good enough to send a short but energetic article on the subject for its following number of November.

I wish I could hope to see you again in Bristol. But though we may not have that pleasure – believe it that you have left impressions of your character which change of place or length of time cannot impair.

God's best blessing be with you, Dear Sir, – I beg my compliments to your brother, who I trust appreciates the value of such society as he has in so excellent a relative as you.

I remain faithfully yours,

George Armstrong

Mr. James[2] will send you a printed copy of our promised address, which I have had deep satisfaction in preparing.

MS.B.1.6. vol. 1 The May Papers [147]
No. 35 Samuel May Jr. to George Armstrong

Geneva. Oct. 9. 1843

My dear Sir,

I received, at Frankfort, your kind letter, & should soon have replied to it, but the rapidity of my journey had rendered it quite impossible. It affords me much pleasure to hear of the deep interest, which so many of the British Unitarians feel in the great question of Slavery as at present agitated in the United States, & particularly in the relation, which their brethren of

---

1. George Armstrong (1792-1857), the Unitarian minister at Lewin's Mead, Bristol, met Samuel May on his visit to Britain in 1843, worked with him over the British Unitarian Address, and remained a firm friend. Born in Ireland, Armstrong was for a time a minister in the Church of England, but early in the 1830's he became a convinced Unitarian, and in 1838 accepted the post at Bristol. He was active in many liberal reform movements, and a central figure in the Bristol group of reformers.
2. William James was the other Unitarian minister at Lewin's Mead, Bristol.

like faith there, sustain to it. – When I landed in your country, it certainly was with no expectation of being called publicly to express in it, my opinion of American slavery. But it did not require a long acquaintance with English Unitarians to convince me that they were not indifferent to the subject of Slavery in the United States; that, on the contrary a deep & inquiring interest was felt in it by many of them.

I heard with much satisfaction, that an eminent American Unitarian minister, while recently in your country, had had his attention repeatedly called to this subject. Under these circumstances, I could not but feel desirous that your views & opinions might be known in my own country. Accordingly, when, at the time of the annual meeting of your West of England Unitarian association at Taunton, I was desired to address the crowded evening meeting, & the subject of American slavery was particularly allotted to me, I expressed the wish that those who were present, & the Unitarians of Great Britain generally, might address an earnest appeal & remonstrance, on this subject, to the brethren in America. I said, I had no doubt that such a remonstrance would be viewed, by some, as an overzealous act on your part; but that I believed the great body of American Unitarians would give it a candid hearing, & that with them it would do good. I was confident, also, that the spirit with which you would put forth, such an address, would entitle it to such a hearing. I believe that you felt, as I did, that Great Britain had too recently given to her own slaves, to warrant her sons in addressing their American brethren in words of bitterness or taunting. I was happy to find that the wish I thus expressed, met with a cordial response from very many present. Subsequently, at a meeting in Glasgow, I ventured to repeat the same wish on my arrival in Dublin, it was with no small pleasure that I learned that the Unitarians there, without waiting for hint or suggestion from any one, had already acted in this matter, & that a committee of several gentlemen, among whom were Rev. Dr. Drummond & James Haughton Esq. had prepared an Address to the Unitarians in America, on the subject of slavery, & had sent it to the care of a much esteemed brother in Boston. It has repeatedly been said to me, that, in order that a document of the kind above spoken of, might be signed with a proper understanding of the question at issue, some further information was needed by the great body of Unitarians in Great Britain. That information, in a thorough & perspicuous manner, I do not presume to think I can give, without a single document or memorandum at hand to which I can refer. But to some points I can speak. Let me however say, that it is to me a most unwelcome & painful task, in my absence from my native land, & from those with whom I have associated, I have taken not only pleasant, but most profitable counsel from my youth, to dwell upon what I deem her faults, or theirs. – ...

Should you, our British brethren & friends think good (as I trust you will) to exert your unquestionable influence on us in this regard, I believe you will have done a good work – tho many minds will be found ready to hear & weigh well what you shall say; they will assuredly view it as the act of friends & they must view it as the act of persons free from those local connexions, which are often thought to warp the judgment, & give it an exclusive or party bias....

Whatever you may address to us, whatever we may receive from you, may it be offered & accepted in that one spirit, which I cannot better express than by repeating the words, "Christo in pauperibus."

Believe me, dear Sir,

With the sincerest respect

and Brother in the faith.

Saml. May Junr.

MS. 960 Webb-Quincy Correspondence [148]
pp. 5-6 Webb to Quincy

Dublin 10th month 16. 1843

My dear Quincy

Things are going on at such a rate with us that I want to let you know something about us. A Cunard liner will sail in 3 days so as it is now evening I have no time to spare, for I cannot write in odds & ends of time being no gentleman "all as one" as Quincy of Dedham – wherefore I must keep "Chapman" contented as well as "Webb", & must mind my business and my creditors.

Yesterday week – Oct. the 8th – O'Connell intended to hold his last monthly meeting. And on *Sunday* the day on which it was to have been held, the shore of Clontarf where the meeting was to have been held – on one side of the Bay of Dublin and within two miles of town was occupied with some thousands of troops, horse & foot, dragoons and artillery. There was no meeting and no *row*. The people were quiet and only looked on and laughed so as there was nobody to fight – the troops returned from the field, and the people of some of them said they had gained a great victory over the black cockles for which the coast is not *infamous*. Two days after out came an address from the Repeal Association to their brother repealers in Ohio, which as you will see is O'Connell's production and the best thing of the kind he ever wrote. He told James Haughton to send as many names of distinguished Abolitionists as he knew to the Corn Exchange Room and that they should all be sent out by the Association to America so James called here in glory to laud O'Connell & the address and by Hannah's help to get the names. She gave him 30. I was from home and when I heard what had been done I sent out about 12 more to America including Nancy Rogers, Nathaniel's mother, for which single circumstance I include her in my catalogue of "gode wymen" – I mean for the circumstance of being his mother. Two days or three – after this address was promulgated, O'Connell was served with an arrest at his house in Merrim Square. He gave bail to abide his trial – so did the Editor of the Freeman's Journal – and the Nation – & I don't know how many more. This morning as I sat in the drawing room warming myself over the fire – for it was excessively cold – and it is now raining like mad – in walked James Haughton – full of something. He wanted to consult me he said. Then he showed me a letter he addressed on Saturday last – the day before yesterday – to his brother Repealers in the Freemans Journal – the great Repeal organ. This consisted of congratulations to the people in the quiet demeanour they had preserved and pretty significant intimations that if they had acted otherwise the government would have had great pleasure in carving them up with gun and bayonet. As I think they would. Likewise he most earnestly counselled them to be as nonresistant as possible – and he preached them a capital peace lecture. Then having read & approved of this missive and expressed my hearty concurrence with it he wanted to know if he were arrested would I be willing to become his bail. To which I in the kindest & promptest manner consented. But it is absurd to think they would always be so silly as to arrest James Haughton for preaching peace which he always preached – and for reflecting on their own cruel and overbearing preparations which were plainly for another purpose than to kill all whom they could, if they were opposed or disobeyed. His friends and relations none of whom sympathised with him (except our little clique) are all alarmed and tell him it was such a shocking thing and so forth. You cant imagine over there the dread which our powerful government inspires. Men are almost afraid to say their soul is their own – when it shows its [iron?] teeth and crooked claws. 99 100s of the people I believe are heartily well pleased with the successful robbery and slaughter of the Chinese – seeing that they have wrung both commerce and gold from the poor celestials my heart sinks in view of the utter endless hypocrisy and want of principle which prevails in the world.

You cannot fail to admire and publish as far and wide as you are able O'Connell's Anti Slavery Address. I wish I could think him what I do not – an honest and a great man. I think that in the interval between the interposition of government to stop the Clontarf meeting and the time of his arrest, he penned & published this great address as a [diversion?] to his mind and from a desire in this crisis of his fate to restore himself to the confidence of a class whom I am sure in his heart he respects – though so lately he half disowned their acquaintance – I mean of course, yourselves, – the abolitionists. The Irish tory papers are now full of the [gall?] of all hatred, hostility, & bitterness against him. They would be delighted to hear he was hanged or to be present at the hanging. The Irish orangemen and ninetenths of all Irish Protestants, who are with few exceptions Tories or conservatives are [elate?] with delight at the interposition of the government, and they actually gloat over the impending prosecutions. They hate him much more fervently than they hate the devil – whatever they may say in their prayers. O'Connell is the darling, the idol of ragged Ireland of the Catholic millions of all who live in Cabins – on the bogs – on the mountain-sides – in the poor houses. Right or wrong they are with him...O'Connell is a wonderful fellow. He is a lawyer – a double tongued pleader – an unscrupulous liar – fond of money – but no miser – he has an extravagant family – but he is simple in his own tastes – for he has no time to spend money – ambition – not pleasure is his hobby. I cant help feeling something towards O'Connell now as a true American feels towards Washington. Though Daniel has none of George's magnanimity – I should rather say, I don't think he has. Yet I would be sorry to see him suffer or crestfallen. I hate English oppression worse than I do his vices whatever they may be. I always feel downhearted with Napoleon in his adversity. His was such a terrible fall – "nor man nor friend hath fallen so far." I abhor the man's military ruthlessness – but his Destiny – the force he carried with him were wonderful. O'Connell is a popular Napoleon with more power over hearts (not over swords) than Napoleon ever wielded. Though I dont *approve* of him it would go to my heart to see him baffled or pinioned in his old days. The Irish people are as ferocious and more bigotted than their enemies – I have no sympathy with repeal which would only be the ascendancy of the most intolerant of sects – still I don't like to see the country held down in this way. We have at this present writing a matter of 6000 troops in Dublin & perhaps 3000 more in other parts of Ireland. And every barracks and fortified place in Ireland that can be fortified is fortified. The green isle is this moment bristling with English bayonets. It is enough to stir the blood of even a nonresistant to be bullied in this manner.

James Haughton among other things read me a letter he has just received from H.C. Wright full of the usual common places that fill his works, written, printed, and epistolary, such as "shooting", "heart stabbing", "Scull splitting"; "brain spattering" and so forth. He congratulates James on the grand moral position of the Irish repealers and of O'Connell. Now I am sure nothing can be less like moral suasion than the bragging, hectoring, bullying style of nine tenths of the speeches made at nine tenths of O'Connell's "monster meetings". The people have no more idea of the meaning of moral suasion than had the infant tiger cat that I saw in the Park Zoological Gardens yesterday. Their notion is simply that by making up a good strong show of physical force, the English will repeal the Union through fear – or else – they – that is Paddy – will take it by force. The universal feeling in England and Scotland is I believe hostile to Repeal – and of at least one fourth of Ireland. I see no prospect of harmony and prosperity for Ireland. Oil and water will coalesce as soon as the Catholic people of Ireland and the High church rulers of England. If Noah's dove had kept hovering over Ireland she would never have found a resting place for the sole of her foot – she could never have plucked her olive branch here....Will you not be sure to tell all people on all hands that it was Daniel O'Connell's personal request that his address would be sent to the Abolitionists of America? Mark how genteely he hath spoken of you – see how plain it is that he has James Haughton at his elbow....

Now it is the 17th...I should tell you that except in the direction of the barracks on the outskirts of the town where of course the slave holders are more abundant you would not know from the appearance of the streets that anything unusual had occured. There has not been a shadow of a collision of any kind with the government. The repression of feeling is complete. Nevertheless O'Connell is in everybody's mouth for curses or prayers. You can have no idea of the discordant elements this people are made up of unless by imagining a mixed population of Garrison abolitionists and McDuffie slaveholders – and even then the comparison would not be complete – for I presume pity rather than hatred would occupy the breasts of "the Clique" and its followers. Perhaps the free and slave population of South Carolina would do as well with the advantage that is in Carolina. The English have the Irish completely down by force of arms – and that the Irish like the blacks will be free whenever they can, I think that the peasant beau ideal of Irish liberty is – the ascendancy of the true Church – the restoration of the Churches to the Catholics – and of the forfeited estates which would include 5/6ths of Ireland to the descendants of the original owners – the expulsion of the absentee – the perpetual tenure of the present holdings on the part of the peasantry on payment of some small rent to be paid or not as they please. And no wonder they should be thus [fierce?] and extravagant when we look back to the past history of their country and the shameful state in which the mass of the people exist. The wonder is not that they think as I say they do but it would be much more marvellous if they had any other aspirations. O'Connell is perpetually making the most fulsome professions of loyalty & love towards the queen – both on his own behalf and on that of the people – and they of course applaud him & cry amen with the whole force of their lungs. Now for my part I cant imagine why or wherefore any such sentiment should exist in Ireland except during the short reign of James the Second & Ireland in 1689...This military repression will undoubtedly keep us down, but John Bull will not make us love him or like him. You see I cannot help a little bitterness though I am neither Catholic, O'Connellite, Repealer, or even a voting politician. I hate the political spirit. It is a bitter bad one – and it stirs up all the evil passions and has no beneficial effect to counterbalance its evil influence. Richard Allen is just come back from a commercial clothbuying tour through England. He says he heard a general expression of dissatisfaction with the arbitrary conduct of the government towards Ireland. But then he moves in a particular circle. Joseph Sturge is one of his great friends – and the dissenting enemies of the government. H.C.W. in his letter to James Haughton remarks that while there is much of a contrary spirit – much bitterness & contempt expressed towards us. These are the worst elements of the ruthless war spirit – bitterness & contempt. They look on us as snakes & will scotch us if they can....

O'Connell has long been fircely opposed to the Chartists. We have a very few in Dublin led on by Patrick O'Higgins. They are not men of much character or ability. At James Haughton's the other day I heard Dr. Madden admit that repeal had no men of mark among its leaders except O'Connell himself. It is the cause of the millions & very few indeed amongst the well dressed feel any desire for its success.

Since writing the above I have been talking to one of *the arrested* – a man of considerable ability & influence and a repealer. I asked him what he anticipated would be the conduct of the Government about the trials. He says he thinks they will spare no money to *pack* juries and obtain convictions – and that if they succeed as he seem[s] to anticipate, they will not be satisfied with less than 2 years imprisonment for the objects of their vengeance. When I feel how bitter my own health is in the expectation of such a doom for O'Connell and his men, I wonder at nothing that I can imagine of ferocity in the bosom of the horny handed Milesian sons of the soil....

Yours affectionately

Rich[d] D. Webb.

No. 37 George Armstrong to Samuel May Jr.

Clifton, Oct. 30 1843

My dear Sir

I thank you most heartily for your deeply interesting and most important communication so obligingly furnished to me, during your sojurn in Geneva, – which I duly received, – and very duly appreciate. You will permit me to make such use of it hereafter, as we shall think most conducive to the great end we have in view; but I must beg you to inform me particularly whether you will object to have *your name* promulgated (in *America*, as well as here) as the writer? – The very same post, or *day* rather, brought me a voluminous and most interesting communication from Miss Harriet Martineau; entering fully on the *American* position of this vast question; & holding out earnest *encouragement* to us to *go on* in our enterprise. She especially desires it for the sake of the heroic young students at Harvard! to whom it will be a balm, & an incitement. Our brethren in England have been more fastidious & shrinking than I could have previously imagined. *All* wish well – *in the abstract* – *but* &c &c &c – the old song! Yet many, very many, have *ardently* aided us, and *signed.*

I send you one of the forms, amended as you will see, in the margin. Having some more names to collect, we shall not be in time to send it by you. But we hope to dispatch it, – by the Packet of middle of November! It is to be engrossed on parchment, with all the names at length. And the original (*autograph*) names &c, if practicable, will be pasted on a blank sheet, and annexed to the same Address, *printed.*

I suppose Wilmer & Smith – of Liverpool, agents for Harnden & Co. Boston, – will be safe channels through which to forward it. Pray give me your opinion as to this point; and also, as the *Address itself;* whether it is of a character such as the occasion calls for.

And now, as the party through whom in America it is to find its way with *best effect* to the Brethren for whom it is intended. Poor Henry Ware, was suggested by you: but now that *he* is gone, *William Ware* has been named by others here, as a very fit person. What think you? And what is his exact address?

Of course, the Address, and all circumstances connected with it, – will be kept *studiously secret* by you until it shall have legitimately arrived at its intended publicity. But I should be glad you would suggest in the mean time, – what particular channels it wd. be desirable to select, whether in journals or otherwise, for the more extensive circulation of our sentiments *among the Unitarian Brethren especially*, – and next among the American public generally – Your deep & virtuous interest in this [great?] question, – will be my assurance that I do not unduly trespass in proposing for you all this trouble – Have you seen the *magnificent* Address of O'Connell to *certain Irish* defenders of slavery, – at Cincinatti? – If not, enquire for it by all means: & do not go to America without it...

Do not think your friends in Bristol forget you; they never can. And that you do not forget us, you will manifest, I trust, in *writing to us* when you can. God bless you, dear Sir,

& ever believe me truly yours

Geo. Armstrong.

MS.A.9.2. vol. 19 pt. 2 1843 The Weston Papers [150]
No. 68 William James to [Maria Weston Chapman?]

Bristol, Nov 1st 1843

My dear Madam,

... I have lately been in correspondence with your excellent friend Miss Martineau on the subject of American slavery, and she assures me that you will readily pardon the liberty I take in addressing you, and be willing to assist me in my wishes to obtain information on this subject that I may make use of for the purpose of placing correct views respecting it within reach of others.

I have been recently co operating with friends and brethren here in order to prepare an Address from the Unitarian ministers of Great Britain to their brethren in the United States of America, relating to slavery, an Address expressive of sympathy with the noble band of Abolitionists in your country and affectionately urging the clergy of the Unitarian church to "stand only amongst those, – yea to be foremost and first of those, – who raise their solemn protest against slavery, as a crime against our common human nature." But many enlightened and benevolent men have witheld their signatures because they did not feel they were sufficiently informed on the subject of American slavery; – on what *had* been done and is *now* doing by, Abolitionists; – or as to what extent the Christian church had failed to do its duty, in the glorious movement you are conducting on behalf of the slave.

Having attended the Anti Slavery Convention held in London in 1840, and seen many delegates from America; and being a regular reader also of our Anti Slavery Reporter, I am tolerably well acquainted myself with the history of your toils and sacrifices, and with the state of public opinion among you. But I want, if possible, to obtain a regular, & pretty frequent supply of American Anti Slavery publications, in order that I may keep the subject before the eye of our friends here, by the insertion in our weekly Newspaper, and our Monthly periodicals of such extracts from them, as may be most useful and desirable:

I write to you, then, dear madam, to assist me in this object, either by sending me such tracts and papers as you can reasonably give me, or by pointing out to me how I may obtain at the least possible cost, those publications of your Society, as you may think best calculated to answer my purpose. [Munroe?] & co – of your city send regularly to John [Green?] of London, and anything sent to him for me, would be sure to reach me.

I am sorry to hear from Miss Martineau of Mr. Garrison's ill health. I had the pleasure of meeting him in London, and have sympathised with him, and with you all, in the trials you have been called to endure, by "false brethren," who have been too successful in prejudicing many minds among us here, as well as in dividing your strength, I fear, in your own land. My heart is with you, and your fellow labourers, faithful as you are amid the faithless, and I feel persuaded, as do you, that the glorious end at which your aiming will be achieved, and that the bread you are casting upon the waters will be found again though it be not until after many days.

I shall feel deeply obliged by a line from you, and count it a great privilege if I can in the smallest degree further this blessed work in which with a martyr's spirit you are engaged.

Believe me,

faithfully yours,

William James.

MS.B.1.6. vol. 1 The May Papers [151]
No. 38 William James to Samuel May

Bristol, Nov. 2, 1843.

My dear Sir,

As Mr. Armstrong has been communicating with you on the subject of our Address, I have not troubled you with a letter in return for your kind epistle to me. But now you are about to embark for your own land I would convey to you the best wishes of my heart for your safe return and that you may find those whom you love well and happy.

You are aware of what we are doing. Our great difficulty is to whose hands we should commit our address in order that the largest amount of good may be done by it. Miss Martineau suggests in this Ware of Cambridge, the Editor of the Examiner. She thinks, she states in a letter to me, that he would do his duty faithfully in regard to it, and give it a place in the periodical which he conducts. Your advice in this particular would be of [essential?] service to us, and I presume you have given us the benefit of your knowledge in relation to it in your reply to Mr. Armstrong. Miss Martineau desires me to convey to you her respects, and to assure you that she would have been most happy to see you if you could have visited in her neighbourhood.

I have enclosed some letters which I hope it will not be troubling you too much to deliver. My letter to Mrs. Chapman relates to Anti-Slavery publications. I want to get some occasional information of the Abolition movement for publication here. There is a lamentable lack of information among us on the subject. The letter to Waterston is on the subject of the ministry at large. Should you see him, perhaps you would be good enough to tell him how glad we should be to establish a regular correspondance with our Boston friends on the subject....

If you are busy, be good enough to give me a line before you leave our shores informing me how you are. Our correspondance must not cease after your return – Mind that! – I should expect to hear from you when you get home and will not prove an ungrateful correspondent...Could we not do some good by the exchange of information as to the state of our causes in our respective countries? Without "telling secrets," we might send each other intelligence which would be interesting and which might occasionally be published as we saw desirable.

I hope I have not seen you for the last time in this world. But if so, may we renew our intercourse in heaven....

Your faithful friend,

William James.

MS.A.1.2. vol. 13 1843 Anti-Slavery Letters to Garrison [152]
No. 82 R.D. Webb to Maria Weston Chapman

Dublin 16th of Eleventh month 1843

My dear Friend

... About O'Connell I have often said as thou hast done that I thought him as honest as so active a politician could be – and I still think so. This to be sure, after all, would be thought faint praise by one who looked upon political life as so corrupting in its influences upon the morals & the feelings of a man, as we do. My remarks upon him, in my letter to you were intended to show what I think of the man as a man – suppose in comparison with Garrison or Rogers – not as a politician or in any other qualifying sense. Since these State Prosecutions have commenced, all my feelings as an Irish man (for I am one of that rate of white nigger) have been roused in his favour. Whatever his faults be and they are many, I dont like to see this leader of the Catholic millions badgered by the vinegar faced Attorney General of a vindictive English Tory ministry whom he has always baffled hitherto, and I hope will baffle again. One of the conspirators now on trial with O'Connell met me the day before yesterday in the streets. I asked him how they fared and what hopes they had. He said "we hope to beat them yet." O'Connell being a first rate lawyer and having some of the ablest men at the bar on his side is of course enabled to do much to worry, postpone, and baffle the crown lawyers which would not be done in ordinary cases. Some weeks since I wrote to H. Martineau (for the first time in my life) – asking for a contribution to the Liberty Bell and pouring forth into her sympathizing (!) ear my regrets & patriotic horror at the Government prosecutions. I wrote at some length – my thoughts suggested by the occasion. She replied courteously that she had sent her contribution to the Liberty Bell to Mrs. Chapman long since – and as to the military occupation of Ireland – the Proclaiming down the Clontarf Repeal Meeting – and the State Prosecutions she thought the conduct of the government so eminently dignified, wise, & humane, that she gloried in it. She thinks O'Connell one of the basest and worst of men for having done what he could to excite hatred between the English & Irish – & has the fullest confidence in the despotism and intention of government to do kindly and justly towards Ireland in the way of inquiring into grievances & the reform of abuses. Mind now this is the same set of men who when in opposition to the Whigs lately in power, used their best efforts and successfully to counteract almost all the measures of reform they did not destroy – They did all this – and Sir Robert Peel at the head of them. Now why can Miss Martineau hope for justice, humanity and kindness to Ireland – except on their own private professions to herself, I cannot tell, I wrote in reply much of what I have now said, and reminded her that as to O'Connells wickedness much might be said but that he had sinned in words, whilst both English Whigs and Tories all the late and all the present ministry, had been the redhanded, blackhearted perpetrators of some of the meanest, cruellest, least justifiable wars in the whole history of the world – I allude to those in the east. That unless we confine our ideas of mens moral obligations within geographical boundaries, these men from whom she appeared to hope so much for Ireland, are some of the most flagitious beings the world has seen – and altogether unlikely to do a good thing in the right way from a good motive. And at any rate if they do good to Ireland, we have O'Connell to thank, & not them. She replied that she was not able for controversy but that she remained of the same mind about O'Connell – that she hoped for measures of great good for Ireland from the government – that she united in my abhorrence of aristocratic aggression and of the eastern wars which she called the crowning disgrace of the Whig ministry – tho' they were equally disgraceful to the Tories who carried them on to a bloody & rapacious conclusion. Her last letter as well as her first was full and courteous – more so than could have looked for in reply to such tirades from an obscure body like myself to one so distinguished as she is. Nevertheless I do not comprehend the grounds of her hopes of sincere and large efforts for the good of Ireland from men who have always acted against her – at least against her Catholic population which includes five Sixths of the people....

thine truly

Rich[d] D. Webb.

MS.960 Quincy-Webb Correspondence 1843-1871 [153]
No. 4 Edmund Quincy to R.D. Webb

Dedham, Nov. 27 1843

My Dear Webb

... You will see by the Liberator that there has been a great meeting held in Faneuil Hall of the Irish, to hear O'C.'s Letter. I was not there but am assured that it was a very spirited & excellent meeting. Phillips made one of his very best speeches, in the course of which he read the Bull of the Pope on Slavery & called for "three cheers for the Pope of Rome," which were given with much spirit....

I did not attend the meeting because it happened not to be convenient, & though I thought it proper that it should be held, still I did not anticipate any good results from it. The Irish in this country are too ignorant & degraded to be abolitionists. They are led by demagogues of their own, who are, of course, pro-slavery & hate abolitionists. Slavery is to be abolished in this country as it was done in the British dominions, not by the highest or the lowest classes of society, but mainly by the middling classes, who are removed equally from the temptations of the rich & of the poor. This is true of the native laboring classes who are much above the generality of the Irish emigrants in intelligence. We have but little help from them. The abolitionists are chiefly made of persons of small but independent means. I mean farmers, mechanics, teachers & persons of small capitals, scattered over the country towns. They told me that at the O'Connell meeting, it was quite plain that the Repeal leaders were ready to throw over not only O'Connell but the Pope himself, rather than run the risk of losing slaveholding help....

Ever thine

Edmund Quincy.

MS.A.9.2. vol. 19 pt. 2 1843 The Weston Papers [154]
No. 81 H.C. Wright to Maria Weston Chapman

Dublin Nov. 28. 1843

Dear Friend –

... Be assured the Irish friends will not be turned from anti-slavery by Leavitt, Phelps & co. Tried spirits are they. They see with anointed eyes. So in Scotland the lines are down – or rather the [t?] ippling Wardlaw & co. now withdrawn from all the interest in this and in everything else that is good. They are all now engaged in running the *boundary line* of the attonement [sic] to settle whether to include the *world* in the territory of salvation or only a few...

Repeal in Ireland – Free Trade in England are all absorbing. Joseph Sturge has been over to see O'Connell to get him to make common cause with Free Suffrage. No go – as yet. The sympathies of many in England are enlisted with O'Connell since the Clontarf Proclamation & the concentration of soldiers in Ireland. The conviction is fast spreading all over both islands that Repeal must come sooner or later if Repealers abide by their *facts & arguments* as their only means...Dublin [is] full of soldiers – The people are quiet and [make merry?] at their awkward predicament of coming over to fight *No fight....*

thine

H.C. Wright.

MS.B.1.6. vol. 1 The May Papers [155]
No. 40 William James to Samuel May Jr.

Kingsdown, Bristol, England.
Nov. 30, 1843

My dear friend & brother,

An opportunity of sending to Boston presents itself in the return to America of my friend that good Abolitionist, whose name may not be unknown to you – James Canning Fuller[1] . I met him at the Convention in London, in 1840, and have had great pleasure in renewing my acquaintance with him here. We have had much communion on anti-slavery subjects, and he is the bearer of our "*Address*" to your shores, which I trust will have all the

1. James Canning Fuller (d.1847) was an English Quaker who emigrated to the United States in the 1830's and lived for a time at Skaneateles, New York. He did much work for the fugitive slaves.

good effect we desire. You will see that some few ministers have withheld their signatures, but this, not from any sympathy with your slavery institution or with the fear of war which keeps back many among you from bearing testimony against the crime of keeping human beings in bondage; but because they either felt that they were not sufficiently familiar with the subject of slavery in your country, and with the state of feeling, and action, among their brethren in the ministry there, or did not like to appear under the character of *admonishers* under circumstances in which they could bear no part of the obloquy and suffering which the course recommended in the Address would involve.

I hope, my dear sir, that you will, when you receive this letter, be once more in the bosom of your family and flock. You are often thought of here, I can assure you, with pleasure, and we are glad that we have made your acquaintance, and hope that our intercourse may be continued, though the mighty seas separate us. I have been thinking that we (I mean you and I) may make our letters interesting to each other, and useful to others, by communicating matters relating to our common cause (which might be from time to time made public, through the medium of our periodicals) and thus contribute to bring about a union between our and your churches which might be productive of the best results. What say you to this?....

yours faithfully,

William James.

MS.A.1.1. vol. 3 Anti-Slavery Letters from Garrison [156]
No. 114 William Lloyd Garrison to H.C. Wright

Boston, Dec. 15, 1843.

My dearly beloved friend–

... Great fears are entertained that Texas will be annexed to the Union at the present session of Congress. It was supposed that President Tyler would strongly recommend the annexation in his message, but he has had the cunning not to do so, knowing that, if he did, a tremendous excitement would ensue throughout the entire North. His language towards Mexico is insulting and belligerent; he intimates that the United States will declare war against her, unless she recognises the independence of Texas, or cease molesting her! There is no telling what a day will bring forth. Congress is corrupt enough to do anything. The right of petition has again been cloven down, and no excitement has followed. This would not be borne in England, but slavery is a more corrupting, more terrible power than Monarchy. Anti-slavery is indubitably lengthening its cords and strengthening its stakes; but it has a mighty work yet to perform. If the abolitionists would only be more uncompromising and more courageous in their dealings with the foe, they would achieve a hundred victories where they now obtain only ten. Multitudes of them yet need to be emancipated from their sectarian and party shackles, and to stand fast in the liberty of Christ....

Yours affectionately,

Wm. Lloyd Garrison.

No. 7 C.S. Toll to Maria Weston Chapman

Old [Steam?] Mill Birmingham Jany 7th 1844

My dear Madam

... 'tis true that the mere *name* of Reformer bears no reproach, while the attempt to act up to it, subjects us to all sorts of contumely – well be it so, we must be prepared to encounter that, if we feel it a duty to make our stand upon the principle with *slavery* in all its hideousness before *you.* I am sure *no* reproach would deter your noble nature from determined and incessant warfare against it, till it no longer disgraces your (otherwise) noble country. If I were in your land, I must join your ranks, I could not possibly be apathetic, neither can I conceive how *any* woman calling herself a Christian and a woman, *can* stand by contented with *professing* herself opposed to slavery.

But I am here in the midst of such poverty, such degradation, such forlon misery – that all one's energies seem absorbed, and a lifetime seems too short to perform half the labour set before us, *one* only cheering circumstance has happened, for a length of time, many good and noble hearts have tried to obtain a *law* against the employment of women in coal mines, I have ardently assisted them, and the legislature was positively *dunned* with petitions signed by 'women of Birmingham' on the subject – at last, we gained our point, and obtained the law, tho' it is still evaded by many...

On the right of suffrage – on the cruelties and horrors of our Poor Law, and on the abject and suffering condition of our labourers, particularly *females,* there is an enormous deal to be done, – in all this, our *best* and most available friend, is the 'Press'. It is indeed our stronghold, extensively open to us – it is also as extensively read, and forms our weapon of amazing strength, in fact, we could do nothing without it...

And what shall I say of my unhappy – torn, country, already you know the fate of poor Ireland, struggling for rights with the bayonet at her throat, occupied by twenty eight thousand armed men – already you know, that goaded by wrongs and oppression, the Welch nightly *break* the Law, and *daily* are *punished* for it, by the sitting 'Special Commissions'. You have read of the rick-burning which nightly illuminate whole counties in England, lighted by the fierce revenge of starving and maddened people in the agricultural districts. You have heard of the tremendous 'Strikes' in the manufacturing regions by which a whole district swarming with living industry, becomes silent as the grave, – and can I add anything – nothing – but that it is *true, all* true, and ten times more misery than rises to the surface, for the world to hear of...

To those good and right-thinking women who act with you in trying to rescue their fellow creatures from the curse of slavery, I beg most respectfully to offer the kind regards of myself and young daughter, who is old enough to appreciate the value of their labours, and to admire the good and virtuous, and to yourself, I present the warm admiration and sincere regard of an old friend: tho' new acquaintance, who will always feel the greatest pleasure in hearing from you, when you can make it convenient,

I remain Dear madam

Yours ever

C.S. Toll.

MS.A.9.2. vol. 20 1844 The Weston Papers [158]
Nos. 8-9 Elizabeth Pease to Anne Warren Weston

Darlington, Jany 27, 1844

My dear Anne

... Perhaps it is as well for us, that, great men shd now & then commit a flaw of this sort, to shew us that none are removed from the imperfections of human nature. I wd not, however, style J[oseph] J[ohn] G[urney] a *great* man, in my sense of the word great, tho' the world call him so, I was thinking more of O'Connell's *mean* behaviour towards our beloved Garrison. I never knew an action, I think, so perfectly at variance with the rest of the character — in many or most respects, O'Connell is a great man, in its true meaning — tho' not *so* great by immensurable degrees, (in my estimation at least) as he whom he affected to despise — I cannot think what sudden fit of aberation seized him — I hardly could believe it possible that he had really said the things he was reported to have uttered.... This is a sad stain on his fame. O'Connell is nevertheless, a great man — he is carrying forward one of the grandest movements that ever was enacted in the theatre of the world. If successful — & if he continues unshaken in his adherence to pacific measures only it will commence a new era in the history of nations — it will be a splendid example of the superiority of a moral over a blood stained revolution. The topic of excitement in this kingdom now is the trials going on in Dublin — the public appear to anticipate nothing but a conviction, for it could scarcely be otherwise, with a jury composed entirely of Protestants... I understand the Attorney General made a poor opening of the case — & brought no charge of conspiracy it was anticipated that the traversers wd commence their defence yesterday — & with it would commence the interest — what would I not give to hear *Dan* in such an occasion! — he will play with them as a cat does with a mouse, in the consciousness of his power & yet his intellect will be brought into full play no doubt, while he grinds them to powder... His sway over the minds of the Irish people is amazing. I am surprised at the tone of H. Martineau, in the question of repeal — that she shd write as Sir Robt. Peel might have written, puzzles me — the expediency or inexpediency of it, is of course a matter open to debate, but, the right of the demand, I cannot see how any honest mind can deny. It was brought about by bribery, corruption & military power, it was forced upon the people in opposition to their wishes, surely they must have a right to ask for its repeal. But O'Connell himself was at the first not desirous of it, if he could have obtained Justice. That is, if Ireland had been put, in all respects, on the same footing as England. A most reasonable demand, surely, but one that never was listened to — his applications were treated with ridicule & scorn & even the reform bill, which was gained by the votes of Irish members, brought no justice to Ireland. Scotland with a population of 2½ millions got an increase of eight members, & Ireland, with a population of eight millions, only got an increase of five, and two of these were enemies, the representatives of the University of Dublin – The franchise in England was continued at 40/-, but in Ireland it was raised to £20, tho' so much poorer a country. When O'Connell applied for the redress of these grievances he was only laughed at, & even Lord Morpeth opposed him. I remember hearing him say in 1838, that it was not repeal but Justice he wanted, but, he found he could not obtain the one without agitating for the other. How, he has been goaded so long it is questionable whether he would accept anything but repeal. Tho' young when the Union was carried, he opposed it, & his first speech in public was made on that side of the question – when, as he says, he owed his escape to his insignificance – for it was a dreadful time. There was security neither to person nor property – the habeas corpus act was suspended, the gaols were full of persons taken upon suspicion & the court martial shed men's blood in the merest mockery of a trial & meetings to petition against the Union were dispersed by military violence. O'Connell contends that it was not a *compact*, because it was obtained by force & bribery – therefore it is *not binding*, & that no union, save the mere act of parliament, has ever existed, else, there wd have been an identification of the inhabitants of both, in political rights & privileges. Instead of which the disproportion in representation is immense. England with a population less than double of Ireland, has about five times the number of representatives – & the franchise as I said before is, is ten times higher in the poorer country. Then again what an intolerable & galling oppression it is, that the whole people shd be required to support the religion of a small minority. Yet they do not ask that the ecclesiastical revenues shd be applied to the support of Roman Catholicism – they are opposed to endowments – & are in favour of the voluntary principle, corporate reform too, was refused for years, after it had been granted in England & Scotland & when it was yielded it was a very insufficient measure.

O'Connell has published a parliamentary paper showing that Lord Castlereagh expended £3,000,000 in direct bribery – the Earl of Shannon, it is said, got £35,000 of it, & bribes of office were given as well – preferment in the army & the church were offered to such as voted for the Union. O'Connell tells a story of Lord Castlereagh & a Mr Carew M.P. The Prime Minister endeavoured to make him vote for the Union by offers of preferment, or a pecuniary bribe but all was in vain – Mr. Carew who was ill at the time observed "well I hope I shall be able to go down to the House of Commons," "to vote for the Union, I hope," rejoined Castlereagh – "No," was the reply – "to state to the House the offer you have made me," "Then" said Castlereagh, "I'll tell you what I'll do, I'll get up in my place, & declare upon my sacred honour, *it is a lie*." This, I imagine, is a fair specimen of the character of him who afterwards died by his own hand.

Pitt filled Ireland with troops, & the expense of the army in Ireland that year was upwards of four millions sterling & the poor Irish were compelled to pay for the soldiers who forced the measure upon them. Even the Tory Attorney General, the organ of the Orange party, affirmed at the time – that the Union might be made binding as a Law, but it never could be made obligatory on conscience – that it wd be obeyed so long as England was strong but, that resistance to it wd be a mere question of prudence. It is said that the state of the country previous to 1800 was remarkably prosperous – & that it has declined almost ever since – be this as it may, can we wonder that the heart's blood of her sons is stirred at the oppression & insult to which England has subjected her? It seems to me, they wd do wrong quietly to sit under it – but, oh! may they adhere to moral & pacific measures only – in that will consist their strength. The people of England have hitherto been culpably indifferent to the wrongs of the sister Isle – the dissenters especially, for whose enfranchisment the catholics of Ireland petitioned before they got their own – yet, hardly a voice, comparatively has been raised, for the redress of their so much greater grievance. But this attempt to [prove?] free discussion – conspiracy, is rousing their feelings & turning the sympathies of multitudes in England towards their Irish neighbours...

Farewell dear Anne, with affec[e] remembrance to thyself & Mrs. Chapman – believe me sincerely thine

E. Pease

MS.960 Webb-Quincy Correspondence [159]
pp. 10ff Webb to Quincy

Dublin, 2nd month 2nd 1844.

My dear Quincy,

Yesterday the regular Cunard left Boston for Liverpool – so that it will be fully a fortnight before we see a new Liberator or Herald of Freedom. Hannah was talking this evening of how long it would be – I dont think there is any reading she cares half so much for, though, as well as myself, her taste is pretty catholic – nothing from divinity to novel reading comes astray to either of us. These four winter months are tiresome because we only hear from you once in four weeks – and anti-Slavery and abolitionists have for years been our world of dreamland. It is a thousand pities the Liberator should go down. If it do, I cannot attribute it to anything so much as Garrison's indolence and procrastination – for I am sure that the talent, fearlessness and enrgy which spread his fame over the world and established his paper when all were against him, need be exhibited in a quite inferior degree to sustain the paper and its editor. We have no such paper as the Liberator in these countries – no such freedom, none such magnanimity – all are more or less the slaves of party or of sect. The idea of a man gibbeting himself as Garrison does in his Refuge of Oppression would never enter the head of any man in the British Islands. I cannot reconcile all I have read of the tyranny of public opinion in America with what I have seen of Americans. Perhaps I know the "choicest spirits" – the most fearless, the most magnanimous – but I see nothing like them here. The fact must be that the anti-slavery enterprise with you has really "tried mens souls," and proved them too – its purely moral, unselfish and elevated nature has raised those who have stood faithful to it beyond the mean requisitions of party and sect that sooner or later expose the hollowness of all their votaries and partizans. Even James Haughton – and I know of no more sincere worshipper of O'Connell than he is (who is at the same time educated, pure minded & intellectual) – even he confesses himself ashamed of him in his treatment of Garrison. He thinks there is a want of magnanimity, and good manners, which he was not prepared to expect. I am not and never was surprised – for I looked for no better. O'Connell would spare no man, and regard no man that stood in his way – no man is his friend any more than while he can make use of him. I am persuaded that while he has a great head he has a cold heart – like Napoleon, he uses men as his tools – he knows how to sway them and control them – and he treats them accordingly. He knows what is great and true and right and he follows them so long as they [answer?] his purpose. I never thought he would answer Garrison's letter. It would be inconvenient. No such a man as O'Connell likes to admit he is mistaken unless he has, when doing so, some open and public opportunity of showing off his greatness of mind. Beside he had a good excuse for not noticing Garrison's letters in the fact that he was in the midst of all the hurry and occupation attending on the preparation for his trial. At any rate if he knows Garrison as well as I know him, I am sure he could not endure him – his spirit of free enquiry – his true love of liberty – his contempt for priestcraft, would all disgust or horrify O'Connell – who, whatever else he be is a staunch Catholic – a hater of infidel and revolutionary France – no republican an upholder and applauder of the old Burbons – the fierce foe of Espartero[1] who was a scourge of the priests. I think him friendly to British connexion with Ireland and a loyal subject to the Queen. If he had been in America I am persuaded he would be no better than Webster or Van Buren – unless he had got a much better moral education than he did get at St. Omer or Doway.

Well the trials of the *traversers* are going on now for 18 days. The counsel for the prosecution have made their speeches and examined their witnesses and the counsel for the defence have been now six days preaching away at the rate of five or six hours per day. I will send you all the papers so far as they have gone. Sheil's was the first. It is very brilliant. The names of O'Connell and Sheil[2] were watchwords during the struggle for *emancipation* – O'Connell was the Demosthenes – Sheil the polished Cicero of that great struggle. Moore, who made the second speech, was generally thought in the time of the Whigs to have been on the high road to the Irish Chancellorship, which office is now so ably filled by Sugden, a very famous English tory lawyer. The other lawyers on the side of the defence are all men of great ability and eloquence. One of them, Pigot was the Whig Attorney General for Ireland, As far as I am able to judge the whole matter I think the government prosecution is a most iniquitous and unconstitutional one, and that if it succeeds it will be a severe blow to the liberties of the Irish people. I fully believe in what Sheil calls the lust of domination or the instinct of domination which prevails amongst all the English of all parties whenever Ireland is in question. They will pity us and patronise us, but they cannot bear to see us standing erect or looking as if we should be well pleased to

---

1. Baldomero Espartero (1793-1879), Duca Della Vittoria, was a Spanish General and politician, acting as Regent from 1841 to 1844.
2. Richard Lalor Sheil (1791-1851) was an Irish politician and M.P. He worked for Catholic Emancipation and then the Repeal movement, but on being made Vice President of the Board of Trade, he became more conservative in his views, though he defended O'Connell at the time of his trial.

set up for ourselves. The English minister may with approbation, or with a degree of indolent remonstrance tantamount to permission, take liberties with Ireland, the fiftieth part of which it is related to England would rouse up a storm of indignant reprobation from one end of England to another. In England on a question like the present justice would be much more likely to be had than in Ireland. The same envenomed spirit of partizanship does not exist there which flourishes here with all the hardy luxuriance of a native plant. With few exceptions all the Catholics of Ireland are Repealers, or at least warm friends of O'Connell – and all the Protestants anti Repealers, or bitter enemies of Dan's. All the jury are known conservatives or tories – sworn foes to O'Connell. Hatred to O'Connell, and loyalty are synonymous ideas in the minds of 19 Irish Protestants out of 20. If they bring in a verdict of not guilty they will crown themselves with immortal honour and prove themselves victorious over the most vehement and inbred prejudices. But of this I have little hope indeed. Of course every body who thinks at all has his mind more or less occupied with the trials and speculations as to its result and the results of the result. – and yet it is wonderful to me how little appearance of excitement there is to be seen in this stormy country amongst this very excitable people. Walk the streets in nothing and see nothing to intimate that the most remarkable man Ireland has produced – the idol of millions of people at this very time on his trial in the Court of Queen's Bench for an imputed crime which may end in his being consigned to a dungeon according to the tender mercy and good pleasure of those very men whom he has thwarted, defied, and baffled for the last twenty years – Wellington, Peel, Stanley, Graham, &c &c. I suppose it was just the same in Jerusalem when Christ was crucified – & in Rome when Caesar was killed. History in books is quite another affair from history in reality. The history we witness and of which after a manner we form a part, feels to us something as Prose did to the man who found he had been writing it all his life without knowing it. I have sent a parcel of newspapers to Eliz. Pease which she will send on to you – and when you have skimmed them you will oblige me by directing them to Miller McKim, Philadelphia, to whom I send them by his very particular request. He wishes for them to tempt the Irish to the Anti Slavery Reading Room. Perhaps he will succeed – but he will not make an abolitionist among them all. They are too ignorant, too bigotted, and their perceptions of human rights and of liberty is altogether too obscure and imperfect. Send us a few thousand blacks amongst us for a year or two and I have little doubt that prejudice against colour and the proslavery spirit would prevail amongst the millions here as they do amongst you. There is no reasoning with the selfishness and prejudice which are at the bottom of all cruelty with which the colored people are treated amongst you. H.C. Wright told me that notwithstanding there are so many abolitionists in Philadelphia, his own home and L. Mott's were the only ones where coloured people were received on terms of equality. I suppose it is pretty much the same elsewhere. Amongst the active Repealers there is not a genuine anti-slavery man, as far as I know, but O'Connell. The rest are angry with him for what he has said and written against proslavery Americans. They cling to the ultimate idea of receiving help from America, and dont like to affront Brother Jonathan. I dont think O'Connell wishes for physical assistance. He is wise enough to know what a successful struggle with bludgeons, pikes and brick bats against the vast military power of England, would be the height of madness – and that it would not be worth the cost if it were successfull. I believe he knows this and feels it. I think he is a sincere friend to moral power as a means of "shaking the world", and that he abhors bloodshed and violence when used for the attainment of revolutionary objects. About ordinary wars between English & French, or Russians and Poles or the like, I dont think he cares. In one of his speeches which I was employed printing last week – it was an extract from one he made some months ago at one of his monster meetings – he tells the people, as something to boast of – that it was by Irish soldiers Chuznee was stormed (in Afghanistan) and that the Royal Irish were the first British soldiers who land in *China.* I cannot imagine a more striking proof of a man's blindness to the atrocity of war than his allusions to these two most infamous and doubly damned invasions of the English within the last two years – and in terms of exultation too, O'Connell's sole and only guide in all his actions I am persuaded is nothing better nor nobler than expediency – strict truth, undeviating integrity, unshaken abherence to principles he has no notion of, except as "rhetorical flourishes". It would be impossible it would be otherwise. He has been all his life a politician in the thick of the struggle – as a demagogue – a statesman – the head of a party. Purity of mind, whiteness of soul, are in my estimation utterly impossible for any one who leads such a life – and if this be so, is it not the most unanswerable proof of the inherent evil of human governments, in so far as man becomes the slave of a party, so far he ceases to be honest and free....

[Letter has no conclusion]

MS.A.9.2. vol. 20 1844 The Weston Papers [160]
No. 36 Richard Allen to Maria Weston Chapman

Dublin 6/2 1844

M. W. Chapman

Dear Friend

I snatch up my pen to scribble a few lines to enclose in my Anne's envelope – though time presses me very closely in a general way we are here now in a state of rejoicing & of mourning & lamentation – O'Connell in prison !! he who stands as the greatest assistor of universal freedom of his age before the whole world – the inmate of a jail!!! Well be it so – posterity will tell on whom opprobbrium will rest. The doings of Sir R. Peel & his government will be lost in oblivion – but the one *broad* – *deep* – indelible blot will remain as a deeply engraved stain on *it & him,* that he imprisoned O'Connell & sought to crush the asserter of the rights of the people by brute force ! But will he achieve his end? History emphatically answers No!... O'Connell, notwithstanding the slips he has occasionally made, deserves the sympathy of the lovers of freedom; he has struggled mightily & I think as a politician stands almost unrivalled for consistancy. I feel little doubt too but that there will be a strong burst of indignation from the true hearts of England – that *moral* power will do its work in the hour of trial... I have said we are in the midst of mourning & joy; the people are mourning, but I question whether they are much cast down: – the tories are rejoicing &

plotting great things. According to them – the Repeal Association is to be put down in a few days...I cannot think the government will be so foolish as to attempt this; but if they do they will part with the lovers of liberty together; & bring a weight of indignation against them which they will be utterly powerless to resist...

Kind regards to all our valued friends

sincerely thine

R. Allen.

MS.A.9.2. vol. 20 1844 The Weston Papers [161]
No. 25 Mary Welsh to ?

Edinburgh April 25th 1844

My dear Friend

... The case of John L. Brown[1] at New Orleans has excited great interest in this country, where the subject has been properly taken up it has been the means of presenting the subject of American slavery to the public and acknowledging an interest not hitherto known. You have ere this I doubt not seen accounts of the Glasgow meeting, one of the most spirited ever held since the days of Borthwick & Thompson,[2] they came out nobly on the subject no mincing of the matter with them. The friendly& faithful resolutions relating to the Free Church in this country taking money from slaveholders in America was good, if they could have been induced to send back the money with a friendly remonstrance to the American church...

The Emancipation Society of Edinburgh exist only in name, there is too much of the aristocrat prevails among them for true abolition. We were in hopes at the time of the Glasgow meeting to get up one of the same kind here, but when the committee saw how the Glasgow society took up the Free Church affair, instead of being stimulated to do likewise they were quite afraid to offend the Free Church & by some stratagem or other they slipp'd the business into the hands of the Town Council, who got up a meeting condemnatory of the sentence passed upon John L. Brown but so far from noticing the Free Church affair, they had Free Church ministers addressing the meeting...

With kind regards I remain your faithful friend in the cause of freedom

Mary Welsh

---

1. John L. Brown was a white man who had helped a female slave to escape. He was sentenced to death for this, but his case aroused a great public outcry especially in Britain, and the sentence was commuted to imprisonment.

2. In 1833 George Thompson had carried out a widely publicised series of debates with Peter Borthwick in Glasgow, in which Thompson made some of his earliest attacks on American slavery. See George Thompson, *Substance of an Address to the Ladies of Glasgow etc.*, Glasgow, 1833.

University Club Pall Mall, East London
May 24. 1844

My dear Mrs. Chapman

... You should know that we have a sort of censorship here & whatever displeases its directors is mutilated or suppressed. George Thompson alluded to this when he spoke in Exeter Hall on the Sugar Duties, all discussion upon which was refused by those who are paid by the abolition society to elicit those truths which nothing but discussion can impress on the minds of men totally ignorant of the principles on which a sound conclusion is to be arrived at. The same specimen of liberality in this tribunal has forever determined me to risk no repetition of the humiliation...

There seemed at last year's Convention[1] to be a rivalry of adulation among the political parties of the day. Ld Palmerston's influence with the Bey of Tunis was set off against Ld Aberdeen's with the President of Texas, & the Whig humanity in the old world was pitted against the Tory humanity in the new. No one had any more doubt of the sincerity attached to these Cabinet professions than he had of the African chief's independence of the Sultan & the French court or of Houston's liberty of action between a free state on one side and slave states on the other. No one asked whether prospective freedom was right in Africa & wrong in America – whether immediate emancipation could be consistently demanded in one part of the world & gradual emancipation be received with thanks in another. Not a voice was raised on behalf of an in-offending ally despoiled of her most valuable province – nor did one of the opponents to a separate legislature in oppressed Ireland hint an objection to the usurpation of every political function by the voluntary subjects of a transatlantic empire. Yet it required no great sagacity to see that the recognition of this new state had done more to injure the cause for which the Convention had assembled than the English government had ever done in its favour. Texas must by the process of assimilation, be incorporated with one of its neighbours. The attraction of free blacks & the attraction of slaves cannot neutralize each other. It must conquer or be conquered. If but a slight acquaintance with the peculiarities of your system had existed where it was both necessary & expected, would our government have been permitted to acknowledge a state of things which had been brought about for the express purpose of supporting what they professed to abominate? Was it not evident to every inquirer that our planters sought in Texas a security for their private property & an increase to their federal prerogatives; – that the revolted province could neither keep a promise of emancipation without offending the people it had left nor break it without attacking the people it had betrayed: & that the maintenance of its separate establishment was equally incompatible with its strength & its weakness? Was it not well known that one if not more, of the proprietors of a paper in the confidence of the Whigs had an interest in deceiving the public proportioned to the lands he possessed in the disputed territory?

---

1. The Second World's Anti-Slavery Convention held in London in 1843.

Were there not agents employed in promoting German emigration to Texas by every act of misrepresentation – the same persons preaching liberty in Europe & slavery in America? Who could doubt that the fear of losing Canada operated more strongly on Downing Street than the wish to save Mexico & that the concession of neutrality in the East was purchased by the permission of aggression in the West? To believe in Whig sincerity on these points evinces little experience & less sagacity. Why does the Morning Chronicle deprecate interference with the American & the Edinburgh Review exhibit such indifference to American abolition? Why has Macaulay, who owes all he has & all he is to abolition, keep aloof from the abolitionists? Why does Ld Morpeth take the chair at meetings for universal emancipation & yet recommend that American emancipation should be left to itself? Has not every statesman of every party endeavoured to make a tool of those who assume to direct public opinion & control of the government? Think for a moment what a combination of mighty interests is arrayed here against an agitation which threatens them with the loss or the interruption of their resources? The English manufacturer cares less for the tears of the negro than for the rise of prices in the cotton market; – he sees insurrection in an abolition pamphlet & waits with philosophic composure till supplies from free labour will enable him to be humane without any sacrifice, all such considerations, & others that might be mentioned, will affect you no further than to instil caution & prepare you for coldness or opposition. The cooperation of legislators may be bought too dearly. They follow their trades; you follow your duty. They obey their masters; you obey your conscience. They work for themselves: you work for others. The labor & the honor may be fairly divided among us – & justice will have no reason to envy expediency...

The London Committee of the Anti-Slavery Society seems somewhat regardless of consistency. They oppose the instruction of laborers into the West Indies & yet demand "protection" for the only interest which is to be promoted by it. They admit immigration will be injurious to the negro, while they represent the Whigs who support it as his best friends. They count the patronage of noble Lords who deprecate the sympathy they themselves profess for the American abolitionist. The economical superiority of free over slave labor is their declared conviction and its inferiority is the assumption of their petitioning to the legislature. They were against slave holding with the money they received from Slave holders (The wrongs of the negro swell out the [Moravian?] subscriptions & the slave-worked mine sharer's contribution on their list of subscribers proclaims their utter disregard of principle. The judge's salary is paid out of the convict's hush-money.) They declaim against the tyranny of the planters while they advocate a line of policy, which by encouraging an unremunerative produce, will leave the black to the mercy of his employer. While the condition of these influences on the national mind is to act in accordance with the national rights & interests, they defend a tariff of duties which robs the people without offering an equivalent enriches bitterest enemies, forces capital out of its natural channels, & depresses labor below the level it would find in the development of its inherent resources. That the West India proprietors, who want "protection" for free labor against compulsory is perfectly consistent. They will know that the cultivation of sugar under circumstances, which require large capital & oppressive bounties, would check the tendency to independence in the growers of produce more adapted to the soil & the climate. They feel that the removal of restrictions would compel them to relinquish all hopes of rivaling the mother country in the enjoyment of a monopoly, based on the degradation of the peasantry & creative of an overbearing oligarchy (They see that Hayti finds it cheaper to import than to grow sugar & they hope to tax us for the whole amount of the difference) abolish the sugar duties & the emancipated negro will be left to make an unimpeded bargain with his employer. Continue them & he will be reduced to his former state of servitude. The Brazilian will not gain freedom & the Jamaican black will lose it. What right, in fact, have we to take for granted the acquaintance of either in the views we are pleased to take of his interest? We may be inflicting an injury in striving to [conferring?] a benefit, & the sum of human misery may be increased by the shape we are taking for its diminution. It is the slave's question in the same sense as the corn-law is the Laborers question.

If free trade, as those of the abolitionists maintain be a natural right, no deviation from its correlative obligation can, as they insinuate, be justified by the pretence of ultimate good. In the one case before us the good is contingent & doubtful; the evil is present and certain. The cry of inhumanity is too absurd to deserve an answer. For my part, I believe that slavery is encouraged by its "abolition".

You will not be surprised then to hear that a schism has shown itself in the abolition Society; & that the doings of the "Privy Council" have not met with the approbation of the general body. So far, indeed, has the impotent indocility proceeded that the committee has been denounced in a printed circular as "not fully enjoying the confidence of the A.S. public as is necessary for the successful prosecution of its labours," & to have "unconsciously adopted a course involving principles of action at variance with justice & humanity." Whether the committee is, like slavery, to have its "phases", I know not. Its present phase, however, looks rather toward an eclipse than a crescent. Let us hope that we may be blessed with a luminary, less encumbered with satellites, less executive in its orbit, & more bright in its inspiration. [MS. ends]

MS.A.1.2. vol. 14 1844 Anti-Slavery Letters to Garrison [163]
No. 35. R.D. Webb to Elizabeth Pease

Dublin 26th of 5th mo. 1844

Dear Elizabeth

... I have seen only a hurried sketch of the B & F Annual meeting. I confess I was somewhat disgusted with G. Thompson's violence and did not think it at all warranted by the provocation he received & which I feel satisfied was not meant as an insult. It seems to me more like the act of a school boy than of a sensible man to take such a huff. How can he think so much of praise or dispraise. What good has praise done him that he need cling to him about the sugar duties. I feel with Joseph Sturge. I say I *feel* – for having but a shallow head for political economy, I dont rely upon my own judgments as to the political bearings of the case – I feel that free trade with Brazil would confirm the reign & extent of slavery there & I dont like to see such a certain evil due in the hope of a great ultimate good. I think O'Connell & Brougham have both forcibly put the matter in this light – perhaps only an able lawyer can – for I have no confidence in the consistency or principle of either....

Rich[d] D Webb.

MS.A.9.2. vol. 20 1844 The Weston Papers [164]
No. 47-48 James Haughton to Maria Weston Chapman

34 Eccles St. Dublin
18th July 1844

My dear Mrs. Chapman

... R.D. Webb & I do not think with you on the Brazilian sugar question,...& yet after all, I don't think there is any great difference between you & us on that matter. Rich[d] & I never asked our Government to do more than tell the Government of Brazil that we could not enter into a new commercial treaty with them unless they emancipated all their slaves; as we looked upon *all* the product of slave labor as stolen goods. For my part, I think it would be just as right for me to purchase goods that I knew to be stolen from a neighbour, as to purchase slave grown produce. You would leave the decision of this point to individual conscience, because any action of Government upon it would be an infringement of liberty of thought & action, & because the laws of Government must be maintained by force; are not all taxes which we pay unwillingly, an encroachment on the former? & do not all civil contracts of every kind imply an ultimate resort to the latter? do you therefore object to all taxation, & to every *bigot* contract in trade, or for the purchase in lands or houses? It is my impression that Government should, in the first instance be, as nearly as possible, a concentration of the voice of the whole people. I would give every man & every woman of full age, & who was not at the time suffering a penalty for a breach of the laws, a voice in the election of representatives, & then, it seems to me that, a Government so chosen, should take cognizance of every matter of public interest or utility, & that on all questions which might arise, & which would be fairly debated by representatives frequently responsible to their constituents, the minority would be morally bound quietly to submit to the judgment of the majority. A fair representation being *the theory* of our Government. I see no impropriety in applying to it to adopt such fiscal regulations as the majority in Parliament would be found willing to adopt. If we were obliged to wait for the consent of every individual to the enactment of every law, there would be an end to all Government, & it seems to me that anarchy would be the inevitable consequence. Neither R.D. Webb nor I, would sanction the use of such force as would endanger life, for the maintainance of our laws; if they could not be executed without such means need be used, nor do I hold myself responsible for the acts of our Government when it resorts to them. It seems to me that a moral influence sufficiently strong to ensure obedience to all good laws, would exist in a well regulated society. Now for the Brazilian question, & for my reasons (in which I believe R.D.W. coincides) for rejecting commercial relations with that people. In the first place I consider all slave grown produce stolen goods, & therefore not a lawful source of commerce — if it were possible, I would reject American cotton wool, but the very fact of the difficulties in which our trade with you for that blood stained article, throws in our way, strikes me as a strong reason why we should decline to trade with Brazil at all, so long as she holds slaves. Our trade with your slave states has created such a powerful pecuniary interest in your country, & in ours in favour of slavery, an interest which has increased your slaves from 700,000 to 2,700,000, should we not be careful to avoid doing anything to produce a similar calamitous result in another land? If we enter into a free trade intercourse with Brazil such as would create an enlarged interchange of our various products, is it not absolutely certain that she will require a greater number of slaves to supply the increased demand, & would we not be accountable to God, unless we protested against the intercourse, for all the additional misery to the poor Africans which would result from it? If we be not guided by the experience which the encrease of slavery in your slave state affords, of what use is experience to us? Can there be any doubt that your increase of slavery is owing to our great trade with you? & is it not equally a truth that, if England, some 60 or 70 years ago, had refused to take your blood stained produce that your slaves would have been then made free? partly from a desire to ensure our custom, & partly because the pecuniary interest in those days would not have been able to overwhelm the moral feeling which then existed; but whether this would have been the result or not, should not we have done our duty? & refused to deal in other goods. I say it is equally our duty in the present day, but we are surrounded with greater difficulties for its accomplishment, millions of our people now live by your cotton wool, & would it not be a fearful thing to say to these, you must lie down & starve, for the thing you live by is dishonestly obtained. It is to avoid a difficulty of this kind, to keep down instead of raise up pecuniary obstacles for our children to have to surmount, in case slavery shall not be abolished in our day, that I ask our Government to say to the Brazilians "we'll have no trade with you." I have appealed to the London Com[e] to cry out against *all slave produce* & thus prove to the world their sincerity, but they have not listened to my appeal, of course. I think their action on the subject is wrong. I do not think your parallel case touching oppression in China & wickedness elsewhere, is to the point. Oppression exists everywhere, but I do not feel that we are bound to enter into a crusade against it in other lands — *Slavery* is a sin so atrocious, that it seems to me to have no parallel, making a chattel of a human being, transcends all other wickedness. Oppression is an evil which depends on many causes over which we have little or no control, on errors in the arrangement of human affairs, arising out of our limited knowledge of the laws of Nature & of our own being...

Our political position almost absorbs all the thoughts of the people; under O'Connell's guidance Ireland is now solving a problem of mighty importance, that is, whether moral power can secure human rights, but I do not think the time has yet arrived when that question will be fairly tried, our people are not only taught to avoid fighting, because it is not [in] their interest to fight, not because it is a wrong thing to fight. O'Connell is the only man of that party, with whom I am acquainted, who has a real horror of & objection to, the shedding of blood. While he lives I believe we shall be safe from the calamity of Civil War, but, if England should be involved in a European war, before she satisfies the wishes of the Irish people, I imagine she will get no help from them, so that I think our agitation is a security for the peace of Europe as I can hardly imagine the English Government so mad as to provoke a war, or even to be very testy on points of honour, so long as our present dislike to her exists –O'Connell & his brother patriots in prison, are the beloved & honoured of their country. I think England is ever in that position in which she must grant our demands or repress them by greater coercion, the latter will be a dangerous policy....

believe me to be my dear Madam with sentiments
of respect & esteem, your friend

James Haughton.

MS.A.1.2. vol. 14 1844 Anti-Slavery Letters to Garrison [165]
No. 44 William Bassett to Elizabeth Pease

Broughton Meadows.
Northampton, Mass. July 22 1844.

My dear Friend

Elizabeth Pease.

... This country is now violently convulsed by the preparations making by the too great political parties for the ensuing Presidential election. The excitement, judging from present appearances, will not be less than that of 1840. The result will probably be the election of Henry Clay to the chief magistracy of this nation. Slave-holder as he is – fully committed as he is understood to be to the support of the infamous system, yet some profesed abolitionists, among whom is our friend D L Child, think they see in his elevation hope for the slave. They consider the Whig party pledged to the rejection of Texas, and in the defeat of that favourite measure of the slave-holding interest they look for great gain to the cause of impartial liberty. We cannot doubt that the result of this, as of every political movement, must have its influence – & it may be for good – upon the cause of emancipation. But it is an instrumentality too impure for true antislavery hands to intermeddle with. To do so, seems like doing evil that good may come....

Affectionately & sincerely thy friend

Wm. Bassett.

No. 45 R.D. Webb to Maria Weston Chapman

Dublin 1st of 8th mo. 1844

My dear friend

... We have not had a finer season for many years. There has been an unusual continuation of fine dry weather – no excessive or very heavy rains. The country looks its best everywhere and there is every prospect of a fine plentiful harvest. As far as my own observations goes, supported by the testimony of older observers I am satisfied that the condition of this country is steadily improving. The houses, the shops, the agriculture, the modes of living, habits of cleanliness & decency, all the appliances of civilization are greatly better now than they were 40, 30, 20, or even ten years ago. The facilities for travelling are greatly increased all over the country & at very cheap rates compared with those in England. A great railway is about to be formed between Dublin & Cashel, 100 miles south – and it will probably be extended by branches to Cork, Limerick & Waterford. One has been opened to Drogheda, 32 miles north, & will be likely to extend to Portadown, from whence one runs to Belfast—the metropolis of the north of Ireland. In a political point of view I doubt if Ireland was ever in a more anomalous condition, or that the rich & the poor were ever more opposed to each other in their opinions and aspirations. The poor Catholics are all repealers – 4 fifths of the nation – the Protestants rich & poor and perhaps 3 fourths of the rich Catholics are Anti-Repealers. The repealers are to be sure generally ignorant, bigotted, and pretty much led by the nose – and would most likely be utterly unable to describe the Repeal they talk about. Indeed I think it would puzzle O'Connell to define the Constitution of Ireland if Repeal were attained tomorrow. Where would our army and navy come from – how we are to escape from the influence of English bribery & unfair influence wherever she had a point to gain in Ireland – how a voluntary church which he has confessed to advocate could be maintained in a country where so large a proportion of the people are members of the most bigotted priest ridden form of Christianity. I fear such scenes as those of Philadelphia would be of frequent occurence. I hear that Irish Protestants form an active portion of the *Native* American Party – This is extremely likely and wherever Irish Catholics and Irish Orangemen get together, they are likely to serve each other as the two famous Kilkenny cats did, which were put into a pit overnight & the morning nothing was found but the two tails. By far the ablest repeal paper in Ireland is the Nation – edited by some young fellows who are sometimes sneeringly called Young Ireland. They acted fiercely Anti-English – they rake up and disseminate all the stories they can gather from history of English treachery, cruelty, rapacity, bad faith, English defeats – They exhort Ireland to stand alone & as plainly as they dare, they hint at the glory & dignity of complete independence of England. They make no empty professions of loyalty to the Queen – They are all for Ireland & war to the knife when ever it can be undertaken against England with the probability of a successful issue. The decision of the English judges on the points mooted in the Writ of Error will probably be delivered some time next month. It will decide whether O'Connell & his fellow martyrs (as they are always called in the Repeal journals) are to remain in jail the remainder of their term – or are to walk out on the whole proceedings being quashed. If they be released the government will be disgraced in the eyes of the people yet more than they are already. If they stay in, the hatred of England will be increased in the popular mind. Nothing that has yet been done has at all resulted in the object aimed at – to lessen the power and influence of O'Connell. I don't think he was ever so dear to the multitude as he is at present moment....

I never hear of George Thompson any more than if he were in India. I presume he is hard at work for the King of Delhi or the Raja of Sattara[1] – & that he enjoys a handsome income and lives near or in London. I dont think he is on the best terms with the members of the Anti Corn League individually. I believe they had some disagreement before he sailed for India & tis likely they are cool enough still. He is a fine fellow – but he is not a rock like Garrison nor a sword from heaven like Rogers ....

Thine very truly

Richd D Webb.

MS. 960 Webb-Quincy Correspondence [167]
pp. 13-14 R.D. Webb to Edmund Quincy

Dublin 17th of Eighth Mo. 1844

My dear Quincy

... We have just now on a visit to my brother James – [met] a very distinguished English Chartist Henry Vincent,[1] once a journey man printer – now an orator & popular agitator of great power. He spoke in our last Exchange Meeting – the room was crammed before he closed his speech & never I saw our people in such extasies with any speaker. There was a good deal of claptrap & ad captandum talk but it was showy & eloquent claptrap much as none but a fluent & quick witted man could put together. About 3 years ago he spent 22 months in prison on account of bits & scraps taken out of his political harangues – he was [14?] months in Monmouth jail – 2 months in London – 8 months in Holkham. for much of the time he was badly fed, badly lodged, & deprived of books, pen, ink & paper – all by the Whig ministry who brought in and carried the Reform Bill. His wife is with him – a bright little woman with a weakly consumptive frame – and a strong heart. I think if she was in Boston she would make a noble abolitionist. She has got two children & a spitting of blood – so that poor thing she is bound for the spirit land. She is pretty & only 22. She reminds me a good deal of H. B. Stanton's wife who is another strong heart in a diminutive cage.

I saw O'Connell this week. I accompanied Vincent & his wife to visit him. I never saw him more ruddy & cheery. His face is almost as rosy as if he were a

---

1. George Thompson, in addition to his work for the Rajah of Satara, was also for a time agent for the Emperor of Delhi.

1. Henry Vincent (1813-1878), one of the leaders of the moral force Chartists, was the friend of several of the British abolitionists, and through them became acquainted also with Garrison.

boy of six years old – his eye is bright & his port erect. He was dressed in a frock coat and wore a cap with a gold band which he affects on procession occasions and whenever he appears in public. He receives visitors three days in the week for 3 hours each day. The place of reception is a large & handsome garden full of fruit trees, vegetables & flowers – on these occasions a word or two is all he has to space for chance customers – so many come and so many more are kept waiting till these are served. Those who want to have a talk with him must make a previous appointment – of course with his consent. The country is as quiet as possible and I am told the ministry take great credit for the means they have taken and the successful result of the prosecution. I think however that it is a treacherous quiet and that they never had less hold on the affections and fidelity of the Irish nation than at the present time. Time will tell. Vincent has had a great opportunity of knowing the feelings & aspirations of the working classes of England & he is of opinion that the tide is strongly towards republicanism and that their hatred of the aristocracy of rank and overgrown wealth is continually increasing. I have no doubt that both the great parties (the Whigs & Tories) are equally hostile to any measure which would raise the condition of the poor in a political point of view or in any way that would give them any real control over the government of the country. From all I can learn the influence of the Tories who have now the ball at their feet, is overwhelming and the Whigs are dying out as a political body. The Tories *have* the power – possession is nine points of the law – and they have plenty of money and no nice scruples to prevent them from doing all they can to [reach?] the position they hold. They overawe the middle classes and buy up the venal votes among the poor. Nevertheless the undercurrent is strong and swelling – habits of self-respect are being formed amongst the working men both in town & country – education is on the increase – political agitation is unceasing – & it all tends to the formation of a more healthy, independent & popular state of opinion amongst the down trodden millions who are the working bees of these three kingdoms....

Thine R D Webb

MS.B.1.6. vol. 1 The May Papers [168]
No. 63 Samuel May to Mary Carpenter

Leicester, Massachusetts, 28th Oct. 1844

My dear Miss Carpenter,

... We have rejoiced with you in the justice done to British Unitarians by the Dissenters' Chapel Bill, and that the Government, particularly, made that Bill one of their own measures. I know no act of any public, legislative body more worthy of admiration and eulogy. Many may be found, more extensively known, more generously applauded, but if any, certainly very few, more honourable and apparently more entirely dictated by a sense of justice. No party in England could hope to benefit itself, in a political point of view, by befriending the Unitarians. So much the more honour is justly theirs, who do so. I can perceive no other reason for the success of the Bill than its inherent, manifest justice. We have much reason to be glad & thankful when justice, common, simple, justice, obtains a victory over its numerous opponents. In your letter you ask me if I will "give you a brief sketch of the state of things" among the American Abolitionists, explaining the ground of their differences, &c. This I have long intended to do, & regret that it has been delayed so long....

The present anti-slavery agitation in this country was recommended about 1830. Previously to that time, sundry publications, giving to the Free States scattered hints of the condition & treatment of the slaves, had been put out.... It was not till 1830, that any deliberate, determined attitude of resistance to slavery was taken. Then it was taken in Boston, by William Lloyd Garrison, in conjunction with another man of great zeal and courage named Isaac Knapp. Him I never knew. Mr. Garrison was Editor of the little paper which started, under the name of the Liberator, without patronage or any subscribers of consequence. He declared, in the outset, his resolution to be plain & bold as truth demanded – I will not give back, he said – I will not equivocate – *and I will be heard.* It is impossible for me now to give any account of the persecutions, to which this determination, fully and honestly acted out, led him, and the cause. He was of course stigmatised, from one end of the Union to the other, as a madman, a fanatic, an incendiary, and regarded by thousands who had no sympathy with slavery or slaveholders as doing a vast deal of harm to the cause. It was all false as time has proved. I saw, and was convinced, 6 or 8 years ago, that this course was as near right as a man can expect to attain to. The most efficient Abolitionists, men & women, have maintained, and now maintain, the same general views of the anti-slavery question which he has held. They are known among us as the old-organized Anti-Slavery party, so far as they can justly be called *a party.* They are the hard working Abolitionists. They are the hard working Abolitionists – those who are aiming to awaken the national conscience, to regenerate the public sentiment; and with wonderful success have their efforts been attended. The cause went on for many years with the most entire harmony on the part of its friends. Opposition, persecution, banded them together. They were too few, to think of dwelling on the differences of opinion existing among themselves *on other matters,* and so Whigs & Democrats, Orthodox and Heterodox, Congregationalists & Presbyterians, Trinitarians and Unitarians, Baptists, Methodists, Quakers and all, united with one heart and mind in carrying forward the great cause. The demon of slavery heard this, and howled, it determined to destroy this harmony. This could not have been affected, had all who pretended to love and serve the antislavery cause been *sincere;* had they loved it, more than they loved sect, and party, and personal advancement. This was unhappily not the case. The cry was raised against Mr. Garrison and his friends that they were *infidels* – they sought the destruction of the Church, the overthrow of Christianity. French Republicanism and Jacobinism were ascribed to Mr. G. and *believed* all over the country, just as the slanders about Unitarianism and its supporters had been spread all over the land, – and by the self-same men, to a great extent – and every where believed then and now.– Many, who formerly ran well, under the pressure of this storm of misrepresentation and abuse, turned their backs upon the cause. They joined in the abuse of Mr. Garrison and his friends, as the surest way of gaining favor and confidence with the proslavery folks, and the best way of covering their retreat. About 5 or 6 years ago, a paper was put forth by several clergymen (all of the Calvinistic order), called the "Clerical Appeal". It was the first note sounded by the deserters, and most meanly & falsely attacked the old abolitionists. One of its principal signers, Rev. Charles Fitch,[1] has since made an honourable confession of the wrong he did.... The *grounds* on which Mr. G. and his friends were attacked thus, and the mad-dog-cry, of infidelity raised against them were simply & solely these – In the prosecution of the anti-slavery cause, it became at length perfectly demonstrated that the *American Churches* were the chief supporters of slavery!.... they openly undertook the defence of slavery, from reason & from the *Bible*. They who did so were not rebuked, or disowned, or in any way opposed by the great mass of Northern religionists. They were still recognised as good Christians, and honourable men. In this state of things, the so-called Church throwing its whole, heavy, dead weight directly on the wheels of the antiSlavery enterprise, embarassing and denouncing it – Mr. G. could not doubt what his duty was. He spoke plainly & strongly in condemnation of this course – he declared that the churches & ministers, who gave to slavery the right hand of fellowship, & could not be, *were not*, the Churches, & Ministers of the Lord Jesus Christ. This self evident truth was denounced as unmitigated *infidelity....*

I have thus named the principal cause of the division. One illustration of it, happening within my personal knowledge, just occurs to me. A Calvinistic minister, conversing with me 6 or 7 years ago on the anti-slavery question, said to me, "If the Abolitionists would only throw Mr. Garrison overboard, they would have a vast accession of numbers and strength from those *who can never consent to act under such a leader.*" I replied to him, "The abolitionists will never do that" (this was before I had any personal knowledge of Mr. Garrison – I knew the estimation in which anti-slavery men held him) "They know Mr. Garrison to be honest, true, intrepid – they could despise themselves to attempt to cast off so faithful a fellow-worker, and would deserve scorn & failure if they did attempt it." "Very well," he replied, "they will not have our support," or something to that effect. The truth is that the Calvinistic party in this country have so long been accustomed to rule, direct and manage, as they pleased, all benevolent enterprises and all moral and religious associations, that they could not submit to join in a cause led by Wm. L. Garrison, and in which Unitarians, Quakers, and Women were admitted to an equal participation....

The word "women" in the last paragraph, leads me to speak of another (alleged) cause, of the division among the abolitionists. At the very beginning of the anti-slavery movement, it was found that to no individuals did this righteous cause make a stronger appeal, from none receive a warmer response, than from certain noble and "honourable" women. Their sympathy, and their labours were warmly welcomed. Some of them were urged to take a more prominent post than they were inclined to take, by individuals who afterwards pursued a very opposite course. Five or six years ago, when it was found necessary to sacrifice Mr. Garrison & his chief supporters, in order to conciliate the *good orthodox folks* and bring them into the antislavery ranks, the action of the women in the cause was thought to be a very good handle for the purpose. Mr. G. and the old abolitionists have always contended for the right of women to act freely, in the Antislavery field, as their conscience and sense of duty should prompt.

---

1. Rev. Charles Fitch was a Boston Congregational Minister who was one of the authors of the Clerical Appeal which condemned Garrison's actions.

They have asked no more than this – This they insisted upon – the mental & moral freedom of woman, as man, in the departmental of moral effort. They refused to put a chain upon woman, while professedly labouring to remove one from the slave. Many abolitionists who would say that, in *their view*, women ought not to assume a public & conspicuous post in the cause, would also say that *their* views were not the measure of *other persons'* duty – that each ought to follow his and her own conviction of right & duty, and that no trammels should be put on any one, who came forward to act, impelled by a sense of duty. This would have been clear enough to the squeamish folks, who dreaded lest the abolitionists should encourage the women to violate St. Paul's rules of female action, had they been willing and disposed to be convinced. This was not the thing. They sought some plea on which the old Abolitionists might be made a proscribed body – and this "woman question" they thought was the very thing. Straightway the alarm was sounded; all the changes on St. Paul's directions about women were rung; a holy horror which the cavalier treatment which the sacred book received at the hands of the ungodly Abolitionists was professed and expressed. – Never did more barefaced, shameless *Hyprocrisy* exist! They, who thus cried out against Mr. G. and his friends, who and what were they? Those very men had urged Mrs. Lydia M. Child, years before, to address a public meeting. Those very men, who now led off on this woman-question, had drawn up and signed papers commissioning Sarah and Angelina Grimké as public agents and lecturers – (two young women of South Carolina, whose father had been a slaveholder, and Sarah G. herself had for several years owned a female slave, as I heard her state). These two women preferred not to become agents of any society, but chose to speak entirely on their own account & responsibility, and did so, addressing many hundreds of audiences all over the Free States. This does not alter, or impair the pertinency of the fact, that their commission as public agents & lecturers was drawn up & signed & offered them by men – the very men who, a few years after, to effect a cowardly & malignant purpose, professed the deepest horror of women acting in public, and who actually, in 1840, seceded from the American Anti Slavery Society, *for no other reason* than that a woman – Abby Kelly[2] – was put upon a committee for recommending Business to the society at its annual Meeting. I was present at that meeting, held in New York, and was a witness to all these proceedings. The woman question is no longer used as a handle. The endeavour to make it a weapon against true anti-slavery has wholly failed, and the blow has recoiled on themselves – returned to plague the inventors. It was found to work so badly for them, that one of the men who had tried to use it against Mr. G. & his friends afterwards called it the "confounded woman-question," and wished it might be forgotten. This was Elizur Wright Jr.,[3] who is now in England – once a fiery abolitionist, and a very able writer – now engaged

---

2. Abby Kelly Foster (1811-1887) was one of the most militant of the women abolitionists, and one of the few to lecture publicly on the subject. In 1845 she married Stephen Foster, another abolitionist, and though both continued to work for the anti-slavery cause, increasingly their attention was turned to the campaign for women's rights.

3. Elizur Wright (1805-1885) during the 1830's acted as Corresponding Secretary of the A.A.S.S., edited the *Massachusetts Abolitionist*, and wrote several pamphlets on slavery. His real interest, however, lay in his work for the development of life insurance.

in selling a translation of Fontaine's Fables, made by himself, & published in a handsomely illustrated edition...

I have not touched upon the *Political* divisions among the Abolitionists. It is maintained by Mr. Garrison and others, – I am inclined to believe they are wholly in the right – that the "Liberty Party" is employed mostly as a cover for those who dare not, or will not, carry their Anti-slavery into their Churches and *religious* bodies. Such, so far as I know the individuals of the Liberty party, is very generally true. They will submit to the greatest indifference to the Anti-Slavery cause in their *Minister*, their *Church*, their denomination, while they demanded that the individual for whom they *vote*, for a secular office, shall belong to *their party;* let him be never so good an Abolitionist, they will not give him their vote, if he is the candidate either of the Whig or Democratic party. – They rely too on political power, and comparatively neglect *moral* – the great instrument by which truth & duty are to be brought home to the slave-holder, and cause him to "undo the heavy burdens & let the oppressed go free." They spend their time & strength in political broils & squabbles, & electioneering, and it is getting to be more & more believed, of the *leaders* of the Liberty Party, that while they talk so loudly of the Slave's good, they mean their own – i.e. their political advancement...

Your friend and – shall I not say – brother,

Samuel May

P.S. You might naturally inquire if there is no prospect of *healing* the differences & dissensions existing among Abolitionists. There is, I fear, little reason to hope that men who have espoused the Anti-Slavery Cause for any but the highest motives who are not willing to lay upon its altar their reputation, their fair fame among men, will ever come to agree in their views, & modes of action with such men as W.L. Garrison, N.P. Rogers, Edmund Quincy, Wendell Phillips, and such women as Abby Kelley, who have made these sacrifices. No! I must say I see no prospect of a cessation of existing differences among those who *are called* Anti-Slavery. Those who *are really such* will not differ so far, as to be hostile to each other. Meantime, as I have already said, these differences are not doing so much harm as at a distance may appear. The good work is advancing – is greatly prospering. There can be no doubt of it.

MS.B.1.6. vol. 2 1844-1849 The May Papers [169]
No. 3 J.B. Estlin[1] *to Samuel May*

Bristol, October 29th, 1844.

My dear Sir,

In a box of *wonderful contents* (which have been exhibited at my

---

1. John Bishop Estlin (1786-1855), a prominent ophthalmic surgeon of Bristol, was a member of the Unitarian circle of that town, and like many of them keenly interested in social reforms. His active interest in slavery began in 1843 with the visit of Samuel May and thereafter he tended more and more to become the leader of the Garrison party in England. His daughter, Mary Estlin, became one of the most active of the British Garrisonites. She maintained a steady correspondence with many Americans, especially Mrs. Chapman, the Weston Sisters, and Sarah Pugh of Philadelphia, she visited America in 1867.

house previously to their transmission to Boston) I have put 12 little papers, each containing a portion, (6 of them a *lock,)* of the hair of the late *Rammohan Roy*[2] ....

That this hair actually was that of the great Hindoo Reformer, you need feel no doubt. I attended him thro' his lamented & fatal illness, cut off some of his hair which has never been out of my possession excepting while in the hands of the lady who kindly tied it up into little parcels....

We shall be much interested, and *you* may be much benefitted on another occasion, by our knowing how the articles we send, sell, & what are the most valuable? Any accounts of the Fair that may be published after, will be very acceptable; and we can dispense them so as to produce considerable interest when there is to be another fair – *"Bazaar,"* we should call it....

We laymen do not think our ministerial *papas* have been very civilly treated as to the notice of their Anti-Slavery Address. I suppose it was unpalatable food, & not easy of digestion? My daughter joins me in kind remembrance to yourself & brother – I am

Dr Sir Yours truly

J B Estlin.

MS.B.1.6. vol. 2 The May Papers [170]
No. 5 Samuel May to J.B. Estlin

Leicester, Massachusetts, Decr 30, 1844

My dear Sir,

... The little packets of the hair of Rammohun Roy, I cannot doubt, will find ready purchasers. Some there are, I know, and doubtless many whom I do not know, who would rejoice to possess one of these undoubted relics of a most extraordinary man. I was in Boston last week, and visited the Anti Slavery Fair or Bazaar....I was much pleased with the very neat manner in which the packets of hair were done up....

The fair opened on Tuesday Dec. 24 at Amory Hall, a spacious & handsome apartment in the principal street of the city. It was well stocked with beautiful and valuable articles, among which the contributions from England, Scotland, & Ireland were as they always have been, conspicuous. Every visitor makes early enquiry for the tables where these contributions are to be found. I saw very many pretty & beautiful things from Bristol, but could not find *all* that came from there; probably some had been disposed

---

2. Rajah Rammohun Roy was a very learned, high caste Brahmin, deeply interested in the study of comparative religion. Although he was claimed by his English friends to have become a Christian, he refused baptism in order not to lose caste. In the 1830's he visited Britain and was closely associated with many leading Unitarians, with whose religious views he had great sympathy. He died on a visit to some of these friends in Bristol, and was attended during his illness by Dr. Estlin; see Mary Carpenter, *The Last Days in England of the Rajah Rammohun Roy*, London, 1886.

of before I arrived. Miss Carpenter's[1] sketches of Rhine scenery were very beautiful & very much admired....

I do not wonder that you and others feel that the British Unitarian Ministers who sent us the Antislavery address have not been "very civilly treated". This however must be *entirely laid* at the door of the committee who were charged with the execution of our purpose to send a *reply*. Our ministers generally, I know, wished to have the reply sent promptly....

Please offer my sincere regards to Miss Estlin, and to all my Bristol friends. My brother is very well – I saw him last week.

Believe me, with sincere respect. Yours Sam.[l] May

MS.A.9.2. vol. 20 The Weston Papers [171]
No. 60 Elizabeth Pease to ?

Bridge of Allan.
Near Stirling

Dear Friend

... I hope our Irish friends have been on the alert to get you some of O'Connell ['s autographs] while he was in prison – the nation is now deeply stirred by his unexpected liberation – every lover of freedom or justice must rejoice at this triumph over the unfairness by which the proceedings in his case were marked – & feel thankful at the triumphant vindication of Lord Denman of the rights of trial by jury – if such a base perversion of it had been suffered to pass this right had been virtually nullified. How wonderfully the evil designs of the Tories for the last year or two have been turned to good. O'Connell has walked out of prison a far greater man (*great* as he was before) than he went in – his unjust incarceration for three months has won many a heart to his side which stood aloof before & the cause of repeal [or ?] full & impartial justice has recd a mighty impulse – and the base attempt of Sir Jas. Graham last year to place education in the hands of the clergy has united all Dissenters in a far more close Union than they ever were before....

With high regards, I remain affec.[ly] thy
friend Eliz[th] Pease

---

1. Mary Carpenter (1807-1877), philanthropist and eldest daughter of the Rev. Lant Carpenter, the famous Unitarian divine, did much work for education of the poor. She was interested also in the social problems of India which she visited.

1. The Home Secretary, Sir James Graham, had tried to conciliate Catholic opinion in Ireland by increasing the grant to Maynooth College, and by setting up colleges, open to Catholics, in the North, West and South of Ireland. These actions, however, provoked strong opposition from Catholics and Protestants alike, – Gladstone resigning from the Cabinet over the issue of the Maynooth grant.

No. 148 George Thompson to ?

n.d. fragment

...I have no expectation that the monopolists of this country will be able to maintain their ground. In all probability the discriminating Sugar duties will be swept away during the next session of parliament, & then, if there be any sincerity in the professions of the Anti Slavery Committee, they will in good earnest do that which they have hitherto so strongly & unaccountably neglected & refused to do. Your election being now over, I earnestly wish you would direct your attention, particularly, to the question which is always uppermost in my mind; namely that of affecting slavery in your own and other countries by means of the development of the riches of the soil of India. I will do all I can to second your efforts in this country....

You will be glad to see the Glasgow Society has taken notice of the conduct of the Free Church of Scotland and its deputation, in the matter of bringing the money of Slaveholders into the Treasury of the Protesting Church.[1] At the meeting recently held our noble hearted friend H.C. Wright made a speech in every way admirable. I am curious to know what the Presbyterian Seceders will say to it, and how they will hereafter justify their proceedings when they see what is going on among various denominations of Christians including their own in the United States. To me it appears they are greatly behind many of their own party on your side and I hope that if they do not relinquish their ill-gotten gains, and bring forth the fruits of a sound repentance, they will be dealt with as they merit by all the churches of America who have dissolved their ecclesiastical connection with Slaveholding professors.

The free-traders are rejoicing over the humiliation of Henry Clay, and are sounding the praises of the Democratic party for their defeat of the champion of Protection.[2] At a great meeting of 5000 persons held last evening/Dec. 11 [?] at Covent Garden Theatre, the Hon. C.P., Villiers and Mr. Cobden referred to your recent election in terms of high congratulation. I think they overrate the zeal of the Polk party in the cause of free trade, and do not look sufficiently close at the views entertained by that large class of politicians on other questions. Will not the Clay party be of more service in the opposition than they were likely to be of in power? – I mean with reference to the [rejection?] of Texas and kindred questions. and will they not be likely to come near to the views of the abolitionists, who if they do not already, are likely soon to hold the balance of power?

The principal part of my time is occupied in attending to Indian matters. In the great field of Indian improvement there are, alas! but few labourers, and I consider myself one, a very humble pioneer in the cause. The day will come I trust when the claims of from 150 to 200 millions of the

---

1. This is a reference to the collection made by the newly formed Free Church of Scotland among the Presbyterian Churches of the Southern States of America. British anti-slavery societies, led by American abolitionists, attacked this action strongly, and throughout 1845 and 1846 the controversy raged in Scotland.
2. Henry Clay, the Whig candidate in the Presidential election of 1844, had just lost the election to the Democratic nominee, James Polk.

human race who are *our* fellow subjects will find audience in Great Britain. What I do is to hasten the approach of that day.

Yours affectionately

Geo: Thompson

MS.A.1.1. vol. 4 1844-1853 Anti-Slavery Letters from Garrison [173]
No. 11 William Lloyd Garrison to R.D. Webb

Boston, March 1, 1845.

My beloved friend Webb:

... I have little doubt that Texas is now a member of the American confederacy. The next mail from Washington will unquestionably bring the last decisive action of the Senate on the subject, and that will be in favour of annexation. There is a bare possibility that the nefarious project may again be defeated; for the vote will be a very close one. But the prize is too great to be put in peril by the sturdiness of one or two opponents, and the will to be bribed to any extent that may be necessary. The history of this Texas movement, from its commencement to the present time, I verily believe has no parallels for villany and inhumanity, connected with the most despotic purposes. We have been betrayed by a party, making the highest pretensions to democracy. It is the shameless defection of the Northern portions of the Democratic party, that has given this bloody and atrocious triumph to the South. But the greediness of the Slave Power will not be satisfied with the annexation of Texas. Its settled purpose is to conquer all Mexico, and on its fertile plains to establish slavery and the slave trade.

Perhaps nothing has operated so powerfully on the public mind, in favor of annexation, as the hue-and-cry which has been so artfully raised against the alleged design of England to subjugate Texas to her own will and purpose, in order to cripple the commerce and manufacturers of the United States, and put in jeopardy our glorious "democratic institutions" – the most cherished of which is the institution of slavery! There is among us a great deal of fear and hatred of England; and it is only necessary for the leading political demagogues to make their appeals to this infernal disposition, and they can achieve whatever feat of scoundrelism they wish to perform. Unhappily, at this juncture, in connection with slavery, the hatred of the Irish population amongst us toward England is of a bitter and most implacable type, and it all goes in favor of the annexation of Texas, through motives of terror or revenge. It is a most deplorable circumstance that, religiously and politically, almost the entire body of Irishmen in this country are disposed to go with the accursed South for any and every purpose, and to any extent. The patriotic and Christian appeals which have been made to them by Daniel O'Connell and Father Matthew, and others of their countrymen at home, on this subject, have not had the slightest perceptible effect on their minds. They are a mighty obstacle, therefore, in the way of negro emancipation on our soil. Truly, they know not what they do....

Yours, with intense affection,

Wm. Lloyd Garrison.

MS.A.9.2. vol. 22 The Weston Papers [174]
No. 146 Anne Cropper[1] to Maria Weston Chapman

n.d.

My dear Mrs. Chapman

...We shall be deeply interested in hearing what is the determination of your government on the important question of the annexation of Texas to the Union – It was a [most?] striking providence which cut off in so awful a manner two of the warm abettors of that iniquitous measure[2].. The accounts of your annual fair is curious & amazing – I shall try if we can send you a few humble contributions to your splendid collection of useful & ornamental articles – Will you allow me again to assure you of the warm sympathy which is felt here in your great cause and of our deep sense of the difficulties which you have to encounter. May you be guided and supported in all your efforts and enabled to unite gentleness, & wisdom; meekness & firmness –

Believe me yours with much esteem and cordial sympathy

Anne Cropper.

MS.A.9.2. vol. 21 The Weston Papers [175]
No. 18 Mary Estlin to Maria Weston Chapman

Park Street March 31 1845

My dear Madam,

... We shall await with anxiety the intelligence of the effect produced in the North, by the final passing of the resolution respecting the Annexation of Texas. Perhaps it may bring to light new friends of Abolition who have hitherto kept aloof, & be the commencement of a more earnest struggle for freedom. At all events we may trust that it will eventually be overruled for good, tho' the immediate prospects are gloomy enough.

We were very glad to hear that the Bristol contributions sold well, & hope another year will not prove less successful.

Believe me, dear madam, with every kind wish for the principle you

---

1. Anne Cropper was probably the wife of John Cropper, James Cropper's eldest son.
2. Thomas Walker Gilmer and A.P. Upshur, two of the members of Tyler's Cabinet, were killed whilst visiting the battleship Princeton, when a gun on board exploded. Both were ardent advocates of the annexation of Texas, and were in negotiation with the leaders of the Texan Republic when they met their death.

are labouring so assiduously to diffuse, & for abundant success to attend your efforts

Yours sincerely

Mary A. Estlin

Mrs. Chapman. Boston.

MS.A.9.2. vol. 21 1845 The Weston Papers [176]
No. 39 Richard Allen to Maria Weston Chapman

Dublin 29th of 7th mo. 1845

My dear Friend

... We seem here, i.e. in Dublin, to be in a profound calm – O'Connell is somewhere, but at least so far as I hear, not agitating vigorously. Still it is evident that "Repeal" is dear to the people's hearts; indeed I believe it grows clearer & clearer, though I think much of what they report is perfectly [Eutopian?] – Some countries however present a serious exception to the general calm – for instance Leitrim & Cavan are in a sad state of tumult, arising mainly from the oppressively high price of land; I fear the fault lies mainly at the rich man's door – We have also had bad work in some parts of Ulster from the revival of the odious party procession displays – in Armagh particularly some lives have been lost, and of course a grievous amount of hatred & ill will engendered amongst the contending parties....

With kind regards to all our friends

Sincerely & respectfully thine

R. Allen.

MS.A.9.2. vol. 21 The Weston Papers [177]
No. 50 George Thompson to Richard [Webb?]

5 Whiteheads Grove, Chelsea;
London August 12, 1845.

My dear Richard

Your letter and its enclosure have just reached me in our new dwelling. Be it known to you that we have left Golders Square, and are now regularly settled in a pleasant detached house near the Thames, with a good sized Garden, and some well laden Pear trees. I can reach my office from hence, in half an hour, (walking) and by the Omnibusses which pass our door, in about 50 minutes. We are all much the better for our out of doors gambols, and shew by our doings at the table, the effects of spade husbandry and horticulture upon our appetites. The Advocates shall be sent you, now and in future. Be assured, I can appreciate the zeal and sympathy of the few good men and true in Dublin, and trust, ever to shew by my public conduct, that I esteem the approbation of such men as yourself, more highly than the patronage & smiles of the powers that be. I have just sent in a requisition to the Court of Directors for a Special General Court of Proprietors, that I may proceed with my charges against Colonel Orans and the Bombay authorities for the dethronement of the Raja. When the debate takes place, you shall have a quantity of the Advocates containing the proceedings. I have been joined in calling this special Court by Sir C. Forbes, Sir Harford Jones Bridges, J W Hume, John Sullivan, General Briggs, & several Barristers. Rungor Bapogee has qualified as a Proprietor, and will second my motion – and speak – in Hindostanee. My legal view of the dethronement of the Raja, which you will find started at the latter end of my late speech at the India House, has been pronounced quite sound, and some wealthy parties here have determined to make it the ground of an appeal, by Petition through the Queen, to the Privy Council. I have another motion on the same subject for the usual Quarterly court on the 24th of next month. I shall not be surprised, if the unjust judges at the India House, wearied at length by my continual [coming?], do something, for the purpose of getting rid of me. They have already sent out orders to India to alleviate the condition of the Raja and his dependants. This is cause of thankfulness, as, while we are working for him, the circumstances of his exile will be more tolerable, and any symptom of relaxation on the part of the Company will give him heart, and awaken such hopes of an ultimate triumph. We recently had a five hour's debate in Parliament on the Case. Hume, Bowring Williams, [?] and Sir Edward Colebrook acquitted themselves well in behalf of the Raja; but the sons of Zeruish were too strong for us. The Government had determined to resist enquiry, and so put up the two Secretaries of the Board of Control (Tennent & Baring) to reply. Hogg, one of our directors (a man whose name is a libel on the whole race of [printers?]) made a wicked speech. I would have given 6 months of my life for an hour to reply to him. I shall however pay him off in our own House. Say to Mrs. Chapman that she shall have a good contribution to the next fair. I have already a good many things prepared, and shall go on accumulating until it is time to despatch the cargo to Boston. All points shall be attended to. I have made all right at the League office, in reference to the sending of a good collection of their pamphlets, which Wendell Phillips said would sell. I regret with you the coming of Remond. He did not shew, when here before, that disinterestedness which we look for in an apostle of the American anti-slavery cause. His number-one-ishness way, as I believe you know, the cause of some little sparring & differences between us; and if he be still the same sort of man, I shall feel but little desire to aid him. Will the Broad Street folks look at the trio, think you? Can this James Buffum[1] make speeches? Do you mean to have them, and keep them, in Ireland? Will you be reprinting the adventures of Douglass?[2] How can a man get H C Wright's last book about Grafenburg

---

1. James Needham Buffum (1807-1887), one of Garrison's Massachusetts' supporters, toured Britain with Douglass during 1845 and 1846.

2. Frederick Douglass (1818-1895) probably the most famous Negro abolitionist, was born a slave in Maryland, escaped, and after some years, became an agent of the Massachusetts Anti-Slavery Society. He wrote his *Narrative of the Life of Frederick Douglass* shortly before coming to Britain, where both he and his book enjoyed great popularity. On his return to America, he began to edit his own paper – the *North Star*, and his break with the Garrison party, first seen during his British visit, became irrevocable. By his writings and speeches, however, he established himself as the

&c &c? I begin to think I shall never see this "kiss for a blow", man; His "*concern*" in the matter of the Free Church, will surely never have an end. Cunningham Candlish & Chalmers[3] must look on him as their thorn in the *spirit.* He did some injury to his cause, by his recent attack upon Wardlaw and others, in a letter to Boston. It was undeserved, and unmitigatedly *bad.* I saw its effect, in the entire absence of a certain party from the late meeting. It is a pity he should do that, which all just and liberal men must condemn. I will add to this the address of the Hilditches when I get to my office.

If I can get away from London after the debates at the India House, I shall have a run to Scotland & Belfast; and if I go to the latter place, I shall see Dublin and you. If I come you must give me the opportunity of having a public palaver about India. I have so little to do now, in the way of public speaking, that there is some little danger of my oratorical powers resting. I must work them a little while away....

With sincere affection,

Yours truly

Geo Thompson

MS.A.9.2. vol. 21 1845 The Weston Papers [178]
No. 58 George Thompson to Maria Weston Chapman

6 Waterloo Place, Pall Mall,
London, October 2 1845

Beloved Friend,

...Do you know that I am getting very restless to see the United States again? I know not why but I am haunted by a strange longing to be among you. If I were not circumstanced as I am I should regard these feelings as a "call", and should soon pack up my carpet bag and be with you. I am more than half an American. My soul cleaves fondly and faithfully to those who have waged the abolition war; and though I write little, I muse much upon all that is going on upon your continent and every day regret the ties that bind me to the spot in which I live. Do not write to me to vindicate myself from any suspicions cast upon my fidelity or consistency by correspondents here or there. As regards the conduct of the [Anti-Corn Law] League, I have always expressed my entire disapprobation of the correspondence with

---

spokesman of his race, and he was to enjoy considerable influence in promoting the cause of the Negro.

3. Dr. William Cunningham (1805-1861), Thomas Chalmers (1780-1847) and Dr. Robert Smith Candlish (1806-1873) were all prominent Scottish ministers and leaders of the Free Church movement, which in 1842 had broken away from the Established Church of Scotland. The leaders of this movement had issued an appeal to American Presbyterian churches for funds, and the Boston abolitionists had protested strongly against their acceptance of money from Southern Churches. Wright, Douglass and later Garrison, led a vigorous campaign to try to force the Free Church to "send back the money."

Calhoun and McDuffie.[1] It was the act of two or three in the Council of Manchester. I had nothing to do with it....The parties who sent presents to the South, are I believe sorry for what they have done. They see their error, but are not greatly chargeable with any intention to fraternize with slaveholders, as such. It was at most an unguarded act, but we cannot expect men who, have never undergone our baptism, to be in all respects[like ourselves. They have at all events encouraged me, times and often, to express my opinions fully upon the subject of slavery on their platforms, & I have followed Cobden, after he has been eulogizing Southern free-traders, with the strongest phillipics against them as slaveholders...

While you are holding your Bazaar I shall be busy prosecuting the prime agent in the dethronement of the Raja of Sattara. I have already indicted him and shall bring forward my proofs at a General Court at the latter end of December. I have got a good many little things ready for you and will ere long despatch them. – I have scrawled this letter amidst incessant interruptions and cannot tell at this stage what I have written. Pardon all its imperfections. Always remember that I am alone in my business and am fighting a battle single-handed with the most powerful monopoly in England.
Ever your own friend.
Geo. Thompson.

MS.A.9.2. vol. 21 1845 The Weston Papers [179]
No. 76 Le Wood [bury?] to Maria Weston Chapman

Manchester Oct[r] 23rd 1845

Mrs. M. W. Chapman

Dear Madam,

Your favour of the 7th inst. was duly received and in reply to your friendly note I would say that on the receipt of yours I conversed with some few individuals here friendly to the cause, and from what I can learn from them I feel it to be somewhat doubtful whether much or anything of consequence can be done here the present season. There are various [reasons?] for this [among?] which is the manny [sic] local calls that have been made on us for the past summer for benevolent objects in our town. This of itself I am fully aware would furnish but a sorry excuse when compared with the claims of the *poor slave.* But on my own behalf I should in candour say that from various (& to me) heavy losses in my business during that trying time for persons engaged in business 1837 to 43. I feel (and I flatter myself it is an honourable feeling) that I must endeavour to be *just* even if it be at the expense and mortification of a disposition to be generous & benevolent. In the effort made here the last season, which amounted to a comparatively small sum to be sure, one half the amount was borne by one individual. I mention this merely to

---

1. Although most of the leaders of the Anti-Corn Law League were admirers of American political institutions and disliked slavery on principle, their sympathies were inevitably drawn to those American Southern leaders who were loud in their attacks on the tariffs which Northern politicians had succeeded in imposing.

show how difficult it is to induce many persons to act in this most righteous cause as they should. But perhaps we may do better than my fears lead me to anticipate. I shall certainly try to do something for that in which you and your self sacrificing friends do so much.

I am yours truly

for right & justice

Le Wood [bury?]

MS.A.9.2. vol. 21 1845 The Weston Papers [180]
Nos. 87-88 John Estlin to [R.D. Webb?]

Bristol, Novr 5th 1845.
(47 Park Street)

Dear Sir,

... No one is more strongly convinced than I am that the American clergy generally do not faithfully discharge their duty in not uttering denunciations of the evils of slavery. Some of them I believe are withheld from coming more forward by the violence of the Abolition Societies – I had much conversation on these points with Rev. Mr. Simmons, formerly of Mobile, who ran great risks there for his A.S. views; but he would not join in any of the Societies – I see his name to the Unit^{n} Protest.

I cannot doubt a ready sale for Douglass's Narrative if copies were sent hither. There is a strong anti-slavery feeling here when it can be made [to] show itself. When N. Keep was here raising money for the Oberlin Institute, 500 guineas were subscribed in Bristol.

Is it possible that Douglass can pay his expenses in England by the sale of his book? I doubt not he has been well advised in not making his tour a money getting one; but I cannot see any good reason, why *after* any of his public lectures, when people's hearts are opened, a collection should not be made at the doors from those who would like to give something either for his private expenses, or for the cause? A room for lecturing in, advert &c must, in some places occasion expenses. I hope F. Douglass will come to Bristol. I have already prepared some of your society the Thomases & Frys to feel an interest in him.

I ought to apologise for addressing you so freely & so amply – the subject however must be my excuse

Yours faithfully

J.B. Estlin

Since writing the enclosed I have had a long interview with a member of the Soc^{y} of Friends, who I found rather prejudiced against the Am^{r} abolition Soc^{y}; from their violence, I believe I satisfied this friend (a very intelligent lady) that we had nothing to do with the specific plans, & peculiar notions of the American A.S. Societies; that they were labouring conscientiously to remedy a dreadful evil, and that our sympathy & encouragement were due to the cause in which they were engaged – She thanked me for having erased the objectionable part in Douglass's

Life, which she could not otherwise have put into the hands of her young people. We have heard that the Friends in Dublin had been scandalized by the violent denunciations uttered by F. Douglass in their meeting House.

I have been invited to meet Joseph Sturge & Mr. [Scoble?] on Saturday next at a party of gentlemen to talk over A.S. affairs, but I know not if my health will allow of my going. If the object of Messrs. S. & S. in coming to Bristol be to favour the ministerial measure of protective duties on sugar, they will not find many supporters here.

J.B.E.

MS.A.1.2. vol. 15 1845 Anti-Slavery Letters to Garrison:on [181]
No. 76 Frederick Douglass to R.D. Webb

Limerick 10th Nov. 1845.

Dear Friend

... I now think my best plan will be to proceed immediately to Scotland from this – ... As to accompanying Friend Wright, I think it unwise to do so. I by no means agree with him as to the importance of his discussing in this country the disunion question, and I think our difference in this matter would prevent that harmony necessary to success. Beside our Friend Wright has created against himself prejudices which I as an abolitionist do not feel myself called upon to withstand. My mission to this land is purely an Anti-Slavery one, and although there are other good causes which need to be advocated – I think that my duty calls me strictly to the question of slavery. I am qualified for this if I am for anything, and it would be idle for me to attempt becoming anything else at least under present circumstances. Friend Wright is identified with doctrines for which I do not wish to seem responsible. He is truly reformer in general; I only claim to be a man of one idea. I should nevertheless be delighted to see him and talk the matter over with him.

Please remember me to Mrs. Webb.

Truly
Yours

F. Douglass.

MS.A.9.2. vol. 21 1845 The Weston Papers [182]
No. 95 J.B. Estlin to R.D. Webb

Bristol, November 13th 1845

My dear Sir

... This brings me to the subject of F. Douglass's visiting Bristol... I think his being here would do much good in making zealous abolitionists. Thorough *Garrisonian* abolitionism is at a discount here. The quakers have long *fancied* they knew something of the subject, and the *Liberty* Party was the true one – Joseph Sturge's visit hither has strengthened this notion – He told me last Saturday that G's was a very small party, that the finest minds among the Abl's in the U.S. ranged themselves under the "Liberty" banner. Mr. Scoble said the same at a large public meeting on Monday. I heard a quaker describing to Mr. S. the bad character of the "Liberator"....

I suspect the great object of Messrs. Sturge & Scoble in coming to Bristol to obtain a Resolution at a public meeting condemnatory of the govt. plan of immigration in the W. Indies. This was obtained at the meeting on Monday, but I have much doubt if the subject were generally comprehended, and then much was said, and the audience much interested in relation to Amer^{n} slavery.

This agitation on the subject of immigration *may* be one of benevolence, but there is nothing *anti-slavery* in it. I wish the B.F.A.S. Soc^{y} would concentrate their energies more upon American slavery until the negros there are as well off as those in the W. Indies. An A.S. feeling is now much awakened here, and if people do not get frightened & disgusted by violent language, & extravagant propositions, I think it will pursue a very desirable course. If Douglass comes hither, I hope he will not offend by his strong views – There is much force in your remark in the circular, that very measured language ought not to be expected from a man who has drunk of the cup of slavery.

Tho' there are rich and generous people in Bristol, I doubt if they would give much towards anti-slavery purposes, as there is no definite plan of proceeding proposed for the abolition of American slavery. I believe hardly any one would give a farthing if they thought any Abolition Soc^{y} advocated as a matter of justice, wisdom, or policy, immediate, unconditional, unrequited emancipation.

I believe I mentioned to you in my last letter, that when Mr. Keep was collecting for Oberlin Institute, he raised in Bristol 500 Guineas. Here was a definite object. What I tell people whom I wish to interest in the subject & to assist in the Fair is, that the great object of the Mass. Anti Slav^{y} Soc^{y} and for which they want funds is, to *awaken the national conscience to the sin & horrors of slavery.*

Our box went off yesterday: it was a very large one, & contained between 6 & 700 separate articles for sale. It was no small labour, though to the Ladies of my family (my daughter & sister in law) a very interesting one, to collect exhibit and pack up these numerous articles – Some were very beautiful

And now my dear Sir, not doubting that you will excuse the freedom with which I have expressed my Anti Slavery opinions but fearing your estimate of my interest in the cause may be somewhat modified, I am,

yours very truly

J.B. Estlin.

MS.A.1.2. vol. 15 1845 Anti-Slavery Letters to Garrison [183]
No. 78-9 R.D. Webb to Maria Weston Chapman

Dublin 16th of November 1845

My dear Friend

... I have no doubt that Henry C. Wright is doing a great work in Scotland – The stirring up he is giving the Free Kirk is just the very thing to excite the Scotch to thought & action – he is forever hammering at "Drs. Chalmers, Cunningham and Candlish" and telling them to "Send back the money" Oh! how grandly he'll bother them. He is a real fine fellow. His heart is in his work....

Frederick Douglass goes on swimmingly in Limerick. He took huff at me while in Dublin for giving him one or two cautionary hints as to his demeanour (which I did much against my will). He is very proud and cant bear anything half so sweetly as praise and petting. I dont mean to give him any more advice – but I think he is foolish to resent it.

You will remark what Joseph Sturge and Scoble say of the Liberty Party and of ours. I think Sturge a well intentioned man, but bigotted and not open enough – and as to Scoble underground is his native place. I think it most likely F.D. will go to Birmingham & Bristol next. He dont incline to fraternise with H.C. Wright who is a far finer minded larger hearted man than he is. It seems to me that Douglass's range is not large and that he dont take half enough pains to extend its limits. Estlin you will see gives a fine account of the contributions from Bristol. Poor Dublin! I cant help blushing a little for our poverty & fewness.

Warm regards to all friends – Yours very truly

Rich[d] D Webb.

MS.A.9.2. vol. 20 1844 The Weston Papers [184]
No. 145 Isabel Jennings to Maria Weston Chapman

n.d.

Dear Mrs. Chapman

... By next year you will better estimate the service Frederick Douglass has done – There never was a person who made a greater sensation in Cork amongst all religious bodies – the Methodists are still (though he is now gone three weeks) as angry about his statements as they were during his stay here.... he has gained friends everywhere he has been – he is indeed a wonderful man – During the three months he spent with us we could find no fault in him – he seems worthy of all the praise of Garrison and Wendell Phillips – He is the first intelligent *slave* who has ever visited Cork and it is only natural that he should excite more sympathy than any of the others – We think we have got contributions from persons belonging to the Church (of England) who never could have been influenced except by a person who had himself suffered – we had no means of approaching them and the clergymen are silent. They have got our old anti-slavery papers and are determined to understand the subject –

and to all who tell them, – "indeed the clergymen are all against slavery", they say, "Mr. Douglass said so and so – his authority is given – and who can know better than he? ...

As yet we cannot judge what sort of Box we shall send this time but we have some fears – Glasgow and Bristol and at some distance we may mention – Dublin – have done well – The two former have put us to the blush – Ireland is certainly not now in a condition to do much – but it is in an improving state. The potato disease appears to have been [?] by the frost – With respect & esteem I shall conclude this long letter – I have often thought myself inexcusable for sending that *very* long one – although you kindly thank me. I feel remorseful I cannot write clearly your affectionate friend

Isabel Jennings.

MS.A.9.2. vol. 20 1844 The Weston Papers [185]
No. 153 Jane Wigham to Maria Weston Chapman

Edinburgh 11th month 24th 1845

My dear Friend

I shall not write much to encroach upon thy time at this busy period – but believe that I forgot when writing before to thank thee for thy letter & the "Liberty Bell" which arose from the hurry in sending off the box sooner than expected. Permit me then briefly to do so now and to say that the others were all forwarded as addressed. Thou wilt receive with this a letter from George Combe[1] which may be published if thought suitable – and two Books as a Contribution from him. There is a parcel from him for Dr. Howe of Boston.

There is an autograph of Joseph John Gurney's and also his wife's – written when they were on a visit at our house on purpose to send to Boston it had been too carefully laid aside till the very last or it would have been put up differently – I know not what value it will be of with you – but it is of much with us.

Having requested contributors to price their own things some of them have done so – and in some instances as we think too high – but [I] leave you to alter as you think proper –

We hope to have Frederick Douglass in Scotland shortly – & H.C. Wright in Edinburgh in a few days – If these two can arrange to have some public meetings together a little fresh interest may be kindled. At all events – we shall immediately begin to agitate for contributions for the 13th Fair.

With sincere regard

Thy assured friend

Jane Wigham.

---

1. George Combe (1788-1858) was a famous Scottish phrenologist whose work was influential on both sides of the Atlantic.

MS.A.9.2. vol. 21 1845 The Weston Papers [186]
No. 122 Mary Welsh to Maria Weston Chapman

7 Monpelier
Edinburgh Decr 1st 1845

My Dear Mrs. Chapman

My last note to you was a hurriedly written one, I thought the mail would be off before it would be possible for me to lift a pen. I hope the boxes sent at that time would reach you safely and that the contents of them will meet a ready sale. I have now the pleasure to inform you that another box is on its way from us, containing articles which were not ready at the former opportunity. The enclosed is a list of its contents with the prices, but we would just say as formerly that you must just make the prices what you think fit, as you are best judge in that matter. There is in this box a very handsome silk patched table cover, which a very excellent young woman of my acquaintance who resides in this neighbourhood has worked for us, the labour in it is immense, I can hardly conceive of the patience necessary for such a piece of work, but she is a devoted friend to the cause of suffering humanity & I believe is just commencing another for next year.... We have tried this year to be guided as nearly as possible by your advice with respect to the kind of article, but in spite of all we can exhort, contributors will just give us what pleases them best, and what they feel most convenient to do.... Our influence here is steadily advancing & it is to us a source of unspeakable pleasure thus to aid the cause of the oppressed. The annexation of Texas is a grievous affair & calls for renewed & increased effort on our part.

Henry C. Wright was here last week & we expect him again tomorrow, he is giving the Free Church no rest, but it seems to do them little good, for their leading men have gained so much influence over the people that they may do anything they choose be it good or bad the people will bear it. I am sick of this world's religion. [Ever ?] yours in the cause of the oppressed. Mary Welsh.

MS.B.1.6. vol. 3 1845-1849 The May Papers [187]
No. 7 Samuel May to Mary Carpenter

Leicester, Massachusetts, Decr. 29, '45

Dear Miss Carpenter.

... I am much interested in what you say of the social improvement of the English working classes. I have intended, & would like to publish extracts from your letters, *without your name*, if you would have no objection. Everything Everything of this sort is valuable here, in addition to its general interest, because it helps to neutralize the slanders of many of our presses against those English, Scotch & Irish friends who help the American Anti-Slavery efforts, These persons are sneeringly told to look after, and relieve their suffering & wronged countrymen at home – as if they did not do this; as if they were not the foremost in measures of benevolence at home. It is a miserably superficial idea which supposes that a heart which feels deeply & truly for human wrongs & sufferings in other lands, can have no benevolence to spare for home claims.... It is indeed very true that many profess a great concern for heathen lands, who manifest none for their brethren at home. It is, I suppose, only too much of this spurious benevolence everywhere. It is the last place to look for it, however, among those who are labouring and praying against multitudinous discouragements & obstacles, on behalf of an unpopular cause, or one from which they cannot by any possibility reap any other benefit than the consciousnes of sincere purposes & honest efforts for the cause of humanity, of truth, of freedom, and of the Gospel. I have no fear that our faithful British and Irish friends will be moved, for an instant, by this sort of heartless & vulgar talk. But everything that goes to silence it here, or show its utter falsity, is valuable to us.

And now I must thank you all for my part of the pleasure derived from your most valuable & acceptable box of contributions for the Annual antislavery Fair. I went to Boston last week, partly for the sake of attending the Fair, — or the *Bazaar*, as I see they have begun to call it. It opened on Tuesday last (Dec. 23^{d}) in *Faneuil Hall*, and is to continue till after New Year's day. You know I suppose that Faneuil Hall is an interesting spot, not to Bostonians only, but to the whole country, from its connexion with our revolutionary history, it being the place where the earliest and most stirring appeals were made on behalf of *Liberty*. It is enlisted now in *a far nobler cause*. This I believe, & avow freely. The cause is as much nobler & worthier, as the sufferings, the wrongs, the outrages, inflicted on our slave-brethren are greater than those which the 13 American Colonies endured from Gt. Britain; and in proportion to the greater dishonour, from playing the tyrant, which falls on those who profess republicanism, & to believe that "all men are created by God free and equal," than on those who make no such professions.... Beyond all controversy, it is the English, Scotch, & Irish donations to the Fair which gives it its greatest pecuaniry value, and much perhaps most of its eclat. At the close of the second day, $ 1500 had been received, indicating a larger sum total at the close than ever before.... With sincere respects to yourself & sister, & brotherly remembrance to your brothers Russell & Philip

I remain, Yours,

Samuel May.

MS.B.1.6. vol. 2 The May Papers [188]
No. 10 Samuel May to J.B. Estlin

Leicester, Massachusetts, Decr 29
1845

To J.B. Estlin Esqr

Dear Sir,

... Your country & ours seem to have been, and yet to be, in very critical positions towards each other, about *Oregon*. A good deal of alarm has actually been felt that there would be *war*. Whether I am apathetic, or what, I cannot say; but I have never been apprehensive of a war between the U.S. and

England. I cannot make it seem any other than a most foolish & almost impossible thing. I know we have utterly unscrupulous men at the nominal head of our national affairs. Would to God New England was forever separated from all connexion with them! With the slave holding states I mean. If we do not cut asunder the tie which binds us, Slavery will be the millstone which will drag us to destruction. To return; I do not anticipate a war. I believe there is too much good sense and right feeling in both countries to permit it. Though I would not trust to what right feeling on the subject there is, in this country, to avert it. But it is well known that the Slaveholding Power dreads a war, and especially with England. It would be a signal for a general Slave insurrection – and they know it; and they will not venture a war, that I regard as certain; and if *they* do not venture, it will not be; for they now have everything completely their own way throughout the land. The talk of Mr. Polk about war &c is universally considered, by sensible men, as only *talk.* It is thought to be the very best way for a man to get popularity, and for *him* to secure re-election to the Presidency....

Hoping that you will soon recover your health and strength, I remain,

Respectfully
yours

Samuel May

MS.A.9.2. vol. 22 1846 The Weston Papers [189]
No. 14 Mary Ireland to Maria Weston Chapman

R[oyal] A[cademical] Institution
Belfast Jany 24th 1846

Dear Madam

An important public cause must plead the excuse of an individual like myself venturing to trespass on your precious time. An intense interest has been excited by the oratory of Frederick Douglass during his late visit to this town and in consequence a female AntiSlavery Society is about being formed just at present. All who have listened to D-- are warm in the cause of the slave many are earnest and energetic and if a fair development of these impulses were permitted I am convinced there is scarcely a lady in Belfast who would not be anxious to join in any means calculated to promote the enfranchisment of the deeply injured Africans. But alas those who usually take the lead in other good works, offended by uncompromising tone of Mr. Douglass in regard to the Free Church of Scotland, are either avowed enemies to the present movement or very hollow friends. Still the cause of the *Bondsman* no one dares to attack openly, but, insinuations, ridicule and every other means which human ingenuity can devise will be attempted in order to chill the warm tide of kindly sympathy and to paralyse further effort.

Thus situated could some decided effort be made to unite *the young especially* in some actual *work* a useful step would be gained.... A few lines from you mentioning a number of articles suitable for your Boston fair will I am certain induce many to make such a commencement as may prevent their being afterwards laughed out of their good intentions.

Besides even your *name* will do much. It was first whispered, but *dare not now be repeated,* that Frederick Douglass was an imposter – it has also been insinuated that C.L. Remond was a white man who had assumed the Ethiop tinge to suit a purpose but, every heart is filled with admiration of Mrs. Chapman. There is a feminine pride associated with the accounts we hear of your untiring efforts which make anyone here feel gratified in following any suggestion that may come from your pen. The Secretary of the New Society will I believe apply to you for advice as soon as there is a regular organisation but during the involuntary delay which must take place I have ventured to anticipate and the dread of our ranks being thinned by the counted influence mentioned above must plead my apology for this and for my request of a few lines in reply. Believe me dear madam with warmest sympathy in your noble efforts.

a very sincere friend to you and your sacred cause

Mary Ireland

Mrs. Chapman
Boston.

MS.A.1.2. vol. 16 1846 Anti-Slavery Letters to Garrison on [190]
No. 13 Frederick Douglass to Francis Jackson

Dundee, Scotland, 1846.
Royal Hotel 29th Jan

My Dear Friend –

... I am travelling in company with my good friend James N. Buffum – Our meetings here have been on the most soul cheering character. The present position of the Free Church in Scotland makes it important to expend as much labor here as possible. You know they sent delegates to the United States to raise money to build their churches and to pay their ministers – they succeeded in getting about four thousand pounds sterling. Well – our efforts are directed to making them disgorge their ill-gotten gains – return it to the slave holder, our rallying cry is "No union with Slave holders and send back the blood stained money" – Under these rallying cries – Old Scotland boils like a pot, I half think if the Free Church had for a moment supposed that her conduct would have been arraigned before the the [sic] Scottish people by such thorough Garrisonians as H.C. Wright James N Buffum and myself she would never have taken the money. She thought to get the gold and no body see her. It was a sad mistake. It would indeed be a grand Anti-Slavery triumph if we could get her to send back the money. It would break upon the confounded slave holders and their [?] like a clap from the sky. We shall continue to deal our [bolts ?] upon her – crying out disgorge – disgorge – your horrid horrid plunder and to this cry thus far the great mass of the people have cried amen....

gratefully yours –

Frederick Douglass.

MS.B.1.6. vol. 2 1844-1848 The May Papers [191]
No. 11 J.B. Estlin to Samuel May

Bristol, January 29th:- Feb. 1st 1846

My dear Mr. May

...With you, I have never been able to believe there *can* be a war between our countries. Whatever may be the notion of who is right or who wrong among those who have studied the Oregon Question, (I know nothing about it) I believe there is the very reverse of a *war feeling* thro' out this country. Our soldiers & sailors might not be displeased to exercise their vocation in *any* quarter of the world in the hopes of getting money or honour in their trade, but even with them I believe there is no war *feeling* against America. I do not believe your Govt. *intend* or *wish* war. In our public national councils a solemn feeling, & dignified conduct seem to prevail on the subject, as far as I can judge, very different from the state of the American Legislative Assemblies. Mr. J.Q. Adams warlike speech surprises me! Did he make it from hostility to the slaveholders, or to serve other party purposes? Is it not unworthy of him if *serious*, or has *senility* come over him?...

sincerely yours

J.B. Estlin.

MS.960 Webb-Quincy Correspondence 1843-1872 [192]
p.19 R.D. Webb to Edmund Quincy

Dublin, February 2 – 1846

My Dear Quincy

...I sent you yesterday a copy of Sir R. Peels speech at the opening of the session. It is considered one of his noblest efforts and is remarkable for its great approach to free trade. In a subsequent exposee of his plans he announces for a gradual abolition of the corn laws in 4 years – immediate removal of the duties from colonial produce – and from the United States maize – and a great reduction of many other duties on articles of food & manufacture. It is thought that when his measure comes to a division after being discussed this day week that he will have a majority in the Commons and that his bill will be thrown out in the Lords. If the Lords hold out against the people, there may be a new election and will certainly be a row of some kind or another. We are tiptoe with expectation – and very exciting times are at hand. There is talk of calling out the militia for no reason I can hear of except the difficulty of obtaining recruits which is greáter in Ireland, than in Scotland, and by no means easy in England, owing to the abundance of unemployment. Do you know I think both the Standard & Liberator are both a little flat just of late. I imagine the time is not propitious – you dont know what to be at. The Anti Texas admission turmoil came to nothing perceptible at a distance. Yet J.C. Fuller says that the abolitionists never had brighter prospects than now. I dont understand why. How shabbily the English deputation have behaved – about as bad as possible. I suppose Mrs. Chapman claps her hands to find how like they all are to what she supposed. Douglass & Buffum go on swimmingly as you will see by the papers they send. They have been in Glasgow, Perth, Aberdeen, & Dundee preaching no union with slaveholders & exhorting the Free Church to send back the bloodstained money. This I think the Free Church Clergy will be obliged to do, to quiet the outcry among the laity. A famine in Ireland is confidently predicted within the next two months by Sir R. Peel and those who have the best means of knowing how the supply of food for the country is circumstanced, but people such as myself, are not able to see the sign of such a catastrophe. If we have a famine for the poor it will surely be followed (as such famines always have been) by a pestilence among the rich & [poor?]. The Hutchinsons[1] succeeded much better in Liverpool, Manchester & neighbourhood than in Dublin. We hear they have gone on to London and I heartily wish them success, though I feel very doubtful that they will get on as well in London as in the provincial towns. Judson was in the habit of "getting sick" in a way that is not common with man at least in these countries. And this was sometimes the cause of heavy loss to them. Here is an extract from a letter that came from Douglass today. Scotland boils like a pot. Things are in a hopeful state. We have held four large meetings in the ancient town of Perth – and the agitation produced is almost without a parallel. We have held three meetings here (in Dundee) and are to hold another tonight. Our rallying cry is "no union with slaveholders" and to the Free Church "Send back the bloodstained money!" Will you tell me the opinion of the Class you are intimate with respecting the Oregon question, &c do you think that if things were amicably settled any way, that the [sic] popular leaders in America would not immediately look about for a new bone of contention to keep their dupes alive and stirring? We have heard nothing of the last Boston Fair – but by the next steamboat we may hope for a great budget of news. Douglass is in great feather. If his brain keeps steady amidst so much flattery, he will show more strength than I give him full credit for. I am printing a second 2000 of his Narrative which has sold remarkably well – and has brought him in certainly £150 nett. To this new edition he is going to add the letter that appeared in refutation in the Delaware Republican with a Reply of his own – clever but swaggering. If he go on as he has begun in Ireland, through Great Britain he will pocket 2500 dollars in twelve months time. Mr. Estlin of Bristol wishes gladly to know what we can do to afford practical aid to your efforts except in the small matter of procuring contributions to the Bazaar....

Hoping to hear from you or some of your faction before long

I remain yours affectionately

Richd D Webb.

---

1. The Hutchinsons were an American family of singers, noted for their singing at religious meetings.

MS.A.1.2. vol. 16 1846 Anti-Slavery Letters to Garrison [193]
No. 15 J.N. Buffum to Elizabeth Pease

Dundee Feb. 10 1846

Dear Friend

... We make slow headway – we are detained in the place where we go much longer than what we expected, owing to the increasing interest in the question of the Free Church and its taking the slave holders money. In all the places where we have gone we have succeeded in convincing those who have come out to hear us, that the Free Church has done an unchristian act, and that the only honourable course now left for her to pursue is to send it back, and disfellowship all slave holders – and then she will stand better than ever before she commit this sin. I am more and more in the faith that they will be obliged to do something to wipe off this stain – their churches are moving in the matter...Perth, Dundee, and Glasgow are boiling hot on the question....

Believe me affectionately thine

J. N. Buffum

MS.A.1.2. vol. 16 1846 Anti-Slavery Letters to Garrison [194]
No. 16 Frederick Douglass to R.D. Webb

Dundee 16th Feb. 1846

Dear Friend –

... The agitation goes nobly on – all this region is in a ferment. The very boys in the streets are singing out "*send back the money.*"...I meet many free Church people who are anxious to have the money sent back. I am certain that the people are right on this point – & if the money is not sent back it will be the fault of their leaders. We shall continue with unabated zeal to sound the alarm – the people shall be informed....

Yours truly

Frederick Douglass

MS.B.1.6. vol. 3 1845-1849 The May Papers [195]
No. 10 Frances Armstrong[1] *to Samuel May.*

Clifton Vale
February 16th
1846.

My dear Sir,

... After the general meeting held in Bristol on the subject of slavery last autumn of which, I suppose you saw the notice in the Inquirer, I was requested to join the Ladies Anti Slavery committee here, which since the emancipation in our own West Indian islands, had been rather a nominal than an active body – and as I have means of knowing the true

---

1. Frances Armstrong was the daughter of Rev. George Armstrong.

position of the American Abolitionists which the other ladies do not possess in the same degree, I thought I might possibly be some little use to the cause by doing so; – and I have endeavoured – both by explaining the views of your Society more fully, and putting in circulation among the ladies of the committee one or two books on American slavery, to increase their interest in your present position – There is some prejudice against "the Garrison party" – but, so far as I was able to collect at our last committee meeting, founded *very much* on *mistaken* notions of their views; – and I so far removed them – that I hope we shall have contributions for your Christmas fair this year from many who have fancied hitherto, – that they would do rather harm than good by strengthening the hands of that portion of your countrymen. –

The great object at which the London Central Society seem now to be aiming both as regards North and South America is the disuse of all slave grown produce; and specimens of cotton goods manufactured from the free grown raw material have been shewn, which do not seem at all inferior to that grown in your Southern States – It will take some time however to have a supply which would make any sensible difference in the cotton market and May is the earliest time at which we are led to expect there will be any at all in the shops – then we are requested to exert all our influence to bring it into general use – before I do so I should be very anxious to know what is your opinion on the subject; you must understand how such a plan would effect your slave states, far better than we can do; and when I see so much misapprehension of the whole question as regards America, as I do here, I can hardly adopt the scheme proposed without making inquiries of you as to its usefulness – Our committee meets next the first week in May, and any suggestions you can favour me with by that time, I should be very glad to lay before it....

We are looking forward with great interest to a visit from Frederick Douglass next month; he seems to be exciting a great sensation wherever he appears. I should think he will hardly be able to return to America with any comfort, as the perfect absence of prejudice against colour here, indeed the interest his colour has excited, would make the return even to New England, painful to him – I think we may congratulate ourselves on the failure of our crops last year, as securing our peaceful relations with America – in how many ways is that calamity working for good – The speedy termination of our Corn Laws – & other restrictions in trade must put an end to *war* among all civilized countries, and hasten the day when *nations* shall acknowledge that "all men are brethren" –

Again apologising for troubling you, I beg you to believe me very truly and respectfully yours

Frances Armstrong.

No. 26 R.D. Webb to Maria Weston Chapman

Dublin February 26, 1846

My dear Friend

... I would be glad if we could call together in London in May or June not a formal convention with much machinery – but a [true?] meeting of all the Friends of your cause who would come – John Murray, Wm. Smeal, Robert Reid, Miss Paton, Andrew Paton[1], Miss Welsh, H. Martineau, Abdy, Estlin, Thompson, Miss Hilditch, E. Pease, H. Bevan, Miss Carpenter, H.C. Wright, Fred. Douglass, James Haughton, J. H. Webb, R. Allen and perhaps a dozen men that I dont know or cant recollect. If all then would sit down together and talk over our position, and consult as to the best means of promoting our views, I am confident great good would be done and a warm union affected between the labourers and zealous friends of the cause. A great deal of money goes to the British & Foreign A.S. Society. It is chiefly subscribed to by friends & is I imagine sent up to London to pay for the Publication of the Report, to defray the salaries of Scoble and like, & to enable them to send vainglorious & untrue deputations to this, that, and the other government. As far as I can learn, the influence this society ever had with the government and the country is almost nothing. I don't think our proposed league would get much money or much confidence – but with a good understanding amongst ourselves we might effect more than with either the one or the other. Union is strength – and this is what the B & F A.S. has not. It is a mere irresponsible oligarchy, and such oligarchs! – You have the pick of them now in Indiana doing their best to induce the Anti Slavery Friends to lay down their meetings and to enter like silly sheep the fold of the proslavery wolves in sheep's clothing...Very few have stomachs for the Liberator...The protestant sects are in their measure fully as much opposed to the [?] of their much vaunted right of private judgment as the Papists. But while this plan of a social meeting of British abolitionists would be delightful and a good thing I fear it would not be very practicable – some of them are poor, some are women who might not readily leave home – some are old – & some very busy. In the other conventions some very rich & bountiful men took a deep interest. It is likely that Samuel Gurney[2] & Joseph Sturge and one or two more put their hands pretty deeply into their pockets to pay the expenses which were very heavy...I think this project first came from George Thompson – now he is one of those who are much more prompt in planning than ready to execute – and as he is up for I think Nottingham in Parliament, he will be likely to have his hands full of other work. I fear this plan cannot be readily brought to bear but I will write to Eliz. Pease, H.C. Wright and a few others and will try whether anything can be done – I will then let you know the results. It would certainly go hard with me or I would go to any such convention if I thought it likely to forward

---

1. Andrew Paton (1850-1884) and his sister Catherine were leading members of the Glasgow Emancipation Society.
2. Samuel Gurney (1786-1856), Quaker banker and philanthropist, contributed generously to the anti-slavery cause, especially to the Liberia colony and the Niger Expedition.

that mutual acquaintance amongst the friends of the cause which is one of my greatest pleasures. It was mainly with the hope of seeing Clarkson and Garrison but chiefly the latter that I went to London in 1840 – little thinking of all that would follow the intimacies formed then and there. The Dublin deputation was the most numerous "faction" there. James Haughton & his 2 daughters, Richd & Anne Allen, my brothers Thomas & James, James' wife, Hannah & myself, Dr. Madden my father (I was near forgetting him) and Robert Moore. When I heard that Garrison had really & truly arrived in London what a fidget I was in till I had seen and spoken with him. I was much more of a hero worshipper than I am now. Many of my idols have been broken since then. Nevertheless I would go as far as ever to take you by the hand...How rejoiced we would be if we could look forward to the prospect of seeing you in Dublin, for I would go farther to see you than any woman in the world – so that it would be a great saving if you would come to see us...

My admiration of Thompson's talents has been greatly exalted by his recent speeches in the India House in the case of the Rajah of Sattara. He is a wonderfully able man – but I think him ambitious and with a good deal of that pliability we attach to our [?] of a statesman...

I think it is evident that your influence is enlarging on this side of the Atlantic slowly but surely. In the last edition of Douglass' Narrative just published I made some addition to the Address to the Friends of the slave and put in some new names. The first edition is nearly sold and he cannot have made less than 750 dollars by it. As H.C. Wright said in a letter to me lately – he is "making money hand over head" which is far from Henry's own case – for he has no combination of interesting circumstances to recommend him. In Belfast they paid D.'s bill at the hotel for nearly a month & made him a present of about 200 dollars beside. I think it 100 to 1 if we get him safe and uninjured – I don't mean personally but in his mind and manners, I have met with some insolence from him such as I was not prepared to meet with from any abolitionist. I think he had no provocation to it except in the headiness induced by the flattery and petting he met with in his travels in Ireland, and which he will not be likely to meet with to anything like the same effect in England & Scotland...

We are all on the qui vive looking for the division in the great debate on Sir Robert Peel's free trade measure. It is thought ministers will have a majority of 75 – Then comes the try in the House of Lords, where they will probably be defeated. If so we shall have a general election, and a great row throughout England, Scotland & Ireland. The balance of all the testimony on the subject goes to show that we shall have a famine in Ireland in a month or two owing to the Potato Rot. The government appears to be taking every precaution to lessen the suffering – and the Irish people none at all. Our people look to Repeal as their panacea. If we get it a pretty hell Ireland would be. They have full reliance & nothing that requires the exercise of their own faculties physical or moral & intellectual. As to their priests, they foster all the vile prejudices of the people & take no pains to make them wiser or better men...

This morning March 2nd –I heard the good news that Sir Robert Peel's Free Trade measure had been carried in a division in the Commons by a majority of 97 – only 240 Protectionists left in a House elected on Protectionist Principles. I send you the Nonconformist.

Yours ever truly
Rich[d] D. Webb.

MS.B.1.6. vol. 2 The May Papers [197]
No. 14 Samuel May to J.B. Estlin

Leicester, Massachusetts, Feb. 26 1846

My dear Sir,

... As to *War*, it is now universally (I believe) granted that it has all blown over. But the thing, as at present viewed, places our Government in a most scandalous and a most mean position. Mr. Polk & Cabinet have evidently tendered to the British Government the abolition of the Tariff of 1842 as an offset or equivalent for Oregon, or the principal part of it. In this way the Slave holding interest – our masters – accomplish two objects of the very first importance to them at one stroke; 1st *They avert a war*, which would be destruction to slavery. 2nd *They gratify their jealousy & spite* of the Free North, by striking (through the overthrow of the Tariff) a deadly blow at all those widely extended interests and that vast outlay of capital, in the North, which that Tariff has caused or created. They would think that the greatest day of slavery's bold, bad career, which should see her dangers all swept away, at the same time that her rival freedom was crippled and cloven down. It appears, by Lord Aberdeen's acknowledgment in the House of Lords, that he and his associates of the government had received a certified copy of the new Tariff projected by Polk, and his right hand man R.J. Walker of Mississippi, Secretary of the Treasury – and this too, before the American people knew aught of it, and before their representatives in Congress knew what that new Tariff was! And this is done by the leaders of a party, who have been the loudest to revile the British Government and people – to call our Whig party "British Whigs", to charge them with being bought by "British gold", etc. It strikes me, who am no statesman it is true, as being one of the most scandalous & despicable acts of which a government, can be guilty... By this scheme, the British Govt., with all its avowed emnity to slavery & the Slave Trade, is to be made the instrument of strengthening and upholding both in America, by co-operating with all the Slaveholders' schemes. This is the position of the War question now. Peace is an unspeakable Blessing, and perhaps can hardly be bought too dearly. But I do think that a price may be demanded which an honest man would blush to give – would rather die than give....

As to the Scotch Free Church, I think myself that their recognition of Slaveholders' funds throws discredit on their whole movement – more throws *suspicion* on their motives. It is only another instance of the old notion that the *End* sanctifies the *Means*. However others may feel, I *cannot* make it out how men can be Christians, i.e. Christ like in a church which defends & sustains ownership & traffic in their own fellow church-members, whom they profess to believe are renewed and sanctified by the Holy Spirit of GOD, and members of the body of Christ; who even make their alleged fact of their slaves' being born of GOD an additional recommendation in their sale, a reason why a large price should be paid. How black, and damning, how defiant of GOD and a Saviour, is this accursed thing? And shall a *Free* Church of old *Scotland*, so stern, so strict, so steadfast as she at least claims to be, trust this accursed thing? and join with it in loving, Christian companionship? It is impossible, without sinking herself to the same level – down to the same abyss. It is *inconceivable* to me, how Dr. Chalmers can say and so as he has on this matter.

I rejoice to hear that you have given F. Douglass an invitation to your house. Such a fact is worth *everything* – it is a *speaking* fact – its influence, with those of every similar deed, tell powerfully in this country wherever known. I mention this fact at the close of an Antislavery Address in this town a few evenings since, not mentioning your name of course, and shall do so at a country meeting which we are to hold next week. I predict great results from Douglass's visit to Scotland. I am sure he will deal unsparingly with the Free Church for its grasp of the monies coined out of the sweat and blood of chattelized men and women. I fear he will exhaust himself before he enters England – I mean his physical strength & health....

My dear sir, do not suffer yourself to doubt whether you are doing, or can do, anything effectual against so remote an evil as American Slavery. It is *remote*, only in its physical and actual locality. Its evil genius demands tribute & homage from all lands & people. A true soul, wherever placed on GOD's earth, can give it mortal wounds. The high-toned, consistent, persevering rebuke of Europeans, and especially of England, Ireland, Scotland, is keenly felt here. The course of such men as Drs. Chalmers and Cunningham, and of the Free Church, raises up a palpable wall of difficulties that are seen and felt, in the path of those who would overthrow slavery, and give liberty to the slave. Therefore in some part, we think & speak of the Free Church as we do– and as I *will not do any* more in this letter, though I do feel indignant, I confess. But, I pray you go on, and encourage every true soul to act and speak out...*Were your influence* (British, Irish, European influence generally) so small and to such little purpose, why should the slaveholdg Presses be so anxious to direct that influence into other channels?...

Believe me,

Faithfully your friend, Samuel May.

MS.A.9.2. vol. 22 The Weston Papers [198]
No. 27 J.B. Estlin to Maria Weston Chapman

Bristol, February 28th, 1846.

My dear Mrs. Chapman,

... The various separations that have taken place in your Societies, & the very strong language employed by the different parties towards each other, appear to us like *quarreling*, but in my letter to Mr. Webb I had, I believe, principally in recollection of the long dispute between Mr. Garrison & Mr. Rogers, who it seems, were once intimate friends. Perhaps you are more *honest* than we are, but if such a dissension took place here between two persons seriously interested in the success of an important object – effort I think would be made to prevent injury to the cause which would be likely to ensue from publicity being given to the disputes of some of the leaders in it.

In the various associations in this country, the "platforms" (as you term it) is I think much narrower than with you: the circles forming them usually consist of those who think alike in politics, & in religion, and these circumstances are so numerous & varied in their objects, that much useful work is done, & done well – in educational & religious projects, the members of the Establishment do not like any other to unite with them in charitable & even literary instit. parties, especially political ones act together, & the management generally falls to the strongest. The Unitarians, to whom we belong, are a small body here though not deficient in intelligence & wordly respectability, they are always ready to unite with others in philanthropic, & unsectarian educational purposes, but are looked upon with coolness, & with absence of sympathy by nearly all other sects...

Were such a paper as the "Liberator" published here, I think very few persons in the numerous committees of our benevolent & literary institutions would like to have the Editor as a colleague. This may appear to you very illiberal, but such would be the feeling very generally, and I mention the fact in illustration.

One point is very certain, & reference to it ought to render us charitable in criticising your efforts, and you for bearing in absorbing the construction we may put on your conduct – no philanthropic movement in England affords a parallel to that for the abolit^{n} of slavery in America. *Our* anti-slavery struggle was very different, & the parties ranged in one side & the other *limited* in comparison with those in Am^{a}: the evil contended against could be but little realized when compared with that in Am^{a} & opposition to it entailed but little of the odium that it brings upon you...

You seem very anxious to know what the precise complaints are against the Abolitionists among those of us who have paid a *little* attention to your movement. They are, a belief that the strong language used against those who do not take your views, argues an *unchristian* spirit. We in Bristol have had much knowledge of W. Indian Planters, & possessors of W.I. property, & should always have been shocked at the supposition of many of them not being as excellent people as any in society: many still firmly believe that our emancipation has been a great *evil* to the islands & to the slaves themselves. It is thought that you do not make sufficient allowances for the motives of those who differ from you – that you do not accord to them that measure of credit for honesty of purpose which you claim for yourselves...

Believe me, my dear Madam,
with much respect,
Faithfully yours

J.B. Estlin.

No. 35 Frederick Douglass to Maria Weston Chapman

Kilmarnock
Scotland
29th March 1846

(*Private*)

Mrs. M. W. Chapman

My dear Madam,

I take up my pen to thank you for the "Liberty Bell" and the kind note which you were pleased to send me by the Cambria. I have not yet found time to read the 'Liberty Bell' but hope to do so soon. My time is greatly taken up with immediate engagements growing necessarily out of my present contact with friends here. I find that in order to make my visit of service to our sacred cause at home, I must as far as possible concentrate my strength upon those circles in whose midst I find myself placed – I am trying to preach and practice a genuine antislavery life – turning neither to the right or left, and I think not without success. I think you may safely calculate seeing some proof of this at your next Bazaar. At the suggestion of Mr. R. D. Webb I have inserted an appeal on behalf of the Bazaar in my narrative, so that wherever the narrative goes – there also goes an appeal on behalf of the old organized AntiSlavery Bazaar. One of the first objects in my lectures has been to make that Bazaar prominent and increase its [success?] by increasing its means. I have done so from no sordid motive, but because I believe it to be a powerful instrument in affording means to carry on our important antislavery machinery. I say this the more freely, because, though I consider myself as forming a humble part of that machinery I have never received any pecuniary aid directly from it. I have never absolutely needed any such aid from it. I have even mannaged [sic] to get on – and keep in the field with very little means...and have followed on with a glad heart and willing mind in the thin but brave ranks of our noble pioneer William Lloyd Garrison. Just before leaving the United States for this country my warm and excellent friend J.N. Buffum – aware of my poverty stepped forward with his characteristic liberality and kindly offered to collect a sufficient sum to pay my passage to this land. He tried and succeeded in getting 68 dollars just 2 dollars short of my expenses in the steerage. I brought with me three hundred, and fifty dollars, money which I had saved from the sale of my narrative – For means to sustain me while here I have relied – and still rely mainly upon the sale of my narration. And thus far I have had reason to complain having already disposed of 2000 copies, I have mentioned these facts and made these remarks – because I have felt somewhat greaved to see by a letter from you to Mr. R. D. Webb of Dublin – that you betray a want of confidence in me as a man, and an abolitonist, utterly inconsistent with all the facts in the history of my connection with the Antislavery enterprise. In that letter you were pointing out to Mr. Webb the necessity of his keeping a watch over myself and friend Mr. Buffum – but as Mr. Buffum *was rich and I poor* while there was little danger but what Mr. Buffum would stand firm, I might be bought up by the London committee... Up to the time of hearing Mr. Webb read that letter I supposed I shared your confidence in common with that of the other members of the Committee at Boston. I am disappointed. I can assure you dear Madam that you have mistaken me altogether if you suppose that either the love of money – or the hate of poverty will drive me from the ranks of the old organized antislavery society. But had I no more confidence in them, than you seem to have in me – I would not take a second breath before leaving them – I have withstood the allurements of New Organization Liberty party – and no organization at home – Why should I not withstand the London committee. You have trusted me or seemed to do so, at home, why distrust me or seem to do so abroad. Of one thing I am certain, and that is I never gave you any just cause to distrust me, and if I am to be watched over for evil rather than for good – by my professed friends I can say with propriety save me from my friends, and I will take care of my enemies".... The cause goes nobly on – Our efforts – that is the efforts of friends Wright and Buffum and my own have been mainly directed toward exposing the conduct of the Free Church of Scotland – in holding fellowship with slaveholders – and taking slave money to build free churches. The Antislavery Committee at Glasgow have succeeded in getting George Thompson to join us in an effort to get the Free Church to send back the money.

Very respectfully

yours

Frederick Douglass.

MS.A.9.2. vol. 22 1846 The Weston Papers [200]
No. 51 R.D. Webb to Maria Weston Chapman

Dublin 16th of May, 1846

My dear Friend

I recd your letter respecting Douglass's tirades yesterday – and as this is the first time that you have had occasion to express dissatisfaction with my course, I feel a little sore and am desirous to lose no time in vindicating myself. The friendly confidential character of your letter has been a source of great gratification to one who esteems you as I do, and I feel vexed that you should be even slightly disposed to withdraw this confidence, from such a cause as this ridiculous outbreak of Douglass. In all my experience of men I have never known one not insane so able and willing as he is to magnify the smallest causes of discomfort of wounded self esteem into insurmountable hills of offence and dissatisfaction. He is in my opinion by much the least likeable and the least easy of all the abolitionists with whom I have come into intimate association. I think his selfishness intense, his affections weak, and his unreasonableness quite extravagant when he is in the slightest degree hurt or when he thinks himself hurt. If I had fifteen minutes conversation I have no doubt I could convince you that there is no occasion for all this absurd & most ungracious fuss he has made. If he had any good feelings you are one of the very last people living that he would dare to wreak his ill temper upon – even if you had, which you have not, done anything in writing to me which it was not perfectly proper and right, and necessary that you should write.

I have looked over your letters and am pretty sure I have found the passage I read to him. It was this. "I earnestly hope he may not yield to temptation. When one work of concession, compromise or even a look marking a line of distinction drawn in *favour* of oneself between oneself and the American Society, will seem to promise so much of personal help and success, how hard not to say it." Now I may not have been quite judicious in reading this to him – but if I were not, it is because he is a very much less sensible & magnanimous man, much less devoted to the cause and much more to himself than I took him to be. And this should be considered a very venial mistake, for I am predisposed to think every American abolitionist who comes here with your recommendation, devoted, magnanimous and sensible. And such I have generally found them to be – but not I think Frederick Douglass.As to his talents I admit them – but personally I care little for great talents, unless they are backed by those qualities which are inseparable from affection and esteem towards the proffessor.

It is my custom when I receive letters from any of my American friends, to take them to a little committee, where our very small "faction" consisting of James Haughton, my two brothers, and sometimes Richard Allen, assemble every Wednesday morning to talk over Anti-Slavery, Teetotalism, Peace &c. There we read aloud such letters or portions of such letters as we have recd during the past week, as bear upon the subject of our deliberations. When we have guests or visitors who are interested in these matters we invite them to our sittings, and of course they hear whatever is to be heard. It was on an occasion very shortly after the arrival of Douglass & Buffum, that they were present at our Committee, and all this terrible mischief was done by my supposing that Douglass was a sensible man and that this advice or suggestion from one of his best friends would be taken in good part.

F. Douglass was a very short time in my house, before I found him to be absurdly haughty, self-possessed, and prone to take offence.

In what I have said of Douglass you understand that I do not mean to say or to insinuate anything to his prejudice as a public man. He has worked well and has not shown any disposition but what is straightforward & upright. In his money transactions he had been most honourable – and I have of late years been disposed to distrust any professions which are not accompanied by a strict sense of the claims of *meum* & *tuum*. But if his balance of mind, his good temper and his forebearance are not much lessened by his visit to Europe, I am greatly mistaken...

As the Irish ballads generally wind up, "I must conclude & come to an end" – Yours truly and all the cliques. Remember me to Pillsbury.[1] What of the Board's Herald?

Rich^{d} D Webb.

---

1. Parker Pillsbury (1809-1898), one of the most devoted of Garrison's lieutenants, was the agent of the New Hampshire, Massachusetts and American Anti-Slavery Societies from 1840 until the emancipation of the slaves. During the 1850's he spent several years lecturing in Britain, but his intemperate manner of speaking coupled with his uncompromising and radical views, made him a difficult guest. Interested in many other social reforms, his later life was given up to the cause of Negro and woman suffrage.

MS.A.9.2. vol. 22 1846 The Weston Papers [201]
No. 53 Mary Welsh to Maria Weston Chapman

Edin.r May 17th 1846

My dear Mrs. Chapman

...We have had a set of glorious meetings here against the Free Church & we are to have more of them this week. George Thompson, Frederick Douglass, James Buffum & H.C. Wright have done wonders in opening the eyes of the public to this enormous iniquity, never was there such excitement created as at present & there is no doubt but great good will be the result, however as you will hear all about it through our newspapers, it is unnecessary for me to enter on the subject, as I cannot do it justice, sufficient to say that we are excited & encouraged beyond expression, & Catherine Paton & myself join in kindest regards to you, & best wishes for your success in this holy work, & Believe us ever

Yours in the cause of humanity

Mary Welsh.

MS.A.9.2. vol. 22 1846 The Weston Papers [202]
No. 45 Catherine Clarkson to Maria Weston Chapman

My dear Madam

...It is not possible that we on this side of the Atlantic can ever forget those on your side who have made sacrifices & at the hazzard [sic] of their lives with such noble self devotion have battled for the right. It cannot be but that you must ultimately succeed & indeed it seems to me that you have made greater progress since what Miss Martineau calls the "Martyr Age of America," to the present time than ever we made in England in the same number of years except when through Joseph Sturge's [exertions?] the apprenticeship was shortened by which he certainly earned Southy's third niche. There is one name among us whom you in America ought specially to honour – Granville Sharpe[1] – for he opposed slavery with all his soul & if it had been possible would gladly have taken it up in conjunction with the abolition of the slave-trade. He broke their shackles on his native soil & whenever you are at a loss for an article for your "Liberty Bell" I think an abridgement of my Husband's account of his labours would furnish a useful one. He was unquestionably the father of the anti-slavery cause in England. Or the inscription on his monument in Westminster Abbey might answer the purpose better as it would occupy less space & is well drawn up by Mr. William Smith –

I should like to be remembered to Mr. Garrison whom having once seen it is impossible ever to forget though I should be glad to forget the subject which brought him here the colonization scheme. I am however pleased to remember that in 1817 when an American Gentleman spent 2 or 3 days

---

1. Granville Sharpe (1735-1813), famous as a philanthropist, pamphleteer and scholar, was one of the earliest Anti-Slavery champions. He was the moving spirit behind the Somerset case, in which Lord Mansfield gave the decision that slavery could not exist under English laws, and was one of the founders of the Sierra Leone Company.

here on a mission of discovery of suitable places for colonizing free coloured people it seemed an inexplicable mystery to me that they could not be provided for at home – They would not be comfortable – why not? to this I could not get an answer though I tried hard for it. They could never mix comfortably with whites. Then give them land to settle on. In time they will form a State and then take them into the Union.

'Twas throwing words away for still
The worthy man would have his will,
And said nay they will be miserable.

Nevertheless to my poor thought it is what America ought to do & then she might emancipate her slaves & have no fear of being in want of free labourers.

I ought to beg pardon for writing in this idle way. I still hope that Mr. C. may be writing to you but I hope he will not make you any promise of writing anything for the press for he really is not fit for it.

Believe me dear madam
Very sincerely your friend

Cath: Clarkson

May 1st 1846

MS.B.1.7. vol. 1 1845-1888 The Estlin Papers [203]
No. 33 Catherine Clarkson to J.B. Estlin

My dear Sir!

I am sure that Mr. Clarkson will very thankfully receive your pamphlet when it comes our & will no doubt if he is pretty well write to you upon it. Our "British & Foreign Anti-Slavery Society" has need of all the aid wh can be obtained for it so that I do not think it would be possible at this time to excite an Interest for any new object in Ipswich. There is too a strong feeling in the minds of many that Boston abolitionists have identified themselves too much with anti-state & (what they deem not merely anti-church but) anti-religious views to make it easy to unite with them though every one feels how much the cause is indebted to them. I have used the word anti-state perhaps anti-government would be a better and anti-scripture rather than anti-religious. It is painful to hear such things nor should I have adverted to the subject but that it renders it impossible to send you any Ladies names from Ipswich where from having resided in the neighbourhood for 30 years it might be supposed that Mr. Clarkson had great influence. I am persuaded however that there is not the slightest disposition to hinder where they cannot conscientiously help but it is a matter of grief to many that there should be any division in the anti-slavery camp in America where the Enemy is so united & so strong.

I remain dear sir wishing you & your family success in your benevolent undertaking

faithfully yours

Cath: Clarkson

May 19th 1846

MS.B.1.7. vol. 1 1845-1888 The Estlin Papers [204]
No. 34-35 Catherine Clarkson to J. B. Estlin

My dear Sir,

I beg that you will not consider what I said in my last letter as coming either from me or Mr. Clarkson. I thought it but honest to state the reasons why it would be useless to attempt doing anything in the way you wished in Ipswich. Our Society lately held a meeting in Ipswich the object of wh. was to rouse attention to the horrors of American Slavery & in the hope of aiding its funds which since the Emancipation it is not very easy to do. I never heard any one express a doubt of Mr. Garrison's Integrity – never heard any one say a harsh word concerning him. It would not be easy for anyone to persuade me that he is an irreligious man but I do most unfeignedly regret that he & some others forced on a separation in the Anti Slavery ranks in America & at a most unfortunate time.

I laid down my pen to read your pamphlet. I admire the spirit in which it is written – since the annexation of Texas Mr. Clarkson seldom converses upon American subjects but I know that he fervently wishes that there had been virtue enough in the Northern States to separate from the southern states immediately upon the annexation of Texas. The truth is that till the strong prejudice against colour is subdued little good will be done in America.

I hope to be able to introduce your Tract to Mr. C. in the course of a few days but for the reasons I have given above I fear that he will not without a good deal of explanation enter into the subject. He has I think forgotten that there has been a separation in America & that there are now two societies instead of one a proof if proof were needed how little animosity there has been on this side the water against old organization even though our society is in correspondence with the new organization. Mr. Clarkson however has shown his good will to both parties – I hope my dear Sir that you will not think me a partisan if I avow myself somewhat shocked at something which Mr. Garrison has brought forward in his own name eg "Tremble Tyrants of the old world" & some that he has admitted into his paper by other persons. Why for instance does he insert in his last paper in the very first page the letter about Mr. & Mrs. Foster's introduction of religious opinions into anti Slavery lectures? It looks to me as if in some way the propagation of these peculiar opinions were thought necessary to forward the anti slavery cause by Mr. Garrison's party in America. I must own therefore that with all the admiration which I feel for the self devotion & all the noble qualities & intellectual powers of the party that I think the cause would prosper more if put forward entirely on its own merits at all events it is a bar to much being done in England especially as a request has been lately sent for and of a similar kind from a Society of Ladies in Philadelphia. It is a very modest request & it expressly states that the society do not wish in the least to interfer with the Boston Fair – Whether it will be taken up I cannot tell but I mention it to you to quicken your diligence on behalf of the Bostonians....

Believe me dear Sir

Sincerely & faithfully yours

C. Clarkson.

June 2nd 1846

MS.B.1.6. The May Papers [205]
No. 12 James Haughton to Samuel May

35 Eccles St. Dublin 28th May 1846

To Rev. Sam[l] May

My dear friend

... A good work appears to be going forward in Scotland through the means of the agitation in the Free Church!! which H.C. Wright, J. Buffum, F. Douglass & some others are keeping up. If the blood stained money be sent back to your Southerners it would gall them exceedingly, & it will be a great triumph of right principles in Scotland. Our O'Connell set the Scotch a good example in that respect, in refusing the contributions of slaveholders to the Repeal funds. That was noble – although I am a Repealer, I do not take an active part in the movement, for I have little faith in the value of merely political agitation. I hope there is not any real danger of a war between us & you on the Oregon question. Yet I have my fears; talk is so big at both sides & there seems a lacking sentiment of hatred which is perhaps after all the great cause of apprehension. Neither party can place any value on the mere acquisition of a territory which must in the long run be the possession of neither. I am satisfied our Government will receive no external stimulus to engage in hostility with yours, as the general feeling is quite averse to a war with America, yet a tone of certainty as to the result, in case of war being declared, prevails which often makes me imagine that some with us feel deeply the mortification of former defeats. But I do hope that Christian sentiment at both sides, will prove the stronger....

I am dear friend aff[ectionately] James Haughton.

MS.B.1.6. vol. 2 The May Papers [206]
No. 25 Samuel May to J.B. Estlin

Leicester, Massachusetts, May 30. 1846

My dear Sir,

The steamship, which (I presume) will carry this, will bear to your country tidings which I deeply feel are most disgraceful to ours. You will hear of us as involved in a war with Mexico, which has already resulted in the loss of many lives, and of our government as bent on prosecuting it further – to what extent, the future only can show. You will gather the particulars of this war from the papers. Briefly, I will say it is a robbery & for slavery. Slavery led to the seizure of Texas, for a seizure of that province it clearly will appear to be, when we go back to the origins of the matter. Texas was [first ?] peopled by the emigration from the U.S., with the view of getting the control there, & then severing that province from Mexico. This was done – how, is a matter of too recent history to need to be rehearsed. Still, gross as was the outrage on Mexico, rapacious & insulting as was the spirit manifested to that *sister-republic* & her functionaries, I do not believe war would have ensued, had not the U.S. committed a farther, and most high-handed, aggression on Mexican territory. The Western boundary of the province of Texas was the river Nueces; after the Annexation of Texas to the U.S. was consummated, Mr. Polk (our wretched Executive) ordered Gen Taylor with some thousands of troops, under the sounding title of "Army of Occupation", to advance into Texas and take a position at Corpus Christi near the mouth of the Nueces. Had no more than this been done, no war would have followed in all probability. Though Mexico felt stung by her wrongs, still in her condition of internal war she would un-questionably have avoided a war with this country or any other. But this was not all. After a period of inaction at Corpus Christi, Gen. Taylor was suddenly ordered to advance to the Rio Grande, (or Bravo del Norte, as also called) some hundreds of miles into the Mexican province of Tamaulipas, a loyal province to Mexico, a region whose inhabitants never belonged to Texas nor took any part in Texas matters. To the very banks of the Del Norte Taylor marched, and there, directly opposite the large Mexican city Matamoras, established his camp, which he immediately proceeded to fortify in the strongest manner pointing his cannon directly at Matamoras, He also fortified Point Isabel, some 60 or 70 miles in the rear of his camp, a place in the coast, as a depot for stores & military equipment of all sorts. Matamoras was previously occupied by a Mexican army, whose strength has been variously estimated from 4 to 12,000 men, & even upwards, at first Gen. Taylor was notified that he was invading Mexican territory, and called upon to retire beyond Nueces, or it would be regarded that he had commenced hostilities against Mexico, and his *invasion* would be repelled. He would not stir, and very soon came into conflict and small encroachments, & skirmishedbetween struggling parties – very pretty beginnings for a livelier state of things. A large body of Mexican troops crossed to the Eastern side of the Del Norte, came between Gen. Taylor's camp and Point Isabel (the depot of provisions, &c), and so intercepted communications & cut off supplies. Gen. T. started with some 1200 men to cut his way to Pt. Isabel; he marched there without seeing a Mexican. They allowed him unmolested passage. While he was gone the camp was attacked from the batteries at Matamoras, and a general cannonading was kept up thro' the day. Flaming reports came to us of the result & that Matamoras was in ashes, 700 Mexicans killed, &c &c. Later accounts show that the town received very little damage, and that but few lives were lost, the inhabitants having generally fled from the place. On Gen. Taylor's return to his camp, with a large train of wagons, he was twice attacked by the Mexican forces, and twice routed them with very great slaughter to them it is said (but probably there is exaggeration here as in the former case), and certainly with some severe losses to himself. Quite a number of officers have been killed; among them Major Ringgold said to be the most accomplished & scientific artillery officer in the U.S. army. During the fight, the fort opposite Matamoras continued to be fired upon (as Gen. Taylor himself reports) for a period in all of 160 hours, during which Major Brown its commander was killed by the bursting of a shell. Gen. Paredes is said to be advancing to Matamoras with 15,00 men. You will see that our Congress has virtually declared war, and put 10 millions of dollars, 50,000 volunteers in the President's hands. Massachusetts has been called on, already, to raise one regiment, and our Governor, to the great sorrow and disgust of many, besides the well known Peace & AntiSlavery men, has issued his Proclamation. Many have hoped he would have the nerve of Caleb Strong, Gov. of Massachusetts in the last war with Gt. Britain, who refused to let the troops, raised in Massachusetts, be marched beyond the boundaries of the States....

It is a very general opinion here that England will interfere in this matter; and this opens a prospect before us which I assure you, my dear sir, I contemplate with unmitigated pain. The danger of war between the U.S. and Gt. Britain seems to me to be imminent. You know, and Mr. Armstrong knows, that I have never fallen in with the expectations entertained by many, of a war between your country & ours. That was was expected to grow out of the Oregon question. I have always been confident that that question would be settled without war; and everything latterly, here, has been tending to that result. But now suddenly & by the wicked management of Mr. Polk, we are deep in a war with Mexico — a war of invasion & conquest — the results of which no man can predict. The prospect of a still more extended state of hostilities opens before us. Dark, almost *wholly* dark as it is, disastrous and awful as it must be, one ray of hope shines through. If England engages with Mexico in a war against the U.S., *slavery must fall.*

One thing more about the Mexican War I should have said. What I stated about W. boundary of Texas is not the one-sided opinion of Abolitionists, Peace Men or Northern Whigs. It has been asserted, & demonstrated, in Congress, by Mr. Benton of Missouri, long one of the leaders of the Democratic party, and by far the ablest man in the Western States; If you see the N.A.S. Standard, you will see his speech. I forget whether it was in the Liberator. He explicitly asserts that to march beyond the Nueces would be an invasion of Mexico, &c. And only see on what grounds Mr. Polk in his War Message to Congress places his justification of ordering the U.S. troops to the del Norte! Why! The Congress of Texas, in 1836 or thereabouts, *voted* that the Del Norte, should be their Western boundary!! and so he, Polk, thinks that is enough! They might just as well have voted to make the Pacific Ocean their Western boundary. This is a sampler of the madness & wickedness of our President & his party I have no words to express my sense of the utter want of principle in all his proceedings.

You will see, also that Mr. Benton has taken an equally honourable & manly [line ?] — the more so because conflicting with the views of his own party, or the majority of it — on the Oregon question. He has declared that the U.S. have no claim to the line of 54° 40′; — that the line of 49° is one on which we may rightfully compromise, and to which Gt. Britain is bound to agree.

I pray GOD there may be no war between England & the United States; but if there should be, may He grant that, with the overflowing scourge and by it, slavery here shall find an eternal grave. But, for one, I protest against war. It is a Wrong too great to be perpetrated – to be resorted to for *any* purpose, unless it be to resist the invaders of our hearthstones. That exception I am not yet quite prepared to withhold....

Pray give my best respects to Miss Estlin. Her note to my little Ade. gave great pleasure to us all.

With respect & affection, I am

Yours ever.

Samuel May.

MS.A.9.2. vol. 22 1846 The Weston Papers [207]
No. 150 R.D. Webb to (Edmund Quincy ?)

n.d.(fragment)

... Will you give me your notion of the prevalent opinion of the rich intelligent classes as to the probability of a war with England. The older I grow the more I am convinced of the immense military power of England – which is I think very imperfectly comprehended in the United States, where the masses are ridiculously befooled by the flatteries and falsehoods of their demagogues....

MS. 960 Quincy-Webb Correspondence [208]
No. 13 Quincy to Webb

Dedham, May 23, 1846.

My dear Webb. –

... You ask what people think here of the probability of a war with England. There are many opinions, but that on which I place the most reliance, viz. *my own*, is that we couldn't be kicked in[to] a war with you on the Oregon question. The question lies in a nutshell. The slaveholders always have had, & still have, the policy of the country in their hands. We shall not go to war without it is their doing. And I do not believe that the slaveholders will go to war with their best customer & ruin themselves for the sake of free territory. Thus much for Oregon. But since this foolish & wicked war with Mexico in which the stupidity of Polk has involved us, I do not feel so sure. We may have trouble grow from them. I doubt whether John Bull will submit to have his bullion cut off from Mexico by our blockade. I do not believe that either England or France will permit an invasion of Mexico. A gentleman recently from Paris (our late Atty. Genl. E.J.T. Austin of pro-slavery notoriety in 1837) says that Louis Phillipe was greatly miffed at what Polk said in his inaugural about our not tolerating European interference on this Continent, & that he is ready to vindicate his right in the first sufficient opportunity. I am heartily in hopes that we shall be well *licked* in Mexico, but am afraid that we have too much of the animal [pluck ?] and bull dog pertinacity of John Bull, not to be more than a match for the Mexicans, at least in the field. In a *guerilla* warfare they may wear us out. The war spirit seems very rife in the country, though there is a strong undercurrent of opposition. But the difficulty here is, what Miss Martineau observe the want of *independence.* Nobody, scarcely, except the Abolitionists, dare to say openly what they say in private. As far as the experiment has worked this far, I cannot think that such Republican Institutions as we have, are favourable to a high national character. John Bull, with all his faults, is a much more respectable chap than Brother Jonathan. There is nothing in this country, except Anti-Slavery that is worth a gentleman's notice. Our politics are a kennel in which the dirtiest dog that rolls in it, gets the most bones. The meanness of our public men, with scarcely an exception, is beyond belief. And it all grows from Slavery. The influence of your aristocracy is elevating & ennobling in the comparison. There is something about such a body that appeals to the imagination & has some at least pretended claims to respect on the ground of historic associations & ancestral service. And there is a certain beneficial influence proceeding from such a body of educated gentlemen, though the effect may be bad. But an aristocracy having no claims but the hereditary one of enslaving a quantity of poor negroes, & yet having a political power vastly transcending that of the British aristocracy, is debasing & debasing only & that continually. We know that what you say of the change which has taken place in the public mind as to American character is true, & we thank God for it. We are dreadfully sensitive, on this side, to public sentiment on yours, & you cannot put it on too fast or too heavy for our deserts. I think we have also fallen in our own estimation at home. That is, I believe, the tolerably intelligent part of the comunity, of all classes, are beginning to perceive the truth that we are not the magnanimous, virtuous, glorious, pattern people that we *cracked ourselves up to be.* (That's a piece of Yankee *flash.*) And this chiefly owing to the Abolitionists.

June 1st Boston. – ... We had a most excellent Convention, the best, I think, that we ever had. Faneuil Hall, the largest in N.E. was always full & generally crammed. There is no meeting that attracts such crowds. Numbers of gentlemen attend them regularly from their love of public speaking. For it is a fact that there is nothing like as good to be got anywhere else. As Emerson says, "eloquence is dog-cheap in the A.S. Meetings." & the reason is obvious. The Abolitionists are the only people who can speak just what thoughts their hearts & heads suggest. All others have to be thinking of something besides their subject, of their party or their sect, or their clique, all which is fatal to true eloquence.... The question of Garrison's going to England was brought up, & the Com. voted that they had heard of the Scotch invitation with pleasure & hoped if his sense of duty permitted that he would go, & pledged themselves, at least twenty, to help toward his expenses. He is evidently inclined to go. Whether it can be made out remains to be seen. It will probably be decided by the sailing of the next Steamer. – At the last Annual Meeting of the Am. A.S. Society we resolved to reduce the price of the Standard to *one dollar,* without reducing its size. We have secured the help of Mrs. Follen[1], James Russell Lowell[2], the Poet, Wm. H. Channing, Wendell Phillips & others in the editorial department. We are resolved that it shall have a very great circulation & have no doubt we shall get it. Everybody subscribes that I ask, proslavery & all. It is so cheap that people are ashamed to

---

1. Mrs. Eliza Lee Cabot Follen (1787-1860) was the wife of Charles Follen, a Harvard Professor and abolitionist. She was also a close friend of Mrs. Chapman.
2. James Russell Lowell (1819-1891), the anti-slavery poet, made his first contributions in 1844.

refuse.... Now I'll tell you what I want *you* to do. It is to be our *"Dublin Correspondent."* That is we wish you to write a letter for the Standard of a column or a column & a half, say one of your sheets full, at least as often as *once a month*, & once a *fortnight* if you have a mind to. Let it be as spicy & entertaining as you can make it; containing whatever anti-slavery news you can pick on your side with public matters of interest, & all kinds of gossip not improper for our columns. No disquisitions & peachment but such sorts of letters as you write to us, with such alterations as will suit them to a public paper. Your letters will be worth a hundred dollars to us in the course of the year— at least....

Farewell. Ever yours.

Edmund Quincy.

MS.A.9.2. vol. 22 1846 The Weston Papers [209]
No. 64 To the Secretary of the Massachusetts Female Antislavery Society

Belfast. 6th mo. 17th 1846.

Dear Friend

... In seeking contributions for the anti-slavery bazaars though our object be directly that of wishing to aid in the overthrow of slavery and the numberless wrongs which crush the energies and embitter the existence of the colored citizens throughout the United States, we hope also through such means to act beneficially on public sentiment at home.

By gradually widening the horizon of that intellectual vision which in its maturity enables man to contemplate the true position of his fellow-man all the world over, we who have committed to us the moral training of the rising generation may surely do something towards improving the tone of public feeling whilst exerting our influence to awaken the sympathies of childhood on behalf of the oppressed. But to do this effectively mothers in the first place must have their own intelligence and their own sympathies aroused – and if rightly aroused they will not fail to communicate in many instances to the moral feeling of man a momentum that shall carry him onward till he reaches the confines of the grave. In the contemplation of this we are especially anxious to see the attention of mothers and governesses directed to an examination of the slavery which exists in the midst of a people who so boastingly talk of freedom.

And if the sons and daughters of Erin ere they leave their own sea-girt isle were intellectually prepared to sympathise with the enslaved and the injured colored inhabitants of your land what a difference might the emigrants who are continually leaving our shores carry with them to the homes and the circles they form in America. As the case now stands we fear that our countrymen reaching your shores more frequently join in proslavery prejudice and outcry instead of seeking to promote antislavery effort.

It is very probable that many who under other circumstances would be prepared to contribute handsomely to your bazaar may in the present suffering state of our own poor send only a mite as expression of their sympathy – but even this contribution mite though it be we do not wish to lose the opportunity of accepting on behalf of those who are in bonds, believing it will tend to keep alive the feelings that have been so sensibly acted on by the eloquent and argumentative appeals of one who himself drank deep at the bitter cup of slavery.

Signed on behalf of the Belfast Ladies Antislavery Association.

Maria Webb Corresponding Secretary.

MS.A.9.2. vol. 22 1846 The Weston Papers [210]
No. 66 J.N. Buffum to Caroline Weston

Perth, Scotland June 25 1846

Dear Friend

I promised that I would write you when I met George Thompson, and tell you how he seemed, and how he stands towards the Anti-Slavery cause... I found him clear on the Liberty party, he has the same views of the Constitution as the Massachusetts Society take, he says that he has red [sic] all that has been said pro and con, and has been more convinced by the absurdity of the arguments of the Liberty Party, than by the strength of the friends of that measure... He has no fellowship with the British and Foreign AntiSlavery Society – they have not asked him to speak in any of their anniversaries for several years – he proposed to me to get up a meeting in London in May next, independent of the "*Broad Street Committee*" – one in which the whole truth could be told, he said that if I would get H. C. Wright and Frederick Douglass to agree to be present – he would in conjunction with Elizabeth Pease get up a great meeeting. I have seen them both, and all the arrangements are made. I expect we shall have a *radical meeting*, one as G. Thompson said "*which we can tell the whole truth as to what sustains the slavery of the U. States as well as what slavery is.*" G. Thompson will make a speech, as well as Henry Vincent & others – we shall see the result. G. Thompson wants to come to the U. States and I had considerable talk with him about it – he has some twenty or thirty Lectures on British India which he says he would like to give in America if he goes. They are exceedingly interesting, and full of the history of that Country and People, he has some others – now the plan that he would like to adopt, would be this, (if it could be carried out) to give these lectures before Lyceums, and in other places and realize money enough to pay his expenses while there, and speak in antislavery meeting as he could. This he proposed, so as not to be burthensome to the friends while there – What do you think of it? Will you mention it to some of the friends, and talk it over among yourselves, and write me – if he goes, he will arrange so as to be over in the fall, and be with us next winter. This I do not wish to be made public – he says he dare not wish, much said, until he shall start – if he goes –

I have met with Elizabeth Pease, spent several hours with her, I am much pleased with her I think her the greatest woman, that I have seen on this side of the Atlantic. She is a woman of uncommon talents as you know, and adheres to principal. You can depend on a fast friend in her, to our cause – I have not met with H. Martineau yet, but expect to go into the north of England in the course of a month, where I shall see her there. I met her brother in Birmingham – I have been very fortunate in all my intercourse with the people my opportunities have been as good as I expected, and the people have treated me and my friend Douglass with the greatest respect – Douglass has had great applause in all the places where he has been, and I think great good has been done... I have I think done some good in this Country, by directing the attention of the friends with whom I meet to you in New England – with a view to future help....

believe me your affectionate friend –

James N. Buffum

Caroline Weston.

MS.A.9.2. vol. 22 1846 The Weston Papers [211]
No. 67 J.N. Buffum to Maria Weston Chapman

Dear Friend

... You can count upon more help from the country than you have heretofore – the people are aroused – Frederick's lectures has done much good to enlighten the people – We are now showing up the *Free Church* of Scotland, and I think the result will be that *the money they took of slave holders will have to go back* ....

I am with much respect your friend

James N. Buffum.

... P.S. I ment to have stated before this that Frederick is not satisfied with a reference you made in one of your letters to R.D. Webb, *that he would* be likely to be influenced by the great temptations in this country and especially that of money – which [he?] says that he has given you no reason to entertain – he is quite *sensative* [sic] on that *point.*

J.N.B.

Perth Jun 26/46

MS.B.1.6. vol. 2 The May Papers [212]
No. 26 Samuel May to J.B. Estlin

Leicester, Massachusetts, June 30, 1846

My dear sir,

... Our war with Mexico is still waged, but with less activity. We have rumours that England has offered to mediate, – these again are contradicted, and it is said England is too large a creditor of Mexico, to allow of her being dismembered of any of her provinces, specially of those of New Mexico, where are some of the richest mines.

I must say I am surprised at the extract you give me from the letter of Mr. James

Martineau. He says "I have found it a disadvantage to know nothing of the parties in America, who originated this scheme (the Annual Fair); the *disgraceful* divisions among the Abolitionists." – How can he call the divisions "disgraceful", if he "knows nothing" concerning the questions on which, and the parties between which, these divisions have existed. Suppose some American, or other ignoramus were to talk of the "disgraceful divisions" in Ireland between the Unitarian and Trintiarian Presbyterians, or between different parties of the Dissenters in England. Perhaps, if Mr. Martineau would think it worth the while to inform himself, he might discover as good reason for these "divisions" as ever exist, for any divisions. And I am, myself, convinced you cannot keep these things out of sight in England more than here. The conduct of the Free Church in Scotland has already opened the door to the most, or all, of them. A rank pro-slavery, once understood to exist in any portion of the Church with you, will lead to comparisons and discussions, which must tend to give you a practical insight into the same controversy which has waged with us ....

My respects to your daughter, and to all my Bristol friends; and to yourself my dear sir,

I am most truly yours

Samuel May.

MS.A.9.2. vol. 22 1846 The Weston Papers [213]
No. 75 R. D. Webb to Maria Weston Chapman

Dublin 16th of July 1846.

My dear Friend

Garrison leaves home today. James Haughton had a short letter from him yesterday, I doubt if he will be received with the same eclat as Elihu Burritt[1] who is more level to the capacity of the crowd – his 50 languages make them stare and nobody feels much difficulty in keeping up with the measure of his philanthropy. The English are especially fitted to be horrified by Garrison's moral courage, independence, plainness, and uncompromising attention of his own opinion. The quakers are almost to a man against him or the likes of him...The people here in Dublin are stagnant – weighed down by Popery & Episcopalianism which would smother the lives out of any people. They are the curse of Ireland...

I dont wonder at Douglass's having met the British & Foreign as he has done. It must be difficult for him to enter into your feelings on this matter, and he is not a man to enter into what he dont comprehend. Joseph Sturge is snuffling, secretive, bigotted, and destitute of magnanimity – but he is benevolent & munificient – and it is only in the latter phases of his character that Douglass has seen him. If J. Sturge had heard Douglass speak as I have heard him he would not touch him with a pair of tongs. I look upon him as an intensely bigoted quaker of the Gurneyite school.

---

1. Elihu Burritt (1810-1879), a self-taught New Englander, was known as the "Learned Blacksmith" because of his mastery of several languages. He is best known for his work for the peace movement, both in Britain and America.

In Belfast a Carolinian Rev. Smith, a Methodist, endeavoured to injure Douglass by calumnious reports against his morality & by imputing infidelity to him. One night the town was placarded with large bills

Send Back
the
Nigger

This could have come from nobody but this diabolical "minister of Christ" – and he will have his regard for he has greatly promoted the cause he tried to injure. A Rev. Mr. Levesey from Providence R.I. tried to palm himself off as an anti-slavery man on the Methodists here – But our indefatigable friend William [Shott?] (a Methodist & a zealous abolitionist) published an extract from the Liberator & circulated it among the Methodists which effectually unmasked him by showing that the R.I. & the Baltimore conference are in full fellowship...

I had a letter from Thompson yesterday. He thinks a private assembly of as many Anti-Slavery people who agree with your views is what is to be desired in London and not a convention. I agree with him. We have not money enough for a Convention & I hate the speech making & splutter which such an occasion would call forth in London – mere self-display. We want to do something or to see what we have [to do?] He only repeats the matter that occurred to me some while since. I [hope?] it will come to this & that a good many will meet about 3 weeks hence in London. truly R. D. Webb.

MS.A.9.2. vol. 26 The Weston Papers [214]
No. 77 William Goodell[1] *to Mrs. Nicholson*

[Honeaye?], Ontaria Co. N.Y. July 30: 1846

To Mrs. Nicholson
Dublin,

Madam...Our good friends in Europe must not think it strange that we in America follow the precedent so unhappily set by our Saxon and Anglo-Saxon ancestors and cousins on the east side of the great water in this same matter of sectarian divisions, and jealousies and strifes. Do they marvel that American abolitionists are *divided?* That mutual criminations and jealousies have taken place? – a sad thing, and injurious to the good cause. But was the protestant faith elaborated and ushered in – or was the deadly [wound?] of the papal beast given without similar exhibitions of human frailty and sin?

Let it be borne in mind, in the first place, that the Antislavery movement found American citizens yea and American Christians already divided into all those multiform divisions and subdivisions which German, Scotch and English dissenters had introduced from one or two or three centuries ago – which have been perpetrated and increased down to the present time along

---

1. William Goodell (c.1792-1878), writer, abolitionist, and temperance reformer, of New York, helped to form the American Anti-Slavery Society, and was editor of its organ, The *Emancipator,* as well as editing another anti-slavery paper, the *Friend of Man.* He was also behind the formation of the Liberty party, and, much later, the prohibition party.

with additional feuds and subdivisions springing up on American soil. Do those who, in England and Scotland are so much scandalous at divisions and schisms among American abolitionists think highly of those schisms which continue to divide British as well as American Christians? Did it never occur to them that American abolitionists should first settle their feuds before they expect British sympathy, might find its parallel in the demand that British and American protestants should first come together, before they may say a word against the despotisms of Rome? Your "Evangelical Alliances" I fear will find much more labor before them, ere they will lay the axe to the root of this evil!

It may be said that English and Scotch abolitionists found no difficulty, notwithstanding their political and sectarian divisions, in acting together in the subject of slavery. As they organised no new political parties, so they founded no new religious sects. There was the best reason for this. The slave power had not in Great Britain so completely subjugated and corrupted the Church and the State as in America. The distance and the colonial dependency of the slave provinces were favourable circumstances in the case. The slaveholder could not overthrow and change the British admiration at their pleasure as in this country, nor could they dictate the actions of every ecclesiastical body as with us! I blush to record this humiliating confession. But truth demands that it be done. Now consider that in America even more than in England you must first agitate, nay, instruct and guide the people, before you can reach the government. Consider too that it is the Church that educates the popular conscience, and that the leaders of nearly all the sects are opposed to the agitation! Then consider that both the [?] national parties in politics (as well as missionary and ecclesiastical boards) depend upon slaveholders money and slaveholders votes. Consider all this, and it will be seen that the agitation of the slave question in America must cut deeper than in Great Britain – must of necessity bring under discussion, the very foundation principles of political as well as church order. Before you can weld either the church or the state against slavery, you have first to regenerate both – a struggle of which but few of our British friends can form any adequate conception, but in slight apprehension of which may serve to convince them that numerous topics may be essential to the discussion here, which would have been "extraneous" in Britain...

Garrison you know was instrumental in first arousing the people. His stirring style, his imprisonment in Baltimore, &c introduced a new era. He has been trained in Baptist views, but was not a communicant, though he appeared devout. His disgust with sectarian exclusiveness probably it was that kept him out of the Church. He was among the ... (MS. incomplete.)

Your friend

Wm. Goodell

MS.A.9.2. vol. 22 1846 The Weston Papers [215]
No. 78 Catherine Clarkson to Maria Weston Chapman

My dear Madam

...Mr. Clarkson had a visit from a fellow countryman of yours the other day Mr. J. P. Buffum. He very kindly came down to take the chance of seeing Mr. C. having only the day before mentioned his intention & enclosed an Introduction from the Poet Whittier to him & for Frederick Douglass.... What an extraordinary man Douglass must be! I wish he were full blood black for I fear your pro-slavery people will attribute his pre-eminent abilities to the white blood that is in his veins.

We are rather drooping just now at our new government equalizing the sugar duties & encouraging the emigration of labourers to the West Indies. On the Irish question there are plausible arguments as on the second none....

Mr. Douglass is making a great impression in this country. We have no pro-slavery party here but too many seem to think that having paid 22,000,000 to redeem our own slaves England has nothing more to do.

Believe me, dear Madam

Your obliged & faithful

Cath. Clarkson.

Playford Hall,
Aug[st] 2nd 1846.

MS.A.1.1. vol. 4 1844-53 Anti-Slavery Letters from Garrison [216]
No. 25 William Lloyd Garrison to Helen Garrison

London, Aug. 18, 1846.

Dear Helen:

This is a beautiful morning, and I lack nothing to complete my enjoyment but your own dear presence, and that of the children. O that I could embrace you all, and bestow upon you as many kisses as my affection would prompt! But here I am, – wide ocean rolling between us, and my work but just begun. It was my hope to be able to leave for home in the steamer of Oct. 4th: but it seems, now, impracticable for me to get away before the 19th. Henry C. Wright is also so circumstanced, that he will not be able to leave till that time. This will make the delay of a fortnight, which will be very long to you, and also to me, but yet it is only a fortnight, and it is better that we should consent to this temporary separation, than that my mission should be left in an imperfect state. It bids fair to be servicable to an extent surpassing my most sanguine expectations. We have formed an Anti-Slavery League for all England, and last evening held a public meeting, which was fully attended by a most intelligent, respectable and enthusiastic assembly. I would have readily given several guineas, if you and the Boston friends could have been spectators. It was a real old organized anti-slavery meeting, such as was never held before in this metropolis. George Thompson was in the chair, and made a brief but earnest speech. in which he referred to me in a very kind and complimentary manner. Henry C. Wright made the opening speech, and it was "a scorcher", and received great applause. I followed him – and on rising, was received by the assembly with a tempest of applause, they rising from their seats, swinging their hearts, and cheering loudly. I made a long speech which elicited the strongest marks of approbation. Douglass was received in a similar manner, and made one of his very best efforts. I never saw an audience more delighted. Henry Vincent made the closing speech, which was eloquently uttered, and warmly cheered. James Haughton, at the commencement, presented a resolution, welcoming us all to England, &c &c Rev. Mr. Kirk, of Boston, was in the meeting, but he found the atmosphere too warm for him at last, and left the room. We began at half-past 6, P.M., and did not adjourn till 12 o'clock, very few having left at that late hour. Everything was encouraging in the highest degree.

Dearest, you have my heart. I shall think of you in the din of public excitement, & the silence of privacy. My health is excellent as I trust yours is. Love to all the dear friends without specification. Write by every steamer.

Yours ever, W.L.G.

MS.A.1.1. vol. 4 1844-53 Anti-Slavery Letters from Garrison [217]
No. 26 William Lloyd Garrison to R.D. Webb

London, Aug. 19, 1846.

My dear Webb:

That plodding, faithful, indefatigable, unparalleled pen-driver, – the fanatical, disorganizing, infidel Henry C. Wright, – is writing to you, at this moment, a sketch of our sayings and doings since you left us, (and your absence is felt by me like a heavy bereavement,) especially in regard to our meeting at the Crown and Anchor, on Monday evening last; so that it will be wholly unnecessary for me to go into the particulars. When I tell you, that it was a real, old-fashioned, old-organized, American anti-slavery meeting, (such, I am quite certain, as was never before held in *England*,) you will understand me to imply all that was bold, uncompromising, undissembling, hearty, enthusiastic. At an early stage of the proceedings, an attempt was made to distract and divide the assembly, by the Rev. John Howard Hinton, who, on the presentation of a resolution by James Haughton, welcoming us to England, &c., rose and declared that he could not vote for it because he went with the American and *Foreign* Anti-Slavery Society! This annunciation elicited not a single note of approbation, and the resolution was adopted by acclamation. Under these circumstances, it was not deemed necessary, by any of us, to say one word in reply; though, if it had not been for interrupting the order of your proceedings, as previously marked out, I should have given such an exposure of that Society as would have caused the reverend intruder to deplore his folly for a long period. Dear H.C.W. made the opening speech, in his characteristic plain, faithful, direct manner, which excited an intense feeling, and elicited much applause. I followed him at considerable length, and was received with the most gratifying evidences of cordiality. Frederick, on rising, drew forth a perfect storm of applause.

His speech was exceedingly happy, both in regard to manner and matter. Both he and H.C.W. excoriated Kirk[1], Patton[1], Marsh[1], et cet., for the deceitful course which they are pursuing in this country, in regard to the anti-slavery movement in the United States. Thus far, "the work goes bravely on."....

Faithfully yours,

Wm. Lloyd Garrison.

MS.A.9.2. vol. 22 1846 The Weston Papers [218]
No. 82 Frederick Douglass to Maria Weston Chapman

My Dear Mrs. Chapman –

... In reply to so much of your letter as relates to my having attended the second meeting of the British and Foreign Anti Slavery Society in London – I must say I have no confession to make or pardon to ask for my conduct in the matter I went there with the counsel and advice of good friends – friends who are as anxious for the emancipation of the slaves as any with whom I think I have ever met. I went for reasons which seemed good – I was not carried there by what you term "money temptations" – no such was offered and I may say (though you may think it an evidence of my self sufficiency) no such temptation would have been availing...My friend George Thompson was in London at the time, I was in Edinburgh he at once wrote urging me for many reasons, most of which sprung out of our Free Church aggetation – to come to London and avail myself of the opportunity afforded by that meeting of striking an important blow in behalf of "sending back the money". I believe Mr. Thompson now regrets having advised me to go. I do not know that he does but I think he does since reading the article in which you refer in the Standard – I must however say that I do not regret his having gone thither or having spoken when I was there.

I do not believe that even the Broad Street Committee admitting them to be all you say of them I do not think them too bad to be preached to – I will speak in any meeting when freedom of speech is allowed and where I may do anything towards exposing the bloody system of slavery – I did not go into that meeting as a new organizationist I distinctly told the meeting just what the Broad Street Committee knew before they invited me – that I was an old organizationist and had I been fully reported you would have seen that I was not there in disguise or at the sacrifice of principles – or friends at home...I attended that meeting for a specific purpose and in doing so compromised no more than did Mr. Garrison Leavitt &c. who last autumn attended meetings and acted on committees together in order to prevent the Annexation of Texas. – I might argue the question if I had time, but I have not. I have said this much that you may know just where I am in this matter – and think this much due to you since you have taken

---

1. Rev. E. N. Kirk (1802-1871), Rev. William Patton (1798-1879) and Rev. John Marsh (1788-1868) were all American Presbyterian or Congregational ministers, active in social reform, who were then in Britain to attend the meeting of the Evangelical Alliance. Their refusal to condemn American slavery outright, drew a furious attack from Garrison and his friends.

so much pains to write me respecting it — I shall not say anything about the matter in any letter I may write for the public as I think enough has.

I recently got a little circle to work for the Bazaar at Boston consisting a few influential young ladies in "Carlile" (Eng.) They will send a box this autumn. Mr. J. D. Carr of the same place will send a valuable contribution to the refreshment table consisting of a large box of fancy buiscuits. I am sorry I cant say more. The lad is waiting to take this to the office.

Very respectfully
Yours

F. Douglass

London. 18th Aug. 1846.

MS.A.1.2. vol. 41 Anti-Slavery Letters to Garrison [219]
No. 33 William Lloyd Garrison to J.B. Estlin

London, Aug. 19. 1846.

Esteemed Friend:

... I wish you could have been with us, at our public meeting on Monday evening last, at the Crown and Anchor; because I am sure it would have given you great pleasure to see how cordially the several speakers were received, and with what bursts of enthusiasm the sentiments uttered by them were endorsed. Never have I seen a more animated assembly. It was highly intelligent, and quite numerous. George Thompson was called to the chair, who made some eloquent introductory remarks. He was followed by James Haughton of Dublin, H.C. Wright, W.L.G., F. Douglass, and Henry Vincent. The meeting began before 7 o'clock, and did not close till midnight — scarcely any having returned, even at that late hour. A pretty full report of the proceedings will appear in the London Universe of Friday. I will endeavour to send you a copy. Nearly all the other city journals have noticed the meeting in respectful terms, and thus have given that publicity to our movement which is so essential to its success.

The Anti-Slavery League which has been formed, if energetically conducted, cannot fail to make a deep impression on the public mind, on both sides of the Atlantic. Whatever it may do toward overthrowing American slavery by righteous instrumentalities, (and it is to be taken for granted that none others will be used,) I feel assured will return in rich blessings on England, and essentially aid, in the most direct manner, the cause of freedom throughout the world. I am happy to know that you are disposed to give it your countenance.

Anticipating much pleasure in my contemplated visit, I remain,

Yours, with much esteem,

Wm Lloyd Garrison.

MS.A.9.2. vol. 22 1846 The Weston Papers [220]
No. 85 R.D. Webb to ?

n.d. fragment

The following Monday we had a sort of open committee at one of the rooms of the Crown & Anchor. We sat from 10 in the morning till *11* at night with about ½ hour intermission. It was extremely interesting. The result was the League. What it will come to I dont know. It is easier to form a League than to carry it on. You must have money & abiding zeal. However if this effort do no more than what I aimed at, to bring people together, & make them acquainted with those who feel with them & for the Am. Society, I shall be satisfied. Great zeal has been roused in Belfast by Douglass & from what I can hear the tables are quite turned on New Broad St. I think we shall go on slowly at first – but the ball will I hope swell into an avalanche. Anti Slavery of the true stamp will be sifted in by degrees.

MS.A.1.1. vol. 4 1844-1853 Anti-Slavery Letters from Garrison [221]
No. 27 William Lloyd Garrison to Henry Clarke Wright

Bristol, August 26, 1846.

My dear Henry:

...Yesterday afternoon, we had a public meeting at the Victoria Rooms, (a splendid building), which was attended by a most select assemblage, the Mayor of the City presiding on the occasion, who introduced us in a very handsome manner. The hall was filled – a considerable part of the assembly being members of the Society of Friends, of the affluent class. Very marked attention was paid to our remarks, and all seemed to be highly gratified; but, to me, it was anything but an animated time. So much formality and *select-ness* takes all the warmth out of me; and I felt as dull and flat as though I had neither perception nor instinct. Frederick seemed to labor under embarrass-ment, but he did much better than myself. I thought he would greatly disturb the Mayor, and our cautious and considerate friend Mr. Estlin – the former by his severe remarks upon slaveholders as "vagabonds" and "villains", (for you will recollect that Bristol is the headquarters of the West India planters in this kingdom, and it was bringing up old reminis-cences not the most pleasant to them and their friends) – and the latter by his "indiscriminate" assault on the American church and clergy. How the mayor really felt at such plain talk, I cannot say; but he concluded the meeting with some commendatory remarks, and, to my surprise, Mr. Estlin took exception at nothing that was said, but seemed to be very much pleased, and declared that he believed a very salutary impres-sion had been made. The more I see of him, the more I am surprised that he means to be a true friend of the cause, and that he is the main spoke in the anti-slavery wheel, in all this region.

Last evening, we had a large circle of persons, of various religious denominations, convened at friend Estlin's, and a most animating con-versation followed, on a variety of topics, but chiefly on *non-resistance* – when I gave them all my heresies on that point. I wish you could have seen us – yes, and been one of the group. I had half a dozen opponents, ministers, lawyers, merchants, etc; but they were so effectively answered that they knew not which way to turn. The discussion, however, was very amicably conducted.

Some would say that it was very poor policy to be talking about such subjects, if I wished to secure aid to the anti-slavery cause, and to make my mission a successful one. Thank God! it is not policy, but principle, by which I mean to be governed in my intercourse with my fellow men, and while I desire at all times to be governed by a sound judgement, and not to be guilty of rashness, I will not desist from declaring "the whole counsel of God", as opportunity may offer, whether men will hear or forbear. As Wendell Phillips once finely remarked – "God has not sent me into the world to abolish slavery, but to do my duty." It seems to me that our intercourse with our fellow men will be to little benefit, if we confine ourselves to the consideration of topics about which we are already agreed, or which are of a trivial character. Phrenologically speaking, my caution is large, and my combativeness not very active; and as I pay no regard whatever to the question of right, I am not very forward in the work of prosleytism.

I have received a very kind note from Francis Bishop[1], of Exeter, in which he says in relation to the coming of Douglass and myself to that place – "I have spoken to several friends on the subject, and they all agree that a public meeting is most desirable. We have accordingly decided on having such a meeting on Friday evening, in the largest and most public room in Exeter. The people only want to know the facts of American slavery, to be heart and soul with you. I trust we shall form an auxiliary to the League in Exeter." We are to meet with a select number of friends at Bishop's residence, tomorrow (Thursday) evening. Thus, you see, our way is fully prepared before us.

Mr. Estlin thinks there ought to be an auxiliary to the League in Bristol. This will probably be agreed upon at the close of our meeting this evening. Thus far, everything here looks auspiciously.

Frederick is stopping with a very wealthy and estimable member of the Society of Friends, who a few weeks since was gulled out of £50 by the Broad Street Committee. What will Sturge and Scoble say to his giving us the right hand of fellowship?...

With assurances of my high regards to William Smeal, John Murray, and to the dear friends at Glasgow; I remain, hastily,
Yours, ever,

W.L. Garrison.

MS.B.1.6. vol. 2 The May Papers [222]
No. 30 J.B. Estlin to Samuel May

Bristol Sept. 1st 1846, Tuesday.

My dear Sir,

... In consequence of communications with my *(corresponding)* friend Rd D Webb of Dublin, I repaired to London on Wednesday Aug. 5.

---

1. Rev. Francis Bishop was another of the West of England Unitarians.

There I was, for the first time, introduced, at Mr. Webb's lodgings to Messrs. Garrison, H. C. Wright, James Haughton, Rich[d] D Webb & brother, & R[d] Allen of Dublin & spent an interesting evening. Mr. Garrison's very cordial meeting, and friendly expressions, made me feel at once with an old friend.

The next morning, Messrs. Garrison & R. D. Webb breakfasted with me at Dr. Prichard's where I was staying, to whom I was glad to introduce them. Professor Retzius, a celebrated Swedish Naturalist, was there. – That evening, an anti-slavery gathering was held at Mr. Allen's lodgings, where the friends before named met, joined by Geo. Thompson, F. Douglass (my first personal meeting with him) & some other friends. Here we had much conversation, & planned an *"Anti Slavery League"*....

Last Monday week, August 24th, I met Messrs. Garrison & Douglass at the Bristol Railway station, & conveyed them to my house to dinner. Several friends interested in the A.S. cause joined us in the evening. Mr. Garrison remained with me & my daughter as our guest. Douglass, I was obliged to surrender to our friend Ed Thomas, who would not allow of my monopolizing both. On the following morning however, Douglass, with some other friends,...breakfasted at my house. At 2 o'clock on that day, Tuesday, we had an excellent meeting at the Victoria Rooms, – a *fashionable* place, the Mayor in the chair.

On Thursday morning, Messrs. G. & D. breakfasted with Mr. Armstrong, and after dining with us Mr. James escorted them in my phaeton to the station on their way to Exeter.

I learn that at Exeter under the auspices of Dr. Barham & Mr. F. Bishop, an immense gathering took place. Douglass remained at Exeter, and Mr. Garrison left for Bath on Saturday. I met with him at the Bristol station, & accompanied him to Bath...Here we dined with Mr. Murdoch, Unit. minr. & then called with Mr. G. upon *Mr. Abdy*. The meeting between them was peculiarly interesting: – it was of short duration – I then attended Mr. G. to the station & saw him start off for London, taking leave of him with much regret, though with feelings of deep satisfaction at having had the pleasure & the privilege of seeing so much of him. If I mistake not, these sentiments were not unreciprocated....

Much attention to American Slavery will be occasioned in Bristol by the present agitation of the question: I hope we shall form an auxiliary to the League: another A.S. socy in this country with new blood in it is quite needed: the old one is getting superannuated – and yet I fear the knowledge of *American a.s. politics* is not so advanced here as to ensure advantage to the cause generally, from the attention which Mr. G.'s being here necessarily attracts to the *divisions* that have occurred....At present, no very influential persons have given their names to the new League – as a right understanding of the actual position & *repute* of persons conspicuous in the a.s. movement is most desirable between the parties on each side of the Atlantic, I do not hesitate to say, that George Thompson's name carries little weight here. An able man & excellent speaker, none deny him to be; but he is looked on as a sort of *adventurer*, trading by his wits in any cause open to him but especially preferring those of a philanthropist; – in a word he carried no *moral* influence with him, & with all the faults of the country, I am happy to say, that in public men, *character* is the sheet anchor of their moral power – ...

With all kind regards from my daughter & the Carpenter family, I am, my dear Sir

Most truly yours

J. B. Estlin.

MS.A.9.2. vol. 22 1846 The Weston Papers [223]
No. 86 Mary Estlin to M.W. Chapman

Park Street, Bristol, September, 1846.

My dear Mrs. Chapman,

I have undertaken to furnish you with the newspaper containing the fullest account of the interesting meetings held here last week but I cannot forward it to Corn Hill...without sending you a few lines to express to you the personal gratification we have derived from the visit of Mr. Garrison & Frederick Douglass...From you, & from Mr. Quincy, & other Transatlantic friends of the slave, as well as from Mr. G. himself in his editorial capacity my father & I had been previously too thoroughly initiated into the hearings of the various points of Anti-Slavery politics – both in their relation to the Churches, the Free States, the Constitution, the secessions from your body with their *real* & their *alleged* causes, & many other debateable matters, to find any new light thrown on the subject by the personal interviews, & spoken eloquence, we have been favoured with this last week; tho' most of our friends – *all* I believe I may say,... have been led to look on some of the relations of this great question in a stronger & clearer point of view, have had some intricate parts made straight, & some difficulties solved & have been inspired with fresh zeal in your cause...He [W.L.G.] has I trust done much good here & dispelled many prejudices by his visit, for great numbers listened to him; & many had private conversation with him; & to be in his atmosphere *must* soften bigotry & disarm unkindly feeling when it existed before...I have said nothing about F. Douglass, for there is but one opinion of him. Wherever he goes he arouses sympathy in your cause & love for himself. He is affecting a great work here, & the longer you can spare him to us the better it will be for us & I believe for you too in the end. Our expectations were highly roused by his narrative, his printed speeches, & the eulogisms of the friends with whom he has been staying: but he far exceeds the picture we had formed both in outward graces, intellectual power & culture, & eloquence. People are looking forward with great anxiety to his second visit, & there seems quite an anti-slavery ferment, wh I hope will result in considerable additions to the Bazaar collections....

With every affectionate wish very sincerely yours

Mary A. Estlin.

MS.A.9.2. vol. 22 1846 The Weston Papers [224]
No. 85 R.D. Webb to (Wendell Phillips?)

Dublin September 1 1846.

My dear Friend

I have just been reading the speeches of Garrison and Douglass at Bristol – They were of course very good. From what I can learn D. was more eloquent everywhere than here. We had comparatively poor audiences here. He had no excitement to stir him up – no opposition worth talking of – no thronging crowds – no great rich people to pique him to effort. The Bristol speech is admirable and he is a fine fellow. It would be a thousand pities that he should go astray – and I think he has not enough to know the side that is best for and [?] creditable to himself. He spoke dashingly in London too. He must go on right. I take back nothing I have said of his defects in the minor points I complained of – but I admire and value him so much for the causes sake that I would bitterly regret if anything occurred to mar his usefulness...

On the 4th Garrison, Thompson & Douglass mean to lecture in Birmingham and I think they look to spending the 6th at Ambleside with Harriet Martineau and then going on to Scotland. At any rate his visit will do good – this I am sure of. I rely greatly upon the Unitarians – the [finest?] & most energetic minds are among them – they are not afraid lest every breath of wind will overthrow their *doxy*.....(MS. ends)

MS.A.1.2. vol. 16 1846 Anti-Slavery Letters to Garrison [225]
No. 85 Frances Armstrong to William Lloyd Garrison

My dear Sir,

I trust I shall not be giving you very much trouble if I request you kindly to give me some information respecting the Philadelphia Bazaar, as many of the Ladies of our Anti Slavery Committee in Bristol have been in the habit of interesting themselves for it, and would wish, if possible, while giving their hearty cooperation to the Boston Society, and joining the Anti Slavery League, not to withdraw their aid from that party which is associated with our British & Foreign Anti-Slavery Society. Did I understand you rightly, to say in answer to a question of Mrs. Tribe's "that the working of that party was inimical to the objects of the Emancipationists, and did real injury to the Abolition cause – " and if so, can you tell me how?

I am aware that you are about to publish a tract on the subject, but I am anxious to have some means of forming a judgment *before* that is likely to come out, as it may greatly influence the contributions to be sent in this month for the Boston box.

Our Ladies Committee will spend next Thursday evening with me, for the purpose of talking the matter over, – and also of deciding if we shall unite ourselves to the League. And I should feel particularly obliged by your letting me hear from you on the subject, before that time. I know it is the opinion of many here, that the two parties may work side by side with each other, and we should certainly prefer living in connection with both, if that can be; but we are in earnest in the matter, and would grieve indeed if, through ignorance, we were in any degree to hinder that glorious end to which our efforts are directed.

I feel I need offer no apology to you for the original request I have made, your heart is in the cause, and I am sure that it is your desire, not to lead blind-fold those who come to you for guidance *how* they may aid, but to give that information which will enable them to see and judge for themselves – not to have mere obedience to the dictation of the Abolition leaders, but that reasonable service which the convinced mind and faithful heart will ever be ready to give.

We have been deeply interested in your and Mr. Douglass' visits to Bristol, and though our hearts were with you in your labours before, we shall feel an additional interest in them for the future, and continually lift up our hearts to that God who made of one blood all nations of men who dwell upon the Earth, that he will hasten the time when all shall be free, and dwell in love and brotherhood together.

Mr. Armstrong desires his kind regards, and I beg you to believe me with sincere esteem.

Most truly yours

Frances Armstrong.

Sept. 3rd 1846.
11 Clifton Vale
Bristol.

MS.A.1.1. vol. 4 Anti-Slavery Letters from Garrison [226]
No. 30 William Lloyd Garrison to his wife

London, Sept. 3, 1846.

My doubly dear Helen:

... You see I am still in London. But you must not infer that I have been stationary here since my arrival in this city. I have been to Bristol; and held two public meetings, – one of them composed of the selectest sort, the mayor presiding – the other of a more popular cast, largely attended, and enthusiastically supported. Douglass was with me, and, of course, wherever he goes, the lion of the occasion. We had a number of private parties, and no pains were spared to make our visit an agreable one. From Bristol we went to Exeter, where we met with a cheering reception, and had a large and glorious meeting. I left Frederick there, to give another lecture, and am to go down to Birmingham tomorrow, with Geo. Thompson, to hold a public meeting in the evening, where Douglass has promised to meet us; I shall then return to London, and spend two or three days in correspondence, and then go to Sheffield and Leeds, to hold public meetings, and perhaps continue on to Darlington, should Elizabeth Pease have returned from her sojourn in the country. Her health is still precarious, but somewhat improving. Hence I shall return to London, to attend a great and final anti-slavery meeting in Exeter Hall, with special reference to the Evangelical Alliance, and its troubled and indefinite action on the subject of slavery.

It will make a deep sensation here, beyond all doubt. Thompson has promised to make one of his strongest efforts, and Douglass will do his part on the occasion. Henry C. Wright will not be able to be with us as he is now in Dublin, superintending the publication of his little work on Non-Resistance.

In addition to addressing a large meeting at the Crown and Anchor, I have spoken at a public meeting, gotten up by Thompson in regard to the atrocious case of the afflicted Rajah of Sattara, (of which comparatively little is known in America, excepting by Philips, Quincy, and Mrs Chapman.) I was cheered to the echo, not so much in consequence of what I said, though that was warmly responded to, but because Thompson told them a few particulars of my labors in the anti-slavery cause in America. Last evening, I addressed a large meeting of the moral suasion Chartists, for the space of two hours, in the National Hall, George Thompson in the chair, and, of course, warmly commending me to the affection and co-operation of the working men of England. I wish you could have been present, to see the enthusiasm that was excited. When I arose to address them the applause was long protracted and overpowering. Peal after peal, like a thunderstorm, made the building quake; and at the conclusion of my remarks, they gave me nine hearty cheers, and adopted by acclamation a highly flattering resolution. I did not appear before them in my official capacity, or as an abolitionist, technically speaking, but on my own responsibility, uttering such *heresies* in regard to Church and State as occurred to me, and fully identifying myself with all the unpopular reformatory movements in this country. This will probably alienate some "good society folks" from me, but no matter. I know that the cause of my enslaved countrymen cannot possibly be injured by my advocacy of the rights of all men or by my opposition to all tyranny....

I have spent a very delightful Sunday at my old friend, William H. Ashurst's, at Muswell Hill, as charming a spot as the earth presents, – *almost.* Thompson and Douglass were with me, and a large social gathering – among whom was the celebrated and eloquent Unitarian preacher, William J. Fox, who, after preaching his forenoon sermon, (it was Sunday), came and spent the remainder of the day with us, engaging in sport after dinner in rolling balls on the greensward, and for healthful exercise. It was a day long to be remembered.

I have twice visited William and Mary Howitt, at their residence in Clapton. They are a remarkable couple, and widely known in the world of literature. I am to spend tonight with them. Mary is kindly preparing for the "People's Journal", an autobiography of my life, which will, no doubt, aid me in no small degree in the prosecution of my mission. It will be published in a few days, and you shall have a copy by the next conveyance.

I shall derive great assistance from the co-operation of William Lovett and Henry Vincent, the leaders of the moral suasion Chartists – the friends of temperance, peace, universal brotherhood. They are true men, who will stand by us to the last – men who have been cast into prisons in this country, and confined therein, (the former one year, the latter twenty months) for pleading the cause of the starving operatives in this country, and contending for universal suffrage. Such men I honor and revere.

I hardly know what I should do without the assistance of George Thompson. A more generous, disinterested, faithful champion of the Right, cannot be found.

He has everything to do – a world of business upon his hands – and yet, he continues to lend me a helping hand at any moment, and to any extent. The indebtedness of our cause to him is immense. Whenever he goes over to the United States, he shall have a reception that shall form a striking contrast to the treatment he experienced in 1835. Mrs. Thompson and the children are well, and all desire to be kindly remembered.....

No conclusion.

MS.A.1.1. vol. 4 Anti-Slavery Letters from Garrison [227]
No. 31 William Lloyd Garrison to R.D. Webb

Birmingham, Sept. 5, 1846.

My dear Webb:

I am now at the house of our friend Arthur Naish, and seize my pen to give you a few hasty lines, in compliance with the request contained in your note to him.

George Thompson came down from London with me yesterday afternoon. Frederick Douglass arrived from Worcester at about the same time. Since I parted from him at Exeter, he has had an enthusiastic public meeting at that place, and another at Bristol, – in both of which places we held meetings together; and in both, an anti-slavery league has been formed, auxiliary to the London League, under very cheering auspices. Our friend Bishop, at Exeter, is an admirable co-worker, and spared no pains to make our visit an eminently successful one. I had an interview with John Dymond, the Quaker Banker, (the brother of Jonathan Dymond,) and, finding that his mind had been tainted by the Broad Street Committee, gave him a full statement of the parties and injurious cause pursued by that Committee, in relation to myself and the American Anti-Slavery Society. I inferred that a favourable impression was left upon his mind, in as much as he seconded one of the resolutions that were adopted at the public meeting.

Our meeting here, last evening, was more fully attended than we had anticipated, and the sentiments that were uttered met with a very hearty response. Thompson went into the subject with his accustomed fidelity and eloquence. It was nearly 11 o'clock before we adjourned. We had no chairman; for the very good reason that no one was willing to occupy the chair, at such short notice. We got along, however, without any difficulty. I regret that I must leave for Carlisle, as we ought to hold a public meeting here. On Wednesday last, I addressed an enthusiastic meeting of the "moral suasion" Chartists, at the National Hall in London, Thompson in the chair. I did not appear on behalf of the American Anti-Slavery Society, or as an abolitionist in the technical sense, but on my own individual responsibility, and gave utterance to some of the "heresies" which I cherish, in regard to the cause of Reform universally. The text which I took was – the effect of American slavery on the progress of liberty throughout the world. I fully identified myself with the struggling reformers against church and State, in this kingdom; and I was equally delighted and surprised to see how warmly my sentiments, however ultra, were responded to. At the conclusion, the large assembly gave nine cheers, and three more for the American abolitionists. You will see a full report of the proceedings, in the London Inquirer, the editor of which has called upon me, and promises to do all that he can to promote the League, both in his private capacity, and as an editor.

The Evangelical Alliance has died, "making no sign" on the question of slavery, though for a whole week it suffered and agonized over it. Its proceedings will excite disgust and indignation, in every true breast. It has been unanimously decided by the friends in London, that we must hold a great public meeting in Exeter Hall, for both sides of the Atlantic, with express reference to the doings of the Alliance; and I have no doubt we shall have an immense meeting. Thompson, Douglass and myself are to be the principal speakers. We all deeply regret that dear H.C. Wright cannot be with us. The meeting is to be held on Monday, Sept. 14, and we intend to make it as effective as possible....

This morning, Thompson, Douglass and myself are to take breakfast with Joseph Sturge, by special invitation. (He was not at our meeting last evening.) I shall try to do justice to our cause. The result of the interview you shall soon learn.

Farewell! – Ever yours, lovingly;

Wm. Lloyd Garrison.

MS.A.1.1. vol. 4 Anti-Slavery Letters from Garrison [228]
No. 31 George Thompson to R.D. Webb (Reverse of W.L.G.'s letter)

Birmingham Saturday 12 o'clock.

Dear Richard. We have just returned from breakfasting with Joseph Sturge, and from a two hours conversation between him and Garrison, on the subject of the conduct of the B. & F. Society. Mr. Garrison went over the main points at issue, and called upon Joseph to support the charges which had been made against him and the American Society. Joseph would do little more than say he wished the matter dropped – Coalition was impossible both parties must pursue their own course. He would not vindicate or explain the acts charged home upon him and his committee. I need not say that W.L.G. was faithful. Douglass was faithful. Douglass returns to Carlisle & Newcastle & thence to meet Garrison at Sheffield on Friday. On Wednesday Garrison will be in Leeds to speak apart of that day and Thursday with Joseph Barker.

G.T.

MS.A.1.2. vol. 16 1846 Anti-Slavery Letters to Garrison [229]
No. 87 Elihu Burritt to William Lloyd Garrison

Frome, Sept. 8, 1846

Dear Friend Garrison

... A few days before you arrived in Bristol I left that city for a short trip in So. Wales. Everything seems to be favorable in this country & on the Continent for a grand alliance of all good men for the overthrow of slavery, War, and all the other great systems of iniquity which have so long oppressed the world. It was one of the principle objects I have in view in visiting this country to form the nucleus of a great League of Universal Brotherhood, which would be to slavery, War, Intemperance, Ignorance, Political & Social Inequalities what the Anti-Corn Law League was to Monopoly in this country.... I am going from place to place on foot, holding social meetings in private houses and trying to interest people in the cause. Thus far I have succeeded beyond all my expectations....

But another plan is in my mind – viz. to adopt the little plan of the Free Labor produce Association of Philadelphia, and expand it to a great system which shoul• finally bring every mother's son of the nonslaveholders of the South into antagonism to their feudal barons of the lash, thus arraying against slavery the powerful interest of free labor right on its bloodstained territory. This I had thought might be achived by the establishment of a cotton factory in America, one in England and another in France, which should manufacture none other than free labor cotton produced in the slave states. These factories should supply establishments in different sections & their respective countries with cloth free from the taint of slavery. These are a few of the measures which I have thought might be commenced on the platform of the League of Universal Brotherhood...

Your friend & brother

Elihu Burritt.

MS.A.1.1. vol. 4 Anti-Slavery Letters from Garrison [230]
No. 38 William Lloyd Garrison to R.D. Webb

Edinburgh, Sept. 25, 1846.

My Beloved Friend:

Your note was received last evening, just as I was leaving the house to attend (with Douglass) our first public meeting in this city. The audience was considerably numerous, but not crowded, but will probably be much larger this evening. I gave a brief history of the American Anti-Slavery Society, and vindicate it and myself from the slanders which had been brought against it; and then proceeded to criminate and rebuke the Free Church, with especial allusions to Chalmers, Candlish, and Cunningham. Frederick took up the Evangelical Alliance, and, as we say in America, "handled it without mittens". The applause was frequent and hearty, though there were a few serpents in the assembly who hissed. An invitation was given to anyone to come forward, and defend either the Free Church or the Alliance; but no one ventured into the lists.

On Tuesday evening, we had a very good meeting in Greenock; but a much longer and incomparably more spirited one at Paisley, on the next evening. On the whole, it surpassed every meeting I have witnessed on this side of the Atlantic. Cheers for the Paisley weavers!

This forenoon we are to address our anti-slavery female coadjutors in this place. "On Monday evening we expect to address a public meeting in Dundee. We are talking about having another public meeting in Edinburgh, on Tuesday evening, but I shall try to evade it and get to Glasgow" preparatory to our great meeting in the city on Wednesday evening. There will probably be another meeting held on Thursday evening on Friday morning, we shall go to Belfast, and address a public meeting that evening, if our friends are disposed to appoint me. I have just written to our friend John R. Neill, to this effect. I hope to be in Dublin some time during Sunday. It grieves me, beyond all expression, to think that I can remain with you and yours, only a day or two, unless I give up my visit to Cork, which place I am quite anxious to see, even as a matter of curiosity. Of course, I shall expect to address no public meeting either in Dublin or Cork, but to enjoy the social circle of friends that may wish to see me. Still, make whatever arrangements you please. If I had better go to Cork, (and I think you will say so,) pray write to our friends there, and say I will be with them on Tuesday evening, Oct. 6th, and remain till Thursday morning , when I must return to Dublin, and leave in the evening packet of that day for Liverpool without fail, to meet Geo. Thompson the next morning at Brown's hotel, and proceed to Wrexham, Manchester and Rochdale, as a public meeting is arranged in each of these places. This plan is beyond alteration, and I must govern myself accordingly....

Faithfully yours,

W.L. Garrison

MS.B.1.6. vol. 2 The May Papers [231]
No. 33 Samuel May to J.B. Estlin

Boston, Saturday, Septr. 26, 1846.

I have had a very particular pleasure, my dear sir, on reading and re-reading your full & interesting letter of the 1st, 2d & 3d inst. .... I was so glad that you had met Mr. Garrison, and that your heart had so kindly warmed towards him. I felt thankful! And I do, for my poor self, most heartily thank you and all the Bristol friends for giving so generous and hearty a reception to Mr. Garrison and to Frederick Douglass....

The formation of the "Anti-Slavery League" is a great event, and full of hope for the cause. I greatly lament, at what you say of the amount of influence George Thompson brings to the cause. He seems to us here so hearty, and so strong, so devoted & fearless, that we can hardly realise his *not* professing an immense influence and especially with the *people. Clarkson* will give his name to the League, will he not? With that name, (unless he is regarded as superannuated), the "League" could afford to do without the Gurneys and the Sturges. I hope Mr. Jay of Bath, Dr. Wardlaw of Glasgow, Mr. John Angell James,[1] and others like them, may join. Is it presumptious? These men have had a prodigious influence over the *religious* mind here; and latterly have spoken very plainly (Jay and James at least) of the cowardice and unfaithfulness of the Churches and ministers of America. – I see, by a letter of G. Thompson's (in the last Liberator) that it is contemplated having American members of the "League"

---

1. Rev. John Angell James (1785-1859), an Independent Congregational minister at Birmingham, England, had many friends in British and American circles. He was the moving spirit behind the Evangelical Alliance.

– I think they will be numerous. I hope the *Unitarian* ministers will join the "League"; *it will have a great effect here,* on the Unitarian body, and much is yet needed to arouse them to their *duty*. I hope William J. Fox[2] may give some time and zeal to the cause. Lord Morpeth's official station will, I suppose, deter him from taking any part in the League; would he not, otherwise? But I might run on so, long. Great things *must* come of the League....

Wednesday Septr. 30.

...The "Evangelical Alliance" I regret as formed to uphold and strengthen the *orthodox* sects, quite as much against the heretical, free-thinking & speaking portions of the religious world, as against the Catholics. It does look, too, as if it meant to take *Slaveholding* under its wing; and, if so, it will be despicable and short-lived. I am thankful that Garrison was in England at the time when so many American Reverend Slaveholders and Pro-Slavery men were there. The fact that they so generously refused to attend the Antislavery League meeting, must be a significant one to British lookers on.

Our shameful War with Mexico still hangs on. We have a report, (but I question its correctness) that Gen. Taylor has commenced his march for Monterey with 12,000 men, provisioned for 30 days. Sickness has been very prevalent and very fatal among the American troops. The issue – so far as fighting goes – will be disastrous to the Americans, I firmly believe; and if there must be fighting, which I do not desire, I hope the United States aims will be defeated. Meanwhile, the Mexican authorities are said to have preferred Pres. Polk's peace proposals to their Congress, which does not regularly assemble until December...

Remember me to your daughter, & believe me,

With respect & affection, yours, S. May.

MS.B.1.6. vol. 2 The May Papers [232]
No. 34 J. B. Estlin to Samuel May

Bristol. October 1st 1846

My dear Mr. May,

... On the subject of the late Evangelical Alliance I can say no more than you will hear from other quarters. The meeting in Exeter Hall attended by Messrs. Garrison, Thompson & Douglass to review the proceedings of the worthy body, was an effective one – On the 7th inst. we have an A.S. meeting in Bristol for the same purpose, when Geo. Thompson comes to lead the attack. A letter to beg him to take up his quarters at my house, is now lying just written, in the desk I am writing on.

To one subject I cannot advert without some regret: it is Mr. Garrison's course of action on this side of the Atlantic. I think he is making a great blunder, & is pursuing a mistaken line. He seems to consider it necessary, for his credit in *America*, to meddle with all sorts of questions that

---

2. William Johnson Fox (1786-1864) was a famous British Unitarian preacher and hymn writer. He was the editor of the Monthly Repository and author of several works.

divide the population of this country – "Universal Suffrage", "the rights of primogeniture," "the observance of the Sabbath," "monarchical form of Govern^{t}." &c &c, are discussed in public & pronounced upon by him. He is thus *going out of his way* to make himself unpopular, & to distinguish his influence as an *Abolition Advocate.* Every man here is expected to *have*, and if called upon, to *express* his opinions upon any of these exciting subjects, but no sensible Englishman who has some important moral or philanthropic object to accomplish, will, *uncalled for*, volunteer to proclaim publicly his convictions upon such matters. Were the middle & lower classes of this country the parties likely to do much for the Am. Abol^{n} cause, there might be some use in courting their favour, even at the risk of offending higher circles.

But these lower, & *lower-middle* classes have not sufficient personal interest in the subject to evidence them to take it up warmly; & if they did, they would do you little or no good. It is not kitchens & workshops that need Anti-Slavery agitation forAmerica's sake, but our *drawing-rooms*, the salons of the wealthy, & the libraries of the learned. And were Mr. G. to confine himself strictly to American Slavery, giving all the *information* he could, & abstaining from every other topic excepting such as which he wished for *information*, it is impossible to calculate the extent of valuable interest he would excite in the A.S. cause. Multitudes *now*, instead of seeking his acquaintance, will shun him as a general agitator. I trust and believe, that his visit to this country will advance the object he, & you & all of us have so much at heart; but I do deeply regret that Mr. G's influence here will fall so much short of what it might have been. Friend R.D. Webb, would probably not accord in my view, but I am sure I have more ample means of forming a judgment on this point than he has. I am fully acquainted with Mr. Garrison's motive for *coming forward* on some of the subjects of contention in England, & I hope it may answer the purpose of increasing his powers of usefulness in the U.S. – tho' it should diminish it with us. Henry Vincent was by no means a choice person for Mr. G. to have fraternized with publicly, unless some point of honour feeling or principle, demanded it.

As nothing is likely to diminish the high esteem & regard I feel for Mr. G. & which I expressed in my last letter, I have no hesitation in speaking freely to *you* on these points. You must take my opinion only for what you think it is worth, but I can assure you mine is the type of the views of very many earnest, intelligent, & calm judging people.

To make you comprehend more clearly in what manner I think Mr. G. is not managing his cause cleverly, I would adduce this as an example. In the National Hall in London, (not a very *choice* place for its appearing in) he said that were it not for American slavery, there would not, at this moment, have been a throne in Europe! Now *if* this were a true hypothesis, 49 people out of every 50 in this country would be very sorry to see its termination. I cannot then see the wisdom, or the advantage to the best interests of the A.S. cause, for Mr. G.'s stirring a host of prejudices against him here from some fanciful notion of raising his reputation for moral courage in America? We, here, need no evidence of his magnanimity, independence, & disinterested philanthropy, and if *you* in America require it, you have not improved your opportunities of studying G's character.

Another evil too of a foreigner's intermeddling with English politics, is, the impossibility of his knowing the sort of persons with whom he must patronise. People here are much influenced by the maxim, that "A man is known by the *company* he keeps." Now Mr. Garrison's intimacy with, & laudation of *Henry Vincent* who has been in prison for some Chartist exploits, would be sure to detract from his power of serving the A.S. cause in England. I say nothing, for I know nothing of Vincent's worth or worthlessness. I know he is only in favour with persons who have but little *power;* (even if they cant be made feel the inclination,) to aid in abolishing American Slavery...

Do not be too sanguine about the new Anti Slavery League, as yet, it has no supporters likely to give it much weight. I am in full expectation of an *open* attack upon it from the B.& F. A.S. Socy – a secret one has been going on I believe for some time. I trust however, it may eventually make a good stand...

My daughter begs her kind remembrance. Believe me my dear Sir

Yours sincerely, J. B. Estlin...

MS.A.1.2. vol. 16 1846 Anti-Slavery Letters to Garrison [233]
No. 113-114 J.B. Estlin to William Lloyd Garrison

Bristol. October 17th – 1846

My dear Mr. Garrison,

... You would not doubt that I have been watching your progress thro' different places in England; I have been pretty fortunate in procuring newspapers giving an account of your public meetings. It cannot be otherwise than that your visit to England must excite a great deal of new-born attention to American slavery. You know that my view was at first, (and observation & much communication with others has confirmed it,) that exclusively confining yourself to the subject of Anti-Slavery was the way to secure a willing attention from a most important & influential class of England Society, who would at once be repelled from an American Citizen who, *uncalled for*, made public statements of his political agitation in this country. It is not that the holding of opinions of any sort is objected to, nor their expression, when circumstances demand their honest avowal; but it is remarkably the case with us, that a person who is a sort of *general fault-finder* and reformer, is little attended to upon any one subject wherein he is particularly qualified & anxious to impart information. American slavery is by no means yet sufficiently understood with us to qualify people to enter into the minutia of what are called anti slavery *principles:* – a year hence, your visit would probably have been more useful. And I think you rather miscalculate the class of persons here who are most likely to benefit your movement, and whom it was most desirable to enlighten. You must bear in mind that your Slavery Institution has remarkably little personal interest with the lower classes of people in England: where their rights & welfare are concerned, movements originating with them are sure to extend upwards; but their *voices,* if ever raised against Am. slavery, will be powerless on the classes above them. It is the wealthy education circles of this country whose desire to assist the abolitionists would do your cause most service.

Still I am quite prepared to believe that the stir you have made, – in spite too of the strength of denunciation which is all but universally condemned, (& regretted by numerous earnest friends of the Aboln. Movt.) will do good, and excite enquiry, tho' less than would have been the case under a different mode of proceedings....

You must not expect much, – for some time at least, from the new League: it has too many opponents, and has not that sort of basis which is needed in this country for giving efficacy to a great *moral* movement, to allow of its producing any speedy results...

(MS.ends)

MS.A.9.2. vol. 22 1846 The Weston Papers [234]
No. 100 Mary Carpenter to Maria Weston Chapman

Bristol Oct. 17th 1846

My dear Mrs. Chapman

... I believe that the visit of Mr. Garrison to England will have been of great importance; – he has formed strong personal friendships, I may at any rate say in Bristol, which will enable us to cooperate with him more than he could have done without knowing him personally. I had long desired to see him, & now I feel it a great privilege to be reckoned among his friends....

Why do you not come over my dear Mrs. Chapman, to stimulate the Ladies in England, & that we may know & love you better?–

I must conclude:– I shall enclose a few memoranda in the Liverpool box respecting the contributions

with very best wishes & warm sympathy

believe me ever yours truly

Mary Carpenter.

MS.A.9.2. vol. 22 1846 The Weston Papers [235]
No. 109 R,D. Webb to [Maria Weston Chapman?]

Dublin Oct 31, 1846

My dear friend

... I am heartily glad to see Douglass go on so well, but I attribute this steadiness very much to Garrison's influence which I suppose would be greater with him than that of any other man... In Dublin owing to the ignorance and indifference that prevail respecting slavery Douglass was little noticed except for a few beyond our circle. But in Edinburgh, in consequence of the stir that has been made there for years, more especially of late – I hear that people of the highest rank in that eminently aristocratic & [concepted ?] metropolis, contend for his company and make him quite a lion... There can be no doubt that much of the sweep of the Bazaar this year may be attributed to him – for from all I can learn the contributions from this side of the Atlantic will be finer than ever. I hear that in Bristol and Belfast they are splendid & doubtless they will be from other parts of England & Scotland. As to poor Dublin it will cut a wretched figure We have neither wealth nor numbers nor anything but the zeal and good wishes of half a dozen – so you must give us credit for the will since we have not the way.

When Garrison was in London and in Dublin I had a good deal of his company and I enjoyed it thoroughly for I had never such an opportunity of being with him. He is truly transparent and guiltless – he bears to be watched & investigated There is no doubting about him – all is plain and clear and straightforward. I never met such a man in this respect – though I think I know many honest men. I dont wonder he is loved and trusted as he is by those that know him. With such a man on my side, I would not regard a thousand enemies. That is, I think I would not, for I have not been tried...

I forgot among the droppers in last night to mention Frederick Douglass who loo stately & majestic – with an air that makes Garrison a mere baby beside him. I had a long talk with Thompson yesterday about the prospects of the League wh thinks might be greatly promoted by Frederick being willing to work heartily wi it & [?], without forgetting himself – but he fears he is impracticable in that he cannot be relied upon. Poor George looks greatly cut up by his recent labour – he was actually quite weak & ill yesterday – but he has wonderful elasticity...

Here is Garrison with his coat off in the agonies of packing away and people congregating below in the parlour to take their last (I [hope] it wont be the last) breakfast with him.

Yours every truly

Rich[d] D Webb

I need not send kind remembrances to our friends – for I never forget them.

You will receive with this the contribution of Mazzini – I hope you will like it. He should be prefaced as the illustrious Italian exile, whose letters were opened by the English Secretary of State, Sir James Graham, & brought down such odium on that functionary. He is a man of noble character & great attainments and his heart and soul are devoted to the regeneration of Italy. I have heard him spoken of as one of the most remarkable men in London.

MS.A.1.2. vol. 16 1846 Anti-Slavery Letters to Garrison [236]
No. 122 John Murray to William Lloyd Garrison

Bowling Bay
30th Oct. 1846

My Dear Friend

... In thinking over what I said to you yesterday of the change in regard to the imprisonment of colored seamen – I rather think that the paragraph which appeared in the Argus & which I gave from the Standard will prevent our Society in the mean time memorialising our Govt. on the subject until we are fully assured that the evil complained of still exists. By writing to the Foreign Office we might ascertain what has been done by Lord Aberdeen the late Foreign Secty – but even that would not inform us what the effect resulting has been – if any – that can only be acquired from the opposite side....

yours truly

John Murray

MS.A.9.2. vol. 22 1846 The Weston Papers [237]
No. 108 S. Hilditch to Maria Weston Chapman

Wrexham Oct. 31/46

My dear Mrs. Chapman

... It is possible the American delegates who came over to the *so called Evangelical Alliance*, (but which proved to be a most unrighteous one when it admitted *them*,) may give *their* reports as to the anti-slavery feeling in *our* country – & alas! they *have*, to the eternal disgrace of the Alliance their side of the question in which to triumph. But it has been proved by the enthusiasm with which our friends George Thompson, W.L. Garrison & F. Douglass have everywhere been received, that the Evangelical Alliance is not the British Public – And they are also aware of it, & now I believe the Alliance is broken up – on the very question of slavery – We feel assured if [?] reorganized its basis will be far different & both the man stealer & his apologists will be excluded from it ...We are going to be very busy in canvassing for members to the League. We are also getting up a petition from our women to their sisters in America & hope to furnish our quota to the ones from the working men. We are not forgetting the Bazaar – our contribution for *this* year is now in Edinburgh & we are again commencing, (with promises from several dear friends to aid us) for our next ....

your devoted & affectionate

S. Hilditch.

Bristol, November 2nd. 1846.

My dear Mr. May,

... The acknowledgement of yourself & Mrs. Chapman of the satisfaction of Mr. Garrison's friends at his reception in Bristol, is some sort of revival to us of the pleasure afforded us by his visit. Of the results of his mission to England time has yet to show. Unquestionably a good deal of attention will be drawn to Amn. slavery. Though many object to the *denouncing* course Mr. G. took in reference to the Ev. Alliance, I am disposed to think it was in the line of his duty to show up the Amn. delegates as he did. His error has been, (and a great mistake I am satisfied it was,) to mix himself up *unnecessarily* with vexed English questions, under some sort of quixotic notion, as it appeared to me, that the more unpopular he made himself with the middle classes of society in this country, the more he should promote the a.s. cause!! Those parties whom he has most pleased, are at least able to do you any service; and the most likely soon to forget all about Amn. Slavery from the pressure of interests nearer to their own welfare; and he has indisposed to hear with attention all he had to say, a most valuable & influential section, who, if once satisfied of the goodness of his cause, would never forget it, & would render it continued & effectual help – I do not mean to say Mr. G. has done harm to his object, or no good: – I trust he has excited much attention & done much good; – but I regret that with such an opportunity as he had, he should not have profited by it to have excited a tenfold tenfold degree of anti slavery feeling to that which he has produced. His situation, however, was a difficult one; and unless he has had wise advisers when he came hither, I hardly know how he could have chalked out the best course. Happily his high moral character, and his unselfish devotion to the great cause secure for him respect & consideration.

You must not be too sanguine about "the League". Mr. G.'s course, has, I fear, been very fatal to its speedy success at least I do not know of a single influential person *anywhere* who has joined it. I believe that the opinions of the supporters or the B & F A S Socy. is, that if let alone, it will soon die a premature death, and I do not expect to find it [?] in the next Reporter. I trust however there will be a certain number of persons really respectable, & influential in these districts, tho' not generally known, who will keep up the League until a strong body of supporters joins it. I mean to do my best, and you may be sure I do not speak to others in the discouraging way I do to you.

Douglass's course is a wise one: indeed he may say what he pleases without being thought uncharitable & intolerant. He is much wanted in some of the central towns of England, where entire ignorance & apathy respecting Slavery prevail....

Yours sincerely

J.B. Estlin

MS.A.9.2. vol. 22 1846 The Weston Papers, [239]
No. 115

To the Secretary of the Boston Female Anti-Slavery Society

Belfast 11th month 2nd 1846

Dear Friend,

... We regretted not being able to get nicer material made from free labour cotton. The muslin is coarse and the only recommendation we can offer for the prints is the fact of being unpolluted by slave labour....

The immediate impulse which set the ingenuity and industry of the ladies of our Association to work for your Bazaar was to give expression to heartfelt sympathy with your philanthropic efforts and also to contribute to a treasury which is expended in seeking the overthrow of the heinous system of slavery. But our Committee has also a collateral object in view which we feel assured you will not disapprove of. We are informed that Irish emigrants with their minds proverbially open to be acted on by prejudice adopting the current sentiments of American society usually join the pro-slavery ranks after crossing the Atlantic; before being exposed to that ordeal we wish as far as possible to have their minds fortified to meet it, hence some of us have long kept an eye fixed on the schools of this country as a fitting theatre for anti-slavery effort; and we rejoice to observe that whilst members of our Association are furnishing you with proofs of their interest in your efforts they are informing their minds by reading and thus preparing themselves to become effectual coworkers in the cause by carrying it to schools which many of them patronize. But if we ever succeeded on an enlarged scale in carrying out our wishes in regard to antislavery principles being introduced into the schools of the British islands and especially of Ireland we must stand forth unshackled by party. We must not present ourselves to the public as the exclusive adherents of the Liberty party but as advocates of the down trodden bondsmen... party spirit has ever been the bane of the ardent Irish people and whenever it has mingled with their efforts whether in Philanthropy or religion it has tended to overthrow all that was good and substitute strife and acrimony in its stead....

Signed on behalf of the Belfast Ladies Anti-Slavery Committee

Maria Webb

Corresponding Secretary.

MS.A.9.2. vol. 16 pt. 2 1841 The Weston Papers [240]
No. 21 R.D. Webb to ?

n.d. fragment

...It is now Monday morning and I am at Brown's Hotel – where Garrison, G. Thompson and his wife have arrived from Glasgow. Andrew Paton is to be here tomorrow and a number of people from Dublin, Sheffield, Wrexham and other places to see Garrison off – so many that I suppose they will be in one anothers way – and in his way too. Before me sits Mr. Farmer[1] a London reporter, a friend of Thompson's, who has I understand accompanied them throughout to tak down their proceedings in shorthand he is just now deciphering the doings at their late last meeting in Edinburgh. As to George Thompson he looks ill and cut up – he has had a very hard work, and complains of bad health. As to his recent course, it has been most admirable – the only part on which I thought he would waver was his attachment to his clerical friends among the dissenters and a probably unwillingness to offend or affront them. But he has shown the utmost boldness and adherence to principle and in the opinion of many has outshone himself as a reformer and an orator atany former time. I should not now be afraid of him under any public circumstances – he is a man of wonderful courage and ability & if kept up to the mark of principle, by such a man as Garrison at his elbow, he would be ready for anything.

As far as I can gather I am disposed to think that the Evangelical Alliance will do very little harm to the Anti Slavery cause in comparison with the good it has done. Amongst people of any intelligence the priests will lose much of the admiration they ever had. In the great public meetings that have been held, the popular feeling, or 99-100 of it, has been on the right side and any who came forward in opposition have only made fools of themselves. Then there is something supremely ridiculous in the contrast of the apologies made by the Evangelical ministers, here on behalf of their dear American brethren, & the statements of the dear American brethren themselves. I never before had so deep a sense of the want of principle of the clerical body as of the trifling degree of honesty their theology has left them. In short the ground was never so well broken up in England before for the formation of genuine Anti Slavery Societies who will do something beside give a yearly subscription, leaving all thought & effort in the hands of a lazy self-constituted London Committee. [MS. ends]

MS.A.9.2. vol. 22 1846 The Weston Papers [241]
No. 131 Catherine Paton to ?

Confidential

16 Richmond St.
Glasgow Novr. 17th 1846

Dear & much esteemed Friend

... The clergy with their supporters who left the Society are still alien as ever & thus we have continually to combat with their opposition. The past year has been one of useful anti-slavery work in Scotland – Henry C. Wright has sown much good seed, which is beginning to spring up in many quarters. The public prints in England Ireland & Scotland have made many malignant attacks & misrepresentations of his views – in his Sabbath pamphlet he has given his own views of that observance – of all the observances in Scotland this is the most reveranced & national prejudice strongest, it was a bold step to attack it. The clergy have made what handle they could of it, but many of the people are beginning to investigate & enquire for themselves – we are a very bigoted people

1. William Farmer became a close friend of Garrison, and wrote an account of his life which ran for seven issues of the Liberator.

in our religious opinions... to be members in a church & assent to an orthodox creed is with many all that is necessary to christian character. Garrison will tell you how much we have of this daily to contend with, to what church do they belong to, is a question continually asked – They cannot see Christ's example followed, his precepts obeyed without the certificate of a church which they esteem orthodox & sound in the faith. Garrison too has been assailed on all sides by the so called religious press & professors with the old bugbear of infidel, but let us rejoice it is opening the eyes of many, & preparing the way for the discussion of many questions hitherto hid from the public mind... his visit was very opportune & will be long remembered by us, we regretted that it was so short, that he was so hurried & overworked; he has accomplished much & we fondly hope that it may not be the last visit to our shore... I am right glad he consented to leave H.C. Wright behind. he is a devoted untiring labourer, without fee or reward, Frederick Douglass & he are together in England at present doing good work on behalf of the Anti Slavery League... I could not aid nor approve of the buying of Frederick as I thought it compromising of principle, & a recognition of the right of property in man; I could not see how Garrison could approve of it – Is not George Thomson's faithfulness above all praise. He has been cutting off right hands & plucking out right eyes all over the country many would receive him but he would go nowhere unless Garrison accompanied, him, he has long stood high in my estimation, but now more than ever...

very sincerely yours

Catherine Paton

MS.A.9.2. vol. 22 1846 The Weston Papers [242]
No. 128 Lucy Browne to [Maria Weston Chapman ?]

Riverside Bridgewater
Tuesday Nov. 17th '46.

My dear Madam

... We shall all be much interested in hearing of the success of the Bazaar, and of the progress which the Anti Slavery cause makes in your country. How far public opinion in England furthers it, or whether its expression may not be regarded by some as an undesirable interference, and thus injure the cause which we wish to promote, you can judge far better than I: but I feel sure that the visits which some of the American friends of freedom (Messrs. Garrison, Douglass, Burritt and Clapp) have made to our country have had a good effect here, in awakening much kind feeling; in spreading a good deal of information respecting the state of your country; in rousing a warm interest in your reforms, which I wish we may not only admire but imitate, and in adding to the list I may almost say of our personal friends, many on your side of the Atlantic whom although we may never, indeed probably shall never meet, we shall always hear of with interest, and think of with affection. Believe me, my dear Madam, to remain

yours respectfully

Lucy Browne.

MS.A.9.2. vol. 22 The Weston Papers [243]
No. 130 M. Welsh to Maria Weston Chapman

Edinr. Novr 17th. 1846.

My dear Mrs. Chapman

... We have a great battle to fight here now, & we are fully determined to gird on our armour, & never yield one inch of vantage ground to the enemy to these Clergy, they are the greatest enemies, [??] has to contend with, however we dont fear them a bit. Our hearts have been refreshed & gladdened by the visit of that noble man Garrison, in the strength of it we shall go for many days to come. H. C. Wright & Douglass are left behind to work with us & truly there is much for them to do & suffer, but they are able for it all. The calumnious reports that are ever circulating against the valuable advocates as well as Garrison, Thompson &c are just so many tests to prove the sincerity of their friends. It is a glorious battle, we are neither ashamed nor afraid of it, success is sure & that I think before long.

Some of us have been very much grieved at Anna Richardson[1] getting that money collected to purchase Frederick Douglass' ransome. We feel it a compromise of principle in this recognising the right the slaveholder had to sell him, & many of us who are the warmest friends the [?] has, both here & in Glasgow took no part in it, from real principle it has grieved us exceedingly. However we are now collecting a little for Frederick himself into which we can heartily enter. There is a ladies society lately formed at Ulster in Ireland, who are advertising themselves as willing to take contributions for both your society & Liberty Party, this has been another source of grief to us, that there should be antislavery friends in this country so truly ignorant of the right position of the question as to ever speak of Liberty Party....

I ever am yours for humanity

M. Welsh.

MS.B.1.6. vol. 3 The May Papers [244]
No. 27 A.H. Richardson to [S. May ?]

n.d. (fragment)

... I have no expectation of reaching the councils of New Broad Street (!) but if, as was the case the other day, its Treasurer, G.W. Alexander,[1] gives me a sovereign to lay out as I please for anti-slavery purposes and Joseph Sturge (whom we know intimately) lends a willing ear, and gives both money and hearty co-

---

1. Anna Richardson (1806-1892), the wife of Henry Richardson of Newcastle, was another of the Quakers who were active in social work. One of her most prominent acts of philanthropy was to raise funds for the purchase of Frederick Douglass, an action loudly condemned by the British Garrisonites. For her family relationship with the Wighams. See Appendix II.

1. George William Alexander, the Treasurer of the B.F.A.S.S., played an important role in the German emigration movement to Texas.

operation when there is anything to be done – and as many of the leaders of the League come under our roof as please to do so when they visit Newcastle, *that* is the kind of Union I mean.

The ground of the Anti-Slavery League was too narrow for my liking – it was avowedly a large auxiliary to the American Anti-Slavery Society, and was expected to uphold to a considerable extent the views of that party. Now in corresponding with America,I should not like to have the least restriction upon the position of the parties with whom we like to hold intercourse. Lewis Tappan is in one place, and William Goodell in another – & we like to have [intercourse ?] with both – I heard the other day from Mrs. Weld (late Grimké) & also from William E. Whiting of the Liberty Party – Most of these are kindly going to assist me with the "Illustrations" &c for which I would equally thank C.L. Remond (whom we know & esteem) or any one else in the opposite side – I see [clearly ?] their own difficulties *as parties* – that the one thinks the American constitution must be pulled to pieces – & the other, reformed & improved – but it seems to me that we in Great Britain may [fairly ?] leave the political view of the matter – We greatly admired dear fd. the candour and impartiality of thy own work – I do not wonder that it has met with large sale – I am sorry to give any one trouble about the "Testimonial", but finding that things from Newcastle were a little overlooked on New Broad Street – I thought it possible that it might gain more notice from a new quarter – & do not often [try ?] them however – We have long since set it down as an axiom that London Societies do not hail provincial associations unless they are more of an *auxiliary* character than would be consistent with our ideas of independence – This makes one think more & more that it is not a parish society that we want with paid officers and an expensive establishment but simply a clear and understanding interest in each others proceedings and a mutual recognition from town to town of each others proceedings, each separate association forming its own plans, & working in the way most adapted to its own local position & circumstances.

We found this out long since in the slave cause & have acted upon it to decided advantage & I think success.

I do not wonder that there would not be a prospect of your doing a *great deal* for the "testimonial" & there is no sort of occasion for anyone to be overtaxed. It is rather the same in Newcastle – or on all events in our immediate circle of friends.

Very sincerely and respectfully thine,

A.H. Richardson.

MS.B.1.6. vol. 2 The May Papers [245]
No. 38 Samuel May to J.B. Estlin

Boston, 1st December, 1846

My dear Sir,

... Mr. Garrison feels that his visit to England has been one of importance and real service to the AntiSlavery cause. It has brought forward, developed and secured some real friends. It has awakened some slumbering fire. I think he was himself surprised at the amount of indifference to the subject, and, still worse, of actual proslavery, which he found in England & Scotland. He thinks many of your countrymen bear away the palm from all on this side [of the] water for ingenuity in planning excuses for slaveholding, and reasons for joinging in social and Christian (!) fellowship with slaveholders & their Apologists. – Whether as you think, he has done some harm, or prevented some good, to the cause, by volunteering his opinions on other subjects, is a question which I feel unable to decide. You must certainly be more competent on this point. But I cannot willingly think that the real advance of any good cause is obstructed by the utterance of the truth with regard to any other. Some timid ones may be offended, go back, and "follow no more" with these plain-spoken advocates of right & justice. But all this shall obstruct the way of right & justice only *apparently;* so I think, and I have almost, if not quite, learned not to regret the temporary loss which is endured by speaking, & labouring for, the right and the true. These people of experience & policies and the like are the very ones who will desert you at a pinch. Is it not to the *entire fidelity and truthfulness* of a few that we owe, under GOD, the progress the AntiSlavery cause has made in this country. Surely, to nothing else; such is the testimony of those whose testimony is best worth having. The principle of the League is a high one, and applies a severe test, I know. But it is the only sufficient basis & corner-stone for the movement. It is making Christ, in the integrity & completeness of his truth, the corner-stone. Many will not indeed accept it. When have *the many* accepted Christ? His Gospel is one of *no compromise with sin & wrong – one* of infinite compassion & forgiveness to the repentant wrong-doers; but it is to him as *repentant,* dating it self to degrees & shades of wrong – and I am sure you cannot; so I need not prove this subject with you...

With affectionate regards to your daughter and all my Bristol friends, believe me,

Ever & most repectfully, yours

Samuel May.

MS.B.1.6. vol. 2 The May Papers [246]
No. 39 Samuel May to J.B. Estlin

Boston, December 4, 1846.

My dear Mr. Estlin,

...I believe I did not, in my letter last Tuesday, say about Mr. Garrison just what I wished to say. I would not appear to dispute your judgment, so much more likely to be correct, as to the *mistakes* made by Mr. G. in England. Assuredly I will not deny that he made mistakes. He may have gone out of his way to give his opinions on "vexed English questions", if so, certainly this was a mistake. But, may it not be, that to him it did not appear to be travelling out of the record? Such is the way in which I cannot refrain from viewing it, knowing as I do, how intimately, & habitually, all questions touching the natural heaven-ordained rights of man, are joined & allied, each to the other, in his mind. I know he wishes to be, not the Advocate of the Slave *alone*, but of every form of injured and wronged humanity; nay, I know he is well convinced that he best subserves the slave's cause, when he makes it identical with the civil, social & individual rights of every human being. This is the view, I confess, which I am strongly inclined to take of his course in England, so far as I am informed about it; and yet I do not wish to question the judgment you form, for the reason that your position gives you opportunities to form such a judgment which I do not at all possess. – I feel that, if he has been injudicious only, the really wise and good will soon get above and beyond that, and the cause will not ultimately suffer; but, if it be that it is because he uttered great truths, essential to be uttered in English ears before they can fully appreciate the antislavery struggle,that many or nay turn away from his, I cannot for one find it in my heart to regret, much less condemn, the course he pursues. – I cannot think Mr. G. wished to make himself "unpopular with the middle classes" among you. It is more in accordance with his habit to make his appeals to, and place his main reliance – upon, these. And would it not be to his condemnation justly, if it could be said of him, on his return home, that he had never protested, in England, against Monarchy as a principle, nor against the social distinctions & awful inequalities among your population, &c &c ? – I have no doubt with you, that Joseph Sturge is a relentless enemy of Mr. Garrison. I suspect Joseph Sturge is something like Gerrit Smith with us; – he cannot forego the distinction, the consideration, which he enjoys, arising from his wealth, & from his position among the Friends. He nurses his dignity, and is forever on the watch to see that it receives no detriment. I have therefore thought him very deficient in candour & fairness....

George Thompson, it seems to me, has entitled himself to the heartiest thanks and respect of every lover of Christianity & Freedom. His labors have been very abundant, very timely, very powerful, and I think must have been very effective, also, I read the report, in the "Inquirer", of his speech on the case of the Rajah of Sattara, and was much impressed by its eloquence & force of argument. I became quite interested in the case. His speech at the "League" in London, on the "Evangelical Alliance" seemed to me a most masterly and unanswerable effort; – indeed all his speeches touching that "Alliance" have been of great ability. I am curious to see how he overthrew Dr. S.A. Cox, at Liverpool. Dr. C. never went near him, I will venture to say....

We are getting members of the "Antislavery League" in this country. Myself, my wife, and two eldest children, have enrolled our names, and taken cards of membership....

With sincere regards to Miss Estlin, and grateful remembrance to all Bristol friends, I remain

Most truly & respectfully yours

Samuel May

Boston, Dec. 19, 1846.

My Beloved Friend:

... You will be pleased to hear, that among the foremost to give me their hearty approval, and to aid me in my mission, were Unitarian friends. I am under great obligations to Francis Bishop, William James, J. Solly, Philip Carpenter[1], George Harris[2], and other Unitarian clergymen, and have formed for them a strong personal friendship, which they appear heartily to reciprocate. By a letter just received from my dear friend Bishop, he informs me that, since I left, his wife has given birth to a daughter, whom they have named Caroline *Garrison* Bishop. This is an indication of their personal regard for me. James Martineau[3] was absent from Liverpool when I was there, and I did not see him. I was told that he is considerably prejudiced against the true anti-slavery band in this country, and sympathises with such men as Drs. [Orville] Dewey and [Francis] Parkman.[4] I meant to have visited Harriet [Martineau], at Ambleside, before my return; but she left for Egypt a few days before I sailed, and I missed the coveted opportunity. I saw her mother and sister at Newcastle. Religiously, the Unitarians in England are regarded as little better than infidels; but I found them to be much better than their revilers and persecutors.

Nothing could have been more timely than my mission. No three months of my life were ever spent more profitably to the cause of religious and personal freedom. The blow that was given to the Evangelical Alliance, by our bold, prompt and scathing condemnation of it, was like a thunderbolt from heaven. If I had not gone to England at that time, there is little doubt that the pro-slavery action of the alliance would have secured in its defence the religious sanction of the evangelical portion of Christendom. You have seen, no doubt, the result of the proceedings of the British Alliance at Manchester. Slaveholders are declared to be ineligible to a seat in that body. Very much is due to the indefatigable exertions of Henry C. Wright, Frederick Douglass, and George Thompson. I trust we shall have all three of them with us next summer....

Your affectionate friend,

Wm. Lloyd Garrison.

---

1. Philip Pearsall Carpenter (1819-1877), the youngest son of Lant Carpenter, engaged in many philanthropic ventures and was the author of numerous articles. His main work, however, was devoted to his collection of and treatises on shells.
2. George Harris (1794-1859) was active in Unitarian circles in Scotland and the North of England. He was a keen radical and deeply interested in social reforms.
3. James Martineau (1805-1900), another Unitarian minister, was the brother of Harriet and author of many theological works.
4. Rev. Orville Dewey (1794-1882) and Rev. Francis Parkman (1788-1852) were both leading American clergymen who gave little support to the abolition movement.

MS.B.1.6. vol. 2 The May Papers [248]
No. 42 J.B. Estlin to Samuel May

Bristol January 12th 1847

My dear Mr. May,

... Our "A.S. League" gets on but little, so far as I can learn: still if they continue to labour at it, – *if Douglass keeps firm,* something may yet spring up to give it impetus. I doubt if F.D. like the uphill work, so swiftly was he before sailing on the tide of popularity. While observing him at Liverpool, I could not but tremble for his future domestic comfort when he returns to the U.S. You can hardly imagine how he is noticed, – *petted* I may say by *ladies.* Some of them really a little exceed the bounds of propriety, or delicacy, as far as appearances are concerned; yet F.D.'s conduct is most guardedly correct, judicious & decorous. I doubt if he forms intimacies much with gentlemen. I should think him of a suspicious turn of mind: but he is most observant of everything, certainly a very remarkable man – My fear is that often associating so much with white women of education & refined taste & manners, he will feel a "craving void" when he returns to his own family, – But of the *League.* No wealthy, or well known high-standing persons have yet joined it: & in this country such leaders are essential to the rapid formation of any new organization. Had I not consented to become Treasurer to the Bristol Auxiliary A S League, it would I fear have died away, but I cannot find any active coadjutors....

Our meeting at Brown's Hotel, Liverpool about noon on the 4th of November after our return from accompanying Mr. Garrison to the Acadia, had, to my view a *solemnity* in it . I know not if it appeared so to others: no one seemed disposed to make a display of sentimentality. At that meeting, F. Douglass, after consideration, firmly declared his decision to be to advocate the "League" – and which I regarded very important, for his influence is very great for the time at least, with every auditory he addresses. Geo. Thompson told me after, in private conversation, that he did not feel at all secure what course F.D. would take on this point, as he was not *a very changeable person.* He firmly discussed the "Principle" of the League as first adopted in London: "*Slaveholding under all conceivable circumstances &c*" and on my suggestion it was unanimously resolved to simplify it, – even more indeed than I advocated. Mr. Thompson even thought the connecting word "all" as in the Bristol card, unneeded, & it was at length realised it would simply be, "Slaveholding is a sin, & ought to be immediately abandoned." I know of no view or proposition this [Major?] does not contain....

I am, my dear Mr. May

Most Truly yours

J.B. Estlin.

Leicester, (Mass.) February 25, 1847.

My dear Sir,

... I am, at times, surprised to find how generally, nay how universally, this slavery question has become the great, national, absorbing question of the time, with us. This winter's session of Congress has been filled up with it. *The War* has "opened up" the whole subject of slavery. The "Wilmot Proviso" so called, by which it is provided that in any territory which may hearafter be annexed to the U. States there shall be no slavery, or involuntary servitude, (save for the crime of which the parties shall be duly convicted) has been passed in the House of Representatives by a vote of 115 to 106.... The Wilmot Proviso annexed to what is called the Three Million Bill is now under discussion in the Senate as you perceive from what Mr. Calhoun says. There is no expectation that the Senate will pass the Bill with that Proviso; no Southern Senator w^d^. vote for it, I presume, and several Northern ones choose to go for slavery, on all occasions, in preference to Freedom. But I trust that the Ho. of Representatives will stand fast, and the Press^dt^. be refused the appropriation without the Proviso. — What a farce (if it were not the greatest of *crimes*) this Mexican War is! This country had a claim on Mexico for a few millions of dollars, 2 or 3 millions, not more; which Mexico acknowledged & was slowly but regularly, paying, up to the time that Mexico annexed Texas which Mexico still claimed as belonging to her, when she very property refused to pay any more. To gain our rights, the country launches into a war, which is said to have cost already $ 70,000,000; and now, to make a peace, the Pres^dt^. asks for $ 3,000,000!!! If this people dont get enough of Slavery's rule, and of James K. Polk's Presidency, before his term is out, then all signs fail...

Great exertions have been making in this country, and are still, to relieve the starving poor of Ireland & Scotland. In our larger cities, the sums are not yet made up... Boston will do largely: it never failed, on such an occasion. Next Monday's ship will carry to England, &c the report of very large sums raised among our citizens for the starving millions of Ireland, &c. I believe that many have felt that the generous aid we have received, from Eng^d^, and Scot^d^, & Ireland, in past years, for the AntiSlavery cause, has added a new obligation for their action in this crisis. — The Irish accounts have caused a very great & deep sensation in this country. The starvation of the body seems to them a horrible thing — so it is!; but the starvation, obliteration, and annihilation of millions of hearts; which slavery has done, by our National sanction during the last sixty years! — oh! what is that! Well, I thank GOD for what good *is* done, and I trust the greater matter will not always be left undone.

I am, as ever, most respectfully, your fellow-servant,

Saml. May

Boston Feb. 28th 1847

My Dear Sir,

... In my letter of the 1st Feb. to Miss Estlin, I suggested the idea of a separate Bazaar in Bristol for the Benefit of the Cause, the remains of which might be sent to us, with such a proportion of the proceeds as should be found judicious. Since writing that letter, the office bearers of our Am. & Masstts. A.S. Societies have unanimously invited George Thompson to visit the U.S. In case of his acceptance the most judicious appropriation of funds seems to me to be for the support of his mission. $3000 would probably support his family, pay his passages, & repay his travelling expenses for Four Months. I could wish he might remain Eight or Twelve. He knows how to adapt himself to the mind of America *much* better than we do, ourselves, and is, above all others, the person to succeed with a New England audience. If he comes, it will be immaterial whether any goods contributed to the cause are retained. The stimulus of his coming will make a market for any quantity, & the knowledge of the additional Expense thereby to be incurred, will act upon American contributors to make them more industrious, energetic & liberal than ever, instead of being dormant, & reposing upon the labours of others. I most warmly concur with the views of our board of officers as to the expediency of his visit. There is really no prejudice against Foreigners here. It is in a man's favour to have been born in England. Second rate Englishmen come here & marry first rate American girls and establish themselves in the first portions of society; – to have travelled in England is a great recommendation. – The attempt to get up a native American party in politics has proved an utter failure. Doubtless the cry of "Foreign Emissary" will be raised against him, but it will be merely a pretence, just as the cry of "infidel" is raised against Garrison, & "woman preacher" against Mrs. Foster & the Grimkés. We are never able to please the proslavery public in our selection of agents. If we send out old & experienced men "they will not be taught the principles of any cause by drivellers." If we send your young ardent men, "it is an insult to put boys to instruct them". Send Garrison & they are insulted because he "was nothing but a printers Devil." Send Wendell Phillips, & they "hate an aristocrat.." These people will of course object to Thompson as a Foreigner; but it is safe to say that the more proslavery for any ostensible reason objects to the man,, is the man for us to sustain. It is no more wise in his holy warfare with wrong than in the iniquitous warfares of the nations, to allow the Enemy the veto power upon instrumentalities. If the man be one that they would admire & uphold as our advocate of slavery, then *we* shall do wisely to retain him as an advocate of Freedom....

hastily but most respectfully

your obliged friend M.W. Chapman.

MS.A.1.2. vol. 17 1847 Anti-Slavery Letters to Garrison [251]
No. 28 William Lovett to William Lloyd Garrison

London,
11 South Row, New Road
March 1st, 1847

My Dear Friend:

I very much regret that many circumstances have transpired to prevent me from writing to you before; but, since I saw you last I have met with very many personal disagreables, which have so fully occupied my time and attention, that I have not been able to do what I anticipated in favour ot that great cause of which you have been both prophet and martyr for so many years. I have, however made a point of attending most of the council meetings of the League, and I rejoic to say that, though our means have been limited, it has proved an instrument of great good. It has helped to purify the ranks of evangelical dissent from the crime of slavery, despite the slaveholders' apologists and abettors. It has also made the subject of slavery plain and familiar to the minds of the millions, and is fast teaching them that slavery, in every land, is but a link in the same great chain of oppression which binds the multitude in all countries and climes. If no other good resulted from your voyage to England, than the formation of the Anti-Slavery League, joined to your plain-speaking appeals, and the numerous addresses of friends Thompson, Douglass, and Wright, be assured that these alone will produce fruit in season to fully compensate you and them for your labour.... Hoping that you and your family are in good health I remain yours very truly

Wm Lovett.

William Lloyd Garrison Esq.
Boston U.S.

MS.A.9.2. vol. 23 1847 The Weston Papers. [252]
No. 11 Mary Howitt to Maria Weston Chapman.

The Elms, Clapton March 2nd

My dear Friend,

And may I call you so without violating truth – I hope so – I believe so & therefore let it stand. I write to you at this moment to ask you respecting an object we have at heart greatly & in which we desire to obtain if possible your kind & valuable assistance. You know that last year we were engaged in the People's Journal & that we endeavoured to make it an organ of good in every possible way & a bond of union & good fellowship between your land & ours. We were fortunate however in our connexion there – the greatest anxiety & distress of mind that ever we endured has grown out of it & now its Editor is endeavouring to do what no one ever dared to do what no one ever dared to do before, to damage our moral characters. He sends a false, very false statement to America to damage us there if possible & he & a tool of his one [Phelph ?], a man of bad character have gained the ear of our dear friend William Lloyd Garriso – Our friend William Lovett was the one to whom Lloyd Garrison proposed the scheme of the international testimony against slavery & now these people – who in reality care nothing about the question – have taken up the idea & are vaunting it everywhere. I believe that these things will in the end all get right, if we had but patience to wait, but it is hard to see the good, & those whom we love & esteem prejudiced against us, & imposed upon by the minority. We have broken ourselves lose from our bad connections in the People's Journal & have begun our own Journal which perhaps you have heard of under the name of "Howitt's Journal" – in this we will still pursue the same honest earnest course that we began in the People's Journal – only as far as America goes, will not you help us? For this purpose it is that I now write to you. We have a very sweet portrait of Abby Kelly – a woman we know – & are in want of a memoir to accompany it. Can we ask this from your pen? It would serve the great cause you have at heart, & oblige us which I trust would not be displeasing to you. We can offer you £1 p page for the Memoir which shall be paid to you through our agent in Boston. I hope we may induce you to do this, & also let me tell you that any information relative to the Anti Slavery cause which you will favour us with shall be presented to the English public & be made as useful to you as possible....

With William's kindest regard
I am, dear Friend,

Yours truly

Mary Howitt.

MS.A.1.1. vol. 4 1844-1853 Anti-Slavery Letters from Garrison [253]
No. 51 William Lloyd Garrison to R.D. Webb

Boston, March, 1, 1847.

My dear Richard,

... As you regularly receive the Standard and Liberator, I deem it unnecessary to say much here, in regard to our anti-slavery doings. We realized from the Bazzar about a thousand dollars more than we did last year. This, on the whole, was an increase greater than we had any good reason to expect. Remember that we are the "forlorn hope" of the anti-slavery movement, and that we are in constant collision with all the religious sects and political parties. Our "Disunion" ground terrifies many, and offends more. There is no transcending it for the overthrow of slavery, and to occupy it requires a good deal of nerve. But it is invulnerable, and must ultimately be occupied by all the non-slaveholding States. A very considerable number of petitions, praying for the secession of Massachusetts from the Union, has already been presented to our Legislature, numerously signed by legal voters. This is encouraging; but a revolution so great, and involving such mementous consequences, is not hastily to be wrought out. out. We must "bide our time". and labor diligently for the result. There is no other question so universally discussed as that of slavery, and within the last six months a most surprising change in public sentiment has undeniably taken place. The cowardly pro-slavery war which our national administration is waging with Mexico is producing a mighty reaction against the Slave Power, and, out of the slave states, is generally regarded with abhorrence. Mr. Calhoun, who is the Napoleon of slavery, is evidently anticipating a "Waterloo defeat", in due season. You will se his speech in the last number of the Liberator. He does not attempt to hide his fears as to the future. Unless Slave States can be added to the Union as fast as free states, his cherished system of diabolism must ultimately be overturned. Mark hislanguage.He is a man who means what he says, and who never blusters. He is no demagogue, but proud, incorrigible, merciless tyrant, though he expresses the hope that he is a kind master! Nicholas of Russia would as complacently expre the same hope.

The horrid particulars of the famine in Ireland have made a wide and profound sensation in this country. Contributions are pouring in from every quarter, and the amount of food, money and clothing, that will be contributed, will be very considerable; yet not a fiftieth part that ought to be done. But we must recollect that the idea of human brotherhood is as yet but imperfectly developed in the world, and that, hitherto, each nation has left other nations to take care of themselves, without being specially concerned for their welfare. Still, enough will be given to save many from starving, and to strengthen the ties of humanity, to the disregard of the selfish feelings of nationality. Boston, I trust, will not be outdone by any other place in the country....

And now I have just begun, I must stop. With the most endearing remembrances to Hannah, and the whole circle of beloved ones in Dublin, I remain, with an overflowing heart,

Yours faithfully,

Wm. Lloyd Garrison.

MS.B.1.6. vol. 3 The May Papers [254]
No. 23 James Haughton to Samuel May

35 Eccles St. Dublin 29th March 1847.

My dear friend

...You [?] hear much about the misery of poor Ireland, our people are indeed sadly afflicted. It is quite impossible, I believe, to exaggerate the woes arising from loss of the Potato crop, which was literally the food of millions in this island. Your subscriptions on our behalf are noble evidence of your sympathy with us, yet I must acknowledge it is cause of sorrow, rather than of joy to me. The gifts of slaveholders will shut our mouths, where our hearts condem &close our eyes so that we will not see the wickedness of man stealing. Only think of it, the Society of Friends here, have accepted a contribution from slaveholders in Charleston & Baltimore, & refused one from ladies in London, because it was produced by a Benefit at a Theatre. Thus declaring to the world that they consider play-acting vile & man stealing no abomination. Some of us will try to oppose this canting hypocrisy, but Public opinion here is so warmed by your magnificence, I fear we shall obtain but little sympathy, but we shall make the attempt....

believe me to be affectionately yours

James Haughton

MS.A.9.2. vol. 23 1847 1847 The Weston Papers [255]
No. 20 James Haughton to Maria Weston Chapman

35 Eccles St. Dublin
1st April 1847.

My dear Mrs. Chapman

...I was battling the cause of the American slave with some of our politicians, today, touching the receipt of slave holders money. One of them who had lived in your country, & was well convinced of the withering effects of slavery on all your institutions, & fully satisfied that it will yet overthrow the Union, if the Union do not overthrow it, was not still, in favour of the measure of the ultra abolitionists – He would not like to be a slave for an hour himself, yet he could not see how violent agitation could do the work. This man is one of our most violent Repealers. He, & many like him who would toil for Ireland, & fight for Ireland, have no sympathy to spare for the poor oppressed Negro. I tell them that, with such feelings it is in vain they labor for the regeneration of their own country. It is not *for* freedom, they fight, but *against* England. So it was the America fought, not for freedom, but against England.

The Unitarian clergy seem to be "tarred with the same stick" as all the rest of the black-coated, & white cravated gentry....

You correspond so regularly with R.D. Webb that you must be well acquainted with all that passes of any movement amongst us. We keep up a steady agitation on several matters of Reform – Freedom – Peace Temperance – Anti-Capital Punishment &c.

The Temperance movement is rather flourishing amongst our poor. We have little drunkenness in our streets, & our meetings in support of the cause are steadily kept up.

... We have a good deal of political action kept up for repeal of the Union between us & England. You will see by the Papers that our once great O'Connell, is great no longer. We have no certain accounts of the state of his mind or body, but I apprehend his mind is broken down, & that this sad result is caused in great measure by the feeling that he has lost the confidence of his country, in consequence of his late errors (errors to use the mildest term) as a politician. His fate is strikingly evidence of the folly of a disingenuous course of action....

believe me your sincere friend

James Haughton.

MS.A.9.2. vol. 23 1847 The Weston Papers [256]
No. 19 Catherine Paton to ?

Glasgow 1st April 1847

Dear and much esteemed Friend

I duly received your kind notes, also the Box containing the Liberty Bells and Books, the former I have forwarded to their several destinations, while

I shall endeavour to make good use of the latter feeling that the information they contain is much wanted in society here, accept my grateful thanks for both. I esteem the Liberty Bell very highly for its valuable contents, the names of its contributors are dear to us as associated in this great cause. We are much gratified with the success of the Bazaar, and read with much interest Lowell's description; we beheld you all in vision – The chagrin of Liberty Party was truly laughable – ... The clergy who deserted in 1841 still retain their enmity, and now that they can no longer control the Society in public do all they can to injure us in private, their vocation giving them great scope in that way, leading captive silly women, not to mention silly men. You know from experience that deserters (clerical ones especially) are always the worst kind of enemies, they refuse to read our notices – but we are learning to get *a weightier member* to take it to them. Then they dare not refuse, being either ashamed or afraid to say nay. Thus we go on *sapping* and *mining* ....

faithfully yours

Catherine Paton.

MS.A.1.1. vol. 4 Anti-Slavery Letters from Garrison [257]
No. 52 William Lloyd Garrison to Elizabeth Pease

Boston, April 1, 1847.

Beloved Friend:

... This country is still prosecuting its murderous warfare against Mexico; but though the American forces have generally been victorious, recently the tide of events appears to be setting in favour of the Mexicans, and confirming the Scriptural declaration, that "the race is not to the swift nor the battle to the strong". We have rumours today of a bloody engagement having taken place, with great loss on both sides, – General Taylor having been compelled to fall back on Monterey, with the loss of many of his officers. I desire to see human life at all times held sacred; but, in a struggle like this, so horribly unjust and offensive on our part, so purely one of self-defence against lawless invaders on the part of the Mexicans, – I feel, as a matter of justice, to desire the overwhelming defeat of the American troops, and the success of the injured Mexicans.

The distress in Ireland continues to excite much sympathy here, and contributions in money and food are daily made in all parts of the country. These will arrive too late to save thousands, now beyond all human aid; but they will prevent other thousands from dying of hunger. It is a singular spectacle we are presenting to the world – with one hand, we are carving desolation and death into a neighbouring republic, and with the other supplying food and clothing to save from suffering and death, those who reside across the wide Atlantic....

Hastily, but truly, yours, Wm Lloyd Garrison.

5 South Gray St. Edinburgh 1/4/47

My dear Friend

... I am very glad to hear that your Societies have again invited George Thompson. If he is able to accept it, his visit would no doubt be useful and I trust his life would be safer than when he was with you before. But he is much engaged with the case of the Rajah of Satarrah – and now that it is beginning to gain, he will not be likely to abandon it – One point for which he has been labouring, has been carried by a small majority in his favour, and he will wish to follow it up closely with more. However if he should go to America – and you still think our contributions of work as needful, I trust we shall not relax in our industry – though many of our hands have been busy for sales in different places in this country, to raise money for the relief of our starving population – ...

But it is high time I should thank thee for thy two letters and also for the Liberty Bell, which keeps up its character well both in contents and outward appearance – we are grateful for the supply sent to Edin^{r} – and we who have been favored to have copies specially addressed to us will lend them as widely as we can among our Anti Slavery friends – this we also do with the "Standards" and "Liberators" – besides reading long extracts from them at our meetings – But we dont approve of private letters being printed in these papers especially with the writers names in full – They fall into hands in this country which makes it very unpleasant to the writers of these letters. I am sure Eliza Wigham[1] had not the slightest idea of ever seeing her *familiar private* letter to W.L.G. again – or it might have been differently worded, though there is nothing in it but what is believed to be true. Thou enquires who she is? She is my husband's daughter and the other Eliza, is Eliza Nicholson the sister of Sarah Wigham who is the wife of John Wigham Jnr. My husband being John Wigham tertius – the two Johns are first cousins – the father of J.W. Jr. was the sen^{r}. but he has been dead a number of years and the others still retain the distinctive adjuncts of Jr. & 3tius – We live within 5 minutes walk of each other and are on terms of the closest love & friendly intercourse...

I have just read a note from our good friend H.C. Wright. He is in Dublin but intends being in Glasgow next week... He is in great concern about his Dublin Relief Committee receiving large contributions from the American Slave States to feed the starving Irish – and think they should refuse to be the almoners of this money – so does a minority of the Relief Committee and so does Wm Fraser – but the majority are for using it. The A.S. Societies in some places are already preparing to remonstrate with them against returning it – but there are many of a contrary opinions – thinking it is a very different case from the Free Church – who *went* to Slaveholders to ask the money – and when found fault with for doing stand up boldly in defence of slaveholding and fellowshipping slaveholders – still there can be no question that great part of these contributions are the price of human beings – and their wages kept back by fraud – I do hope the Committee will act rightly in the matter – We were told yesterday that another £500 has

---

1. See Wigham family tree – Appendix II.

just been received from the Southern States by the Free Church – perhaps sent now to keep them quiet over next Assembly – I hope they will not be able to do that – We (the Ladies Society) are preparing a remonstrance to the Assembly – and we hear of some other place also doing the same –

... hoping to hear from thee soon remain with dear love thy affectionate friend

Jane Wigham

MS.A.9.2. vol. 23 1847 The Weston Papers [259]
No. 26 Lucy Browne to Maria Weston Chapman

Riverside Bridgewater
April 14th 1847

My Dear Mrs. Chapman

... Some of us are already at work for the next Bazaar, and we shall do what we can to get contributions for it; at the same time I fear that we shall have much less to send you than we had last time, chiefly on account of the very unusual exertions which have been made here for the relief of the starving Irish and which have monopolized the time and thoughts of many of our fellow-townsmen; besides this the last contributions were made in the midst of the enthusiasm excited by Mr. Douglass in his visit to us in the beginning of September – Now although he has inspired not a few with an interest in the cause which will not pass away, yet I do not know how far it will be permanent in many who shared in it strongly at the time...

With respect toEnglish influence on this question, it should certainly be used in destroying that slavery which was first introduced by Englishmen, and long encouraged if not enforced by our government. At the same time I think that every censure and remonstrance addressed by our nation to yours, should be sent in no spirit of self satisfied virtue but with the full consciousness of the many sins which still nationally disgrace us and with the sad remembrance of how few years have passed since, by the persevering & life long efforts of our best country men, that direst oppression ceased to find a sanction in our statute book and a place in our dominions. ...

Yours very faithfully

Lucy Browne

MS.B.1.6. vol. 2 The May Papers [260]
No. 46 Samuel May to J.B. Estlin

Leicester, Massachusetts, April, 29th 1847.

My dear Mr. Estlin,

... When I wrote to you last, I spoke of the state of the Antislavery question in Congress, and the hopeful action on what was called the *Wilmot*

Proviso; did I predict, in my letter to you, the way in which that would be defeated? I did to many others here, who afterwards (some of them) spoke to me of the exact fulfilment of my words. It needed, indeed, no ghost to tell an Abolitionist that slavery would find ways enough to make the North succumb & retreat. The "*Wilmot Proviso*" had a majority of 9 in the House of Representatives. The Senate, as everybody knew they would, rejected the "proviso"; – in order therefore to secure the 3 million dollars to Mr. Polk, to which the Proviso was attached, it became necessary to coax, bribe or otherwise induce *five* men – this was the least number that would do it – and become traitors of the worst sort; and this was my prediction, viz that efforts would be made to bring over *5 men.* And it happened to turn out first so. Five men of the majority turned about and voted to throw the Proviso overboard, and it was done. Many understanding how the thing had gone, did not vote at all, at last; so there were some dozen or more majority to throw out the "Proviso". The President got his 3 million dollars, to make peace with!! Now we are told that there is no likelihood of peace at present – The American arms have been quite successful in Mexico, as you will have seen; but it is a most dishonourable & ignominious success. Reverses may come yet; I should be glad to see the American army driven out of Mexico for my sympathies are all with the people, who are fighting for their native land & their homes and emphatically for liberty, and not for the blood thirsty army which has gone forth from his land in the service of Slavery. I wish no life lost, on either side; it gives me no pleasure, but quite the reverse, to hear of the destruction on either side. But I would rejoice in the expulsion of the American arms from Mexico, and in the humiliation of the despotic and grasping spirit which sent them there....

With my kind regards to your daughter, Believe me to be, yours, with sincere respect,

S.May.

MS.A.9.2. vol. 23 1847 The Weston Papers [261]
No. 28 Jane Carr[1] *to Maria Weston Chapman*

Eden Bank, 5th mo. 1st 47

Dear Friend

Maria Weston Chapman

... I sadly fear that we shall not have very much to forward this year, not owing to a diminution of feeling on the subject, but owing to several circumstances over which we have no control – the large subscriptions which have been made at different time for the '*Irish*' – the high price of provisions and a Bazaar being [to ? form ?] here for our Infirmary. This is to to be open in about two months and the Ladies of Carlisle and the country are greatly engaged in providing for it. Then we have now no *Frederick Douglass* to rouse the dormant feelings of many,

1. Jane Carr was the wife of J. D. Carr, the Quaker biscuit manufacturer of Carlisle. See Appendix II.

who in this land of real liberty of mind & person are too apt to forget the far off suffering bond men & women ....
thy sincere friend

Jane D Carr

MS.A.9.2. vol. 23 1847 The Weston Papers [262]
No. 29 R.D. Webb to Maria Weston Chapman

Dublin June 12 – 1847

My dear Friend

... Just now James Haughton who loves popularity, is extremely unpopular for the usual no-reason. He is a corn factor & has lined his purse pretty well this hard year, like all the dealers in provisions. He is accused as a forestaller, a monopoliser, a grinder of the faces of the poor, a destroyer of provisions sooner than that prices should come down. James is a kindly man and is a good deal mortified – much more than he should be – I suppose the storm will blow over...

I believe you are right about the poor Irish too – it is a work of immense difficulty to do anything for them except to keep them alive. And it is impossible to see them die while we have enough & more than enough for ourselves. The people are liars, and lazy, & demoralized to a very great degree. Their religion is eminently demoralizing. Their priests are a bad set – all liars and all opposed to any real elevation of the multitude. All classes in Ireland with little exception are demoralized, grasping, needy, & mean. The law of landlord & tenant in both England & Ireland is hostile to the tenant – but in England custom & usage throws a shield over the tenant which protects him from the landlord. In some parts of the country the people are horrible ferocious – the peasantry thinks nothing of shooting a man for anything or nothing. Injurious as some of the laws are, they would have little effect in depressing an energetic, self-respecting civilized people. My prevailing feelings are those of disgust and helplessness. You can have no idea of the suffering, starvation, nakedness, filth and degradation. You see nothing like it. Our "comfortable farmers" are flocking to your shores, and well you may ask if these be the comfortable farmers, the elect of the peasantry, what sort of wretches remain behind. A large part of a priests income is derived from marriage fees, and accordingly the landlord for the sake of his tenants' votes and the priest for the sake of the fees have (the former until within about 20 years and the latter until the present year) done all they could to increase the number of marriages, so that Ireland would be better off if her population were less by millions provided the remainder were a respectable, industrious, enlightened people. I tell you it is a miserable country for a man to be in, and I would be heartily glad to be well out of it. The burden of poor laws and so forth are expected to be very great and most kinds of trade are now particularly dull...

Mazzini got no Liberty Bell – & I have not one left. If you send one, you should write something in it with your own hand. Be sure to pester Garrison until he writes to him of [Dublin ?] Castle – or I'll be destroyed.

Yours very truly
Rich[d] D. Webb.

No. 35 Catherine Paton to [Maria Weston Chapman ?]

Roseneath – July 15/47

Dear and much esteemed Friend

I wrote you by F. Douglas and have waited anxiously, for a letter from you, respecting our contributions to the last Bazaar; and would esteem it great kindness, if on receipt of this, you would say whether the articles were suitable – particularly the embroidered black satin aprons, also the check ones, and the embroidered Baby cloaks; and if so, we would begin immediately to prepare similar ones, or if you can suggest anything more suitable. A letter from you is highly valued and very encouraging to the Society....

I learn from a friend who was in Perth last week, that a number of contributors there, are rather discouraged at not receiving a letter from you, with particulars about their Box. Their articles were all marked Perth, and I hope that you may be able to recall to your memory, some idea of what they were, as to be able to say to them, whether, in general, they were suitable. I thought them unexceptionable, and told them so, amongst the number was a large patched silk table cover elegantly lined and finished, with a knitted tidy to suit....

They are rather a vigorous society, composed of sterling people, but they are but young in the cause, and need a little encouragement, I hope that you will not mistake the spirit that has impelled me to write this, the interests of the cause, and being as jealous of your reputation as of my own, are my only motives....

HC W[right] left us this week for Dublin to say farewell to his kind friends there, he has become very much endeared to us, and it is a real sorrow to us to part with him, he has done invaluable services here, his labours have been most abundant, in every good cause, and done in the most disinterested manner. It is of great value, to the antislavery cause, that its advocates should be of a self denying, self sacrificing spirit. This he has proved himself to be, in his mission thro' this country, and he does merit a warm welcome home from the American Abolitionists. We have had a Henry of a very different stamp, trying to sow discord and misunderstanding; I meant Clapp he had not the slightest effect on the old & well informed abolitionists. There is another traitor to the cause here, a Mr. Gloucester a coloured minister from Philadelphia – on a mission to raise money, to clear a debt of £1200 on his chapel. Here he has been chiefly patronised by the Free Church, and at a sermon which I heard him give in Glasgow last week, he said not a word on behalf of the slave, but stated that he had got £400, and did not wish to leave the country till he got the full sum... George Thomspon is a candidate as M.P. for the Tower Hamlets, a district in London, and has issued a noble address to the electors. I do not know whether I should wish him success or not. Best love to all the true hearted.

Ever yours

Catherine Paton

MS.A.9.2. vol. 23 1847 The Weston Papers [264]
No. 40 Jane Wigham to Maria Weston Chapman

Edinburgh, 15th of 8th month 1847

My dear Friend

We feel very sorry to part with Henry C. Wright, or rather to have sent our farewell wishes to him at Liverpool, instead of seeing him once more as we expected before he sails for America, – he leaves many warm friends and ardent admirers of his Anti Slavery & Peace principles – and this country is much indebted to him for leaving behind the labours of his pen on these subjects. His visit to this country has been of great service, and will *tell* long after he has taken his departure from it, and from this lower world...

We have had a proslavery minister from Virginia last week lecturing on religious subjects – but he has been well questioned and proves himself very bad and in the opinion of many establishes the truth of all we have been told by our American friends of the, ministers in the Southern States, – There is a public meeting called for this evening at which his lectures and proceedings are to be reviewed, but he has left town – having been first invited to attend a public meeting to explain himself, and also challenged by a respectable citizen to a public discussion – both of which he treated with contempt – but go where he will in Scotland he will find his character has preceeded him. The city was well placarded with large bills warning the public to beware of him – and on what account – copies of these bills have been sent on before to be posted in every town he intended to visit – a list of which has been obtained from a friend at whose house he staid – Scotland is thus becoming too anti-slavery for American slaveholders or their apologists to travel through publicly preaching or lecturing, & we may & ought to thank H.C. Wright for this – as he was the man who first roused us to the position of the free church – and reawakened public attention to the subject of American slavery – after several years during which the subject except in two or three towns had slept in Scotland. – but now that he and others have so well informed the people of the character of the oppressors of our fellow beings, and what they can do to help to put an end to slavery, I trust Scotland will never again be allowed to fall asleep on the subject.

Hoping to hear from thee soon I am thy affectionate friend

Jane Wigham.

MS.A.9.2. vol. 23 1847 The Weston Papers [265]
No. 39 Isabel Jennings to Maria Weston Chapman

August 2. 1847

My dear Mrs. Chapman

... Of the state of matters in the West you heard from R.D. Webb but he was not in Cork or in Skibbereen. Elihu Burritt only told the simple facts about the latter place[1] – we have seen the children lying dead in their mother's arms but we could not – writing as he did with the desire to gain sympathy – tell you of the *general* state of the country west and south of this city – every year numbers die of want – this did not prevent the people marrying nor did it cause them to lay by anything for the future – all they cared for was – enough of potatoes – education was unknown – when they came into Cork you knew they were human beings but so very low in the scale that you could not *feel* they were your brethren. This may be wrong but if we had known them even to care for any intellectual enjoyment we wd have been a thousand times more unhappy at their fate. What we felt most sorrow for, was those who are reduced from being a comfort by the dearness of all sorts of provisions – and who had to look for support from others instead of independently finding their own – poor work women & such like....

We shall be delighted to have it in our power to see you face to face – I should like to speak to you of all the topics of the present day – of 'communities' and of 'associations' (not that these are spoken of in Ireland yet awhile) the Physical Force men, alias the Young Irelanders absorb public attention to the exclusion of better things) and to ask you whether the failure of the Total Abstinence Pledge to enforce Temperance in Ireland has at all altered your faith in pledges – it has mine. I think I see that there is nothing inconsistent in a truly religious and conscientious man partaking *occasionally* of wine or porter – or even spirits – perhaps part of this has been caused by a very wonderful clairvoyante telling my sister Jane that a little wine is useful for a weak and delicate person in the cold stage of fever – it was tried on herself in the fever a few weeks since by my sister who was with her constantly and found admirable....

If Jane has time she will I think send you some of her clairvoyante's remedies but she is now with our brother-in-law who has been rather severely attacked with fever. He has a hydropathic doctor – but one who allows the clairvoyante's remedies to be used in this case however she cannot [?] – it is not wished – and now with every good wish for you and all your friends I remain at length

your affectionate friend

Isabel Jennings.

MS.B.1.6. vol. 3 The May Papers [266]
No. 38 James Haughton to Samuel May

35 Eccles St. Dublin
30th Augt. 1847

Rev. Saml. May Jr.

My dear friend

... I do fear that the contributions from America for relief of Irish

---

1. Elihu Burritt, *A Journal of a visit of Three Days to Skibbereen*, London, 1847.

distress have done lasting injury to the moral sentiments of our people. There is, no doubt, a strong feeling of abhorrence of the cruelties resulting from your system of slavery, but our people have been taught to love the Americans on the ground that you are the enemies of England & your contributions have been received with grateful feeling as much from the belief that you sympathise with us on account of our political wrongs from England, as from the conviction that they are the spontaneous expressions of benevolent sympathy with us in our late starving condition. There are a great many Irish in America, & these carry with them the dislike of England which is so general amongst our population. Englishmen contributed largely to relieve our wants, & yet there is no such general expression of thankfulness for their munificience, as has been offered for much less pecuniary aid from your side....

The past year was a remarkable one for poor Ireland but we are now gathering in a fine harvest, which will, for a time at least, give plenty to our people. You have sent us generous contributions from America, but I am one of those who fear they have done us injury instead of good. A grateful feeling towards America has, to a great extent, destroyed our hatred of slavery as it exists amongst you. You have bought off our condemnation of your wicked system.

Yours sincerely,

James Haughton.

MS.A.9.2. vol. 23 1847 The Weston Papers [267]
No. 43 R.D. Webb to Maria Weston Chapman

Dublin Sept. 16 1847

My dear Friend

... I was not sorry to see the Game Law Letter in the Refuge of Oppression which E.Q. also castigates with such severity. It proves in a striking manner how people become so accustomed to an evil that they cant see the harm of it. It passes my comprehension how the Americans can cherish slavery as they do, so that when ever so friendly a remonstrance is made against it by personal friends & fellow professors of religion, the interference is resented as impertinent & rude. Surely if it be wrong for an Englishman to protest against American slavery, it must be at least equally so for any preacher from this side of the Atlantic to preach to an American audience on any subject. I am sure that any amount of remonstrance from America against the English game laws – if a bona fide remonstrance – would be hailed with gratitude by a large majority of the English people – including I should think nine tenths of the Unitarian body. I don't suppose a Unitarian minister in England benefits by these laws or would be otherwise than delighted at their repeal. And they will surely be repealed or greatly modified before long. Things were never before in so fair a way for mending in England as they are now – and the popular will was never before in so sure & safe a way of being so obeyed in all its reasonable demands...

What do you think of the Pope? In my opinion he is the greatest man in Europe. I am quite enthusiastic about him and contrary to my wont, I read the newspapers regularly for the purpose of seeing what the day [has ?] brought forth to affect his interests. I look on him as a man of extraordinary wisdom, largeness of view, intelligence & benevolence– and it is grand to see the probable regeneration of a nation in consequence of the resurrection of such a man from the abyss of degradation in which poor Italy was sunk beneath the repressible, soul benumbing policy of Austria, that incubus of the Nations.

With cordial good morrows to all the clique from my domestic clique
I remain yours every truly & respectfully,

Rich[d] D. Webb

MS.B.1.6. vol. 3 The May Papers [268]
No. 46 Samuel May to R.D. Webb

Boston, March 7. 1848

My dear Mr. Webb,

The Antislavery Cause, I believe is going steadily onward. We never had plain antislavery so talked in Congress as during this winter. Never did the question so enter into all political machinations as now. It is indeed true that the political parties were never so seemingly bent upon cringing to the Slave Power as now. Zachary Taylor, the bloody leader in the Mexican War, and the first man to advise the employment of Cuban bloodhounds in the war against the Florida Indians, is almost sure to be the Whig candidate for President. Of what stamp the Democratic candidate will be, we need no Ghost to tell us. The most hardened, unscrupulous, & selfish politician to be found in their ranks, he will be their Candidate. The so called *Liberty Party* – Heaven save the mark! – have already attached themselves to the skirts of a man who never has pretended to be an Abolitionist! who has indeed done well as a Democrat, and as a Seceder from the Democratic ranks rather than go for the annexation of Texas, and the *Extension* of Slavery. But his Antislavery has this extent – no more.

John Quincy Adams is dead, as you will have learnt before you get this. And the Nation is almost crazy with the enthusiasm of its admiration, both of the man, and of the place & manner of his death! He has done great service for many good causes. He has manfully fought the South on many occasions. But he is not entitled to the name of an *abolitionist* save as a general respect for the movement, and not a care to abuse its friends, but occasionally to encourage them a little, may entitle him thereto....

With kind & respectful remembrance to your brothers, to Mr. Allen & Mr. Haughton, I am, very truly, yours, Samuel May Jr.

MS.B.1.6. vol. 3 The May Papers [269]
No. 48 William James to Samuel May

Bristol, March 24. 1848

My dear Mr. May

... Ere this letter is received by you, the intelligence of what is passing in Europe will have reached your shores. During the last few weeks, we have been literally astounded by the rapidity with which the nations of Europe, one after another, have arisen to cool off the despotism and oppression under which they have groaned. And the end is not yet! God grant that the people may be kept from excesses which would stain the sacred cause of liberty, as in the first French Revolution. Of course America will rejoice greatly that France has got rid of her perfidious king: that Russia has put down her military despotism; that Austria has made Ferdinand feel, and quail before, the power of the people, and that the Italian states will probably soon successfully assert their rights. But until they shall learn to go justly at home, their republican institutions will only serve to make the conduct of your people towards the blacks, both enslaved and free, appear more inconsistent and wicked, in the eye of reason and religon. I am glad to see the stand you have made against the Mexican War, and that you raise your voices against oppression and iniquity in all its forms – I am sure that this course of conduct is what Christianity requires....

Faithfully & affectionately yours

William James –

Rev. S. May

[270]

MS.B.1.6. vol. 2 The May Papers
No. 70 J.B. Estlin to Samuel May

Bristol, Friday,April 7th 1848

My dear Mr. May

...But I must not conclude without one word on what is engaging everyone's thoughts here, (& time too with spelling the papers) – the eventful state of *Europe!* Good I doubt not will be the result, but I tremble to think what may yet be in store for the agitated countries – I grieve over the present monarchical condition of France. The welfare of that country has long been exciting increasing interest in English minds. I should like to have seen a Republic fairly & freely tried there: but there seems no chance of this – I doubt if the majority of the nation are favourable to one, & I by no means think them *fitted* for one. A Civil Monarchy I think, would best suit the desires, as well as the genius of the people. Bloodshed must follow the present disorganised, lawless & *idle* state of the working populations. Lamartine has certainly conducted himself in the noblest, bravest & perhaps *wisest* way, considering the torrent he has had to stem, & his violent, (*unprincipled* I fear as regards Ledu – Rollin & Marast) coadjutors.

Only think of *men, grown men, "Nativists"*, employing their time at such a moment as the present at Paris, in going about planting little *poplar trees!!*

It is interesting to see the general good feeling & wishes of the English press towards the French, & the determination to let them alone Lamartine's speech to the Irish deputation who expected his full sympathy with them against the English, has offered great satisfaction in this country – I hope you do not judge of the actual state of *Ireland*, & Irish feeling from the violent speeches allowed to be made by a few of the intemperate leaders there. It is however by no means improbable that the excitable Irish will be stimulated to some violence which will occasion bloodshed, & defeat the true interests of the country. I wish O'Connell instead of advocating so questionable a measure as repeal of the Union, had taken up the *State Church* question & urged a separation of the Ch. from the state in Ireland:- *there* he wd. have carried with him the sympathy of large masses of English: everyone here almost, believes *Repeal* would be more injurious to the Irish than the English.

I saw last night a friend (Mr. R. Norris) who had been with Jos. Sturge to Paris to present a peace address, from a London Meeting. He saw all the members of the Provis[l]. Govt. heard Mr. Lamartine's address & was much interested in his visit. He hopes more favourably of the French movement, than I am able to hope. I will send you a newspaper left here by my brother-in-law yesterday, the "Economist" Anti Corn Law League paper; edited by some able men, Mem[bers] of Parliament &c You will see their fears for France. Our papers are now exceedingly interesting.

If for no other means I regret that a Republic is uncertain in France, because the Provl. Govt. so promptly denounced the absurdity of a Republic holding slaves. I wish M. Lamartine had hinted this to the American deputation that went to congratulate the new Govt. Disturbances are apprehended in London on Monday next in consequence of a large assembly of Chartists determining to march to the H. of Commons with their petitions. I do not expect we shall altogether escape the infection of Continental agitation.

My daughter joins me in kind regards — other friends do not know of my writing. I am my dear Sir. Sincerely yours J.B. Estlin.

MS.A.9.2. vol. 13 1840 pt. 1 The Weston Papers [271]
No. 34 Eliza Nicholson to Maria Weston Chapman

Eden Bank, Carlisle 3 '7

Dear Friend

M.W. Chapman

I write on behalf on my beloved sister Jane Carr & myself to thank thee for thy kindness in sending us each a "Liberty Bell"; which we do highly value both on account of the cause it advocates & for the sake of the kind Donor. We were very sorry to send so few things but really no one seemed inclined to help us, and there was so much to do within our own borders that we could not urge it... We receive regularly the "North Star" edited by our beloved friend and *Brother* Frederick Douglass, we are exceedingly interested in them, and are quite encouraged to hope & trust they will answer admirably His friends here are much pleased with them, amongst *them* there seems to be but one opinion. What stirring scenes in France just now, how instantaneous seems to have been the revolution, and what varied scenes the ex king of France has experienced in his lifetime. Some noble acts of the Republic are already being passed, one glorious resolution they have come to, has come to our knowledge only this morning, their noble intention of setting *Free the slaves in their dominion.* It is not this a fine example for Republican America? Surely they will be ashamed not to follow the example set them by the French...They have also abolished capital Punishments for political offences, which gives great satisfaction. Many in ths country are most anxious to have them entirely done away with, for every offence, for surely no man has a right to take the life of his fellow man; and there are labourers most earnest and zealous in the cause, who I hope may accomplish their desired end....

I remain thy sincere & affectionate friend.

Eliza Nicholson.

MS.B.1.6. vol. 2 The May Papers [272]
No. 74 Samuel May to J.B. Estlin

Boston, Tuesday Eve.g May 2d. 1848

My dear Mr. Estlin,

...The European News has been most exciting & most interesting to us all. The arrival of the last ship was awaited with an intense anxiety, on account of the apprehensions & anticipation respecting the Chartist *demonstration* in London. I had felt, & said repeatedly, that I believed there was too much good sense in the English people, too much progress already made towards free & just institutions, and too fresh a remembrance of the victory gained by the Anti Corn Law agitiation, to allow of a brutal & bloody contest between Government & People. Very many here expected, & some doubtless wished, a bloody overthrow of the Throne, the Aristocracy & the State Church of England. *We* rejoice & thank GOD that this thirst for blood & love of violence have been disappointed....

Believe me, with sincere respect

Yours

Samuel May Jr.

MS.B.1.6. vol. 2 The May Papers [273]
No. 75 J.B. Estlin to Samuel May

Bristol May 26th 1848 to June 9th Friday

My dear Mr. May

...The present state of France is most unpropitious for attention to American slavery. The condition of that country is lamentable: how bloodshed is to be avoided I know not! How truly some of your papers expose the absurdity & hypocrisy of the Americans sympathising with the French on ridding themselves of *despotism!* What was Louis Philippe's despotism to theirs! Events on the Continent appear to be attaching this country more & more to our monarchical form of government. Gradual reforms here must take place. The ultraviolent *mischievous* party (there is none respectable enough to be termed *revolutionary)* is ascertained to be most contemptible in their numbers & their aims. And even in Ireland the discontent is not so extensive as the activity of the more violent party would lead distant countries to suppose. That there are real grievances there, and a most indolent, uncivilized, & intractable population to manage, none will deny; the best friends of Ireland & the most noble & liberal minds, see full well this difficulty of dealing with Irish evil. Our friend R. D. Webb, who is anything but an aristocrat, or lover of oppression, says that the separation of Ireland from England would be an act of the greatest cruelty:— that 1,500,000 of the best portion of the population would be ruined by such measures as the Repealers call for....

believe me sincerely yours

J. B. Estlin

MS.B.1.6. vol. 2 The May Papers [274]
No. 79 Samuel May to J.B. Estlin

Boston, Mass. Septr 5, 1848.

My dear Mr. Estlin,

...We have had a busier summer than I believe is common in this Antislavery warfare; during that season, our lecturing agents have usually rested awhile but not so, this summer; while the whole community is astir, in no small measure with reference to slavery, its usurpations, its audacious claims, and its enormous Power, it has been no time for Abolitionists to be long idle, or absent from, their posts. Last week our agents at Harwich, Barnstaple Co. (I did not happen to be at that Convention) were set upon by a ferocious mob, *led on by Church members,* who could not bear the exposures and rebukes, of which their different sectarian organizations were unsparingly made the objects, and it was with great difficulty that they were kept from serious injury, S.S. Foster had his clothing badly torn; W.W. Brown[1] was taken up by two men, and hurled from the speaker's platform over the side railing, (the convention was held in a Grove, & several thousand people were in attendance) — the yells, & oaths, have been described frightful & hideous beyond what our agents have ever heard before, and that is a bold word, for Foster & Pillsbury have looked on many a fearful scene where the mob-law (*la loi de lynch,* as Miss P. translates it) had undisputed sway. They were protected in this instance by a strong, stalwart body of men, but the meeting was entirely broken up, and of the *platform* no two pieces were left together, so you see the spirit of pro-slavery and of mob-ism has by no means been exorcised from old Massachusetts — the most civilized upon the whole, of any American State. We are just about entering upon our Fall Campaign and with renewed vigour. Our agents will go into the States of Maine, New Hampshire & Rhode Island, as well as Mass; under authority from the New England Yearly Convention. And as the Presidential Election comes

1. William Wells Brown (1826-1884), a fugitive slave from Kentucky, made a name for himself as an anti-slavery speaker before coming to Europe in 1849. In that year he represented the U.S. at the Peace Congress of Paris. He remained abroad until 1854 working for the anti-slavery Cause. He was the author of several works and histories championing the Negro.

in the 7th of November, and the different parties are waxing every week hotter & fiercer, I look forward to pretty warm & arduous work for the 2 coming months. There is, as you are aware from our Antislavery papers, a *New Party* in the field called the Free Soil party. Their cordial principle is *No-Extension of Slavery into New Territory*. On this, they are at issue with *all the slave states* – I ought to do them the justice to say that a very considerable number of men in these States – chiefly the more Northern of them, but appealing even in Mississippi – sympathise warmly with this No-Extension cry, and stand ready – (such is the testimony of Southern men) – to go even for the entire abolition of slavery. It will not be long, I think before these become the controlling power in Maryland, Virginia, & Kentucky. Delaware is pretty nearly *Abolitionised* now; an Anti-slavery paper, outspoken too, is freely published there; so also one, which is little more than a Free-soil paper, I believe, in No. Western Virginia, – called the Crisis. This Free Soil party has put in nomination, for the Presidency, *Martin Van Buren*, of New York, once Presdt. for 4 years 1837-1841, – but rejected from a nomination for a 2d term, by the command of the South because he opposed the Annexation of Texas. Mr. Van Buren will receive unquestionably a very large votem – very many of his old political opponents will now go for him, having got their eyes well opened to the utter profligacy and proslavery meanness of their party, the so-called "Whig". The Democratic party, for a long series of years, has not pretended to be anything else than the slaveholder's Jackal I think it most probably that an election, *by the people*, will be prevented....

How complete seems the submission of Ireland, and how general the awe of the superior military force of the government. A crazy scheme, most will call that of O'Brien & his confederates, now that it has so emphatically failed; and it could hardly have failed so suddenly & utterly, if it had not been a crazy scheme, ill-arranged & wholly immature. It is quite an interesting question here what will be done with O'Brien,[2] Meagher,[3] & others; and a general hope expressed, on account of all the many hearings & relations of the thing, that your Government will not proceed to extremities with them, – but rather be lenient! ....

Wednesday a.m. Sept. 6

It is not for me to understand the present condition of France, nor what may probably ensue there. I cling strongly to my confidence in Lamartine's integrity. Have you seen any evidence, that satisfies you, that he had any participation in the late insurrectionary movements, or in the profligate course of some of his associates in the late Provisional Government? Is Cavaignac – for I can get hold of nothing which shows his past history – equal to maintaining the post he holds? If so, he is a wonderful man, & should have greatly distinguished himself before this, I think....

The "Free Soil" men of this State hold a great Convention today in his city,

2. William Smith O'Brien (1803-1864) joined the Irish Repeal Association in 1844 and became leader of the Young Irelanders. Under his leadership they adopted more revolutionary tactics, and attempted an armed revolt in 1848. Smith was tried at Clonmel, and later transported to Tasmania.

3. Thomas Francis Meagher (1823-1867) was a friend of O'Brien, and active with the Repeal cause. He joined in the 1848 rising and was deported, but escaped from Tasmania to New York in 1852. During the Civil War he supported the Union, and helped to form an Irish Brigade, which he commanded, rising to the rank of Brigadier General.

to nominate State officers, & to prepare for the November elections. John Van Buren, son of the ex-President, is to be present....

The hour is at hand for the steamer's departure, and I must close –
with sincere respect,

yours

Saml. May Jr.

MS.B.1.6. vol. 2 The May Papers [275]
No. 80 Samuel May to J.B. Estlin

Boston, Tuesday Eveg. Sept. 19. 1848

Dear Mr. Estlin,

...The "Liberty Party" of this country has gone in solid phalanx, with only an exception here & there, into the ranks of the so-called Free Soil party, supporting candidates who have never showed any regard for their opinions or their cause, but who have done much to counteract & embarass both.[1] They are utterly annihilated as a party, and their leaders, (such as Leavitt, Stanton, &c) who have traded them away several times now, will soon fall to their true level of shame; the more they are known the less will they be trusted. I must cease, and am

With sincere regards, yours

Sam[l] May Jr.

MS.A.1.2. vol. 18 1848-49 Anti-Slavery Letters to Garrison [276]
No. 38 George Thompson to R.D. Webb

Manchester Oct. 19. 1848

My Dear Friend,

...Does not the formation of the Free Soil Political party in the U.S. prove beyond all question the great effect which has been wrought by the labour of the Abolitionists? I trust our own friends will stand aloof and maintain their uncompromising dissolution principles. In proportion to the spread of anti-slavery doctrines & the professions of an antislavery creed among politicians will be the necessity for watchfulness and integrity among the original champions of the cause.

Believe me,
Very truly yours

Geo. Thompson.

---

1. The 'Old Organisationists' had never supported anti-slave, political action, whether conducted by the purely abolitonist Liberty Party, or by the Free Soil Party which was broader in its aims.

MS.B.1.6. vol. 3 The May Papers [277]
No. 51 Samuel May to Mary Carpenter

Boston, September 19, 1848.

My dear Miss Carpenter,

...You speak of the Chartists, and of the sympathy which, you suppose, is generally felt for them in this country. It is true that much sympathy is felt here in their cause, or rather in the objects for which they are contending; but there is, I think, but little sympathy in their violent plans for accomplishing these objects. So far as I understand the objects of the Chartists, I think them just, equal, what is due to them as men, & what is absolutely needful to elevate them to a social position where they will learn to respect themselves, & so become worthy of the respect of others. – There is a class in this country – not very numerous I suspect, but rather noisy & quite persevering, who will approve & aid any movement got up by anybody whatever, which looks likely to embarass the British government, and cripple British power. The defeat of the Irish revolutionary schemes was a terrible extinguisher upon the hopes & plans of these men – it really "put them out" entirely! Scarce a word has been uttered by them for many weeks; and there is no encouragement, clearly, for them to be very talkative. But I hope England is not going to be content with *crushing Irish rebellion.* Irish misery ought to be well considered, relieved, & measurably prevented. You have a *strong* government, as is plain from its triumphant success in several most critical seasons, and in a year when nearly every other European throne fell, or at least was *shaken awfully.* If so strong to suppress violence, to dispose & scatter legions of disaffected men, it must have strength to benefit them, and to open a way for their ultimate rescue and relief....

With sincere regard, I remain,

Yours Sam[l] May Jr.

MS.B.1.6. vol. 2 The May Papers [278]
No. 81 J. B. Estlin to Samuel May

Bristol, Oct. 2nd 1848. Monday

My dear Mr. May

...My last letter to you was sent by Mr. Jas. Heywood, dated August 30th. I hope he did not consider it a letter of introduction to be delivered or not according to his convenience. In that letter I said a little about Ireland. But there was an excellent leading article on the subject in a late A.S. Standard, & in the same paper most wise remarks of Mr. R.D. Webb's in his letter to the Editor. You may always depend upon R. D. Webb. There is in this country a universal sympathy for the real suffering of the Irish, & a great desire to relieve them: but no clear way seems obvious, for they will not help themselves. There is no fear of the Govt. being harsh with Smith O'Brien &c, even should a jury be found to convict them. The general opinion is that the Govt. have hitherto been too lenient in not earlier taking strong measures. Unmixed evil must befal the men deluded by Smith O.B. Meagher, Mitchell &. The measures urged by some were horrid, – throwing vitriol about &c &c. The Catholic priests are most hostile to the Govt. & sadly mislead their deluded flocks. The manner in which they have encouraged their followers to sneer at the assistance afforded by the generous people of this country in the last famine, has done much to destroy similar sympathy should a second one occur. I see no amendment in Irish affairs, & the prospect seems one of increased difficulty –

This country is really very tranquil though you may hear of Chartist [toils?] & occasional disturbance. But there is a vast amount of good sense in the country: it is too, generally known, that evils will be increased not remedied by violence: a highly well considered appreciation of our form of Govt. prevails: the Queen is personally liked, and a sort of instinctive attachment to Monarchy exists. Besides this, our people have a thorough knowledge of all that is going on in other countries; talk of them with freedom, & judge them impartially. All the changes that have yet occurred seem to warm, rather than allure to imitation. I do not believe the slightest ill-will or jealousy is felt towards America and while very willing for you to have the form of Govt. you like best, as an *example* to us, I am satisfied that your Republic acts upon the mass of people here repulsively. And yet we have an immense amount of poverty here, & a super abounding population. Emigration on a large scale must I think take place.

You can judge of the French as well as I can. I have no respect for them – Lamartine did nobly *for a while*, but his mission was a short one, & he was unequal to his high duties he has probably plenty of French sentiment, but I fear a small amount of high moral principle. He is an extravagant & needy man. Cavaignac seems clever & brave, but I do not expect a great deal of him. Orago, I have good reason to know is a man *reckless of truth.* I wish I could see the ten honest men to save France! No one I believe has any idea of Lamartine's being implicated in the insurrection. He certainly staved it off for some time, but had not the courage to shake off, or withdraw from the colleagues who were by their measures laying the foundation for a bloodier contest than he, at the daily risk of his own life, was keeping down. I doubt if it would not have been better for the fighting to have occurred in Feby. But these speculations of mine you will consider as waste of time & paper....

sincerely yours

J. B. Estlin.

MS.B.1.6. vol. 2 The May Papers [279]
No. 83 Samuel May to J.B. Estlin

Boston Tuesday Eveg. Octo – 31 – 1848

My dear Mr. Estlin,

...Your letter of Octo. 2d reached me the 21st. It was several months since I had heard from you. That sent from Mr. Heywood I had not received. Six daysafterwards, Mr. Heywood came into our office, presented your letter (of Aug. 30,) – also one from you to F. Douglass. Mr. H. stopped but a few moments. He seemed not to have taken a favourable view at all of the British West India movement for Emancipation. I suppose his view is a very common one in Lancashire, among the Cotton-spinners, who probably look upon slavery with the same complacency and do not care a straw whether slavery continues or not and would not lose $ 10,000 to prevent its being extended over all Mexico, and all South America to boot. At Mr. Heywood's request I made up a small parcel of Anti-Slavery documents for him, and hoped to have seen him again. As yet I have not. 'Tis but 4 days since I first saw him.

The Presidential Contest waxes hotter & hotter; and it is almost idle to attempt to get the ear of the people for any other subject. One week from today the Election takes place throughout the country. You are, I see, quite "at fault" with regard to an expression I lately used that I thought "an election *by the people* would be prevented". It is simply this, – that if no one candidate receives a majority of all the votes cast there is then *no election by the people*, and the choice devolves upon the House of Representatives of Congress. This year there are 3 prominent candidates; Zachary Taylor, of the Whig Party; Lewis Cass, of the Democratic do; and Martin Van Buren, of the "Free Soil" party, or Party opposed to the extension of slavery over soil now free. (This last as a party, goes for maintaining the existing *compromises* of the Constitution, as well as the other two; and therefore the old Abolitionists cannot join with them.) I send you a little pamphlet, containing the U.S. constitution from which you will see, (pp. 12.24) if you think it worth while to take the trouble, how this matter of electing the President stands. In 1825 it happened there was no President chosen by the people; Genl. Jackson had the most of any one. Mr. Adams (J.Q.) had a party, Henry Clay a part, & W.H. Crawford of Georgia the rest; but, in order to a choice, some one must have a *majority* of all the votes thrown, more than all the others put together. This year Mr. Van Buren will, very probably, receive so many votes as to defeat the election of either of the others; in which case the Ho. of Reps. must vote by States, & choose a President; i.e. in taking such a vote, the members of each state meet by themselves & cast their ballots; the one who has a majority is considered as having the vote of that state. As there are 30 states now, 16 votes would be the least number which could elect a Pres^{dt} in Ho. of Reps. At the election in 1825 (above referred to) the friends of Mr. Clay united upon Mr. Adams & carried him *in* – You will notice by the little pamphlet aforesaid that when the people vote, they do not vote directly; but choose, if they can, *electors*, who meet in the several states, cast their votes, & transmit them sealed to Congress. Possibly I may have made out a blind matter of this business of electing a President. It is, notwithstanding, very simple when you get the thing clearly before you. – These Quadrennial Elections throw the people into a perfect state of intoxication, and they are all incapable of reasoning on the subject as brutes would be. There can be no direct bribery – the offer of money, if known, would invalidate the vote – but there is a system of measures put in operation which has the same effect; men are overawed, or wheedled, or cheated, into doing the very thing they have denounced with loathing. Mr. Garrison today said that he should consider the regular visit of the Asiatic cholera to our shores once in 4 years, a much less evil than the Presidential Election is. The former cannot *demoralize*, & reconcile the mind to lying, fraud & time serving. This is done by the latter on an enormous scale. – The number of abolitionists, or other persons, who for conscientious reasons do not vote at all (about which you inquire) is very, very small. The propensity to vote is an absolute *mania* in this country, and few stop to weigh the moral character of the act. Prove to them, as plain as the nose on their face, that the Constitution is made vile by its guarantees to slavery, prove to them so that they will acknowledge the thing as perfectly clear, that, by voting, they send a man to go & swear to uphold the Constitution, in all its parts & provisions, & of course that *they* are responsible for the acts of their organ, & are themselves through him supporting a pro-slavery Constitution & Union, and 999 of 100 will go and *vote*, under Election day. – There is a sect of religionists in the Middle States, called Covenanters, few in number, who have always consistently refused to vote, or hold any office, under the existing U.S. Constitution, because of its slavery & war provisions, & its atheistical character, as they deem it. They, and a small company, scattered through the Non-slaveholding States, of "old-organized Abolitionists", make up the whole of those who refrain, in principle from casting a vote.

I have read your remarks upon Ireland with much interest – as also upon the state of Europe generally. Surely the prospect, for France, is gloomy enough. How old Louis Philippe, and Mons. Guizot, & their adherents are chuckling over the strange work made in their old haunts! Is it impossible to supply the defect in the French character? Are they of necessity so vehement, impulsive, volatile, hasty, headstrong? They seem to learn very slowly. Yet it cannot be denied there is a decided improvement upon the methods of doing things there in 1790 & onward....

As ever, respectfully, yours

Samuel May Jr.

MS.B.1.6. vol. 2 The May Papers [280]
No. 84 J.B. Estlin to Samuel May

Bristol. November 30 – 1848.

My dear Mr. May

...I do not suppose Mr. Heywood was adverse to the W. India Emancipation, but some members of his family had large W. India possessions, & he probably referred to the wide spread ruin of planters, merchants &c now existing in the W. Indies, & especially in Jamaica. Certainly, on immense numbers who once had to do with slavery, a heavy visitation is now come. I *know* of people in Jamaica, bred upon luxury, now wanting clothing & nutritious food. Estates are fast going out of cultivation. Still, I believe *generally* the *Negros* themselves are not badly off; and after the present severe storm is over, I trust that a peaceful & prosperous condition will ensue. But present evils are by no means the result of emancipation, tho' that measure may have hastened a catastrophe that had been year after year obviously approaching. I am glad you gave Mr. Heywood some a.s. tracts: he is a kind-hearted man, but not likely I think to be a "*violent abolitionist*".

Thank you for your explanations about the election of President; I hope soon to master the subject, which I doubt not is a very simple one to those who understand it. I do not think any of the eager desire for *voting* exists here, which you speak of; and were any important political or philanthropic purpose to be served by the avoidance of voting, I am satisfied that not few would be the number of stubborn, unwavering Englishmen, who would disfranchise themselves in the most determined manner. Nothing is more common in our elections of Members of Parliament, where a borough returns two members & each elector can vote for the 2, for him to give what is called a *plumper*, – that is a vote for *one* member only.

I could not have supposed any of my crude remarks upon continental policies could have interested you. I have now done with speculation as far as *France* is concerned. I lose almost all interest in a country that contemplates so aimless a project as electing Louis Napoleon as President, – a thoroughly stupid man, with no recommendation but his Uncle's *name!*

I much fear events on the Continent – the horrid massacres of *citizens* by their *fellow-citizens* in Paris, Berlin, Frankfort, Vienna, Naples, & now in Rome, will tend to make people submit with unusual contentment to "strong" Government for the purpose of being secured from the violence of those who have much to gain & nothing to lose by anarchy & confusion. Accustomed as I have always been to mix much with those whose sympathies are with freedom & liberal Government, I could not but be struck with remarking while the contest was going on at Vienna, how general the hope was, that the cause of *order* would triumph in the success of the *Emperor* over the insurgents! – However, I feel satisfied that Providence will overrule all for good, and I cannot but hope that Roman Catholic priestcraft will receive some deadly blows in the struggles now going on, so much confined to Catholic populations. The visit of many hundred French Natl. Guards to London lately was a curious & amazing circumstance. John Bull really cordially welcomed them, & they are said to have been astonished & delighted at their hospitable reception. An English grenadier who robbed one of the Natl. Guards, while they were drinking together of a few shillings, tho' interceded for by the forgiving Frenchman, has been tried, found guilty, & expelled from the service with much ignominy...

Ever sincerely yours

J. B. Estlin.

MSS.Acc. 2705 [281]
William Lloyd Garrison to Samuel May Jr.

Boston, Dec. 2, 1848.

My dear friend May:-

...As for the "Free Soil" movement, I am for having it as a cheering sign of the times, and an unmistakable proof of the progress we have made under God, in changing public sentiment. Those who have left the Whig and Democratic parties, for conscience sake, and joined the movement, deserve our commendation and sympathy; at the same time it is our duty to show them and all others, that there is a higher position to be attained by them, or they will have the blood of the slave staining their garments. This can be done charitably, yet faithfully. On the two old parties, especially the Whig Taylor party, I would expend – *pro tempore* at least – our heaviest ammunition.

Hastily, but faithfully yours,

Wm. Lloyd Garrison.

MS.B.1.6. vol. 2 The May Papers [282]
No. 85 Samuel May to J.B. Estlin

Boston, Massachusetts
Monday Eve$^{g.}$ Jan. 8. 1849

My dear Mr. Estlin,

If it were not that I feel that you *ought* to have a letter from me by the best steamship from this country – (which sails by the way day after tomorrow from New York) I should not have chosen this time for one; for I am still feeling the worse for a heavy cold I took at the clearing up of the Hall, and the re-packing & safe storing of goods after our Bazaar was over, – together with what I suppose is a sort of nervous reaction from the excitement caused by the scenes, labours, & anxieties of that occasion....

We commenced actual work at Faneuil Hall on the 14th Dec^{r}...[and] the Bazaar opened the 20th and remained open until Saturday night the 30th – just 10 days exclusive of the Sunday. During the whole 10 days there was *scarcely one pleasant one* – certainly not one, after the first, when both weather & walking were favorable for ladies to be abroad...The whole sum realized, during the two stormy or otherwise unpropitious days was $3000, something over $1000 less than last year. This is, I think mainly to be accounted for by the weather, but other causes may be mentioned. It is a very pinching time for money in Boston – has been so for an unprecedented length of time, & is likely to be so for much longer; then again the Whigs of Boston, who include in their number nearly all the wealth, have been much enraged against Abolitionists on account of the Free Soil movement, & for the hostility to the Slaveholder and Man of Blood Zachary Taylor, whom the Slave Power, with the servile complaince & help of Northern doughfaces, has made our next President. Against all these elements of opposition we have a right to feel, and we *do* feel, that the taking of $3,300, at our Fair this year was a great thing. My father who is an experienced man & knows Boston pretty well, thinks it the best, the most successful & encouraging work, under the circumstances we have done at any Bazaar.

For all this success we are mainly indebted to the comparatively new British Abolitionists. Fervently & sincerely do I pray, GOD bless them all – for their noble perseverance, for their unstinted liberality, for their so much needed encouragement to us, may he bless them all. And, friends, think not that ye labour in vain, think not that our movement, scandalized, denuded, feared, hated as it is – scarcely less so than the Gospel of Christ was when he first preached it – has been untimely, or ill-advised, or badly managed, or is in any danger now of suffering shipwreck...I will not say, confidently, that our Anti-Slavery movement could *not* have been more wisely or well conducted but I am free to say that I go *very near thinking so.* To err is human; and no one of us is blind to the infirmities which have not been wholly absent from our Enterprise; but the great *principle*, on which the cause has been carried forward, of speaking right out the honest truth of GOD, without reference to who might be condemned, who might be stripped of his lofty pretensions, who showed to be morally & religiously deformed, who made to start up & show himself a derision – the principle, in other words, which insists upon testing every man, and every sect, and every institution, in a professedly *Christian* land, by the great law of *Christianity*, and nothing *more* than this, & nothing less, has been the pervading principle of the A. S. movement. – This principle I say is right, & is the *only* right one, and *results* have shown that the faithful adherence to it of the Anti-slavery leaders, martyrs, & saviours of the age have been most signally blessed of GOD. Eighteen years ago darkness, moral death, reigned over the land; slavery was in the ascendant *undisputed* – not even a dog dared wag his tongue, or impugn its rightful authority. When that silence was broken, and one, and then a few voices were heard boldly denouncing Slavery as a *wrong, as a sin,* of which this present & living American people was guilty, before Man & GOD, then came forth a howl from every quarter as if Hell had given up her own. For years, to *speak* upon slavery was an inadmissable thing anywhere and everywhere. Slowly, but without intermission, the pioneers toiled on, never flinching from mobs, or excommunication, or loss of reputation, or loss of the means of winning their bread, or from death even: and now where are we? The question of slavery is the one great, & everywhere prevailing topic of discussion in every part of the land – Free States, Slave States, – Legislatures – Congress – Gubernatorial and Presidential Messages – Ecclesiastical Synods, Conferences, Associations. No longer is a man threatened with loss of life who stirs the question on the floors of Congress. Bowie knives have striven in vain to banish it thence. Mr. Palfrey of Massachusetts moves the measures be taken to abolish slavery in the District of Columbia – Mr. Giddings of Ohio moves that question (the continuance of slavery) be left to the *inhabitants* of the District, *black* as well as white – Mr. Gott of New York moves to instruct a Committee to bring in a bill for the suppression of the Slave trade in the District, and though the South resist, and manoeuvre, and fawn, & supplicate, & scold, no bowie knives are threatened, no expulsion is dreamed of; noise & vaporing & [slang?] have succeeded. The Slave Power is a great big bully; and I believe the Northern people now understand that pretty thoroughly; so well that they will never be bullied down again. Many men from Slave States, and chief among them Thomas H. Benton of Missouri, have given great countenance to the entire exclusion of Slavery from all new Territory. You have perhaps the fact that a Convention of Citizens of New Mexico (now a territory of the United States) petitioned our Congress not to allow Slavery to be introduced there. Two Senators from slave-holding states, Benton & Clayton, introduced this to the Senate, & gave it the weight of their countenance & general concurrence. Calhoun madly & bitterly denounced the Petition as insulting and wished to throw it out altogether. The South are divided – are at issue among themselves on this question – the North is rising, and fast withdrawing its sympathy from the Slaveholder – the new territory stands ready to cast back with loathing the infernal system of human chattelism; and the wretched, GOD-forsaken South, must die in cursing & agony, or, ceasing to defy GOD & to outrage man, must *repent*, and cease from its iniquity, & do that which is lawful & right, and so *live*, and not *die.* – This is the result, as at present seen; the result of faithfully laboring in the direction which conscience & Christianity alike indicate, the only direction where we have any right to look for GOD's blessing, and the very direction where we may be *sure* to *have* that blessing.

I have not exaggerated a single point of the sketch; very many encouraging features have been left altogether unnoticed. True the political potsherds & leaders, by chicanery & sophistry & fraud have put an ignorant, coarse old slaveholder into the Press chair; but his power for mischief is less than James K. Polk's was, because he will not dare to proceed in defiance of a popular sentiment much more intelligent, & much better knowing its strength, than was the case when Polk assumed the reins 4 years ago. A strong effort will be made to seize, or buy Cuba; but it will be defeated, I believe, or will be made itself the means of the destruction of this Union, which is only another word for the downfall of slavery. Two years ago I should have hoped that England could interfer, by her government, against the occupancy of Cuba by the U. States. Now I hope otherwise; I think the Union will receive a blow, from which it will never recover, if Cuba is annexed; whether annexed free or slave matters little – the slave power will be humbled & defeated by the former, intoxicated & hurried to its destruction by the latter, – Such being the state of things, have we any reason for despair, or for distrust? Altogether the reverse. We address ourselves to the use of the same weapons, the same measures, with a new confidence & spirit; *to have no fellowship with the unfruitful works of darkness* whether they come in the guise of a church or of a Political party, to speak the truth with all compassion for the suffering, the ignorant, & the penitent – & with all due plainness & severity to the wilful & determined wrongdoers....

Tuesday a.m. Jan. 9th

... – It is true that Van Buren had not a single vote, i.e. not a single *Electoral* vote. Each state chooses *Electors* of Prest. & V. Prest.; as many as the whole no. of Senator & Representatives it is entitled to have in Congress. Massachusetts accordingly choose 12 Electors, & Mass. has 12 Electoral votes. The Van Buren party threw 36,000 votes in Mass^{tts}, & prevailed any election of Electors by the People. The Legislature was called together in Boston the 1st of December, & was Whiggish & Taylorish enough to choose the 12 Taylor Electors. The Free Soil vote in the whole country was an immense one, under the circumstances, – some 3000,000 and tho' not resulting in a single *state* going from Van Buren it has had an important warning effect upon all parties in the Government, & Congress, both North & South. The Free Soil men have elected several strong men to the next Congress as Representatives...

– I see gladly that a new Postal Treaty has been agreed upon between your Govt. & Ours, by which postage will be about 10 pence each way. – And now omitting several matters, & with sincere respects to Miss E. I am. affectionately yrs. S. May

MS.B.1.6. vol. 2 The May Papers [283]
No. 86 J.B. Estlin to Samuel May

Bristol, Jany. 30th 1849

My dear Mr. May,

...Our French neighbours, you see, are going on such as might be expected with their King Log. What but confusion can ensue? The idea of a Republic of *Frenchmen*, is almost as ludicrous to my mind as of an Emperor of America. Never was there a nation less fitted for self-government. And I believe the *desire of the Nations* is for a limited monarchy, which I doubt not they will in time obtain. Happily "Red Republicanism" has not succeeded in Germany. A people so badly governed as the Austrians, would be quite unfit for entire liberty: I trust & believe that kings will have learned a valuable lesson as well as their *subjects.* I doubt not the late storms will clear the moral atmosphere. I often think that the two Presidents elected last year do not do any great credit to the wisdom & the morality of the American & French nations –

The Howitts I hear are going to America. With them goes, as I learn by a letter from her, Miss Julia Griffiths of Beckenham, Kent. I think I have before mentioned her to you as Douglass' devoted friend, & as (so at least I fancy), identifying anti-slavery with him alone. I do not know her personally. She is a great friend of Mrs. Richardson. I question her having any accurate knowledge of the A.S. Movement, & she has probably undefined prejudices against "the Garrison party" – but I do not know this....

Ever sincerely yours

J. B. Estlin.

MS.A.9.2. vol. 24 The Weston Papers [284]
No. 81 R.D. Webb to Anne Warren Weston

Dublin – July 5 – 1849

My dear Friend –

...I entirely agree with you about the Philadelphia effort – I have always thought that more harm than good would be done by attempting to do more than direct all the help we could give to the Boston Bazaar. When applied to on behalf of the Philadelphians and others I have told them what is the simple truth that if we who feel deeply interested in the cause were to direct our efforts to the support of one Bazaar we would dissipate our strength & fatigue our supporters. This however I think might be done. If the Philadelphia people saw as you do – if they could be made aware of the superior importance of your efforts & would make use of their influence to help you, I would suggest that they should take all the English are willing to send them which they wont send to you – and then let them divide the proceeds so as to help the cause both in Philadelphia & New England. If it be really the case that no Liberty Party or other clan of abolitionists who do not sympathise with you, is now in existence in the Union States, there will be many of Joseph Sturge's friends at a loss how to deepen of their bounty – for I dont suppose they would like to soil their fingers with the Garrison party whose staunch adherence to principle in spite of all the thunders of Church & State, they have never shown themselves able to understand. The more is the pity – for those Sturges & Gurneys have long purses and are very bountiful – The fact is there are few respectable English people prepared to sanction the lengths to which abolitionists have been compelled to go by their determination to follow truth leading whenever she might lead the way. You have made yourselves of no present reputation. Reputation is the darling of the quakers – and the quakers are the backbone of all philanthropic efforts in England. They are liberal with their money, unsparing of labour – zealous in good works – but extremely cautious & careful of their good name.

It would be difficult to give you an idea of how very little I am able to do for you – All that goes in the Dublin box is contributed by very few persons and the number of our helpers is not increased but diminished from year to year. Human nature is the same everywhere – and after all that has been said of British abolitionism I dont imagine when pushed to extremities as you have been, there are many more than with you who would imitate your heroism. The times are so depressed that I dont hope we will be able to do much this year. I always feel ashamed when I see a small donation going, for there is no class of benevolent effort so near my heart...

I am every yours truly

Richd D. Webb.

MS.A.9.24 1848 The Weston Papers [285]
No. 82 R.D. Webb to ?

Brooklawn – near Dublin
July 8 – 1849

My dear Friend –

...I wonder what is the end of this French invasion of Rome. For my own part, and as far as I hear others express their opinion, it is looked on by all commonly honest people as one of the most disgraceful and outrageous pieces of tyranny ever perpetrated. I dont know how the French take so quietly from Louis Napoleon, a graver act by far than any ever committed by his uncle or by Louis Philippe – far meaner – far more inconsistent. I cant see a Frenchman in our streets without thinking he ought to be ashamed of himself.

About the Philadelphia people I think Mrs. Chapman judges them a little too sternly. Beside the fact that they cannot see things so clearly in their operations and consequences as they see them, it is, I think, the case that whilst an application for assistance to a Philadelphia fair for Philadelphia anti-slavery efforts (keeping Hicksism out of view) would meet with some success amongst English Friends, no application for the Boston Bazaar would have any chance. The ideals of heresy, nonviolence, women's rights, Garrison, Bible & Sabbath (Conventions & such like are inextricably mixed up with the latter – whilst a purely anti-slavery application from Philadelphia friends, believed to be orthodox would be sure of sympathy. The English friends I believe sincerely abhor slavery but not so much as they dread these things I have mentioned or any risk to the good name of their society – or to its integrity. For instance when the split took place in Indiana they at once gave *the go by* to the seceders, who had followed their advice, and seceded only because they were not allowed to continue to be consistent anti-slavery men. Considering the course the leading members of the Am— A.S. Society have been compelled to take – the wonder with me is not so much that the orthodox hold back from it as that any are found to adhere to it. Of what consequence is the abolition of slavery to a man who thinks he is labouring for it at the risk of the eternal salvation of his fellow labourers. If orthodoxy be right, how are Garrison, Wright, Quincy, Mrs. Chapman, L. Mott, and others who have thrown overboard the doctrines of the eternal damnation of the majority of mankind, & the special inspiration of the Bible – to be saved? I cannot imagine, can you? I know there are excellent abolitionists with Calvinistic views – but I don't see their consistency. And I think the natural result of thorough going abolitionism is to make a man an infidel to the popular religion. I know this is what it has done with me. But what has all this with the Philadelphians asking English people for help for their anti-slavery efforts instead of for the Am. a.s. Society? Simply this, that I would not object if they can spoil the Philistines, and do any good with what they get for I am quite sure that those same Philistines wont let you spoil them. If I thought they would get anything that we would be likely to get, I would object – but I do not. Garrison and Wright are not much better than Rousseau and Voltaire in the estimation of a great proportion of the wealthy, munificient, easy going, orthodox anti slavery men & women of England...But I am often really ashamed of the little we can do – Our influence contracts from year to year, the better we, and the people on whose behalf we labour, are known...It would amuse you to see how solemn the words *antislavery* or Garrison would make a whole company of Quakers. The portrait of Garrison which has hung over my drawingroom mantlepiece and that of Lucretia Mott (the Hicksite preacher) in another part of the room, are looked on as flags of defiance to the whole society. What good can come out of Galilee? I think it likely that much which your sister attributes to baseness, meanness, treachery, and hostility to the cause in the conduct of many who abhor fighting well for a time have withdrawn from the old organization, has in point of fact resulted from inability to follow the path of duty which fidelity to the slaves cause required, and at the same time maintain their allegiance to their creed and escape its terrors. Your course is clear – the course of the people is not clear. They are in a terrible dilemma. I have seen many succumb even in my own circle. It takes great nerve – at least I think it does – to conquer the terror of the mockery... I wrote to Sarah Pugh a few days ago my ideas of the necessity of unity of labour among abolitionists – that the cause and not sections of individuals should be nearest to all – and that if by their influence with any particular classes or persons they recd. help from England they should look on its distribution chiefly to the good of the cause. If Joseph Sturge who is one of the most orthodox and most obstinate of men, could be brought round so as to cooperate willingly with any section of the Am.A.S. Society I would be exceedingly surprised. He may see clearly enough that no others are doing any good – but how could he countenance infidels – anti-sabbatarians – people who dont believe that Solomon's song is an address from Christ to his Church – or that David's ferocious denunciations are all as worthy of respect as the Sermon on the Mount?

We should condescend to each others weaknesses. I am sure that much that was wrong has been done by new organizers through bigotry, ignorance and mistake without half as clear a conviction of the turpitude of their acts as was felt by those who had greater light & more clear moral perceptions. For instance Joseph Sturge is known to be bigotted & pigheaded – exceedingly self-willed – yet he has shown great liberality of cash & general kindness to those who have needed his assistance. His zeal and devotedness doubtedly were principal means of the overthrow of the West Indian apprenticeship. When a man thinks that you and I hold opinions which are damnable and dangerous, is he not excusable in taking any means in preventing the spread of our heresy by discountenancing us? If the devil is not so back as he is painted, neither I hope is Joseph Sturge as dark as Edmund Quincy portrays him. This I say not from any intimacy or acquaintance with J. S. for I have not spoken to him or heard from him for years – but because I think it only just....There are rumours in our papers of a restoration of the Bourbons – what do people think about you? It is deplorable to see France so disgraced in the eyes of the world.

I suppose you know that the English Peace Society are to hold a Convention in Paris in August and that a good many Americans are to be there. I had a letter inviting my attention to the subject. I think all that is done in this way does some good – and it is certainly the case that public opinion in England is rapidly altering in favour of peace principles.

With best wishes for all your circle & hoping to hear from you shortly
I remain ever yours truly

Rich[d] D. Webb.

MS.A.9.2. vol. 24 1847 The Weston Papers [286]
No. 84 R.D. Webb to ?

Dublin August 3, 1849

My dear Friend

...Within the last few days William Wells Brown arrived – he is now our guest and we like him very much. He is very intelligent & easy, full of anecdote and staunch to his colour. I have no doubt he will make his way. He is not so great a man than Douglass – but neither is he so haughty and impatient. It is quite a luxury to have one to talk to who is so up to the progress of the cause and who has a fellow feeling with myself for those who are labourers in its behalf. I am about to print an edition of his narration from the sterotype plates, & I hope to be able to do the job to his satisfaction, & that he will be easier to deal with than Douglass was who appeared to be eaten up with suspicion.

...This is Friday – the Queen is expected on Monday to make her entry into Dublin, & there are to be illuminations in the evening. Meanwhile there are multitudes in extreme misery in the West of Ireland. There is great talk about loyalty – and there will be an immensity of display & an abundance of smiles on the faces of unhappy people. The prevalent depression is very great in business & I dont understand how the Queen's coming can be of the slightest service to us. John Mitchell, Smith O'Brien & their companions now in banishment were rash men in a worldly sense– but they loved Ireland & sacrificed everything for Ireland. What does the Queen care for us? This is a miserable, degraded, divided, distracted country – and whilst one cannot but feel for it, no sensible man has reason to be proud of it. I cannot hope that England will ever be really united in heart & feeling. The English despise us. Their arrogance knows no bounds. And yet all or nearly all the evil that afflicts us is the will of their forefathers – who did their best to grind us down & degrade us. I half hope the people wont make great fools of themselves on Monday – I know they wont if they act then as they feel now. But who can answer for a mob?

But the Queen coming or going is a small matter compared with the substantial fact that the harvest prospects are unusually fine – such as we have not had for the last 4 years – and there is no report of potato blight. The potatoes will be a fine crop and as good as in old times. This will bring us round if anything can, If Ireland were ruled for the people, and not, as is the case, for a thoroughly selfish & heartless aristocracy we should yet see good times.

With warmest good wishes for all your circle.

Ever yours truly
Rich^d^ D Webb.

MS.B.1.6. vol. 14 1848-1865 May-Estlin Correspondence [287]
No. 4 Samuel May to J. B. Estlin

Leicester, Massachusetts, Sept. 7, 1849

Dear Mr. Estlin,

...You will have seen what our Southern *brethren* are doing about Cuba; a very extensive plan has been laid, *ostensibly* to aid the people of that island in throwing off the Spanish yoke (!); *really* to seize the island, and, instead of casting *off* yokes, fasten tighter the *yoke of slavery*, and in a worse form than even the slavery now existing in Cuba, upon the present black population there with as many more as American cupidity and 'enterprise' can add to the number. This is all a piece with the Texas, New Mexico, and California business; immense thefts, done up in half picaroon, half-pedlar fashion. Genl. Worth, it is said, had agreed to conduct the expedition, provided the aid of United States citizens was requested in Cuba – all of which would have been arranged easily. Genl. Worth was carried off by cholera, or something like it – Was it not remarkable that Polk, Worth, Gaines, all prominent men in this high-handed plunder of Mexico, this "act of unparalleled outrage on Mexico" as Col. Benton called it, were so suddenly struck down, and so near to each other? It recalled the equally striking & more sudden death of Upshur, Gilmer, & other conspirators in the Texas business, who, you will recollect, were killed by the explosion of a monster cannon, which they had blasphemously christened the "Peacemaker". The long suffering of GOD with this nation is beyond all human imagination; only the Father of *Infinite* Mercies could have borne so long with so hypocritical and so corrupt a people. Other nations are awfully involved in guilt, in their treatment of the poor, the weak, the helpless. It remained for America to belie herself, and to outrage all her own professions & pledges to the world, while distancing or at least equalling all other nations in her acts of oppression and cruelty towards those whom she was chiefly bound to protect. Our President, Zachary Taylor, has issued a Manifesto, or Proclamation, forbidding all citizens of [the] U.S. to take any part in this movement; – I do not believe that the present Administration will "sit up o 'nights," as the saying is, to carry the procl^{n} into force. One of the principal S. Carolina journals has already openly defied the President, his Proclamation, & his Cabinet, and declares that no American citizen will be deterred by it from giving aid to the struggling cause of Liberty and Independence in Cuba – or words to that effect.

You are rather severe, Sir, in what you say of my "brother-republicans" (of France) "bombarding Rome, & murdering its noble citizens," &c I think you will recognize Lamartine, and those who were chiefly instrumental in the Revolution of 1848, as of quite a different stamp and character from President Bonaparte, and his backers, and his tools. Under *their* administration, Guizot has gone back to Paris, I see, and I see not why all the others, excepting perhaps Louis Phillippe himself may not do the same. France is in a bad way. Her course towards Mazzini and his noble Romans is detestable for its meanness & trickery, as well as for its baseness. I entirely agree with you that "history *does not* record a more contemptible and disgraceful transaction". But you will not identify Lamartine & his friends, I think, with this transaction. Since the election of Napoleon, my hopes & expectations for France for the present have been quite overthrown. It remains to be seen how long it will take to free the French nation from their absurd infatuation for Bonaparte, military glory, & mere names. Each successive revolution has shown a decided advance; perhaps, for the cause of true liberty, the falling back on Pres. Bonaparte is not *worse* than the taking up with Louis Phillipe was in 1830. The latter was cunning, and long deceived the people; the former appears to be weak, & at any rate exhibits at the very first his character, as a foe of popular freedom.

– Since writing the last sentence, the mail has brought us papers from Boston of this morning, giving the sad intelligence of the defeat of the Hungarians, their submission to the Russian power, the flight of Kossuth, &c. The cause of Hungary, & the resolute character of Bem & Kossuth, had excited a very deep & general sympathy in this country....

I know very little of the New York Vigilance Committee, to which you refer; but I do not suppose it to be a *Society for assisting Slaves to escape* in the sense in which I think you understand it. They employ, so far as I know, no travelling agents, & use no means to induce slaves at home to run away. These

Vig. Comtees are local bodies, so far as I am acquainted with them existing quite independent of each other in the cities and larger towns, with a view of giving aid to fugitives as they pass along; They are to a considerable extent, and in some places entirely sustained by the colored people. We have thought them a very useful instrumentality; and something of the kind seems absolutely necessary in places on the great routes which fugitives must take, or *near* which, at least, they must go. It is no part of their plan, so far as I am acquainted with them, to set on foot schemes like that of Capt. Drayton and the "Pearl"; but to see that actual fugitives, when in their vicinity, receive the aid, shelter & protection they need, and also, in case of any law-proceedings, to to see that the fugitives are suitably defended. I do not consider that these Associations or Committees "involve the practice of deceit". They are openly announced, hold public meetings, &c. It is obvious however that they afford facilities, to such as may be inclined to use them, for setting schemes on foot to "decoy", as the word is, slaves away. And, in view of a strict morality, it would not be easy to show wherein the act of aiding a fugitive at your own door, differs from that of going to his to furnish the means of doing what they nearly all eagerly desire to do. – In justice to these communities I ought to say, I do not remember ever to have heard of their engaging in any *general* measures for getting slaves away; they confine themselves, so far as I know, to the *particular cases* which come directly in their way. Moreover, they are not possessed of funds to enable them to carry on any very extensive schemes....

Respectfully yours, Samuel May Jr.

MS.A.9.2. vol. 25 1850-61 The Weston Papers [288]
No. 8

ANTI-SLAVERY CAUSE

Glasgow, May, 1850.

We the undersigned, have been long connected with the efforts made in Glasgow to aid American Abolitionists to wipe out the foul blot of Slavery, which disfigures their constitution, and curses their soil. But of late we have been surprised and grieved, by the discovery that many zealous labourers in that country have – by resolution adopted, and speeches and letters published – been making powerful efforts to propagate infidel notions:– repudiating the Holy Scriptures, trying to abrogate a weekly Sabbath pouring contempt on the ordinances of Christ, and utterly renouncing connection with the Christian Church – as if all has been held sacred constituted an impassable barrier in the way of our achieving liberty to the captives. With the points noticed, as religious questions, we do not now intermedole. Our object is not to infuse a sectarian element into the Anti-Slavery movement, but to protest against this, as exemplified by some of our American friends, who openly advocate Abolition on infidel principles, and thus entail on all in this country who cooperate with them, no small share both of the odium and the responsibility which attach to their religious views.

We will yield to none in the strength of our religious desires to see the slave emancipated, and elevated to the highest privileges cherished by the whole population; but we will not consent to sacrifice any part of written Revelation for this or any other benevolent object – we will not abandon Divinely-instituted ordinances – nor, while resolved to have no connection with Slave-holding churches, will we allow ourself to be mixed up with infidel attacks on the Christian Church even in America, in order to realise emancipation, – if for no other reason than this, that such reckless procedure is absolutely necessary, and abominably wicked. If Churches in that country, to a very large extent support Slavery, none know, better than our Anti-Slavery friends in America, that many Churches have renounced all connection with Slavery and Slave-holders, and that there are Churches which had occupied the same ground long before the present race of abolitionists came upon the stage of action. We cannot submit, therefore, that our names and our influence, and, through us, that Christianity in our country, should be associated with those Advocates of Anti-Slavery principles in America who, in public articles referred to, employ universally sweeping condemnations...

Besides, the accredited and paid lecturers, sent out by our Boston friends, assist at public meetings, in discussing and passing resolutions, embodying principles hostile to Christianity, under the gratuitous assumption, that it is antagonistic to liberty; instead of labouring according to the law of kindness which is ever on their lips, to obtain its emancipation from pro-slavery influence, wherever this lies with a blight upon it. Our contributions have hitherto gone to the support of this Society connected with the National Anti-Slavery Bazaar, at Boston; and Christian friends, in Glasgow and throughout the country, have long regarded our connection with them, as an indication rather of ill-judged generosity, than of Christian discernment; and from what they suspected of their infidelity they have refused to cooperate with us, and thus the Anti-Slavery Cause has become exceedingly weak in this country.

From the prominent position which some of our American Emancipationists occupy in this and the Peace Movement, and their readiness to take advantage of that position to disseminate their sceptical principles, we, with many zealous friends of the slave, feel ourselves justified in terminating our cooperation with the Boston Society, which we have hitherto aided. But we would not cease from well-doing in this wide field of benevolence; and we earnestly solicit the attention of our friends to the objects of "The Vigilance Committee of New York", which involves no sectarian bias. Their efforts are directed to the protection of fugitive Slaves; they find their food and clothing, and secure for them employment, while they provide for their safety in that, and other Free States, or in cases where their seizure appears to be imminent, by forwarding them to Canada. Fugitives, from the Slave States, average at present about 2500 per annum; and very many of these come direct to New York. To consult the interests of these, is a most humane and Christian duty, in which all may co-operate without imperilling any sacred principle...

We expect shortly to lay before you the constitution of a Ladies' Society, and will be glad of your countenance and support.

We are, &c.

(Signed)	MARGARET SMITH	ELIZA SIMPSON
	JANE BARCLAY	MARGARET McGREGOR
	ELIZABETH TURNER	MARION SLIMAN
	AGNES ROBERTSON	MARY MUIR
	ALEXANDER HODGE	

MS.A.9.2. vol. 25 1850-51 The Weston Papers [289]
No. 11 R.D. Webb to Mrs. W.C. Barclay

Dublin June 3rd 1850.

To Mrs. W. C. Barclay

Madam,

I have long been under the impression that nowhere on this side of the Atlantic was there to be found a greater number of persons than in Glasgow, who possessed deep antislavery convictions & an intelligent knowledge of the American abolition enterprise & the difficulties they had to contend with. Presuming that you & the other ladies whose names are signed to the circular you sent me, [no. 8] are of this number, I am amazed at the conclusion you have come to. Pardon me if I say that it seems to me a virtual abandonment of the anti-slavery cause; & a diversion of your efforts into a channel which has nothing whatever to do with the abolition of slavery. The New York Vigilance Committee is, I doubt not, well employed, – but it is the much higher mission of the Am. A.S. Society to denounce slavery, to unmask its meanness, immorality & cruelty, – to point out its impolicy, & to diffuse such information as shall arouse & enlighten the public mind. It is to support this society that the Boston Bazaar is held; & in withdrawing your aid from *it*, you are surely, however unintentionally, acting as the enemy of the slave....

...As a member of the Glasgow antislavery Society, you have cooperated with quakers, who observe no ordinances. Their opinions on the Sabbath are nearly the same as those of H. C. Wright, & they differ world wide from Knox & Calvin on many other important tenets. I would say, persevere in this wise toleration; the antislavery cause has nothing to do with the discussion of these questions. Leaving their members to their own religious political or scientific opinions, the Am. A.S. Society joyfully welcomes the assistance of all who believe slaveholding to be a sin. In working for the Boston Bazaar you assist the antislavery cause, & *no other....*

Yours respectfully,

Richd D. Webb

No. 49 Henry Wigham[1] *to [William Lloyd Garrison?]*

Edinburgh 16/7 m. 1850.

My dear Friend

...Thou wilt I doubt not through our Glasgow Friends, have been furnished with a Copy of a Circular, issued by some ladies in Glasgow suggesting that the friends of the slave in this country, shd. withdraw their assistance from the American Anti-Slavery Society & transfer it to the "Vigilance Committee" – To the misstatements in that Circular able replies have been written & published by Maria W. Chapman & Dr. Estlin of Bristol; & by those not hopelessly biased by a sectarian spirit, have been considered conclusive as to the connection subsisting between the American A.S. Society & H. C. Wright & thyself. As an individual, whilst disagreeing with some of thy theological sentiments – thy Anti-Slavery efforts have my warmest sympathy & I will gladly continue any little support I have been able to give to the A. S. S. Society – as I hold that every one has a right to have his own private opinions, & to give utterance to them by whatever means he may see fit – & that whilst agreeing with him on the pursuit of one philanthropic object I do not commit myself in any respect to sentiments extraneous to, & totally independent of that subject – in this opinion, I think I may say, I am joined by several of the warm abolitionists of Great Britain; those who have laboured long in the cause & to whose judgment I have ever looked up. I will not withhold from thee however, that some of the best friends in this land, whilst perfectly recognising the *right* have doubted the good policy of a line of argument, more especially taken up by Henry C. Wright, – of setting aside the authenticity of the Old Testament, in order to controvert the arguments of proslavery Professors of Christianity. They are of opinion that such a line of argument is unnecessary to prove that slavery is sinful – they wd. rather take their ground on the firm basis of Christianity, whose precepts are so diametrically at variance with Slavery. It is not my purpose in this letter even if I felt myself competent to do so, to enter into a discussion of this point – but simply, & I think with a full appreciation of the peculiar position in which you are placed, to let thee know the opinions of some of thy warmest friends & well wishers – & amongst the rest of myself one of the least influential though not least interested....

Thy old opponents the Free Church are in a state of pious rapture at having succeeded in shutting up the Post Office on the 1st day of the Week, but I fear before long their joy will be turned into mourning as the public are beginning to feel the serious inconvenience of the step, & to see that the present arrangement will tend to aggravate what is called the desecration of the Sabbath, instead of decreasing it. In London, Liverpool, & Manchester private individuals have undertaken to deliver papers & parcels as usual on the Sundays & employing a much larger number of men than were required under the more complicated machinery of the Post Office....

I am thy sincere friend

Henry Wigham.

---

1. See Wigham family tree, Appendix II.

Of "Expression of sentiment tendered by members of the Edinburgh Ladies Emancipation Society to the Meeting of Committee, held August 1st 1850."

"We have long cherished a most ardent desire for the emancipation of the slave in all quarters of the Globe; of late years especially we have been earnestly desirous of aiding every effort made for the liberation of those millions of our fellow creatures held in bondage within the United States of America.

Convinced that no principle was right in itself or could strike the root of the evil, except that of immediate emancipation, we have given our humble, but most cordial support to the Boston society, through this association; but deep & ardent tho' our love to the slave must ever be, there is a still higher principle than that of anti-slavery, viz. the honour of our God and Saviour which we dare not compromise.

With sincere sorrow of heart therefore we feel ourselves compelled to withdraw from connection with the Boston Society for the following reasons.

1st Because sentiments we conceive derogatory to the character of the Bible have been brought forward in the anti-slavery platform, & published in the papers supported by the anti-slavery society; – for in some of the resolutions passed at the New England Convention, particularly resolution 19th, the word of God has been spoken of in a manner that must fill the soul of every sincere Christian with alarm.

2nd Because the leading advocates of that society in America have given utterance to sentiments which in our opinion, are infidel in their nature & blasphemous against the Most High God.

3rd Because by holding such fellowship, we could not expect the blessing of God to rest upon our efforts"

Minute of the Edin^r Ladies Emancipation Committee August 1st 1850.

"The foregoing expression of sentiment, being that of many members of this Committee: – It is resolved, though with deep regret, that no box of contributions be this year sent to the Boston Bazaar under the auspices of this committee.

"The Secretary is directed to forward a copy of this minute to the Council of the Boston Bazaar. –

E. Wigham Sec.

MS.B.1.6. vol. 4 1850-1853 The May Papers [292]
No. 6 Samuel May to Mary Carpenter

Leicester, Mass; Aug. 2. 1850.

My dear Miss Carpenter,

We have been enjoying a very pleasant visit from your brother Russell.[1] He thinks you have been somewhat troubled by the Circular Letter of the Glasgow friends. It appears to me that a document so clearly unfair & malignant, as that is, need not occasion us a great deal of alarm or trouble. I call it unfair – most grossly so – to single out a single writer in the Liberator (a paper notoriously open to the discussion, pro & con, of every important moral and social question, so long as that discussion is maintained in good faith), and make that the basis for judging of the *character of the Liberator;*– how much more, for an attack upon *the American Anti-Slavery Society*, which has nothing whatever to do with H. C. Wright, save as he is an earnest devoted labourer in the anti-slavery field. – Mr. Wright's opinions are far from being the singular or new ones which some persons try to make it appear; they are coarsely & often offensively expressed, I admit, (& I regret it) but they amount to this, & they go no farther, viz. That the GOD he worships, the Father of Jesus Christ, He who is Love, never did & never can command or justify War, or Slavery, or any other oppressive & inhuman act; – that they who worship a GOD, who does allow & sanction these, worship a false GOD, a heathen idol, or a creation of their own corrupt & cruel hearts, a GOD whom He will never acknowledge. Is this shocking, impious, infidel? If so, I could wish to be called by those names, as essential to a genuine, heartfelt reverence for GOD & true religion....

Believe me most truly yours,

Saml. May Jr.

MS.A.9.2. vol. 25 The Weston Papers [293]
No. 18 Eliza Wigham to ?

5 Gray Street Edinburgh 8th month 30th 1850.

My dear Friend,

It is with great pain that I forward to thee the enclosed copy of a minute &c inserted in the book of our society. I could have wished that the connection between the two societies (yours & ours) should have had no interruption of however short duration, feeling as we do that yours is the truest & most disinterested association in America for the help of the slave, & the only one in which we can fully place confidence as far as regards the interests of the cause as strictly anti-slavery; we are much grieved that you should have brought forward arguments & sentiments in your advocacy of the question, which we deem unnecessary, inexpedient, & dangerous. – We

---

1. Russell Carpenter, one of the sons of Lant Carpenter, the famous Bristol Unitarian minister, took a more temperate view of slavery, and so came in for some severe criticism from the Garrison abolitionists.

do not think this great cause at all requires such arguments as have been lately used by the agents of the American A.S. Socy. – on the contrary, we think they weaken our hands, for where did the enterprise ever stand so firmly as when the faithful Garrison placed it in "the Bible & the Bible alone"? The more you weaken human faith in the precepts & the authority of the Bible, the more we think will you withdraw a firm foundation from the arguments & efforts & hopes called forth to our aid in this great cause. – Thus much I have thought it needful to say on behalf of my mother, myself & several of our friends here, because while in some measure differing from the determination of the larger number of the committee, we wished to state clearly that we unite in their feelings of uneasiness respecting the mode of argument in question. – We do not however see it right to withhold the little help we may have been able to render to the slave through you, and shall probably send through our Glasgow friends, as we cannot at all expect to fill a box of our own; – we shall do our best, however, to send all we can, but it must of course be considered as a *private* contribution.. My dear friend, I trust no hardness of heart may creep in between us on account of these things! – let us rather yield some things to the conscientious convictions of our friends & if any change may be made without compromise of! let us all be willing to concede even to what some may term united views in others....

Thine affectionately & sincerely for the slave

E. Wigham.

MS.A.1.2. vol. 19 1850 Anti-Slavery Letters to Garrison [294]
No. 86 George Thompson to William Lloyd Garrison

Matlock, Derbyshire;
England, October 3, 1850.

My Dear Garrison,

Start not when I announce to you that I have engaged a passage to Boston by the "Canada", Mail Steamer, which sails from Liverpool on the 19th Instant, & that should no accident happen to me or the vessel, I hope to take you by the hand on or before the 1st of November.

Now for the objects I seek by this trip for the Second time to the Shores of the United States.

1. I have an ardent desire to revisit your country, and to renew my acquaintance with those who were my friends in 1835 – and to become acquainted also with those, who, since that eventful period, have become the friends and champions of the cause I advocated, and may therefore be disposed to give a not unfriendly reception to one who, like yourself, was early in the field, and did not shun, either the reproach or the danger to which the abolitionists were exposed during the reign of mob-supremacy. Believe me, it will be most refreshing to me to mingle with the whole-hearted reformers of your City, and of the old Bay State. I gave you some reason to expect me more than two months ago. My visit at that time, however, was impracticable. Parliament was not up, and when it did rise,

some other engagements, as well as the state of my domestic affairs, prevented me from carrying my wish into fulfilment. I now think I see the possibility of my being for 5 months without the disregard of any claim upon my time or labours in this country.

2. In addition to my desire to see you and the friends of our Common Cause, I have a project to carry out of which America is the field. For some years before I entered Parliament, and at the time I entered it, I had been, and was, [in] the receipt of an income insufficient to meet all my wants, & to supp[ort] the position to which I aspired. In less than three months after I became a legislator, that income wholly failed me, and for three years I have been supporting myself and my family upon that which I had hoped I should be able to leave behind me. I am now poor; but hopeful, with unimpared mental energy, with a constitution yet sound and strong, and a character unassailable by any imputation of selfishness or corruption.

In these circumstances [MS. incomplete]
land in Liverpool next Spring with the reflection, that I was master of enough to carry me over the session of Parliament, and keep the pot boiling at home, while I rebuked the minister from my seat, as the representative of the people.

Well, in the prospect of my being speedily with you, what do I ask of you, as an old friend. First, that you will receive me as the friend who, when the road to fame and fortune was open to him at the bar of England, cast in his lot with you, and took joyfully his share with you in the perils of the old campaign. That you will believe me as warmly as ever the advocate of the cause of the slave. This, let the last refuge that has come to our shores testify. That you will not believe me mercenary. I could sing in a garrett, with a crust before me, if I had but myself to care for. That you will believe it is only the love of independence and of my family, and my desire to be, here, the incorruptible & *unpaid* advocate of the people, that makes me devise this scheme for putting money in my pocket, that you will not think the worse of me, because I do not come to them myself as, I did before, into the Antislavery cause, *exclusively;* but to discourse on topics that will bring those to hear me who will not refuse to pay their 25 or 50 cents for the opportunity. Finally, that you will aid my plan. I authorise you to communicate the contents of this letter to Francis Jackson, Wendell Phillips, and Edmund Quincy and to such others as you or they may think fit to take into your counsels. I authorise you to make it known through the most convenient channels, that I shall be willing to give lectures, if invited to do so, on the terms of other foreign lecturers. I authorise you to arrange for my beginning to lecture within one week of my landing. Perhaps it may enter into your minds to give me some public reception. If it should, & that can be turned to account, I authorise you to take steps to do it. I can remain with you till the last day of February. If careful, I shall be equal to three lectures a week, *in* or *out* of Boston. These I should like to be able to give, & not more to be delivered in such places, and under such circumstances, as promises the best results. I should be glad to have associated with me some congenial friend (to be remunerated for his services) who should relieve me of all the details of arrangements, money – talking etc. Another friend in Boston who would be my Treasurer, and remit, week by week, or mail by mail, my gains to this country, to my host Sir Joshua Walmsley,[1] who will not refuse to perform the friendly office of dispenser to the wife & children. [Letter ends.]

MS.A.1.2. vol. 19 1850 Anti-Slavery Letters to Garrison [295]
No. 93 Joseph Barker[1] *to William Lloyd Garrison*

Wortley, near Leeds, Octr 24, 1850.

My Dear Friend,

I am glad to learn from the *Liberator* that you are well, and able to labour in the cause of freedom. I hope you will like to see the great object of your wishes and the great end if your' labours accomplished. I feel exceedingly desirous to see the spirit of liberty & righteousness triumph over the spirit of oppression and wrong. Nothing on earth would rejoice me more than the abolition of American Slavery. It is, so far as I can learn, the most notorious form of iniquity, the most revolting piece of inhumanity with which the earth is at present dishonoured and cursed. It is, besides, one of the strongest props of European tyranny, and one of the greatest obstacles to the spread and triumph of European Liberty. No men on earth are engaged in a more important enterprise than you and your fellow Labourers. Most devoutly do I pray for your success, and most gladly would I aid you in your arduous and god-like labours....

I have felt most keenly since the passing of a new Law for the capture of fugitive slaves.... If the Law be not speedily abolished, there is hardly a man in Europe that will not look on America with disgust & loathing. No one in England, perhaps has spoken more favourably of the free states of America than myself; but if they allow this Law for the capture of fugitive slaves to be executed, I shall have to retract every word I have spoken, and mournfully acknowledge that America is the basest and most inhuman of all the nations upon earth. I have lately been in Ireland, and I saw such forms of misery there as pained me most acutely. The indignation I felt against the tyrants who had created such fearful scenes of misery was greater than I can describe. I felt as if I could have found in my heart, if I had had the power, to tear them in pieces and destroy them from the face of the earth. But on reading in the *Standard* the account of the capture and carrying away of James Hamlet, I felt, if possible, more keenly still, I felt that there were human beings in a worse condition than even the plundered and starving Irish. I saw no Irishman that was not at liberty to run away from his wretched country and seek a living and a home elsewhere. I saw no Irish landlords with whips and bowie knives,

---

1. Sir Joshua Walmsley (1794-1871) was a noted radical politician. He had agitated for the repeal of the Corn Laws and was a founder of the National Reform Association.

1. Joseph Barker (1806-1875), preacher and writer of pamphlets and articles, dabbled in radical politics and reform movements. A controversial and rather unstable figure, he supported Garrison and in 1857 he emigrated to America, where he continued to lecture on anti-slavery.

with pistols and rifles, with bloodhounds and kidnappers, hunting the runaway paupers in order to bring them back to their wretchedness and rags. I could not help but feel, while reading the papers which I have received from your country, that notwithstanding the excellency of its laws and institutions in many respects, and the comparative happiness of the middle and labouring classes in the free states, the country is disgraced and afflicted with a curse more terrible than the most miserable and down-trodden country I have seen in monarchical Europe.

This passing of the Fugitive Slave Bill has produced a most discouraging effect on the minds of my wife and children, as well as on my own. We are looking forward to America as our future home. We had made up our minds to leave England for one of your Western states in March or April next, with the intention of settling there. The news which we have received by the last post has obliged us, most reluctantly, to suspend or modify our resolution. We shall probably come to your country, and spend some time in it; but if the northern people do not render the iniquitous law inoperative, and insist on its speedy abolition, we shall, if permitted, return to England, and end our days under its monarchical and aristocratical institutions, the people of England are a more enlightened, a more manly, a more god-like, a more respectable and worthy set of people than the inhabitants even of the northern states of America.

But I cannot believe as yet that the Northern States will allow the law to be put in force, or even to remain in the Statute-book. It will be one of the greatest disappointments and one of the bitterest mortifications and humiliations of my life, if they do not act in such a way as to render the law of non effect and secure its speedy abolition.

I wish I could spend a few years labouring with you in the cause of abolition. I must contrive to assist you in your labours in some way. There are many of my readers who would like to help you, if they only know how to do it. We must endeavour to find out some means of giving you assistance, and of hastening the downfall of that revolting and inhuman system that so fearfully dishonours and curses your country.

With kindest regards to all your fellow-labourers, and with most earnest prayers for your success & triumph in the cause of human freedom .

I am,
Yours very affectionately,

Joseph Barker,

W. L. Garrison Esqr.

MS.A.9.2. vol. 25 1850-51 The Weston Papers [296]
No. 33 J.B. Estlin to Anne Warren Weston

Clevedon nr. Bristol; October 31 – 1850

My dear Miss Weston,

...I am curious to know what Geo. Thompson will do, & say in

America. It seems to me a matter of questionable propriety for a British member of Parliament to take an active part in any of the political movements of a foreign country which he may visit? Mr. Smith writes anxiously about him.......

MS. incomplete.

MS.B.1.6. vol. 14 1849-1865 May-Estlin Papers [297]
No. 22 Samuel May to J.B. Estlin

Boston, Massachusetts, Nov. 10. 1850.

My dear Mr. Estlin,

...And now I must tell you what I have been doing this last 2 or three days. When you know what unprincipled legislators we have in this country – I speak now of the National legislators – and what infamous laws they enact, you will not be much startled, I presume, to know that I have been violating the Law of the Land. You have seen, before this, accounts of a desperate attempt, by two fellows from Macon, Georgia, to seize William and Ellen Craft and take them back to slavery in Georgia. The U.S. Judge resident here – Levi Woodbury – on application from these men, (I hate to call them *men*) issued a warrant to the U.S. Marshall for the arrest of W & Ellen Craft.[1] For about 6 days these men remained in the city, during which time the writ was in the Marshal's hands. No attempt was made to serve it! It was said that Judge Sprague (of the U.S. Court) instructed the Marshal that he had no right to force the outer door of a dwelling house, in order to execute the warrant; – this has been denied. However this was, it was generally known that Wm. Craft was effectually armed, with knife, revolving pistols, &c &c. and would resist to the death any attempt to take him into slavery again. *The whole city was in great excitement.* The more active part of the inhabitants to a great extent expressed the determination not to suffer Wm. or Ellen Craft to be taken from the city. The Vigilance Committee (appointed at a late meeting held in Faneuil Hall for the purpose of denouncing the new Fugitive Slave Law) enlarged their numbers, held an almost permanent session, and appointed various sub-committees to act in different ways. One of the committees called upon Messrs. Hughes & Knight the Slave-Catchers – and requested and advised them to leave the city. At first, they refused peremptorily to do so, and said they would never leave till they got hold of the d-d niggers. On the complaint of different persons, these two fellows were several times arrested, carried before one of our county courts, on the charge of *conspiracy to kidnap, of defamation* in calling William & Ellen Craft slaves, &c &c. At each time they were held to

---

1. William and Ellen Craft, a Negro couple, had made a notable escape from slavery, but with the passing of the Fugitive Slave Law, they were forced to continue their flight to Britain, where they soon became popular lecturers supported both by the Garrison Group and by the Stafford House Party.

bail in heavy sums. At length, they became so alarmed that they left the city by an indirect route, evading the vigilance of many persons who are on the look out for them. Hughes came very near losing his life, at one time, at the hands of an infuriated colored man. While these men remained in the city, a prominent Whig gentlemen sent word to William Craft that if he would peaceably submit to arrest, he and his wife should be bought from their owners, cost what it would. Craft replied (in effect) that he was, in a measure, the representative of every other fugitive in Boston, some 2 or 300; that if he gave up, they would all be at the mercy of the slave-catchers, & must fly from the city at once, at any sacrifice, and if his freedom could be bought for two cents, he would not consent to compromise the matter in that way. Having thus manfully stood his ground, while the danger impended over him (Ellen in the meantime had been taken to a retired place out of the city) – when the kidnappers had gone, the friends of himself and Ellen felt that they must not stay in Boston nor in this country; for it appeared that the U.S. Government determined to try its hand in enforcing the Fugitive Law, and we knew that Wm & Ellen C. would be prominent objects of the slaveholders' vengeance. On talking with Wm. we found that, more particularly in his wife's account he had been thinking it best to leave the country. For myself, I had been advising the *going to England*, ever since the successful seizure & delivering into slavery of James Hamlet in New York. It was, after consultation as to ways & mean, & the expediency of the think, determined that they should go to England, and seek there, under the British Monarchy, the home, the Liberty, the chance to live and get a living, which in this *Free Republic* (!) are denied to them. What a humiliating conclusion for Americans, whose fathers fought against Gt. Britain in order to be free, to be compelled to come to.

William and Ellen Craft are now on their way to England. We did not like to run the risk of putting them here on board the Steamship which leaves this port next Wednesday. Accordingly they took the Railroad, on Thursday last, to Portland (110 miles to the N.E. of us) in the state of Maine – out of the jurisdiction of the Marshal who held the warrant against them – designing to take Steamboat that same night for St. John's New Brunswick, thence to Windsor, Nova Scotia, & thence (by stage) to Halifax – there to await the arrival of the British Steamship from Boston on Thursday next & proceed in her to Liverpool. Most unfortunately, on arriving at Portland we found (for I accompanied them in this flight) that the steamboat had been so much damaged, on her last trip, by a collision with another vessel, that she was hauled up for repairs, and would not sail that night, nor until Saturday morning at the earliest. I took them to a friend's house in Portland, where we were most hospitality welcomed & sheltered. At their urgent request I remained in Portland until Sat. P.M. It then had become a matter of reasonable certainty that the boat would sail in the evening – I saw the repairs completed, and the Boat afloat and getting ready; – and then I left them, in care of their friends at P., and returned to Boston, it being quite necessary I should do so, and nothing being left for them to do, but to go on board the boat when she was ready to depart – However, I am sorry to say I left Ellen C. suffering very much from a severe headache, the consequence of her protracted alarm & anxiety; and I confess I feel somewhat concerned for her, that she may have become more ill, and been unable to proceed. But she did not think it would be so, and I hope the best. I expect to hear tomorrow. I trust GOD will grant them a safe deliverance from the hands of their pursuers, and will guide them to a peaceful home. I gave to Wm. a letter of introduction to yourself, knowing that whatever your health would allow you to do for them, you would most gladly do. They have also letters from George Thompson to friends in England. I think, on their arrival in England, they will make the best of their way wherever Wm. W Brown is. On my return to Boston, I found at the AntiSlavery Office, to which place I first turned my steps, the letter from Mrs. Thomas, with the enclosure from your daughter for Mrs. May.

Leicester. Tuesday noon, Novr 12th ... George Thompson, you know, is now with us. I was very happy to become acquainted with him. I saw him once, & heard him speak briefly, in 1835. I have already become very much interested in him. On Friday evening next a Reception Meeting is to be held for him in Boston; after which, he proposes a brief course of Lectures, in compliance with urgent request, on British India, &c and will also, from time to time, during the winter lecture on various topics, Slavery included, as he may be invited to do. He told us, (as we were inquiring about Wm. W. Brown) of the aid you had afforded him, in getting out his Panorama. B. has sent me a copy of the little descriptive pamphlet and I think it promises well for the Pictures ... Every Abolitionist here feels that the Antislavery Cause owes a large debt to George Thompson, and had they wealth at their command, I am sure he would be a sharer of it. As it is, he will share what they have ....

I must say a few words about the recent Women's Rights convention at Worcester – a subject in which you, perhaps, feel an interest no more *lively* than I have done, although I am & have been, well convinced that many of the existing social & civil relations are established in a tyrannical spirit towards woman, and even where we may not suspect any sinister motive, we see an oppressive result. I think little of women having an opportunity to mingle with men in public affairs – but in all matters of business, occupation, and ways and means of getting a living reputably & sufficiently, I think they are much wronged. I do not however *object* to a woman being Governor of the State, or President of the Country, if she is qualified for it; and I do think that an infusion of *honest* women into our National Congress & Councils (I fear we couldn't get such there, any more than *honest men*, in any considerable numbers) would have saved us from the shame & baseness of the last Congress, and of our Government generally. The Convention at Worcester was one of the most interesting assemblies I ever attended. Women were the principal, though not the only speakers and showed themselves in no wise inferior, as good reasoners, acute expounders of Scripture, and eloquent speakers to our best men ....

I am, &c &c.,

Saml May Jr.

MS.A.9.2. vol. 25 1850-51 The Weston Papers [298]
No. 45 Andrew Paton to Anne Warren Weston

Glasgow 15th Nov 1850

Miss Anne W. Weston
Boston

Dear Madam

I forward to Liverpool on the 12th inst. one Box sent to my [home?] from Jane Wigham Edinburgh, to be shipped for you by the steamer which sails for Boston tomorrow, & which I hope will reach you safe.... It has been found impossible to send off the Box from Glasgow until the steamer from Liverpool on the 30th when it will be sent – my sisters cannot as yet say what may be the value, but that it will be pretty considerably injured by parties who have set up a new female anti-slavery Society here on acct of the want of *orthodoxy* in our American friends, & have endeavoured to withdraw contributions – in this they have been assisted by a coloured man named Dr. Pennington,[1] who is said to be a Minister of a Presbyterian Church at New York, & has suggested the New York Vigilance Committee as the proper party to be supported. I intend writing Garrison about this affair; my sister desires to be remembered to yourself, Mrs. Garrison & other friends

I am dear Madam

yours very truly
Andrew Paton.

MS.A.9.2. vol. 25 1850-51 The Weston Papers [299]
No. 46 Catherine Morton to Anne Warren Weston

Perth 26th Nov. 1850

Miss Weston
Boston

Madam,

I take the liberty of acquainting you, as requested by the Committee of the Ladies Anti-Slavery Society here, that a Box of articles was sent from this [place] to Liverpool to be shipped on board the 'Europa'...

May I request the favour of your acknowledging receipt of the above so soon after the sale as convenient, which we fondly hope will be a successful one, and at the same time you will please insert in the Gazette the parties

---

1. Rev. J. W. C. Pennington (1809-1870) was born a slave in Maryland, escaping when he was twenty-one. He later became a minister in the African Congregational Church. He represented Connecticut at the London Anti-Slavery Convention in 1843, and was again in Britain at the time of the Fugitive Slave Act. Due to his origins, this Act placed him in some difficulties until friends raised sufficient money to pay for his purchase. He was then sold to a third party who liberated him. His later life was spent as a minister in various Negro Presbyterian Churches.

who, have favoured us with Donations, as it communicates a pleasing feeling and acts as a stimulus to future exertion, especially upon the young when they see their labours thus acknowledged in connection with so benevolent an object.

I regret to say that a report is in circulation here which has caused no little annoyance to the Society, and has this year paralized its efforts to a considerable extent, and caused divisions amongst its members. Viz. that certain members (lecturers) in America, are persons of unsound religious views:— how far individuals may be justified on these grounds in withholding their support is a question on which I do not enter, but it must be a matter of deep regret to every lover of humanity that the society should suffer in consequence, and the cause of freedom be thereby affected. — We would fondly hope however, that the present effort feeble tho' it be, will have its weight, accompanied by our prayers, in hastening that longed for period, when slavery shall cease, and the oppressed go free.

I am, Madam,
yours faithfully,
C. Morton.

MS.A.9.2. vol. 25 1850-51 The Weston Papers [300]
No. 47 Mary Welsh to [Anne Warren Weston?]

78, Apsley Place Glasgow Nov[r] 29th 1850

My Dear Friend

I have much pleasure in stating that we have sent off Per Steamer our contributions for your Bazaar, as the large box would not take all the things we had to put the remainder in a small box, so that you will receive 2 boxes, a large one & also a small one.... We are happy to be able to state that our contributions, are nothing behind last year, but rather better, as you will see by the list, and that the opposition started against us has not injured us at all....

The fugitive Slave Bill is exciting great interest here there was a meeting got up the other night by the working men in America who have gone from this country, it was a real hearty thoroughgoing meeting. What an infamous Bill that is, just too bad to work, it will be the death blow to slavery I hope.

With kindest regards and every wish for your success

Believe me ever to remain yours for the cause of the oppressed
Mary Welsh.

MS.A.1.2. vol. 19 1850 Anti-Slavery Letters to Garrison [301]
No. 106 James Hoey to William Lloyd Garrison

Glasgow, Decr 12th 1850

To W. L. Garrison

Dear Friend

The enclosed as you will see, is an address and appeal from the the working men of Glasgow to working men in the United States relative to their connection with slavery and the infamous fugitive Slave Bill, the report which I send is from the Post, the Sentinel has given us a good report of the meeting, some of the friends will have furnished you with a number of that journal, the regular reporter of the Post could not be present, and the person who was in his place clamoured for the manuscript of the remonstrance which was handed to him, both journals being published in one day, and want of room has made things just as we find them.

Yours sincerely

Jas Hoey.

MS.A.1.2. vol. 19 1850 Anti-Slavery Letters to Garrison [302]
No. 106

FUGITIVE SLAVE BILL
AND
MANHOOD SUFFRAGE

A GREAT PUBLIC MEETING of Working Men and others friendly to Slave Emancipation, and a just measure of Political Reform in the British House of Commons, will be held in the CITY HALL, on TUESDAY Evening, the 26th inst., when resolutions will be submitted condemnatory of Slavery and the Fugitive Slave Bill, recently become Law in the United States, and also against an Exclusive Suffrage in this country.

Doors open at half-past Seven – Chair taken at Eight precisely.

N.B. One Penny will be charged at the door to defray expenses.

FELLOW – WORKMEN,

We appeal to you on behalf of the objects above stated. To all who earn bread by the sweat of their face, the hideous injustice of Slavery must be a subject of peculiar interest. The depots of both hemispheres are again at their iniquitous work, of crushing the rising spirit of freedom in their midst. The infamous Fugitive Slave Bill in America, and Cossack Despotism on the Continent of Europe, with aristocratic domination at home, are just so many links in the chain by which multitudes are fettered to a hateful system of oppression and misrule. Be it ours, therefore, to make the forthcoming demonstration a magnificent display of fraternal sympathy for the poor slave.

and likewise a dignified protest against our own exclusion from political privilege.

(signed) MATTHEW CULLEN, Chairman of Interim Committee.
JAMES HOEY, Convener.

P.S. Please to give the above as wide a circulation as possible.

Sir,

You are respectfully requested to meet with the Committee in the Ante-room at Half-past 7, and to accompany them to the platform. Entry by South Albion Street.

M.C. & J. H.

MS.A.9.2. vol. 25 1850-51 The Weston Papers [303]
No. 50 William Smeal to W.W. Brown

Extract from a letter from Mr. Wm. Smeal to W. Wells Brown, in reference to his visiting Glasgow to hold a public meeting, to exhibit his Panorama &c &c

Dated Decr 12th 1850

'On consulting with our mutual friend Andrew Paton, about thy coming to Glasgow, it appears to us desirable to make an effort for a *real*, good good, & *bold Anti-Slavery Meeting* at this crisis; not having held a *Public Meeting* of the Glasgow Emancipation Society for about 4 years, – the reason for wh. is, that our agitation of some years against the *Free Church* of Scotland, for receiving the contributions of slaveholders to build churches &c entailed upon us a load of debt. wh. is not yet quite paid off, altho' very much reduced.

Secondly – some months ago, on Dr. Pennington coming here, certain parties male & female, mostly the latter, have become dissatisfied with contributing to the Boston A. S. Bazaar, because identified with W. L. Garrison & H. C. Wright, whose religious views they could no longer be held as virtually approving, they formed a new female society, termed the Glasgow Female Association for promoting the Abolition of Slavery, 'Limiting their support to the Vigilance Committee' of New York. They issued circulars also exposing the ultra of W. L. F. & H. C. W. &c & altho' their circular has been replied to by M. W. Chapman, these said parties have not only taken no notice of M. W. C's refutation of their statement, but have succeeded to some extend in showing division in our Antislavery camp, not a little aided as we apprehend by Dr. P, who it is understood is connected with the 'Vigilance Committee' of New York, & is to be correspondent in that city, of this New Organization in Glasgow. An attempt has not yet been made, so far as I know, to institute a new *Male* antiSlavery Society; but the friends of the New Female one are to hold a public meeting to-morrow evening to protest against the New Fugitive Slave Bill, at wh. Dr. P. is to assist, in conjunction with certain Dissenting & Free Church clergymen. This will be the second meeting these sowers of division in our ranks have got up; & we of the *old society*, wh. had fought the battles of freedom for the last 30 years, have made no effort to *take the shine out of them.* In this we have been actuated by motives of *prudence*, that we might not unnecessarily show to the public there was division in the camp; & partly because being still in debt disabled us in some measure from what I may term *offensive* war, preferring rather to act in the *defensive*; & thirdly, becuase ever since I saw thee in London we have fully intended making an *imposing demonstration* when thou arrived.'

'Thou will be pleased to hear, for all the opposition to the old society I have noted, that a capital Box of Work for the *Boston Bazaar* has been sent off, & I hope is by this time arrived.'

MS.A.1.2. vol. 20 1851 Anti-Slavery Letters to Garrison [304]
No. 1 Elizabeth Pease to William Lloyd Garrison

Darlington 1st mo. 18. 1851

My Dear Friend

Wm. Lloyd Garrison,

...This last act (the Fugitive Slave Law) – the last expiring effort, as I fondly hope, of the slave power, while it primarily affects but one nation of the human family, in fact imperils the liberties of all, so flagrant an outrage on the heaven bestowed gift of personal freedom cannot be offered to one portion of mankind without the liberties of man universally being placed in jeopardy. It is then a world's question & you who are fighting a world's battle, are entitled to the sympathy of every human heart, the wide world over, which prizes the right to "life liberty & the pursuit of happiness" as the choicest of earthly blessings & glad, ah! glad should I be could a world's convention be assembled to ratify the verdict passed last week, at a meeting held in Glasgow – a verdict which placed beyond the pale of civilization and ranks among savages, the originators & supporters of the Fugitive Slave Law....

Ms. incomplete.

MS.A.13.1. The Thompson Papers [305]
No. 11 George Thompson to Anne Warren Weston

Portland, Maine;
Thursday night,–
11 p.m.

My Dear Friend,

My meeting here is over – I have had some stewed oysters & milk for my supper, and have returned to my bedroom for the night – My *AMERICAN* bedroom – for everything reminds me that I am here. I write by the side of an *air-tight stove* – with the light of an *explosive spirit lamp* – sitting in a *rocking chair* – at the foot of a *curtain-less bed* – before a window covered ¼ of an inch thick with *ice*, and a *fire-bell* ringing in my ears.

My lecture tonight has been something peculiar, owing to the following circumstances. At tea time a friend put into my hand a copy of a little daily penny paper, containing the enclosed article, informing me at the time, that the Editor had for two months been throwing mud at me in true Jonathan Jefferson Brick style, and doing all in his power to stir the sediment in this city. I cut out the editorial, and carried it with me to the meeting, & in the course of my introductory observations, took such notice of the attack as I thought it deserved. It served me, too, as a peg on which to suspend some remarks upon the whole tribe of American literary scavengers – I then proceeded with my lecture, and toward the close, drew a picture, of the progress, & present sublime aspect of the anti-slavery cause, notwithstanding the blue bottle and carrion crow attacks of such insects and obscene birds as the "*News*". At this stage, a person cried out, "the writer is here, and is not ashamed of what he has done." This set me afire, and away I went, running amuck at all the papers that for the last 15 or 16 years had been inciting the people to mobs and violence – all the while belabouring the unfortunate Editor of the News – to the infinite diversion of my audience. I assure you, I obtained wonderful relief from the throwing off of a vast quantity of long accumulating bile. To the audience, this was the best part of my discourse, and sent them away in the happiest possible frame of mind. My meeting was held in what is called the *Christian* church – a very comfortable and eligible building. It was remarkably well filled at 12½ cents per head. They have rewarded my castigation of their townsmen with $ 50. The audience was the best known at a ticket meeting, except when Mr. James came amongst them, to take snuff for an hour, and read them a portion of one of his printed works, touching the ancient Britons, which they will have it was inferior in information to the answers of a school girl in the 1st class. I got here a little before one, much jaded, and have spent most of my time in my bed-room, trying to doze, I have been strongly entreated to remain over to-morrow, but have resisted and I am now going to my pillow to prepare for a start at ½p. 8 for Boston, where I shall post this.

Peace be with you & yours, whether at home or *abroad.*

Ever gratefully,
& sincerely Your's

Geo. Thompson.

To
A.W.W.

MS.A.1.3.1. The Thompson Papers. [306]
No. 17 George Thompson to Anne Warren Weston

New Bedford, Mass:
Sunday Evening, ½ past 11 P.M.
February 2. 1851.

My Dear Friend,

...Yesterday morning Wendell Phillips called upon me to say he could not accompany me owing to the state of his wife's health. Garrison though he might have been excused resolved to share my labours & we started at 4 P.M. accompanied by Dr. & Mrs. Taft. Mr. Robeson met us at the Cars at ½ past 6 and brought me here. At ½ past seven we held our first meeting in Liberty Hall and had a moderately full attendance. The Chairman, a Mr. French, gave me a suitable introduction, and to believe Garrison I spoke most of the evening, he having to say but a very few words when I sat down. There had been rumours of opposition and a disturbance but all went off most peaceably.

This morning at ½ past 10 we met again in the same place. I was first called upon, and speaking till 12 oclock the meeting was adjourned till ½ past 2. Almost every seat was occupied at this meeting.

In the afternoon the house was too small and we had to resort to many contrivances to find the ladies who came late, accommodation. Garrison spoke till about ½ past three, after which I talked for ¾ of an hour and we then adjourned till half past six.

Our last gathering was a bumper.Wherever a human being could be stowed away there was one. The sight was grand. "The people" of New Bedford were present. Garrison commenced and continued the discussion of the great theme till nine. The audience departed very slowly and apparently very reluctantly. They seemed to "want some more." The very best feeling has prevailed at all our meetings. The addresses have been solemn searching and uncompromising but I think discreet and unexceptionable in their tone. No misconstructions were possible. Garrison though unwell & in pain has spoken well. Tonight he was animated, fluent, impressive and at times eloquent. Besides our speeches there have been none save the introducting remarks of the chairman and a short address today from an aged colored minister of this city....

We leave at ½ past 7 in the morning for Boston. We have every reason to be gratified with the result thus far of our visit. May our bread appear after many days! For myself, though my body as been weak, I have been in the spirit of my work and have been able to go through it without any difficulty I trust I shall not feel much the worse tomorrow – today for the clock has just struck 12.

Accept my heartfelt thanks for all your kindness. Believe me it is felt and appreciated. You might easily extend it to one worthier – You could not to one who valued it more or is more grateful than your attached friend.

Geo. Thompson

Love to *all*

MS.A.13.1. The Thompson Papers [307]

DAILY EVENING NEWS

WEDNESDAY, FEBRUARY 5, 1851.

GEORGE THOMPSON, M.P. – We see by a notice in the Argus and Advertiser, that this notorious personage is coming to Portland the present week to lecture. We had hoped that this member of the British Parliament and emissary of the foreign abolitionists, sent here to get up agitation and excitement on the question of domestic slavery, to array different sections of the country against each other and promote a dissolution of the Union, would keep away from this state and not come here to scatter abolition fire-brands and preach political incendiarism. When he was in this country on a similar mission in 1836, he declared at Andover that *"the slave-holders ought to have their throats cut,"* and at that time, as now, he was hissed and hooted in Faneuil Hall and not allowed to speak there on account of his mission, his impertinent interference with our affairs, and vile abuse of this country. His associates and colaborers here are Garrison, Douglass, Abby Kelly, etc., persons who hold that the American Constitution is *"a covenant with death and an agreement with hell,"* and who are deadly foes of the Union. Such is the person who is announced as coming here, to enlighten and instruct our citizens in regard to their moral and political duties.

MS.A.1.2. vol. 20 1851 Anti-Slavery Letters to Garrison [308]
No. 3 Andrew Paton to William Lloyd Garrison

Glasgow 7th Feb. 1851.

Private & Confidential

My dear friend,

I wrote to you by last Steamer, & y'day got a copy of the Report of the Edinburgh Ladies A.S. Socy. for last year, which is sent you by this mail. Lest it should not have been sent you otherwise – I am greatly grieved to see the terms in which the proceedings, regarding the withhold contributions from the Boston Bazaar are narrated – they are in my opinion very offensive & could scarcely be more so, were they expressly framed for the purpose of strengthening the new Socy. here – the writer I have no doubt is Henry, Eliza, or Jane Wigham, as there is no mistaking the Quaker style in which they are written; "slippings" &c, for instance; 'tis certainly very strange that they could not state the bare truths, that tho' a majority of the Committee withheld contributions, yet that a considerable minority had forwarded contributions as before – this is the more strange from the expressions of regret that Jane Wigham has used when she has been stating to me & others that altho' the Socy, as such were not sending this season, yet that herself & some would send contributions – & then you will see that the report recommends for their support the ensuing year, the free Labour Movement, fugitives in Canada &c & not a word of the Amn. A.S. Socy. – the *Quakers* are in many respects a strange set, & beyond being fathomed in their motives & conduct – my opinion is that this move is produced at the instigation of Anna H. Richardson of Newcastle who is related to the Wighams – at least to the Wighams of 10 Salisbury Road, & they to the other Wighams of 6 So. Gray St. I will endeavour to get our staunch friend Mary Welsh to visit Edinr. & see those of the Comtee there whom she knows to be sound & have them decide that if the Amn. Socy. is to be thrown over, that they will themselves labour only for the Amn. Socy. – I think you had better mean time not notice this report publicly, until it can be learnt what the Wighams intend to do. You will perhaps recollect that Jane W. is sister to Wm. Smeal

& stepmother to Henry & Eliza. It was most shabby conduct to get Wm. & Ellen Craft to give interest to a meeting which had taken such a position with regard to you.

Pennington has not yet replied to the letter of Wm. Smeal & myself enquiring after the proposal to raise money to buy him, we have written him again & he must say something immediately which I will communicate – he called on me a week ago & told me a very improbable story but which it is needless to relate here no doubt he wishes to get off answering us in black & white this however he wont do....

Regretting that my communications at present are so far "not pleasant but grievous" but trusting that soon "a better time is coming" with best regard for yourself Mrs. G. & all anti-Slavery friends.

I am yours always

Andrew Paton

Mr. Wm. L. Garrison
21 Cornhill
Boston U.S.

MS.A.13.1. The Thompson Papers [309]
No. 18 George Thompson to Anne Warren Weston

Union Village, Washington County:
Friday morning, Feb. 21. 1851.

My Dear Friend –

Let me hear of you to the Care of S. J. May, Syracuse "This far into the bowels of the land" – as Richmond says, I have penetrated unobstructed.

The incidents by the way have been but few. After our party I was soon at the Station. When there, I sent Putnam[1] get three tickets for Albany – for *himself*, *Sojourner*[2] and *me*. While he was gone to the office, I walked leisurely towards the cars, passing on my way some 8 or 10 men of an Equivocal aspect. Presently, an egg passed me, and fell on the platform. I returned – stood before these men, and said, "Will the miscreant who threw that egg shew himself, and say; "I did it." All were dumb. Behind me I heard a voice say, "You had better be quiet." I turned to the person, and said, "Tell those cowards, and dastard Americans, to be quiet." "I was not speaking to you, sir," said the person. It was the Superintendent, who, as I afterwards understood, made these men immediately quit the platform. From one end of the route to the other, I was the stared at of all starers. The chief business of the conductor seemed to be, to point me out to spread the news at the station – and to lend his passengers the Republican of the day. *Two* o'Clock saw us on the banks of the Hudson. The scenes of Springfield were forgotten amidst the glorious scenery of America's finest river. "No poetry," I hear you say – "Give us facts – stern, Buffonian facts," I hear, and obey. We changed cars, and got to Troy, – where Helen

---

1. George W. Putnam was Thompson's secretary during his second visit to the United States.
2. Sojourner Truth was a Negress, active in the Underground Railroad.

was not. Arrived, a meek-faced man entered our car, and stood near the door, silently surveying the crowd – for we were very full. "Putnam," said I, "who is that?" "A *Shaker*" said he, "I could swear it by the cut of his jib." "He might be" said I – "cravatless, – a huge broadbrimmer, and all the *etceteras* of the tribe." Presently the vision spoke, and said, – "Is a person of the name of *William Lloyd Garrison,* of Boston, in this car?" It was enough. "Putnam," said I, "that man's no *Shaker,* he's a chip of the everlasting rock; speak to him."

He was friend Wilmer, who had brought his waggon and team to convey us nearly 30 miles to this place. Behold us in our triumphant car. Boxes, bags, buffaloes, broad-brim and narrow-brims, all stowed away, and a couple of bay horses doing their work in thorough free labour style. We kept the bank of the Hudson for 12 miles. The consternation below was great, the "*Citizens*" came in succession, but finding I was in "*the harms of Murphy*", went off saying, each as he left a farewell ejaculation of juice behind him, – "Well, I guess I'll see him start in the morning." I had 11 hours of bed! Precisely at past seven – breakfast having been secured – we were again in our waggon. The citizens lined the piazza of the Hotel (!!) I had already acknowledged, in suitable words, – few, impressive, and Websterian – their meditated compliments.– We were off, and the citizens remained to catch a glimpse of the team, as it turned the corner, and conveyed perhaps forever, the illustrious stranger from their view. The rest *had* restored me. A pretty Irish maid, who had waited upon me (her looks cost me 50 cents) – had put me in good humour, & I enjoyed the 12 miles drive. At this village, I was received into the mansion of Mr. Gibbs, a wealthy man. At 11, the Convention organised – Abby Foster spoke & at one there was an adjournment. In the afternoon I spoke an hour and a Quarter. In the evening I had *all* the time, and spoke 2 hours, and more. This morning we recommence. The place of meeting is a new school, reformatory, Orthodox Church – recently founded. The building, though not large is neat. All is clean, comfortable, & pleasant to the eye. The congregations have been good. The people are Seward Whigs, or Gerrit Smithites, I think we shall leave many of them Garrisonians. Pardon, very dear friends, this incoherent narrative. Let it at least prove, *you are not quite forgotten* by your's affectionately, George Thompson.

MS.A.1.2. vol. 20 1851 Anti-Slavery Letters to Garrison [310]
No. 6 J.B. Estlin to William Lloyd Garrison

Bristol. Feby. 21st 1851

PRIVATE

My dear Mr. Garrison,

...This mail will bring you, I hope, a "London Morning Advertiser" in which is an *editorial* (not a leading article) of mine headed "*The Slavery of America – her clergy at the Gt. Exhibition.*" This newspaper has a large *London* circulation. My object is however, to have an easy & effectual way of sending to persons I wish to read it, the article in question.

I want to make the clergy in this Country, (not those of the *Establishment,* for they will attend to nothing out of the Church) – be upon their guard in respect to their "*Amn Brethren*"; and for those in America to feel a little uncertain as to the reception they may meet with here.

I have just received 400 copies of the "M. Advert." for my own distribution, & with the help of friends, – (many orthodox,) I hope to make a good use of them. You will probably think it worth while to insert the article in the Libr. to help its warning voice....

I am particularly anxious that *my name* may be in no way connected with this effort: for it would detract from the effect of an Editorial article from a *London* paper; – some too of the Boston Unitarian Ministers are now so well acquainted with my anti-slavery tendencies, that their supposing me to have written the warning, wd. detract from its influence with them....

Believe me dear Mr. Garrison, sincerely yours

J. B. Estlin.

MS.A.13.1. The Thompson Papers [311]
No. 20 George Thompson to the Westons

National Parliamentary and Financial
Reform Association
Offices

½ p. 9. a.m.

Rockton, Valley of the Mohawk.
Feb. 24. 1851.

My Dear Friends, –

I wrote you on the morning of the 20th (Thursday) from Union Village, on the Hudson. In the afternoon I attended the Convention and in a speech of upwards of an hour I introduced the Foreigner to the notice of my audience (a very good one) and told them as much about him as I thought it expedient they should know. My friendly speech seemed to win for him the good opinion of the majority and many were the smiles he got while I was speaking and the greetings when I had finished. In the evening the emissary ascended the desk, and after singing,* occupied the whole time (more than two hours). Though I did not think much of the speech the people pronounced it a *non such* in their part of the country and that is enough. What can you expect from the descendants of Rip Van Wincle in the way of judgment on oratory.

Friday 21st spoke in the morning meeting. Spoke also in the afternoon and retired to lie down while I was away S.S.F. turned the milk to curds by an attack upon all church organization wh did some harm. (Confidential!) In the evening Abby made a masterly (no *mistressly*) speech on the growth and Bohun Upas influence of the slave power. Then I rose and delivered a valedictory & the Convention adjourned *sine die.*

Saturday 22. Started at 9-30 a.m. for Troy – 29 miles, in a stage & accomplished the journey in *8* hours reaching the Washington Hotel at ½ past 5!! Oh

* There was an accomplished choir who with the aid of melodeon and a bass viol gave us some very sweet & well executed music.

that ride! Heaven preserve me from another such. At Troy, had to wait till 7 in a *pisunus* (pestiferous) bar room newly painted with a red hot stove in it. Oh my head! At 7 took the cars and arrived here a little before midnight. Too unwell to come down on Sunday morning the 23rd. A meeting held at which Putnam & the Fosters spoke. Place the Rechabite Hall. In the afternoon I went in and spoke at length. After my address a young Patriot rose and took the stand. Vindicated the Fugitive Slave Law – The North had nothing to do with Slavery – The Colonization Society had done more to promote abolition than *we* (you) had done. Mr. Thompson did not seem to understand that we were 31 separate states with individual Sovreignty & reserved rights &c &c &c. Mr. Thompson replied – the audience in extasies. The patriot used up. The applause vociferous. At the close the principal citizens offered a word of advice to the young man, vizt. that before he attempted to lift an *ox* he should practice himself by lifting a calf everyday.

In the evening we had no meeting, but instead, held a leave at our hotel which was numerously attended.

We are now off to West Winfield some twenty miles – all but 6 miles by waggon. Pray for me that I be not left in fragments on the road for the shaking is awful and the danger of dislocation is imminent. Can you put up with these epistles? If you can you shall hear more concerning the rambles of an incendiary. Ever yrs. G.T.

MS.A. 13.1. The Thompson Papers [312]
No. 19 George Thompson to Anne Warren Weston

N.Y. Peterborough, Friday,
February 28. 1851.
10-15 am

My Dear Friend,

I have just come hither, from the residence of Gerrit Smith, which is about a mile and a half from hence. I am now at the house of his daughter, Mrs. [sic] and am sitting in her parlour. This is the day for the Commencement of the convention here, which will extend over tomorrow, while it is organized, I am remaining under this roof, and shall not go in, until the afternoon, unless much needed, I will attempt a rapid sketch of our journeying since I wrote you from Rocktown, (or, Little Falls).

Monday 24 at 11 a.m. took the cars for Herkimer, 6 miles, and there remained till one, when we started in a waggon, under a heavy rain, for W. Winfield – a distance of 16 miles, with the roads in a dreadful state. Had the weather been fine, the ride would have been delightful, and we passed through the finest scenery I have yet looked upon in the United States. Soon after leaving Herkimer, we entered a pass through to the hills, which are well wooded from their summit to their base. A rapid stream flows along the bottom of the valley. The road has been cut along the bottom of the hills, and in some places looked dangerous, but we met with no mishap. This romantic defile is 7 or eight miles long. It is called, the gulf, by the people in the neighbourhood. I would travel any distance to see it in fine weather. We were five hours accomplishing our 16 miles, and at last alighted at the house of the friend who had driven us, a Mr. Thomas, who keeps a Temperance hotel at Winfield – has been a deacon – but is now a come-outer, and Garrisonian abolitionist – one of the many converts of Mrs. Foster, who labours in this state 8 years ago have produced much fruit I found a most comfortable room prepared for me, and went to it for the rest of the day.

Tuesday 25. First day of the Convention. Had a quiet morning in my room. In the afternoon, spoke nearly two hours, upon the present aspect of the country, in relation to Slavery. Had great freedom of utterance. In the Evening, took the speech of Mr. Clay, at the late Colonization meeting at Washington, for my text, and spoke not only of the expatriating scheme, but of Mr. Clay's views, generally, on the Anti-Slavery question, and his scheme of gradual emancipation by natural causes. Went home – had a basin-full of Thompsonian hot mixture and then to bed.

Wednesday 26 The Convention today, was held in the village of *East* Winfield, in a larger house, and was well attended. In the afternoon I had a controversy with a Methodist Minister who undertook the defence of his religious body. The debate excited great interest. In the evening made the closing speech. Went home and had apple pie and Thompsonian mixture for supper.

Thursday 27. At nine a.m. left W. Winfield for this place. Mr. Smith had sent his waggon the day before for us. These waggons are open conveyances, with three seats. We accomplished our journey in seven hours, reaching Mr. Smith's a little after seven. Our reception was most hospitable. Mr. Smith is a noble looking man. Quite American in his apperance, but the best looking American I have ever seen. On our arrival, Mr. Putnam was put to bed, to nurse a fever, and Mrs. Foster returned, to administer to herself for the removal of inflammatory systems on the chest. Stephen seems to bear all things without injury. My worst complaint was fatigue. I sat till 10, conversing with Mr. Smith and then went to bed, and rested till eight this morning. We have left Mrs. Foster & Mr. Putnam behind us. You will be happy to hear that Mr. Smith's daughter in whose house I write this, has adopted the Turkish costume – a short dress, and full trousers, drawn just above the ankle. Mrs. H. B. Stanton has also put on the same dress & both appear *a la Turque* in public. I shall anticipate with much pleasure the appearance of the *Westons* at my next anti-Slavery meeting in Mass:– in similar dresses. If you will consult a copy of an Illustrated Byron, which contains pictures of Gulnare, the Corsair's wife, the Maid of Athens, the Bride of Abydos, &c &c you will be able to compound dresses that will be picturesque, and I have no doubt that, *pari passu* with the revolution of public sentiment on the question of Slavery, there will be an upturning on the question of petticoats. The reformers referred to say, that until now, they never had the use of but one arm in walking in wet weather, or in "getting up stairs" now (in the matter of Clothing) they are as free – as the Men. Your visit in New York will enable you to prepare for a coming out that shall astonish the Natives.

I must now proceed to what (to me) are more serious matters than Ladies Pantalets – to the work before me in the Convention. I am *well.* I will write you again from Syracuse, for which place I shall leave on Monday, going from hence by waggon 9 miles to Oneida, & thence by *rail.* Your own friend, G.T.

Boston March 9, 1851

Dear Sister,

...The Garrisons and ourselves were delighted to hear again from you, and see your welcome handwriting. We had talked you over often with George Thompson, and squeezed out of him all the news we could: little enough I am sorry to say, at the best. But your own handwriting was better than all. G.T.'s visit, by the by, has had a wonderful effect: calling out into something of activity some who were alive during his former stay, but had fallen off, or fallen asleep, in the long & hard trials of the years since; and some who were awkwardly conscious of having ratted when trouble lowered, and longed for some occasion that would open the door for a return without imposing too palpable a confession of repentance. Then his name gathers immense audiences, the fame of his former achievements still haunting our towns, the plebians of the cause (the converts since 1835) hankering after the sound of that voice whose echoes had reached them in the stirring tales of the nobles of earlier conversion. It is generally voted that he has not grown a day older since 1835, though the dissentients are not few. Then many scold, more laugh, at his snuff; but his vivacity, brilliancy, and variety of accomplishment in private life charm everyone that has the good luck to get near him. He is a universal idol. His project of lecturing on general topics would, in my opinion, have been a failure even had no disturbance intervened to prevent it. Your English mode of lecture is so totally different from ours that, lacking the impetus of being abused, he would have got on but poorly in his voyage. As it is he has delivered his India course in five or six towns, and with tolerable success, owing to the extra exertions of friends, and the wish of many to hear the "Great Unheard", without compromising their dignity by being seen in an abolition meeting. In our anti-slavery gatherings his speeches have been grand and eloquent beyond all description. We hope his visit will not have been wholly vain to him in a pecuniary point of view....

Garrison was to have gone West with Thompson (who, by the by, intends to see Montreal, Quebec, and the fugitive slave settlements in Canada before he returns): but W.L.G. has been for a fortnight, confined to the house and part of the time to the bed, with severe pains in the spine. He is now better, and will take the *Liberator* again. His health has been unusually good the past winter, and he has done an immense amount of lecturing....

In Boston all is activity never before so much since I knew the cause. The rescue of Shadrach has set the whole public afire.[1] We have some hundreds of fugitives among us – The oldest are alarmed. I had an old woman of seventy ask my advice about flying – though originally free – & fearful only of being caught up by mistake – but in others it is horrible to see

---

1. Attempts to enforce the Fugitive Slave Law roused great public outcry in the North. In Boston, Shadrach, alleged to be a fugitive, was rescued while his trial was proceeding and quickly taken to Canada.

the distress of families torn apart at this inclement season & the working head forced to leave good employment & seek not employment so much as the chance of it in the narrow unenterprising & overstocked market of Canada. Our Vigilance Comee. meets every night. The escapers have been providential — since Shadrach's case nigh a hundred have left the city. The way we get news of warrants is surprising. One officer was boasting to one of our members, whom he did not know to be such, that now they had a fellow in sight, and he would be arrested by 1 o'clock. Our friend lounged carelessly away, told what he'd heard, and by 12 the poor fellow came out of his employers store, saw his old master before him, heard him *whistle*, thought that was as much music as he cared to wait for, dived into the cellar, up the back door, and "has not been heard tell of", as Baillie Nicol Jarvie says, since. Three have been several as close escapes as that, and there are still quite a number of Southerners here. It is said privately that all they want is *one from Boston* to show the discontented ones at home that *it can be done;* and our merchants groan at the trade they lost by the hatred the South bears us because she has not brought Boston under. Our business streets are markedly quiet. But we hope the same spirit is alive as laughed to scorn the mother country shutting up our harbor to starve us into compliance. Webster, too, (like your Lord North), the infamous New Hampshire renegade, threatens to line our streets with soldiers. We've seen none, opposed to us, since the redcoats; the Government, which wishes to succeed to the hatred they earned for their employers, had better send us their successors....

goodbye with dearest love from

Ann & Wendell

MS.A.13.1. The Thompson Papers. [314]
No. 23 George Thompson to [the Westons?]

Waverly Hotel, Rochester;
Monday Evening
March 10. 1851.

My Dear Friends,

I fulfil my promise, by sending a line from this place. I left Auburn at 10, after waiting in the anti-room at the station rather more than an hour. The train was due *here* at two, and had I arrived at that hour, I should have had to have gone to the Lecture room at *three*. The cars however did not reach this city till four, I was met by some gentlemen, who informed me that 700 ladies and gentlemen had been waiting for me for more than an hour in Corinthian Hall, and I must go immediately to them. Wearied and faint with my journey, I protested against this, but agreed to lecture at 3 tomorrow. They returned to the Hall to announce this, and I came here, to the quarters which had been provided for me. The gentlemen came back to say, that the audience had returned contentedly. I dined at ½ past four. I have got a very nice sitting room, with a bell in it, and shall be comfortable I have no doubt. I am writing this in the parlour of Mr. Pratt, a very respectable merchant of the city who with his lady, (no other family) boards here. I am to be his, and his wife's guest. The latter is at this moment my only companion, & I am scribbling this on my knee, while talking with Mrs. Pratt about England, where she travelled three years ago, and where I had the opportunity of shewing her husband some slight attentions.

I am informed there has been reaction here and that I am not to be mobbed. The *Advertiser* drew in his horns on Saturday, and disclaimed any intention to incite to violence. The only advice he now gives is – "Stay away and let the ill-begotten apology for a man speak to empty benches". You shall hear from me as frequently as I can find a few moments to write.

I am more than delighted with all I have seen in this state. The numerous lakes add much to the beauty of the country. I am now above 400 miles from your city of N.Y. and can form some idea of the extent magnificence and resources of this Empire district. I have travelled today with a frank & free hearted Montrealian who has gone forward to prepare the way for me in his city. Adieu!

All blessings be yours!

Geo. Thompson.

MS.A.13.1. The Thompson Papers [315]
No. 14 George Thompson to Anne Warren Weston

The Waverly Hotel, Rochester,
Wednesday March 12. 185[1]

My kind and thoughtful friend,

Not till this morning was I aware of the treasure which lay concealed under the rude exterior of the parcel you sent me while I was at Syracuse. This morning I determined to explore the bundle, when lo! Alton Locke and a Canister bearing the true imprint of the celestial world met my astonished and enraptured view. I have already held sweet and refreshing communion with my angelic visitant and shall not suffer a section of the day to pass without an interview, as long as the dear messenger remains. Alton Locke will be grateful at all times & will soothe one in these brief intervals of repose which occur between my public appearances. Are you thanked. If not receive my assurance that three times a day I will think of you and bless you as I quaff the precious cup – "Which cheers but not inebriates." (Milton)

Oh! what a magnificent triumph we have gained here. On Monday, about 600 persons were assembled in Corinthian Hall to hear me. The cars did not arrive till 4 the lecture hour was 3. – I was too unwell to speak and the lecture was therefore postponed till the following day (yesterday) About 1000 were present to listen to me a very great audience for the day time. When I rose, the aspect of the meeting was cold, solemn, and uninspiring; but as I proceeded, suspicion and prejudice gave way; the frostwork melted; and it became animated, enthusiastic and touching a scene as you ever witnessed.

At the close I was surrounded by a crowd eager to shake hands with me and not a few of them frankly acknowledged that they have been prejudiced by the report and articles in their papers. Alas for the *Advertiser*! this paper had been assailing me with a degree of malice & scurrility almost unexampled, and continued down to yesterday. To make its humiliation complete, it had prophesied as well as vituperated; when lo! my audience was the largest ever known at the hour – my reception cordial in the extreme – my vindication triumphant – and its prediction, like its charges, were proved to be *lies*.

In the evening I went to the house of the Posts (warm abolitionists of the true *stripe*). There about 50 persons spent several hours with me and I did my best to gratify their desire to hear me talk.

I thank God for this result, for the friends here were very apprehensive, and a disturbance would have discouraged them greatly. I was yesterday unanimously invited to give another lecture, at my convenience & promised to do so. I am resting today. The Convention begins tomorrow.

I shall, probably, remain here all next week, for though I am working hard, I am not well, and feel that it is quite necessary I should relax a little.

My course from this will be to go from this city to Lockport, near the Falls, & from thence over to *Hamilton*, & Toronto on the British side; then return and visit Seneca Falls and Waterloo and perhaps one or two other places, and revisit Auburn & Syracuse, & then return to Massachusetts, via Springfield. At a later period, if I remain in this country, I shall go to Montreal, by way of Vermont; and also to Quebec, and then *ascend* the St. Lawrence, & look upon some of the scenery of that glorious part of this continent.

I write amidst interruptions & therefore badly. I will conclude and send this as it is. I shall not write again before Saturday.

A thousand things strike me as topics for my letters but alas! I have no time even had I strength for writing as I should like. Accept my barren scrawls as a proof of my affectionate recollections and believe me,

Everywhere, and always,

Your's and Lucia's
sincere friend

Geo. Thompson.

MS.A.13.1. The Thompson Papers [316]
No. 24 George Thompson to ?

Waverly Hotel, Rochester;
Saturday March 15. 1851

My Dear Friend,

I think it was on Wednesday last that I scribbled my last to you. The two succeeding days have been busy eventful and triumphant ones. On Thursday the Convention assembled here & was tolerably well attended the majority however I believe influenced rather by curiosity than love for the cause. I spoke in the afternoon to a Hall comfortably filled and was heard with the most gratifying attention. After I had concluded my speech a copy of the Advertiser (the Evening paper here) was placed in my hands. It contained a scurrilous article, founded on a letter sent to the Advertiser by the Editors of the Springfield Republican!!! This letter was intended to increase the excitement here and represented me as "a vile *lowbred* blackguard who had throughly disgusted the citizens of Springfield who would not allow me again to pollute their town," &c &c. This tirade from the kindred editors brought me again to my feet and led me to give a full account of the Springfield affair. I converted the whole proceedings into an *impromptu* farce and acted all alone the several parts. Scene 1. The green on Sunday morning The effigy swinging in the breeze on the green.

Scene 2. Monday. Hampden Hotel. The interview with Foot, Stearns and Smith.

Scene 3. The parlour at night. The mob under the window. The Lord shall lay his hand upon the wipers &c &c. *Our* merriment &c.

Scene 4. Dwights Hall. Effect of my address.

Scene 5. The Free Church. The Senior Editor & Deacon. "Let him alone" &c &c.

Scene 6. The Evening mob, Triangle; Effigy; Tar Barrels; Band; Broken windows; &c &c.

Scene 7. Departure, Egg thrown &c &c &c.

I was in a happy mood at the time I went through these scenes. They came vividly before me. I was able (as Phillips says to) "project myself" into the men I represented; and as a consequence, the audience were convulsed. I at once rose to the pinnacle of popularity – not only as an *orator* but as an *actor.* "Is he not a wonderful man". How great he would have been upon the stage." "Did you ever see anything so fine." "Did you really think he studied the parts" &c &c Dont you admire *my modesty*, as much as these good Rochesterians admired my versatile talents, and deemed me a male Siddons who was painted by Reynolds seated between the Muses of Tragedy and Comedy – wooed alike by each and great in both. Oh, it was a treat to my auditors, and a rich treat to me, also; for what greater pleasure, than to feel at ease, & be able to take such a sweet and innocent revenge upon ones adversaries!

In the evening I was at a large party at the house of a Mr. Porter here who is a wealthy Baptist – a munificent supporter of a College in this city and a tolerable abolitionist. (No, that was the night before. On Thursday night I went to the house of F. Douglass, where some fifty friends were present, and we had a pleasant evening irradiated by the mild splendour of a certain Julia[1] – (not *Byron's*) We had music from the presiding spirit of the scene – stories from some – songs from others – thanks from all.

Friday. It being advertised that I should speak twice in this day the Hall was well attended in the morning and I extemporised for more than an hour. Afternoon. Corinthian Hall crowded to its utmost capacity. Every device adopted to find seats for admission. This was the invention of the Fosters. I spoke for two hours. Concluded by doing justice to the citizens

---

1. Probably Julia Griffith, Frederick Douglass' English helper. There was a certain degree of scandalous gossip attached to the friendship with Douglass [see below].

of Rochester – and the curtain dropped. Returned home – took two blue pills & have written this and other letters under their influence which is anything but pleasant as they are operating on my bile. More anon. Alton Locke distresses me, but I must read it. Ever, yours, G.T.

MS.A.13.1. The Thompson Papers [317]
No. 25 George Thompson to Anne Warren Weston

Waverly House, Rochester; N.Y.
Monday Evening, March 17. 1851

My Dear Friend,

As my last letter to you made its *exit*, your welcome one to me made its entrance. It was instantly devoured, for it reached me at a moment when I was ravenous for news – from you. I have nothing out of which I can hope to fabricate a readable letter. My motive for writing you just now is low, selfish, and unworthy. I am stupid from confinement in my room all day, and for a change of occupation, I am scribbling this to you. There you have it. I've made a clean breast. While I write, some 200 citizens are feeding in the long room, opposite mine, in honour of Ireland and Ireland's patron saint. A band is at my door, stunning me with "Hail Columbia"? "St. Patrick's day in the Morning", "The lass o'Gowrie," and "Yankee doodle." Toasts sentiments & speeches are to follow, and I have resigned myself to four or five hours of torment, – for I am not in a state of health that will permit of my extracting amusement from the noise of an after supper assembly.

Today, the *America* is out against me, & the *Advertiser* will therefore be in high glee tomorrow. I enclose the article, and will only say, that it is a gross misrepresentation of what it affects to talk about. I treated "Harry of the West" most respectfully and dealt only in calm criticisms upon the doctrines and views put forth in his late speech. The other quotations – wrenched from their contexts – are unfairly used. But, all is right. Several thousands of persons have heard me – and while these reports may injure me elsewhere – they only injure their concocters here. How would you feel, if you were daily vituperated as I am, and made to stand before millions a very devil? Would you not lose all faith in public writers, and learn to loathe the very name of a newspaper? Could you avoid coupling the *people* with the *press;* for it is written in *Alton Locke* "as with the *people* so with the *priest*, is the everlasting law." Editors are as much priests as parsons. I long to reach Niagara, and to forget, amidst the sublimities of nature, the depravity of man. Oh, if for one hour, nature should *depart from truth* as far as man," chaos would come again." Why is it we love nature so much? Is it not, because in nature there is *truth* – falsehood, in man alone. I have found many well-meaning persons here, but not one congenial spirit. I long for a companion. I do not wonder at the low condition of our cause here. It is almost altogether in the hands of the *Rappers*, and their vagaries are most ludicrous. A word in your ear. The principal members of the Western New York Antislavery Society were lately enquiring of the rapping spirits; and these instructors, having told the eldest of the party (Mr.

Pest) to go home, told the rest (a goodly number) to turn into *one bed* together. This could only be done by the contrivance of placing several beds side by side, which was accomplished and the "believers" tumbled in side by side!!!!

Down to the last period there was great uneasiness felt on account of the peculiar relationship of a certain English lady to a certain distinguished orator and editor of this city; but counsel having been taken of the spirits, they replied, that *the lady was in her right place.* Since then, the lady referred to has been the oracle of the true believers. I mourn greatly over the state of things here, for this is a fine city and there are elements in it worth moulding; but, alas! I have not found more than three persons who appear to possess any force of character. The rest are full of the "spirit world", though for the life of me I cannot discover what they have obtained from it that does them any good in *this.* I should much like to spend a month here, and have strength to keep lecturing all the time I have won upon those who have heard me marvellously & I should like to have the opportunity of preaching the whole Gospel of Abolitionism to the people here. A great work might be done with an effective agency. Mr. Foster occupied a hall here yesterday, but had few hearers. Where agents cannot obtain hearers, the influence is necessarily small. Mr. & Mrs. Foster I believe to be most valuable auxiliaries. They are faithful, indomitable, unwearied; – and under most important service; by locking up the friends of the cause, & keeping them together, and confirming their faith, and pointing out to them the various ways in which they can be useful. They are genuine and devoted friends of the *American Anti-Slavery Society* – quick to scent a plot & to unmask false friends – good financiers – and enjoy the unlimited confidence of the entire household of faith. I believe they do a good work, and heaven forbid, such true and noble friends would be aught but loved and cherished. Stephen, however, is not attractive. He has not the art of "winning souls." He has a plan & a theory of his own, and will give neither up. he must "e'en gang his ain gait," and do his own work. Abby has wrought wonders in her day. Her children are found wherever she has laboured, and her zeal burns with a strength and clearness which, not time nor persecutors can impair. I love her dearly for her works sake, & could I invest her with some attributes – but nonsense – she is made to be a missionary in the anti-slavery cause, not to be a companion for a sentimentalist like me. She has a nobler work than to amuse my weary hours. We (that is, S.S. & A.K. & G.T.) have a project to form *a New York State Anti-Slavery Society* the headquarters to be at Syracuse, where there is, the stuff necessary for the organization, and whence the sound might go out into all the region round about. Mr. May, will I believe be my companion next week to Lockport, the Falls, and Canada, and we shall talk the matter well over. It would be a grand move if it could be properly effected, and this scene to be a most favourable juncture. More of this anon,...

I am a special favourite among the Rochester ladies – *for a few days.* Locks of my hair – autographs – & likenesses are in great demand. Of course they are supplied, though candour obliges me to say, I have felt no disposition, in any instance to return the compliment. I have four evenings parties before me this week. Pray that I may have a safe deliverance.Those Those I have hither to attended here have been suffocating affairs, and in every case I have been to take my station between two rooms, that I might at least be heard, if not seen, in both. I have done my very utmost to acquit myself creditably – at all events to amuse my kind friends. Were all I have met in parties here of the same stuff I have met in Boston, this city might soon be revolutionised today, the ladies have called upon me in considerable numbers. In my room – which is parlour, bedroom, study and all, I have received them in my dressing gown, – paste brush in hand; and have tried by best to do the agreeable. I have looked in vain for one I should care to see again. What is it, the absence of which in the fair sex in this country, occasions this strange indifference? Perhaps you cannot tell me, as you have not seen your sex in other lands. Till now, I though myself impressible, and mourned over my quick susceptibilities, which were the cause of innumerable regrets amidst my short-lived acquaintship; but now – no matter. So it is, and yet as Othello says – I am not old – at least in heart. I am tired – stupid – worn out. I have scrawled this while all kinds of noises have been going on. Excuse its blunders, and burn it, least it should appear in judgement against me: I will to bed – though not to sleep, for these Irish Democrats I fear will keep it up till morning. I can trace the effects of what they drink, and can tell how they are going on, as well as if I counted very glass. I shall not be surprised to hear that I came in for a share of their eloquence as a mischievous foreigner!

I have received and read the proceedings of the AntiSlavery Meeting recently held in Toronto, and also the rules and regulations of the Society formed at the same meeting. I recognise in the officers of the Society some friends I have known at home. Charles Stuart is, I see, one of the Corresponding Secretaries, when I last met with him, he was a great Garrison hater, and I am afraid he remains so. I expect therefore to find the folds prejudiced against old organization. There are 9 ministers on the list of officers including several D.Ds.

I must now leave off. I have added this since I got up this (Tuesday) morning. My head is very bad. I scarcely ever feel else than ill until I have been up several hours.

It is now just a month since you got to New York. How much longer do you mean to remain under the guardianship of the Union & Safety Committee? Let me know how long. Could you not join us at Syracuse on my return from Canada, and go back via Springfield. This would be a good move. Think it over. We hope to have a great gathering at Syracuse by and by.

Yours affectionately (& Lucia's)

Geo. Thompson.

No. 26 George Thompson to [Anne Warren Weston?]

Lockport, Western N. York;
March 26. 1851.

My Dear Friend/

I am most heartily ashamed of myself for having so long neglected to write you. My last letter was laid aside to be posted the following morning – was forgotten – and only turned up as I was packing my things to leave Rochester.

Rochester! I shall long remember my visit to that city. My operations there were as follows:-

1. My lecture on British Reforms on the afternoon of Tuesday the 11th.
2. A speech on the Convention on Wednesday Aftn. We had no Convention Meeting in the evening.
3. A speech on Slavery on the morning of the 12th.
4. Lecture on Clay's views in the afternoon of 12th.
5. 1st Lecture on British India on Tuesday afternoon the 18th.
6. 2nd Lecture on India, Wednesday afternoon the 19th.
7. Lecture on Slavery Sunday Eveng. 23rd.

Thus, I made in all, seven speeches. At every meeting the audience approved and and applauded. The lecture on India and reform netted me $225 dollars and the the lecture on slavery ------ 127 -do.
total $352

The net proceeds of the Convention were I believe about 100 dollars, which the Fosters claimed for the American Society, – to the annoyance somewhat of the members of the Western New York Association.

On Sunday night 159 dollars were taken for admission at 12½ cents each, so that I had an audience of at least 1300.

These meetings have done much good in Rochester which is a very important city. There are now the elements I think of an extended organization and I am deliberating in my mind respecting the steps I should adopt on my next visit to turn the present state of things to account.

On one subject I have thought much; and I have arrived at a decided opinion. That subject is the next annual meeting of the American Anti-Slavery Society. I have come to the conclusion that this year it ought not to be held in New York City; but in Syracuse. That city would be an admirable locality for it. At that city the meeting would be accessible to the friends in Philadelphia and New England and we should have the fruit of all the recent labours in the Western part of this state – a delegation from Canada &c &c. We should have a quiet business and effective meeting and accomplish far more than by going to New York City.

I have a very earnest desire to attend the next annual meeting to take part in its deliberations. This I cannot do; and would not attempt, in the city of N.Y.

I want you to think the matter over. I should be glad to find my advice acted upon. It is not often I tender counsel – distrusting my own judgement; but on this subject I see clearly and am decided.

Talk the matter over with Mr. Gay.[1] If the change be made the intimation should be given early in the anti-slavery papers. I left Rochester on Monday evening for Buffalo. Slept in that city – and yesterday came to Niagra. I saw the falls from Goat Island. This is all I can say. I can hither in the afternoon and gave a lecture on British India before the Literary Association. I had a very good audience – the largest but one that has ever been known. The bell for the Convention here is ringing as I close this letter. If you can pick up some more good tea for me do so. All you gave me is gone and I am drinking poor stuff here. I will gladly pay the carriage to Buffalo, where it should be sent to me at the *Phelps* House, where I staid the other night, & won the favor of the Proprietor who is a *gentlemen*. Ever affectionately

Geo: Thompson.

MS.B.1.6. vol. 14 1849-1865 May-Estlin Correspondence [319]
No. 30 John Bishop Estlin to Samuel May

Bristol, May 2nd. 1851

My dear Mr. May,

...Wm. & Ellen Craft with my sister in law Mrs. Mitchell, were around my hearth when your letter came, & you may suppose how eagerly the C.'s listened to its contents. Poor Ellen sighed deeply at Sim's fate.[1] Craft regretted that he had not killed the policeman to have secured the *merciful punishment* of being hanged at Boston, instead of being sent back to slavery! What a comment upon the transaction.

The Crafts have been with us for the most part of 3 weeks, & W. W. Brown a good deal of the time. We seemed to have known but little of the iniquity of slavery till hearing Ellen's quiet, tea-table, incidental details of her experience. She has not had the tranquillity and free communication with friends that she had with us, since she left Boston; and often has she spoken of our house as *home*. Brown has been backwards & forwards, very energetic & efficient in what he does. But for the fortunate meeting & arrangement of the C.'s with him, they wd. have been lost to the a.s. world. Their union is a mutual advantage. Brown has made liberal terms with them. They had kind, but not judicious, (& some vulgar) advisers in the North of England, neither their interest nor *respectability* (Ellen's espy) being properly consulted. Some of their hand-bills have been headed "Arrival of 3 Fugitive Slaves from America" !!! as if 3 monkeys had been imported, and their public appearance

1. Sidney Howard Gay (1814-1888), journalist and abolitionist, was one of Garrison's more critical friends. From 1844 to 1857 he edited the *Anti-Slavery Standard*, but after this date he gave up active anti-slavery work and joined the staff of the New York *Herald Tribune*.

1. Despite the efforts of Theodore Parker and leading Bostonians who formed the Vigilance Committee to prevent the return of fugitive slaves – Thomas Sims, a young Negro boy, was captured in Boston and returned to slavery in the south – an action which roused bitter feeling in the North.

has been too often of the *exhibitive* kind. Neither B. nor, of course Craft, was quite *up* to the sort of position they ought to take, Ellen's *instincts* made her view the whole matter in its precisely correct light, & most thankful is she for the way in which *we* have spoken to Brown & Wm. The proceedings of our Bristol meeting on the 9th April, (which were entirely arranged by us) will show you the sort of position we think our coloured friends ought to take. 8 or 10 ladies accompanied Ellen to the platform. The Crafts left us after a most interesting visit on Wednesday for Plymouth. After clearing all expenses the Meeting & Lectures here, realized £23 8 0. besides what was got by a large sale of Brown's narrative, & Ellen's picture.... They go on very harmoniously together. Craft has none of Brown's energy: my impression is that *he* is a little indolent. Ellen is quite the reverse. She worked hard at reading & writing while here....

I have had numerous interruptions Post time is come, so with a hundred things unsaid, I must subscribe myself

Ever yours

J. B. Estlin

MS.A.1.1. vol. 4 Anti-Slavery Letters from Garrison [320]
No. 108 W.L. Garrison to Elizabeth Pease

Boston, June 23. 1851.

My dear Friend,

...It is more than eight months since George Thompson came among us, on a second visit to this country, and if you have kept the run of his movements, during that time, as detailed in the Liberator and Standard, you need no special information in regard to it. It constitutes another era in his eventful life, and by no means an unpleasant one; for, with only one or two very slight exceptions, he has been everywhere received, – from Maine to Upper Canada, and from the Lakes to Pennsylvania, – in a manner truly gratifying. His labors have been almost without intermission, and though he has never failed to speak of slavery and its abettors in the strongest terms of reprobation, he has never failed to commend himself to the respect, admiration and good will of the thousands who have listened to this addresses. His presence has been a quickening and purifying influence, nationally; and it has proved how great is the change which has been wrought in public sentiment, on the subject to slavery, since his first visit. A Farewell Soiree was given to him in this city, on Monday evening last, at which more than a thousand persons sat down to supper, constituting an imposing array of intellect, moral worth, and philanthropy, such as I have never seen before on any occasion. Addresses were made by Quincy, Thompson, Phillips. Theodore Parker, Remond, myself, and others, sketches of which will be given in the next Liberator, G.T. spoke at great length, and in very happy strain. It would amply have compensated you for taking a voyage across the Atlantic, to have witnessed the scene. And, pray, when are you coming? What is such a voyage now, but a mere pleasure excursion? In twelve days, you can be with us in Boston. Only think of it, seriously, not as a matter of fancy, and see whether you cannot come over, and spend at least a few months with us. – There are multitudes longing to take you by the hand, and to extend to you their friendship and hospitality. I have no doubt your health would be benefitted by the voyage, and that you would derive much gratification from the visit. Let me know whether you dare to cherish the hope that you may yet see New England, and tread on the soil of the Pilgrim Fathers....

With unbounded regard,

Your faithful friend,

Wm. Lloyd Garrison.

MS.A.9.2. vol. 25 1850-51 The Weston Papers [321]
No. 102 W. Farmer to Maria Weston Chapman

28 Charlotte Terrace, Barnsbury Road,
Islington, July 24th, 1851.

Dear Madam,

Before this reaches you, you will probably have learned from the Daily Papers the fact that Mr. Thompson passed through his first ordeal with his constituency successfully. I fear however you are likely from that source to learn little more than the bare result, the spirit of the meeting will not be fairly described. At the very outset there were strong symptoms of dissatisfaction and oppositon, which ultimately displayed themselves in the shape of a hostile amendment. A resolution was moved approving of Mr. Thompson's past proceedings, and pledging the meeting to his future support in the Tower Hamlets. An amendment was passed declaring Mr. Thompson an unfit and improper person to represent the borough. The speech which Mr. Thompson had prepared, as in the case with him upon all occasions of unexpected opposition, went to the winds. He was an intellectual giant, clad in the most invulnerable armour which a man can be arrayed in, the moral greatness of the cause in which he had been engaged, and for the advocacy of which he was then publicly arraigned. His speech was short but one of the most manly, eloquent and effective I ever heard him deliver.... There was no cringing before the democratic power here any more than there was before the slave power in America. He stood before his constituents, but not cap in hand. While paying them all due courtesy he never forgot his own self-respect. He rapidly sketched his own career as an Anti-Slavery advocate, describing his visit to America in 1835, the reasons which led to his second visit in 1850, the circumstances attending that visit, his being compelled to vindicate the right of free speech, his successful assertion of that right, the result of his mission on both sides of the Atlantic, his repudiation of all narrow or sectarian views in the advocacy of the cause of liberty, his hope that their own feelings corresponded with his in reference to American slavery, but whether that were so or not, and whatever might be the verdict they pronounced upon that occasion, he announced his firm determination never to abandon the sacred cause of negro emancipation, with which his name is so intimately identified. If his decision was hostile he would retire from the representation of the Tower Hamlets, but he should do so with the proud satisfaction that in that which they had condemned him he had done his duty in a great and glorious contest. The effect was irresistible; the audience nearly 3,000 in number were almost mad with enthusiasm. Not a single hand, not even those of the mover and seconder was held up for the amendment, and the original motion was carried with only one dissentient. The speeches were decidedly and strongly anti-slavery. The Tower Hamlets may now be considered formally and emphatically to have censured American slavery, not only before the American visitors to England, but in the presence of her representatives of the whole world...

Tonight another meeting is to be held at the Edinburgh Castle, Rhodeswell Road, Limehouse.

I am, Dear Madam,
Yours most truly,

W. Farmer.

MS.A.13.1. The Thompson Papers [322]
No. 27 George Thompson to ?

128 Sloane Street, London,
Friday August 15, 1851.

My Very Dear Friend,

Yours from Clifton S. Isd. was delivered to me when your sisters and niece were surrounding me in my sanctum, and its bidding, so far as concerned your brothers, were most welcome to them. To me, every part of your letter, which I have learnt almost by heart, was deeply interesting. I will rely upon you for the future, and will endeavour to prove, even though my letters should be dull and profitless, my desire to reciprocate favours....

My unworthy self, This is my first to you since I wrote you from H'fax. I very much enjoyed the voyage. I landed, cheerful and robust. A London life has pulled me down. My first business was with my constituents. Enemies has been industriously sowing tares. My course was bold and open. My tone, respectful, but independent. Five times I have entered the crucible, and five times have come out triumphantly. I have been treated *better* than *well.* My absence in the U.S. has not been *forgiven*, it has been *approved.* The Anti-slavery cause will gain largely in the Tower Hamlets from the circumstances of my having to explain my course in America, and therefore to go into the history and aspect of the cause there. Great is the indignation already excited against the Broad Street obstructionists. Innumerable are the questions I have to answer, referring to parties on your side. A good work is progressing. Without an open declaration of war against Scoble and co., on my part, I am effectually unveiling the hypocrisy and sham that have so long sat enthroned here. The 1st of August meeting was a happy idea. It has told well.

Scoble I am informed is off to Boston, with Henson[1], to go thence to Canada. Let him have *no quarter.* Tell Garrison to expose him unsparingly. Let Quincy do the needful in the *Standard. I earnestly desire* that he may be scorned as he merits, by every true friend of our cause. He will probably show signs of repentance, or presume to talk of reconciliation & cooperation. Let him be despised the more, if he should do so. His malignity can do no more *harm* – his pretended friendship, if accepted, would bring a *disgrace* and a *curse* upon us. The more he can be shewn up on your side, the better for the right cause *here.* Look well to this. Now is the time to send over some hot shot, directed to the Broad Street Committee. The *Liberator* is at present read with avidity. Let it contain the case against the new organization party here, and suitable advice to the honest and sincere amongst us, who now only want light...

Mrs. Chapman & party will be in Bristol shortly. I intend to go and give an address while they are there. From that city I will try to write you.

The speeches at Worcester (4 July) were drybones. Accursed politics, how they sap the soul of all that is pure, or elevated, or just! In this connection I am forced to exclaim, Poor Douglass! how changed he is. The North Star, rayless and extinct, & in its place *"F.D.'s Paper"* with its herculean attempts to wash the Ethiop white. How has the fine gold become dim! What a worse than waste of time this controversy about the Constitution is! It is treason to the Slave, to be prating about words, when the *thing* is before one, & be the meaning or construction of the words, this or that, the fact is undeniable. Why talk about the Constitution, when the Bible itself and the Tables of Stone, are claimed by the robber & the priest as on the side of slavery. The *thing* must be attacked. The nation is diseased. The defeat is not so much in the letter of the instrument, as in the depraved heart & perverted vision of the people. The weekly Commonwealth, that came with your letter, caused us to clap our hands with joy, for that it was no longer wedded to that "body of death" the Emancipator. So perish whatever is not of the true stamp! Send me when you can a paper from the camp of the Philistines. All the scraps will be *precious,* though *vile.*

I cannot see very distinctly into the future either near or distant. I have said nothing of resigning my seat in Parliament because I had to gain a victory over my political opponents and to circumvent the sappers miners & engineers who had been at work in my absence. A word in thine ear for thou art discreet and I am somewhat ambitious. Malicious tongues had said, "Thompson has lost his seat." "He cannot again face his constituents." "Should he do so, they will call upon him to resign." If he stands at another election he will be beaten." &c &c. Say then, who in thy true friendship for me, value my fame, and wouldst not see me the scorn of my adversaries will it be nothing to be able to say (for *you* to say) He saw his constituents face to face in every part of his district – in open public free meetings he placed himself voluntarily on his trial declaring that he would not re-enter the House of Commons unless again elected by the people. In every such meeting he was

1. Josiah Henson (1789-1883), a fugitive slave who did much to further the cause of other Negroes, visited Britain after 1850 mainly on behalf of the Manual Labour School at Dawn, Ontario. He was very popular in Britain, and roused much public interest as the original "Uncle Tom", and was received at Windsor by Queen Victoria.

received with enthusiasm: his conduct approved: his labours in the U.S. commended: his election reaffirmed; and a pledge given, to support him, and bear him victoriously into Parliament, at the next general Election. More; would it not be well to test again with every prospect of success, the attachment of the hundreds of thousands in the Tower-Hamlets, & to be a *second* time elected to the H of C even, if I soon afterwards gracefully resigned my trust to come to you? Under other circumstances, might not slanderous tongues amongst thine own nation, say, I was the rejected & spewed forth of a constituency whose confidence I had lost, & to whom I dare not again appeal?

Between now and the reassembling of Parliament I shall probably throw myself into the reform movement and for four months *Oct. Nov. Dec. & Jan,* traverse the kingdom with a view to a Union amongst all classes in favor of a real reform Bill next Session. These journeyings will afford me the opportunity of sowing the good seed of Anti-Slavery and of preparing the way for some proper organization of the elements that have long lain dormant.

And now, very dear friend, as post time is near, I must conclude. All you tell me is noted. God grant I may live to re-enter your loved and well remembered abode. Blessings on it for the sake of those in it. My affectionate & dutiful regards to your esteemed parents. A brother's love to Deborah, Lucia I will write to. Remember me to Mr. Byfield & the Dr. Say that the "Gables" & the Scarlet Letter are great favourites her[e] & I shall cherish them as gifts; Ever, your own honoured friend,

Geo. Thompson.

MS.A.9.2. vol. 25 1850-51 The Weston Papers [323]
No. 124 Mary Estlin to Miss [Caroline?] Weston

Bristol Oct. 3 1851

My dear Miss Weston,

...The Resolution of our Ladies Antislavery Committee which I enclose will I hope satisfy you that we *mean well* at present, & are full of love & gratitude to you all, & determined to carry on the work which your sisters have entrusted to us to complete, of tearing away the veil which has so long been separating the English from the American Abolitionists. I have been drawing up a *bill of indictments* against the Broad Street Society, on the grounds of which our Bristol committee means formally to withdraw from all connection with it, & to publish the statement & send it together with the letter of J. Sturge & Mr. Thompson (of which I forward you a copy) to every auxiliary A.S. Society, & every independent one & each of the Broad St. Come, & any Quakers or others whom we suspect of sympathising with them. Dont you commend our spirit? I must not boast yet lest the courage of our members should fail at the next meeting when the matter is to be settled, but at present their state of mind is such that they are prepared to declare their sentiments in the most decided terms, & take the consequences of the wrath of J. Sturge & his whole community. You will I think give me credit for having taken some pains with the *education of my pupils*, of whose ignorance on my first introduction to them 8 months ago I think I gave you a picture. Happily the visit of the Crafts, & Scoble's misdemeanours in claiming our doings for himself, helped open their eyes, & prepared them to appreciate fully the benefits of Mrs. Chapman's & Miss Weston's lucid details of the rise & progress of New Organization, with which it rejoices my heart to be now in a position to contend openly. The spirit of *Anti New Organ*[n] was kindled within me as early as that of Anti-Slavery, for the destruction of the first appeared essential as a precursor to my effective attack on the last, from the first moment I looked into the history of the movement in America; so that it has been a great trial of patience to wait 6 years for weapons with which to assail the enemy. Now that they have *themselves* forged *some* for us, & that your sisters have furnished us with others, we will take good care to wield them with effect...I do believe if your sisters could have spent as many months with us as they were able to spare weeks & had bestowed an equal time on a few other strongholds, such as Glasgow, Leeds, &c we should have accomplished the victory....The good people here, whom Mrs. C & Miss W. have been successfully indoctrinating, are so fully impressed with the facts that the American & *Foreign* A.S.S. is a "humbug", & Lewis Tappan a thief, that they call the latter by the title of "*the man that took the money*", & are importunate for some such clear statement of his misdeeds & of the origin & subsequent course of the A & For Socy. to be put forth in print....

Most affly yours

Mary Estlin

MS.B.1.6. vol. 14 May-Estlin Correspondence [324]
No. 41 Samuel May to J.B. Estlin

Boston, November 4. 1851

My dear Mr. Estlin;

...We hear, with great pleasure, of Kossuth's arrival in England, and of his generous & cordial reception at Southampton & Winchester. – I *hope* a great deal of Kossuth. Whether he will disappoint us, remains to be seen. – I am greatly encouraged in my hope by seeing that the journals here, generally, which are in the interest of the slaveholders & of the present Administration, are making an insidious & steady effort to prejudice the public mind against him. All their accusations come *anonymously*, and though couched in high sounding phrases really amount to nothing, – i.e. nothing discreditable to him. The heaviest charge is, that he has not abandoned as hopeless the cause of Hungary, & desires to obtain pecuniary aid, in this country & elsewhere, to sustain it. – Excellent reasons for *republicans* to cast him off, truly! But, without irony, it is doubtless a sufficient reason why the slaveholding powers of this land, and their minions should dread & dislike Kossuth. There was a time & spirit manifest in his Address to the people of this country (published here about 6 weeks since) which indicated that he would not be a *silent* spectator of the gross and petted tyranny of this false Republic; and I believe it is therefore their wish to keep him out of the country, or if that cannot be, to neutralise his influence in it, as far as possible....

Very respectfully yours

Samuel May Jr.

MS.A.1.2. vol. 20 1851 Anti-Slavery Letters to Garrison [325]
No. 156 George Thompson to R.D. Webb

128 Sloane Street, London;
December 22, 1851

My Dear Friend

Yours of October has been lying over in the hope that I might be able to fix a time for visiting Dublin in an Antislavery Mission. That hope is now extinguished. My engagements on this side the Channel extend to the period at which parliament reassembles, and then I shall be a prisoner in town during the Eventful Session.

I need not talk of the Transatlantic news as you know it as well as myself. Garrison's infidelity is keeping our Scotch friends (and foes) employed, and I have brought upon myself the ire of a Morrisonian parson at Greenock, who is gratifying his *Cacoethes scribendi*, by filling columns of the Glasgow Christian in reply to my charge against him of being a "false accuser".

I enjoyed a month at Paris with the Chapmans and Westons very much. I wish you had been with us.

I have recently had a long letter from them describing their Situation in their state of seige. They are satisfied as long as they do not get orders to quit.

Yours most truly

Geo. Thompson,

MS.A.9.2. vol. 25 1850-51 The Weston Papers [326]
No. 60 R. D. Webb to Maria Weston Chapman

Dublin, 31st December, 1851.

My dear friend –

This is the last letter I am like to write this year. I need not say that within the last month you have all been very often on my mind. As soon as we heard of the events in Paris we could not but feel anxious about you, and yet I did not think the danger even to quiet people like yourselves was so great until I was favoured with a sight of the letter you wrote to the Estlins which they very kindly forwarded to me. You have indeed been almost eye witness of one of the shocking and soul sinking events in all history – one which seems to put back indefinitely the hope of the world & of the progress of humanity. This change seems to have been brought round in the most cruel and ruthless ways and to have opened the door and set the example for an indefinite amount of crime & misery in the future. I know that those who live at a distance cannot readily put themselves in the position of people who are actually on the stage where such events are going on as you are witnessing. Still, judging from my own feelings I would suppose there must be a great deal adherent to your feelings in the actual presence of a nation throttled, plundered, blind folded and disgraced as France is and by such agency. I cannot see what hope or heart there can remain in those brilliant coterie of wily, intelligent, high minded Frenchmen & women which you have hitherto so much enjoyed, or what good for the Anti-slavery cause or for any cause can be expected from a nation that has lost all power to protect itself from the most fearful injustice & insult. The general impression that prevails in England & Ireland as far as I have the means of knowing is that a coalition of the four great despots of the continent is extremely probable – that a demand will be made to expel all the political fugitives and that this will be as I hope successfully rejected and then – the end of the world will come. For my part I have no fear for England if she had the whole world against her provided her rulers act with upright motives and with energy. The more I see of other countries the stronger my hope is in the English people – It has turned out with Kossuth as most people feared. I got a Sun from New York yesterday filled with his speeches to the New Yorkers – he praises the Union declares against all interference of any kind with themselves – and earnestly entreats them to go on crusading against Austria. His speeches are as clever as usual – but the determination to be all things to all men is too apparent. It is disgusting to see such praises lavished on the greedy, conceited, slave-hunting New Yorkers – who say liberty exists nowhere else – we are the only people who understand government – we must teach the world. It is hateful to have to take down one's idols – and to find that Kossuth is but common clay after all. If the abolitionists alone are right, what a very minute grain of mustard seed compared with the gigantic oak of violence and cruelty that is rising & spreading on all hands....

I got a letter from the North of England last week containing a capital letter from a learned friend of mine now in Paris respecting the events of the time. It gave a very full review of the president's writings & opinions and showed that his present policy is a legitimate deduction from them – One feels as if the night of tyranny & darkness were settling down again upon the Continent. It is difficult to think of Europe as if the sun shone there and people enjoyed themselves as usual. Above all things I wonder how such people as you can ever be happy in a country under such deplorable circumstances....

We have been a good deal interest by a Novel or Anti-Slavery tale now in course of publication in the National Era, called "Uncle Tom or Life among the Lowly" by Mrs. Harriet Beecher Stowe. Do you know the lady. It is all about slavery and slave holders and is very ably & racily written. There is a good deal of evangelical religion in it – and the hero Uncle Tom an old Negro, is a miracle of piety, goodness, & spiritual refinements – But a great many examples of the negro race are introduced & ample allowance made for all the influences of slavery upon them. I will be greatly surprised if the book do not attain an extreme popularity....

Ever truly yours

Rich[d] D. Webb

MS.B.1.7. vol. 1 1845-1888 The Estlin Papers [327]
No. 54 Maria Weston Chapman to Mary Estlin

Paris Jan. 24th 1852

My dear Mary,

...Poor Kossuth! The advocate of the rights of nations! But rights of nations are nothing but consecrated rights of men, & he cannot advocate these, it seems. The anti-slavery cause is dearer to me than other things because its principles include all other things. If it were *only* the freedom of the the Negroes, or *only* the Freedom of Hungary, I could not honour it so much could I go into Austria & obtain aid for my cause by keeping & promising to keep a studied silence about Hungary? Neither ought Kossuth to take the parallel course in the U.S. It is not a party question. It is the fundamental one. The identical question to present wh. he is in the U.S. Were it a different one, he ought not to sacrifice right to expediency, i.e. do a crooked thing today in the hope of [going the more uprightly?] for it tomorrow....

I am ever yours most cordially

M W C

MS.A.9.2. vol. 15 pt. 1 1841 The Weston Papers [328]
No. 4 A.W. Power to Maria Weston Chapman

n.d.

My dear Mrs. Chapman

I send you a Daily News I received since I sent you your books, as besides the account of the meeting at Stafford House[1] there is much in the leading article which I think will please you – I return you at the same time with my sister's and my best thanks "The Liberty Bell" which interested us both exceedingly – I only wish the attack on Kossuth had been left out – He is too unfortunate and owes too much to America not to be spared such severity – Great as is the crime of slavery in your country that of Austria is one of as deep a die, and had Garrison only lived some time under her iron yoke he would have seen how it penetrated into the homes and bosoms of all classes – there are three millions of suffering fellow creatures in America, in Italy alone there are twenty millions under the last of Austria, for her baneful influence extends to the furthest extremity of the Peninsula, to say nothing of all the horrors of Galicia &c &c. Had Garrison reflected he would not I am sure have spoken so highly as he does of the

1. This meeting, sponsored by Lord Shaftesbury and the Duchess of Sutherland, was prompted by the popular anti-slavery enthusiasm which *Uncle Tom's Cabin* had roused in Britain. It resulted in the Stafford House Address, signed by about half a million English women, petitioning American women to work for the slave, and roused great resentment in American circles.

sufferings of the Hungarians. Pray give my kindest remembrances to your circle and believe me my dear Mrs. Chapman

Most truly & sincerely

Yours

A. W. Power

Rue de [Monceau?] 11
Friday morning.

MS.A.1.2. vol. 22 1852 Anti-Slavery Letters to Garrison [329]
No. 32 J.B. Estlin to William Lloyd Garrison

London June 7th 1852
Private 22 Cecil St.

My dear Mr. Garrison,

...I have been immersed with A.S. affairs during the week I have been here. On Friday & this morning there have been meetings at my lodgings, of Messrs. W. Wells Brown (who lodges in this house) Geo. Thompson, Farmer & Robt. Smith. We have organized a humble A.S. Society, solely as yet, for getting out an a.s. paper the socy. to be called "*the Anglo-American A.S.Assocn.*" – the paper the "A.S.Advocate". The latter is to be double-column large 8vo sheet, to come out on the 1st (2nd Aug.) at a London A.S. meeting to commemorate British Emancipation. We have no "prospectus", no advertisements: the paper is to be its own herald & *puff*. We send it forth with a determination to try it for a year, & ask for but little support until our article is seen & judged of. But we are resolved *it shall be interesting*, & it will test the amount of A.S. friends here. I fear they are few. I have been deputed to write the first, & introductory article. It will be a short, unsentimental, cool, (*cold* perhaps) businesslike *English* production. G.T. will begin a history of the Abn. movt. We do not mean to *begin* antagonistically. The "B. & F.A.S.S." & the "Reporter", we mean to ignore *at first.* Brown will tell how the Amn. Abols. are met & attacked by the pro-slavery people of the U.S. with the cry of "infidelity" – R.D. Webb, I hope, will furnish a monthly leader – though all our original articles will be *leaders & headed....*

Your faithful friend

John Bishop Estlin

MS.A.1.2. vol. 21 1852 Anti-Slavery Letters to Garrison [330]
No. 99 George Thompson to William Lloyd Garrison

London, September 24, 1852

My Dear Garrison,

...For more than two months you have known of my defeat in the Tower Hamlets. No one has been less annoyed by this event than myself. Nearly 5000 of the independent, the free and the virtuous amongst the Electors recorded their votes in my favour; but these were not enough to ensure success against a combination of Publicans, Brewers, Distillers, Gin-Shop Keepers, Magistrates, Monopolists and great corporations; to say nothing of my unpopularity with the "hunkers" of all parties, whether Whigs, Conservatives, Churchmen, Anti-Reform Weslyans, and spurious non-conformists. The great body of the unenfranchised class was with me, but the elements I have specified, in close coalition, could not be withstood, and although I polled more single votes than any other candidate I had to resign my seat in Parliament to the nominee of the Tavern Keepers.

The result of the late general election has been favourable to the radical interest. Some twenty additional men, going the length of the principles of the National Reform Association, have been returned. Many of the old supporters of the Reform movement, who have been recently rejected, will be sent into Parliament within a year of the meeting of the two Houses. It is possible that the *Ballot* will be *the* measure first insisted upon by the radicals. The system of vote by ballot, if established, will make thousands of voters who are now enslaved, free, and secure, to a great extent, fair play for those who are unable or unwilling to resort to bribery and coercion. Mr. Cobden and his followers in Manchester intend to agitate vigorously for this point in the People's Charter. Two hundred men in the present parliament are, I should say, prepared to vote for the ballot, while the pressure from without may be relied on to influence as many of the rest as may be necessary to secure a majority in the House of Commons. I do not expect that this or any other measure of Electoral reform will be carried speedily. Some financial change will first be made, then will come the renewal of the East India Company's Charter; and then, perhaps, the ballot.

Uncle Tom is doing a great work here. Between 400,000 and 500,000 copies (varying in price from 6d to 7/6) are already in circulation. Two of our metropolitan theatres are nightly crowded to overflowing by persons anxious to witness a representation of its most striking scenes on the stage. Hildreth's white slave[1] is also finding a rapid sale. Another volume called "Uncle Tom's England" has been published. Ten thousand copies were taken by "the trade" the first day. There is just now an unprecedented demand for Anti-Slavery Literature. Behold the fruit of your labour & rejoice....

Our prime Minister, the Earl of Derby, and his colleagues may be considered fortunate in being in office at the time of the death of the Duke of Wellington. This event has placed the office of Commander in Chief, the order of the Garter, the Wardenship of the Cinque Ports, the Constableship of the Tower, the Rangership of the Parks and many other good things at their disposal. They will also appropriate the *Eclat* of a public funeral in St. Pauls, and by resolving that the interment should not take place until after the sanction of Parliament has been obtained to the programme, they have provided for an animated discussion of the military and political

---

1. Richard Hildreth's book, *The White Slave*, first published in 1836 and reissued at this date – was a very popular fictional work on slavery.

career of the great captain, instead of a debate upon the claims of the present ministry in the confidence and support of the nation....

Yours ever sincerely

Geo: Thompson.

MS.A.9.2. vol. 26 1852 The Weston Papers [331]
No. 61 S.F. Dawson to Mary Estlin

Coastguard Cottage
Teignmouth
Devon
Oct 6/52

My dear Miss Estlin

...What about Fred. Douglass & Rochester Bazaars? – & Boston partizanship? I do wish people wouldn't quarrel over straws when there is such a quantity of corn to be cut & carried! If *you* know *Julia Griffiths* I have only to say – I do too! But it is of no use for me to say *that*, to Mrs. Edmund Sturge when she comes with her catlike quaker-velvet tongue & tells me Julia & Fredk. Douglass send things to Boston Bazaar, but Boston people won't or at least don't help Julia. What is this about?

I did not like Garrison's speeches here in England – *his words;* & his collected works strike me as very scanty of facts or suggestions to deeds, – they are chiefly *epithets;* all very well in their way, but usually *lumber* when *work* is to be done – & worse than lumber where Prejudice is to be conquered.

I fell in love *on hearsay* with Mrs. Chapman though I laughed at her "Women's Rights Women" companions-in-arms.

So that in my own doubts as to whether Garrison with all his real worth & hardy doings is not doing mischief to his own cause – & my certainty that Julia Griffiths would weary out the most determined of believers – I am in a cleft stick – .... All anti-slavery papers & tracts have left a void in me. I know "all that" – but what is to be *done?* The only things I see now, are, a chain of frontier settlements to receive fugitives – (& that is not for you & me) & a set of resolutions like those famous ones of the Congregational people. Really I begin to think there is some of the real old *stuff* left in English Dissent yet! ....

Oh! – concerning the Bazaar I couldn't get anything this year, because I was too idle to walk out when Katie's answer came – to seek out the leisurely young ladies, – & the few I saw want to know "what becomes of the money got at the sale?" Can you answer that? I said – salaries of lecturers & was answered "where do they lecture?"

Uncle Tom is doing your work effectually; but I want to turn the tears that are shed over it, to *pearls* of value & enduring workmanship....

Yours right truly

S.F. Dawson.

MS.A.1.2. vol. 22 1852 Anti-Slavery Letters to Garrison [332]
No. 121 Henry Wigham to William Lloyd Garrison

Edinburgh 17/11 mo. 1852

Not for the Liberator

My dear Friend

...I am glad to say there is an increasing interest in the anti-slavery Cause here & in the Country generally principally caused by the publication & extensive circulation of Uncle Tom's Cabin – Indeed from the Peer to the Peasant the whole country seems boiling with indignation at the oppressors of the poor slave & their hearts are overflowing with sympathy for his wrongs. Edinburgh has taken the lead in the attempt to turn this excitement to something practical & not let it die away & leave no prints behind. A large Public Meeting was held about 10 days ago presided over by our Lord Provost at which it was resolved that a Penny subscription should be instituted from all the readers of Uncle Tom's Cabin – of course not limiting it to a penny but naming a sum which would be within the reach of all (to be devoted to anti-Slavery purposes & to be placed at Mrs. Stowe's[1] disposal with that object) Another proposition was to send to America a "National Remonstrance against Slavery" – Both of these projects are going on & likely to be warmly taken up by the Country generally – Last night there was a large meeting in the City Hall Glasgow presided over by our friend William Smeal – at which they resolved a similar action to ours. I also hear they are moving in Birmingham & Newcastle Tyne. One of the speakers at our meeting (Rev. J.R. Campbell) did ample justice to the claims of the Members of the American Anti-Slavery Society to public approval for their steadfast & constant adherence to the cause of the slave....

MS. incomplete.

MS.B.1.6. vol. 4 The May Papers [333]
No. 54 Samuel May to R.D. Webb

Boston (Mass.) November 11. 1852

My dear Mr. Webb,

Long before you receive this, you will probably have noticed what I said in the Liberator of the *AntiSlavery Advocate.* It fell to my lot to do that service, in the absence of Mr. Garrison, who had gone to Pennsylvania, to the annual Meeting of their State AntiSlavery Society. You may be sure we were right glad to see the little sheet, so compact & neat, & so judiciously made up. We are now looking for the 2^{d} number, which a few days will undoubtedly bring us. – I wish you might have a circulation commensurate with the importance of the topics it treats of, & with the merit of the treatment; I know not how this will be; I have my fears for you, but I

1. Harriet Beecher Stowe (1811-1896), author and abolitionist, was the daughter of Lyman Beecher and wife of Calvin Ellis Stowe. As the author of *Uncle Tom's Cabin* she enjoyed considerable popularity both in Britain and America, and her book exerted an enormous influence on popular opinion.

have no fear or doubt but that good will come out of it. I know there must be a good deal of labour in forming even a moderate-sized subscription list, but with Scotland to back you, and scattered friends in England & Wales to co-operate, I have my hopes also....

With sincere regard Yours

Samuel May Jr.

MS.A.9.2. vol. 26 1852 The Weston Papers [334]
No. 71 Jane Wigham to Anne Warren Weston

Edinburgh 18/11/52

My dear Friend

We have just packed up two boxes, which we intend to send by the next steamer, and hope they will arrive safe at Boston in good time for the Bazaar – They are later than we intended, but had they been sent by last steamer they would have been less worth sending. There was an anti-slavery Bazaar at Glasgow held the last week of last month, and many who used to contribute to our box sent their things to it this year, – being determined not to give anything more while such objectionable matter still appears in the columns of the Liberator, – which though not the organ of the American Anti Slavery Society, – is conducted by its President – who I am sure cannot be aware of the injury he is doing to the cause of Religion and humanity, by inserting the writings of Foster – Barker – Pilsbury – and H. C. Wright regarding the Holy Scriptures – or I am sure he would not do it. I wish if thou hast any influence with W.L.G. thou would advise him to leave the Bible alone – If all acted accordingly to its instructions there would neither be war nor Slavery – and it has outlived all its enemies & will I trust never be either mutilated or set aside. – What should *we* be without the Bible?...

The great excitement caused by "Uncle Tom's Cabin" – is unlikely to do much good, and we were grieved to see H.C.W. trying to undervalue the book – we should be thankful for every auxiliary – even though it be not entirely according to our standard. I believe that book has awakened an interest that will never settle down again while American slavery exists....

I am thy affectionate friend
Jane Wigham

MS.A.9.2. vol. 26 1852 The Weston Papers [335]
No. 75 J.B. Estlin to Maria Weston Chapman

Bristol Decr 1852

My dear Mrs. Chapman,

Many thanks for your letter of – date, I should have answered it before had I been in better health, & had not the subject about which you wrote been "perfunctorily" (as Mr. Quincy says) disposed of, by the starting of Ld Shaftsbury's Memorial, before the arrival of y^{r} letter. Miss

Cabot has previously announced to us the other intended Address, but the time had not arrived for our being consulted about it, and I never knew exactly what was the intended course. I am quite sure that in the present temper, & present *ignorance* of the English A.S. Public, any Address containing Garrison's name or especial Notice of the Am. A. S. Soc^{y} w^{d} not only have obtained few signatures, but would have opened the flood-gates for a torrent of mischievous invective which we have been long endeavouring, & with some success to keep in check, & with the hope of eventually turning its course. I never clearly understood what was meant by collecting "Millions of Shillings from signers of the Memorial"? A quarter of that number of pence would never have been obtained throughout the three kingdoms from A S people. The Duchess of Sutherland's Address amuses me: [1] it is useful for exciting discussion; it is too very satisfactory to see people of the Established Church condescending to think & speak, if not very sensibly, on Am AntiSlavery Another Memorial & subscription for Mrs. Stowe is on foot. Of course we *oppose* none of these harmless amusements. "Mrs. Richardson's Slave Trade" (as Mr. Webb calls it) we felt it a duty to oppose....

I took the "Church Question" & the M. Adv. article.... I hope in the next we shall say a word for Garrison, tho' not professing any especial following of his leadership. The Quakers were never more bitter against W.L.G. than they are now. Mrs. R[ichardson] as far as we have the means of judging, always fanning the flame of opposition to him [Spite?] however of their continual efforts they have been unable to prevent, I believe an unusual amount of aid from this country to the Boston Bazaar....

I hear G.T. has been delivering some A.S. lectures but I see no great opening for his doing much in this, his best sphere of action. I have had to defend him against some undefined accusations, in a correspondence with Miss Lushington. The insuperable prejudice against him arises from every one's inquiring, & no one's knowing "*how he lives!*" Such an anomalous position has long been, & will continue a bar to G.T.'s taking any high stand in public estimation....

Affecly yours

J. B. Estlin.

MS.A.9.2. vol. 27 1853 The Weston Papers [336]
No. 4 Mary Estlin to Maria Weston Chapman

Park St. Jan 10th – 1853.

Dearest Mrs. Chapman;

...Never was there such an A S ferment over the land; & such openings for truth to enter & find acceptance, but alas the laborers are not forthcoming, & unless some from America who can speak in public as well as Miss Pugh does in private will come to our aid I fear the enemy will soon take advantage of this newly ploughed field & sow his tares in. Mr. Webb calls "all this fuss about pennies & memorials, *soda water*", which is true, but until the angel had troubled the pool its healing properties were not near

1. The Stafford House Address – (see above).

enough the surface to benefit by them. *Now* I dont like for "another" to "step in" & deprive us of them, but I long for some Wendell Phillips to come while the agitation lasts & proclaim the *whole truth* to the eager multitude. A few weeks of his labors amongst us would defeat the machinations of the pro-slavery clergy to retain the English ecclesiastical sanction that they have hitherto relied upon....

Yr. ever affect^{e} & grateful

Mary Estlin.

MS.B.1.6. vol. 14 May-Estlin Correspondence [337]
No. 56 Samuel May to J.B. Estlin

Boston, February 28, 1853.

Dear Mr. Estlin;

...I know that "heresy" and "radicalism" are even worse hated in England than with us – being regarded, for the most part, as rather low & vulgar, beside criminal. I know that 'Society' with you is much more sharply divided – classes & ranks more strictly defined, than with us. I suppose that you have not a well-educated and thinking *labouring*, *farming*, *mechanic*, class, to anything like the extent that we have in the Northern States. You yourself suggest that, with you, reforms must commence with the higher classes, at least, that it is of primary importance to get those classes right. With us, it is exactly the opposite; and I should have said, much more so in your country than I understand you to admit. Whence, for instance, came the Repeal of the Corn Law System? Certainly Cobden, [Wilson?], and even Sir Robert Peel may have devised the measures, & arranged the details; but did not the whole thing lie first in the hearts of the simple-minded peasantry and working people, including that vast class which labours with its hands for daily bread – and did not the *demand* for that repeal come first from them? This Am^{n}. A.S. question is not, I know, altogether parallel – it being a question, in one sense foreign to your people and country, – and one which depends, so far as your country can influence & determine it for good, very much on the judgment of the educated & thinking portion of your people. But what is to excite & render active that judgment? Archbishop Whately, Lord Denman[1], Lord Shaftesbury, the Earl of Carlisle & all his relations, have known for years, just as well as they know now, what slavery is and does, what *American* slavery is & does. Why have they not testified before, as strongly & eloquently as of late? Some few of them have. But most of them give tongue now for the first time. Is it not owing to the fact, that the *popular* heart and conscience of England were touched & roused, in God's providence, by that simple tale of Mrs. Stowe's, that we are now having the testimonies, the remonstrances, and the intercessions of these distinguished ones? They speak, because England

1. Thomas Denman, 1st Lord Denman (1779-1854), Lord Chief Justice and a friend of Brougham's, was noted for his interest in liberal and social reforms as was Lord Shaftesbury, the great nineteenth century social reformer.

expects and *demands* it of them; & because they know they will be sustained — which even the loftiest peer, & the wisest doctor, likes, as well perhaps as another....

I am, yours

Samuel May Jr.

MS.A.13.1 The Thompson Papers [338]
No. 15 George Thompson to [Anne Warren Weston?]

(4th March 1853)

"Lord! How oft shall my brother sin against me and I forgive him? Till seven times? I say not unto thee, until seven times, but until seventy times seven."

These blessed words have been uppermost in my mind ever since the receipt of your letter dated from Weymouth on the 5th Feb. It is now the 4th of March the day of your President's inauguration[1] — it is the afternoon. I have just turned from a visit to Rochester, in the county of Kent, where I have been trying to revive the anti-slavery feeling in the city where I delivered by first antiSlavery Lecture. I have put a light to my study fire — have counted the minutes from now till past time, and will spend them all in scribbling to you, my own dear friend. It is difficult to communicate with you, for I am dreadfully oppressed by the recollection of my shamefully ungrateful conduct.You have promised me an act of oblivion. I joyfully accept it. You will perhaps expect me to give the reasons why I have not written. I cannot send you any, for I have none. Your own letter contains the best apology that could be offered for my silence. I adopt it....
Since the late General Election my own pursuits have been of a quiet and, generally private character. If disposed to relinquish the platform & the business of an agitator, I might find sufficient employment, and some profit besides, in an assurance company with which I am connected, and to the concerns of wh. I have recently devoted a good deal of my time. I cannot say, however, that such business yields me much satisfaction, or appears to me my most "appropriate sphere". While engaged in it I am still waiting for the "way to open" that I may renew my labors in the cause of the slave.

Within the last three months I have accepted a number of invitations to lecture on American Slavery, and have had large and enthusiastic audiences. On the 7th and 8th of this month I shall be lecturing on the subject in the town of Basingstoke, in Hampshire. I have intimated to my friends that I am willing, to the extent of my opportunities, to deliver addresses on slavery, and I dare say I shall be very often called upon. You may be sure that as often as I speak upon the question of Am. Slavery I shall aim to do justice to my friends in Boston, and their friends everywhere.

The Estlins have been in town & I have had some pleasant seasons with them. Last Sunday Sarah Pugh joined the circle, and reported progress in Leeds.

---

1. The inauguration of President Franklin Pierce.

I am superintending the construction of a large sketch map, designed to illustrate Slavery and Anti-Slavery in the U.S. – the progress of the slave power – the Underground railway, &c. One of my recent lectures has been published. I will try to get it to you.

Lewis Tappan I perceive announces a new work from the prolific pen of Wm. Goodell – "The American Slave Code, in theory & practice." If well done, this book will be of service to us. I have seen "Slavery & Anti-Slavery" & do not like it, save in one particular, namely, that it confirms my statements of the *nothingness* of *Am. & Foreign A.S. Society.*

I have read with intense pleasure, as far as published, the proceedings at the Annual Meeting of the Mass. Society. The Resolutions struck me as peculiarly excellent & well timed, and the speeches as more than usually appropriate and of high merit. *Your* annual address was *very good....*

We cannot complain of indifference to the American slave question in England, just now. The subject is discussed in a thousand forms. Even our Quarterlies are entertaining it, and Blackwood, for many years the champion amongst the monthlies, of the Proslavery party, has an article to which with some exceptions, Garrison might well put his name. Mrs. Stowe and her brother Charles Beecher[2] will I fear be almost wholly in the hands (on this county) of those who have sought to depreciate & even destroy the true anti-slavery party in the U.S. Let our consolation be this – Uncle Tom's Cabin has awakened the sensibilities of thousands of persons who can never be made to feel any interest in past or present controversies, and who will in one way or another contribute to increase the amount & power of that public opinion on which we rely for the overthrow of the system.

I would say something about the folks at 27 New Broad Street, did I not know that your faithful correspondents, the Estlins, are in the practice of supplying you with needful intelligence of matters in that quarter. Things have been managed rather better since the exodus of John Scoble. I hear Scoble left his family in New York & preceeded himself to survey the promised land beyond Jordan. Have you obtained any tiding of the man?

The result of your Bazaar gratified & surprised me. When I found you were going into the Horticultural Hall, I fear your receipts would fall below recent years, but by your statement it appears you did well....

A repentant brother's best love [to] you all. You live in my heart of hearts.

Geo Thompson.

---

2. Rev. Charles Beecher (1815-1900), a Congregational minister and author of several books, was the youngest child of Lyman Beecher and brother of Harriet Beecher Stowe.

No. 31 William Smeal to William Lloyd Garrison

private Glasgow 4th March 1853

Mr. Wm. Lloyd Garrison
Boston U.S.

My dear Sir,

It is considerable time since I had the pleasure of writing you. I do so at present in relation to Mrs. H. B. Stowe's proposed visit to Scotland. You are I dare say aware that some time since the *new* antislavery Societies in Glasgow sent her an invitation, written on their behalf by Rev. Dr. Wardlaw, to visit Britain, & especially themselves in Glasgow, they bearing all expenses of her visit in testimony of their approval & gratitude to her as the author of "Uncle Tom's Cabin"; & that they might have the opportunity of personal conference with her to learn what she considered the most effective way in which they could exert themselves for the abolition of American Slavery, & with whom they should cooperate in the U.S.

You are also aware that the originating & chief object of the parties who started & direct the movements of these new A. S. Societies here, is the desire to withdraw cooperation & assistance from the old American A. S. Society, & especially from the Boston annual A. S. Bazaar – on the grounds of the infidelity of the leading members of the Am^{n} A S Society especially of yourself as manifested in the Liberator &c – now these parties whose bitter hostility time seems to increase, in place of lessening, I have no doubt intend to make the most of Mrs. Stowe to further their views – they will not probably inform her, at least fully of the ideas that animate them in regard to yourself & the Am. A. S. Society; & that they wish the sanction of her name to enable them to make the British public believe that by aiding the New York Vigilance Committee or the Am^{n} & Foreign A. S. Socy (Tappan) they will be effectually & in a Christian way adopting the best means of abolishing slavery whilst to countenance & assist the Am A. S. Socy & the Boston Bazaar is to aid *infidelity* as much or a great deal more than to abolish slavery.

It has occurred to me that it is proper to make known to Mrs. Stowe before she leaves America the position of these *new* A. S. Societies here who have invited her, & also of the *old* Glasgow Female A. S. Socy, perhaps this may be best done by putting into her hands the statement issued by the *new* society on its formation with the replied thereto of Mrs. Chapman & J. B. Estlin with the report of the *old* G.^{w} Female A. S. Soc^{y} of Jany 1851 all of which I have sent to your address by this steamer & which I will thank you to forward to Mrs. Stowe, – could one of the Boston friends who understands the position of parties call on Mrs. S with them & have an interview with her, it might be useful & insure her perusal of them. I observe from our newspapers this week, that Mrs. Stowe has accepted the offer of a Free passage from the owners of the Screw Steamer "Glasgow" which is advertised to sail from New York for Glasgow on the *26th inst....* In the present present state of feeling regarding Mrs. S. in Britain it would be of most essential service could she be induced to recommend the Am^{n} A. S. Soc^{y} &

particularly the *Boston Bazaar* as an efficient a.s. instrumentality, by contributing to which, British Ladies could essentially benefit the cause....

MS. incomplete.

MS.B.1.6. vol. 15 1849-1872 Additional Letters to Samuel May Jr. [340]

Dublin March 11, 1853

Dear Mr. May

...I believe the new editor of the B & F A.S. Reporter is far from an enemy to Mr. Garrison or the American A.S. Society. This I think will soon appear, and I quite believe that the people who allowed that base John Scoble to lord it over them and the cause are now aware that they have therefore served neither the cause nor their own character. I am happy to believe that the stir that has been made in many ways within the last year in various ways has greatly stirred the dry bones. How much Mr. & Miss Estlin are to be thanked for all this I need not tell you.... You may be sure I will lose no opportunity of placing the Am. A.S.S. in their true light before the public. The older I grow the deeper if possible becomes my veneration for that society & its American supporters. From all I hear I fear Mrs. Stowe's influence in England (which will unquestionably be very great for an individual) will not serve the true labourers. I think she has not been magnanimous nor even quite mannerly towards them. But from my reading of Wendell Phillips last glorious speech, I feel the most assured confidence that all the powers of bigotry will not avail against the final success of your glorious principles. How I wish that speech could be widely disseminated through these countries. It is the most complete exposition of the deeds of the American Society I have yet seen.

Yours ever truly
Rich[d] D Webb.

MS.B.1.7. vol. 2 1846-1865 The Estlin Papers [341]
No. 67 Andrew Paton to Mary Estlin

Glasgow 20th April 1853

My dear Madam

...Enclosed is the first number of a proposed monthly entitled "Friend of the Fugitive" issued by the Glasgow *New* Fem. A. S. Socy. taken up I suppose in imitation of the "A.S. Advocate" in which you will observe that the same cry of infidelity of the Amn. A.S. Soc. & Mr. Garrison which they have hitherto resorted to, is continued. I also send newspapers containing a report of the Soiree, to Mrs. Stowe held under the auspices of the *new* Female, & *Gentlemen* A. S. Socy. – From these you will see that the Speakers at the first & chief Soiree pursued a very disingenuous course whilst knowing that *the infidelity* of the Amn. Socy & Mrs. G. is in the *watchword Reason* assigned for the existence of the Soc. in whose behalf they spoke, they venture not one word of allusion to it. Had they common honesty they wd. have done so fully, & had their allegations been confirmed

& sanctioned as true by Mrs. Stowe, her husband & brother. I am disposed to think that having by previous conversation learnt that Mrs. S. & her relatives did not coincide in their sentiments respecting the Amn. Soc. & Mr. G. they had concluded their best move was to be silent regarding their charges against him. – John Guthrie of Greenock a dissenting minister of no note, connected with a small body called Morrisonians, the writer of the article on the infidelity of Mr. G. in the "Friends of the Fugitive", who spoke last at the soiree, was as silent as the others.

The conduct of Professor Stowe & Rev. C. Beecher in ignoring Mr. G. & the Amn. Socy. under any circumstances cannot be approved as fair or honourable, or such as reformers of any sort adopt towards the pioneers & best known men in the same cause – as there is room for doubting that they must have been aware of the sentiments of the parties in Glasgow who brought them here, regarding the Amn Socy & Mr. G. – omitting to testify in favour of slandered absent friends was uncandid & ungenerous, & playing the game of the parties here in whose hands they were, against those in America whom they still call friends. Mr. Thomas Brown who spoke at the so-called working Men's!! Soiree to the great surprise & mortification of the managers of it, acted nobly by Mr. Garrison & some passages of his speech were hissed by some on the platform but applauded strongly by the meeting.

The Glasgow Fem. a.s. socy also presented an address to Mrs. Stowe; she cd. not from illness, as stated, personally receive a small deputation with it, & her reply, in the circumstances of parties in Glasgow, of which I believe she is quite informed, appears to me, not to be by any means such as she being a friend of W.L.G. might have been expected to have given.

I will send you a copy of both in a day or two as I have to leave town immediately until Friday. Could you send me a copy of Mrs. Stowe's letter to Mr. G. in which she states that she fully sumpathized with his treatment of the Amn. churches & clergy &c – if it can with propriety be made public I wd get it inserted in our newspapers & it might do much good to our friends....

My sister unites with me in kindest regards to your Father & yourself. I am very sincerely yours

Andrew Paton.

Miss Mary Estlin
Bristol.

MS.B.1.7. vol. 2 1846-1865 Estlin Papers [342]
No. 66 Mary Estlin to ?

47 Park St April 29th

This letter contains an Extract from Frederick Douglass' paper: April 15th.

"We feel a deep interest in Mrs. Stowe's visit to England. It is an interest arising out of no sectarian or partizan unity, but the very opposite of this. Were Mrs. Stowe's visit to England on behalf of any anti-slavery society, state or national, much of our interest in it would instantly subside; for in that case, we know that time and energy which should be given to the cause of the oppressed would be consumed in an almost useless debate, as to which a.s. Society is doing much to promote the a.s. cause. There is the "American A.S. Society", and the "American & Foreign A.S. Society", both of these societies have *antecedents,* which the representative of either would be called upon to justify and defend. Too often has the cause of the slave been compelled to give place to the cause of a society. Anti-Slavery as well as Christianity, has often seen the means apparently exalted above the end – the latter greater than the spirit – the "alter" above the 'gift which sanctified the alter" – Mrs. Stowe goes to England untrammelled and free. She goes for the cause, and judging from what she has already accomplished, there never went from our shores ones whose labors will compare with hers. She will do more than has ever yet been done to present and diffuse among Englishmen a correct understanding of the *men* and the *measures* opperating [sic] for the downfall of slavery. She will not exalt the *non-voter* up to heaven, and cast the *antislavery voter* down to hell; nor vice versa; but will recognize the *virtue* and value of both. She will not make Lewis Tappan a Saint, and William Lloyd Garrison a Satan, but will see in both these men, honest, and devoted friends of emancipation. Nor have we any fear that she will be at the pains (like another American lady) of trying to convince English abolitionists that our paper is unworthy of support. But enough of this." *quite enough.*

MS.B.1.6. vol. 15 1849-1872 Additional Letters to Samuel May Jr. [343]

Dublin June 3, 1853

Dear Mr. May –

...I was in London lately in company with Mr. & Miss Estlin. J. Miller McKim, Sarah Pugh, the Crafts, Geo. Thompson, W. W. Brown, Edw. Matthews[1] & others. I saw a good deal of the new secretary to the New Broad Street Society. I think him an honest straightforward, well disposed man – most desirous to help the cause – but I think his employers are too old to mend, & I hope little from them. They are always humming, hawing, managing, and manoeuvering, trying to keep their consistency & their character – and looking on the cause as a very secondary thing to their own reputations. Then the orthodoxy of the members of the Committee makes cooperation with the heterodox irksome and difficult. Mr. Chamerovzow[2] will find his position unpleasant unless he is more compliant and less honest than I think him. He must either swim with the stream or give up his situation which is I should think tolerably comfortable and one that confers some patronage and importance – for the London secretary of a philanthropic society is to a great extent *the Society.* No such thing is known in London as the free speech, & individual action of your Societies. Mr. Estlin has been entertaining the idea of a system of cooperation with

---

1. Rev. Edward Matthews, a Baptist missionary from Wisconsin, spent several years in Britain, lecturing on American slavery.
2. Louis Alexis Chamerovzow, writer and journalist, was the newly appointed Secretary of the B.F.A.S.S. The Garrison party thought him a very much more suitable figure than Scoble.

the Broad Street Society. I am almost sure he will be disappointed. What do you think of my remarks in the Standard upon the insinuation in its columns and in the last annual report that the New Broad St. people were muddling & foolish in protesting against the Stafford House Address for its insinuation against [the] immediate emancipation principle? We all thought this unjust and unwise and that we should put an [advertance?] in the right in this manner. G. Thompson & Mr. Estlin were decidedly of my view. And Mr. Cham. was greatly pleased to find we were so. He said "Now I feel I have fair people to deal with"....

Yours ever truly
Rich[d] D Webb.

MS.A.9.2. vol. 27 1853 The Weston Papers [344]
No. 40 Sarah Pugh to Anne Warren Weston

London – June 6 – 53

My dear friend

...It is now more than three weeks since Mr. & Miss Estlin & myself came to London. Here we were most happy to meet my good friend Mr. McKim who arrived here the day before us. We were soon settled in comfortable lodgings together – when W. W. Brown, George Thompson, Mrs. Follen – "Charlie" Miss Cabot[1] – W. & E. Craft – Professor Allen & lady[2] – Mrs. Massie Mr. Chamerovzow &c &c – frequently clustered around us – holding long & interesting conferences respecting "the cause" – and all that might be feared & hoped for it in the present "crisis" – You know that *we* are always in that condition – but it is emphatically so now in England – under the Stowe excitement – & the new Secretary in Broad St. The papers will tell you of the "Exeter Hall meeting" – & the "Stowe soiree" – and your practised judgment will enable you to detect much not discerned by the public eye – You will notice "the straws" which denote a change of policy in the ruling anti slavery powers of this country – for a change most certainly there is, – under the new Secretary, – but to what extent remains yet to be seen. From what has been, many of our friends are hopeful of much more, others are not so sanguine; – all are willing to wait for a time – the results, which as yet none can foresee....

yours most cordially
Sarah Pugh.

---

1. Susan Copley Cabot (1794-1861) a sister of Mrs. Elizabeth Lee (Cabot) Follen. Eliza Lee Follen (1787-1860) was the widow of the Rev. Charles Theodore Christian Follen, who had been killed in the destruction of the Steamboat Lexington in Long Island Sound, on the night of January 13th-14th, 1840.

2. Professor William G. Allen was a coloured professor at Central College, McGrowsville, New York who came to Britain in 1853 with his wife, a white student, whom he had married after much public outcry. He settled in Britain and never returned to America.

MS. 960 vol. 2 Webb-Quincy Correspondence [345]
pp. 58-59 Webb to Quincy

Dublin, July 22, 1853.

My dear Quincy – ... Among other things Thompson talked to me of his wish to go to America again. He has since sounded McKim, and Sarah Pugh on the same subject. He seemed to wait for an invitation from them, but this they were to cautious to give.If he went he should go upon invitation. He should go with his wife's consent, and on such terms that his family could live in his absense, or they should go with him...

I look upon Thompson as a man of genius, with great gifts and a generous chivalrous dispostion – just the man for the abolition ranks in America. But with his careless habits of expenses, his want of punctuality, indifference to his appointments – and dubious position here – his fiery temper – and the readiness with which he blazes up against the purse proud conceited, rigidly righteous quakers who would do anything for him if he were ready to be their humble servant and clothe them in a mantle of philanthropy – he is not the man for philanthropic England. Here it is too much a dilettante affair to take part in anti-slavery efforts. Except to give a little money; and not much of it at any time, there are very few indeed take the matter to heart and do anything. With you the greatness of the necessity has [?] the noblest powers and dispositions of the true labourers – I think I have now unreservedly told you all I know about Thompson and quite enough to enable you to form a decision as to your course. I will rejoice if you can [wisely?] invite him over. I think it would be the best thing for him & for his family. I think it is what I imagine he would greatly prefer himself. He cant live without excitement and with you he would have the kind that suit him best and which he turns to the best account....

Perhaps you are right in saying that the Sutherland Address should have been accepted with exceptions as an honest effort of new & important allies who could not have been expected to fall into all the notions of abolitionists at once. Still I think you need not have set down the objections to a wrong disposition. I think New Broad St. was in the right and meant well. Bigotry, narrowness, bad rearing and old age will account for a hundred foolish or wrong things. I think it is more Sturge's misfortune than his sin that he is so crooked & cant walk straight...

Yours ever truly

Richd. D. Webb

MS.A.9.2. vol. 27 1853 The Weston Papers. [346]
No. 63 Ellis Gray Loring to Anne Warren Weston.

Boston: September 9, 1853

Dear friend,

Some days before receiving your letter, I had a conversation with Wendell, in the Railroad cars, as to the expediency of George Thompson's visiting this country as an Anti-slavery lecturer; and told Wendell, that although my own impressions would be opposed to it, I should of course acquiesce, willingly, in the Society's so employing him, if they thought proper; in as much as I never would differ, unkindly, from the other friends of the cause, with respect to the choice of measure.

While therefore I cannot find fault with those who would promote your object, and would not be overconfident of my own judgment, I yet do not feel, in respect to his coming, that assurance of its benefit to the cause which would induce me to give freely for that purpose.

My doubts mainly touch these points: 1. When Mr. Thompson *first* came to this country I considered his labors to be of doubtful advantage. Doing full justice to his singleness of purpose, and ability as a speaker, I yet thought that the question discussed involved pretty delicate political considerations. And although I had no objection to hearing the truth from any quarter, I yet doubted whether he did not give occasion to more prejudice than he dispelled. Still, in the attitude our Society *then* maintained, our action was almost exclusively moral; addressing itself to our individual consciences as *men;* – more than as citizens: – and we had a right to reply to all gain-sayers, that Mr. Thompson has as good a right to appeal to us, on a purely religious and moral question, as Dr. Judson has, to preach Christianity to the subjects of the King of Ava. But now, our Society, and the leading friends with whom Mr. Thompson would be identified, have taken up a new line of action, and avow themselves, and are chiefly known to the nation, as aiming to disband the Union and overthrow the government. You will understand that I do not blame them for this: they act according to their light; – perhaps a clearer light than mine, altho' I dont see it. Now I do not say, positively, that Mr. Thompson, if here, would, formally & expressly, preach disunion; – though I think it highly likely: – but his position, on this subject, would be perfectly understood. He would of course closely fraternise with our principal disunionists, – Nor loving and esteeming them, as I do, would I wish him to do otherwise. But I think it a false position for him and for the cause. I might be very willing to pay a missionary to preach Christianity in Siam, – although well assured that its reception would work the most important political changes in that Kingdom, but I should greatly hesitate about sending thither an emissary, whose *primary* purpose were to induce the people to upset their government – even though it were, as a first step, towards the introduction of Christianity. And my reluctance to such a measure would certainly not be weakened by my knowledge, that at least nineteen twentieths of the people were, whether right or wrong, devotedly attached to the existing government. – Dropping comparisons, however, I would say, in one word, that I cannot but conclude that, in the present state of the controversy, Mr. Thompson would be likely to harm – more than help us.

2. It might, perhaps, as well stop here, – because I have gained no right to advise; but you will not take it amiss if I should say to you, that many of our speakers appear to me to have more weight & adaptation to our American audiences than Mr. Thompson: setting aside, wholly, his position, as an Englishman. I heard him, two or three times, during his last visit, and saw several others who went to his lectures and meetings with the most friendly

prepossessions: I would instance, among several others, T. W. Higginson[1], of Worcester, and John King. I think that with these, and, generally, with the best judges of speaking, there was a very considerable disappointment, which I shared with them. He talked a great deal of himself; he amplified the common places of our cause, at great length; but I did not find much depth or maturity of thought, nor ever force or elegance of diction. He spoke rhetorically of the wrongs of the negro, and the crime of imbruting the immortal Soul; but I did not find that he handled, vigorously, the topics or difficulties which were haunting the American mind. In briefer terms, he did not (like Garrison & Phillips,) hit the nail on the head: at least, so it seemed to me.

I have said, dear Anne, enough, – possibly too much – on this topic: but pray remember, that your kind letter gave me plenary indulgence, in advance..

Give my love to the dear girls, until they hear from us more particularly, and believe me, dear Anne, with all frankness, your sincere friend:

Ellis Gray Loring.

MS.A.9.2. vol. 27 1853 The Weston Papers [347]
No. 77 Lucretia Mott to Anne Warren Weston

Phila. 11 mo. 18th. 1853

My dear Ann

Come to the second Decade, and hear all I can say to thee, in reply to thy spicy answer to E.M. Davis, & self, relative to the encouragement proper to give to our friend George Thompson's coming to this country, as an agent for our cause. I would rather talk than write about it. Miller McKim & Sarah Pugh thou knows I presume are both favorable to his coming in the way proposed. I know not whether they have yet had an opp[y] to talk with Edw[d] & hear his objections. I could not recollect which of us named his being a foreigner, as forming one objection, not however to his being welcomed on our platform, but only as to the expediency of making choice of him as an agent, for this & other reasons. Thou says "this would shut the mouth of Miller McKim in England". No – as a parallel, the English sh.[d] raise the cry of "down with the aristocracy' – when it might be a question of expediency, whether their money sh.[d] be used in employing an American Republican as an agent, or one of their own countrymen equally well qualified. But more of this hereafter....

In great haste, & with my husbands best regards

thine, Lucretia Mott.

---

1. Thomas Wentworth Higginson (1823-1911) was a Unitarian minister and author, and active in social reform in Massachusetts. He supported the radical wing of the abolition movement and commanded the first coloured regiment during the Civil War.

No. 3 F.W. Chesson[1] *to Maria Weston Chapman*

34 Windsor Place, Cheetham
Hill Road, Manchester
17th January 1854.

Dear Madam

Today I send you a copy of the *anti slavery Watchman* by which you will perceive that we, who have been termed "the Happy Family", have had a quarrel about a Yankee parson, which has ended in an eternal separation. "Happy" we have never been in the *Manchester Anti-Slavery Union.* My anti-slavery life during the last few weeks has been one series of "squabbles", as Chamerovzow terms them. – But some of us who have been compelled to secede from a majority who neither understand the principles of abolitionism; not comprehended the duties of gentlemen, have in the slightest degree compromised ourselves as the sworn and faithful friends of the *American* Society. The Ladies Society (which since 1847 has made extensive contributions to the Boston Bazaar) has enlarged its basis in order to receive us; and under the designation of the *Manchester Anti Slavery League* we trust to originate a movement in the manufacturing district which shall assist, in a voice that shall be heard throughout the country, the principle of thorough abolitionism, and whose influence shall be felt in the remotest plantations of the slave-holding South. We wish to unite in the new Manchester Movement all the friends of this American Sy. in the country, and to commence active operations at once.

Miss Estlin suggested to me the propriety of my writing to you to request your kind and able advice, especially with regard to the leading points of our address, and constitution. We shall be very glad indeed if you will aid us in this manner, and if, also, you will consent to become a member of our corresponding Committee.

Our friend George Thompson was, I deeply grieve to say, compelled hurriedly to return to town the other day in consequence of the serious illness of his lovely little girl Edith –

Earnestly requesting an early reply, believe me,

Dear Madam
Very Respectfully Yours
Fred. W. Chesson.

Mrs. M. W. Chapman.

---

1. Frederick William Chesson, George Thompson's son-in-law, was the editor of the *Dial* and the *Morning Star.* He took a leading part in anti-slavery organization.

No. 12 Samuel May Jr. to R.D. Webb

Boston, Masstts., Feb. 12. 1854

Dear Mr. Webb,

...Feb. 13 We (i.e. the country) are now in the midst of another *crisis. You* know that a number of them we have passed through! an agitation is springing up, which at present looks healthy & hopeful. Stephen A. Douglas, of Illinois, a Senator in Congress from that state, one of the numerous aspirants for the Presidency of this *Republic (!)* recently had the hardihood, hitherto unparalleled even in this slavehunting & heaven daring land, to propose, in his place in the Senate, a bill for rendering void what is called the Missouri Compromise of 1820 (by which, in a deliberate compact entered into by all the States, North, South, East & West, it was agreed that slavery & involuntary servitude should be forever excluded from all Territory of the U.S. north of the line 36° 30′; the effect of Douglas's Bill would be to open to slavery the vast territory of Nebraska, occupying an extent of half a million square miles, and universally considered until now as guaranteed to freedom; this is a pitch of audacity that no statesman, North or South, has ever ventured upon before. This proposal for yielding up, by the North, of an arrangement which secured so large a Territory to Freedom, is Senator Douglas's bid for the Presidential Nomination in 1856. No one but an accomplished villain would have ventured to father a scheme of such perfidy. Hundreds of thousands of square miles, now free & untainted, to be yielded up to all the woes & horrors of eternal slavery, to gratify the ambition, for a short-lived honour, of one such wretch as Stephen A. Douglas! – It is because I am naturally hopeful, that I faintly hope for the defeat of this iniquitous scheme. But Douglas, like other selfish political schemers, is wary, and would hardly have ventured in so bold a move, had he not carefully looked over the field, and counted his men. It is already a moral certainty, that three-fourths of the U.S. Senate will vote in favour of Douglas's Bill. There remains the chance that Douglas & Pres. Pierce, with all the Government patronage to back them, cannot bribe or intimidate men enough in the H. of Representatives, to carry their point! A slender chance indeed, leaving scarcely room for *hope!* Oh, what a Nation is this; and to what wickedness & baseness has it not given itself up, in obedience to the demands of Slavery. – The Northern States are speaking out, quite manfully, against this nefarious measure. Many meetings have been held, or are to be, held. Petitions & remonstrances are going in. – I believe the South will rue the day that sees the Missouri Compromise rescinded, in part by her votes. So barefaced a fraud will never be forgotten or forgiven, by those who have any soul left – and, GOD be thanked, our people are not utterly soul-less yet....

Believe me gratefully & sincerely your friend

Samuel May

MS.B.1.6. vol. 5 1853-1855 The May Papers [350]
No. 27 Samuel May to R.D. Webb

Boston, 21 Cornhill,
July 21, 1854.

(A Postscript)

...Congress is about to adjourn; and the President has asked for Ten Millions of Dollars to make war with Spain, for Cuba, if he can construe a pretext for the same.[1] That there will be no difficulty in picking a quarrel, we may be very certain. I send you a little slip, showing that measures are in train for a treaty of amity, or something of the sort, between the *United States & Russia!* Russia will keep England & France busy, while the U. States rifle Spain of Cuba. This is evidently the meaning. In return this slaveholding Govt. will help the Czar in some way, – perhaps by a loan of money!

MS.B.1.6. vol. 14 May-Estlin Correspondence [351]
No. 72 Samuel May to J.B. Estlin

Leicester, Mass. July 30, 1854

Dear Mr. Estlin;

...We are watching the European War with no little interest. It would now appear that Russia means to fight it out. I think Austria will take very good care not to fight against Russia. And we had pretty reliable evidence – indeed the Washington Government organ as good as admits, that a treaty of some sort has lately been entered into between Russia & the United States. Highly probable – nothing more natural, indeed. Gt. Britain, & even France, are *too free* for our Government, the vile tool of slaveholders as it is, the organ of the vilest despotism the sun ever shone upon. Russian Czarism & American slaveholding are one in spirit, and we have the European war to thank for developing the fact so that all may see it. Is it not a singular state of things? The United States nominally neutral, virtually fighting for the most Absolute Government, & complete Subjection of the people! Such is slavery's work! But I believe all will work for the best. – Meanwhile if the U.S. will favour Russia now & in the future, Russia will agree to keep England & France busy, while the U.S. Govt. seizes upon Cuba. This is to be the game, I doubt not. And when Spain finds she has *actually lost* Cuba she will consent to take $100,000,000 as a soother of her wounded dignity, and a sort of offset for her loss.

But I will now relieve you, & finish with a few lines to Mary – Ever affectionately, Yours. Saml. May.

---

1. In 1854 Southern ambitions to annex Cuba to the United States reached their height. That President Pierce was unable to force such a plan through Congress indicates the unwillingness of Northern politicians to support an adventure which could only have benefited their southern neighbours.

MS.A.1.2. vol. 24 1854 Anti-Slavery Letters to Garrison [352]
No. 106 Wendell Phillips to Elizabeth Pease Nichol

August 7 1854

Dear Lizzie,

...I would say something on the Burns case[1] if I did not know you saw the Standard and Liberator, from whose columns you get so many particulars that a note like this can add little. 'Twas the saddest week I ever passed. Men talked of the good we might expect for the cause, but I could not think then of the general cause, so mournful and sad rose ever before me pleading eyes of the poor victim, when he sat and cast his eyes on our consciences, and placed his fate in our hands. I could not forget the man in the idea. Time has passed since, and I begin to think more of the 3,000,000 and less of the individuals. The effect of his surrender under this infamous law has been like 'Uncle Tom' and all such spasms, far less deep and general than thoughtless folk anticipated. We always gain at such times a few hundred and the old friends are strengthened, but the mass settle down very little different from before.

Indeed, the *Govt.* has fallen into the hands of the slave power completely – so far as *national* politics are concerned we are beaten – there's no hope we shall have Cuba in a year or two, Mexico in five – and I should not wonder if efforts were made to revive the slave trade, though, perhaps unsuccessfully, as the Northern slave states which live by the export of slaves would help us in opposing this. Events hurry forward with amazing rapidity. We live fast here – The future seems to unfold a vast slave Empire united with Brazil & darkening the whole West – I hope I may be a false prophet, but the sky was never so dark. Our union, all confess, must sever finally on this question – It is now with 9/10 only a question of time....

With best love to your husband, & yours most affly.

Ann & Wendell Phillips.

MS.B.1.6. vol. 15 Additional Letters to Samuel May Jr. [353]

Dublin, August 16, 1854

Dear Mr. May –

...About the *Advocate* I never felt any surprize that more was not done for it in New England. I rather wondered that you sent in so many subscribers. I know how many claims must be made upon the abolitionists – so small a handful in presence of so great a work, and I would be sorry to add to them. Sending an anti-slavery paper to American abolitionists is like sending coals to Newcastle. Still, I know it must cheer you on to feel and see that you have hearty sympathisers on this side of the Atlantic who see eye to eye with you, and are proud to bear even so small a share in

1. Anthony Burns, an escaped Negro slave, was arrested in Boston and returned to slavery, in spite of the most violent protests throughout Massachusetts. As a climax to one of the meetings of protest Garrison held up the Constitution of the United States, denounced it as "a Covenant with Death and an agreement with Hell," and then publicly burned it, with hardly a dissenting murmur.

your labours. I have no doubt the numbers of them will increase, though the result of our experience is to show how dark & prevalent is the ignorance of anti slavery affairs in their countries, and how much there is to be done, before much can be effected for you here. Among the very first things that arrested my attention when I came into the cause were the gross ignorance & apathy of the majority of the anti slavery people of England as to the real merits of the cause in the United States, and the many ramifications of its bearings....

The heads of your friends here are full of Mr. Chamerovzow at present. Mr. Cham. took offence at P. Pillsbury not responding more cordially to his nomination of him as a speaker on the British & Foreign platform. P.P. informs Mr. Cham. that he wrote him from Paris declining the nomination – that he sent the letter to the care of Wm. W. Brown. Brown says he sent it off immediately to New Broad St[reet] – Cham. says he did not get it for 10 days after the meeting – & accuses Brown of holding it over – for some crooked purpose of Brown's own. This leads to a thorough sifting of the whole affair – which ends in Cham[w] admitting he was quite mistaken as to facts & conclusions, & writing an apology to Brown, who accepts it very good naturedly. Geo. Thompson, Mr. Chesson, Mr. Steinthal, W. W. B. and Miss Estlin have had a deal of writing about it. This day I received from Mr. Steinthal, a letter from G.T. to him giving chapter and verse for the whole story – and an excessively damaging one it is to Mr. Cham[w]. He seems without any provocation from Brown or apparent benefit to himself to have accused him wantonly in a way that might have cast a slur on him for life – on one who had never injured him & whose only dependence was his unsullied character. – Mr. Estlin was extremely desirous for a fusion with the New Broad St. Society – Cham. was apparently a very great improvement on Scoble – free from his antipathies, & his bigotry and malevolence. He placed such unlimited confidence in Mr. E. & I may say in myself, that I was greatly won in his favour – and so were the Estlins. He seemed most anxious for a good understanding with the Am. A.S.S. & its friends and to think if he was only given time enough if people would have enough patience with him – he would muzzle the demon of bigotry, conceit, & exclusiveness at 27 New Broad St. and would bring about a heaven of halcyon days, peace, and good humour, between Joseph Sturge & W. L. Garrison & their respective adherents. I never expected this – I never thought it possible – but I admire the disposition of Mr. Cham. and the desires of Mr. Estlin and I knew as I was a bad hoper, it was possible I might be in a degree mistaken. However this Brown letter affair is a very sad one, and shows an amount of duplicity, meanness & unscrupulousness that leaves one no room to hope for a continuance of the *entente cordiale* with Mr. Cham. or with New Broad Street – and so we must do the best we can without them. To the best of my knowledge & belief W.W. Brown's conduct has been altogether respectable & unexceptionable since he first landed in England, & he has the warm good wishes of all the friends of the Am. A.S. Society on this side of the ocean & of many others besides amongst whom he has been during his antislavery tours.

The papers will tell you all about the Manchester Conference which seems to have gone off very well though they attempted to do too much in the short time they could devote to deliberation. Owing to matters of business I was prevented from attending to my own very great regret....

As to Pillsbury in Scotland, I do not think he could do much good in the way you suggest. The Scotch are I believe the most intensely bigotted of any educated people in existence. They are past praying for. They are so early and carefully crammed with the most intense Calvinism that their judgment on such points is overwhelmed before they have had time to use it. And so they continue bigotted & conceited to an extraordinary degree. I look upon orthodoxy as a great enemy to abolitionism, and the reason is simple. Bad as slavery is, it is not so bad as damnation. Better that the slaves continue slaves than that I be damned. If the orthodox faith be true, it is of the first importance that I keep sound in it – that I run no risk of any sort – that I avoid all unitarians, deists, infidels, all philosophy & vain deceit, all heresy and heretics. Some such train of thought, I am persuaded is constantly operating against the spread of abolitionism amongst the so-called religious world – so sure do I feel this, that I never think it worth my while to waste much labour with people we think in this direction. I dont think it either fair or reasonable to expect it....

Yours ever truly

Rich[d] D. Webb

MS.B.1.6. vol. 5 The May Papers [354]
No. 28 S. Alfred Steinthal[1] *to Samuel May*

Bridgewater, August 17th 1854.

My dear Mr. May,

...Our conference in Manchester went off very well, with one untoward circumstance. Joseph Barker wished to speak, but was not permitted, from what appears to me to be a wrong view of a point of order on the part of several of our friends, and from religious bigotry on the part of many ministers who were present at the meeting....The meeting has however been very useful. It has diffused much information and has brought the American Anti-Slavery Society prominently before the public. Parker Pillsbury was truly eloquent....George Thompson's morning speech on the West India Question was perhaps the most useful oration he ever delivered, so full of facts to prove that Emancipation has been even a greater blessing to the West Indies, than its most sanguine friend could have expected. You will not be surprised to hear that his facts were clothed in language well calculated to warm the heart with generous enthusiasm. – The effect of the Conference will, I hope, manifest themselves at your Boston Bazaar....

yours most faithfully

S. Alfred Steinthal.

1. Rev. S. Alfred Steinthal was a Unitarian minister and became an active Garrison supporter.

MS.960 vol. 2 Webb-Quincy Correspondence [355]
pp. 62-64 Webb to Quincy

Dublin August 21, 1854.

My dear Quincy

...A very good Anti Slavery Conference was held in Manchester on the 1st of August. The only interruption to the harmony of the proceedings was caused by Joseph Barker who was in haste for a train trying to speak for a few moments, whilst another man (Ward,[1] the Black minister,) had the floor before him, and was also in haste for the same train. As far as I can learn Barker was decidedly out of order – though he was opposed in a still more disorderly way and in a bad spirit by some of the orthodox people present. I hope he may not make a grievance of this; I fear he allows himself to be served by the opposition to which his fearless antagonism renders him liable....

Richd. D. Webb

You ask about G.T.'s present means of making ends meet. I do not know. It is and always has been a great puzzle to me how people who have no apparent property or means of earning, manage to get on. It is a great difficulty in T's way on this side the water, as such a man is always looked on with contempt or suspicion. He is a fine fellow, noble, magnanimous & chivalrous. It is a pity he should go to waste [still?] however he may do with a popular audience, I greatly wonder people should think of preferring him to Wendell Phillips whose speeches as read are in my estimation much finer productions – more original – more profound – more intellectually brilliant than Thompsons. I look upon Phillips as morally and intellectually a very great man. It is said that Chesson, a very good fellow I am sure, but I suppose very poor, is going to marry Thompson's second daughter – and this accounts to me for the active part Thompson has taken in the Manchester Conference which was got up solely by the energy of Chesson. As far as I can judge, Barker who made an unseemly interruption to get himself heard in the Conference, was quite wrong, although he was discourteously opposed and put down by some orthodox ministers. He should have taken care to have time to be heard and to put his oponents entirely in the wrong if they had objected to hear him. He delights in a storm, and I fear does not make enough allowance for the hatred which his fearless outspeaking naturally [?] on the part of those whose craft is in danger from his labours.

MS.B.1.6. vol. 5 The May Papers [356]
No. 29 S. Alfred Steinthal to Samuel May

Bridgewater – September 29th, 1854.

My dear Sir

...I was rather amused, & perhaps a little annoyed at a letter

---

1. Samuel Ringgold Ward (1817-1866), born in Maryland of slave parents who escaped shortly after his birth, was educated in New York, and helped by the Tappans and others of the A.A.S.S.. He went to Britain in 1853 through the aid of the A.S.S. of Canada where he had been active in work for fugitive slaves. He left Britain about 1855 for Jamaica where he finally settled.

which I see in the last Liberator (No. 1052) signed "one of your subscribers ever since 1835" in which our good friend Parker Pillsbury is rather blamed for his silence about the wickedness of the English government and people. I think that some of our good friends in America have rather strange notions about England & English Institutions & fancy that we are suffering under some sad oppression. Letters like those that Joseph Barker send you are perhaps calculated to keep up the tension, and yet we that live here do not find such great reason for complaint. My friends here never gave me credit for much Toryism; I dare say I am rather too much of a radical for such a suspicion ever to be raised against me, & it has never been my habit to speak of our English Institutions in Church and State as the model of a Constitution. I have left that to Republicans of the United States pattern. I grant we have many things that can bear improvement, & I could perhaps reckon up as many things in the present state of affairs that need that amendment, as the old subscriber could. But there is one great difference in our English grievances and the one great grievance of the United States. We have nothing that denies the humanity of any being that breathes upon our shores; our state church never tells its members to send Bibles to the heathen, like your voluntary churches do. Our government although it has carried on unjust wars enough never pledges its whole power to keep in servitude, men born upon our soil, because they have a shade of darker colour in their skin.... the direst wrong committed under the sanction of England's time honoured name, can not compare with slave holding as practiced in the model (?) Republic....

Let me say one word about our Anti-Slavery friends here and their relation to English wrongs. Of course we being brought up under monarchical rule, do not look upon that form of government as many of your Republicans do. We have seen in our past history that many disadvantages arise from our constitution & with reform in parliament, in the civil service & general patronage, all of which we shall obtain, we do not hesitate to say that we are satisfied with our government and are loyal to our Queen. Some of the prominent Anti-slavery men belong to our aristocracy. They naturally hold even stronger views than I have expressed: but it can never be said of men like Lord Shaftesbury, Lord Brougham and others I can name that they have been indifferent to the improvement of their fellow countrymen....Descending to those who hold a lower rank, look through the list of English Abolitionists they are ever to be formed among the active workers in reforms at home. Indeed let me ask is it not natural they should if they are at all governed by principle. The very reason that causes them to work for oppressed humanity when they hear its cry for help coming across the Atlantic, fires them to hear that same voice when lifted up in England....

Most faithfully yours

S. Alfred Steinthal.

MS.B.1.6. vol. 5 The May Papers [357]
No. 31 Parker Pillsbury to Samuel May

Belfast Oct 5 – 1854.

Dear Friend –

...The thing which troubles me most here, is, to find so many of all sorts of creatures travelling in the name of American Anti Slavery, and picking the people's pockets for *vigilance Committees, Canada Missions, Chaplain funds, colored schools* in the West, & colored churches in Canada. And now another movement has sprung up in the name of the Tract Association, that proposes to do the work by spending Anti slavery Tracts all through the South. The Agent of this scheme is a Mr. Vincent – I have seen him, and heard him – and he "put the *licks* into the American churches," as James Buffum says, with a will, and seemed true hearted man. But as to Pennington, Garnet,[1] Ward, Hemming, Henson, Gloucester, & that fry, they are an outrage on all decency, & a scandal to the name of anti-slavery. I have published a long letter about their deeds in several papers, a copy of which I will send to you.... I spent September in Scotland, visiting Glasgow, Edinboro', Aberdeen & various smaller places – though seeing but few people. Abolitionists of our stripe are scarce as comets there. Mrs. Stowe in Scotland did us no good....

I am going up to London next month to see Chamerovzow's "*Conference*" – I could write you a volume about him – *pro & con* – particularly *con*.... But I have time for no more today, & must close this hasty and desultory note by subscribing with unabated friendship & affection for you & yours –

Parker Pillsbury.

MS.B.1.6. vol. 5 The May Papers [358]
No. 32 Samuel May to R.D. Webb

Boston, October 25. 1854.

Dear Mr. Webb –

...Day before yesterday I had a very welcome letter from Pillsbury, dated at Belfast....He appears to feel quite apprehensive of unfavourable results from the projected union of *the true* anti-Slavery forces of Great Britain with those of New Broad Street, London. I appreciate his views of that subject, and I share his fears as to the result of such an experiment. The idea of obtaining strength from an alliance with those who have been seeking our ruin, – and in every mean and covert way too – for fifteen years, is to me simply preposterous. What does this Broad Street movement mean followed up so indefatigably? – ...The Abolitionists of Gt. Britain, of the more free and

1. Henry Highland Garnet (1815-1882), born a slave in Maryland, escaped to New York where he entered school and later the ministry. He spoke for the A.A.S.S. and was a serious rival of Frederick Douglass. His fame as a speaker having spread to Britain, he was invited in 1850 to make a tour of the country, and remained for three years lecturing. He then went to Jamaica as a missionary for the United Presbyterian Church of Scotland. He later served as pastor in various American Negro Churches before being appointed Minister to Liberia, where he died shortly after taking up his appointment.

genuine stamp, have been assiduously labouring for a dozen years and more, to find a place to stand upon, and get their cause *recognized* by the people. At length it is, in a measure done....A most encouraging Conference is held, wholly independent of Broad Street patronage or dictation; – and the Broad St. gentlemen, and even their very friendly and courteous Secretary, feel offended & displeased, even somewhat indignant, at the *liberty taken* to hold any such meeting at all, – when everybody knew that *Broad St.* was intending to hold one in another place – 200 miles off & more – some three months later! But the Confce was held, and was in every respect successful. It proved that British Anti Slavery had a place to stand upon, and abundant material to work with, without being at all indebted to the B. & F. Anti-Slavery Society, or to any of its machinery and appliances. – At this juncture, Broad St. comes forward, & renews its solicitude for *a union* of forces. Had it done so, when our friends were struggling against their hostility and tyranny for dear life, – or even when W. W. Brown and other friends of ours appeared in England after *the strife* had somewhat abated, – it would have been quite another thing. But, *at present*, and with such restrictions and limitations as are evidently to be laid upon our friends if they listen to the *peace* propositions – I am totally distrustful....I believe the exclusive Broad St. power has been waning for the past five years, or more; and that nobody understood this better than themselves, and that that was the reason for Mr. Scoble's departure. A totally different policy is now pursued, with the purpose of regaining the influence they have lost, and with the hope of obtaining the control of the newly-awakened anti-slavery feeling which the long labours of the faithful abolitionists, and Mrs. Stowe's book, have been instrumental in producing....I hope our friends will not be hasty, and that they will meet with the Broad Street gentlemen only on the most equal terms, and even then in the most cautious manner. And above all that they will merge nothing of their own in the old Broad St. Society....

In haste, & with sincere regards to Mrs. Webb and to all Dublin friends.
Aff'ly yours
Samuel May

MS.B.1.6. vol. 15 Additional Letters to Samuel May Jr. [359]

Dublin, November, 7, 1854.

Dear Mr. May

I have recd your letter and...think it better to write at once to ease your mind about the danger incurred by a union of the friends of the American A. S. Society, with the New Broad Street people. In my opinion & I think my opinion is a good one on such a matter, there is very little danger of any such union. I think Pillsbury has charmed you on this head. What he may have been at home I cannot know, but I do think this way of receiving almost everything here partakes of a morbid character. He is sensitive & touchy, he requires to be managed & carefully approached & takes very exaggerated views of things....The truth is the warm intelligent friends of the Am. A.S. Society are very few and they are not likely to give up anything to New Broad Street. The only persons of any consequence who would be suspected of any such disposition are the Estlins and all they want is to make the best use that can be made through the friendly dispositions of the Secretary of the only Society that stands before the public in the position of a national A.S. Society with a staff, an office, and money at command. From the Society I hope nothing. Its leaders are too old, too proud, or too indifferent to change. I think Cham.[w] would like to display his talents as a mediator & diplomatist by bringing his friends & the Garrisonian abolitionists into friendly relations subject to his supervision, advice & patronage. I dont think he will ever begin to do anything of the kind. I think Cham.[w] is honestly anti-slavery and would be with us as far as consists with his bread & butter. He has astonishingly good temper – but is too much of a manoeuverer to make a good abolitionist...I feel confident he will never make much of his favourite scheme of a happy family of abolitionists of the Garrison & Lewis Tappan kind living & working harmoniously together. I am told the conference in New Broad St. is hardly likely to come to anything – Joseph Sturge cant (wont) come – others cant (wont) come – they dont wish to be part of the happy family – and Cham.[w] will make nothing of his scheme. Mr. & Miss Estlin expect far more from such unions than I do or ever would do. The moral materials on each side are as wide as the poles asunder....

Yours ever truly

Rich[d] D. Webb.

MS.B.1.6. vol. 5 The May Papers [360]
No. 86 S. Alfred Steinthal to Mary Estlin

Bridgewater. Nov.[r] 10th 1854.

My dear Miss Estlin

...I suppose we old Englanders never shall fully enter into all New England mysteries, but I am sure New Englanders never seem to understand us completely. And this is not surprising: we are such a queer mixture. Look at men like Sturge and Alexander: they are I firmly believe well intentioned men, but their goodness is covered on one side with such a mass of bigotry and unconscious intolerance that it only shines out by accident now and then to us, towards whom the bigoted and intolerant side is turned. To their good, orthodox bretheren they are all light. We Unitarians have a good training to appreciate such men: we meet this contradiction in every question, so that we understand it better when we hit upon it in Anti Slavery matters. Our American friends do not know what powers these orthodox gentry have, and how much good can yet be done by them in England, which we can never accomplish. It is nothing but right therefore for us to work with them as far as they will go with us, only let it be clearly understood by all parties, we do not limit ourselves to cooperation when we think it useful to exceed their bounds....

MS. incomplete.

MS.B.1.6. vol. 14 May-Estlin Correspondence [361]
No. 78 Samuel May to J.B. Estlin

Boston, 21 Cornhill, April 17, 1855.

Dear Mary Estlin;

...We hear from sundry quarters of the great probability there is of a Revolution in England – a *social* revolution, not (probably) a bloody one. Joseph Sturge, who has just returned to this country, talks in this way I understand. His authority will not, I presume, be very weighty with you. I do not give much ear or credit to these stories, for there has been so much wisdom in the counsels of your Governments – for the past generation at least – that these coming storms have been foreseen and averted by timely measures. But I have felt, for many years, even before I went to England that your State Church, with its enormous & absurd monopolies, ought to be abolished. Now it seems absolutely indispensible that the Aristocracy – the Nobility – should also be abolished, and every man stand upon his own character, merits & abilities. I do not at all expect, as one man (a German) told me the other day, that "Victoria will have to pay a visit to these shores very soon."! – but I do *hope*, & expect, to see material & radical changes introduced with the structure of your Government ere long. This war with Russia must prove excedingly burdensome to the English people, and they will, I think, exact a severe reckoning of the men who have brought them into it, and then do so little to uphold the British honour, or secure the ends which were desired, in carrying it on. –

Meanwhile, *our* Government, never foreseeing the triumph of the Right, never desiring or meaning to yield in ever so partial a measure to its demands, never aiming to secure the end of justice or of Freedom, is plotting & scheming, by every insidious and treacherous act, to possess itself of the island of Cuba. That obtained, they will after securing their victory, prepare their plans for seizing Hayti. Doubtless they look forward to seizing Jamaica, and the whole W. India group, as necessary to their plan of spreading slavery through the American tropics. They are driving forward now, with all the industry and craft they can, to secure the possession of Cuba, while England & France have their hands full of this Russian war; and they are secretly fomenting difficulties in Cuba, and inviting insults to American citizens for the purpose of resenting them, in order that they have some ground for a war with Spain, and a seizure of the island. – So [you] will see how much reason the American abolitionists have, apart from general grounds, to desire the end of this European war....

Very truly yours

Samuel May Jr.

MS.B.1.6. vol. 5 The May Papers [362]
No. 74 Samuel May to R.D. Webb

Leicester, July 24, 1855.

Dear friend Webb,

...I have wanted, a score of times, since we heard of dear Mr. Estlin's death, to write to you; – you knew him so well, you valued him so truly, that you can well understand our feeling, at his departure, and will estimate our loss, in him, just as we do. – and so indeed you do, as your note expresses. It is true, as you say, that in this country G. Thompson's death (had it occurred) would make a wider impression because he has personally been here & become known to very many; but, even in this country, with those who knew both men, not even G.T.'s death w^{d} be regarded as the loss the cause, which it now sustains in Mr. Estlin's. But he has done his work so well – so judiciously, so carefully, so thoroughly – he has so wisely prepared for his departure – & left his various testimonies so clearly registered, – that, whatever could be done to abate the loss, we shall find to be done. We can always refer to him, as the best authority, wherever authority is needed; and his example will cheer & help us to the last....

We shall be glad to know, when you see fit to tell us, what are now the prospects of the *Advocate.* Will it go beyond its present year? and what shall be done for its support & continuance? This must, to a large extent depend on you; for what with its editing, printing, & distribution, no small share of your time must be required by it. It must be, I am sure, a serious question with you, whether you can continue to give this amount of time and effort....

Politics are in a strange chaotic state. The *New York Tribune*, as I have been telling Miss Estlin, is working assiduously & powerfully to unite all the anti-slavery of the North, oblivious of all past distinctions & divisions – into one great party, to recover Kansas, restore the Missouri line of 36.30 (not 33½ as you have it in the *Advocate)* – & then proceed to resist the Slave Power in other respects. But it wont do. Disunion is our *Wisdom & Safety*, as well as our Duty. Faithfully yrs. S. May

MS.B.1.6. vol. 5 The May Papers [363]
No. 76 George Armstrong to Samuel May

The Nooks
Durdham Park, Bristol
Aug. 14. 1855.

My dear Friend

...I wish I could show you a correspondence I have had with *Kossuth!* On this subject, I was the first Englishman to convey [to] him the impressions of a hatred of American slavery – through the hands of that *true* man Mazzini on his first landing at Southampton. I never concealed from him my views. I *shouted* them to him at the Guildhall in London. I stated them in an Address & in conversation with him at his residence in London. And when he besought my exertions to procure him contributions to his *Hungarian fund*, while for the sake of his *country* I did what I could (for which he thanked me very heartily), – I could not allow the opportunity to pass without expression of regrets that we differed so essentially as to the course it became one to take in dealing with American Society. And so things remained; until the appearance in the "Anti-Slavery Advocate" of an extract from New York paper containing a letter from Kossuth to the Editor (I think) – taking the *right ground*, and offering that *many advice* to the slaveholders, – the *suppression* of which while he was in *their presence*, we might have forgiven had he not sinned so egregiously agst. all right principle & right feeling, by positively *flattering* them, & proclaiming them as the most generous, most heroic, of the human race: model men, in short, for all the rest of the world!!!...

Yours most truly

Geo. Armstrong.

MS.B.1.6. vol. 1 1837-1845 The May Papers [364]
No. 11 Joseph Mazzini to George Armstrong

Copy of a note from M. Mazzini to G. Armstrong

Thursday
Cromwell Lodge
Old Brompton

Dear Sir –

I have transmitted your letter handed over to me by Mr. Ashurst, to Kossuth. Whether he will or not acknowledge it, is a matter of time; but I feel sure that once away from our shores and at rest on the wide sea, he will think of its contents, and profit by them(?!!!)

I avail myself of the opportunity to thank you for the book which you were so kind as to send me a copy of. We are moving on the same path, and endeavouring to relink Earth to Heaven by substituting a truly devoted, religious spirit to all worship of idols and orthodoxy by trying to realize the sense of the only prayer which is worth God & Man, "Let O Father, they kingdom come, and they will be done here down, as in Heaven."

We are brothers & friends in this faith
very faithfully yours

Jos. Mazzini

The Secretary of Kossuth, Hadrian Lemmi,[1] an Italian, is an intimate friend of mine; and I should wish very much to have him introduced in America to such men who can sympathize with, and act in some way or another for our national Italian cause.

May I venture to ask you if you can lend me your support in this wish of mine? Can you give me the address of Mrs. Chapman whom I had the pleasure of meeting here in London some time ago?

1. Hadrian Lemmi was the go-between of Kossuth and Mazzini.

MS.B.1.6. vol. 6 The May Papers [365]
No. 1 Eliza Wigham to Samuel May

5 Gray Street, Edinburgh – 4.1.1856

My dear Friend,

...We are earnestly watching events to know what the next issue will be, Kansas, the slave insurrections, the Walker expeditions all betoken yet more important events – We are very much interested in the African Slave trade question. I believe the attempt to reopen that trade will more than any other movement arouse the spirit of indignation in Britain; – thus it is a striking circumstance to witness the difference of sentiment on this subject in the states themselves, & to understand something of the motives for this difference. Some of our friends have been much interested for the sufferers in Kansas & have subscribed a sort of testimony against despotism to the amount of £35 (perhaps a little more) for the relief of the distress, this money they thought it well to send to Professor Stowe as he had the charge of Lady Byron's & Miss Murray's contributions....

Yours sincerely

Eliza Wigham.

MS.960 Quincy-Webb Correspondence 1843-1871 [366]
No. 23 Quincy to Webb

Bankside, Dedham.
Feb. 12. 1856

My dearest Webb:

...I am happy to find that the probability of our going to fighting with one another is diminishing. It would be very bad economy. Though, perhaps, a black army from the West Indies landed in South Carolina might be productive of good results. It is part of our demagoguism here to bully England and to make believe to want to fight her. Even Seward and the Free Soilers fall into this beastly snobbishness from the fear of the Democrats turning all that sort of capital on their own account. But the slaveholders will never let us go to war with England, unless it be for Cuba or some slave territory immediately necessary for their purposes. An English war would materially interfer with the invasion of Europe by the Yankees which is all the time going on. Pretty much all Yankee-dom is either in Europe or just setting out or just returning....

I am, my dear Webb, your loving, though unworthy friend,

E.Q.

MS.B.1.6. vol. 6 The May Papers [367]
No. 20 Samuel May to R. D. Webb

Boston, February 25. 1856

Dear Mr. Webb,

...Our papers & people without exception are thinking that the aspect of affairs between your country and ours is a very critical one. I am rather sorry to see some of the Eng. papers, and especially the *Times*, dwelling upon the terrible scourging which England will give to the U. States, should it come to war. It is the very sort of language to stir bad blood. So far as I have looked into the Central America matter, and the so called Clayton-Bulwer Treaty, I think England has a fair show of right, and has not infringed upon the treaty. In the matter of enlistment for her army, on our soil, it is otherwise. I think England was wrong in that matter, and very indiscreet – but that no hard was done, & that for the wrong (such as it was) she has made the *amende honorable*, most amply. I am very sure the American *people* are perfectly satisfied on that point, and would scorn the idea of going to war for that. But if defiant language is resorted to, – especially with such head-strong and shameless National administration as we have, reason & good feeling will be supplanted by anger and violence. There is a great use and need of hard language; but it is not the time for it, when two nations are on the verge of a quarrel, – which is all known well eno' to you; – excuse my *seeming* to think otherwise – I put great dependence on the Commercial Interests of the 2 countries binding them to keep the peace. The only good thing, likely to come of a war with G. Britain, would be its disturbing, & perhaps destroying influence on Slavery.

The great quadrennial Presidential turmoil is now just commencing here. The "Know Nothings" have given new proof of the correctness of their name by making Fugitive Slave Law Fillmore their candidate. There was an extensive *bolt* of Northern members from Convention....

Kanzas matters are full of interest to us. The President sides, most decidedly, with those who are striving to make a Slave State; and the U.S. troops will be employed to crush any opposition to the same. I think there will be a contest; the Free State men are a very large majority in the territory. The slavery-ruffians are nearly all outside of it. Large supplies of weapons and ammunition have been sent from the Free States to Kanzas. The beginning of the End appears. Truly Yours

Saml. May Jr.

MS.B.1.6. vol. 15 Additional Letters to Samuel May Jr. [368]

Dublin, March 13, 1856

Dear Mr. May –

...Do you know that on account of what you said of the prevalent feeling in your country respecting a quarrel with England, I sent your letter to Lord Carlisle (the Lord Lieutenant here) thinking that the opinion of one on whom he can rely is important for our government to learn. Nothing can be further from the notions of the English people than a quarrel with the United States. I am satisfied that a friendly feeling is as nearly universal as it is possible for a feeling to be. I sent your letter because it guaranteed its own genuineness....

Yours ever

R D Webb

MS.B.1.6. vol. 15 Additional Letters to Samuel May Jr. [369]

Dublin, May 8, 1856.

Dear Mr. May –

...One consequence of Lord Carlisle's call upon me was that P. Pillsbury left his card at the castle and received an invitation to an interview next day of which he will give you all the particulars. He was most kindly & cordially received and seemed to have enjoyed the visit very much. You asked me what Lord C. said to me about the cause – nothing very special except that he considered it one of the most important if not *the* most important movement of the day. As I suppose a private call from the viceroy to an ordinary tradesman is to say the least very uncommon – I took care to let him lead the conversation and to answer rather than to ask. I mean I wished to avoid anything like inviting him to commit himself by saying anything that from his official position he might wish unsaid. I talked a great deal for I saw that he wished to hear what I had to say about the abolitionists, our own country, the priests & many other subjects on which I have very decided opinions – I suspected after he left me that Miss Martineau had something to do with the call, and accordingly giving her credit for this, I wrote to thank her. She sent me word that she had written to Lord Carlisle about me – I think it probable that my sending your letter to him gave him an opportunity which he might have otherwise wanted. But this is very egotistical & I wd. not have written it had you not asked me....

Yours ever truly

Richard Webb

MS.B.1.6. vol. 6 The May Papers [370]
No. 30 Samuel May to Mary Carpenter

Boston, April 22d. 1856.

Dear Miss Carpenter,

...For ourselves, we are still contending with the mighty powers leagued in the support of Slavery. It is as great a marvel to me, as it was at first, now and why men *and women* of prominent and 'reputable' position, Church members professing to be renewed by the spirit of God, ministers claiming to be set for the defence of the Gospel. – all suffer themselves to be more or less committed to the justification (or at least excuse) of a system of such bare-faced wrong, such cruel oppression, such unbridled lust and villainy, as American Slavery pre-eminently is. I fear that the most undoubted charity cannot deny that it is the power of *money*, and the *love of money*, in the last resort, which moves the whole. Northern merchants, Northern manufacturers, Northern mechanics, make 'good livings' & often large fortunes out of Southern trade, – especially in cotton and tobacco, and in the supply to the South of the innumerable articles (as has been said, from a steam-engine to a threepenny nail) which the North furnishes. The women are easily reconciled to a system of things which supplies them with comforts and sometimes luxuries; most of them take care not to get in the way of learning, or rather hearing much of the atrocities of Slavery; and as their church and their minister, & the distinguished Rev. Dr. So and So, of the neighbouring city, all say that slavery is not sinful, that it has always been permitted by God for His own wise purposes, and that the Abolitionists are Seditious Men, Infidels, and Enemies of the Church of Christ, their Consciences, too sensitive, are soon lulled to sleep, – God help us! What a heavy work remains to do! But it does advance. Let us be glad & give thanks! With affectionate regard, Yours,

Samuel May Jr.

MS.B.1.6. vol. 6 1856-1858 The May Papers [371]
No. 33 Samuel May Jr. to R.D. Webb

Leicester, Mass. June 10, 1856
(Tuesday)

Dear Mr. Webb,

...We are living in stirring times, and amidst painful scenes. Kanzas is subjugated to the Slave Power. It is given over to all profanities, indecencies, outrages, & enormities, which never fail to herald, accompany & follow the march of slavery. A large company of desperadoes, gathered in Alabama & Georgia, and receiving accessions by the way & led on by a Major Buford, arrived in Kanzas a month or 6 weeks since. They came with the avowed purpose of driving out, by force, the Free State Settlers, and of subjecting the territory to the exclusive dominion of the slaveholders. On arriving on the borders of Kanzas one of their number was, *by President Pierce*, appointed United States Marshal for the District of Kanzas!! a ferocious, bloody minded, & desperate character, as a slave holder, on such a mission needs must be. He immediately summoned the rest of the Alabama gang to act as his *posse comitatus*, and caused them to be armed with *United States musquets!* But you will see in the American papers, fuller particulars than I have time to write. This man with his posse marched to Lawrence, took several leading men prisoners – cannonaded the hotel & burnt it to the ground – destroying 2 printing offices with all their contents – burnt Gov. Robinson's house – entered all the houses, stealing everything they could carry off, – stealing horses, &c – destroying large quantities of property not easily movable, – and driving off the inhabitants, killing several, and (it is said) violating some of the women. We shall have fuller particulars, bye & bye. All this is directly & entirely chargeable to Franklin Pierce & the U.S. Government. Had he protected the Kanzas settlers, *in their persons & property*, nothing of the kind *could* have happened. Had he & his Govt. done nothing, stood neutral, folded their arms & looked on, it would not have happened. Against these poverty stricken & half-starved Alabamians, and against the Border Ruffians of Missouri, the Kanzas people, both men and women, were prepared to defend themselves and I sincerely believe would have made a firm and probably a successful resistance. But when these hungry and desperate blood-hounds came clothed with *United States* authority led by a *United States* officer and armed with United States weapons, – what could they do? Resistance was entirely useless. Moreover, the wretched Pierce (I cannot, if he is President, speak of him in any milder terms, for none such would describe him) has ordered from Fort Leavenworth a considerable body of regular U.S. troops to Lawrence. Their commander would give – said he *could* give – no help, & no protection even, to the citizens of Lawrence. His orders were to act, when called upon by Governor Shannon (a poor creature of F. Pierce's) and he could do nothing until said Gov. S. directed Gov. S. positively refused to order them to give any protection to the people of Lawrence. It was well known that, if the Lawrence people *lifted a finger* to resist the U.S. Marshal, or Sheriff Jones, *or the lawless doings of their infamous posse* (for said *posse* was transferred from U.S. Marshall to the Territorial Sheriff, as found convenient) the Governor would *then* order the U.S. troops to sustain the U.S. Marshal. Such was the scheme ('tis useless to apply *epithets* to such conduct) concocted at Washington, emanating from such Northern men as Caleb Cushing, Stephen A. Douglas, and Franklin Pierce, and readily accepted by the desperate & unprincipled Southerners, whose leaders in the bloody work are Atchison and Stringfellow of Missouri, Judge Lecompte, & others.

The Committee of the House of Representatives Messrs. Howard, Sherman & Oliver – have been in Kanzas, perhaps two months, collecting evidence as to the election of Gen. Whitfield, returned to Congress as Delegate from Kanzas, and well known to have been *elected* by hordes of men from Missouri, going over into Kanzas, at the time of the election, and out-voting the regular inhabitants, – driving away the citizens, taking possession of the polls, &c. – This Comtee has collected a vast mass of tesimony, & transmitted it to Washington, and it will be published, – but all too late to effect anything, I fear. Should the H. of Representatives take any effective step, (and I have not the least belief that they will), the Senate is utterly pro-slavery, and would refuse to co-operate; and, if otherwise, Pierce would of course veto anything that displeased the Slaveholder, the most that the House will do, I presume, is to reject Whitfield, & order a new election, – a barren triumph, under the circumstances; for the territory being now utterly subjugated, and the avenues to Missouri voters everywhere opened, he would be immediately re-elected. The triumph of the Slave Power in Kanzas is complete. How long at last, is yet in the future. The Committee have been insulted, browbeaten, threatened in every way by the Ruffians.

Meanwhile, comes the case of Charles Sumner, in the United States Senate[1].

---

1. This was the attack on Charles Sumner by the southerner, Preston Brooks, in the Senate. Sumner, the Senator from Massachusetts and a spokesman for extreme Northern and anti-slavery interests had just spoken in the senate on "the crime against

You will have read all about it long before this reaches you, and I will not attempt any particulars. I am happy to inform you that he is recovering, though very slowly. Three weeks have now elapsed, and he has not yet been allowed, by his physicians to leave his room. He has had a very narrow escape with his life. *This is certain;* though the administrations prints have, many of them, pretended to believe that he was not seriously hurt. They know they lied.

No two men could have behaved better in the circumstances than the two Massachusetts Senators have behaved. And it is most pleasant & encouraging to see how extensively they are sustained and thanked at home & through the Northern States. The Northern feeling is more than ever aroused, and the North is coming, by slow degrees, to the point of definite action. Thousands are aroused, who never were before. Men who have been very much opposed to Mess. Sumner & Wilson, now speak of them in terms of respect & even admiration.

We are now vigorously circulating a new petition for dissolution of the Union. Our people, strange to say, have not got ready for this point yet; – at least, their prominent & so-called 'leading' men have not. But the mass of the people are far ahead of them. The seeds of truth are now rapidly germinating in a soil fast warming – and something great & good will, I think, burst into sight & life ere long.

As one indication, in the political world, of the coming Event, look at the fact that, at the great Democratic Presidential Nominating Convention, (which met at Cincinnati last week), *Franklin Pierce,* who has laboured like a dog, & prostituted all the powers of the Government for 2 years past, to get the nomination for himself, was *rejected – cast aside – pushed out of the way;* – Stephen A. Douglas who has been manoeuvring and labouring for himself in the most desperate manner – the author & mover of the whole Kanzas-Nebraska Fraud, – fared no better, – he also was pushed aside, and James Buchanan of Pennsylvania (late minister to England) has *received the nomination!*

Buchanan is as servile as either of the others, and his administration (if elected) will be as corrupt as F. Pierce's has been, every whit; but he has not been mixed up with the villainies of the last 2 or 3 years set on foot by Cushing, Douglas, & Pierce, and so they are dropped and he selected. Oh! what gnashing of teeth on the part of Douglas & Pierce! and they cant either of them enjoy *each other's* sympathy even; for they both know that the other has been doing all in his power to supplant him.

Our people are now going through another mad whirl of political excitement in electing a President. John McLean of Ohio will probably be the Candidate of the Republican party. He will be taken as most *available,* but is not a man that an honest abolitionist can honestly vote for. His decisions, on the U.S. Supreme Bench, have been uniformly of a pro-slavery type, and his admini-

---

Kansas", in which he denounced the Kansas – Nebraska Bill and attacked several leading politicians, including the absent Senator from South Carolina, Andrew P. Butler. A few days later Sumner was violently assaulted in the Senate by Butler's nephew, Representative Preston S. Brooks – an attack which heightened tension considerably both in the North and the South.

stration would be one of compromises, and fawning to the South; Col. Fremont stands a good chance of the nomination, and is a cleaner man; still I think McLean will get it. The nomination is to be made in a Convention at Philadelphia, the 17th instant.

But I must stop, dear Mr. Webb, assuring you that I am

Most truly yours

Samuel May Jr.

MS.B.1.6. vol. 6 The May Papers [372]
No. 34 Samuel May to S.A. Steinthal

Leicester (Massachusetts), June 23/56.

Dear Mr. Steinthal;

...You will see that the Democratic National Convention threw aside Franklin Pierce, as you anticipated, in making their nomination for the next Presidency; & that they took James Buchanan, as you did not anticipate, – but as I predicted, in some letters to an English correspondent, 2 or 3 months since. Pierce's administration has been so utterly contemptible and has so outraged every decent man in its reckless disregard of honour, faith, justice, & right, that it would have been madness to set him up. Douglas, too, is so notorious in his villainies, that it would have been no less mad & foolish to take him. The field, or "course", was then fairly open to Buchanan, a facile man, cautious, and known to be ready for easy moulding to the will of the Slave holders, but who has not yet committed any great, glaring act of National fraud to prejudice the Northern mind against him. To be sure, he has planted himself full upon the vilest platform that even the American democratic party ever raised, & said it met his most cordial approbation; but the Northern democrats argue that this is *a thing of course* & to be reduced to practice only if absolutely *necessary*. So Buchanan is taken, although, I apprehend, a very indifferent statesman, and a very inferior man. Virginia had agreed with Pennsylvania that he should be the man. This was, to Pierce, the unkindest cut of all; for to none has he been so obsequious as to Virginia. Ever may such reward attend such traitors – Millard Fillmore has just landed on our shores again, adding another heartless and selfish tool of the Slave Power to the number here already. He is the candidate of the pro-slavery Know-Nothings, and will have (I fear) a considerable vote, although much behind the others. Col. John C. Fremont is the candidate of the National Republicans, in which the anti-slavery Know-Nothings (or "North-Americans") have concurred. This is a very fair nomination – I expect that Judge McLean of Ohio would get it, which would have been the ruin of the party. Now they are on the advance; they tie themselves to no old and committed conservative. They take a man, new, vigorous, with a principle (as he avers) of opposition to slavery, whose life has been adventurous, daring, & successful, with an indomitable spirit, and without personal enemies. He may be considered the Pioneer of the Way to California! – and this is a great glory with our people! He may disappoint and cheat his friends; as Pres. of this proslavery Union, he must trim & compromise, either according to his nature or against his nature. Such are the 3 candidates – among whom Buchanan's chances are decidedly the best, and he will – I fear and expect – be elected. Yet I dont know why I should *fear* it; great as the shame and the degradation would be, it would be a part of the humiliation thro' which this land must go, – a part of the heavy atonement, she must make for her numberless sins, for her terrible transgressions against God & man – an atonement she must make, a penalty she must pay, a discipline she must undergo, before her sight & sense, her heart & conscience, will be so purged & cleaned that she can build up the temple of Freedom. Through this discipline the land is now going, – with many pains & throes, & must reluctantly, but stern necessity drives her on. You have seen the accounts of the foray into Kanzas of the ruffians & tools of the Slave power – of their burning, robberies, & murders; – of the base course of Prs. Pierce in countenancing & allowing these things; and of the conquered condition of that territory. I am happy to be able to say that the spirit of the Free State men is not yet wholly subdued, and that there is a widely-spreading & already very great sympathy with them, throughout the Northern States. Large companies of men are going to their aid, and large subscriptions of money are already made. I cannot go into particulars; – of the difficult escape of Ex. Gov. Reeder from villains thirsting for his blood, of the imprisonment of Gov. Robinson & six or seven other leading Free State men, of the attack upon Lawrence, the blowing up of the new (stone) hotel, & the destruction of 2 printing offices with all their types, presses, & apparatus, & of a multitude of equally infamous details, you will have seen accounts in the anti-Slavery papers. If my envelope allows it, I propose sending you an authentic account of the "sack of Lawrence", written to Dr. Webb, the secretary of the N. Engl.[d] Emigrant Aid Co., & published in the Boston *Atlas*, one of the best papers of the city, formerly (and for 20 years at least) the leading Whig paper of the State, but which is now fully & thoroughly committed to the National Republican movement, & to the nomination of Fremont. – I have not yet mentioned Charles Sumner. You can hardly believe what a revolution there has been, in the minds of multitudes at the North, in his favour. His brave and powerful speech, his dignified & manly course under insult & cowardly attempts at assasination, his perilled life, his unconquered spirit, have all endeared him greatly to his old friends, and created for him a host of new ones. Massachusetts is feeling very proud of her two Senators now. *Wilson*, in his way, has been consistent, manly, and bold, speaking plainly, & evidently prepared to act. His refusal to fight a duel with that miserable Brooks, the ground of his refusal, & his proclaimed purpose to defend himself from all assaults, have met with almost universal approval at the North. The struggle for the expulsion of Brooks from the house is soon to come on. As it requires a two-thirds vote, it will fail; but a majority may inflict some penalties, if they choose. We shall see what stuff they are made of – & whether they tamely submit to the insult & disgrace of the presence of Brooks, & of the Murderer Herbert.

I am happy to say that Mr. Sumner is recovering though it is very slowly. I fear that it may yet be many months, before his brain can recover its natural & healthy action; the last exertion, at present, fatigues him, & causes severe pains in the head.

The Anti-Slavery papers will also inform you of *our* saying & doings; of our Annual Meeting in N.Y., and N. England A.S. Convention (a very interesting gathering & discussion), & of the Reception given to Parker Pillsbury. There was universal pleasure in seeing our good friend P again and to find him in better health, apparently, than we had anticipated. He has resumed his labours with us; – cautiously, at first, till we & he know what he can bear. His visit to your country has been of manifest advantage to him, and the connexions & friendships he formed there will be to him a never ceasing source of satisfaction & pleasure....

Yours ever S. May Jr.

MS.B.1.6. vol. 6 The May Papers [373]
No. 40 Samuel May to R.D. Webb

Boston, October 5, 1856.

Dear Mr. Webb,

...In 4 weeks from tomorrow will come the Presidential Election. The nation is completely absorbed by it. It is very generally conceded now that nothing can prevent Col. Fremont's election but a coalition between the Democrats & Know Nothing parties, hitherto open and bitter enemies to each other – a coalition between the Catholic and the foes of the Catholic, between the foreigner & those who hate him & have created a great party in order to crush him. Such a coalition seems impossible. But it is being attempted now; and either Mr. Buchanan or Mr. Fillmore will be called on to withdraw, in order that slavery may not be baulked of its triumph. – There are, alas!, only too many signs that, if Col. Fremont succeeds, his administration will be one of proslavery compromises, a continual mortification, sorrow, & reproach to those *antislavery* people who have toiled so hard, & stretched their consciences so far, to secure his elevation. – American Politics is a most deceitful & desperately wicked game. *Vide*, N.P. Bank's speech to the New York Merchants. Mr. B. is speaker of the Natl. Ho. of Representatives, one of the most important & influential posts in the Government. You will observe he says that if Col. Fremont is elected, the question of Freedom or Slavery will no longer agitate the land, – but it will be *the Pacific Rail Road (!!!)* and the trade of the Pacific Ocean! Alas for him. He is deceiving somebody most grossly. We shall soon see who.

I am, dear Mr. Webb, most sincerely yours

Samuel May, Jr.

MS.B.1.6. vol. 14 May-Estlin Correspondence [374]
No. 79 Samuel May to Mary Estlin

Boston, March 24, 1857.

Dear Miss Estlin,

...The Antislavery cause is destined never to want abundant cause of agitation. We have recently had a decision of our United States Supreme Court (full bench of nine judges) which, if possible, transcends all the other frauds, cruelties, and intiquities which the Slave Power of these

United States has heaped upon its degraded and too patient victims. I refer to the decision in the Dred Scott case, of which you will see, I presume, a history in some of the papers which come under your eye, and on which I will not therefore enlarge. Scott was a Missouri slave, & was, years ago, taken by his *owner*, who was a U.S. military officer, to a U.S. fort situated in free territory, & there kept many years – where he married & had children. By all former decisions & rulings, Scott was made free by *being taken by his master* into free territory. But he was taken back into Missouri, and as might makes right with many men, he was again claimed as property. He brought a suit for his freedom in Missouri – The decision was against him. He appealed to the U.S. Supreme Court; and they, in their might, magnanimity, democracy, and justice, declare that the said Scott is a slave – that being a slave, he cannot sue or appear in a U.S. Court – that no slave or descendant of a slave, or man with African blood, is or can be a Citizen of the United States – that the colored man '*has no rights which the white man is bound to respect'* – the very language of the Court!! (just Heaven, where are thy lightnings!) By this decision, the whole African race in this country, with all their descendants, however commingled with Saxon, Spanish, French, or Indian blood, is given over to the unliscensed, irresponsible dominion and powers of the 'white' race – the larger proportion of whom in the Southern & Southwestern States are the vilest, lowest, of the species. The effect of the decision upon our Northern people remains to be seen. I am not very sanguine of the result. Our people have become so heart-hardened, so callous, so demoralized by their long connexion with slavery; and what is as bad as to its immediate effects upon freedom, they have been so deceived by their own northern political leaders, even by such as chiefly professed & promised to guide them into the contest with slavery, as to have lost to a great extent courage and hope for further resistance to the compact, and cunning forces of slavery. – *We* have long seen that there is *no remedy*, save in entire separation of ourselves from our corrupting and fatal connexion with the slave-holding states; but the people are stupidly slow to get their eyes open to the same. You will perceive that Rev. S.J. May, of Syracuse, N.Y., who laboured so hard for the Republican party and for the election of Col. Fremont, now says that he 'is glad' the Republican party *did not succeed*, for that they are not prepared to go into power with any useful results, their own standards having become so lowered and their objects so be-littled. Nevertheless, the Dred Scott decision will have a very great effect upon the country, and will rapidly hasten the downfall of this false republic. The republic began in a most dishonourable bargain with dealers in human flesh. As a very few foresaw, it was not only a dishonourable but a most disastrous bargain. It has proved *destructive* to the great principles and noble ideas which many of our fathers supposed were firmly grafted into our national system. Our alliance with the 'sum of all villanies' has crippled & made cowards of the best of our people, & villains of the the rest. There is no possible chance of the salvation of either of them, save the cutting loose from the corruption with which they now are linked in. Some – indeed many – are seeing this to be true. God speed the day when American may have a genuine Republic, free from all connexion & taint of slavery....

Affectionately your friend,

Samuel May, Jr.

Anti-Slavery Office
Philada.
Apl. 19th [1857]

My dear friend R. D. Webb,

...I like the *Advocate* however, & I hope you will keep on without any abatement of heart or hope in its publication. It serves to bind together the friends of the cause on both sides of the water; it helps to preserve the unity of our movement. It is one of the instrumentalities – albeit an unpretending one – which is now successfully at work for the overthrow of slavery. I say successfully, for the indications of our final [triumph?] are beginning to manifest themselves even to our opponents. The event is looking up visibly in the distance, and we are moving toward it every day with a steady & undeviating step. On every hand there are evidences of our progress. At Washington the slaveholders find that the tables are beginning to be turned upon them. Instead of having *everything* their own way they have thus far during this session of Congress had *nothing* their own way. The proslavery lobby which had been ridden so successfully in all previous political races, proves now to have had barely sufficient strength to carry Mr. Buchanan [to] win the Presidency. The wind-broken man has since been hardly able to stand on *his* legs, and it is quite evident that he will never be able to win another Presidential Seat. The Advocates of slavery are a minority in the House and are not overstrong in the Senate. Moral agitation kept up by the abolitionists is revolutionary, politically & religiously the public sentiment of the Free States, and is now making itself felt on the other side of the border. Missouri bids fair to be a Free State and today Delaware. There is a hopeful state of feeling in Kentucky, and the people of Western Texas talk of organising themselves into a separate commonwealth, & coming into the Union as a Free State. The abolition of freedom in Russia is exciting quite a sensation in this country, & cant fail to be productive of good results. The same is true of Emancipation in the Danish colonies. If now, the rumour which has just reached us but which seems too good to be true, should be well founded, that the Spanish Government has taken steps for the abolition of slavery in Cuba, what a glorious consummation it would be! It would bring to a sudden end the infamous slave trade & give the *coup-de-grace* to the whole American system. If your new ministry had the power & the will to bring any influence to bear on the Spanish Government sufficient to secure the abolition of slavery in Cuba, they would render a service to the world the value of which no human mind could compute, & whose lustre would invest their names with imperishable glory....

Yours ever truly,

J. M. McKim.

Boston,
21 Cornhill,
January 25, 1858.

Dear Mr. Webb,

...Kanzas affairs are in a state of extraordinary complication, and as the Administration has no wish to disentangle the web, and does not dare to cut through the knot, and give liberty to that much-abused territory, there seems little prospect that justice will be done or the popular vote (which went by an immense majority in favour of making it a free State) regarded & carried out. The latest telegraphic report – I cant write *telegram* yet – is that the President of the Kanzas ('Bogies.') Senate has set aside the votes given on the 4th January (when the people gave a vote of 10,000 majority for a free state) as irregular, illegal, & therefore *void*. Thus giving the Territory & the incipient State into the hands of the Border Ruffian Pro-Slavery Democracy; – as clear a case of usurpation, of despotic rule, of tyrannical trampling on the popular will & Sovreignty, as ever existed. President Buchanan is running himself down and out, more rapidly than any President the country has seen. His measures have distracted the counsels of his own supporters. He has promised opposite things to opposite parties, and his knavery must ere long be plainly visible to the sight of all....

I am, as ever, yours,

Samuel May, Jr.

MS.B.1.6. vol. 15 Additional Letters to Samuel May Jr. [377]

Dublin 26th Feb. 1858.

Dear Mr. May,

...As to the Standard I know this that for years past, since Oliver Johnson[1] & Quincy have had to do with it, it has been an infinitely better paper than it was in Mr. Grays dark days of despair – then it was decidedly dry & heavy. Latterly it has been a spirited & an admirable paper. I hope in the changes which are taking place this character may not leave it.

As to Mrs. Chapman I do not think she would make a popular paper. She flies too high, and revels in allusion, quotations, parenthesis, & involution which drive common place readers to despair. I am fond of good, clear, plain English and dont relish Carlylism or Emersonism or transcendentalism generally. The leaders in the Standard of late years I regard with admiration both for matter and manner.

As to this move about the Bazaar I have not met with a single person who regards it otherwise than with apprehension. Unless those who live in their

1. Oliver Johnson (1809-1889), an original member of the N.E.A.S.S., edited various anti-slavery papers, including for a time the *Liberator* and the *National Anti-Slavery Standard.* He was the author of *William Lloyd Garrison and his times*, Boston, 1880, a useful study of the Boston anti-slavery movement.

country & have had the chief burden of anti slavery for years past are mistaken in their estimate of those with whom they have had to do, Mrs. Chapman is quite astray in her estimate of the money that is likely to be got here. As far as I know very few hand out the ready money – or are likely to do so.... The best gifts come from Scotland – the fruit of Mrs. Wigham Seniors direct begging. She begged as few could or would beg for the cause – but the money could not be had as goods wd. be – either as direct gifts or at a greatly reduced price. I know how much rubbish was collected – how much was wasted in freight & in duty how shocking & lamentable the loss of time & health & effort to raise the Bazaar money. So much so that probably less money got with less pain might do more real good. Still I fear the falling off in receipts will be very great. Of course those who have hitherto given money – or goods bought with their money will give no less – perhaps more in future – and that will be clear cash in hand. But if the Bazaar contributions be no longer collected, the dropping off of interest connected with such offerings will be a great loss to the cause, so far as anything we landed here can help you...

When we bring your dollars down to pounds sterling it has always been a subject of amazement to me that the whole United States & Great Britain can contribute at the outside no more than £1200 to this great cause by all the efforts of the mangers of the Boston Bazaar. Of all the British workers those who do the most are the Wigham family – that is Mr. & Miss Wigham in Edinburgh & Mrs. Edmondson in Dublin. Miss Estlin gives money & advice, Miss Waring (my sister in law) gives largely of her means – but the Wighams are real workers.....

Since these hard times have come upon you Miss Estlin has sounded me about giving up the Advocate and sending the money to your treasury. I have told her as I have always done that the matter was in her own hands & that I had no will in the matter except as she saw best. Miss Wigham has had correspondence with her on the subject. It is her opinion that the Advocate does great good – that it is liked in Edinburgh – that giving it up would be a confession of defeat, especially in connection with a giving up of the Bazaar at the same time.... Miss Estlin has little opportunity of knowing what the Advocate does where it chiefly circulates – She is told it is little read by those who take it for the sake of doing something & she concludes that it is so everywhere I have as little means of judging as she has & my opinion is of no value. I never recommended its establishment & I only took the matter up at Mr. Estlin's earnest request, – & have continued it sometimes at the cost of a good deal of personal inconvenience, which I only mention to indicate that I was disinterested in the affair. I cheerfully did & do whatever I can....

Ever yours affectionately,

Richd D. Webb.

MS.B.1.6. vol. 6 The May Papers [378]
No. 88 Samuel May to R.D. Webb

Boston, 21 Cornhill, March 30/58.

Dear friend Webb,

I feel that I ought not to lose any time in communicating to you the mind of our Executive Committee on the subject in your last letter. In compliance with your request I send to them in full what you said about the *Advocate*. The result of the matter (in a full meeting) I have stated, as you will find, on the other sheets. I need not add my private assurance that the feeling as expressed was cordial & hearty — and it was unanimous. It would be a real grief to some of us to have the *Advocate* disappear and we *know* with the assurance of those who believe in the operation of great and unchanging laws, that the *very existence and presence and regular utterance* of an agency or instrumentality against a flagrant wrong must have a powerful influence to check the base, to awe the evil disposed, and by bringing their evil deed to the light to shame them before the people. We are not deceiving ourselves into thinking that the *Advocate* is a widely-known and an acknowledged power. We know better than that. Its power never will be *acknowledged*, even to the extent that it is felt; and it will be sneered at by many who really dread it. No matter for that... In our cause, of all others, we cannot afford to dispense with any means of getting this truth before even a *limited* audience. No one can calculate how fast or how widely a great truth will spread, although at first told to but two or three. — This is the entire secret of the progress of the AntiSlavery Cause in this Country. It was indeed but as a grain of mustard seed. It now moves the entire mass....It is like a terrible Doom or Destiny hovering over Presidents and Administrations, and ever will be, until Justice takes the place of all Injustice, and this monster Wrong is righted....

As to the *Bazaar*, so far as Mrs. Chapman and her sisters are concerned it is no more. They will do no more for it. Such is my clear conviction. But I am not prepared to take it therefore for granted that it *is* no more. I feel that it would be wrong for the rest of us to abandon it, *simply because* Mrs. Chapman can do no more for it....I *do not know of a single person*, amongst all our friends, who approves of her course, in undertaking to determine and decide this important question herself, and without any consultation with any of the ladies of the Committee, or with any friends of the cause, so far as I can ascertain....I am perfectly sure she meant no slight or disrespect. I doubt not she saw so clearly (or thought she saw) that the Bazaar had done all its work, and would no longer help but under our enterprise, that she is perfectly justified in her conclusions, *so far as her own action is concerned.*

But she should have remembered there were some 30 other ladies, not one of whom perhaps saw the matter as she did — certainly the vast majority of whom did not, and it was due to them, on every ground and by every consideration, to have had the whole case fully & fairly laid before them, and their opinions & their judgment taken, before any decision was made.

I therefore think that it is not to be taken for granted that the Bazaar is dead, *because* Mrs. Chapman says it is. I think it very probably (this is between us) that there may be before long a meeting of ladies and others *to consult and agree* what is best to be done. I cannot say I think it likely that they will decide to go on with the Annual Bazaar. But they may do so. I am sure, this valuable instrumentality ought not to be abandoned suddenly or lightly. Its value to the cause — 1. pecuniarily — 2. morally & socially — has been very great. I firmly believe its power & value have not gone. I know that, to take away Mrs. Chapman and her sisters, would be like cutting off its right arm. But the maimed and mutilated body might yet be instinct with life, and do much with its remaining limbs, while its *will* and *spirit* would be as good as ever. I ask myself, *why should it die?* Mrs. C. has some great plans to supercede, & wholly eclipse, the Bazaar. But what it is she does not tell us,— or gives such indistinct and uncertain glimpses, as are of little satisfaction....

Samuel May Jr. Secy.
pro. tem.

MS.A.9.2. vol. 29 1857-1859 The Weston Papers [379]
No. 54 R.D. Webb to ?

Dublin, March 31, 1858.

My dear Friend,

...About the cause you know how the Bazaar is doomed & the reasons for the sentence. They are many and conclusive. But it took us some time to take them in and the intelligence fell like a bombshell into our little camp. With very few exceptions which we only heard afterwards, as far as I can find, it is feared that very little will be had in cash compared at least to the estimated value of the goods that we annually collected. I know all about the charges & clippings of all kinds to which the proceeds were liable – and how much there was that did not sell, and I think that less money would be more valuable if it cost less in valuable time & strength that might be so much better expended/on behalf of the cause. However you need not be troubled with this talk. I hope you got the last Advocate which will tell you all we thought on the subject and how resigned & dutiful we are. Indeed jokes apart, it is well that the little handful of workers in this side are so fully persuaded of the superior wisdom & better means of judging possessed by our friends in Boston.

As to politics you know that our Derby ministry owes its existence to the unpopular deference of that unprincipled Lord Palmerston towards Louis Napoleon – & that the general sentiment here is that your illustrious & high minded sovreign has played a foolish game. Everybody thinks that [Orsini?] gave him the best chance he ever had of strengthening his position & that he has made the worst possible use of it....

MS incomplete.

MS.B.1.6. vol. 15 Additional Letters to Samuel May Jr. [380]

Dublin 16/April 1858.

My dear friend May,

I have but a few minutes to say that your last letter grieved me very much. You told us that Mrs. Chapman had decreed the end of the Bazaar. You now say that this conclusion is by no means approved of & was come to without the advice & consent of the rest of the committee. We had the intelligence from Mrs. Chapman in such a multitude of letters that the only thing we could do was to do the best we could by inviting contributions for

Philadelphia that they might not go to Rochester, & meaning to send whatever money we could gather to Boston. The feeling against the giving up the Bazaar was almost universal on this side. But I greatly fear it will be very difficult to mend all the mischief that has been done & to bring round the contributions to their former amount... I do not think Mrs. Chapman would have thought anyone else entitled to act in this highhanded way....

Yours ever affectionately,

Rich[d]. D. Webb.

MS.B.1.6. vol. 7 1858-1859 The May Papers [381]
No. 1 Samuel May to R.D. Webb

Leicester, Massachusetts, June 6 1858.

Dear friend Webb,

...Our *cause is alive* you may be sure of that, and likely to be, while such galvanic shocks are given to the people as are now being administered by Buchanan's government, by the American Tract Society, and by the efforts of Southern Statesmen to give the New African Slave Trade the protection and aid of this Government and Country. A great deal of windy talk has been recently uttered at Washington and elsewhere, on the subject of the search and visitation of American vessels by British armed cruisers. The national feeling on this subject is invoked, and cunningly used by the Slave trading gentry, to further their ends. But I trust that Great Britain will not be in the least deterred from prosecuting her purpose of breaking up the Slave Trade. Let her hold the United States firmly to their agreement to participate in the work – let the eyes of the whole world be turned upon the spectacle, – if it must be so – of England engaged in suppressing the Traffic in Slaves, and the American *Republic* in upholding & protecting it and *God defend the Right*, say I. I have no love of country, if my country deliberately upholds villainy, piracy, and all infernalism. But I believe it will not follow Buchanan in this last villainy.

Love to you all,

Saml. May Jr.

MS.B.1.6. vol. 7 The May Papers [382]
No. 18 Samuel May to ?

n.d. 1850s?

...I have not left myself room or time to speak as I would wish on the important question at issue – if I may say it is still at issue – between your country and ours; viz[t] the *African Slave Trade*, and the Right to Visit to vessels on the high seas to determine whether they are, or are not, engaged in that Traffic. *What is to be the position & course of Great Britain on this momentous subject?* Is the question which we are anxiously asking. Too suddenly your Government seems to have yielded the Right of Visit & Search, at the blustering, bullying demands of the New Orleans fillibusters, as your *Saturday Review* well says. It may be, that, according to principles of International law, as your Crown Advisers say, there is no legal right inhering in any nation to visit the ships of another power. But does it follow from this that they may visit no vessel, which chooses to hoist the flag of another power? Of course not, for, if such were the fact, Great Britain would be utterly powerless to prevent her own subjects and her own ships from engaging in the African Slave Trade. Yet now she is to do this on the ground now taken by your government upon the advice of the Crown layers? Suppose that ships should again be built by British capital, manned by British seamen, and sail from your ports, ostensibly in a lawful business, but bye & bye at some Cuban, or other American port refit as slavery, and with the same owners, and the same (or a different) crew, proceed to the coast of Africa and fill their holds with their live African cargoes again, as in those paling days of the last century. Proceedings on their return voyage to Cuba, – or Texas, – or the Mississippi river, they meet a British Man of War; of course they have provided themselves with a complete and handsome set of American colours, and they instantly, at the first gun from the Man of War, hoist them conspicuously. Surely there is nothing improbable, nor likely to happen, in this supposition. What follows? Why – the British Man of War hauls off, – does he not? He must, according to the advice of your crown lawyers, and the position of your present ministry, if we rightly understand it here. The Man of War is not to be allowed to overhaul that slave-ship, nor send a single man to board her, because the American flag floats over her. Such a doctrine is suicidal; it opens the whole ocean to pirates and marauders of the worst description, and it cannot stand for an instant in the eye of reason of right or common sense. If it is law, it must be superseded, and better law be found or made. Such will be the Universal cry, – not perhaps, however, until the sea is swarming again with buccaneers and redrovers, and none can sail the seas with safety, and all commerce is reduced to running the gauntlet of pirate-crews. To be sure we are told that your government proposes to appeal to the Government of the United States not to allow their flag to be disgraced by being made cover for the African Slave Trade, – I could hope, for England's honour, that she would stoop to no such appeal, will the American government pay any regard to such an appeal, when it has no impulse itself to protect its flag from this shame? Or indeed can any deeper disgrace be added to that flag, which is even now the symbol of the bondage of four millions of human beings of all colours & ages, & both sexes, and the pledge that all who are united under it will join at any moment to trample to death any effort of those slaves to obtain their 'inalienable rights', and to reduce them again to slavery and chains. If such is the position of the English Government, Heaven grant it may soon be superseded by a ministry which better understands the honour of the Empire, the heart of the Sovreign, and the will and principles of your People. If Britain is pledged to anything, before God & the Nations, it is to the suppression of the African Slave Trade on the High Seas. In this work she was nobly contended – has given her strength and her wealth, – and has met with glorious success. Let her then mark the men, in Parliament, or in Ministerial places, or in Editorial chairs, who would betray her honour and sell out her birth-right for a contemptible mess of pottage. We look anxiously, but calmly, for what Great Britain shall do. Farewell for the present. I have taxed your time enough.

Affly. yours.

S. May Jr.

Dublin June 25, 1858.

My dear Mr. May,

...You see the Right of visit & the Right of Search are both abandoned on a legal opinion of the Crown Advisers – so that the American pirates & slavers have full fling. A man has only to haul up the Stars & Stripes & he may do as he pleases. Read what the Saturday [Review?] says in the next *Advocate*. It is very good. I am confident in the good faith of our government. I have none whatever in yours. The character of the American government is rapidly making republicanism stink in the nostrils of the English people. As far as I know nobody pleads for republicanism unless he is also ready to cover up or apologise for slavery. As you will see by the Advocate a proslavery Journal has really been started in London. I am pulling off one copy to send you by this post. The rest will not go till next week. Will you please forward the letters for me & add a line to P. Pillsbury to the effect that nothing of his for the *Advocate* was ever omitted but in one case, where it came to hand too late. I am always rejoiced to get contributions but of course must use my judgment as to their actual fitness – you know he is touchy....

Yours ever truly,

Rich[d] D. Webb.

MS.B.1.6. vol. 15 Additional Letters to Samuel May Jr. [384]

Dublin 9 of October 1858.

My dear Friend,

...For some time past I have felt as the old Friends used to say on a low plane about Anti Slavery matters. The charge about the Fair threw cold water on any efforts we had been used to make here – and people act so much from habit that when they are put out, it is hard to get them into the same disposition for any effort again. Beside I have felt small in myself. Mrs. Chapman dont understand England or English efforts & has been finding fault with the Advocate (very gently) for countenancing Mr. Matthews. It seems to me as if she wants one to make brick without straw. We can only work with the tools we have. Very few are so high minded as she is, & as we will hav[e] nothing to do with none but angels, I can see them and may as well sit down. The almost total want of sympathy or cooperation are difficult to *[work?] & to hope through....*

Ever yours affectionately,

Rich[d] D. Webb.

MS.B.1.6. vol. 7 The May Papers [385]
No. 18-19 Samuel May to R.D. Webb

Leicester, Massachusetts, No. 7. 1858.

Dear friend Webb,

...I do not share in your feeling that the 'cause seems flat', amongst us here; or I should not, at least, so describe the state of things which you advert to. I own there is not, at present, that excitement, or stir, which has sometimes marked the cause and its progress. There are reasons for this, and such reasons as to comfort us, and encourage us greatly. *The South is dismayed* at least, – palpably so, and with great reason. It ventured everything on a few desperate throws, – the repeal of the Missouri Compromise, and the Dred Scott decision especially, – and hoped by hold playing, and a definite, cut-throat attitude, to carry its point. It selected a crafty, popular old Northern politician to lead its forces, and he promised them success, and the thorough routing and annihilation of their enemies.... He has met, face to face, in every move he has made, in every position he has taken, and has been himself defeated & humbled in the most ignominious manner; and, what he feels most sorely of all, his own original friends, his own party, and *his own State*, have to a great extent deserted him. The Slave holders were not prepared for this, and now stand aghast. They do not repent, neither do they own their shame and their guilt, but at present they are quiet. Their talk of seizing Cuba, and re-opening the African Slave Trade, is hushed for the present. The North is very generally of the opinion that, by the October and November elections, it has given the South a very powerful dose indeed, and it too is waiting – to see the operation. That seems to be the present position of the parties North & South: they are *antagonist forces*, and the loudest brawler for *Union* cannot deny it, nor make anything else of it. They have long been preparing for a contest. The North has now (to use the language of prizefighters, which I do abominate in that connexion....) the north has now struck the South one of the heaviest blows the latter has ever received, or the former ever roused itself to give. The South is staggered – it plainly reels under the effects. The North is no wise damaged by said blow, but seems wonderfully refreshed – all the better for it. Now they stand – both rather quietly, each looking at the other, and considering what the next step must be....

Truly & aff'ly, your friend

Sam. May, Jr.

MS.A.9.2. vol. 11 (1) 1839 The Weston Papers [386]
No. 33 William P. Powell to M.W. Chapman

123 Field Street Everton
L'pool 21 Jany 1859

UBI LIBERTAS IBI PATRIA

Dear Mrs. Chapman,

...You will have learnt ere this of the safe arrival of our devot[d] colaborers Rev[d] S.J. May and Miss Sarah P. Remond[1]. Mr. May has gone to the Continent – Miss Remond is at present in L'pool, and will lecture tonight at the *Tuckerman's Institute.* Rev. W[m]. H. Channing in the chair.

You seem somewhat pleased with the *crest* which I have adopted as my *motto.* It is a very significant one, and speaks for itself, and for me as well. Indeed Madam I never knew I had a country until I crossed the Atlantic ocean. . . . In old England Liberty is not an empty name, as the American democratic cradle robbers would have us believe – on the contrary it means that. 'In all things that hath beauty, There is nothing to man more comely than Liberty. Give me the liberty *to know, to think, to speak, to argue* and to act freely above all liberties.'

Now as regards myself, what are the facts? I came to this country a poor despised outcast – outlawed American negro – driven from my native country for no 'color of crime' but for the 'crime of color' And here in monarchical England I seek one asylum from the storms of American persecution & negro hate. In this strange country I am regarded as a *man*, and invested with all the rights of a British born subject, without even the *farce* of *naturalization.* Taxation & representation are together alike awarded to every subject who conforms to the provisions of the Reform Law of 1832. 'It matters not whether an African or an Indian sun may have burnt upon him, the moment he sets his foot upon British soil, that the ground which he treads is Holy and consecrated to the genious of Universal Emancipation.' Here I exercise my right as a voter – sit on juries, and am eligible to hold office under the government – municipal or otherwise. Can I say as much in favour of Republican slaveholding America, the land of my birth? ...

I am madam
Yours faithfully,

Wm. P. Powell.

MS.B.1.6. vol. 7 The May Papers [387]
No. 33 Samuel May to R.D. Webb

N.D. (fragment).

I have read the *Advocate* for February with very great pleasure. Please tell me who Mr. Stephenson is, who writes about the *League.* I liked his letter, and heartily wished it were possible to form a stronger and effective A.S. League. You doubtless remember that this was tried, some 15 years ago. I recollect becoming a member of it, and making a small subscription at the time. Mr. Estlin, I think, took some part in its formation; but he had never much faith in its value, or rather in its success. He did not very highly appreciate Geo. Thompson's labours in the cause, – and it was G.T., if I rightly remember, who was mainly active in efforts to form the *League.* I do not doubt that the considerations, which you state, are pretty conclusive

---

1. Sarah Parker Remond was the sister of Charles Lenox Remond. She lectured in Britain in 1859 and 1860, receiving several public addresses. She was again in Britain during the Civil War, finally settling in Florence, where she obtained a medical degree in 1871.

against the probable success of such a measure, at the present time. Yet, I cannot but remember how much A.S. work has been done in G. Britain in that 15 years – what an impulse has been given to the Cause the world over – and I confess to feeling a strong desire that some living association might spring up, to take the place which the B. & F. Society ought to fill, but does not, and never will. A League, or Association, with the Earl of Carlisle at its head, and with both men and women on its committee – yourself, Armistead,[1] Jos. Lupton, the Patons, the Wighams, Prof. Nichol and wife Mary Estlin, Mrs. Stephens, Mrs. Turner, Miss Whitelegge, Philip Carpenter, Steinthal, W.P. Powell, Francis Bishop, – to which add all the orthodox men I *don't* know, who are true to the principle, and a very vigorous committee might be had. Would not E. Matthews lead up a great many of his Baptist brethren? – And I have ommited many – such as Thomas Sturge, & Edward Baines,[2] and F.W. Chesson, & several in Ireland. – These are all, or nearly all, Dissenters, I suppose, excepting *the Earl.* The thing looks to me worth trying. If it did no other good, it would make it needful for many persons to show their colours....

I am, with sincere respect, yours

Saml. May, Jr.

MS.B.1.6. vol. 15 Additional Letters to Samuel May Jr. [388]

Dublin, March 10, 1859.

My dear Mr. May,

...As to your idea of a League it wd. be a charming thing if it could be brought to bear – but I am very sceptical. I will give your list and my opinions of them.

Armistead – I have sent him valuable a.s. books for years & when I ask for them, he writes me letters but forgets to answer my questions respecting them. I have never seen him – but am prejudiced against him on this account. I think he is a somewhat dry quaker & very cautious & timid.

Joseph Lupton – Have never seen him. Believe he is a good fellow – but not active in the cause – & a little 'high & mighty' as a rich man.

The Patons – Excellent but great stayers at home. Andrew not fond of writing. His sister dont write at all.

The Wighams – Mrs. Wigham, Eliza, & her sister in Dublin Mrs. Edmundson all as good as gold. The brothers in Dublin somewhat dry & not active in a.s. matters. Great Maine Law men.

Prof. Nichol – In my opinion very small in our way. The wife is a jewel – but is a good deal swallowed up in him. She is a fine woman – but has little time for anything not immediately connected with the Dr. as she calls him.

1. Wilson Armistead (1819-1865) was a North of England Quaker who took an active interest in the anti-slavery movement, and edited several works dealing with the lives of prominent Negro leaders.

2. Sir Edward Baines (1800-1890), M.P. and journalist, was for many years editor of the *Leeds Mercury* and active and influential in liberal reform movements.

Miss Estlin – She does not like much personal publicity – & looks on the maintenance of the Advocate as her peculiar province.

Mrs. Stephen of Bristol – I hardly know – she is I believe a good woman – but is also a [warm?] wife.

Miss Whitelegge – very good– but wd. be hardly like to help much in council.

Philip Carpenter – You know & I dont. He is I believe a saint in his way. Mr. Robson has a very high opinion of him he is high principled – a hard worker – but greatly swallowed up by conchological pursuits. About 18 months ago he was in Dublin & expressed a wish to see me. I addressed him one day in a meeting & said I was myself. He looked at me with a blank expression, said nothing, turned away, & I saw him no more. My wife was with me at the time.

Mr. Steinthal I have no intercourse with beyond an occasional short note perhaps once a year. He never writes to or from the Advocate, & is I believe greatly absorbed by his engagement as a missionary to the poor. He is a friend to the Am. A.S.S. but beyond this I hear nothing of him. It was in his hands the Philadelphia contributions went astray. I imagine he is not much up to business.

W. P. Powell is a poor man in the employment of others. His heart is excellent – his judgment very small. He once brought his wife and 5 or six children on a visit to me uninvited at a very inconvenient time. The poor woman is a born lady and was greatly distressed by the move of her lord. He has a son a surgeon, very intemperate, & one of the stupidest men I ever met with, in whose social position his father takes great satisfaction.

Francis Bishop – I was informed by Mr. Robson took no part with the abolitionists in America when he was there. This amazed me for I had the highest opinion of him.

E. Matthews has never had in my opinion a warm feeling for the Am. A.S.S., but as he never opposed it that I could hear of, I did my best to keep him in countenance as an a.s. man diffusing useful information. Mrs. Chapman scares him, & meted by her high standard perhaps with justice. But this would be an unfair test for most of us, myself included.

Thomas Sturge is a good rich man, very odd & very generous, whom I have never seen.

Edward Baines patronised & assisted the Leeds Young Men – but when Dr. Pomeroy came he snubbed them & patronised him. You can hardly ever trust any one who lives by an orthodox reputation.

F. W. Chesson is poor, fussy & not his own master. I have never seen him but have always found him friendly in correspondence.

On the whole these are a most incongruous medley in everything except a mutual friendly feeling towards the cause. Except in a few cases, it would be too much to speak of a strong interest. I mentioned the fact that many of them are poor to show that their [?] & circumstances forbid the chance of their being able to do much in the way of personal cooperation. One great advantage as it seems to me in the U.S. over us is that as you earn more easily you spend more freely & are less afraid of the future....

A real working meeting, deliberating, acting League would be delightful – but I see neither the people, the circumstances nor the money that would make such a scheme practicable. In all such efforts in England, very large sums have generally been handed down by a few rich men like Joseph Sturge who were very zealous in the cause they aimed to promote....

Yours ever truly,

Richd. D. Webb.

MS.B.1.6. vol. 15 Additional Letters to Samuel May Jr. [389]

Dublin, May 3, 1859

Dear Mr. May

....As to what Eliza Wigham writes to you about G.T. I do not understand it. She has probably some knowledge that is not acceptable to me. G.T.'s affairs are a puzzle & have been for many years. The worst thing about such difficulties is that it is so impossible for any ordinary efforts to relieve them unless the man can help himself. His recent speeches in behalf of reform I don't understand or sympathise with. He is not in a position to devote time or strength to political contests–unless he is well paid for what he attempts....

Miss Remond writes beside me. She had an interview with Abp. Wately & his family & a group of friends at the Palace today & along talk on a.s. matters. She is really very clever–the most so of all the coloured people I ever met, except Douglass, & is a very much more sensible & thoroughgoing person than he. Except Wendell Phillips I don't think you could have a more effective agent here. She is far less crotchety than Wright or Pillsbury. She has more common sense–& her devotion to the cause & its friends is thorough. We like her very much....

Yours ever truly

Richd. D. Webb

MS.B.1.6. vol. 7 The May Papers [390]
No. 57 R.D. Webb to Samuel May

Dublin, 22 of July, 1859.

Dear Mr. May–

...This peace has not increased Louis Napoleon's prestige.[1] Like you & almost everyone else, I have no faith in him. He is utterly unprincipled & has the Bonapartean selfishness in full measure. But I was full of hope that the Austrians would be expelled from Italy & that the poor Italians would

1. This was the agreement between Louis Napoleon and Franz Joseph at Villafranca which brought to a close the Franco-Austrian war in which France had aided the Italians in their move to drive the Austrians from Italy. Though favouring Italian unification Britain remained constantly suspicious of Louis Napoleon's aims.

have a chance. I have no patience with the insolent way in which the English (& I have heard the Americans) have been in the way of talking of the unfitness of the Italians for Liberty. These nations are apt to forget how many of their advantages are due to their geographical position. I think that amongst the Italians will be found living men as noble as any of their illustrious heroes of former days—what finer men than Manin, Mazzini, Garibaldi, Poevio, & Cavour . . . .

Yours ever affectionately

Rich[d] D. Webb

MS.B.1.6. vol. 7 The May Papers [391]
No. 62 Samuel May to R.D. Webb

Leicester. Mass. Sept. 13/59.

Dear friend Webb;

...I hope something may come of the new A.S. movement in London. I think Chesson will *work*. I fear G.T. will not be able to do much. Was glad to see that the *Reporter* had, at last, got so bold as to publish a speech of W. Phillips....

I see Fred. Douglass is going to England again. He will do mischief, of course. I think he will not have as much to say of the American a.s. society and its members *in public*—he will carefully avoid anything beyond insinuation and implication, at which he is a master; but in private his malice will have full swing, I do not doubt. You will have an eye upon him, unquestionably....

With respect to Mrs. Webb,

Ever truly yrs.

S. May Jr.

MS.B.1.6. vol. 7 The May Papers [392]
No. 73 & 64 Samuel May to R.D. Webb

Leicester, October 31, 1859.

Dear friend Webb;

...The papers doubtless will have told you into what consternation our Slave-holding States here, & especially Virginia, have been recently thrown by a very daring & extraordinary attempt, by a mere handful of men, to seize the United States armory & arsenal at Harper's Ferry, Virginia, on the border adjoining Maryland, with the avowed (and, doubtless, actual) purpose of setting free the slaves, first in that vicinity, & afterwards in a wider territory. Nothing has happened, for a long time, to excite the whole country, indeed, so much. On the night of Saturday, October 15th, a small, armed band of men, 22 in number only, quietly marched into Harper's Ferry, and without a show of resistance, possessed themselves of the Arsenal, & all the

Government workshops there. Setting a guard in that place, they proceeded to visit several neighbouring farms, summoned the slaves to join them who did so, some willingly, the most (it is said) reluctantly,—took the masters prisoners, together with several prominent citizens of Harper's Ferry, & marched them all to the Arsenal. They also obtained complete possession of the whole town, a place of over 1000 inhabitants! and no attempt at organized resistance was made there. They stopped the R.R^d trains (they afterwards confessed that this was a mistake), cut the telegraph wires, & endeavored to prevent the news from immediately spreading. But in vain. On Monday, some companies of Virginia militia, from the neighbouring districts, marched into the place. They accomplished little or nothing save to shoot at some stragglers, a portion of whom were unarmed, but endeavouring to escape. Soon after troops arrived from Baltimore, and a large body of United States Marines from the Navy Yard at Washington. The officers of the latter held a parley with the force in the arsenal, who offered to leave if they could do so with their arms & prisoners, and have a few minutes clear time, when they would release their prisoners in safety, and the troops then might pursue. But these terms were refused, and a violent attack made on the arsenal. Its heavy gates were burst in, and after a brief fight the little party within were overcome, & killed or taken prisoners. One marine only was shot.

The leader of this daring and desperate attempt was an old man, pretty well known here of late years, John Brown[1] of Kanzas. He was for many years a resident in the State of New York, where he reared a very large family. They were all earnest antislavery men; and when the Kanzas question arose, & a large rival emigration of men from the Free & Slave States rushed thither, to determine the question whether it should be a free state or a slave state, old Brown & his sons were among the first to go thither. They settled on good land, but were very soon set upon by the "Border Ruffians" of Missouri, who insulted them, stole from them, and at last killed one of Brown's sons, a fine young man. From that time Brown's whole soul seemed bent on doing what he could against slavery. He organized a company, for protection against the 'ruffians', and he soon made his very name a terror to those brutal men, who fled alarmed when they *heard* of his approach. In one of his expeditions, he drove out a band of these men from the town of Ossawatomie, routing them completely, and has since been known by the name of 'Ossawatomie Brown'. Little had been heard of him recently until this Harper's Ferry affair. In the contest there, two more sons of his were killed, and he himself badly wounded. The trial of the three or four prisoners is now going on. The Virginians are completely panic-stricken, and are hurrying the trial in a most unheard-of way, and will doubtless hurry the prisoners to the speediest execution which the forms of law here allow, and they allow *anything* the slaveholders want, as against their slaves, and all who would set them free. Their real *policy*—as even the most pro-slavery journals of the north, such as the New York *Journal of Commerce*, are telling them—is to

---

1. John Brown (1800-1859), the leader of the famous raid on Harper's Ferry was eulogised by the abolitionists and his scheme had been planned with the foreknowledge and some help of certain of the Massachusetts' anti-slavery leaders, though probably not Garrison. As a consequence, neither this letter, nor subsequent ones give an unprejudiced or accurate account of Brown's career.

treat these men with moderation, at least to spare their lives, and to inflict no greater punishment than imprisonment; but they are too much alarmed & infuriated for this, &, will doubtless have nothing short of their lives. Brown has behaved with the utmost selfpossession and dignity through the entire trial, and the unanimous testimony of all who have seen him from the beginning of the affairs that he has proved himself a man of great capacity, of cool judgment, & of indomitable spirit. Towards his prisoners he was courteous & respectful. To all he proclaimed his purpose to be that of liberating the slave, and he should touch no life or property, save what he deemed absolutely necessary to secure that end. His great mistake was in supposing that the slaves of that section were bold enough to fight for liberty, and ready to fly to arms against their masters; besides the news of his seizure of the arsenal could not possible circulate among them rapidly, and they could not be sure, when they heard of it, that the men were their friends. Had the slaves risen in considerable numbers, and joined Brown as he evidently expected, none can foresee what would have been the issue of the contest—possibly a general servile war would have ensued. For Brown had it not only in his power to distribute among them all the arms & ammunition of the U.S. armoury at that place, but had collected in the neighbourhood a large quantity of weapons, &c. among them, it is said, 1500 spikes or spears, for arming the slaves, not skilled in the use of fire-arms. It would seem that he had long been planning their attack. It was surely a very daring one, in many respects planned & executed with great judgment, & its secrecy well-kept; but it utterly failed, on account of defects obvious enough now, but which he seems to have been deceived about, or to have deceived himself. His plans appear even to have looked to seizing the reins of the United States Government, expelling Buchanan and his pro-Slavery Cabinet, and settling up an AntiSlavery Government! Alas, for his delusion! His object was a noble one; for if ever a resort to physical force and bloody means can be justified, it surely is so in the case of the slaves of this country, & their friends. Slavery is itself a continual state of war, violence, Bloodshed, and cruelty insupportable, and is itself a reason and a justification of any amount or kind of resistance to it, according as one believes in one kind of resistance or another.

What the effect of this daring, but unsuccessful, effort against the Slave Power will be, it is too soon to say. Some Republicans who are alarmed for their political success in the coming Presidential contest, predict all manner of evil. The *Democratic* Party which is now nothing but an appendage to the Slave Powers, and ready for the most servile work, so they get the offices & other pay,—is in high spirits at the affair, believing they can make it the means of saving their party, which they had before quite despaired of. My own opinion is that if the Republicans are such fools as to flinch before the Slaveholders in this matter,—apologise, and disavow all sympathy, & join in the execution of Brown,—they will make themselves despised, & throw away their own victory . . . . For as Thomas Jefferson himself said, Virginian and slave holder as he was. "I tremble for my country when I remember that GOD is just, and that His Justice cannot sleep forever, for one hour of the slave's bondage is frought with more misery than ages of the Oppression which our fathers rose in rebellion to throw off; and, in the contest which must come, God had no attribute which can take sides with the Slaveholder." Let the just issue be made up....

Kindest regards to all yours,

Sam[l] May.

MS.A.9.2. vol. 29 1857-1859 The Weston Papers [393]
No. 76 R.D. Webb to Maria Weston Chapman

Greenfield–Kilgobbin–Co. Dublin
Nov. 10. 1859.

Dear Mrs. Chapman–

...As to our friend Garrison coming to England, you know how I love & honour him & that there is no man I would rather see under my roof. But I doubt whether he is as likely to make an impression on the British public as a much less remarkable man. He is so apt to say whatever he chooses upon every subject (many of them regarded with great distrust by the leaders of public opinion or a majority of them) that I would fear his pulling down with one hand what he built with the other. This is only for yourself. If he comes no one will more rejoice to see him than I will or will be willing to do more to make his stay pleasant and useful to him....

I am ever truly yours

Rich[d] D. Webb

MS.A.9.2. vol. 29 1857-1859 The Weston Papers [394]
No. 79 The Duchess of Argyll[1] *to Maria Weston Chapman*

Nov. 25. 1859
Argyll Lodge
Kensington.

My dear Mrs. Chapman,

...The great experiment of Free Labour in the South, which seems to be so successful in Texas, and elsewhere is very important and encouraging –as to the *feeling* in England you cannot doubt that it is *entirely* with you. There may be sad want of faith as to the possibility of Right being done, here and everywhere.

We have been painfully interested in the Harper's Ferry Affair and are still very imperfectly informed on the subject.

I was very sorry not to see Mrs. Stowe when she was last here.

My uncle Lord Carlisle writes me "Pray tell Mrs. Chapman how entirely I appreciate her letter, but as I feel that I cd. not as a member of the Govt. express myself with complete freedom on the subject, I think it better to refrain fr. writing at all."

---

1. Elizabeth, Duchess of Argyll (1824-1878) was the daughter of the Duchess of Sutherland, and shared her mother's philanthropic interests.

We shall be anxious to hear how our dear Friend Mr. Sumner bears the work, and the excitement at Washington. He is a noble standard-Bearer of a noble cause . . . .

Believe me yours very truly

E. Argyll.

MS.B.1.6 vol. 7 The May Papers [395]
No. 82 Samuel May to R.D. Webb

Boston, Dec. 7. 1859.

Dear friend Webb;

...In my last I gave you a brief account of a very remarkable man —though with the very unimposing name of *John Brown*—who, by a sudden inroad into Virginia with some 17 white and 5 colored men had taken possession of the United States arsenal at Harpers' Ferry, Virginia, had held for some two days possession of it and of the considerable town adjoining, and had sent a conscience-stricken fear throughout the State, and to a great degree through the whole slave-holding South. Every day since his capture, the public interest in him has increased. There has been a genuine outburst of admiration throughout the North of his character, his courage, motives, principles, and his self-sacrifice although very many disapprove of the means he employed. He underwent a wretched mockery of a trial before a Virginia Court, his case prejudiced from the first, and his doom pre-determined, and was condemned to be executed on the 2 of December. He had finally been taken prisoner by *United States troops* upon *United States territory*, having kept all the military force of Virginia at bay, and ought to have been tried in a United States court. But Virginia meanly seized him, after the United States had disarmed him and fettered him, and has now, as our best lawyers declare, "judicially murdered" him, contrary to law as well as to right; our present national administration were only too willing to have it so, having neither spirit nor inclination to resist any demand of a Slaveholding State. And Brown knew, from the first moment, that his fate was sealed. During the six or seven weeks from the time of his capture to his execution, his whole course has been thoroughly manly, brave, and consistent. It was obvious to every one that his composure was not assumed nor forced—that his claim to be activated by a high sense of duty, in his effort to liberate slaves on a large scale, was in strict accordance with his known principles and purposes—that he really felt, as he declared, himself to be called of God to set free the slaves of America, or to be offered up a willing sacrifice in their behalf. Moreover, a tender heart, a kindly feeling towards all around him, an unaffected simplicity to speech and manners have been strikingly conspicuous. His jailer Mr. Avis became warmly attached to him, and has proved his friendship by many considerate and kind acts,—sometimes allowing him the freedom of his own house, unfettered, sure that his confidence was not misplaced. You will see published some of Brown's simple but admirable letters, written from his prison—especially those to his wife and to his old school-master; also accounts of his interviews with various persons, and particularly with slaveholding clergymen, who came to offer him their help in his brief remnant of life.

These, from the first, he showed no respect for; to one he said, "I am willing to treat you as a gentleman but it must be as a *heathen* gentleman." And he said he would rather have some little slave-children, and an old slave mother, go to the place of execution with him, and ask blessings on his head, than all the slaveholding ministers in the States. To one, who offered some argument on behalf of slavery, he said that he knew nothing whatever of Christianity, and needed to learn the A.B.C.s of its first lesson. To the last, he never blenched nor faltered, but died with a perfect, and unquestionably most sincere, trust in God. He has left the lasting memory of a most heroic character. His name will be a watchword and signal for still more devoted and determined efforts against the Slave Power which rules and curses the country; and it shall yet be seen and felt that John Brown's unselfish consecration of his life to the cause of freedom has been the most powerful blow struck for many a long year at that "sum of all villainies"—American slavery.

Very numerous meetings were held throughout the Northern States on the day of his death. The one in this City, which was held in the Tremont Temple, consisted of not less than 3500 persons, crowding the hall in every part, and great numbers going away, unable to gain admittance. It was addressed by Samuel E. Sewell, Esq., who presided, by Rev. J. S. Martin,[1] and Rev. J. F. Clarke,[2] of Boston, Messrs. Griffin and Davis of the State Legislature, and by Mr. Garrison who spoke with great power and effect. You will see a full report in our papers.

In my previous letter to you, about John Brown, I think I alluded to the terror which his name inspired, in Kanzas, in the ranks of the Border Ruffians, and I believe I gave you to understand that he was connected with some very harsh retaliatory acts, wherein the lives of several of these marauders were taken. I have since seen evidence which convinces me that these stories of John Brown are without foundation, and are indeed the malicious charges of men who, both for their personal enmity to him and their base determination of the Free State cause in Kanzas, are unworthy of belief. Indeed it appears that the evidence before the Congressional Kanzas Investigation Committee exonerates Brown entirely on this head, and shows him to have been at a place 18 miles distant at the time of the Commission of the murders alluded to; while it appears that he stands charged with these acts only by some evidence taken before an *ex-parte*, and wholly pro-slavery, committee.... Certain it is that this man has manifested, to the conviction of both enemies and friends, as well as of persons heretofore wholly ignorant of him, some of the very loftiest, noblest and most truly Christian characteristics, which have ever adorned, or which can adorn, our human nature. So widespread has become the popular interest, and even admiration, that the pro-slavery men in various cities of the North are getting up Counter-meetings with a view to "reassure our Southern brethren" that the North means strictly to observe all its obligations to them & to the Union. A meeting of this sort is to come off in this city tomorrow supported almost entirely

---

1. Rev. James Sella Martin was a Negro minister. He visited Britain in 1867 and was present at the Breakfast held in London in honour of Garrison.

2. Rev. James Freeman Clarke (1810-1885), a prominent Boston Unitarian clergyman, was active in social reform.

by men either in the pay of President Buchanan and of the Proslavery Democracy, or who are striving to become so, and wish to commend themselves by their fawning. Their movement is pretty thoroughly & generally understood and is despised, as it deserves to be, by every honest lover of freedom....

Aff'ly yrs:

S. May Jr.

MS.B.1.6. vol. 7 The May Papers [396]
No. 84 Eliza Wigham to Samuel May

5 Gray Street Edinburgh
22.12–59

My dear friend,

...Thou mayst be sure we have been watching with no common interest the history of noble, but mistaken, John Brown. We had believed in the reprieve & were full of hope that some way of escape might yet be found —when on the 16th came the news that his precious life had been taken two weeks before.—His death seems to have caused great excitement everywhere, nothing that has taken the murder of this man whom all must admire, & whose bearing throughout has been worthy of a martyr....

thine affectionately

E. Wigham.

MS.B.1.6. vol. 8 The May Papers [397]
No. 2 Samuel May to R.D. Webb

21, Cornhill, Boston
January 10, 1860.

Dear Webb,

...The John Brown "raid", as the foolish Republicans call it, is taking up this nation by the four corners, and shaking it to its very centre. The agitation is tremendous, but healthy. It is developing the diabolism of Slavery as it never appeared before—or, not least, as it was never seen before by any but the handful of abolitionists. John Brown knew a great deal, but he has worked and builded "better than he knew". All honour to his Example. 'Tis a glorious one, and wonderful to have happened in this land, so dead in its trespasses and sins—its conscience so seared by its long persistence in cruelty and fraud—so drunk with the intoxicating wine of slavery. His death is proving a mighty teacher of what slavery is, and of what the human soul can bear and do....

With sincere & affectionate regard—

S. May Jr.

MS.B.1.6. vol. 15 Additional Letters to Samuel May Jr. [398]

Dublin 29th of May 1860.

Dear Mr. May–

...I am glad Garrison did not come with H. C. Wright who though I doubt not an honest upright man–is by no means in good odour outside of a very small circle. His want of manner, tact & taste are all against him & would be injurious to any one in whose company he might come. Personally I have nothing but kindness & good feeling towards Wright–but I cannot shut my eyes to the facts. Such men as Wright & Pillsbury who cannot conform to the company they meet with–who are in no sense men of the world, & who learn nothing here, do not do as missionaries to the fastidious, censorious & not too zealous or sympathizing English. These people must be won & not repelled. I know of no man I would so like to see come over with Garrison as yourself, unless it were Wendell Phillips. If I were speaking behind your back I would say I do not know which is to be preferred on public grounds. Speaking for myself there is no one I would rather see with him than you– & I should be rejoiced to see you together–and do most earnestly hope to see you....

George Thompson was in Dublin a few weeks ago for a short time. He stayed with Mr. Edmundson & was made much of there. He is really delightful & I do not wonder that people are fascinated by him. If he had got a wife worthy of a proper sense of the value of money, he would have been a great man as a good fellow. He is true to the cause & its friends–and no man is better suited for our platforms on this subject. His knowledge, his industry, & his systematic comprehension of the whole question are admirable & enviable....

Ever yours affectionately

Rich.[d] D. Webb.

MS.B.1.6. vol. 8 The May Papers [399]
No. 39 Samuel May to R.D. Webb

Leicester, Masstts. Nov. 6/60

Dear Mr. Webb,

....This day (Nov. 6) is one of somewhat unusual interest & importance here. It is the day of the Presidential Election, including that of Members of Congress throughout the Union.... The great bulk of anti-slavery men will vote with the Republican party. A consistent, thorough, uncompromising political Antislavery party, is an impossibility in this Union, and under the present Constitution, and all attempts to form such a party have proved miserable failures, as the American Antislavery Society, from the outset, foretold. Our Union with slaveholders, our joining in a common government with these robbers, plunderers, adulterers, and murderers, is a wicked union, under any kind of constitution such as they will accept no matter what interpretation be put upon it.... The abolitionists of the

American A. S. Society stand therefore disfranchised by the very terms of the Union. They cannot vote,—for that would make them accomplices. They will lend no aid to getting up political parties, whose nominees, if elected, must write in a common government with slaveholders, and take the oath of support to a Proslavery Constitution. Nevertheless, as between the existing parties, we cannot but desire the success of that one which the slaveholder most fears, and which will do the most to check the growth of slavery, and promote the interests and spread of freedom. In the present contest this party is undoubtedly the Republican party, although its issues with the slave power are the fewest possible, and its controlling purpose anything but that of extirpating slavery from the land. If Mr. Lincoln is elected President, his administration will undoubtedly be an exceedingly cautious and conservative one. No abolitionist will be in the least surprised to see him go [to] great lengths in conciliating the South. It is greatly feared he will make unmanly and cowardly concessions to them. If, as many of the Southern fire-eaters threaten, a forcible resistance shall be made to his inauguration or administration, it is to be hoped that he will not hesitate to treat the ringleaders as the Laws require that traitors and public enemies should be treated;—otherwise he will be despised, both North & South....

I am, truly yr. friend

Samuel May Jr.

MS.B.1.6. vol. 7 The May Papers [400]
No. 54 Samuel May to R.D. Webb

n.d. fragment 60/61

Dear friend Richard Webb,

...Of course *you* will understand, and I hope all readers of the Advocate will understand, that the abolitionists are not at all disconcerted at the secession of South Carolina and her sister cotton states. We would not put a straw in the way of their leaving the Union, but only regret that the North had not virtue and self-respect enough to leave their fellowship long since. We would speed their parting—but would demand to have it done decently, with a certain courtesy, and decidedly that they should not dishonestly lay their hands upon U.S. property as they go. It is my belief that their unmolested experiment of self-government would be one of the most instructive lessons & most complete failures the world ever saw. Indeed some of them already confess incompetency, by proposing to establish a monarchy (!), and to invite over from Europe some Prince of the Royal House of Hanover perhaps, or some other (!!) I think this has been *seriously* suggested. Was ever such folly.

Yours, still for Liberty and Justice—
for God & Humanity—
No Slavery—No Slave Trade—
Freedom forever!—affectionately

S. May Jr.

Copy of a letter from Mrs. Maria Weston Chapman to Mrs. Mitchell

[Jany. 1861].

I do hope you have received it [the AntiSlavery Standard] for it has been the work & the record of an unparalleled year—the year when all our subterranean labors have burst into open day, The long concentrated enormities, the long denied outrage of the Slaveholding community, are now open & undeniable, & every newspaper now trumpets horrors which when we began our work we were obliged to seek long & often vainly to get authenticated in such books as Weld's "Testimony of a Thousand Witnesses," published by the Am. A.S. Socy. at a time when our Southern brethren had succeeded by the masterly *Calhoun* plan they followed (of *masterly inactivity*) in getting the subject of slavery completely laid to sleep; forgotten by the whole community. This, tho' not the "year of jubilee" itself, is that "acceptable year" which brings us an assurance of not having wrought in vain, & which by announcing to the world the truth of our statements, & the value of our methods, & of our persistency will bring us an amount of co-operation, I trust, by which the days of the slave's sufferings & the nations' sins shall be shortened. You will have seen by the Standard the whole history of the situation. The rage of the South when the balance of power was shifted by the election of Lincoln;—the previous treasons of Buchanan, the *reigning* President, in getting all possible advantages into the hands of the South in preparation for the Coup d'detat; the secession of South Carolina, & the falling into line with her of the rest of the Southern States, with their threat of secession also the consequent interruption of business relation, & the ensuing commercial panic—the fall in the price of Southern Stocks & Shares;—the sympathetic spasm felt among the slaveholder's tools in the Atlantic cities, as the South surged away with her puppet's purse strings in her hand: the riotous demonstrations, & the threat of assassinating Wendell Phillips (who having the ear of the people, is extremely, obnoxious to the defeated northern minority, since they acknowledged that they *are* such, & *that* irremediably;)—the firmness of the Republicans in Congress up to this time—the becoming silence of the President-elect as to his future course, while every emergency of the press has been brought to bear upon him, & every screw turned of public & private effort, to make him put forth some programme of his purposes before taking his seat:— and, having seen all this, I need not enter upon this domain of news that makes history. Once, & that not long ago, I had the comfort in writing of being able to tell what was unknown, to the rest of the world. It is so no longer. *Our* affairs are now the universal concern. Still it is our mission as of old, to break the way for others,—to take the mobbing, & see the coppers going into some miserable by-player's pocket that are needed to sustain our enterprise.

We are well & in high spirits. Civil War, if we are to have it, (which I do not think) is not so bad as slavery. Public opinion is so rapidly consolidating under the recent & present revelations, and I augur nothing but good.

MS.A.1.2. vol. 31 Anti-Slavery Letters to Garrison [402]
No. 12 W.H. Herndon[1] *to Samuel Sewall*

Springfield, Ill. Feb. 1 [1861]

Mr. Sewall,

Dear Sir,

Though I am not personally acquainted with you, still I feel that I may say a word or two to you. I am happy to know that you are opposed to the repeal of the Mass. Pers. Lib. Law[2]. The South really do not care about it: they want a Southern Republic—nothing else. They scorn you, i.e. the Northern man who rolls in the dirt. A Southern fire-eater has just left my office, come, I suppose, to learn how Lincoln feels, & to the question "Do you of the South care about Northern Lib. Bills?" He said "Do you suppose we are fools? We are striking for a Southern Republic, & we mean to have it or die."

This is the whole truth, & nothing but the truth. The Northern men must learn this faet, & bite the dust no more—must not cower more. We ought to die, every one of us, if we crouch & shirk away from duty. The slavery question *must be met & met* now. I am afraid we are not yet prepared to meet & frown down or *fight down* this blustering, this Southern bullying. Thank God we will get ready sometime. The Anti-Slavery sentiment is prevailing in the West. We are not yet ruled by cotton. Cotton is not king—but *Conscience* is. The West is true & will so remain. Why does Adams act so, i.e. why did he? Is he a coward? Bye the bye, Phillips' last speech rings gold-like—has the chime of true metal in it. How different is this speech from Mr. Seward's. I do not agree with Phillips about Disunion, though I see that Disunion is liberty to the slave, & God speed that day.

Mr. Lincoln yet remains firm as a rock: he is true game & is strong in the faith of Justice, Right, Liberty, Man & God. He has told me, not only once, but often & often, that rather than back down—rather than concede to traitors, his soul might go back to God from the wings of the Capitol. I believe it. He & I have been partners in law for 13 years & I know him. Say to the Mass. boys "Stand firm—keep your convictions true to your soul."

Yours truly

W. H. Herndon

MS.B.1.7. vol. 2 The Estlin Papers [403]
No. 116 Samuel J. May to Mary Estlin

New York Feb. 12 1861

Dear Miss Estlin.—

I should not have been so silent towards you so long—had I not been engrossed by the alarming and perilous condition of our country. You

1. William Henry Herndon (1818-1891) was Abraham Lincoln's law partner.
2. In an attempt to frustrate the operation of the Fugitive Slave Law, Massachusetts had passed a Personal Liberty Law, an example which was followed by other Northern states.

have been partly informed of it by the newspapers but one must needs be here in the midst—to realise how every day's report brings some tidings that take possession of one's thoughts—and unfit him for everything else but to do or say something that shall guide to a right issue the great struggle in the midst of which we are.

I sent last week a newspaper to Rev. Edwin Chapman in which my Bristol friends may find some account & the violent doings of the pro slavery party in Syracuse, on the 29th & 30th ult^{o}—The character of our city must not be inferred from these transactions—not withstanding the spicy and spiteful article in the last AntiSlavery Standard signed M.—(C.D.B. Mills).

There are many humane people—friends of the slaves—in Syracuse. But the Democratic Party hoped to make political capital by breaking up our Convention—and insulting and denouncing us—and the Republicans were not prepared to stand up in support of a meeting—which [them ?] deemed inexpedient at the time—But there will not be a reaction there.—My own Church took the matter bravely up—Sunday before last—without any intimation from me—and their final action was had last Sunday. I have not heard what it was, but have not a doubt that it was honourable to them.

The tidings from the South yesterday and this morning are somewhat more favourable. But it is impossible to foretell what course will be taken—until after the administration shall have been inaugurated.—Mr. Lincoln left his home yesterday in Illinois for Washington. He will come through New York State and perhaps go to New England. He will reach Washington by the 20th of this month—and be inaugurated on the 4th of March. He is called to his high position on a day of utmost trial—if he shall prove to be the man for the Hour—he will stand in our future history, next only to Washington.—I must confess that I fear—with Mr. Seward as his chief Secretary, he will adopt a compromising course—which may possibly (tho' not probably) heal the breach for a little while—but do nothing to extirpate the root of bitterness—and so have us liable, at any time, to a worse explosion—

I know how deeply you will sympathise with us—and how unjustly you appreciate the great reforms we have undertaken.—It must ultimately be affected—but whether in our day we are to witness any mitigation of the wrongs of Africa and of her American descendants is extremely doubtful. You will be grieved to hear that Mr. Garrison is still quite unwell. His disability at this time is a sore bereavement to our little host.—But God reigns—and those who—however few—are on his side, are in a mighty majority —though the whole world be against them.—

Yours very sincerely & gratefully

Saml. J. May

Miss Mary Estlin.

MS. 960 Webb-Quincy Correspondence [404]
pp. 74-75 Webb to Quincy

Dublin, March 7. 1861.

My dear Quincy

...If I were once more safe across the vasty brine with my stomach entire, I would dearly like to be a looker on for a while upon the Terrified Democracy. Here I think the opinion grows that a permanent Dissolution of the Union is the most probable solution of the present difficulty. Like the little cabin boy who was impelled by the rope's end to his devotions—"You may make me kneel if you like, but damn me if I pray"—so the Southern whites, both mean & mannerly—may be dragooned back but they will never again cohere to the Free States. It is a wonder to me how low the Northerners are ready to stoop to their former masters to induce to take their seats on their necks as before— but there is no accounting for tastes—and for the tastes of the swinish multitude least of all. A wealthy Dublin merchant tells me that the effect of the new American tariff will be to put an end to the exportations to the Free States & the Times (who care nothing for slavery) say that this Tariff is a more portentious measure than the recent secession itself.[1] Of course they mean to English commercial interests though I greatly doubt if even this be true. The Tariff must at any rate additionally disgust & alienate the South. But I need not go on with this talk. Doubtless you get plenty of it all around you. At any rate the abolitionists have good reason to congratulate themselves for they have proved the true prophets—whilst all the wise men, all the great politicians are no better than fools. If the South were fairly set adrift and the North were content to be free from the burden she has hitherto borne what a glorious destiny lies before the Free States. I wish the people generally were not so readily led by the nose, & that they had some better right to call themselves free & enlightened....

Yours ever truly

Richd. D. Webb.

MS.B.1.6. vol. 8 The May Papers [405]
No. 56 Samuel May to R.D. Webb

Boston, 22 1 Washington St.
Friday, May 3, 1861.

Dear Webb,

...There are times when we wish that John Brown and Theodore Parker were living.—They are very hopeful times indeed—*Never before* has the North been so united! In one purpose to punish the South soundly and thoroughly for her turbulent, insolent, and traitorous course, the North may be said to be *absolutely unanimous.* What a wonderful change! There is *a North* at last, and the Southern people are absolutely confounded at the

---

1. This was the Morrill Tariff, enacted by the Republicans as part of their promise further to increase tariff barriers in order to protect native industries. It was resented not only by the South but by free trade Britain as well.

sight. It is in a large measure the result of the antislavery Education it has led. There are now some 25,000 troops in Washington and its immediate vicinity; probably at least 25,000 more within 1 to 2 days march, *Northern* troops I mean; not less than 10,000 already at St. Louis, Cairo, (Ill.) Pittsburgh, &c is still going on with the greatest eagerness. From a state of profound peace, and a total inexperience of any other condition, we have suddenly burst out into a great enthusiasm for a thorough fight with the Seceding and "Rebellious" States, and there is every prospect that it will be had. It took Ft. Sumter, 8,000 men against 80, & crowed over it, as it were something wonderful. It confesses itself entirely foiled as to Ft. Pickens (on the Gulf of Mexico)—and certainly is so,whether its confession is sincere or not. Ft. Monroe, wh. commands the approach to Richmond, Virginia is amply garrisoned by U.S. Troops. The rebels have lost the golden moment for an attack on Washington, & are daily getting more & more shut up. A thorough blockade of all their posts will be at once established. The Administration have not only been abundantly sustained by the Northern people, but are urged on by them to vigorous & decided measures. We trust that the overruling Power will now accomplish the Deliverance of the Slave.

Affectionately & truly yr. Friend.

Saml. May Jr.

MS.B.1.6. vol. 8 The May Papers [406]
No. 60 Samuel May to R.D. Webb

Leicester, Mass., June 3. 1861.

Dear friend Webb,

...Much anxiety is felt in some quarters at the course which England will take, and by some of our papers the Queen's Proclamation[1] is criticised sharply. For myself, I liked the Proclamation. I understand it as prohibiting any participation in the War here, by accepting privateer commissions or otherwise; and expressly warned that no protection or redress would be afforded by the Brit Govt. for any harm or loss incurred by such participation; but all our people do not so interpret it. — I feel great confidence in the sympathy of the *British people* with our position, as against the Seceding Slaveholders & slavetraders. Should the Brit. Govt. give the least encouragement, or show the least favour to the Confederate States, it will be dishonoured & disgraced before all people; for nothing could go so far as to convict it of hypocrisy in its profound desire to put down the Slave Trade, and Slavery. I believe the Brit. People will not suffer their Govt. to betray them.

Truly & every yours,

Saml. May Jr.

---

1. The Queen's Proclamation of Neutrality of 21st May, 1861, announcing the official British attitude to the contest between North and South.

Greenfield, Kilgobbin, Co. Dublin
July 16 1861.

My dear Friend,

...I own that the outbreak of the war in America has caused me many surprizes. I wonder greatly at the unreserved exultation on the part of many out and out friends of nonresistance among the abolitionists at the opening of a long and bloody struggle. I dont wonder that they should be glad at the prospect of the overthrow of Slavery at almost any price: but I am surprised that it is such unqualified gratification... I think there was no sufficient provocation for the outbursts of anger in the United States at the neutral position of England in this affair – since the struggle on the part of the free states has never yet taken the aspect of an anti-slavery struggle on the part of either the government or the people. On the contrary great pains have been taken to show that it is no such thing. Slaves have been repeatedly returned to their masters and neither Lincoln nor Seward has yet spoken an antislavery syllable since they took office. As far as professions go, the war on the part of the north is only an armed attempt to punish traitors and to restore the Union to its former dimensions. Now we have always heard from the abolitionists that the Union was one of the chief bulwarks of the slave system, and as we heard nothing except from the abolitionists of this war for its maintenance being likely to weaken slavery it is not surprizing that no general interest was felt amongst us. At the same time my full belief is, that the great majority of the English people who had any opinion on the matter were and are in favour of the free states. I never doubted that the war will immediately weaken and eventually destroy slavery. In a country like England with a free press it would be absurd to expect that there should not be a great variety of opinions and that people should not try to make those opinions heard. The cotton interest is powerful & important & to these an unlimited supply of cotton is of immense interest. To these people this object is more near to their hearts than any other. A great many think that the attempt to subdue the South so far as to return the Union is unpracticable, & that if successful such a Union would not be worth retaining. Great offense has been taken at what the Times has said – at the views of the Anti Slavery Reporter – and at the silence of Exeter Hall. As if the English people were any more dependent for their opinions on these papers than the Americans are upon the New York Herald or the Tribune – and as if it was the custom (which it is not) for the English people to assemble in Exeter Hall & pass authoritative resolutions upon the internal affairs of other nations in matters of peace and war. If the war had been at the first or if it became even now an openly antislavery war the result would have been altogether different. If it became an antislavery war indifference would be inexcusable. As it is not one, the course that has been taken is readily accounted for. I am persuaded that much of this anti British oratory has had its origin in the policy of the New York Herald & other democratic journals to turn the odium for their traitorous complicity with the South from themselves by turning it against England. A strong feeling prevails in England that no matter what her course may be, some way will be discovered by American editors to pick a quarrel with her – & that this quarrel will as a matter of course become popular. I do not wonder at this so much since so large a portion of the American population are Irish who hate England, and who have always been accustomed by their priests to follow their spiritual leaders blindly, and without regard to reason or common sense. These priests are at this present hour the chief impediment to the rapid progress of the people in education and prosperity. It is owing to them and not to any natural deficiency of will or intellect that such a very small number of the poorer class amongst us fight their way upwards by any means except sordid saving and money getting....

With my kindest regards to Caroline & Lucia,

I am every truly yours,

Richard D. Webb.

MS.A.9.2. vol. 16 pt. 2 1841 The Weston Papers [408]
No. 20 R.D. Webb to the Westons

n.d.
Greenfield, Kilgobbin, Co. Dublin

My dear Friend

If any one had asked me yesterday morning (Monday) when I went into my office in town, who I should be best pleased to hear from I should have said 'Caroline Weston'. And then, if I had been asked why, I should have said 'Because I have a very great regard for her, & I used to hear from her – long ago – not infrequently. But of late since she has been with [? ?] of me – since this war broke out in America – & the world having gone [?], every one has opinions of his (& her) own, I fear she looks on me as a political heretic & has cut my acquaintance – which is extremely uncomfortable. Accordingly I was so much gratified by the receipt of your letter, that like a child with a cake, I only nibbled a scrap at a time through the day – at long intervals – & only finished it when I was seated at home comfortably by the fireside this perishing cold weather.

I have known some very clever women in my time – & I think nearly every one of them was remarkable for extraordinary fixedness & uncompromising tenacity of opinion – not given to making allowances, & perhaps inclined to draw unreasonably large conclusions from insufficient premises. Now as you are in my estimate one of this class you must not be offended if I attribute to you some of their infirmities. I think you are not altogether fair when you pronounce judgment upon tens of millions of your fellow creatures. This whole Civil war is eminently calculated to mystify that prodigious majority of the British nation who have had little previous knowledge of or interest in American politics. American politics & the whole framework & constitution of the American political system are so intricate & complex – that I can't wonder that 99 out of 100 Englishmen are confused and confounded & mistaken when they attempt to form or pronounce an opinion.

It cannot be too often insisted on that by far the most influential & numerous class of teachers on these subjects have been our American visitors – of whom an extremely small proportion have been abolitionists or favourable to abolitionism. You know better than I do that as gentlemen at ease, as moneyed men, merchants, divines, planters, &c &c 99 out of 100 Americans in England have defended or apologised for slavery & have represented abolitionists as foolish, irreligious, intermeddling fanatics. And they have been generally believed. The English people take an absurb pride in their practical turn of mind – their contempt for theory, their disposition to mend piece by piece, & their dislike of violent revolution or any revolution. Then again the U.S. owed their existence as a nation to a successful insurrection – which they have never done lauding & celebrating – it was successful rebellion against England which Englishmen have often been invited to commemorate in London – & besides the American people have almost invariably shown a hearty sympathy with other rebellions against England and other constituted governments. I don't wonder that a great number of all informed, misinformed Englishmen, whose knowledge of America & American politics & chattel slavery was derived from American travellers – I dont in the least wonder that they should have a small vindictive pleasure in seeing that the U.S. had a rebellion on their hands even though the rebels were slaveholders – more especially when the uprising of the north for the maintenance of the Union did not effect to be for the overthrow of slavery, when the government anxiously disclaimed such an object, when slaves were repeated[ly] returned to rebel masters by Northern officers, & when many northern newspapers used all their influences to denounce such a thing as abolition & were particularly dishonest & malignant in their condemnation of abolitionists.

I never doubted from the time of the attack on Fort Sumter that the death blow of slavery in the United States was struck at the same time – & that the consummation was merely a question of time – but when we consider that the number of tolerably-well-informed-as-to-American-affairs-Englishmen is very small, and that the number of Americans who had no notion that in fighting for the Union they were also contending for abolition was very great, we ought not to be angry, or surprised the English who care nothing for the Union regarded both sides as nearly equally proslavery, & that the Northerners aimed at conquest and the South at independence. Many thought that the North would become really opposed to slavery if the South established a union of their own – & that the South standing alone would be unable to maintain a system so opposed to the public opinion of the rest of the civilised world. I have no doubt that many Englishmen who were tired of the quarrelsome tendencies of American statesmen, & the disposition to pick quarrels with England which are so apt to fill the columns of American newspapers, really thought that if the North & South were separate empires they would have so much to do in settling their own differences that they would have no time for remoter quarrels, and as many who thought so, really believed that as to hostility to slavery there was not much to choose between the two sections, I am not much surprised that they should have looked without regard on the probabilities of the success of the attempt at secession.

You will understand that I am not at all expressing my own opinion but merely my notion of the probable notion of others – and in this way I .

account for the existence of views which you look on with great disgust & disapprobation, but which under the circumstances would be both natural & reasonable.

The whole subject always has been heretofore & still is filled with difficulty in my mind. Until lately I thought the North would hardly succeed in conquering the South until after a long and desperate struggle. I still doubt whether the conquest when made will be worth the trouble whilst the feelings of the people, either through ignorance or self-interest – either as mean whites or slave holders, are filled with such bitter hostility to their conquerors. As far as I know there is no such hatred between any two European nations as that which prevails on the part of the South towards the North, for the extracts in the Abolition papers entitle us to think that many Northern editors of Democratic papers with many democratic politicians and wire pullers detest the abolitionists far more than they do the secessionists, and would gladly have the status ante bellum with every gaurantee for slavery if they could then undo what has been done. I never could see my way to the existence of two republics in the room of the United States – for the possession of the Mississippi & the Gulf of Mexico would create immense difficulties – not to speak of the impossibility of enforcing any treaty engagements in connection with the recovery of fugitive slaves. It is not fair to call people on this side of the Atlantic *proslavery* because they have felt and expressed themselves puzzled by such difficulties as these which have created great differences of opinion among the foremost of the abolitionists. I have had letters from many of them and the variety of sentiment is most remarkable & such as should teach us all a lesson of charity. When they differ, who know so much & feel so much – surely people here who know so little, may be allowed to have a great variety of views on matters so complex....

How about Harriet Martineau. This is a tender subject.[1] Knowing how heartily you dislike her, it takes some courage for me to approach it. A very dear friend of her own – not your sister Maria, who is I believe her dearest friend – told me she thought her isolated life, living nearly alone with little or no opportunity owing to her delicacy & her deafness, was very unfavourable to her way of viewing things – & that this was the cause of the 'arrogance' of her American letters. I greatly regret this. I also regret that Mr. Phillips' attacks upon England (which were I think unjust & unprovoked) havemade her unjustifiably unfair to him. I admit her faults – I think she has her full share of them – as most of us have – but still I maintain that for many years past and at to the present time there is nobody in Europe who has done so much to promote anti-slavery views and to uphold the northern cause in

---

1. Harriet Martineau, as befitted an intimate friend of Mrs. Chapman, was an ardent abolitionist and extremely partizan supporter of Old Organization. Her knowledge of America and her American connections encouraged her not only to defend American actions in Britain, but as a Correspondent for the *Anti-Slavery Standard*, to lecture to Americans on their shortcomings in their own country. She welcomed the coming of the Civil War as justifying her belief in the corrupt and tyrannical native of Southern Society, but she was dismayed that it was not an outright struggle against slavery; she deplored the Morrill Tariff, and she berated the Americans for their action in the Trent incident. It is scarcely surprising that her views met with little sympathy, or understanding in America.

England. No, not George Thompson. General Thompson, John Bright & Richard Cobden rolled into one. Her articles in the Daily Sun, [sic] her notices of American books, &c are full of wonderfully able writing – all in favour of the efforts & principles of the abolitionists & antislavery Americans. And the snubbing she has got from the Standard has not in the least affected her. I believe her principles are quite superior to personal feelings. I think it a great feather in her cap that Mrs. Chapman loves & respects her so highly, for I regard Mrs. Chapman as the largest minded mortal of whom I have any knowledge.

I have been diverted & saddened by observing the facility with which reputations are lost & won under present circumstances in the United States. To think of Harriet Martineau being cast out and John Bright elevated into a hero – he who never said a good word for the anti-slavery cause or for its advocates until the war broke out & obliged him to declare himself. Many years ago he & the Anti Corn Law League placed busts of Calhoun & MacDuffie in their board room, as good staunch Free Traders. But indeed after all in their great struggles the feeling is forced upon us that individual men & reputations are of small importance – men are swept away like motes in the sunbeam – and the results of their acts are all that remain....

I dont like national hatreds. They are unwise & they do no good. No one civilised nation that gets fair play is very much worse than another. See what the Italians have become. Look at Garibaldi what a grand old hero is he – and yet a few years since he was 'only an Italian.' There are good people in England & it is not wise for you Americans to regard us as sinners above all that dwell in Jerusalem.

I am ever yours affectionately,

Richd D. Webb.

MS.A.9.2. vol. 6 The Weston Papers [409]
No. 40 Maria Weston Chapman to Anne Chapman

Weymouth July 28.

Dear Anne,

Henry [Chapman], Eleanor and the two fabulously good and beautiful babies are all here, with two nursery maids. so you may imagine there is not much time for writing. Still I had written you an immense letter. But as it is overweight, in every sense of the word, all things considered, I send this sheet instead. Your Aunt Mary has just left us after a visit of a day. The recruiting goes on slowly. Hesse[1] has enlisted, & 45 others:— offering of 250 dollars bounty tells upon the patriotic mind. A third of our quota have come very slowly up. Things look very blue Henry says: but to me, who judge by the progress the pressure makes in squeezing pro-slavery into an anti-slavery [?], things look better than ever before. I do not believe England will interfere – simply because her settled [and usual?] policy is, *non*-interference. But I do hope the [call?] of our people about it – seeing

---

1. Hesse was their handy man, who became a gunner in the 9th Massachusetts Battery and was wounded at Gettysburg.

they would never [be?] mad about it, will continue till they are sane again, & help to make them emancipate. Little Henry Cowing is off again to camp of instruction in Maryland. When he got there, no preparations, had to sleep on the ground, but rations have begun & he will soon have quarters. So far from finding books and professors, he has sent home for yellow-covered literature to while away the time with. So we sent him on all we could spare, & I slipt in a rejected cornerstone of Moncure Conway.[2] They tell me you are getting to be an heiress. A hundred thousand men & a thousand million of dollars to make my daughter an heiress. Such is life & such its concatenations. I am grieved to hear you cant wear Monitor hats & Lincoln clothes in England. But it is no more than I know must be, when I heard Cassius Clay Ambassador playing into the hands of an English war-party by threatening through 'the Times' that the U.S. would [sow?] Great Britain with salt. Everything in the way of hostility between nations has causes:– and I disapprove all this Cassius Clay rhodomantade:– it is like an insane baby. I desire to bless my stars for our incapacity to entertain national hatred.

I am thankful to think of you all safely housed in a no worse place than England – *although* you cant sport Monitor Ribbons, without making yourselves unpopular. I [am] dreadfully sorry for the loss of the twenty pounds duty on silver, and think all such duties are disgraceful to any country, more particularly to England, where the bulk of the people know better than to be fleeced to protect Rundell & Bridges.[3] I think our West will not forever be fleeced in a similar way out [of] her corn trade, to enrich a couple of small privileged classes in Pennsylvania & Manhattan. But I cant make it out to be a cause of war when people say they like free trade & mean to have it & cant get it as soon as they want it. But between nations nothing is considered so hostile as to put up obstacles to intercourse, I observe, and so I always go against putting them up. I wish you could hear people talk here. 'Fe-fi-fo-fum' – is the low lived burden of their low lived song. If you have a wicked party in England, we have a set of fools playing into its hands, to the great vexation of dear good Abe Lincoln, who had no such political coxcomb's notions as Seward had, – of meeting a proclamation of neutrality with threats of annexing Canada.

We have Victor Hugo's book.[4] Very fine certainly. One of his phrases made me think of V. Vandemeyer's Manners 'politesse proportionee.' You see a great deal of it in a Monarchist country, as yet unshaken by revolution. Don't be vexed by it. Nothing should be permitted to vex good hearts, by their owners. Such vexations are the beginning of hatred, which is a thing utterly cut out. Let the sight of its damnableness be a warning to you against

---

2. Moncure Conway (1832-1907), an American preacher and author, became a radical abolitionist in the 1850's and wrote several articles and pamphlets on the slavery question. In 1863 he went to England to lecture on behalf of the north, and while in London was offered the pastorate of South Place Chapel, Finsbury, a post which he held for many years.

3. Rundell, Bridge & Co. were a famous London firm of goldsmiths and silversmiths.

4. Possibly Victory Hugo's defence of John Brown.

indulging it. I see enough of it here to sink a nation. And if the U.S. *do* sink it will be because they cherish such perilous stuff.

Will – and must close,

Your loving parent,

M.W.C.

MS.B.1.6. vol. 8 May Papers [410]
No. 78 Samuel May to R.D. Webb

Leicester Masstts. Octr. 11. 1861

Dear friend Webb,

...Of course we know where the sympathy and good wishes of all true abolitionists must be, in England as elsewhere; at any rate, where *it will not be*, viz. with the South, in the mad and cruel war which they are waging, with characteristic methods and spirit, on behalf of 'the sum of all villainies' But the number of genuine, thorough, and intelligent abolitionists in England, as you have always declared, is small, – and this is perhaps not very much to be wondered at; such is the fact in this country also. With regard to the great mass and bulk of the British nation, they are doubtless to be classed as anti-slavery.... And yet the antislavery of this large mass is rather historical and hereditary, than personal & vital, – arising from an established habit of thought & feeling rather than from a study of, and thorough acquaintance with, the man-stealing and man-destroying institution itself. So, at least, I understand it, guided to this opinion by the words of the most capable English judge of the matter I know. Then there is the class, strong numerically & very strong by wealth and commercial position, who see little else in this difficulty but the fact that business is deranged, that the supply of cotton to their mills is diminished and its price for the time very much enhanced, with the prospect of the stopping of the manufacture with its consequent suffering and other evils; a very serious & important aspect of the question, all will admit; yet it is not of that importance as to demand the sacrifice of Right, Justice, Freedom and the abandonment of all moral Principle. This last class is that which chiefly controls the Press, the daily and weekly journals, is it not? Now it is not to be denied that these journals have for the most part spoken coldly, derisively, or adversely of our Government's war against the slaveholding Rebellion (after a most long & patient waiting to avert if possible the bloody issue) and that they have spoken apologetically, and in some cases approvingly, of the Southern Movement.... And I may say your own letter, reciting as it does the several causes which for many years past have been producing a *pro-slavery* effect upon the English mind, and admitting the pro-slavery tone of leading journals, is to some extent an admission that the American complaints of England's attitude & influence at this time are not ill-founded....

Ms. incomplete.

MS.B.1.6. vol. 9 The May Papers. [411]
No. 6 Eliza Wigham to Samuel May

5 Gray St. Edinburgh n.d.

My dear Friend,

...Thou wilt see that we have much less to send than last year – we are very sorry for this especially because the reason alleged for it in many quarters is that you have rather deserted the high ground & been swayed by the general movement which has been for the restoration of the Union. Some have deplored your leaving the peace principle & some have grieved over your bitter feeling against England – but I have told thee these things before, & now I hope there is a subsidiary of the contentions, & between us we are coming to a better state of things....

Thine very sincerely & affectionately,

Eliza Wigham.

MS.960 1843-1871 Quincy-Webb Papers [412]
p. 25 Quincy to Webb

Dedham, Oct. 25, 1861.

My dear Webb,

...The War is a dreadful thing in many points of view, but by no means so a bad thing as the state of which preceded it. Had the slaveholder been willing to have everything they ever asked or could have under the old Union, they could have had it, if they would only have kept the peace. The spirit of civil Liberty seemed to have died out. Seward and Charles Francis Adams seemed as ready to surrender at discretion as the worst of the Democrats. The cowardice and meanness are dreadful to contemplate. But the insolence of Jeff. Davis and the slaveholders would consent to nothing that did not secure them much more than the old Constitution. I don't believe they intended absolute secession: but only to compel a reconstruction of the Union on the basis of slavery which should give them the control of the government and of the press and platform in the Free States as in the Slave. A plot was ramified through the Free States and especially in the Cities, to help them. Hence came the revival of the Mob Spirit at the North. They and their tools at the North verily believed that the moneyed classes, who had always been ready to buy peace at any price, would help them overthrow the government and that their battles would be fought in the streets of Boston, N.Y., and Phila. And we thought so too. Their astonishment was utter at the effect of the bombardment of Fort Sumpter. A Boston gentleman of my acquaintance was off Charleston at that time accompanying Mr. Appleton, the M.C. for Boston, who went for his health. As they listened to the cannonade, they said to one another. 'As soon as this news reaches N.Y. the Tribune and Evening Post Office will be sacked, and the Custom-House seized for the Confederates. 'Everybody thought so, of all shades of opinion. On landing at Charleston, everybody there of course was of that opinion. The first N.Y. Herald, which was almost the only Northern paper read there, recd.

after the news confirmed the opinion. That day, you remember, Bennett had to turn his coat in a hurry. My informant said he was in the reading room of the Mills House at C. when the next Herald came, which called for halters for Jeff. D. and his associates and the utter destruction of Charleston and the Abolition of Slavery. He said their utter bewilderment and rage was excessively comic, the rather that *he* was as much astonished as they. Neither they nor we understood the certainty with which the instinct of capital would point out its true action. The very men who were willing to let the South have everything it could ask and who did actually furnish the money that bought Pennsylvania in 1856 and so elected Buchanan, provided it would only be quiet and let them make and spend money in peace, as soon as peace became impossible were just as resolute to put it down, seeing that such a state of things was not tolerable which should put the Govt. at the mercy of the minority at every election. It was bring Mexico and the South Am. States home. So they rose as one man, and the [?] sympathizers disappeared as if they had never been. Such a War is a much more wholesome and more *moral* a state of things than that which went before it. As to the way the War is to end, *qui sait? Quien sabe?* Perhaps, the Lord. Certainly, nobody else. Only of this I feel assured that it can't leave this nation in as bad a way as it found it. If Jeff Davis and his crew were willing to give over and come back on the old terms, there are no conditions they could not command from Lincoln and Seward. And it is the hope that the Rebels would grow tired of the War, and compel a peace of their leaders, and the overweening opinion of the importance of keeping Kentucky and Missouri that has made the war so shilly-shally in its conduct. But, thank God, this is a vain expectation. They hate and despise us heartily and their means for maintaining the War are much more than our newspapers will allow. A hundred-fold greater than we had in the Revolutionary War. The difficulty on our side is that we have not 'got mad', as you Irish and we Yankees say, enough with them. We must hope for reserves enough to put us into this frame of mind, not Christian perhaps, but most essential to fighting. It seems to me that these can be but two ways of ending the war. If we do 'get mad' enough, I believe we are strong enough to conquer them; that is, to seize all their seaports and command all their rivers and occupy their most important inland towns. But it will go till after a desperate struggle and desperate losses, and then I dont believe we shall be content to leave Slavery behind us. We shall be educated by the war up to that point by that time. But should we fail of doing this and get tired ourselves first, then we must recognize their Independence and have a Free Nation on one side the Potomac, and a Slave on the other. And this would be worth all the War costs, and it would end indirectly in the Abolition of Slavery in the Confederate States. One thing the War has done, it has shown the North how strong and rich it is. I doubt whether England or France would have raised so fine an army as we have now in the field in three months, on the heel of defeat, as we have since the middle of July. The Commissariat and the Contracts are all put on an honest footing and no complaints are now heard about them. As to the effect of the War on Northern prosperity, I imagine it is nearly as great as on your side the water. The depression of business has never been anything like what it was in the Fifty-Seven. Indeed, business is now growing good, and next winter will be better than it has been for years. The war has taught us how small a matter Southern trade was to us. The N.Y. Times says it is only *five per cent* of N.Y. trade, and that the trade of Massachusetts was worth more to N.Y. than all the Slave States put together in the best years. This does not include the cotton which we used to buy and pay gold for – but the merchandize with which we supplied them. The West is our profitable customer. In 1857 we had the Southern trade undisturbed and they were prosperous and able to pay, but it was but a drop in the bucket, to stay the ruin caused by the failure of the West. Now the West is running over with its crops, and the United States war furnishes it with the currency which it has always wanted. The curse of the West has been a vicious Banking system which devoured all the profits of the former. Now the U.S. Treasury notes and certificates answer the purpose of a National Bank, so that they can move their crops and receive remittances as good as gold, which comes back to us for all kinds of articles which we import and manufacture, and of which they are entirely bare. In fact, I should not wonder if the War should become as popular as Pitt's war with Bonaparte was in England. *We* hear of distress and no doubt that there is enough of it, but there are no outward signs of it yet. I have had fewer applications for assistance than in the average of years. The streets are full as ever. The lace shops and jewellers' shops swarm with customers. The theaters are doing a fine business here in N.Y. The Cotton manufacturers are the worst off, but even they are kept along by the rise of their goods in hand. The woolen Mills are running night and day for the Arms, so there are two sides even to this picture....

Most truly yours,

E. Q.

MS.B.1.6. vol. 15 Additional Letters to Samuel May Jr. [413]

Greenfield, Kilgobbin, near Dublin.
Sunday, Oct. 27. 1861.

My dear Mr. May,

...I have read part of your letter to a friend of mine, a Dublin merchant of the first rank, who is also an intelligent & clear headed a man as any I know, and of an eminently impartial & judicial turn of mind. He says you are quite mistaken (& I agree with him), in attributing so much influence to the cotton interest in England – that they are far from possessing the overwhelming weight in the control of affairs which you attribute to them. Although an important class, they are vastly inferior to the landed interest in weight & importance – and irrespective of their relative power, the fact is that it does not appear they have attempted to use it for the purpose of breaking the blockade – or in any was marring the national policy of nonintervention.

He says his conviction is that though such a thing might not be openly proclaimed by any body, there is probably so much jealously, or dislike of the manufacturers in the mind of the landholders (including the aristocracy & country gentry) that they would perhaps not be very sorry to see them a little put about by this American difficulty. He says that Americans find it almost impossible to apprehend the extent to which affairs in these countries are controlled by the variety & interests which exists amongst us.

With respect to the ship laden with stores for the Confederates that ran the blockade & escaped into Charleston, he says that she had regular papers for some export not in the United States, and that our government had no power in interfere. My son has just returned from Huddersfield in Yorkshire. The general depression of business is very great there as well as elsewhere, chiefly owing to your civil war. Yet one of the great woolen factories will be kept busy all the winter with an order for 120,000 pairs of blankets supposed to be for the Federal Government. Should our Government stop this order? In point of fact our rulers are strictly bound by law in all their proceedings – and Lord Palmerston is just as open to an action at law for contravening his legal powers as I am. During the Russian war I believe it is well known that warlike supplies were furnished by the citizens of the United States to the Russians & it is unquestionable that sympathy for the Emperor Nicholas as against England & France was freely expressed. Yet that war succeeded in its object of crippling the Russian power, and putting down the autocrats hardly concealed intention to strangle all manifestations of liberty in Europe. If he had lived, Italy, Hungary & Poland would not have had even their present chance. Just as there are traitors in Washington, New York & Boston, who care for nothing but themselves, so there are money getters in England who care for nothing but money – but it would be as fair to include in our condemnation all the people of the Free States as all the people of England on account of the conduct of individuals in these matters....

Yours ever affectionately,
Rich[d] D. Webb.

MS.A.9.2. vol. 30 The Weston Papers [414]
No. 82 R.D. Webb to ?

Dublin 6th of November 1861.

My dear friend,

...Ever since your last letter reached me rather more than ten days ago I have been trying to pluck up courage to answer it. A strange expression for me to use when talking of writing to you with whom I have so much enjoyed all chances of communication. But as I perceive that you think me greatly astray on the American question I shrank from the idea of entering into controversy on a subject so difficult to [treat?] satisfactorily by letter or in any other way except amid the ease and leisure of social intercourse. I never claimed that the English people generally were abolitionists in the sense which we affix to the word – or that the difference between them was any other than that inevitably resulting from differences of circumstances. But the difference of circumstances has been very great & quite sufficient to make the American maintenance of slavery very wonderful & incomprehensible to that vast majority of Englishmen who are imperfectly acquainted with the ascendancy which that institution has attained over the minds of the American people. As far as the more intellectual and intelligent portion of our population evince a proclivity to pro-slavery views I think it must be admitted that we have Americans to thank for the circumstance – since a very large majority of travelled Americans do their best, whenever they have the opportunity, to inculcate views favourable to slavery or to make apologies for slaveholders. For one word spoken in England by American abolitionists, more than 100 are spoken on the other side by their opponents. This being so it shd be wonderful that any antislavery feeling was left in England, were it not for the triumphant result of our own antislavery experiment or achievements.

From all the testimony I can gather there is on the part of the North a war for the maintenance of the Union in which the right is entirely on the side of the North, & in which they have my hearty God speed – since it must weaken the slave power – it is not so as far as I can learn either in profession or intention – and it is therefore expecting too much to look for English sympathy. The English dislike slavery. But they dont care for the Union – and from the dislike so generally felt by Americans to England I do not wonder that John Bull should regard the probable termination of the Union with some complacency, since instead of one indefatigable & powerful opponent, two nations will be constituted who will have enough to do to watch another without quarreling with him as heretofore.

As far as the American government has been a grand Republican experiment which was a glory to the earth, you as an abolitionist will admit that it has been grievously marred within the last thirty years, & that nothing that has been said or done by the Northern people of late shows that they contemplate any improvement in the matter of slavery.

With regard to myself I am conscious of no change for the worse in my feelings as an abolitionist except that I despair of the Northern people being converted by moral influences or by any thing but the terrible teachings of adverse circumstances. You think my letters show that I take a [narrow view?] of American affairs. I can only reply that Mrs. Chapman has of late repeatedly thanked me for the tenor of them & that in the very last of several which I have recd from her she said she wished H. Martineau was the editor of the Standard & that I was the European correspondent. I by no means think so highly of myself – but she is a clear headed & an honest woman & would not say what she does not think. Several of my American friends have in a like manner approved of my letters on very gratifying terms. I am not in the least huffed that you dont agree with them & if you will give me the particulars of your objections I will endeavour to mend & will heartily thank you for the hints.

I have no special love for England, but I like fair play – and I do think the prevailing American feeling towards her is more like an unreasoning & quarrelsome antipathy than an objection founded on reason. I think most Americans are rather sorry not to have an opportunity of snubbing & find fault with her – which I regard as a state of mind unbecoming a great and magnanimous people – & one which is likely only to create a kindred feeling on this side of the water....

With my wife's love I am ever truly,

yours,

Rich[d] D. Webb.

Leicester, Masstts, Decr. 20. '61.

Dear friend Webb,

...Last Monday we received the first intelligence of the English thundering about the Slidell & Mason affair.[1] Your people have generally accused *us* (Americans) of being specially impulsive and hasty in our utterances; but I think no American precedent can be found to outdo this exhibition of English indignation. Without getting *half the facts*, or the *ex-parte statement* of the officers of the Trent (who, as *we* understand it, were very abusive & violent to the American officers, who, on their part, from the best information we have, conducted themselves with coolness, judgment, and civility, forebearing to retort the abuse heaped upon them) and without waiting to consider the *International Law*, or look into the course *which the English Govt. & Nation has itself taken heretofore in similar cases*, the whole press, nation and government of England seem to have come to the conclusion that, in taking the rebel envoys from a neutral ship, the American captain and his government were utterly without precedent or justification. *We* universally understand it just the other way; and instead of thinking it an 'outrage', we think it a just proceding, fully warranted by the example of England herself, fully sustained by her highest law authorities, which are cited & published in full; and instead of thinking it a 'folly', we deem it *a right*, and *a duty*, to intercept & take the officers, agents, & other means employed in furthering the rebellion against our Government. A Queen's Messenger has arrived here, with dispatches to Lord Lyons.[2] What the substance there of is has not yet transpired. – Of course if the English govt. & people want a war with America, they can probably have it; and their great haste in this matter (taking their public journals now as the evidence) would seem to prove they *do* want it, else, why not wait to know the stand which our government will take in the affair? Why not take the necessary time to look into the subject, and see what the law and practice of England herself have been. This hot haste to decide, to demand, to issue Queen's proclamations prohibiting the export hither of salt petre, arms, lead, &c, to threaten a large additional military force to be sent to Canada, – and the thousand other menaces with which the British ministerial & other presses teem, looks to me strongly like a determination to use the 'Trent' affair as the pretext of a quarrel already desired & all but determined on. I see some of the French papers interpret it as evidence of a purpose in the Eng. Govt. to take a favourable opportunity to break down the American nation, whose progress in wealth & power the last 40 years has been they say, too rapid to suit the ideas of England. It looks so, I must say.... Will England take this 'opportunity' to rush into a war with us, and

---

1. John Slidell (1793-1872) and James Mason (1798-1871) were confederate agents on their way to Europe on board the 'Trent', a British ship, to seek support for the South. The 'Trent' was stopped at sea by the U.S. Navy and Slidell and Mason were removed and returned to America. This caused a diplomatic quarrel of the first order between the two countries and nearly precipitated a war. The matter was only settled when the two men were released and allowed to continue on their way to Europe.
2. Lord Lyons, a prominent British diplomatist, was the British Ambassador to the United States during the period of the Civil War.

so strengthen the Slaveholding Empire at a time, when, *but* for that aid, she must speedily despair of carrying out her oppressive plans? – I do not allow myself to say all I think of England's course towards the United States since the breaking out of this War; but I have been unspeakably astonished at it. At first, a just and righteous Proclamation of Neutrality was issued. But how has it been respected by English subjects? how enforced by the Government? It has been violated in your ports at home, continually, violated in your provincial ports with the same knowledge; great quantities of British goods, contraband of war, arms, ammunition, clothing, medicines, &c have been run into Southern ports in violation of the blockade (the blockade has been insufficient, that is true, but advantage was taken of the fact that our Navy, scattered & weakened as it was by the villainy of the last administration, could not thoroughly & at once blockade over 200 miles of coast;) it has been violated by suffering the Rebel privateer 'Nashville' (a vessel stolen from her owners, in part residing at the North) to enter & lie in an English harbour, after having sailed & burned an American merchant ship within a short distance of your coast, – and instead of ordering her to sea, suffering her to remain in the harbour, & refusing to the Captain of the burnt ship the requisite authority to go on board the privateer to search for his own property, stolen from him & then believed to be in the privateer's possession. And now this attempt of ours to take Rebel Envoys, in a manner strictly in accordance with established international law & England's own example, is to be made a cause of War! It is true that we have had some scattered testimonies, here and there, in England, in behalf of the Northern States, and their cause of established government as against Slaveholders' rebellion, but the vast mass of British speech, writing, and action has gone steadily & strongly *for* the South, and against the North. England may, and very likely will, temporarily succeed in this course. But assuredly the day is not far off, when she will bitterly regret it, – I believe so at least. For remember, *as between your Nation & ours*, this is not a question whether the U.S. Government is or should be pro-slavery or anti-slavery. I freely admit, *as an Abolitionist*, the shortsightedness, the weakness, the folly, of the policy of our Government. But neither England nor any other nation has a right to make any condition for us of this sort. To speak plainly, *it is none of their business* whether, as a Government, we are anti-slavery or not. The Eng. Govt. made a treaty with us when we were not only just as pro-slavery as we are now, but a thousand times more pro-slavery; – when, in the whole nation scarce a voice was raised against the iniquity of slaveholding, – when indeed, England herself was slaveholding. Will England observe her treaty obligations, or not? That is the question. Will she observe them or will she foment a rebellion against the nation, whilst openly pledged to a contrary course?... We – as a Nation – have never asked aid of England not any sort of participation with us in this war. Her absolute & honorable neutrality we did ask and expect, – and she freely promised it. But how has the promise been kept to the ear, and broken to the hope! I lament over this state of things, even more than I feel indignant. It fully confirms what you & others have long told us –... that a rank, unqualified pro-slavery feeling was as prevalent and outspoken in England as in America. Nothing short of that can explain the amount of open and secret aid which this slaveholding rebellion has, from the first, received from England – the utter coldness with which every Northern effort has been treated – the undisguised joy and satisfaction and merriment even.

Tuesday, Dec. 24... Since I wrote, we have had 3 arrivals from England, – all bringing accounts of extensive naval and military preparation in England, troops & armaments getting ready for Canada; – and in Canada itself, the Government paper calling the people to arms, & the government itself calling out a large force of the militia. Does this mean less than a purpose or position of our Government, all these various menaces are held out over us, – and *at what a time!!* – Unless the tenor of English despatches (of which, as yet, we know nothing positively), and the tone of the Eng. Government, toward us, prove far more considerate & fair than we now have reason to apprehend, the good feeling which universally prevailed through our Northern States amongst the intelligent and solid classes towards England will be utterly alienated, and a nation of friends and well wishers deeply embittered....

Ever truly yrs.,

Saml. May Jr.

MS.B. 1.6. vol. 15 Additional Letters to Samuel May Jr. [416]

Dublin, December 21, 1861.

My dear Mr. May,

...It is quite wonderful how decidedly the American & the English people have taken their stand on the Trent affair. I never knew such unanimity in England, and the general sentiment is that the conduct of Captain Wilkes[1] was both illegal & unwise & that if the President & government stand by him they show a total incapacity to look at the affair as the United States would have done had the San Jacinto been our ship & yours the Trent steamer. I hope the matter may be ended without war – but it will be almost a miracle if it do – considering the antecedents of the two countries and the great exasperations & vast preparations of England for the defence of Canada. The Royal Guards have gone out – & this is always a sign that our government is in earnest. Mason & co are doubtless great villains & a great prize but I doubt if they will be worth all it may cost to catch hold of them in such fashion.

I think a great deal of the misapprehension resulting from the fact that that [sic] ships have fitted out for the service of the North & the South in England, has arisen from the mistakes you make as to the limits of law in England. As I am assured it is not the business of our government to interfere with the ordinary operations of trade & commerce in our ports for the defence of belligerents in other countries – & that there was nothing to hinder ships taking in arms for any port say in South America or in Europe on the presumption that they would take them to the United States North or South.

---

1. Capt. Wilkes was the commander of the American warship San Jacinto, which stopped the British ship, the Trent, took off the two Southern Commissioners James Mason and John Slidell – who were being sent to Europe to gain support for the Confederate cause. The Trent incident provoked strong feeling in both Britain and America and there was a very real chance that Britain might have declared war against the U.S. had the Commissioners not been released and allowed to proceed on their journey.

If they attempt to run the blockade on your shores that is their own affair & they will get no protection here. Every antislavery paper I get exhibits on the part of the individuals & parties & even of the Federal government an amount of virtual pro-slavery complicity & want of antislavery principle at once sorrowful, disheartening & amazing....

All the friends of peace are making active efforts to reach the ears of the Government & the country to [sic] as to stay the hand of war. It is felt to be every way deplorable that there should be war between England & the Free States more especially now that you are committed to the side of Freedom & that our real interests as well as general sympathies are on your side. The general feeling is that if the affront put on one by Captain Wilkes were papered over we must give over any idea of British dignity & national independence. Tell me how it strikes you....

Yours ever affectionately,

Richd D. Webb.

MS.A.6.1.2. The May Papers [417]
No. 12 Samuel May to Samuel J. May

Leicester, Decr. 22nd. '61.

Dear Mr. May,

...I have been exceedingly surprised and disappointed at the attitude & course of England, from an early period in the War. The antislavery feeling of England seems to have oozed out in Remonstrances and Rebukes sent to this country – never themselves backed up by any great A.S. faithfulness when the American culprits appeared in England, with their pious phrases & sanctimonious looks – 'round, fat, oily men of God'; and now the remnant of that feeling seems quite overslaughed by the power of the Cotton Lords, the Money Exchangers, and Small Politicians. The Queen's Proclamation of Neutrality – very good in itself – has neither been respected by her subjects, nor enforced by her Government; on the contrary has been openly & grossly defied – & with impunity – in her principal ports at home, & in her American colonies....

We *all* send love to all of you,

affectionately,

Yr. Cousin,

Saml. May Jr.

MS.A.9.2. vol. 30 The Weston Papers [418]
No. 89 R.D. Webb to Miss Weston.

Dublin, Dec. 31, 1861.

My dear Friend,

...I have always thought that owing chiefly to the circumstances of their education there was infinitely less international hatred towards America in England than there is towards England in America. I firmly believe that if the war had been a bonafide anti-Slavery war instead of a war which may turn out on the slave's [?] by accident & against the intention of the Northern people, a degree of enthusiasm would have been called forth in England like that which attended with breathless interest & sympathy the progress of Garibaldi from Marsala to Naples....

Yours ever affectionately,

Richd. D. Webb.

MS.B.1.6. vol. 15 Additional Letters to Samuel May Jr. [419]

Dublin 7th of January – 186[1 ? 2].

Dear Mr. May

...As to the Trent affair I am told that Thurlow Weed[1] who is now in London has expressly admitted in a letter to the Times that 'the bottom had fallen out of the best precedent' by which that act was attempted to be defended in the United States. I do not believe that a desire to take you at a disadvantage had the remotest connexion with the almost unanimous disapprobation which followed the act of Captain Wilkes – no – none whatever. In no other way could the tenderest point be touched by which you could arouse the English people. On no other points are they more sensitive than on that which asserts a right of asylum for English land & English ships. I believe that 19 out of every 20 of us wd. much rather the captain had been any one else than Southern commissioners. That Mason & Slidell were the men was generally felt to be a drawback to the determination to stand by the honor of the flag. As to taking you at a disadvantage when we thought ourselves very badly used, do you really think that your having acted so while you had another quarrel on your hands was a good reason why we should submit to it without remonstrance? You remember that when we were hard pushed during the Russian war, you insisted on the removal of Sir John Crampton[2] because he was in some degree implicated in an attempt to obtain recruits in the United States. It was universally felt then that the conduct of the U.S. government was offensively haughty, overhearing, & intentionally humiliating to us. Our government has so often succumbed in this way from a dislike to a quarrel with yours that on your side it was generally attributed to fear & to a notion that without your cotton, your corn,

1. Thurlow Weed (1797-1882), politician and Whig party boss of New York State, had for long had close ties with William H. Seward, who became Lincoln's Secretary of State. Weed, together with Archbishop Hughes and Bishop McIlvain, had been sent on an unofficial mission to Britain and France to conciliate public opinion after the Trent affair.

2. Sir John Crampton (1805-1886), the British Ambassador to Washington during the Crimean war, had fallen foul of the American Government because of his attempts to raise troops on American soil. The demand for his recall, however, was made as Webb rightly points out, in order to stir up popular anti-British sentiment in the United States, which might win support for President Pierce at his next election.

& your dollars we felt that we must cease to exist. Nothing like your hatred to England, the all pervading dislike of England & everything belonging to her which with you is a popular superstition has any existence here. We think that the American nation is boastful & has an extravagant idea of its own gifts, graces, power and destiny – that it is freer, happier, better, & more enlightened than any other. Their notions are generally regarded as arising from the youth of the country & the small opportunity the people have had of really measuring themselves with other nations. Whether we are right in holding such opinions it is certain that [there is] no such natural antipathy against you here as your masses hold against us. It has been felt as a foolish & utterly uncalled for insult that such men as Seward & W. Phillips should talk of annexing Canada. It is not in the spirit of menace that the troops were sent to Canada after the Trent affair. We did not know how your government would regard our interpretation of it – & lest Canada should be left defenceless, it was perfectly right that we should send troops over. We have as good a right to send 20,000 troops to our territory as you have to keep 500,000 on your own soil. I have no question that any application that may be or may have been made by England in this matter will be stated with an anxious desire to avoid giving offence & to prevent the danger of war. The public acts of our statesmen are never shaped for merely popular ends and are liable to be severely criticised – and any heat or precipitancy which would lead to a war with America would be unpopular; as any cowardly submission would certainly be. I find in the letter of my American friends that the idea of 'wanting a war' is repeatedly suggested. Now we know how much war costs in blood & treasure – we know it injures trade & is a blundering remedy – and therefore a general feeling of satisfaction exists in the prospect of peace which we now have before us.

However the abolition of slavery may result from your civil war it is really most puzzling to know what to deduce from even the abolition newspapers. Such dissentions in the Cabinet – such contrary conduct on the part of the generals – some for – some against slavery – such demands for 'conservative' caution on the part of the editors – such declarations that the war is for the Union – not for abolition. All this is most confusing & confounding & very great allowance should be made for us when we are unable to that which may appear clear to you. The American proclivity to anger against the Aggression comes from our side as in the case of the supposed interference with the slave ships – or from yourselves as in the Trent affair. We are equally wrong whatever we do. This is too bad....

Yours ever affectionately,

Richd. D. Webb.

Phila. Feb 1, 1862.

R. D. Webb, Esq.

My dear friend,

...You express surprise at the 'want of candour' on our side in not admitting the fact that the pro-slavery sentiment of England, whatever may be the extent of its existence, is due mainly to American influences. We on the other hand are impressed that you should dwell upon this, as a fact of any pertinance to the point in dispute. Of course we know and are ready to admit to the fullest possible extent the culpability of American slavery in demoralising European sentiment. The question between us has not been the cause, but the fact of the proslavery feeling in England. You think we overestimate, we think you underestimate the extent of its prevalence. The fact admitted with all the 'candour' possible that we are the guilty cause, does not affect, in the least, the other fact of its existence, in the extent or criminality of its existence. One of our grave charges against Southern slavery has been that it contaminated everything it touched, that it demoralised New England and corrupted the pure fountains of old England. It has seemed to us that you were quicker to see the signs of corruption in this country than in your own. In this you intimate we are mistaken: and I am sure you have the right to know.

You are under a mistake in supposing that we have objected to a 'remonstrance' from England in the *Trent* affair. If such objection have existed at any time I have seen no sign of it. On the contrary the expectation was absolutely universal that England would 'remonstrate'; nay in one that she would be angry. We expected to be called to account for Commander Wilkes' procedure, and we held ourselves ready to explain. This was the universal expectation & state of feeling. *But we did not expect what happened.* You call it 'remonstrance' that's a 'more tenderer word' than the phrase we wd. apply to it; but let that pass. Time & reflection will make manifest who is right & who is wrong; or rather who is nearest right, and who furthest wrong.

You will have noticed that in the subject of our domestic strife & our international dispute, the abolitionists here are all of one mind. The matter is so plain, or seems so plain to us, that we are all of one opinion. You must have noticed that on certain points you find yourself opposed not only by all the abolitionists of all classes on this side, but by many enlightened people, abolitionists & others in your side of the water. This does not prove I admit that you are wrong, but it is a strong suggestion against the certainty that you are right.

I fancy that if you were, in political principles, more of a democrat your views & ours would more nearly accord on questions which now seem to divide us. The distrust of the people your language implies seems to me the *proton pseudos* to which is to be traced your divergence from what we would consider the proper view to be taken of our difficulties. But enough said. The war that seemed imminent between your country & mine is happily averted; let there be no controversy – at least no alienation between your British abolitionists & us Americans. Our cooperation heretofore has been one of the words that has bound the two countries in amity. *Esto perpetua.* With love to your family I am yours ever the same.

Miller McKim.

MS.B.1.6. vol. 15 Additional Letters to Samuel May Jr. [421]

Greenbank 8/1mo 1862.

Dear Richard,

I cannot but feel grieved for the distress which the recent proceedings have caused to a man of such evident warm heartedness & good feeling as Saml. May, yet the transactions themselves appear to me in a very different light from that in which he looked at them.

He looks on Mason & Slidell as rebels, whom they were fully justified in seizing wherever they could. We dont at all deny that they are rebels, but we consider ourselves bound to protect every one, no matter what his previous conduct may have been, who see our protection & attains our shores or the deck of one of our vessels. The Austrians look on Kossuth as a rebel. Mazzini is a rebel, & we have harboured him while engaged in plots, in which the people of England had little sympathy, & which the 'Times' strongly denounced. The plots against Louis Napoleon's life were hatched in London and much as we hate assasination, we refused in any way to interfere without *complete legal proof.* We look upon the duty of affording an asylum to any one who seeks it as imperative & never to be surrendered but with the independence of the country itself; and I feel confident that the people of the United States look upon it in the same light, and would feel the same indignation that we have done, if a British man of war had stopped an American vessel, & taken out of her John Mitchel & Thos. F. Meagher,[1] whether the bearers of despatches from a rebellious government, or simply traitors who had tried to get up a rebellion & failed in the attempt.

As to the rapidity with which troops & munitions of war have been sent to Canada, it should be borne in mind that, unless sent off at once, there was no hope of finding the St. Lawrence open until May, and although I trust and believe that whenever Canada wishes for a complete separation and asks it through her *legal official* organs, no shot will ever be fired by Gt. Britain to prevent it; yet surely, so long as the Canadians wish to remain united to the mother country, the latter is bound to protect her, and 30,000 or 40,000 troops are not many in view of the chances of a war with a country which has 600,000 men under arms.

As respects neutrality, our idea is that our government should treat both parties in exactly the same manner, therefore as our people have full liberty to

---

1. John Mitchel (1815-1875) and Thomas Francis Meagher (1823-1867) were Irish nationalists who had been sentenced to transportation because of their seditious activities. Both escaped from Van Dieman's land to America where they were received with great popular acclaim.

trade with the Federal States, not only in clothing & the necessaries of life, but also until the late proclamation in warlike stores & all the munitions of war, so no restrictions could be placed on our trade with the Southern States, except that arising from the blockade, and therefore, when a Southern man bought clothing in Manchester or rifles in Birmingham, the Government had no right to interfere. He shipped himself or an Englishman shipped them for him, the vessel cleared for the coast of Africa, in order that her destruction should not be known, and then sailed for America, & tried to run the blockade. If unsuccessful, she was taken & condemned as a prize, & our Government, which had previously warned all owners of ships of the risk they would run in such an attempt, of course made no objection to the ship thus taken being condemned.

Whatever our Government might wish to do in such a case they could not prevent ship owners & merchants from engaging in such a trade if they wished, no more than the Government of the United States could prevent your citizens from doing the same under similar circumstances.

The very same principle of treating both parties alike was adopted in the case of the 'Nashville', which was allowed to refit, in the same manner as the 'James Adger' had done a few weeks before. And this is the same principle on which the Governor of Martinique acted in the case of the 'Sumter & Iroquois' and on which the 'Sumter' has just been allowed entrance into the harbour of Cadiz.

Things look very differently according to the point of view from which we regard them; but I feel confident that if there were now war between Ireland & England, or between France & Algiers, and that Canadians or Irish or Algerines had been seized on board of an American Packet ship the people of the United States would have felt precisely the same indignation which the people of Gt. Britain just now felt.

Thine very truly,

Jno. Pim.

Richd. D. Webb
Gt. Brunswick St.

MS.B.1.6. vol. 9 The May Papers [422]
No. 7 Eliza Wigham to Samuel May

5 Gray St. Edinburgh 24. 1. 62.

My dear Friend,

...We are not at all surprised that your Govt. is not Anti-Slavery. I think you have taught us too much about it for that, & we could expect no miracle in this matter, but if any surprise exists, it is that the Govt., in *self-interest* does not see how greatly to its advantage an Emancipation policy would be – it has hitherto *resisted* every advance in this direction & yet we do rejoice with you that so many advances have been made, & as the people rule the Govt. I hope the people may gradually move right & compel the administration to move right too; & may you abolitionists who lead them keep still on the highest ground....

This matter of the Stone Blockade of Charleston Harbour has created intense disgust here – & has given rise to the proposition of France to raise the blockade – It has such a financial aspect – that labour to destroy in all time coming a harbour of refuge & commerce as it was represented to us, that a feeling of revulsion took place in regard to the perpetrators of the cruel deed, – but our minds are altering when we know it a little better....

MS. incomplete.

MS.960 vol. 2 Webb-Quincy Correspondence [423]
pp. 77-79 R.D. Webb to Edmund Quincy

Dublin, January 31, 1862.

My dear Quincy,

...No circumstance that has occurred since the rebellion broke out has amazed me more than the wide divergence of opinion between you and me on many points on which I thought you (being a sensible man) could have been sure to agree with me. For example do you in the least doubt that if the Trent & the San Jacinto has changed nationalities the Americans would have cried our at least as loud as the English did? I wish it to be particularly understood that in this affair the British people were as nearly & as promptly unanimous as I have ever known them to be. Their unanimity was not the result of any wire pulling on the part of sect, party, class, or caste – of cotton broker or aristocracy. It was touching the country on its tenderest point – & would have been just the same if Mason & Co. had been black slave instead of proslavery commissioners. The outcry resulted not from a determination to attack you when your hands were full – but because it was felt to be an affront which ought not to be put up with, & that if we did so, no other nation, certainly not yours, would any longer respect us. I fancy a great many Americans had really made up their minds that Englishmen had no rights which you were bound to respect – and were really angry that this was not our opinion. In no other way can I account for the furious outburst of offended pride on the part of Mr. Lovejoy because we refused to submit on this occasion also.

The general sentiment here is that there is a very small chance of Southern submission very little approach to a strong & hearty antislavery opinion at the north – & little likelihood that (even if there were, at this time) it could have much power in affecting the liberation of the slaves by direct action at an early day. I think the slaves' chance is now pretty much what it would have been if the former proportion of the Abolitionists for 'No union with slaveholders' had been peaceably adopted by the secession of the North instead of the South from the Union. I most earnestly hope the European powers may not interfere in any way that could be regarded by the North as hostile to their interests or on any pretence. They wd. do themselves great harm & would do you no good. The hostility of the President, of many of the generals & of a great portion of the Northern Press to manumission makes it most improbable that any such thing will be attempted now — since they abstained when it might have been successful. If the South establish their independence they will not have so good a back for slavery as they had while supported by all the strength and national pride of the Free States. As to the recognition of the Slaveholders as belligerents which have such offence to the North, nobody that I know of has attempted to show us how we could help it unless by going to war to help you which you would certainly not have thanked us for. I know there are millions in the North who wd. find fault with any turn we might take — but I would not have suspected you to be one of the number. I admit & have admitted the ignorance of many of our writers for the press — but is not this equally true on your side, & should not this also be allowed for, when estimating the value of the opinions & conclusions of your editor? In your article on 'The Golden Moment' you very fairly claim an equal right for Americans to adopt protection principles as for us to stand up for Free Trade. It is not more than 40 years since Free Trade began to gain ground with commercial men in England, & with the former nothing but the prosperity which followed the abolition of the Corn Laws, could convince them that they were not ruined by Cobden & Bright. It is the simple truth that the benefits of free trade are looked upon as so decided, that a man might as well say that 3 & 3 are 7, as propose a return to our old world ways. But we have no right to dragoon you into our opinions so long as you think them the best for yourselves. — I was a good deal struck with your comments on the different views taken in England from those which you take as to the relative guilt of offences against property & those against the person. All you said I heartily assent to. I am continually horrified by the contrast between the leniency of magistrates towards perpetrators of the most bastardly, ferocious & brutal outrages, compared with their severity in punishing comparatively trifling thefts. Our criminal law is a mass of absurdity in this respect & I was glad to see you hold up the mirror as you do.

The remarks in English papers on the 'ferocity' of your 'fratricidal' war are sheer nonsence. This kind of talk goes on about all wars in which England takes any interest. The Russians were cruel, the Hindoos were cruel — only the English never admit that they were cruel. I think them far more cruel than the Northern Americans — but they cant see it — for their interests are engaged. I would very much like to have your opinions of the probabilities of the war, if France & England keep quiet, as I fervently hope they may. The struggle & the expenditure have been terrible — but the circumstances are without parallel except to some extent in your revolutionary war and it is now clear to me that your success at that time was partly owing to your possession of a good general & to the fact that you fought on your own soil pro aris et focis. The South hates the North more than the Colonists hated English. They are more numerous & they have millions of slaves to do their hard work. These slaves would now be your helpers but for Lincoln's loyalty to that absurd Constitution which has a strange power to dazzle & befool nearly all Americans. What Gerritt Smith says on this point is very well said....

Yours ever truly,

Richd. D. Webb.

MS.B.1.6. vol. 9 The May Papers [424]
No. 7 Eliza Wigham to ?

n.d. [fragment]

...As for the Mason & Slidell difficulty – we are too thankful for its termination & the hopes of Peace it brings to dwell on the misunderstanding of the case – men may differ on points of law & on the measures required for their own protection without *wishing* to go to war with any one nation. – I am sure the desire for peace here was general – & the thankfulness for its assurance too.

MS.B.1.6. vol. 9 The May Papers [425]
No. 5 Eliza Wigham to Samuel May

5 Gray Street, Edinburgh.
12. 2. 1862.

My dear Friend,

...I hope the overruling of Providence will soon be made bare for the emancipation of the slaves & the preservation of your guilty nation:– but God has so long called & *it has refused*, that we cannot but fear the judgments that may yet be in store for you. I see a proposition again before Congress, to emancipate slaves of rebels & secure some territory to which they may be sent '*if they are willing*' the latter proviso is a great improvement – but why should a nation send away its most productive class of labourers? it is not usual when countries seize & subjugate other countries that they send away the labourers. But this problem will work itself out if your Govt. would only proclaim emancipation to all to whom such proclamation can reach....

Thine very sincerely & affectionately,

E. Wigham.

MS.B.1.6. vol. 9 The May Papers [426]
No. 10 Samuel May to R.D. Webb

Leicester, February 25, 1862.

Dear friend Webb,

...We were both surprised and disappointed to see how quickly (how seemingly spontaneously) and how furiously the flame of war-feeling against the country burst forth in England. It was a revelation of an unexpected fact. We had always heard, from England, how strong & inimical was the feeling of our country against yours. We were very little aware of it, ourselves, and didn't really believe in it; and yet had got in the way of supposing it must be so, until the visit of the Prince of Wales, and the cordial good feeling towards him, his royal mother, and people he represented, expressed universally by all the people & journals, city & country, of our Northern States, afforded a proof which must have convinced any but a stubbornly unbelieving mind of the non-existence among us of any considerable enmity to England. I am bound to say, that the same thing could not be said now, with equal truth. Our nation and government were treated, in the Mason and Slidell case, as tho' an international insult to England had been planned and executed. Nothing could further than that from the truth. *No insult, or discourtesy, to England was imagined....* (&) injury, and great injury, was done to us by their being received on the Trent at all....

Yours very truly,

S. M. Jr.

MS.B.1.6. vol. 15 Additional Letters to Samuel May Jr. [427]

Dublin March 12, 1862.

Dear Mr. May,

...John Bright's speech at Rochdale was able & generous – but until your trouble began I never looked on him as friendly to the abolitionists. The League had the busts of Calhoun & Macduffie in their Board Rooms though well aware of their atrocious character as High Priests of Chattel Slavery. Cobden & Bright are benefactors of their country in the great inauguration of the Free Trade System by which we benefit so much -- but they have not done the hundredth part so much for your cause as H. M[artineau] who is the writer of the numerous leaders in the Daily News on American subjects – & the D. N. is the most respectable daily paper in London....

I am yours affectionately,

Richd. D. Webb.

MS.960.2. Webb-Quincy Correspondence [428]
p. 80 Webb to Quincy

Dublin, March 12, 1862.

My dear Quincy,

...I had a long talk yesterday with a a friend of my own, an old school fellow, and now a wealthy merchant of the highest standing as to transactions, ability, & general intelligence of any in Ireland. During the famine he was repeatedly consulted by Sir Robert Peel, Lord John Russell, & the Earl of Clarendon. He is a remarkably modest, even clear-headed man & would have made a first rate judge. He agrees with me in my opinion that enmity to America or a desire to take a shabby advantage had nothing to do with the Trent affair.

On the contrary the prospect of a war was looked on with dislike on every account – on account of the help it would give to the slaveholders – the fact that the war would be with our nearest kindred nation and must sow the seeds of ill will & hostility for generations – & in short on every ground that could make a war abominable, besides the cost of blood, tears & treasure.

He also agrees with me that no overt act (notwithstanding what we might naturally expect, & not withstanding assumptions which with you have become solidifi[ed] into facts) can be pointed out showing that the aristocracy, the commercial & manufacturing classes or the operatives have evinced any desire to embarrass the North or to deprive them of their fair chance to suppress the rebellion — perhaps with the exception of the dinner to Yancey[1] by the Fishmongers Company in London.

My friend thinks the aristocracy would *a priori* be hostile to the rebellion because they dislike all rebellion as interfering with vested interests & with that stability of public affairs which is the best guarantee for the undisturbed possession of their own property & privileges.

He regards the course of the Times as an indication of the existence of a large amount of sympathy with the rebellion among the readers of that paper, and this sympathy he accounts for in the following way. For years past the American journals have led us to regard the American people as ambitious & aggressive in no ordinary degree — We have heard of the Monroe Doctrine, of the Ostend Manifesto, of the rapid increase of your 30 millions to 50 millions, 70 millions, 100 millions within the lifetime of people now in coats, waistcoats & trousers. We have been threatened with being swallowed up. We are not in the least afraid of you now — but our grandchildren may be. It is not pleasant to think of being ridden over roughshod, of being swallowed up or of our posterity being subdued by the Yankees. If you were split into two powers you would [have] enough to do to watch one another and would be less disposed to set about absorbing us. As to the slaves, the South if hemmed in cannot support their system, which must speedily die out. Whilst if the North subdue them & retain their fealty to the Constitution along with their dislike of the blacks, the slave will be apparently as badly off as ever. The leaders in the last Standard show that you feel far from confident that this will not be the case.... We both think that our government are sincerely desirous to keep out of your quarrels, & to act so as to give no real ground of offence to either side. As to the character of the Southern leaders or the objects they proclaim, there is no second opinion — but it is felt that they must fail in establishing & extending a slave empire if hemmed in by a hostile North & opposed by the public opinion of the world. — It is thought that the North & the South can never be welded together to any good purpose. Very few on this side at all comprehend your attachment to the Union or the crime involved in breaking it up although the shabby conduct of the traitors in doing as they have done is well understood. It is not like a Yorkshireman rebelling against the Unity of England — or a Prussian against the Unity of France. The Northerners & Southerners are looked on as essentially different people. These however are only speculations & I maintain that an earnest desire generally prevails to give no reasonable ground of offence to your people — & that the great majority will [?] to the North as those with whom their sympathies naturally go. I find that the ablest book on the Southern side[2] (that by James Spence of Liverpool) — a very well written volume full of facts & fallacies is from the pen of a leader in the cotton interest. — the man who took the chair at the only [?] meeting held in England on the Mason & Slidell affair....

---

1. William Lowndes Yancey (1814-1863), a leader of the Southern cause, was sent to England and France as a Commissioner of the Confederate States of America.
2. *On the Recognition of the Southern Confederation*, London, 1862.

It was repeatedly said that we wanted to pick a quarrel in order to go to war with you. Nothing of the kind. No minister could keep his place who should venture to plunge the country into a war with the United States on any pretence that was regarded or contrived for that object.

Great offence was caused by our sending troops to Canada. Suppose there had been a war how would Lord Palmerston have looked if he had left Canada undefended? Had we not as good a right to defend Canada as you had to defend New York? As you did not go to war with us our troops did you no harm. We could not say what the result of the negotiations would be & you could not fairly object to a little prudent precaution on our part.

That some of our people should not be sorry if you had something to fight about at home instead of falling foul of us is not more blameworthy than the desire that prevails on your side for the overthrow of our crumbling thrones & falling dynasties. With the exception of the newspapers editors & writers of leaders who are (you know) a mischievous race on your side as well as ours – I see no indication whatever variety of opinion there may be of anything but a desire to act loyally & fairly towards you – & certainly no hostility or bitterness exists here such as prevails *there....*

It is very hard for us here to know what to make of the tenderness of your government for the slave property of the slaveholders – How can they think to pacify the cruel enemies of the North & of liberty by any such contrivance? Heartily wishing your nation out of her troubles I am ever truly & affectionately yours,

Richd. D. Webb.

MS.960 Quincy–Webb Correspondence [429]
p. 28b Quincy to Webb

Dedham – 1862.

My dear Webb,

...One thing is very observable as to the state of the American mind, and that is the indifference to English and Foreign opinion which has succeeded to the sensitiveness of a year ago. The subject is seldom mentioned and whereas the leaders of the London papers were eagerly copied into ours and Russell's[1] Letters were greedily reread for the first few months, it is next to never that we ever see one in our papers now. I doubt whether one in fifty of the readers of newspapers have known for the last six months whether Russell was in this country or not. I am sure I did not until I saw the account of his being turned out of the transport with as little ceremony as if her had been a negro pedlar. A year ago we had no army, no arms, (so to speak) an empty treasury, doubtful credit and we were keenly alive to the state of

1. W.H. Russell, "Bull Run Russell", first won fame as a war Correspondent in the Crimea, and was at this time the American Correspondent for the London *Times.* His letters to the *Times* were widely read and his account of the Northern Cause after the battle of Bull Run convinced most British readers of the probability of a Southern victory – and caused such personal attacks on him in the American press that they were used as a pretext for his recall to London.

feelings and probabilities of action in Europe and especially in England. Now we have the finest army in the world, splendidly equipped, with vast reserves of artillery, small arms and munitions of war, the Secretary of the Treasury has as much money as he wants and declines further loans and all Government Stocks are above par and with a rising market, and this without a dollar borrowed out of the country. Of course we don't care what you think of us. We were concerned about your Navy until the Monitor demolished all your Wooden Walls with its two guns and now we regard ourselves as your watch at sea as well as on land. We have not the least doubt about Jonathan's always being six months of John Bull in any invention for peace or war. You will pardon me if I say, what seems to me the fact, that a general feeling of contempt has replaced the anxious interest with which we used to regard England. She has sunk fathoms deep in American opinion, whether from just cause or not. I think full justice is done to our friends there, and we admire the independence of John Bright, and his party and its organs. But we know that he is not in a majority and that the leading influences have been unfriendly to us. We have looked fairly at this side of the shield, but we also have looked at the other. All that you say of the state of feeling in England is true, of course, as to the people you see and hear. But you have not the entree of Lady Palmerston's and Lady Russell's receptions in London or of Lady Cowley's in Paris. I know from persons who have, what is the atmosphere there. It is all but intolerable for American lungs. The sympathy with the South, thinly veiled by politeness or by insolent pity for the North and the assumption of our necessary defeat, the whole tone of society in the highest political and fashionable circles in fact, show what aristocratic feeling is in our direction. And that does govern the squirearchy and the rich merchants and manufacturers who look down upon John Bright and his party as much as on us Yankees. And it is this feeling that overflows in the *Times*, *Punch*, *Blackwood*, *the Saturday Review*. At any rate, the feeling here is that the government influences were entirely with the South, that they did all they dared to help it, and it was only fear of hurting themselves and the hope that the North would soon have to give in, that held them back from openly assisting it. The latest advices, I see, say that England and France are about ready to interfere. Of course, the news of the opening of the ports of Beaufort, Norfolk and New Orleans and the certainty of the opening of those Charleston, Mobile and Savannah in a very short time, will put a stop to any such purpose, if it really exist. But there would not be a moment's hesitation here about engaging both matters, if they should provoke a fight. Indeed there are many people who think that a few years' war with you would be the best thing for the U.S. as it would build up our manufacturers in every direction and make us entirely independent of Europe. Observe, I don't think so. But there would be no such disinclination to a European war as used to exist before we knew our strength and when our trade was at its height. However, that is out of the question, I trust. Whatever the abstract truth of Free Trade doctrines may be, our Protective System has had the effect of making us independent of all the world. We depend on England absolutely for nothing that I can think of. We make everything necessary to eat, drink and wear, furniture, the most beautiful glass and earthern ware, we supply your colonies with agricultural tools, we have all kinds of manufactures in iron, from columbiads to the most delicate surgical instruments, mathematical and astronomical apparatus and everything I can think of necessary for subsistence, luxury or science. Silks and wines are all we depend on France for. Silks we can do without, if we should not introduce the culture, and we are not getting excellent qualities of wine from California, which is going to be one of the great wine-growing countries of the world. Wine has always been raised there from home-consumption and the manufacture is greatly increasing and improving. *The Times* I see continues to prophesy natural bankruptcy and general insolvency. And the moon-calf Charles MacKay[2] confessed to his astonishment at finding Boston apparently as prosperous as ever, and no bread riots in the streets! I know nothing, personally, about trade; but there are all the external signs of business here and in New York that are usual in the best of times. The streets and shops are full of people, carts and drays are going in every direction, private carriages are just as many and there are no signs of poverty anywhere. The hotels here and in N.Y. are as full as they can be, and this though the Southern custom is *nil.* As to failures there have been none of any consequence here and few in N.Y. excepting those of houses in the Southern trade. And the war has taught us how much we had exaggerated the importance of that. The N.Y. *Times* affirmed last autumn that the Southern trade of N.Y. was not more than *five per cent* of its business and that in an average of years there was more lost than gained by it. This did not include, I take it, the cotton we used to buy and pay gold for, but the merchandize with which we supplied them. It said further, that the business of Boston was worth more to N.Y. than that of all the Cotton States and that of the six New England States with a territory no bigger than Great Britain, worth more than all the Slave States put together, a territory greater than all Europe, excepting Russia. Indeed, knowing ones affirm that there was never so much money made in the Northern States in any one year as in the last one. The capital which was diverted from trade was lent to the government, and put into the various manufactures the government needed. Every cent of the loans was spent in the country, or nearly so. All kinds of manufactures have been doing excellently well. The wool traders have made fortunes. (Tom Mott of Phila. among the number). The Cotton manufactories have made larger dividends than usual – owing to the rise in prices and the stocks they had in hand the banks never were as prosperous, for, investing the money not wanted for commerce in government securities at the first price and selling out now. Of course all trades and manufacturies connected directly with the war have been doing a profitable business. The main depreciation has been in the price of real-estate and in rents. But as this chiefly fell on the rich, it is not of so much consequence. They seldom actually suffer in consequence. Persons with capital invested in good 6 per cent. securities have had no diminution of income.... The earnings of the last year have been immense and this is the reason government stocks are so high and Mr. Chase[3] can get all the money he wants at five per cent. And, I am told, trade is improving and real-estate looking up. Wendell Phillips says that they told him at Chicago and those western cities trade is in breadstuffs that their business was never so good as now, and that they knew nothing of

2. Charles McKay, a British journalist and traveller, was another Correspondent of the London *Times.*

3. Salmon Portland Chase (1808-1873) was then Secretary of the Treasury.

the War, excepting through the newspapers. And I see that the Western traders came in this Spring for their stocks bringing cash funds and asking no credit.

(MS. ends)

MS.B.1.6. vol. 9 The May Papers [430]
No. 33 Samuel May to ?

n.d. (fragment).

I am told by Mr. Garrison that Lord Palmerston's organ in London had openly aspoused the side of the Southern Rebels. I have not myself seen the journals, and he could not lay his hand upon them. At all events, the opinion is certainly growing stronger here that England is at this time, in spirit and policy, hostile to the United States Government. I wish there were not the reasons & grounds, which I believe there are, for this judgment. The case of the 'Bermuda' steamer, *sold in England to the Rebel Goverment, openly loaded in an English port with supplies of the most valuable & abundant character, and carried into Savannah, Georgia, in violation of the blockade, & herself fitted to act as a privateer on Northern commerce* is a most marked evidence & proof in the case, provided the above publicly asserted facts are established. Let us hope they may be disproved. Meantime let us still more strongly hope that the reserved voice of the British people will yet speak out against the Slaveholders and their Desperate Attempt to establish a Slaveholding Empire.

I am, in haste, very truly yrs.,

Saml. May Jr.

MS.A.1.2. vol. 31 Anti-Slavery Letters to Garrison [431]
No. 115 Oliver Johnston to William Lloyd Garrison

Anti-Slavery Office,
New York, 18 April, 1862.

My Dear Garrison,

Have you not been happy in the last few days over the great event of the abolition of slavery in the District of Columbia? Will not even the workers now be willing to confess that our cause has made progress – that the present, however dark, is brighter than the past – and that we have good ground for hope as to the future? Will not our friend Pillsbury be able to discern a ray of light stealing over the dark picture that seems always hanging before his mind's eye? The work yet to be done is mighty and will task our energies to the utmost; but ought we not to catch a new inspiration from the thought that the capital is free at length from the crime against which we have been so long contending? I hope our Anniversary will take from this even a tone of cheerfulness and deep assurance of victory nigh at hand; for I am sure that in this temper our labors will be far more effectual than in any other....

Yours faithfully,

O. Johnson.

MS.B.1.6. vol. 9 The May Papers [432]
No. 32 Samuel May to R.D. Webb.

Boston, Tuesd. Eveg. May 27. 1862.

Dear Friend Webb,

...Our President has again sorely disappointed the antislavery portion of the country & the army, – which now has grown to be a very large portion, – by overruling General Hunter's Proclamation of Emancipation in the States of Georgia, Florida, and South Carolina, as he did General Fremont's in Missouri.... To you, & to multitudes abroad, it will again seem, I doubt not, to indicate an anxious regard for *Slavery* in the President, an unwillingness to touch it, & more, a determination not to touch it. You will think it most unreasonable, & so do we; – short-sighted, & so do we, an act of over-weening caution & timidity, & so do we.... Sad as I am, at the President's failure to do the right & wise thing, I would do justice to his act, his words, & motives. I do not believe he has any love of Slavery, or seeks to conserve it. He has publicity declared slavery to be at war with the best interests of the country, & has called on the slaveholding states to cooperate with the Northern in removing this fruitful cause of dissension and strife. Congress under his advice, have offered pecuniary aid to any State adopting an Emancipation policy.... If we thought the President corrupt, & Pro-slavery, we should despair of the country, so far as any human help is concerned. But we believe him an honest man and a friend to his country; who aims at the good of all its people; and that his policy, if weak, is not designedly wicked.... No more critical or perilous time has ever come to us, I think, than the present. The miserable Northern sympathizers with the rebels are rejoicing at the President's cause, and at the refusal of Congress to confiscate the slave property of rebels. Such facts should open his eyes. But it would seem that our Government is smitten with judicial blindness, and is leading us all astray. May light look upon us, soon....

Yrs. ever,

S. May Jr.

MS.B.1.6. vol. 9 The May Papers [433]
No. 39 Samuel May to Charles [Burleigh?]

Leicester, July 17/62.

Dear Charles,

...If Lincoln vetoes the Confiscation Bill, – passed as it was in both Houses near 2 to 1 – I believe I shall entirely give him up. – My confidence in his capacity & fitness for the place has been much shaken in the past few weeks; – at the time that he nullified Hunter's proclamation, it began indeed to be empaired. Accounts of his talk & sentiments are conflicting – *both may be true*, and so he would be a trimmer & double-tongued, which I am loth, I confess, to believe him to be. – C. Sumner, in his letter to the great N.Yk. Meeting, does not *hint* even anything of the confidence in Lincoln of which his former letters have been so full. Ruin stares us in the face, – i.e. as a united country. If we cant be united, *and free*, may we never see a union again. It will be hard after the holocaust of life which the North has offered in this War, to find ourselves outwitted, defeated, beaten at every point, Lincoln is the criminal. – McClellan has been no hypocrite, at least. He has never pretended to fight the battles of freedom, but the contrary; & Lincoln & Seward & all of them have known it from the first. Lincoln's running to West Point to get old Scott's advice was, as I now look at it, humiliating & of evil omen. –

Truly yrs.

S. May Jr.

MS.B.1.6. vol. 9 The May Papers [434]
No. 46 Samuel May to R.D. Webb

Boston, Sept. 23. 1862.

Dear friend,

This morning I can write you on but one topic, for I can think & speak of no other. This morning's journals bring in *President Lincoln's Proclamation*, dated at Washington yesterday (22d) and now published all over the country, wherein he declares that on the 1st day of January next all slaves in States, or parts of States, which shall then be in rebellion against the Government shall be *'thenceforward and forever free'*. Laus Deo!...

MS.A.1.2. vol. 31 Anti-Slavery Letters to Garrison [435]
No. 150 Oliver Johnson to William Lloyd Garrison

New York, 25 Sept., 1862.

Dear Garrison,

...How do you feel about the Proclamation? Of course it is not all that justice requires, nor all that we could wish; but hope springs up in my heart that it will save us. The Democrats are very bitter, and show a determination to fight, but I am confident that they will be overwhelmed – that the vast majority of the Northern people will sustain the President. That it is possible to coax or drive back into the Union before the first of January, I do not believe; and I am sure old Abe, having set his foot down, will not yield. It remains to be seen whether the North will have the pluck to put the war through on this basis, and carry freedom from the Potomac to the Gulf. My hope that she will is very strong....

Yours with exultation,

Oliver Johnson.

No. 157 Wm. A. Jackson[1] *to ?*

London November 6th / 62.

Mr. Editor, Dear Sir,

I now take the friendly opportunity of writing to you. I know that you and the friends of liberty would like to know of my arrival in Europe. I haste to tell you I come on my own responsibility, which you and the friends all know. I arrived in Liverpool on the 5th inst. at one o' clock P.M. by the steam ship City of New York, making the voyage eleven days and four hours. She brought over a good many passengers. They put off a good many at Queenstown – a good many of Irish – all of which were anxious to go home, and see their mothers, fathers, brothers, sisters and some of their friends that had been sick and lame for years. But they never thought of them at all till Father Abraham commenced drafting, and then they began to take off to Ireland, and think of their friends that they had left behind. There was one who said, 'Faith, I have a bounty, and I will go and see my father.' I have often wondered why the Irish had such a prejudice against colored gentlemen, because I am under the flag of Queen Victoria, because I know a colored man can come here, and in this land be free. Here you do not hear the word 'nigger', like you do among the low, degraded Irish of the North, who pretend to support the Constitution and the Union, and get their bounty, and go off till the war is over. Then they all will want to come back, and then they will talk about the constitution better than George Francis Train[2].... I am stopping at Mr. Thompson's for the present. I feel that I will be sure to get along, if I look to God, and do not forget to pray; though I would rather be with the Union army, if I could help to kill some of the rebels, and my people all go free. I have done all that I could to get a chance to go, before I left the United States, but the Government would not accept the regiment that Governor Sprague was raising at Providence, Rhode Island, which I joined. But, nevertheless, I hope it will all come right bye and bye, I know my people will be free. I was offered the chance to go to Washington, the day that I arrived in New York from Boston to take the steamer; but then it was too late, for I had made my arrangements to sail for Europe.... I have no more to write, but it is getting late. I will always stand up for the Constitution and the Union as it ought to be.

Very respectfully yours,

Wm. A. Jackson.
Ex-coachman of Jeff. Davis.

---

1. William Andrew Jackson, an escaped slave, had been Jefferson Davis' coachman.
2. George Francis Train (1829-1904), eccentric and chauvinistic businessman and author, was in Britain at the beginning of the Civil War, and strongly defended the Northern cause.

Leicester, Mass. Nov. 18 / 62.

Dear friend Webb,

....I am particularly obliged to you for sending me Prof. Cairnes's[1] Lecture at Dublin, & to hear of what you say of it & of him.... We are, as a country, indebted to Prof. Cairnes. Had such candour & good sense as he displays, had a modicum of his *immortal* spirit (impartial, not partisan, or biased towards us) prevailed among the leading men, classes & journals of Great Britain towards this country, during our bitter, still bitter struggle to free this continent from what Lord Carlisle well calls 'The hideous grasp of slavery', our land would not be pervaded, as to a great extent it is, with a feeling of abhorrence for England in the selfish course she has pursued, of mortification in the example she has set of repudiating her own best history, & of resentment at the narrow spirit she has exhibited towards us. *I* feel it the more, because I had entertained such different opinions and views of England, I see, indeed, that there is a contest in England no less than here in our own Northern States. I see that there, as here, the sober judgment, the settled convictions of the intelligent & disinterested masses, the conscience & principles of the high-minded, lean to the side of Freedom. And I see that there is an immensely wealthy & powerful class, (or rather classes), who feel (some of them) that now is their time to cripple the American Republic and pay off old scores of Revolutionary and later times. To feed this old grudge of theirs they are not too nice or scrupulous to take the slave-trader's & slave-holder's bloody & dirty hand in their aristocratic & dainty hands and to give him such countenance and assistance as may be needful to compass their own objects. Others of them – the cotton men – with a shortsightedness which is the invariable characteristic & accompaniment, I believe of selfish greed, think the cotton producing states must be upheld in as much as they can serve their turn the best. With these join the Trading and Shipping classes who see in the Slaveholding States a race of people very dependent on others for all the comforts & luxuries & many of the necessaries of life; all to be supplied (they trust) by British manufactures, British shipping, & British free trade. To men bent on mere success in the scramble for money, these last considerations are a most powerful temptation. Similar considerations have been operating here under our own eye for scores of years, and the political & moral democratization of this country, of which Prof. C. speaks, none too strongly, has been largely caused by their influence. Now these several classes in Great Britain, for the first time, have been acting cordially & vigorously together, since the Southern Rebellion broke out. *Their action* has inspired not only the masses of the American people, but more impartial & dispassionate observers abroad, (among whom I think the Count Gasparin may be named) with – I must say it – a *contempt* for their spirit, motives, & object, which any language of mine is feeble to express. Whether these aristocratic and trading classes combined are to rule England – is the question now. We hope not; we hope it (as we believe) as much for

1. Professor John Elliott Cairnes (1823-1875) was an Irish economist whose work, *The Slave Power*, 1862, was one of the most important British attacks on the South.

England's honour & her ultimate interests, as we do for our own sakes. For we, as Americans, feel that we have an historical & a personal state in England's honour & character; & her good, or her evil, deeds reflect their own spirit & character in some measure upon us. But we are not the custodians of England's honour, nor in any position now to be very calm judges in the matter, I suppose. But we have not lost our moral discernment; and we now look with a most eager (to me painful) interest to see whether Principle or Selfishness, Justice or Spite, Self-Respect or Self-Aggrandisement, shall carry the day in the counsels and action of Great Britain towards us. Amongst her solid, educated, thinking people we fully believe the former of these prevail and actuate; but the latter bear sway, we see, amongst her aristocratic & her moneyed classes, with those who usually hold the reins of Government. Hitherto these classes have been the noisy, the demonstrative, the busy ones; & under their incessant appeals, the Government, though not yet turned from its original purpose, appears to be well-nigh palsied as to any *action.* Immense supplies for the Rebellion go from British home & provincial ports, & meet with such large pay of some sort that they can afford to lose many ships & cargoes by capture. Iron clad vessels of war for the Confederates are built in British ship yards, the most effective armament put in them, & they openly leave to do their work of destruction upon American commerce, (and that too under the British flag!!) while an American vessel of war is not suffered to enter a British port for any supplies, even of fuel. What kind of neutrality is that? Is the British Govt. going to succumb to the vile influences I have referred to? We are constantly assured not. You assure me that we need not fear intervention. And I know that if these questions are decided upon established British rules and principles, intervention *cannot* take place in favour of the Slaveholding South. But there is the very difficulty. Will they be decided on these principles? If Prof. Cairnes, and J. Stuart Mill,[2] and John Bright, & the Daily News & a few other journals are regarded, all will be right. But what is the outlook of the matter now? Taught by so fair & candid an example as Prof. C., I will not pre-judge the case of England's future. She has much to do to wipe out the record of the past eighteen months. I hope the appeal wh. the *Daily News* has just made to the Eng. Govt., to stop the building of Confederate vessels of war in British dockyards, or else rescind the neutrality proclamation; and that either the one or the other will be done....

Ever yours,

S. May Jr.

MS.A.1.2. vol. 31 Anti-Slavery Letters to Garrison [438]
No. 162 George Thompson to William Lloyd Garrison

London, Dec. 5, 1862.

My dear Garrison,

I am so worn down by much lecturing upon the American question, that I am not fit for writing, and can do no more than give you a general idea of what is doing. Our London Emancipation Committee has

---

2. John Stuart Mill (1806-1873), the famous liberal philosopher and economist, was one of the most important Northern supporters in Britain during the Civil War.

merged in a Society, the object of wh. you will learn from a circular and an Address which I enclose. We have an active Executive Committee, and a general Committee, which already numbers about 200; composed of good men and true in all parts of the kingdom. We are making daily additions to it. We have commenced holding meetings in the metropolis, and shall multiply them as rapidly as possible.... You will not have forgotten my campaign in the 'Send back the Money Question'; nor the one on the conduct of the Evangelical Alliance. The present is like unto those; but my strength is not as great now as then. Nevertheless, I am doing all I can and, with God's blessing on the efforts of myself, and other and better men, England shall be saved from her delusion....

Ever most truly yours,

Geo. Thompson.

MS.A.1.2. vol. 31 Anti-Slavery Letters to Garrison [439]
No. 164 George Thompson to William Lloyd Garrison.

London, December 12. 1862.

My dear Garrison,

I have just returned from Staffordshire where I have been holding meetings at Hanly, Burslem, and Newcastle upon the Emancipation question in America. In every place I had large and enthusiastic meetings and although I heard of many persons with Southern sympathies & though at every meeting I invited opposition no antagonist appeared....

I am looking with impatience & nervous anxiety for the appearance of the President's message. I have been encouraged by what I have seen in the American papers to believe that it will be satisfactory on the slave question but I want the assurance of the document itself. My disappointment would be great, and the sorrow of the slave here most poignant if it should show any infirmity of purpose in reference to emancipation.

Too much praise cannot be awarded to our unemployed and suffering population in the manufacturing districts for the patience & uncomplaining fortitude with which they have borne their privations consequent on the stoppage of the supply of cotton. Many & evil have been the attempts made to stir them to utter a demand for interference on the part of the government with a view to the recognition of the rebel states and the opening of the Southern ports. But they have been proof against all temptations and have found amongst themselves able spokesmen to answer the arguments of the Enemies of the North & of the cause of freedom....

Our Emancipation Society has issued a circular to ministers of all religious denominations urging them to call attention to the president's proclamation. I send you a copy and hope you will approve it....

Always, most sincerely yours,

Geo. Thompson.

Evening of Christmas Day, 1862.

My Dear Garrison,

While reading the Antislavery Standard of the 13th Instant, my eye has lighted on an extract from the Thanksgiving sermon of the Rev. H. W. Beecher,[1] in which I find these words:—

'The public sentiment of England has rapidly become pro-slavery.' 'She has stood forth as a proslavery nation' And this, because 'her factories and ships, her commerce and manufacturing were touched.'

England, thus described, is contrasted with England at the time Mrs. Stowe was here, when half a million of signatures were attached to a document beseeching America to take immediate action in reference to slavery, and do away the great and crying evil.

My answer to Mr. Beecher is, that the Spirit prevailing among the men of this country, connected with 'ships, commerce, factories and manufacturing', has always been that of indifference or opposition to the anti-slavery cause. That this spirit has been manifested during your struggle with the slaveholding states, is no evidence that this country has apostatized from the principles which so signally triumphed thirty years ago. As for the half million of signatures furnished by 'the ladies in England, including every principal woman excepting the illustrious Queen', I would undertake to obtain double the number now, to an Address praying Mr. Lincoln and the Congress to give immediate and unconditional freedom to every slave in America, and to compensate them for past injustice by dividing amongst them the confiscated lands of their enslavers. I would not promise that in *my* record of the names of my countrywomen would appear as many of the titled & aristocratic as were contained in the volumes exhibited in the drawing room of the Duchess of Sutherland; but I think I might guarantee that these should be the names of at least two hundred thousand women, who are at this moment heroically & uncomplainingly suffering from the suspension of our supply of slave-grown cotton, and who are willing to continue to suffer, rather than see the triumph of the slave holder, or a compromise of the principles of liberty on the part of the Northern States.

On New Year's eve a great meeting of the working classes will be convened in the Free Trade Hall, Manchester, to consider & adopt Resolutions, and an Address to your President, on the subject of the abolition of Slavery. The meeting will be, *bona fide*, one of operatives, — of persons plunged into the deepest distress by the want of cotton. Yet I venture to predict that these will be an all but unanimous expression of sympathy with the American slave. The spirit of ship's commerce and manufactures will not reign there, but the warm, generous unselfish spirit of the industrial population of the seat of the cotton trade of this country. I have received

---

1. **Rev. Henry Ward Beecher (1813-1887), one of the most prominent clergymen and public figures in his day, defended the Northern cause in Britain, and attacked British neutrality in a series of lectures given throughout the country.**

a copy of the Resolutions & Address which will be submitted, and enclose them to you for publication. You shall have the best account I can furnish of the proceedings. I shall not be there, having promised to be present at a similar meeting in Sheffield at the same time.

In the endeavour to arrive at a sound & unprejudiced judgment on the true state of public feeling in this country, certain facts should be kept in mind.

The sentiments of our leading journals of a portion of our public men, and of the aristocratic circles, at the present time, on the subject of slavery, and precisely similar to those which prevailed in the same quarters during the struggle for the emancipation of our own slaves. In this respect, England is neither better nor worse Blackwood's Magazine and the *Times* of to-day, are the same as they were in 1832 – the one of the essence of Toryism, the other of Mammon. In the years 1831, 32 and 33, when petitions from all parts of the kingdom were being poured into the House of Commons in favour of abolition, if the Times, the Quarterly, Frazer, Blackwood, the John Bull, and a host of our other 'public instructors' had been taken as the Exponents of English sentiment, we might have been pronounced a proslavery nation. Mr. Beecher visits upon the heads of the masses of our people the sins of certain classes in our country, with which classes we are always in conflict when promoting any object connected with the elevation or freedom of the many. On the vital question of slavery, *the heart of the people is sound.* It would be impossible to carry a proslavery resolution in any unpacked assembly in the kingdom. I could obtain a vote of censure from the constituents of every man who has vindicated the cause of the slaveholding rebels. The *Times* could not obtain an endorsement of its sentiments in any open meeting in the city of London, or elsewhere, where an opportunity was afforded of speaking the truth. The mention of its name invariably calls forth 'a groan.' It should always be remembered, too, that our people are very imperfectly acquainted with the powers of your Federal Government. They know little or nothing of your constitution – its compromises, guarantees, limitations, obligations, &c. They are consequently unable to appreciate the difficulties of your president, or to comprehend the caution, forbearance & tenderness which he displays when speaking of slavery, slaveholders, Slave States, &c. Then, again; our anti-American journals have been careful to conceal the truth. They have exposed every blunder; blazoned every proslavery act of general or officer in the army; have republished the harsh criticisms of abolition speakers; and above all, the repeated declarations of members of the Republican party, that the war was *not* for the abolition of slavery. But I must close my letter. I have an engagement, and must keep it. For those who have misrepresented & maligned the North, I have only contempt and condemnation. For those who have ignorantly erred & who have withheld their sympathy through a misunderstanding of the facts of the case, I have much forgiveness, and at the same time faith to foresee their repentance and amendment. None know better than you and I how much the Northern people themselves have done to furnish occasion to the adversary and to justify the taunts & reproaches he has hurled against them. *You* can understand the difficulty of my position during the first year of the War, when so many ugly facts came out illustrating the proslavery tendencies of your public men. You know how many plagues it has needed to bring the North to hear the command – wh. is not even yet obeyed – 'let my people go!' You know how impossible it is at this moment to vindicate as one would wish the course of Mr. Lincoln. In no one of his utterances is there an assertion of great principle – no appeal to right or justice. In everything he does & says affecting the slave, there is the alloy of expediency. The slave may be free – if it should be *'necessary'* or *'convenient'* or 'agreable to his master'. What we want to see him do, is to take his stand upon the doctrine of human equality, & man's inalienable right to life liberty & the pursuit of happiness. All else is [palterings ?] with conscience & with truth. I sometimes feel unutterably indignant when I see the liberty of four millions of God's immortal children made contingent upon the inclinations,' loyalty & advantages of their tyrants. I firmly believe that Mr. Lincoln might, if he would, extirpate, root and branch, the accursed system; and that both God & man would support him in the deed. Oh, that he would do it – and thereby secure the peace of his soul, the blessing of the slave, the applause of mankind, the verdict of posterity & the approbation of heaven!

Ever, most sincerely,

Geo. Thompson.

MS.A.1.2. vol. 32 Anti-Slavery Letters to Garrison [441]
No. 4 F.W. Chesson to William Lloyd Garrison

Emancipation Society,
Offices – 65 Fleet Street,
London E.C.
9th January, 1863.

My dear Sir,

I send you a copy of the *Saturday Review* which contains an article on the Emancipation Society's address to the clergy. Do not, however, mistake this, or any similar, ebullition for an expression of the real opinion of the English people on the slavery question, or on the issues between the North and the South. The great meetings which have been held in London and various parts of the country, during the last six weeks to express sympathy with the anti-slavery policy of the American governments, indicate what is the true state of public feeling on this side of the Atlantic. We have endured the misrepresentations of certain organs of our press too long; and we have now determined to endure them no longer. But always remember that from the beginning the best of our journals have remained true to the anti-slavery cause, that the *Star*,[1] *Daily News*,[2] *Westminster Review*, *Spectator*, *Nonconformist*, *British Standard*, *Dial*, *Birmingham Post*, *Manchester Examiner*, *Newcastle Chronicle*, *Caledonian Mercury*, *Belfast Whig*, & host of other representatives of the fourth estate, have never departed from the pure faith. The working classes also have proved to be sound to the core whenever their opinion has been tested. Witness the noble demonstration of Manchester

1. The *Morning Star* was owned by Samuel Lucas, a brother-in-law of John Bright, and edited by Charles and Justin McCarthy.
2. Harriet Martineau contributed regularly to the *Daily News*.

operatives the other day, when three thousand of the worthy sons of labour, (many of whom were actual sufferers from the cotton famine,) adopted by acclamation an address to President Lincoln sympathising with his proclamation. A friend of mine who was present on the occasion tells me that the heartiness and enthusiasm of the working men was something glorious – that he had heard them say to one another that they would rather remain unemployed for twenty years than get cotton from the South at the expense of the slave. Mr. Thompson has been in the ports of Lancashire lately, and the meetings he has addressed have been attended with the same results. Our experience in London has been equally satisfactory. It would have done you good, if you had heard Baptist Noel's[3] speech; or attended the great meeting of the Working Classes which was held on the 31st of December – the eve of freedom. Newman Hall's[4] speech on this occasion was one of the best I ever listened to. He stated, in the fairest manner, every conceivable argument which had been urged in favour of the slave confederacy or against the policy of the Federal government; and then replied to them *seriatim*, demolishing every sophistry and gibbeting every falsehood, until the slaveocracy had really not a say left wherewith to conceal the revolting defects of their odious cause.

The Emancipation Society includes, as you will have seen, some of the best men in the country, without distinction of sect or party. The name of John Stuart Mill – one of the greatest in England – stands at the head of the list. We are now arranging for a demonstration in Exeter Hall to take place on the 29th inst. Our friends in Manchester and Birmingham are organizing branch societies in those important towns; and applications for meetings and deputations are pouring in from all quarters. Our friend Mr. Webb, who is doing such good service in the *Advocate*, and in other ways more private but not less useful, tells me that Professor Cairne's admirable work[5] is about to pass into another edition. As a proof of how extensively it is read, I may say that I have made two unsuccessful attempts to obtain it from Mudie's circulating library (the greatest in the world,) where there is a large number of copies. The answer on both occasions was, that every copy was in the hands of subscribers. Mrs. Stowe's eloquent and beautiful address to the women of England is exciting great interest, and cannot fail to do much good. It was published by Sampson Low & Co. on Wednesday, in the form of a small volume, and it has since been printed *entire* in the columns of the *Morning Star* and the *Daily News* – a remarkable tribute to the popularity of Mrs. Stowe in this country, as well as a proof of the earnest interest which these journals take in the good work. It would not have appeared at a more

---

3. Hon. & Rev. Baptist Noel (1798-1873) a noted London preacher, Baptist Noel had for many years been a clergyman of the Church of England. He had close relations with Evangelical Nonconformist ministers, and in 1848 as a result of the Gorham case (dealing with the doctrine of baptism), left the Anglican church to be reordained the following year as a Baptist minister. He was as active in his new ministry as he had been in his old, championing social reforms and attacking the links between Church and State.

4. Rev. Christopher Newman Hall (1816- ?) another noted Nonconformist London preacher, was also the author of several hymns and devotional works. During the Civil War he visited the United States and preached before Congress.

5. *The Slave Power: Its Character, Career and probable Designs: Being an Attempt to Explain the Real Issues Involved in the American Contest.* The book was published in Dublin by Richard Webb whose knowledge of American slavery greatly aided Prof. Cairnes.

favourable moment, for on Tuesday last the *Times*, with a maniacal folly, which is often linked with malignity, published an article pleading Biblical sanction for slavery, and actually suggesting that it was perhaps a religious duty on the part of the slave to refuse his freedom, even if it were offered to him! Nothing could be more calculated to stir up the religious sentiment of the country against the cause of which the Times has made itself the principal champion. This is another example of the manner in which the devil sometimes overreaches himself.

Very truly yours,

F. W. Chesson.

William Lloyd Garrison Esq.

MS.B.1.6. vol. 9 The May Papers [442]
No. 2 Samuel May to R.D. Webb

Leicester, Masstts.,
Jan. 12. 1862 [? 3].

Dear friend Webb,

...We have much comfort & satisfaction in the changed aspect of affairs in G. Britain – not in any *change* on the part of those who have been pro-slavery all along; *they* remain as they have been. But the old, solid antislavery feeling is stirring. I hope we may yet hear the unmistakeable voice of *the English people*, the genuine roar of the British lion, (so long asleep), at the infernal, blasphemous attempt, in the middle of the 19th Century, to build up a Slave Empire, & get England's friendship & alliance. You may think & say, that this sentiment did not express itself in G. Britain before, because the *North* & the *U.S. Govt.*, have not until recently taken an anti-slavery position. Allowing this to be literally & exactly true, (which it is not – witness the suppression of the Slave Trade – abolition in the District of Columbia – the prohibition of any more Slave States – the recommendation of Emancipation to the sl:holding States, & promise of Pecuniary Compensation –) but allowing it to be literally true, it does not touch the case; because, whatever *the North* did or did not do, there could be no mistake as to what *the South* was about, & what she meant to do, nor that her purpose was to build up her new Confederacy upon Human Slavery.... Norwithstanding all this, England has, in the most forcible and ready way in which it can be done, – short of an open alliance – ministered to, helped, & fed the slaveholders' rebellion, & their project of a Slaveholding Empire, from the first. This is a fact which can never be wiped out; just where the responsibility rests, cannot now be fully determined; but it will come to light, in time I fervently trust the *English people* will fully exonerate themselves. Most nobly have the Lancashire people vindicated themselves & cleared their skirts – *most nobly!* The statement of their case as given by Mr. Bright at Birmingham is touching, in the extreme. More generous & disinterested conduct we never hear of. Nobly has Prof. Newman[1] written to that

1. Francis William Newman (1805-1897) scholar and author of several works of political and social affairs, was a brother of Cardinal Newman, but when he became disillusioned with Anglicanism turned instead to Nonconformity and in the later years of his life joined the Unitarian Association.

hypocrite Gladstone – Well, too, did Bright rebuke him. Nobly did the speakers at the Lambeth (London) meeting hear their testimonies. And George Thompson, from the first, had uttered no uncertain sound....See, (too) what Mr. Bright says of the affair of the 'Alabama'; nothing more emphatic has ever been said in America; & surely nothing less creditable to the Eng. Govt. than its behaviour in that case, can be easily imagined. It seems to me (tho' I am not a diplomatist, not versed much in international Law) that the U.S. Govt. has a good claim on the Brit. Govt. for every shillings worth destroyed by Semmes in that vessel....

I trust the Manchester meeting will prove all that Alfred [Webb] anticipates. If the English *people* speak out, as they did at Lambeth, at Birmingham, & have done in Lancashire, we shall care comparatively little for the Government, for we know *their* career will be checked....

How truly you will rejoice with us in our President's great Act of January 1st, 1863, – by which he gives full and unconditional freedom to more than Three Millions of Slaves. Henceforth they are legally and constitutionally free; & will be so practically, just so far & fast as the Rebellion is subdued. The rejoicings here are very great, & very deep. But, on the other hand, the opposition to the measure is bitter, and the newly-inaugurated Governor of New York is striving to lead off in measure of *resistance.* This will, & must, soon come to a head, and we shall know whether treason and anarchy are apt to get the upper hand or not, at the North. But time is up....

With sincere affection to you all,

Yours truly,

Sam[l]. May Jr.

MS.B.1.6. vol. 9 The May Papers [443]
No. 58 Samuel May to R.D. Webb

Boston, 221 Washington St.
Jan. 16, '63.

Dear Mr. Webb,

...I am troubled, in myself, to think how differently England has looked to me for the past year & a half, from what she used to do. And herein consists my answer to your inquiry.... 'how it happens that more anger has been shown to England, for refusing to interfere with your (our) affairs, than with France which proposed to do so.' It lies just here – we have felt that *England* was our kindred, of the same family – stock, brothers, (or 'cousins' at least;) – and that – having a common language & literature & faith – a common origin and a closer connexion that between nations generally, we had a right to look, nationally, for more consideration at her hands than from others. I don't say we had any right or claim which can be justified in any court of appeal, and perhaps there *was* no such right at all. But very few persons, with whom I ever came in contact, during my life, have entertained other than kindly & respectful feelings towards England; I speak of times before this War. – It has been well enough *proved* that the bulk of the jealousy, & hostility, in this country, towards England, was of *Southern* origin. The rout made in England about the 'Morrill Tariff' was wholly misplaced – the motives to which it was attributed has no (or almost no) existence – *absolutely none*, that I ever heard alluded to, until they heard the denunciations from H.M. & others in England – which took us back completely – We *have* felt worse about England, I admit it; but it was not because of E's *refusing* to interfere, &c but because she *has*, practically, & most mightily, interfered, in *behalf of the South*, & to our great national detriment.... But we *have* felt duty, & deeply, indignant towards France, also; – yet all other nations combined have not *practically*, or to our detriment, interfered in this war, to the extent of one half that England has done. – The damage the 'Alabama' (or '290') is now weekly doing, is continually aggravating the ill-feeling – chafing a sóre place.

But to go to a more agreable topic. Who wrote the Manchester Address to the President? It is *admirable*, for clearness, for dignity, for a generous view & estimate of our National policy (perhaps more generous than is deserved,) and for full & sagacious perceptions of the real merits & difficulties of the case. It is really above my praise. 'Tis a most noble document, and presents that meeting of Manchester workpeople in a most honourable light. These men, *I* say, are the *real nobility* of England, & put her lordlings & wealthy aristocracy to an open shame....

Very truly yours,

Saml. May Jr.

MS.B.1.6. vol. 9 The May Papers [444]
No. 59 Eliza Wigham to Samuel May

6 Gray Street, Edinburgh, 16. 1. 63.

My dear Friend,

It is a very long time since I heard from thee directly, & so I am very glad to embrace this annual opportunity of cummunication so as to keep up our acquaintanceship, which I certainly do not wish to lose. The matters in your country are of such intense interest that we are kept very close to you in sympathy & anxious watching & we eagerly read the newspapers from week to week – & grieve over the terrible losses in battle – the young hope & promise & all the broken hearts & desolated homes that these losses involve – It is dreadful to contemplate even from far, & what must it be to you! We sympathize with you very affectionately – & when there is cause for rejoicing we rejoice with you. These 'terrible things in righteousness' seem to have driven your nation to the contemplation of their cause & we are very thankful that the slave is now recognised throughout the Republic as having certain rights, the withholding of which has brought down the vengeance of the Almighty in such calamities as have prevailed. I hope before long the nation will see a little further, & liberty to the slaves will be granted, not as a measure of self-preservation but as a measure of justice & righteousness . In the meantime we are glad to have the President's Proclamation such as it is, & we hope it will work well for the slaves. We are tremblingly anxious for the next tidings. May God rule all! and avert the sufferings that may possibly arise by the revenge of the Southern slaveholders.

I am very glad the President does not in so many words exempt *loyal* slaveholders from the Proclamation, although it is done virtually *'at present'*, it does not read so grossly as when the right to hold slaves was plainly set down as a *premium to loyalty.* We were & are exceedingly grateful for the supplies sent to Lancashire, such generosity & the noble forbearance of the sufferers there will do more to foster, a right feeling between our two countries than all the red tape in the world – and, my dear friend, let us do all we can by word & prayer & kindly thought to promote love & friendship between us ; – we may be of very little significance, but one word added to another makes up a public voice & it is very important to have the public voice on the right side.... I hope our Lancashire distress is a little abating & that much good has come from the fearful lesson we have had. If we had taken the advice of G. Thomson [sic] & other farseeing philanthropists in 1836 & 7 & prosecuted the cultivation of cotton in other parts of the world we should not now have had these sufferings & possibly the war in America might have been averted, a commercial motive having been given for the abandonment of slavery long ago. – We have of course a little more difficulty in collecting money this year on account of the Lancashire distress & so our little donation to the general funds in response to the appeal is but small, but we send it in token of our sympathy in your past & present labours for the slave....

Sincerely & affectionately,

Eliza Wigham.

MS.A.1.2. vol. 32 Anti-Slavery Letters to Garrison [445]
No. 9 George Thompson to William Lloyd Garrison.

London, Feb. 5, 1863.

My Dear Garrison,

Since I last addressed you, I have attended meetings in the following places, viz: Sheffield, (three times) Heywood, Dumfries, Kilmarnock, Greenock, Dumbarton, Paisley, Glasgow, Stirling, Perth, Aberdeen, Dundee, Edinburgh, Galashiels, Gloucester, Cheltenham, Bristol, Bath, Stroud, Kingswood, and London. The mention of some of these towns will bring old scenes to your remembrance, when we were companions and fellow-labourers – as thank God, we still are.... Since I left Scotland, on the 22nd ultimo, my meetings have been all on the American question – and such meetings! They have reminded me of those I was wont to hold in 1831, 1832, and '33, – densely crowded, sublimely enthusiastic, and all but unanimous. The opposition has been of the most insignificant & contemptible kind. Before this reaches you, you will have seen the report of the meetings above and below, and in the open air round, Exeter Hall. I was the same evening engaged in holding a meeting at Stroud, which did not conclude till midnight. Three nights ago I held a meeting near my own residence. Thousands were excluded for want of room. These outsiders were addressed by competent persons, and the cheers raised by the multitude found their way into the meeting I was addressing, and increased the excitement of my audience. I shall not rest till the 10th, and then recommence my labours, which are in great demand.

This anti-slavery movement is assuming gigantic proportions, and, if wisely & energetically conducted, as I trust it will be, will have a powerful, and at the same time beneficial influence upon the counsels of your public men. It will be of vital importance in this country. It will teach a salutary lesson to our public men. It will mould the decisions of our government. It will neutralise the poison diffused by our journals. It will enlighten & stir up our ministers of religion. It will create the anti-slavery sentiment of the new generation. It will impregnate with the true fire the masses of our people. In a word, it will put England in her old & proper position.

The arrival of the President's Proclamation, of the 1st of January, gave me a degree of satisfaction and joy wh. words cannot express. It confirmed the hopes & fulfilled the predictions in which I had indulged. In spite of all prognostications and appearances to the contrary, the cherished a confident belief that Mr. Lincoln would execute the decree of Sept. 22. Nevertheless, the suspense was painful. My anxiety is now at an end, as respects the *fiat* of Emancipation, and I am waiting to see its fruits which I hope will be abundant and peaceful.

On New Year's day I addressed a crowded assembly of unemployed operatives in the town, of Heywood, near Manchester, and spoke to them for two hours about the Slaveholders' Rebellion. They were united and vociferous in the expression of their willingness to suffer all the hardships consequent upon a want of cotton, if thereby the liberty of the victims of Southern despotism might be promoted. All honour to the half million of our working population in Lancashire, Cheshire, and elsewhere who are bearing with heroic fortitude the grievous privations which your war has entailed upon them! The four millions of slaves in America have no sincerer friend than these lean, pale-faced, idle people, who are reconciled to their meagre fare and desolate homes by the thought that the trials are working out the delivrance of the oppressed children of your country. Their sublime resignation, their self-forgetfulness, their observance of the law, their whole-souled love of the cause of human freedom, their quick and clear perception of the merits of the question between the North and the South, their superiority to the sophisms of those who would delude them, and their appreciation of the labour question involved in the 'irrepressible conflict', are extorting the admiration of all classes of the community, and are reading the nation a valuable lesson....

Ever sincerely yours,

Geo. Thompson.

MS.B.1.6. vol. 9 The May Papers [446]
No. 85 Samuel May to R.D. Webb

Boston, February 17 – 1863.

Dear Mr. Webb,

I will not let tomorrow's mail leave our shores without a word to tell you how much we feel cheered and strengthened, in our labours to save this fair country from the jaws of Slavery and destruction, by the tidings which come thickly to us, the last two days, of the splendid great meetings in London on the 29th of January; it cannot be said to have been in Exeter Hall, so much *as in all that neighbourhood;* so that even our steadfast friends amongst you confess that its multitudes, its enthusiasm, its unanimity, took them fairly by surprise. To us it seems like a resurrection to new life. The sleeping & smothered fires of British anti-Slavery feeling and purpose have at last burst out into a glorious flame, lighting up the horizon, reassuring us in our difficult and dangerous path, and promising to shrivel up, in its devouring way, the dastardly, cowardly disgraceful cords with which slavery and the tools of slavery have so long been seeking to bind & hold fast the conscience and principle of England....

– And now one word on another subject – a sore one to us, not so much for the material damage inflicted, as for the evidence afforded, of unfriendliness to us, nay of hostility on the part of your government towards ours, & towards us as a people, – I speak of the pirate Alabama, fitted out in your principal shipping port, & sailing thence to devastate & prey upon our commerce and the lives of our people. I will not touch now upon those points. Clear as we deem the proof against your Government of a more inexcusable delay. I only now allude to the fact that that pirate-ship is allowed to enter your colonial ports, discharge her prisoners & obtain supplies of coal & other necessaries, – that her pirate-chief is received by Jamaica merchants with honor & congratulations, – and that no orders from the British Government have forbidden any of these deeds! Surely, when the career of the Alabama on the ocean became known in your country, the *least* your governmet could have done in the premises was to have said to all her colonial officers, *Give no aid or comfort to this vessel.* But, while our men-of-war have no such privilege, it seems to be freely & gladly extended to Semmes and his pirate crew! Let the spirit which showed itself at London on the 29th of January, and which is being evoked in every part of Great Britain, as we trust & believe, call upon your Government to *act* in the matter, or else that Government will grossly belie the spirit of your people, & show itself false to all its declarations of neutrality.

I am, ever sincerely, yours

Saml. May Jr.

MS.A.1.2. vol. 32 Anti-Slavery Letters to Garrison [447]
No. 14 George Thompson to William Lloyd Garrison

London, February 27. 1863.

My Dear Garrison –

...It would be impossible to give you a list of all the meetings which have recently been held, for the purpose of expressing sympathy with the Anti-Slavery movement in the United States, and commendation of the Abolition policy of the Government and Congress. My own strength has been taxed to the utmost, and has been seriously impaired, by the effort I have made to keep the demands made upon me; but though the spirit is willing, the flesh is weak; and were I never so strong, I should be unable to accept half the invitations which are sent me.

The men who a few months ago were so bold and blatant in the advocacy of the cause of the Southern Rebels, are now silent. Though some of them are in Parliament, they have thus far been silent mute, and we hear nothing of motions in favour of recognition, or proposals for mediation. We have now an organization which will enable us to furnish an antidote to an proslavery person that may be diffused through the press or the legislature; and there are men in the House of Commons who are now so thoroughly conversant with the merits of the question, that any misrepresentation of facts would be met, at once, with an ample and overwhelming refutation....

As ever, & for ever, your friend & fellow-labourer

Geo. Thompson

W.L.G.

MS.B.1.6. vol. 9 The May Papers [448]
No. 86 Samuel May to R.D. Webb

Leicester, Mastts., Feb, 28/63

Dear Mr. Webb;

...At last that deep, full, distinct, unmistakeable utterance of long-established British opinion & conviction ... is heard. The sentiments, both in behalf of freedom as against every form of slavery and also of genuine good-will and sympathy to this country, appear to be extensive and emphatic. The Manchester meeting & Address were the first opening, and have been frankly followed up at London, Glasgow, Bristol, &c .... May the good work go on in your country, and may our people & government also go on, & justify the friendly regards and the generous confidence of the great souls of Europe....

MS. incomplete.

MS.A.1.2. vol. 32 Anti-Slavery Letters to Garrison [449]
No. 17 George Thompson to William Lloyd Garrison

London, Mar. 16, 1863.

My Dear Garrison –

I am about leaving home, to hold three meetings in Lancashire this week – at Preston, Blackburn, and Bury. After which I hope to have a few day's rest, preparatory to meetings in Liverpool, Birmingham, and elsewhere.

The meetings to which the enclosed advertisement refers, to be held in St. James' Hall on the 26th[1], will be a great one: the name of John Bright will attract, & the Trades' Unionists are a very numerous &

---

1. One of the most famous of the pro-northern meetings, it is possible that Karl Marx was the guiding hand behind this organization. See E.D. Adams, *Great Britain and the American Civil War*, vol. 2, pp. 291-2. New York, 1925.

powerful body, with branches throughout the kingdom. I attach great importance to the Demonstration, and have long desired to see it made....

Believe me, as Ever,

Sincerely yours,

Geo. Thompson.

W. L. Garrison Esq.

MS. 960 vol. 2 Webb-Quincy Correspondence [450]
p. 81 Webb to Quincy

Dublin, April 3 – 1863.

My dear Quincy

It seems a very long time since I last heard from you. I wonder how you "get along" these times and what you are thinking of. American affairs are never long out of my thoughts. It has always seemed to me that the fear of European intervention was greatly beyond any probability that appeared to us here. Such a source never had any shame of that kind of popular favour which carries the day in all public measures of moment with us. Even the Times published a series of able letters by Unitarians denouncing any such course. The feeling among the English working classes has always been in favor of the North. As to the Irish working classes I really do not know & it is not of much consequence – for they have little political weight – and 19 out of 20 of them are such slaves to their priests – that it is more important to know the priests opinion than those of their flocks on any subject of importance. I have been and am continually amazed at the avowals I hear from estimable, sensible, benevolent men – never from abolitionists – of a wish that the North may not succeed in conquering the South. Very many of them say they think slavery will thus be more easily abolished by the necessity of circumstances than by the rule of the North. Many dread the mercenary power of the U.S. and say it is better you should be occupied at home than in picking quarrels with England – others doubtless think England would largely share in the trade of the South after the South had escaped from the anti free trade impediments so popular in the North. After all it is hard to speak for such a large & varied population as ours – composed of such an infinite variety of classes, cliques & interests. Nearly all the most reputable of the English, Scotch & Irish provincial papers are for the North and I feel confident so are the preponderating mass of Englishmen. That the aristocratic classes utterly abhor your republic, or any republic which is able to exist apart from an aristocracy I firmly believe & have believed for years. If your anger with England should tempt you to go to war with us – it is your best friends amongst us who would suffer, and the aristocracy who would not suffer at all, would heartily rejoice.... On the whole I dont think people on this side are much better or much worse than they are on your side of the water. But I do confidently believe there is no country in the world where so large a proportion of the inhabitants have a good chance for education, food, clothing & fair treatment as in the Free States – and for this reason all my warmest wishes are in your favour.

Yours ever affectionately

Richard D. Webb

Edmund Quincy, Esq.,

MS.A.1.2. vol. 32 Anti-Slavery Letters to Garrison [451]
No. 22 F.W. Chesson to Oliver Johnson

Emancipation Society
Offices – 65, Fleet Street, London, E.C.
7th April 1863.

My dear Sir,

I have received your very important letter respecting Mr. Wendell Phillips and have read it to the Committee of the Emancipation Society. They are unanimously of [the] opinion that a visit from Mr. Phillips to the country would, at the present time, be of great service to the cause; and they would gladly assist to the utmost of their power in promoting the success of that visit by holding, and inducing their friends to hold, public meetings in the chief towns of Great Britain and Ireland. This fame of Mr. Phillips's reputation as an orator has long since spread throughout this country, and his position as an advocate of Emancipation is well understood. We who so often feel obliged to criticise the action of our own government can fully appreciate the value of Mr. Phillips's censure of President Lincoln's administration, but you will readily understand that in this country we have made a generous allowance for defects which appear to us to exist from the very nature of things, and have not cared to afford even incidental assistance to the enemies of human liberty who would have rejoiced at any admission on our part that your government was indifferent to the cause of Emancipation. If then Mr. Phillips should honour us with a visit we hope he will kindly bear in mind this broad distinction between the circumstances of the two countries. He will be associated with those who have defended not only the institutions of America, assailed by Southern treachery, but the men who have been invested with supreme authority, and who, despite their errors of judgment, have, we believe, endeavoured to perform their duty to their country and to mankind.

With regard to the expenses incidental to the visit of Mr. Phillips (should he conclude to undertake the mission) will you write me frankly on the subject. The expenses of the meetings, travelling &c are as much as I can see my way to just now; for our movement has been a costly one thus far, and our resources are heavily taxed. But with the prospect of having Mr. Phillips amongst us our friends will, I am sure, make an extra effort. I hope if he comes *he will not lose a moment* in throwing himself into our ranks and assisting to secure us that moral victory which I am sure we shall gain.

You will be glad to learn of the seizure by our government of a confederate gunboat at Liverpool. This evidence of vigour is a tribute to public opinion.

In haste, I remain,

My dear Sir,

Very truly yours,

F. W. Chesson.

Oliver Johnson Esq.

MS.A.1.1. vol. 6 Anti-Slavery Letters from Garrison [452]
No. 57 William Lloyd Garrison to Elizabeth Pease Nichol

Boston, April 10, 1863.

Ever Beloved Friend:

...While the course of the English government towards our own seems to be, if not flagrantly hostile, at least very unfriendly, in allowing so many piratical vessels to be built for the use of the Southern Confederacy, and to destroy our commerce, we are cheered and strengthened by the many popular demonstrations made in our behalf, these showing that the heart of the people is right, however perverse may be the tory and aristocratic element. Nevertheless, unless your government put a stop to the furnishing of iron clads for the piratical Confederates, it is to be feared that public exasperation here will culminate in demanding of the government a declaration of war against England, sooner or later. Such an event is to be contemplated with horror; for both countries would be able to inflict the most frightful injuries upon each other, and cause immense suffering throughout the civilized world. God grant that none may be permitted to see a spectacle so revolting and unnatural! England can have no possible interest in the success of the Southern Confederacy. Slavery is as commercially unfruitful, as it is morally unjust and atrocious. Freedom is the life of the universe....

Your much attached friend,

Wm. Lloyd Garrison.

Elizabeth Pease Nichol

Leicester, Mass. Apl. 21. '63.

Dear Mr. Webb,

...As to our National affairs, – we hope & think progress is making; yet it is slow. The rebels do not abate their purpose nor improve in temper & spirit, though doubtless they are feeling very keenly the dearth of food, & the pressure of financial difficulties. They made an overwhelming demonstration against our nine iron-clads when they entered the harbour of Charleston 2 weeks ago today. For a time the discharges of heavy rebel artillery averaged 200 a minute. It was for some time one unbroken, continuous roar. The quantity of metal showered upon those devoted vessels was enormous, – and much of it proved to be ammunition of English origin. For myself I believe they not only had the very best cannon & ammunition which England could furnish, in heavy quantities, but the aid of the ablest English gunners hired & sent there. This may not be quite susceptible of proof as yet; – I have to thank you for a 'Daily News' containing report of parliamentary debate on the 'Alabama'. Mr. Foster did bravely. Mr. Baring's censure of the ministers, though very carefully expressed, must have been felt by them deeply. Mr. Laird's speech was simply infamous. The Solicitor-General (who is he?) made a most sophistical speech also, if I can judge at all, and one particularly calculated to stir up feelings of strife. 'Tis really the most lamentable thing about this Slaveholder's rebellion – the amount & extent of hostile & vindictive feeling in England to this country, and the eagerness with which multitudes there 'jump at the chance' of crippling & subjecting us; – and to think of Britain alliance with *these Slaveholders* for such a purpose! the very men who have cheated England, insulted England, & attributed every low & selfish motive to England all their lives, and who used the U.S. Govt. (when they controlled it) as long & as much as they could for the purpose of defying & opposing England. With these men it is that the Lairds and their like deem it proper to associate, to associate, to accomplish their selfish & spiteful ends. Do these men fore-see (& with satisfaction) the state of things they are bring about? If there is conscience & manliness enough in the British people to listen to Bright, & Newman, & Hall, & Baptist Noel, & Mill, &c &c instead of Palmerston, & Gladstone, & Gregory, & Laird, &c. we shall be saved, both sides, a multitude of woes. But my time is up nearly, and I must write a line or two to Miss Wigham.

With sincerest regards to all yr family, – & yourself

Ever truly yours

Saml May Jr.

MS.B.1.6. vol. 9 The May Papers [454]
No. 93 Samuel May to R.D. Webb

Leicester, Masstts, May 23/63.

Dear friend Webb,

...I have been very sorry for the course taken by our Minister Mr. Adams in giving the safe conduct for the London vessel to Matamoras; not that I can see that he did anything strictly wrong, but he seems to have stepped beyond his own record and jurisdiction entirely in doing it, and in the present critical condition of affairs between your country & ours, & us & France, should in an especial manner have been avoided. Besides, it looks as if the British Govt. lacked the will or the power to protect its own commerce, and that nobody here believes; & it was surely very unwise to afford any ill-disposed person the pretext for asserting that Mr. Adams, or his government, designed to intimate anything of the kind. I see that Mr. A. has given some explanation – what, I know not; but cannot doubt it will be an honourable & satisfactory one; for it is a comparatively trifling matter, to us of no consequence whatever, and should not be allowed to grow into any importance. – France has no cause or right to bluster about it. Having been allowed (I regret to say) to purchase in this country & ship from New York many necessary military appliances & aids for her invasion & War upon Mexico, she has no great right to complain if our diplomatic agents should give some help to the other side.... Our Govt. will not, probably, "send Lord Lyons away," but I almost wish they would. He is too palpably partizan, & I wish he might be recalled....

Very sincerely & ever yours Saml May Jr.

MS.B.1.6. vol. 15 Additional Letters to Samuel May [455]

Dublin, Saturday
May 30, 1863.

Dear Mr. May –

I heard today with hearty satisfaction that Vicksburgh is in the hands of the Federals & that Port Hudson is likely to follow before long. With the whole length of the Mississippi in possession of the Free States, the power of the slave-holders & the existence of slavery must soon be suffocated for want of breathing room. No European power could have borne such a strain as that which the North has been put to by this tremendous struggle, or borne with such cheerfulness & elasticity so many severe disappointments. My confidence in the value of popular institutions has been vastly strengthened by what I have learned of the endurance, humanity, & the confidence in their elected rulers of the great majority of the Northern people since the war began. How I wish I could talk to you instead of writing about these things.... I do not in the least wonder at the bitterness that exists amongst you against England for you have been greatly disappointed in her – but in Ireland I think the whole northern feeling is just as widely expressed & is in my mind more shameful – for the north is the great asylum of the poor Irish. However the number of our poorer classes who have any correct information or any political opinion of their own is very small & I dont include them in any censure – but only the reading & writing portion of our countrymen. I dont like to see in the American papers (though I do not wonder at such language) the covert threats that when you have opportunity you will turn your attention to England in a martial way. War is a clumsy expedient and it is one which must injure both sides, & should not be resorted to unless under the compulsion of something more imperative than mere vindictiveness. I wish American too well to wish to see her engaged in a war that must do her more harm than good, even if she should be entirely victorious & successful to the utmost of her [?] in a struggle with England. The position of the English nation which has suffered most from the civil war are your best friends, the operative classes of Lancashire. There were the great consumers of Irish agricultural produce & their inability to buy, combined with a succession of three cold, wet summers & bad harvests have caused such a prostration of all kinds of business, & of many failures & bankruptcies as I do not remember at any former time. Every one I speak to have the same complaint of bad trade, and so forth.

The Advocate is dead. I did not think it right to go on with it at Miss Estlin's expense as the circulation was small, & I have been unable to get any settlement from the London agent for the last 17 months. Besides the truth is that a great number of the best provincial English papers & the most widely circulated, with many of the most respectable & ablest London ones are strongly Northern & there was no use keeping alive our little farthing rush-light....

A prodigious emigration goes on from Ireland chiefly to your shores – it is said to be nearly 5000 a week – I wish the imigrants were likely to add as much to your moral strength as to your material ability. With kindest regards to you all.

I am ever yours truly
Rich^{d} D Webb.

MS.960 Quincy-Webb Correspondence [456]
p. 27 Quincy to Webb

Dedham June 1863

My dear Webb:

...As to the diminution of the former contributions to the A.S. cause from your side, the reasons were well understood here. We did not think it consistent with self-respect, in the existing relations of the two countries, to make our usual applications and especially considering the calls upon you at home. We thought you owed all you could spare for God's poor to those at your own doors. You speak of the prostration of all business with you. The effect of the war has been strangely different from all our expectations. Two years ago when it began, we all made up our minds that we were to be ruined. Trade was to be at an end, fixed investments would cease to make dividends, crime and poverty would increase and multiply and the devil was to be to pay, generally. The result has strangely contradicted all these anticipations, thus far. Real estate in cities was affected more permanently than any other kind of property. Tenants demanded a reduction of rents on the assumption that business was to decline and they did not recover themselves (the rents) for an undue time. My father's income was cut down to a third, I suppose in this way, and some people in N.Y. and Phila. especially were deprived of all income from their tenants' failing as as to be rid of their rents. But this was in cases of most exorbitant and absurd ones which our fair business could afford. But this has gradually righted itself, and should the war last another year with no worse luck than we have had this far, rents will be higher than ever. There is no reason why they should not, as business is immensely increased. The streets and shops are crowded as they never were before, here and in N.Y., and mercers, lacemen and jewellers say that they never sold a fifth of what they do now. There were never so many diamonds, camel's hair shawls and laces sold as now, and so of all the luxuries of life. This is caused in a great measure by the sudden fortunes made by contractors and other persons supplying the army and navy. But there has been no real diminution of incomes from actual fixed investments – rather an increase. Cotton factories it was supposed would be good for nothing. On the contrary, they have never made such good dividends. Some of them which had large stocks on hand, have made immense ones. Two or three have made *100 per cent extra* dividends, besides the usual earnings; several more 50 and 30 per cent extra. Persons lucky enough to hold shares in these companies have had from $ 100,000 more money than they counted on, and so down to smaller sums. None, I believe, have passed more than one dividend. I and my children had no stock in any of these fortunate companies: but our property is mostly invested in various kinds of joint-stock companies and we have had more from them the last two years than many previous two years, and this with the income tax of 3 p.c. paid by companies and not deducted from the dividends. There was one class of persons utterly ruined by the war and that was the merchants engaged in Southern trade. These disappeared like Jonah's gourd, in a night. Many persons, especially in N.Y. where the chief Southern trade was, who had lived in fine houses, and kept carriages and [?] in [?] were reduced to absolute poverty, by the confiscation of the debts due them and the property they had trusted to their Southern Correspondents. But they met with small pity, and were besides, a very inconsiderable number of persons. The N.Y. *Times* in a statistical article at the opening of the War. declared that the Southern business of N.Y. was only *five per cent* of its transactions and that the business with Boston was worth more to her than that of the seven Cotton States and that of New England than that of all the Slave States put together. This did not include, of course, the buying of cotton which was always paid for in gold, but only the furnishing of merchandize and supplies of all kinds. Boston had next to none of this business, and so suffered but little in that way. Then we have had no poverty, so to speak, – none arising from the war, and half the usual crime. The natural tendency of the idle fellows to the army and the demand for labor consequent on the draught made by it on the industrious, has kept everybody employed at good wages. The families of the soldiers I suppose were never so well off in their lives. For, besides arrangements made for allotments of their pay to their families, all the work that the class of woman could so, was second to them in this wise. The ladies in all the great cities made associations, some gentlemen took the contract for shirts, drawers &c and bought the materials, the ladies, including those of the very highest standing, and wealthiest families, worked by reliefs, at cutting out the work, which was then given out to the soldiers' wives and daughters to make up so that they got the entire profits of the contract. There was never so little suffering from want in any two winters as in the two last. The returns of the criminal would show a remarkable diminution in the average of crime, owing to the many of that class of men having gone into the army, doubtless. The final average of crime, I am sorry to say, is about as usual. In fact, I am afraid that a prophecy of money, which I remember you copied into the Advocate, at the beginning of the war, has become true, and that the War has become as popular here as that with Bonaparte in England. The operation of the depredations of the Alabama and other "*British Pirates*' as we call them, is very odd. There is a sense of humiliation at the Government's not taking proper measures to exterminate them, or letting us do it for ourselves, which the merchants have offered to do but the losses seem to be inappreciable. I asked an old merchant how it happened we hear so little about them. He said the principal effect was on the rates of insurance. That the losses were thus spread over a large surface. "Besides," said he, "we are fast selling out our ships to the English and taking bills on England. These we sell, pocket the exchange, and invest in building new ships to be ready to take the sea, as soon as the war is over." In fact, there never was such an amount of ship-building going on as at present. And terrible as has been the loss of life in battle and by disease in this war, there never was so little in any former war in proportion to the number engaged. The annual mortality in the army for the last two years has been only *six per cent*, while yours in the Crimea was *23 per cent* and in the Peninsular War *sixteen and a half per cent.* And there never were hospitals so well provided for. And this by the people, to whom the Govt. has virtually given them up. The organization of the Sanitary Association is so perfect that the supplies of everything possible to alleviate suffering are always ready and despatched to the point where needed. A bare statement that such and such things are wanted is all that is necessary to bring in more than enough. A constant supervision of the hospitals is kept up and I suppose there were never any so free from abuses as ours. I thought these statements might be interesting to you, and perhaps some of them new. You may rely on their strict accuracy....

Adieu, my dear Webb, and believe me ever most truly yours,

Edmund Quincy.

MS.B.1.6. vol. 9 The May Papers [457]
No. 98 Samuel May to R.D. Webb

Leicester, Mass. July 14/63

Dear friend Webb,

...Very unpleasant tidings come to us of a riotous combination in New York City against the Draft for the Army. It has taken place all over New England, including Boston, with the utmost quietness & no spark of opposition. This outbreak in N. Yk. is a most unpleasant fact. The Govt. ought to have been better prepared for it, than it seems to have been.

Our successes at Vicksburgh, and against Lee's great army, have been very great, & are most important....

Yours with sincere regard

Saml May Jr.

MS.B.1.6. vol. 15 Webb-May Correspondence [458]

Co. Dublin
Aug. 3. 1863

Dear Mr. May –

...I am glad to find from the enclosed extract from the D. News that my suspicion is confirmed that those horrible N. York riots were the act of Catholic Irish & not of Americans. A more fanatical unreasoning people there does not exist than my Catholic countrymen – they are priest ridden & ruled by passion & prejudice to the last degree. As these riots were clearly instigated by the democratic leaders I am in hopes that they may be extinguished by the disgrace which will be the certain result of their successful efforts to rouse the mob against the Government. The London Spectator applauds the President for the promptitude with which he took effectual measures for the suppression of the riots. Within the last year we have had movs. in Cork & Dublin which would [have] acted precisely in the same way if they had not been promptly put down. I like to see the poorer Irish go to America for their own sakes – but I regret it for yours – for they are the most dangerous element in your population. As to Archbishop Hughes & his clerical bretheren they abhor a free country like yours which is sure to undermine the despotic influence of the Ultramontane clergy.

MS.B.1.6. vol. 9 The May Papers [459]
No. 99 Samuel May to R.D. Webb

Leicester, Massts. Septr. 8/63

Dear friend Webb –

...The *Times* containing full report of the debate on the motion of Mr. Roebuck came duly to hand. I am very glad to get it indeed, &

to possess it. It is astonishing how much deception, misrepresentation, & fraudulent statement can be for into one speech of the length of Roebuck's. By this mail I have sent you an *Evening Post* – containing a recent letter of President Lincoln, which had been anticipated several days with a great deal of interest, & had disappointed only the "Copperheads", and traitors. If our Northern, our National cause, is ruined and lost, it will be by the means of these Northern scoundrels, who are now stirring up *hell itself* to defeat the Government in its measures of Emancipation and the Employment of Coloured Troops, and by the intrigues, and powerful help otherwise to the Confederate States, of England and France. Napoleon is showing his hand at last. I trust he will ere long bitterly rue the day he ever thrust it into American affairs. In the paper I send you are some good articles on that topic....

In the Roebuck debate nothing offended me so much as the position taken by Palmerston and the tone & style (contemptuous & sneering) in which he spoke of the American war, & our affairs generally. When the pirate-ship-builders and outfitters can set and listen to such speeches as that from the very head of the British Cabinet, they need ask or want no further encouragement or spear in their mean cowardly business. They may be pretty sure of complete immunity to it, so far as Lord Palmerston goes....

I am,

Very affectionately, Yours

Sam[l] Nay Jr.

MS.B.1.6. vol. 7 The May Papers [460]
No. 74 Samuel May to R.D. Webb

n.d. (fragment)

We have been agreably surprised of late at the altered tone of of many of the leading English journals towards America, and at the manifest change in English feeling generally towards us. I say *surprised*, because it was hardly to have been looked for that the *London Quarterly Review*, so soon after its article of *Democracy on its Trial*, should have published another so eminently dispassionate, sensible, fair, & appreciative of the ten thousand difficulties etc. Our unmilitary country was obliged in a sudden to encounter, (& which it has done so much to surmount,) as that entitled *The Struggle in America....* Its estimate of the Southern character is true & just, & contrasts well with the abominable false and very pro-slavery article in *Blackwoods* magazine. Its rebukes of the London *Times* are severe & I think must have been telling. It deals with the whole 'Trent' affair in a cool & dignified way, so unlike that of the English journals generally, and interprets reasonably, & fairly, the motive of the American captain and the feeling of our people in that case. Not once, I think, in the whole article, is the American people stigmatized as "a mob" – the current name for us, the year past, with the bulk of English writers and speakers. And tho' the article is not free from errors... it is (with a few exceptions) very correct, eminently candid, & must do much to allay the bitter feeling which has grown up here. The London *Times* itself has seemingly gone about on a new tack, – under what influence I don't pretent to know. We, here, are inclined to attribute a good deal of influence to J. S. Mill's article in Fraser's Magazine on "The Contest in America"... and think that he and Mr. Bright and George Thompson (with others doubtless) may fairly divide the honour of saving England from rushing blindfold upon a career which, however harmful to us it had been, must have in the long run been very much more to her own loss and dishonour.... I have had little disposition to complain that England showed our government and People, no more sympathy, but I have contended that her lack of moral discrimination in regard to an entire struggle – its origin, history, progress, & conduct – was absolutely *astounding* and *confounding*, while the spirit in which the 'Trent' affair was *generally*, (as we had reason to think) received, resented, and seized upon as an *opportunity*, certainly fully justified the very courteously expressed but still keen rebuke of the Count de Gasparin.... The course of the English Government for the past few months has been more impartial than we had been led to expect, & leaves us nothing of material importance to take exception to. At one time we supposed it was about to make a serious disturbance about the sinking of the stone-laden ships off Charleston. I do not know just on what grounds that question now rests, and so perhaps had better say nothing – except that, in such a matter as that, I do not think the American people would consent to any European interference or influence.... With every emotion of my heart warmly grateful to England for what she has done in the past centuries for civil, social, & religious freedom, and especially for what she has so perseveringly sought and successfully accomplished, in abolishing the slave trade and Slavery itself wherever her power extended or her influence would reach, – with every prepossession of my mind firmly engaged in behalf of the English people as a steadily progressive and truly liberty-loving people, I must nevertheless testify against her course, as a nation, towards us as a nation, since the present slaveholding rebellion broke out; and must declare my deep conviction that the words of Mill, Gasparin, & others of like tenor are not a jot too strong, – and that the injured and indignant feeling which has nearly universally prevailed agmonst us, towards England, has had *only too much foundation.* But I repeat, as I began, that we rejoice and are exceedingly glad at the numerous evidences we are now receiving that the sober judgment of the thinking and right-feeling portion of the people is getting expression, is having a marked effect, and is making itself felt even in quarters little accustomed to yield such influence. Every such expression, when obviously sincere, does great good in this country. There is no deep-seated animosity to England in America, as had been charged. The feelings engendered by the wars of 1775 & 1812 had almost wholly been obliterated & forgotten: but a bitter remembrance of them was forced upon us, when we came to see & understand the policy of England & the feeling of so many of her people toward us. May the future be such as to send all such....

[MS. ends.]

8 Clayton Place,
Kennington Road
London Oct. 3 63

My Dear Garrison,

...The news of the Scotia is not such as we were anticipating & desired to receive. But we see nothing in it of a disspiriting character. The Confederates have, doubtless, obtained a temporary success; but we shall look to see the late disasters repaired, & to hear of the defeat of Bragg, Polk, Longstreet, & their co-conspirators. The events of the last three months have wrought a great change in the feelings, convictions and views of the people here. The fall of Vicksburg & Port Hudson – the absolute freedom of the waters of the Mississippi & its tributaries – the continuous success of the Northern arms in the South-West – the expulsion of Lee from Pennsylvania – the suppression of the Copperheads; Irish riots in New York – the firm and effectual enforcement of the Draft, – Wood, Seymour, Vallandingham, & the *World & Herald* to the contrary notwithstanding – the Letter of the President, so full of assurance on the subject of the proclamation – the position taken by Negroes in the grand drama now developing in its final acts – the Elections in California, Maine, Vermont, & elsewhere – the evident overthrow of the malevolent & pro-slavery schemes of the traitorous peace party – the masterly exposure of our English government by your noble Senator in his recent magnificent oration – the display of power made at Charleston, and the certain doom of that wicked city – these, and other things, have wrought a striking result here. The miscreant Mason has fled to his rebel associate at Paris – Earl Russel has been forced to defend his past conduct, & so brand the cause of the South as infamous – the *Times* has been brought to see in the North "a mighty nation", destined to be "a first rate power", whatever may be the form of its future government – journals of lesser make and inferior powers of evil, are following its example – the once blatant traducers of the North are [delivered?] & humiliated – the Lairds, Lindsays & Roebucks are mourning over the fate of the Steam Rams, & find their occupation gone – and the friends of the Republic, of Freedom, & the slave, are full of hope & confidence, & are cultivating magnanimity towards the base & venal tools of Jeff Davis, & the perjured hero of the 2nd of December. You will henceforth see all changed here. The word has gone forth – the cure has been given – the priests received its instructions from head quarters; & for the future it will be *The United States*, *England* & the *Czar*, against *Napoleon & Jeff Davis* – Anti-Slavery Britain and the north against... the flesh mongers of the South and their allies in the plain of Mexico.

In much haste;

Ever yours,

Geo. Thompson.

MS.A.6.1.2. The May Papers [462]
No. 28 Samuel May to Samuel J. May

Leicester,
Nov. 8/63

My dear Sir,

...Has not Henry Ward Beecher done well in England? What think you? So far as I have read the reports of his speeches, & the testimonies to their value of many able & competent judges, he has acquitted himself bravely, wisely, and most beneficially to his country. The encomium of the *Evening Post* that the services of all our national representatives at foreign courts, ordinary & extra-ordinary, put together, have not equalled in value, & efficacy, the recent labours of Mr. Beecher, does not seem to me very much exaggerated. He seems to have laid aside the inclination to mere jocosity and theatrical effect, and to have given his utmost strength and powers to the most careful and well-considered efforts for the Cause. He really "fought with wild beasts" at Liverpool – with the most violent & unmitigated blackguards which Rebeldom & Liverpool combined, (and that is a bold word) could get up....

I am

Very affectionately yours

Saml. May Jr.

MS.B.1.7. vol. 2 The Estlin Papers [463]
No. 119 Samuel J. May to Mary Estlin

Syracuse, Dec. 13. 1863.

My Dear Miss Estlin,

I should not have allowed your very interesting and most acceptable letter of Nov. 5 to remain so long unanswered, if I had not been wholly engrossed by my many and various duties. It was well that I had the season of recreation & enjoyment, that I spent in England and on the Continent just before our Civil War commenced. If this terrific national trial had come upon us, when I was in that low state of health wch. made it necessary for me to travel, I could not have endured the excitement and the great increase of labour which this public calamity has brought upon me.

No part of my visit abroad was quite so grateful to me, as that that [sic] which I spent with you in Dublin, Wales and Bristol. I long to see you again, and when our terrible civil war is over, if you will but come to our country, I shall delight to do all I may be able to make your visit here agreable to you. Many, besides myself, know well how constant and consistent you have been in the cause of the enslaved – how just and generous in your appreciation of the embarrassments that have beset our government in the management of this war with slaveholders. The relation of the States to the Federal Head of our nation had never been clearly defined. Deference to the Constitution of the U.S. has always been the cherished loyalty of our citizens – so that very many sincere opponents of slavery have refused to do anything for its abolition, in violation of the provisions of our Magna Charta. But the emergency, created by the persistency of the rebels, has compelled our excellent President to resort to that power, which must be latent in every government, and superior to all written constitutions. With that he has struck the blow, which has severed the legal chains of three millions of bondsmen, and which if our armies triumph, will break every yoke, and give freedom in its glorious reality to all the bondsmen in the land.

We are grateful to you, and to our other faithful friends in England, who have never faltered in your adherence to the American Abolitionists – nor doubted that the war, which was forced upon us by slaveholders, must end in their discomfiture, and the utter subversion of their "peculiar institution".

Some of our Anti Slavery fellow laborers are so sure the end of Slavery is at hand, that they are giving themselves wholly to the relief, guidance and improvement of the freed people. But it was determined at our great meeting in Philadelphia last week, on the 30th anniversary of the American Society, not to disband our organization until that gigantic wrong, against which we united ourselves, shall have passed away utterly.

Meanwhile we are doing all we can to help the freedmen. In this city we have an active Association, auxiliary to the Nat. Fr. Relief Association, of which I am the general Agent. We have sent six excellent teachers to Florida who have done, and are doing, a good work. Some of them have instituted an Asylun for parentless children and our Association have contributed largely to fitting and furnishing it. If our fund were larger, we could greatly extend our operations – and I am confident we are working to good purpose. But for a few years it will put in requisition all the enterprise, energy and pecuniary resources of the friends of our colored people, to answer the just demands of the millions, who have come and shall come out of the house of bandage, stripped by their oppressor of everything but their human nature and its wants.

But never did a people make more ample or prompt returns for all that is done for them. I send you by this mail two of our reports – and will hereafter send you more and fuller accounts of the results of the experiments that have been made in South Carolina & Florida.

It seems to us, that the statements explanations and arguments made by Mr. Henry Ward Beecher, in his several addresses in England and Scotland must have *relieved* the minds of all in your country, who are not willing to be so perplexed by the action of our Genl. Government and the conduct of the free states, as to see, or think they see that the right in this contest, is on the side of the rebels. Much more does it seem to us, that the logic of events must, ere this, have convinced all those whose will are set against conviction, that a war, wagedby slaveholders, for the express purpose of perpetuating and extending slavery, if those slaveholders shall be conquered (as they obviously must be) will subvert the iniquitous system which they have vainly attempted to establish.

We are very grateful to all those in G. Britain who, from the first, have taken pains to understand the nature and complicated difficulties of our controversy with the Aristocracy of the South, and to explain them to your countrymen. We are much gratified by the manifestations of a more friendly feeling towards our nation, and by the altered policy of your government towards us. We earnestly hope and pray that the fraternal relations, which subsisted between our two nations before this war, may be restored, never again to be disturbed. –

We are expecting the arrival ere long, of Mr. Geo. Thompson. Many who have not been hitherto known as abolitionists will unite with us to do him honor as one, who has rendered us important service in this day of our trial. If Mr. John Bright, or Mr. Cobden or Mr. Mill, or Prof. Cairnes, or Mr. Foster, or Newman Hall should visit us, their reception would satisfy them and the world, that we know our friends and appreciate their services – If you and Miss Cobbe will come over to us, you shall be received with something warmer than gratitude – yes with hearty affection....

Please give my best regards to my Bristol friends, especially, Mr. Edwin Chapman, Miss Mary Carpenter, Mr. & Mrs. Thomas, Rev. Mr. James, Mr. & Miss Palmer and Judge Hill – and be assured of my very sincere and affectionate regard for yourself.

Samuel J. May.

MS.A.1.2. vol. 33 Anti-Slavery Letters to Garrison [464]
No. 3 George Thompson to W.L. Garrison

London, Jan. 9. 1864.

My Dear Garrison,

I this morning received the Standard & Liberator & read in the former the resolution passed at Philadelphia in reference to myself. I am deeply grateful to you as the proposer of that resolution and to those who so unanimously adopted it. Such a notion of my humble labors by such men & women as composed the assembly at wh. it was passed richly recompenses me for any exertions I have made during my past life in the cause of freedom & humanity.

My passage is taken in the Asia wh. will sail on the 23rd. I have several anti-slavery meetings before me. On the 12th I speak at a great meeting in London. On the 13th I give a lecture on the approaching triumph of the cause of liberty in America. On the 14th I speak at Oxford. On the 16th I am to be entertained at a farewell soiree given me by the London Emancipation Society. On the 21st I am to be entertained in the City Hall of Manchester & on the 22nd at a breakfast in Liverpool. Here will end my public speaking in England. All these meetings will I trust more or less promote the great cause in wh. we are in common interested.

I trust the arrangements of the Parker Fraternity committee will not have been seriously disturbed by the postponment for a fortnight of my departure. I suppose I shall not really reach Boston before the 5th or 6th of Feb. If on my arrival I can render any service to the good cause by speaking in public I shall be happy to do so to the extent of my physical ability. One appearance a week would I think be as much as I ought to undertake. The rest of the time I shall require for rest from speaking & business instead of making engagements for myself I wd. prefer that they should be made for me by yourself & such other friends as you might like to act in concert with. I shall need your counsel as to the course I ought to pursue. If you will render it you shall find that I will strongly follow it.

I have written to Mr. Sewall by this mail and should like you to see my letter for this is written very hurriedly & I have no time to repeat the contents of the letter I have already dispatched. My kindest regard to your family and all friends.

Ever most sincerely,

Geo. Thompson.

MS.A.1.2. vol. 33 Anti-Slavery Letters to Garrison [465]
No.12 Oliver Johnson to William Lloyd Garrison

Anti Slavery Offices,
New York, 15 Feb., 1864.

My Dear Garrison,

I feel a strong desire to go on to your Reception, but fear it will be impossible or at least very inconvenient, to do so. I am anxious that he [George Thompson] should have some sort of reception here, and can't help hoping that the example of Boston may set our Loyal Leaguers at work for the accomplishment of that result. Meanwhile I hope he will not at present accept the application of any individual or association to come here *merely* as a lecturer. It would be a pity to have him make his *first* appearance here under any other than the right auspices. *Let the example of Boston have time to work.* If your reception goes off well, I think something can be done here. I suppose Mr. Thompson has letters of commendation from Bright, Cobden and others of our English friends, to conspicuous Union men here, and I want to have an opportunity to honor him if they will.

Pray remember me very cordially to Mr. Thompson, and assure him of the gratification I feel in view of his safe arrival in our country. My kindest regards, dear Garrison, to your wife, of whose convalescence I hear with heartfelt satisfaction.

Yours faithfully,

Oliver Johnson.

MS.B.1.6. vol. 10 The May Papers [466]
No. 1 Samuel May to R.D. Webb

Leicester, Tu. a.m. March, 1. 1864.

Dear friend Webb,

...I am sorry...at the number of *discontinuances* of the "Standard" – far less on act of the paper itself, but because it betokens a failing interest in the cause on the part of the British people, & seems to give a degree of support to the charge that much of the professed "anti-slavery" of England was largely the result of an "anti-American" feeling which was glad (or not sorry) to find so conspicuous a blot & stain on our national character, as slavery, & was very willing to spread tho' England the knowledge of the atrocities perpetrated by it, & with the consent of the Nation. That such men & women as Dr. Thoresby, Dr. Montgomery, R. Gaskell, Jas. Haughton, Mrs. J. Stephens, &c &c &c should allow their moral support & countenance to the American Anti-Slavery Society to cease & be withdrawn, at this critical hour, is passing strange, & carries many sad thoughts through my mind. When our enemies assail us, we can grow the stronger for it; not so, when old & trusted friends grow cool & desert us....

You would rejoice to hear George Thompson, as he speaks to every audience here, & always in private. He never loses an opportunity to cultiviate, so far as he possibly can, a good understanding a feeling between England & America. And he takes the wise, & the only course to do it. He shows to us how essentially friendly to our country & everything good in it, is the great mass of the working, labouring, mechanic people of England, including with them a very large body of the middling class, & not a few of the best-educated minds. In his speech at his Boston reception, the best I have heard from him since he arrived with us – he brought against the *London Times* the double charge, of grossly misrepresenting the American people, (& their present great struggle with the Rebellion) to the British nation, and of quite *as* grossly & wickedly misrepresenting the real sentiments & feelings of the British people to us. He made a very strong point of it. *Should you fully agree with him?...*

S. M. Jr.

MS.A.1.1. vol. 6 1861-1865 Anti-Slavery Letters from Garrison. [467]
No. 72 William Lloyd Garrison to Oliver Johnson

Boston, March 14, 1864.

My dear Johnson:

Your letters, if not always promptly answered, are always duly appreciated.

On mature thought, I have changed my original purpose of accompanying Mr. Thompson to Washington, in as much as I wish him to be the one sole object of attention, and to have concentrated upon him all the honors that might be divided between us, provided we were together. I want him thus to be individually and conspicuously noticed for various reasons – especially for international ones: it will tell well in England, and help to strengthen the ties of friendship and amity between both countries. Possibly, but not probably, I may conclude to visit Washington before the final adjournment of Congress.

In your last, you diffidently propose accompanying us to Washington, should there be no objection, and provided you could make the necessary arrangements – with regard to the Standard, I suppose. Your overture was very gratifying to us both, and all the more so to Mr. Thompson, after ascertaining that I thought it the best policy to remain behind. He has doubtless, talked the matter over with you; and I trust you will be nonetheless disposed to go to the Capital with him, because I shall not make one of the party. I am quite sure that Wendell and Theodore would be willing to look after the Standard during your absence for two or three numbers; and I am not less certain that G. T. needs some one to accompany him as a friend and caretaker, and I know of no one he would prefer to yourself.

It may be that, on second thought, the expense of such a trip would be greater than you can well meet at the present time. If so, I know Mr. Thompson would gladly cover any part of that expense, or the whole of it, rather than go without you. And you need not hesitate about his paying the bill, as he is now receiving a good income from his lectures, which will be steadily augmenting, as he is receiving applications in every direction. So do not hesitate to be frank about the matter, and everything shall be arranged according to your needs and your wishes.

The Washington overture is certainly remarkable, and, headed as it is by the Vice President of the United States, and backed up by a long list of prominent Senators and Representatives, indicates how cheering and general is the change in public sentiment. I trust the Hall of the House of Representatives will be granted to Mr. Thompson, and presume President Lincoln will indicate by his presence at the meeting his appreciation of the generous and indefatigable labours of Mr. Thompson to vindicate and uphold his administration, and to cover with infamy the traitors who have seceded from the Union for the most nefarious purposes.

So far as the weather was concerned Mr. Thompson was unfortunate in regard to this reception at Mrs. Beecher's church on Friday night; still, I doubt not there was a large attendance, and an interesting meeting. The sketch of the proceedings, in the Tribune, was a brief and unsatisfactory one. Perhaps some one of the Brooklyn papers made a fuller report: if so, it (or, perhaps, a still better one) will appear in the next Standard Mr. Thompson is not always equally eloquent, and does not sustain so even a flight as Mr. Phillips, though he often soars much higher; and he writes to me that he has not felt well about the head since he left Boston. He cannot endure much labor continuously and has lost a great deal of his early fire and strength. Besides, his deplorable habit of snuff taking is doing his once marvellously fine voice serious injury. I despair of his ever conquering it....

Ever faithfully yours,

Wm. Lloyd Garrison.

Leicester, Masstts., March 29/64.

Dear friend Webb,

....George Thompson is having a series of glorious meetings in his country. The Boston meeting – perfect of its kind – gave the key-note, – New York was no whit behind in power or moral effect; Springfield, (Mass.) which mobbed him in 1850, when the Boston mob howled him down in Faneuil Hall, the Mayor & City Police encouraging them) gave him their welcome, in a most handsome manner. My wife & daughter, & several other Leicester people, were there to see, & hear; and Thompson spoke with more fire, & *intensity*, than I have heard at any previous time on this visit. I have been writing a little acct. of it to the *Standard*, and so will not go right over the ground again. But his great point was to exhort & stir the Amn. people to *finish* the work they have in hand, & make a complete end of slavery. He said that the solid worth & strength of the British people had sided with us, from the moment that Mr. Lincoln's Procln. of Jan 1/63 gave unmistakeable proof of an anti-slavery purpose in our Govt. & people; that their support was *sure*, & would increase, & might be thoroughly relied upon, if the U. States would take a bold & uncompromising stand for the destruction & eternal prohibition of Slavery. We all feel, & know, that this is our *duty*, as well as our best policy, & that, whether England comes to our side, or stands with folded arms, watching, or joins our enemies. We feel quite sure, with G. T., of the moral sympathy of the great body of the English common-place, & of the wisest & noblest among her educated classes; & we know that their influence is a very marked & strong one with the Govt. & with the governing classes, – as Thompson well proved last night. But those same governing & wealthy classes have so many ways, with their money & other means of influence, of helping the slavery & rebel side, that they make easy shift to defeat the policy of the Government & the choice of the bulk of the people, and in fact have rendered England's still-boated neutrality a complete misnomer in many respects. But is is no small thing to be assured of the cordial & steady moral support of the great body of the nation, and we shall have faith in this, & hold on to it as long as we can. Napoleon is a scoundrel. He has been quietly & steadily working, from the first, as I now believe & think I can see, to help the Rebellion, & at the same time further his own schemes of power & personal aggrandisement. Maximilian – if he ever gets to Mexico – is of course to be only the tool of Napoleon & the Catholic Church; & the Slave-holding Secessionists will do *anything*, yield anything, submit to anything, no matter how humiliating, at the hands of European imperialists & priests, rather than acknowledge themselves beaten by the "damned Yankees", whom they have always affected to despise as their inferiors, & fit only to do their dirty work (have had reason enough to think so of very many Yankees, too, – dirty dogs, who have lied to the people, deceived & misled them, & *for pay* worn the Southern collar, & 'umbly accepted the Southern scorn & contempt,) the Southerners (the leaders, & slaveholders) look upon the Northern uprising, just as they would upon an insurrection of their own slaves, – insolent &

unsufferable, – & would treat it in the same way if they could. For one, I hope Napoleon & Maximilian *will* show their faces plainly for slavery; & believe 'twill be their sure defeat to do so....

I am, Ever truly yrs.

S. May jr.

MS.A.1.2. vol. 33 Anti-Slavery Letters to Garrison [469]
No. 38 George Thompson to William Lloyd Garrison

Washington Wednesday night.
April 6. 1864.

My Dear Garrison,

I have just retired to my bedroom after delivering my address in the Hall of Representatives. Mr. Pierpoint and the Vice President Mr. Hamlin, waited upon me to conduct me to the capital. In the Speaker's room I found Mr. Lincoln who gave me a hearty greeting and accompanied me into the House taking a seat immediately in front of me. The audience was very large & the *tout ensemble* extremely brilliant. There was a very large attendance of Senators Representatives Judges Generals &c &c. My emotions were very strong on rising but my embarrasment wore off as I proceeded. Mr. Johnson will tell you the rest when I mentioned the names of yourself & Phillips the applause was loud and general. The name of John Brown was loudly cheered. The persons introduced to me would be too numerous to mention even if I could remember them all. The whole affair has passed off remarkably well & I am very thankful. The President has invited me to the White House and I go to him tomorrow. It will not be long I trust my dear friend ere you shall stand where I have stood tonight. God knows how delightedly I would have given place to one so much more worthy, & competent besides, to address the assembly I have just left.

On Friday morning O.J. and myself go to Wilmington. Love to all. Good night.

Ever your's.

Geo. Thompson.

MS.A.1.1. vol. 6 Anti-Slavery Letters from Garrison [470]
No. 79 William Lloyd Garrison to his wife

Baltimore, June 8, 1864.

My Dear Wife:

I arrived here in the evening train on Monday, and met with a very kind welcome from the Needles, who were expecting my coming, with George Thompson as my companion. Since then, I have been constantly occupied in seeing the city, which has almost wholly grown out of my recollections. It is ahead of Boston in population and extent, but has not as many good residences or handsome stores. The old jail that I once had the honor and happiness to occupy for a time has been torn down, and a new and handsome prison erected upon its site; so the charm was broken, and it was useless to think of visiting my old cell: —

"High walls and huge the body may confine;' &c The city is very quiet and very clean; and the general appearance of the people, including the colored people, is creditable.

Yesterday and today, I have attended the National Convention for the nomination of President and Vice President of the U.S. It has been a full one, and its proceedings have been such as to gladden my heart, and almost make me fear that I am at home dreaming, and not in the state of Maryland. Even my friend Phillips would have been highly gratified with the tone and spirit of the Convention. In the speeches made, every allusion made to slavery as a curse to be extirpated, and a crime no longer to be tolerated, had been most enthusiastically responded to; in several instances the assembly rising to their feet, and giving vent to their feelings in rousing cheers. The result has been the nomination of Mr. Lincoln by a unanimous vote, (529), and of Andy Johnson, of Tennessee, for the Vice Presidency, by a large majority. It was unanimously voted that slavery ought to be abolished, the Constitution amended, black soldiers employed and protected; &c. It was richly worth coming to the Convention to see and hear what has been said and done. Each evening there has been a mass meeting held in Monument Square, addresses made, and the most radical sentiments rapturously applauded, without a single copperhead daring to peep or mutter. This evening there will be an immense ratification meeting held in the same Square, with speech-making, &c. &c....

Heaven bless and protect you all!

W.L. G.

MS.A.1.1. vol. 6 Anti-Slavery Letters from Garrison [471]
No. 82 William Lloyd Garrison to his wife

Freedman's Relief Association,
No. 424 Walnut Street, Philadelphia
June 11, 1864.

Dear Wife:

It is now 3 O'clock, P.M. I left Washington this morning, and have just arrived here — very dusty and tired, but in good health and spirits.

Yesterday noon, Tilton and I had an hour's private interview with the President at the White House, and it was a very satisfactory one indeed. There is no mistake about it in regard to Mr. Lincoln's desire to do all that he can see it right and possible for him to do to uproot slavery, and give fair play to the emancipated. I was much pleased with his spirit, and the familiar and candid way in which he unbosomed himself.

Last evening I spent with solicitor Whiting, (the brother of Aaron) and had a good time.

I shall stay here over Sunday — but have no time to add more.

Love unbounded to you and the children.

Farewell, for a few days!

W.L.G.

MS.B.1.6. vol. 10 The May Papers [472]
No. 8 Samuel May to R.D. Webb

Leicester, Masstts., July 12/64.

Dear friend Webb;

Always your debtor in the epistolary line, I seem especially so just now, for I frequently receive proofs of your remembrance, & interest in our affairs, in notes & newspapers of value. A few days ago came a Manchester paper, containing Semmes's lawyer-like & sophistical argument in his defence & the editor's reply, quiet but sufficient; and about the same time, your own little note....From one sentiment in your notes we dissented generally, – I believe without exception, – as I had myself done on first reading it, viz. that we, (the U.S. Govt.) were "probably to blame" in the matter of the enlistment of British subjects. I see no evidence of it whatever. Our government claims that it has scrupulously abstained, from the first until now, from everything of the kind, and I believe it is strictly so. The Govt. offers its inducements to men to enlist voluntarily, its pay & its bounty – money, to which the several states add aid to families, & often additional cash bounties. If these inducements are so strong as to attract men to our shores and our service from foreign countries, that is an affair of their own, for while they are unanswerable to no Govt., and with which ours has nothing to do, and no candid person can complain of it, I have no doubt it is true that agents of private manufacturing & other business corporations, & of emigrants & societies, have gone to Europe to obtain workmen & labourers for our mills, shops and farms, all of which are suffering from the scarcity of labour caused by the numbers who have gone into the Army & Navy. This too, I take it, is perfectly legitimate; and even if some of the emigrants, thus aided to our shores, should elect to go into the Army instead of into a cotton-mill or a machine-shop or upon a farm, – and I dare say there have been some cases of this, – yet this is a matter with which no Govt. has any call or right to interfere, because it is one for which ours is in no sense responsible, having no hand in it whatever, & having given no authority to any person or persons thus to act. The wages now paid in this country for the commonest labouring hand, even in the farming districts, are as high as $2 per day, in the cities, higher; and the labour of good mechanics & mill hands of all sorts is paid double, & more than double, when it formerly was paid and we need many more hands in all departments of industry now, than we have so that, although the cost of living is larger than it was, yet the rise in wages, of labouring men, mechanics, &c &c has advanced in even a greater ratio, and the inducements to emigration hither are as great, perhaps greater than ever. Of course it suits such men as the Marquis of Clanricarde to keep *any* question open & stirring, whereby the American cause may possibly be damaged and the Slaveholding Rebellion helped. Earl Russell's reply would have silenced an ordinarily fair man, I thought, viz. that, whenever *proof was adduced* of any enlisting on your shores by our Govt., her Majesty's Govt. would attend to it. But the best answer to that large class in England, to which the Marquis of C belongs, is that which the "Kearsage" gave to the "Alabama" lately in the British channel; and Semmes's[1] declaration that "*his best gunners were men trained on board her Majesty's ship "Excellent"* (!!) will not tend to make that answer any more palatable to them. How the haters of America, in England, must writhe & curse under the results of the hours fight during the "morning service" which the *Times* tells about! I cannot conceive of a more pitiable set. "Exceeding mad" hardly will describe them; and the Eng. Government will, I believe, have its hands full to suppress the overflow of bile, and spleen, and what not, which thereby have been engendered. Of course they (the Clanricarde set) will fit Semmes out again with a ship, and a fleet too, if only to sink the "Kearsage"; for they cannot eat, drink, nor sleep in peace & quietness while that ship floats, I am very sure. And how manly it was in that English yacht, – *so accidentally present*, – to pick up 30 or 40 of the "Kearsage's' prisoners, & run off with them; & how remarkable that "Capt. Semmes" happened to be of the number! This is the way in which the seeds of trouble are so often getting sowed, which are to spring up in a future crop of difficulties between this country & England. It is declared here that the yacht belonged to Fraser, Trenholm & co. of Liverpool. Very likely; but whether so, or not, her presence in Cherbourg harbour, & going out to be near the contestants, were of course pre-arranged; & her making off with Semmes and the others was an atrocious violation of duty & propriety.

Our cause at home makes progress, yet slowly. Gen Grant has forced Lee and his army steadily backward, and now he beleaguers the city of Petersburg the most important outpost of Richmond, & has cut off the principal channels of supply and communication of the latter city. Just now a considerable Rebel force is in Maryland again, and its advance threatens Baltimore. Strange to say, the Govt., & the people of Maryland & Pennsylvania, seem no better prepared to repel such an invasion than they have heretofore been, to their unspeakable disgrace. Had there existed, – as there easily might have, – a well-drilled body of minute-men, or militia, in Pennsylvania & Maryland, organised to resist invasion and raids, the whole thing would have been speedly crushed, – or, more likely, would never have been attempted. This rebel force has already done much mischief, & created much alarm – has cut off rail-road & telegraphic communication in some instances, and even, it is said, burnt to the ground the residence of the Governor of Maryland within short distance of Baltimore. You will get later tidings than any I can now write, by the steamer which takes this. I have no doubt it will work well, even if our people have to suffer tenfold by it what they have suffered....

Ever truly, yours Saml. May Jr.

---

1. Captain Semmes was in command of the Alabama.

Ambleside
August 10/64

Dear friend

....If there was any way in wh. I cd. publicly express my own views in the matter, I shd. be very glad to hear my testimony to what seems to me our entire agreement on the question of Mr. Lincoln's character, deserts, & claim to re-election; & to express my hearty admiration of the magnanimity of your conduct, as well as of the justness & clearness of your views in the most critical hour of the history of your Republic. All who know me here know what I think; & if it cd. be of any use (which I hardly suppose) its being understood on your side of the water, I shd. be glad that it was known....

Prof. Cairnes & I were anxious each to know what the other thought of Mr. Lincoln, & of your course; & it was pleasant to find how entirely we agreed.

It strikes me that you may be more or less surprised that we have been so quiet, on the subject of Wendell Phillips & his clique. My own judgment is in favour of taking no notice whatever, in any public way, of the split among the old abolitionists: & my reasons are these.

The Abolitionists are lost sight of here in the overwhelming interest of your present national affairs. I believe that they are revered as having brought about the national repentance & amendment; & that they are merged in the nation, in people's view, & taken leave of with congratulations on the nobleness first, & next on the success, of their work. It wd do great mischief, in our (your friends') opinion, to set the abolitionists before the world as breaking asunder & wrangling, now when their exceptional work is done; & it seems to be due to your own dignified quietness & forbearance to keep *your* name clear from all associations with strife & insults, if it can be done. There is no occasion to tell people here that you have been insulted by any but slave-holders & copperheads. – Nobody but Mr. Newman's own friends (& they are very few) will hear of his letter to you; – & *they* will see your answer. We judge it best to avow on all reasonable occasions our wish for Mr. Lincoln's re-election, & our respect for the patriotism & wisdom of abolitionists who are forebearing with *his* human frailties, for the sake of the national welfare.

I need scarcely add that Wendell Phillips's crazy denunciations of "England' deprive him of all public influence here. People don't care a straw what a passionate man says of "England"; but of course any movement which is led by him is simply set aside as of no importance....

I say as much as circumstances permit in honour of Mr. Lincoln in the "Daily News" & I shall try my best to work in that the best possible direction. It wd. only damage the cause & yourself to introduce the Phillips [?] & spread the knowledge of a strife wh. is nobody's business here. Your reputation is in no danger, never will be.

Your Dear friend, affectionately

H. Martineau.

MS.A.9.2. vol. 22 The Weston Papers [474]
No. 90 Elizabeth Pease Nichol to ?

Huntly Lodge,
Nr. Edinburgh
28th of Sept.

My dear Friend

...The friends of the anti-slavery cause here have seen with regret the opposing views taken by Garrison & Phillips on the Presidential question – differences of opinion must arise with freedom of thought & I rejoice to hear from Geo. Thompson what I believed must be the cause, that whilst differing on the platform they are still the best of friends in private...to me it seems that Garrison is right & I hope that the re-election of Lincoln is pretty certain. The recent successes in the federal side will doubtless have a favourable influence. To us here it is incomprehensible how any friend of freedom can desire *McClellan* should fill the highest office in the nation – he makes no secret of what his policy wd. be on the slavery question.

This has been & is a dreadful war & heartily do I wish it were at an end – but still more is a compromise regarding slavery to be dreaded – altho' this seems a strange sentiment from a person holding the peace principle – and indeed would it be that all this blood should have been shed & slavery yet survive!...

With kindest regards to yrself

I am ever

Yours most truly

Eliz. P. Nichol.

MS.A.1.2. vol. 32 Anti-Slavery Letters to Garrison [475]
No. 91 George Thompson to William Lloyd Garrison

London, Dec. 4th

COTTON NOT KING

My Dear Garrison,

I have made several speeches lately for the purpose of showing how completely the sceptre has departed from king cotton.

Great Britain is at this moment absolutely independent of the Southern States for the supply of the raw material of her cotton manufacture.

The rebels may burn their cotton, or export it, as they please, for it is not necessary to the present or future prosperity of our cotton trade that we should receive another bale of their produce; not only so, but it wd. be greatly to the advantage of our distant dependencies and of the world at large that we shd. not.

The effect of the stoppage of our supply from America has been to impart a mighty stimulus to the exertions of the inhabitants of other parts of the

World, the climate & soils of wh. are adapted to the cultivation of the cotton plant.

I have given much attention to this subject recently, & upon the most authentic and trustworthy data – much of it official – I am able to state with confidence, that our imports of cotton for the coming year (1864) will be at the rate of at least, 45,00 bales per week, and will be more than sufficient to give employment to all the hands then available.

From India we shall receive about 1,600 bales; from Turkey about 375,000 bales; from China & Japan 250,000 bales; from Turkey & Greece 220,000 bales; from South America 200,000 bales; from Southern Italy, Sicily and the Mediterranean 50,000 bales; from the West Indies, Cuba, Africa, Australia & other sources 70,000 bales; and to all this stock on hand on the 1st of January, – say 250,000 bales; and we shall have more than three million bales of cotton; from which, deduct 600,000 bales for exportation, & we have still the promise of an amount, which if not adequate to the full & constant employment of all our *machinery* will be as much, and more than as much, as we shall be able to find *hands* to work up, & as much as can be brought into consumption.

The countries wh. have evinced the greatest eagerness to meet our demand for cotton, have been Egypt, Turkey, and Italy. The Governments in these countries have in every possible way encouraged the cultivation of the plant, & have shown an energy & steadfastness of purpose altogether unlike their former apathetic modes of administration in matters relating to commerce.

I am over sanguine when I express my belief, as well as my hope, that in a few years our supply of cotton from the shores of the Mediterranean alone will be equal to two millions of bales of cotton a year.

During the last six years a body of gentlemen in Manchester, acting under the name of "the Cotton Supply Association", have been directing their attention to the acquisition of information from all parts of the world, on the subject of an increased supply of cotton for the English market. During the same period they have sent to a great number of places assortments of the best descriptions of seed, together with machines for cleaning the cotton. The result of their labours has been, that they have not only obtained a large amount of most valuable information, & formed a cotton museum filled with specimens of cotton from all cotton growing countries, but have received cotton, in various quantities from fifty *new places*, & have been able through their committees and correspondence abroad, to render great service during the late crisis. It was fortunate that such a society was in existence & efficient operation when that crisis came upon us.

True it is that our operatives in the North have been called to pass through a season of deep distress, in consequence of the closing of the mills, and the stagnation of all branches of the cotton manufacture. But this distress has been pretty greatly alleviated by the spontaneous benevolence of all classes of the community; also, by the parochial [rates ?] wh. although they have fallen very heavily upon the rate payers have been borne uncomplainingly; also by a parliamentary appropriation of £1,500,000, sterling, for the employment of the able bodied men, in works of public & permanent utility.

Though doubtless, our working classes have suffered great privations (which they have borne with heroic fortitude & resignation) there has been no increase or mortality in the distressed districts, & even less disease than in other parts of the country.

To give you some idea of the diminution in the distress prevailing in the cotton districts, I may refer to the last report upon the subject. The number receiving parochial aid, in the shape of out-door relief, was, in the third week of Novr. 1862, 249,836, while in the corresponding week of 1863, it was 111,298; being a diminution of 138,538. The money paid in the former week, was £17,773, while in the latter week it was 8,216; being a decrease of £9,557. To meet the distress of the approaching winter months, there is remaining of the fund in the hands of the Central Relief Committee, about £250,000; of another fund, called the Bridgewater House fund, £80,000; of the Liverpool Fund, £60,000 and at the hands of the Parochial Boards £100,000 – total £490,000, to wh. add £1,500,000 for unemployment in public works and you will see that, exclusive of the ordinary parochial rates, we have nearly two millions sterling to be applied to the relief of distress, pending the arrival of our expected supplies in cotton, and the resumption of work at our mills!

The value of the works wh. are being carried on in the various town-ships most severely visited by the distress, will far exceed the amount of money expended upon them. The result in the improvement both of the public property & the public health will be immense. Miles upon miles of streets will be sewered and paved; parks for the people will be laid out and planted; wasted lands will be drained & brought into cultivation, and all who are employed in these and similar undertakings – having their physical wants provided for while so engaged, will be more likely to enjoy robust health, than they wd. be if immersed within the heated rooms of a cotton factory.

After a sober & thoughtful review of our domestic conditions during the last three years, and an equally deliberate estimate of our prosperity for the future, I have arrived at the conclusion that the failure of our supply of cotton from the Southern States has done us no serious injury, & that in its results to us it will be one of the most fortunate events that could have happened.

The spell by wh. we were bound is broken – the enchantment is dissolved. England no longer bows her neck to the yoke of Slavery. Her cotton is no longer stained with blood.

Previous to the breaking out of that wicked rebellion, wh. at this moment is alike convulsing & regenerating your country, so prolific were the plantations of the South, so excellent was the quality of the fibre grown, so comparatively bare was the field of production, & so established the trade, exchange & correspondence between England & America, that 85% of all the cotton we consumed came from your Slave Cursed shores. While this was the state of things, there was the slightest possible encouragement to other countries to grow cotton in competition with the produce of the Southern States. Hence our bondage to the slaveholders seemed complete & inexorable. By their own act, we have been emancipated, & shall never again be enthralled. The cunning have been taken in their own craftiness. Vaulting ambition hath overleaped itself.

How marvellously have events, evil in themselves, worked towards the furtherance of ends beneficient and good.

From England I turn to American. Instead of peace, industry and union the dogs of War have been let loose, & twice five hundred thousand men have been summoned to the battlefield. War has brought with it its invariable incidents – derangement of trade, the substitution of destructive for peaceful and productive arts, waste of money time & energy, excess crimes and blood, bereavement mourning & dissolution. Through these things I look to the *results.* A renovated North. The press, the pulpit, & the mart delivered from the pollution & chains thrown around them by the South. The Slavepower – bloated with success, arrogant, ambitious, insolent, intolerant,grasping – filled with dreams of universal dominion; assuming to give laws to the world; confident of the recognition & cooperation of the countries it has bound in coils of cotton; this haughty tyrant is today prostrate. He may well possess strength, & hate, & malice, and an unsubdued spirit, but he is powerless for further mischief – the monster has been brought low. And what of slavery-the minister to his wealth – the nursery of his lusts – the foundation of his empire? By the act that has given independence to us, he has given death to the creature of his idolatry. I could almost thank God for the rebellion. What I had never dared to hope to see has come to pass – freedom to the slaves of the cotton plantations of the South. The slave of yesterday the free man of today – a man, a citizen, a patriot soldier!

How I have longed to see the day when free Labour Cotton from other countries would take the place upon our wharves, and in our mills, and upon our counters of the cotton raised by the forced labour of American slaves. I see it now. It is already here, and the cry is, "Still it comes," It is coming in millions of bales from India; in hundreds of thousands from Egypt, & Turkey, and South America; & tens of thousands from the emancipated islands of the West Indies; from Southern Northern and Western Africa, from Austral-Asia, and the South Sea Islands; – It is blessing him that grows it and it will bless the (shore lands) that will manufacture & consume it....

There are cheering facts, and may lead the friends of humanity on the sides of the water to rejoice that *cotton is no longer king.*

Ever steadfastly yours,
In the cause of the Enslaved,

Geo. Thompson.

MS.B.1.6. vol. 10 The May Papers [476]
No. 13 Samuel May to R.D. Webb

Boston Mond. Eveg. Jan 2d. 1865

Dear friend Richard Webb;

...You know how utterly disappointed I have been *in England*. – while I cannot say but that you, & Dr. Estlin, always warned me that I was counting too much upon the Antislavery reputation of England. I knew that the great Antislavery acts of England were in the past, and yet not wholly so. Still she kept up vigorously her efforts to suppress the Slave Trade, and the great West India Emancipation was engineered by men still on the stage, and in public life. I could not believe that England would ever so unblushingly, so obstinately, espouse the side of "American slavery, the vilest the sun looks upon," .... The position and courses of Englishmen, the almost unobstructed opposition of all that British wealth and ingenuity could supply, have been the most powerful aids and levers which the Southern Rebellion has ever had; another long protraction of the war is directly traceable to what England has done to supply to the Rebels the materials and sinews of war....

Yr. friend

Saml. May.

MS.A.9.2. vol. 32 The Weston Papers [477]
No. 35 R.D. Webb to ?

Dublin, April 21, 1865.

My dear Friend –

...My interest in the anti-Slavery cause or in the cause of America has never abated – & I am generally regarded as a fanatic in these parts by those who know far less of their importance than I do.

After all it remains a fact that the bulk of the English working classes and the great majority of the most eminent Englishmen – men of real not conventional eminence – have been all along on your side – and I think much of the unfriendly feeling here which from ignorance, with the exception of the aristocratic & clerical parties who have felt that the success of a great Republic was dangerous to the permanence of their own parties. Cobden the most eminent man in the nation was always a staunch friend of the North. So are Bright, Tennyson, Mill, Hughes,[1] Professor Newman, Hughes & many more than I could name. Cairnes came into my office yesterday in a most unusual fever of excitement & exaltation at the fall of Richmond & the expulsion of Lee, Davis, &c. I believe if England, Scotland & Ireland were polled as large or nearly as large a majority would be found in favour of the North as could be had in the North itself. When condemning one on this side for the conduct of our governing classes you should remember how

1. Thomas Hughes (1822-1896), the reformer, writer and leader of the Christian Socialist movement.

erroneous has been the multitude of your own Democrats since the War began. At any rate I rejoice for the sake of the United States, of the slaves & the civilised world that the right side has won....

With kind regards to all your circle I am yours ever truly

Richd D. Webb.

MS.B.1.7. vol. 2 The Estlin Papers [478]
No. 124 Miss Weston to Mary Estlin

Weymouth, Massachusetts.
April – 1865.

My dear Friend,

I write today from the midst of a National sorrow deeper & more bitter than can be told, & which seems more intense as the weary days go on & the terrible event of last week is more distinctly realised. I shall send you by this post some American newspapers containing some particulars of this last dreadful crime, the completion of an iniquity that was already beyond precedent. You will have seen already the accounts furnished by your newspapers, but as they are with a few exceptions friendly to the rebels you may not get clear ideas from them of how the event is regarded here or what is the real aspect & the true feeling of the country under these exciting & afflicting circumstances I was thinking of you during the brilliant rejoicing over our recent victories & the prospect of the termination of the war, & intended to claim the sympathy I knew you were feeling for us while you read of the fall of Petersburg & Richmond & the surrender of Lee – events wh. virtually ended the Rebellion – for they left the rebels without seaports, supplies, or means of transport, and best of all *without slaves;* left all who were weary of the fight to go home to their families – & set at liberty thousands of prisoners, – not to speak of the emancipation of hosts of Union men shut up in southern cities. Joy was in all hearts & everywhere flags were flying, glad bells were ringing, cannon roaring, & everywhere was the voice of thanksgiving to God who had given the victory. Then came this last overwhelming blow. It is heartbreaking. *Never* I think has any man so associated himself with all that is honest & noblest in a nation's life as President Lincoln had done with ours. He was beloved in every home as a personal friend is beloved. Never have we ourselves felt so deep a sorrow except when death was under our own roof. The integrity, elevation, fearlessness & tenderness of his character were widely & deeply felt. No selfish purpose – no low ambition deformed his large & generous nature. I believe God had made & trained him for the great emergency to which he was called, & for which his rare qualities so singularly & it would almost seem miraculously fitted him. He was a man endowed with uncommon wisdom, & wonderful equanimity of character, & his solemn sense of the vast responsibility of his position was accompanied with a consciousness of corresponding ability. How he had been beloved & trusted in his Western home, before his public services made him known to the whole nation you will read. He was a great & good man murdered by those on whose souls rest all the righteous blood spilt since the beginning. For this is no chance shot of a madman, no private vengeance for fancied wrongs – it is the last expiring effort of slaveholding Barbarism ignorantly thinking to distract & perhaps destroy the country by this blow to the Government. No doubt is entertained that it was intended to murder not only the President and Secretary of State, but Mr. Stanton and Mr. Sumner, as well as the Vice – President and other important men. Happily the opportunities of the courage of the other ruffians were insufficient. The telegraph caused, on that fatal morning of April 15, a shock to every home in the wide loyal United States. There was grief and mourning in every house as when a beloved one lies dead. The mourning was deep, and universal, and spontaneous, as, by common consent, dwellings and public buildings were covered with emblems of mourning. The grief of the people everywhere found a religious expression. There was prayer in the dwellings of the citizens; in the churches; on " 'Change" – everywhere wherever two or three were gathered together by chance. The people seemed now to bow as in one agony of prayer and supplication, as they had a few days before united in a joyful thanks giving. It was a strange time for such a great blow. The land was full of thanksgiving however triumphant might be its feeling in view of a country redeemed from a great sin and a great danger, was singularly free from any sentiment of animosity or revenge on those whose wickedness has brought in so dreadful a trial. Everywhere the wish to restore the South as speedily as possible with the rebels, was paramount. Even till now many were saying, "Forgive them who knew not what they did." This spirit of forgiveness seems to have a sudden increase, as the obvious termination of the war opened such a happy prospect for the future. All felt that the reorganization of society at the South & the new state of things – with the element of *free labor* and freed *men* and *women* – present many diffucult problems. But there was a perfect confidence placed in the President and his Cabinet, and all trusted that things would work well. Never shall I forget the hour of that day which brought us the news of the assassination: there was no early train to our village, and a dreadful rumour reached us early (brought by someone who had seen at a distant station a passenger by the New York train) that "the President has been stabbed, was *in extremis*, but not dead;" then another report followed that Mr. Seward had been attacked. We passed two restless hours, and then our own train came bringing confirmation; but we passed all the first part of the day in painful agitation, as the telegrams reported both the President and Secretary mortally wounded, and then at last came tidings that *both were dead.* The news happily was untrue as regards Mr. Seward, but for two hours we thought both were no more! No one can tell what was it, and as we felt so felt all. I saw everywhere men and women in tears, and a gloom like that of the grave was in every house. In Boston not only all place of business and amusement, but all public-houses and dram shops were shut, and the city has been hushed these last nights like a city of the dead.

With all this grief and mourning came no thought of fear, no doubt of the safety and stability of the Government: the strong foundations of a nation resting on so broad a basis can be shaken by no one on earth, no single man's loss, however wise and great and good. Lincoln will be missed as never man was: but there was no fear, no panic; no public function was left unfulfilled at Washington; financial affairs were unaffected by it; it had no other effect on the gold market than that the brokers, with one consent, closed their places of business, and it was felt to be no time for specualations. Expressions of sympathy with the Vice-President, so suddenly and awfully called into office, came from all quarters. I believe there is little doubt of the existence of a conspiracy as extensive and as formidable as that which threatened Mr. Lincoln's life at the time of his first inaguration. Though the proper measure for safety were taken, yet I suppose that men living so long in the midst of war did not at every instant remember that rewards for the assassination of our chief men – Lincoln first of all – have been repeatedly inserted in the rebel newspapers. Lee, Davis, Benjamin, Floyd, &c, have seen, under their own eyes, and by their own orders, thousands and thousands of our prisoners dying a state too horrible for description – of cold and hunger, devoured by vermin, without water, and *shot* down if they dared approach the narrow window of their crowded prison for a ray of light or a breath of air. Multitudes died in prison of these horrors. Multitudes, exchanged for strong and hearty men, died after reaching our camps – many having forgotten their own names, and returning to their comrades in a state of idiocy, soon followed by death. Others gained strength, by tender and careful treatment, to reach their own homes and die among their kindred. Two such funerals passed our door last week. For these things is the man whom the London Daily *News* calls a "fine soldier", a "gallant gentleman", &c, accountable. They express admiration of a rebel who has betrayed his country and fired on his flag. What would they say of a British officer who had done these things? I regretted that Gen. Grant & his advisers, among them probably the good Lincoln himself, shd. have given Lee the terms accorded to an honourable foe – for vain is magnanimity & generosity when one deals with men whose life has been spend in the constrained indulgence of the basest passions, to whom truth & faith & honor are unknown. Lee who flogged a helpless woman with his own hands, Jefferson Davis who has been making a fortune by Blockade running while his dupes were starving and dying of cold and hunger. Benjamin who was in his youth a detected *thief* at Yale College – saved from public punishment only by the generosity of his college class, Floyd the robber of the public money and all the rest – loaded with crime and treason are not proper objects of sympathy. If however there had been any thought of amnesties that shd. include the leaders & officers of the Rebellion it has I think passed away. All these men who do not get out of the country will be brought to trial for their crimes. Mr. Seward's escape is truly wonderful and I am astonished that at his age and in his situation he had not yielded to the shock – think of an old man helpless from the accident of the preceeding week, attacked and repeatedly stabbed in the face and neck, and aware of a death struggle going on in his room between his brave servant & the assassin! It seem his presence of mind never deserted him. As soon as the man grappled with the murderer and forced him away for a moment, the Secretary did the only thing left for him. He rolled himself from the bed and when they went to him & thought him dead or dying as he lay in a pool of blood, he roused himself to give the necessary orders. "*I am not dead* send for the police & a surgeon & close the house" & then he spoke no more for a long time. That Mr. Seward's life was spared we feel to be a special providence, for his wisdom, & ability, & devotion was never more needed than now. I suppose that danger from these desperate to representatives of the "Confederacy" is still apprehended as a guard is placed round Charles Sumner's house…. The Ruffians are supposed to be connected with the St. Alban's raiders as Mr. Seward was warned by a letter from Canada of an attempt about to be made on his & the President's life, but in consequence of the dangerous accident which confined him to his bed he could not give the letter the attention it deserved. It will be remembered the gang in Canada procured evidence from Richmond (before the capture) of the Rebel govt. and authorization of their proceedings, on which shewing they were discharged, the presumption is that *this* murderer had a similar warrant.

But I have no more time or space. Think of us troubled but not despairing – cast down but not destroyed. Our great grief is that Abraham Lincoln could not live to enjoy the safety & prosperity which he has done so much to establish & the love of a people who understood him & valued him as he deserved. He will be missed in every way, but no doubt or fear darkens the future of the Republic. Never since we were a Nation were we so strong as now when all the strength, ability & virtue in the land, pushes by a natural law in the right direction....

[MS. incomplete]

MS.A.9.2. vol. 32 The Weston Papers.
No. 36 R.D. Webb to Mary Estlin [479]

Dublin
April 27 1865.

Dear Miss Estlin –

What sorrowful news this is about poor Abraham Lincoln – next to Washington the greatest of the American presidents and in integrity and absence of self seeking inferior to none. It is difficult to guess at the probably results. The present President Johnson is an intemperate man, a man of ability, but uncultivated & of a far less gentle character than Lincoln. I hope they may put such a man as Sumner in a permanent & powerful position. It is impossible to estimate the probable results of the crime upon the United States & alternately upon the whole course of history....

Yours ever

Rich^d D Webb.

MS.A.6.1.2. 1860-1870 The May Papers [480]
No. 44 Samuel May Jr. to S.J. May

Leicester,
Sund. Sept. 17/65.

Dear Cousin S.

...The State Republican Convention here last Thursday did a good work, especially in placing Charles Sumner at its head. Genl Butler next, & in giving to the State & Country two admirable & characteristic speeches of those two men. I trust you will find time to read both of them. – I was glad to see Gen. Slocum's order, staying Govr. Sharkey's hand in forming military organizations thro' Mississippi. If there's need of any military in Mississippi at present, it shd. be *United States* military, as I take leave to think, the Presdt. to the contrary notwithstanding. I was therefore proportionally chagrined to see the Presdt.'s despatch to Gen. Slocum to rescind his orders, & to Carl Schurz,[1] virtually snubbing him for meddling. Sorry was I, again, to see Gen. Slocum's letter, expressing what I thought dangerous, and in him, inconsistent haste, to have civil govt. substituted for the military, throughout the Rebel States, – and also to see his readiness to take office from the Democratic party in New York. – If the coming Congress does not present itself, like an immovable wall of adamant, to the encroachments of the Southern managers & their friends, in and out of Government, we shall be left in a most singular position, & the culmination of our terrible struggle & of the terrible sufferings of the land will be a most lamentable, & at the same time a most farcical one. – I am not, however, one of the party of doubt, distrust, & denunciation. I hold that *the people* are right, – have again & again & with the greatest force & clearness, expressed their will, and that neither President Johnson, nor the South, nor any cabal of men at the North, shall dare attempt to overthrow or to controvert that will. Let him who ventures to give Slavery, or its infamous supporters, whether in South Carolina or in New Jersey, in Pennsylvania or in Mississippi, a new opportunity for acquiring power & control in the United States, look out for a fearful reckoning. Assuredly he will hear thunder, not of the dismal & muttering kind, but of over-whelming majesty & irresistible consequences....

– all send love to you.

Yrs aff'ly

S. May Jr.

MS. 960 Webb-Quincy Correspondence
p. 90 Quincy to Webb

[481]

Dedham, Oct. 16th 1865

My Dear Webb,

...The alienation of Wendell Phillips is indeed most lamentable, but it has been of his own doing it is certainly what I never expected would accompany the success of the Movement, It shows that a man may be a great orator, probably the greatest living orator, and yet be lacking in common sense & proper feeling. I think it grows out of a personal animosity to Lincoln & a determination to defeat him, in which he was opposed by Garrison and the Standard. His conduct towards Oliver Johnson can only be called ungentlemanlike & insolent, as an humble man whom he could kick out of existence with impunity. The course of this personal hostility to Lincoln I divine to be this, though it is capable of only presumptive and inferential proof. The first winter after Lincoln's [accession ?] W.P. went to Wash.[n] & was very well received by all the big-wigs. The Prest. went to hear him

1. Carl Schurz (1829-1906), born in Germany, was active in liberal reform movements on the Continent before going to America. His work for the newly formed Republican party made Lincoln appoint him United States Minister to Spain, but by 1862 he had resigned his post and returned to America, where he was active in the ranks of the Union Army. His later career as a journalist and Senator was equally famous.

speak & treated him with much personal kindness. During the two first years of Lincoln's Administration, when we were all in the greatest doubt & feat as to what he was going to do, W.P. lauded him to the skies & stood by him thoroughly. When the Emancipation Proclamation was issued, he went again to Washington & I have no doubt thought the time had come for him to take part in public affairs. I don't believe he expected or desired any office, but that he believed he should be taken into the Presdt.'s councils & be the power behind the throne. And I apprehend the first thing he demanded was the removal of Seward. And then I have not the least doubt that the President snubbed him roundly, & told him, virtually, to mind his own business. From that time forward he seems to have been animated by the bitterest personal hostility to Lincoln. He could do & say nothing right & the lies of the press were caught up by him & set forth with all the clearness of his eloquence as authentic facts. This want of exactness to the facts on which he has grounded his diatribes has very much diminished the confidence & regard of the public towards him....

Ever affectionately yours,

Edmund Quincy.

MS.960 vol. 2 Webb-Quincy Correspondence [482]
p. 92 Webb to Quincy

St. Ann's Hill, near Cork, Dec. 8. 1865

My dear Quincy—

...There is an awful affair in Jamaica & indicates in a remarkable degree how little mercy a colored population have to hope for either of justice or mercy at the hands of a race of white planters who have full power in their hands. It has excited & is exciting great attention in England & the government will be obliged to make immediate inquiry & to act with mercy in consequence. There are few events in the history of civilized nations which show more unmistakeably how skin deep is our Christianity. Yet all the gentlemen here who have any opinion on politics are on the side of the planter with the exception of Mr. [Arthur ?] & myself. Indeed if the British power were to leave Ireland without striking a blow the whole island would soon be one scene of bloodshed & anarchy — for as politicians neither side has much regard for humanity or appreciation of constitutional laws. I am told indeed that most of those whose names are before the public in connection with these events, from the governor downwards are Irishmen. And yet it is a fact that *in Ireland* the family & social virtues, the chastity, the security of property, & the general freedom from great crimes are far away above the English standard. I have been assured on good authority by one who has known this place for 8 years that nothing has been lost by theft although the number of servants is large, and the property of the inmates scattered through at least 50 years is greatly exposed. I would very much rather live in Ireland than in England for the poorer classes are pleasanter & less brutal. Owing to the dread the priests have of knowledge the spirit of intellectual improvement is almost nil, and except in the way of [saving ?] , and trading there is little disposition to elevate themselves among the Catholic population – at least, the great bulk of them....

Yours ever truly

Richd. D. Webb

MS.B.1.7. vol. 1 The Estlin Papers [483]
No. 30 Anne Warren Weston to Mary Estlin

Oct. 17 1866

My Dear Mary

...But I must give a little space to public opinion in my own home. Though the President is making so scandalous an exhibition & tho the prospect may look dark to foreign observers, I assure you all is going on quite as well as any reasonable person could have expected. Had Lincoln lived there would have been much less *individual* suffering. The poor blacks would have fared better & the reconstruction of the country would have been much sooner accomplished. But the *ultimate* national results will prove the same. The present constitutional amendments, the one now under consideration will be adopted, & sooner or later negro suffrage will come. *Here* I differ with some good people. The question of negro suffrage is attended with some difficulties & perplexities, constitutional & otherwise, & I should not make its adoption a *sine qua non* by the Republican party. As a party the abolitionists no longer exist. For all practical purposes they are merged, as they should be with the great mass of their fellow citizens. I have been very sorry that Wendell Phillips has pursued the course he has, but it is purely on his own account, perhaps I must confess that when I saw the time arrive, when he might naturally & properly enter on a course of political renown, such as his talents & position made natural, I was sorry to see him thrown away all his prospects, from an entire want of clearness of judgment & an inability to understand the situation. Perhaps it was as much as could be expected that one man, even Garrison, was found quite equal to the occasion. I dont believe in any impeachment of the President or anything of that sort. Probably matters will [wear ?] along for the next 2 years, & then Gen Grant step into the presidency.

I am a good deal shocked at finding such a party here in favour of Gov. Eyre;[1] it does certainly seem as if the negro question was to be a perfect test, trying both nations & individuals, I do not of course wish Eyre hanged, tho' speaking popularly he deserved it, but I do think he should be tried for Gordon's murder....

yours every affectionately – A.W.W.

---

1. **Edward John Eyre (1815-1901), colonial governor and explorer, was Governor of Jamaica in 1864 and put down a rising there with great severity. George William Gordon, a coloured politician, was accused of being responsible for the Rebellion, tried under martial law and hanged. The circumstances of his arrest, his sentence and the severity of Eyre's treatment of the affair, created a public outcry and Eyre was recalled.**

MS.A.6.1.2. 1860-1870 The May Papers [484]
No. 48 Samuel May Jr. to S.J. May

n.d. fragment

P.S. Thousands of times, I might almost say, have I thought of you during the past trying 3 months. How have I longed to talk with you, – to hear your views. "Never despair" is my word. A traitor in the camp – and at the head of it, too, – a turn-coat – an apostate, – is a hard case to deal with; and the American people & their Govt. are summoned to a new conflict, to one demanding the greatest Patience, Coolness, Endurance, Firmness & Sobriety. Thank God all these qualities are with the North, and are not (certainly not the first 2, and the last,) with their false President. But do you know that, bad as that man's policy & behaviour are, it is a *New Yorker* who is the author of the former, and who steadily upholds the latter? I mean Wm. H. Seward. Do you believe this of him? I do, – for I have such positive, direct well-authenticated testimony to that effect, corroborated as it is so strongly by his whole course since he became Sec. of State – that I cannot help believing it Mr. S. tried to bring Mr. Lincoln to adopt a similar policy, – and for a considerable time not wholly without effect: but Mr. Lincoln was far too honest & patriotic to go the lengths of condescension, coaxing, and insinuation, that Mr. Seward wd. have him; but in Andrew Johnson he has found an easy, willing & suitable accomplice. *Never despair*, I say – Congress is brave, and I believe is true, – (Although some few Republicans have so badly swerved, like Doolittle, yr. Senator Morgan (& is Harris much better?) and *yr. Repr.* Davis! – to say nothing of Raymond) the people are intelligent, clear-sighted, and determined, and more than all, God reigns. We must avoid another war, if possible; for it would not be so well to have *our* "President" (1) the leader of the *Enemies* of the Country! – I fear that the "Civil Rights Bill sis really open to some serious objections; but if so, & loyal & honest Presdt. wd. have pointed them out specifically instead of killing the whole measure, Some leading Republicans I meet in Boston say the Bill *would* necessarily produce a state of *Civil War*! But one would think such men at Washington as voted for that Bill would see that feature it there, & remove it; – or whatever was justly liable to such a charge.

We hear from you only occasionally, indirectly, & rather meagrely. *We* are pretty well. My wife has been thro' March quite poorly; but better now. Father keeps mostly up-stairs – prefers the quiet– but is comfortable. – Did you see the magnificent eclipse last night? Truly yrs. Saml May Jr.

MS.A.9.2. vol. 16 pt. 2 1841 The Weston Papers [485]
No. 25 R.D. Webb to ?

n.d. (fragment)

The general feeling in England is that Ireland is essential to the safety & greatness of England, & the English are determined to keep us while they probably have little love for us. As an Irishman I reciprocate this state of feelings exactly. Ireland is in my opinion in every way better in union with England than she could be alone. Ireland was never so rich, so prosperous, so well cultivated, so well governed, so well off in every respect as she is at present time. But between the priests until lately, & the Fenian sympathisers at present the ignorant [?] peasants & lower middle class of catholics are kept with their eyes continually looking backwards to the unquestionably evil times behind the last 50 years, when the government of this country by England was utterly bad & utterly selfish. Indeed I think the English as a nation quite as selfish & insolent as any other. But taking in Irish as we are if left alone we wd. be like so many Kilkenny cats – we are a nation of bigots, Catholic & Protestant much alike. The proportion of really liberal, large minded for truth a[re] lamentably small. Then our national temperament is utterly unintelligible to the English & they are continually ignorantly, foolishly & unpolitically treading on our corns & wounding our great susceptibilities....

I remain yours affectionately

Rich[d] D Webb.

MS.B.1.6. vol. 6 The May Papers [486]
No. 70 Samuel May to R.D. Webb

21 Cornhill Boston Dec[r] 1.

Dear Mr. Webb,

...When I was a boy, Boston had a great many fine gardens in it, which have now, *(every one of them I believe)* been given over to Goths & Vandals & filled up with brick & stone in various sightly & unsightly shapes. Formerly we had no Irish here – not probably a 1000 when I was 10 years old; now there (are) thereabout 70,000, and Boston has suffered terribly under the invasion. I suppose you will bear this from me, Irishman though you be. God knows I wish we had any number of such Irishmen as you amongst us. But the "Corkonians" and "Fardowners" (as they call themselves), invaluable & indispensible as they are for all labour, are terrible to live among or near. They defile and desecrate everything they touch, & hundreds of tidy neighbourhoods & quiet spots now reek with vile sights & smells, where they swarm....

MS.A.9.2. vol. 32 The Weston Papers [487]
No. 70 R.D. Webb to ?

May, 23 1867.

(fragment)

...All that you say about the follies of the Fenians in running their heads against a stone wall is quite true. Still they represent the feelings of millions of the poorer classes and if the government hang any of them they will make a great mistake. In my opinion England is not loved by any of the Irish Catholics who are not placeholders in fact or in expectancy. Nor do I think that the English sentiment of loyalty exists here. The English are an insolent nation and have abused & ridiculed us so persistently through the times that I think a very general feeling is one of alienation. I am utterly destitute of any feeling of pride in British citizenship... When I see how the North has behaved to those cruel, bloody, Southern rebels I wonder that the English government should be such fools as to hang any of these poor foolish Fenians, considering that many of their own aristocracy did their best to help the Proslavery rebellion....

Ever & yours affectionately
Rich[d] D. Webb

MSS.Acc. 2705 [488]
William Lloyd Garrison to Samuel May

Roxbury, March 10, 1867.

Dear friend May:

...Yes, it is true that I am seriously thinking of going across the Atlantic this summer – for four reasons. First, because, though I expect to be sea-sick, I believe the trip would be decidedly beneficial to my health, and therefore to my future usefulness; for, though I am much better than I was last summer and fall, I am still lacking in my usual strength and spirits, and need a total change of surroundings. My previous trips to England have always given me renewed vigor. Second, it will be something – I think a great deal – to see the Paris Exhibition of the World's industries; but this pleasure will be immeasurably enhanced by meeting there Fanny and her husband and Frank, and perhaps ultimately returning with them all. Third, as a World's Anti-Slavery Congress is to be held at Paris about the middle of June, it is fitting that I should be present; and, understanding that I contemplate going to it, the Executive Committee of the American Freedmen's Commission have already requested me to appear as a delegate in its behalf. Fourth, I wish to see my old Anti-Slavery friends in England, to rejoice with them face to face over the abolition of American slavery, and in all probability to take to them a final earthly farewell. You know, my dear friend, that, for the last three years I have had such a project in view. First we talked of going over together, but that failed. The next year George Thompson and I speculated about going across, but he could not see his way clear to do so. Last year I was utterly broken down by my falls. This time I trust it will not prove a failure; but I shall not think of going if, at the last the health of my dear wife should seem to be precarious. She is now very comfortable, and has decidedly improved under her magnetic treatment; but she has now a troublesome sore on her paralysed limb, about which we have all felt a good deal of anxiety; but is looking less inclined to gangrene than it did, and we are hoping it will in the end prove advantageous. With her characteristic self-abnegation, she desires me to go and join the children, and seek thereby the renovation of my health. I shall have an excellent person, a relation of hers, to be with her during my absence. She will almost make Fanny's place good. I shall engage passage in the Great Eastern for 16th of May. George Thompson will go with me, probably.

Yours indebted friend, Wm. Lloyd Garrison.

No. 30 W. Robson to William Lloyd Garrison

59 Mornington Road
Regents Park
London N.W.
June 10, 1867.

My Dear Mr. Garrison,

Miss Remond called here on Friday last and made me quite happy by telling me how well you are looking after the multifarious labours and trials & painful accidents of the past nine years. She says you are scarcely looking any different from when she saw you in America – and she also told me what was quite news that Frank & Fanny[1] were with you & that you were all coming to London on Saturday next. I need not tell you how glad I should be to have you all for my guests at any time & for as long as would suit your convenience.... The only objection to it that I know is the great undesirableness in *your* case of putting yourself in personal relations that would suggest to the outside world your connection with any of our political or religious parties in England, which would damage your position here very much. But this could hardly exist in any case because in London I am just nobody, and utterly unknown. Still as you now occupy a very prominent position in the world's history, a fact that your bitterest enemy would not deny, I think it exceedingly desirable that you should enter the mixed arena of English Society, just as *William Lloyd Garrison, the Abolitionist* of America, indebted to nobody & nothing but your own recognised position for your entrance into English social life. Believe me there will be many (I cannot help saying it) who will try to make social capital out of their acquaintanceship & personal friendship for you. Be on your guard against this and quietly put it down. We that is the English nation are in the throes of a new birth, and I see great good in your mixing without any of our conventional restraints amongst all the leading men of the age now in London. I think you might do much to improve public opinion in England on all the great questions of the day by coming face to face with those who form it, which in this country more than in any other perhaps is the work of recognised leaders in the various social political, religious, scientific & literary walks of life. But then party & class feeling is so strong, that your recognized association with it would in great measure shut you from all chance of freely meeting with [?] whom for national purposes it is equally desirable, perhaps more desirable that you should see & influence.... I want you to come in close personal contact with our wealthy great men and the leaders of public opinion, without ministers of State, with our leaders of opposition, and most prominent men of science. Without religious bodies you can do nothing and all time spent amongst them would be wasted. But amongst the leaders of the political world you might do a world of good. Of course I cannot help you in this, and there are not many who can, out of the highest circles themselves. But I have faith in the instincts of my countrymen, that they can & will recognize true greatness when it comes amongst them, & so I will hope & believe that

---

1. Garrison's son and daughter.

your coming to England at this juncture will not be without great good and abiding consequences & results in which we shall rejoice....

faithfully & affectionately

W. Robson.

MS.A.1.2. vol. 35 Anti-Slavery Letters to Garrison [490]
No. 33 W. Robson to William Lloyd Garrison

59 Mornington Road,
Regents Park, London N.W.
June 13, 1867.

My dear Mr. Garrison,

...The outlook for England just now does not seem pleasant to me. Of all the charlatans who have held the office of premier in this country for many years, I think "Disraeli" must be awarded the most prominent place. I regard him as a clever unscrupulous man, an atheist of the Jefferson Davis School, who would willingly help God to govern England on Tory principles, provided he may be premier. On any other condition he will do all that lies in his power to make cosmos a chaos; truth, honor, morality, being all to be measured by the cardinal fact of their subserviency to his own selfish interests and supreme dignity. I should have liked to bring out great men face to face, were it only for an hour, with the diviner faith in the Eternal right, that has imparted strength for a lifelong combat with sin & wrong. I thought and still think it would do them good, and the world might reap the benefit of it. The Eyre business has openly shown the fearfully corrupt state of English feeling with regard to the rights of the black race; and we have not, alas! the faithful few to stand in the breach, and reprove the nation for its sin. I look & wonder. There were plenty of men to condemn the conduct of Eyre and bring him to the verge of trial. But when an English jury refuses to put the man on his trial, instead of the sectional zeal & faith rising higher and higher to the assertion of the Everlasting right & truth, the righteous end is looked upon as impossible of attainment; and faith collapses in an instant and dies. Where would have been the slavery question now if such cowardice & blindness had filled the Anti-Slavery heart of America, five & thirty years ago?...

W. Robson.

MS.A.1.2. vol. 35 1867 Anti-Slavery Letters to Garrison [491]
No. 88 Andrew Fyfe to William Lloyd Garrison

21, St. Andrew Square
Edinburgh 17, July 1867.

My Dear Sir,

I have the pleasure to announce that the Council have agreed to offer you the Freedom of the City in the Council Chambers tomorrow at 12 o'clock. If you will have the goodness to come to the Council Chamber tomorrow *a quarter before 12* I shall introduce you to the Lord Provost, & the Members of Council.

If Mrs. Nichol & her friends including your son & daughter will come at the same time I will take them into the Council Chambers. I remain my dear sir yours very truly

And.w Fyfe.

Wm. Lloyd Garrison Esq.

MS.960 Quincy-Webb Correspondence [492]
No. 33 Quincy to Webb

Bankside, Dedham,
Apr. 7th 1870

My dear Webb:

...I really don't know what Goldwin Smith means by the hostility to England in this country. I believe it to be a morbid delusion. As to Virginia being more like N.E., I believe it to be absurd. If there be any national prejudice against the English, I imagine it will be found among the old slaveholding states. Richmond was the only place in which the Prince of Wales was insulted in this country.

There he was all but mobbed. Mr. Smith, I believe to be a very well meaning sort of person, but he has not always the wisdom profitable to direct.

I know nothing whatever of Miss Forten,[1] excepting that she is well-looking and well-mannered. You did well to urge the money question upon her. The abolition of slavery has put an end to the prejudice in *favor* of *color* in England and black people must make their way like white ones. And I imagine the visitations of Miss R[emond] will not make the English Abolitionists very swift to welcome one from Miss F. She should be made to understand that she should not go abroad without funds enough to pay her own way and the reasonable amount stated....

MS.B.1.6. vol. 9 The May Papers [493]
No. 44 Samuel May to R.D. Webb

fragment n.d. [1870 ?]

A previous "Spectator" had the brave & honest article, which you (or some reader before us) had pencil lined in margin, exposing the savage & abominable treatment of O'Donovan, [Rossa?], & other Fenian prisoners, in English jails. That is a villainous trait in England too, – the way it (i.e. its

1. Charlotte Forten was the daughter of James Forten (see above) and had in her earliest youth taken an active part in anti-slavery work, both in Philadelphia, where her family were prominent among the prosperous free Negro citizens, and in New England. In the years preceding her visit to Britain she had worked as a schoolteacher among Negro children in the South. See R.A. Billington, *A Free Negro in the Slave Era. The Journal of Charlotte Forten.* New York, 1961.

Govt. & leading, governing classes, whoever they are) stands by its servants through thick & thin, no matter how bad they behave. England is a dishonoured land, today, for letting off Eyre, Gov. of Jamaica; and what has she done, or will she, to punish that wretch who ran down the U.S. ship "Oneida", (coming out of Japan). Something, I trust, she will feel compelled to do yet if not for justice' sake, yet to keep peace with the U.S. That was a cold blooded, fiendish act, – to cut down (meaning to cut *into*, I believe,) a U.S. ship, & then deliberately keep on her course without stopping to see if help were needed. Can England expect such things will be forgotten? She is laying up too many rods for herself, too abundant cause for fearful retribution to burst on her head yet. And now will she hold a strict, just hand with those jail governors who so tortured the Fenian prisoners? Small sympathy have I with that blundering, stupid, absurd Fenian *Movement;* yet, much with the deep-seated feeling, in their inmost being, of the contemptuous, insulting, oppressive treatment which England had dealt out to them and their fathers and Ireland so long. But is it true...that it had not been the real *Celtic* men, but men of England & Scotch origin and religious faith, who have stirred up the worst feeling in Ireland, & made England the most trouble there?

I read aloud to Ade, last week, the report of the Dublin meeting, at which Alfred offered his resolution, and made his speech, receiving such warm & ample support by the vote. We are glad to see it...I will remember his foresight in the time of our war, and his prompt judgment and the wrong England had done us in the case of the "Alabama". Few in Ireland even, – almost none in England, – then would have agreed with him. Now, nearly all do, & there is even an *eagerness* to make full reparation for the losses inflicted by that pirate, – with such wonderfully just retribution sent to the bottom of the sea, in the English channel itself. – English nobles, & others of the first prominense, are even now on the ocean, coming to our country, to sit with American Commissioners, on *American soil,* to settle that business; how, remains to be seen but assuredly in a very different tone & style from that of 6 to 8 years ago.....

S.M.

APPENDIXES

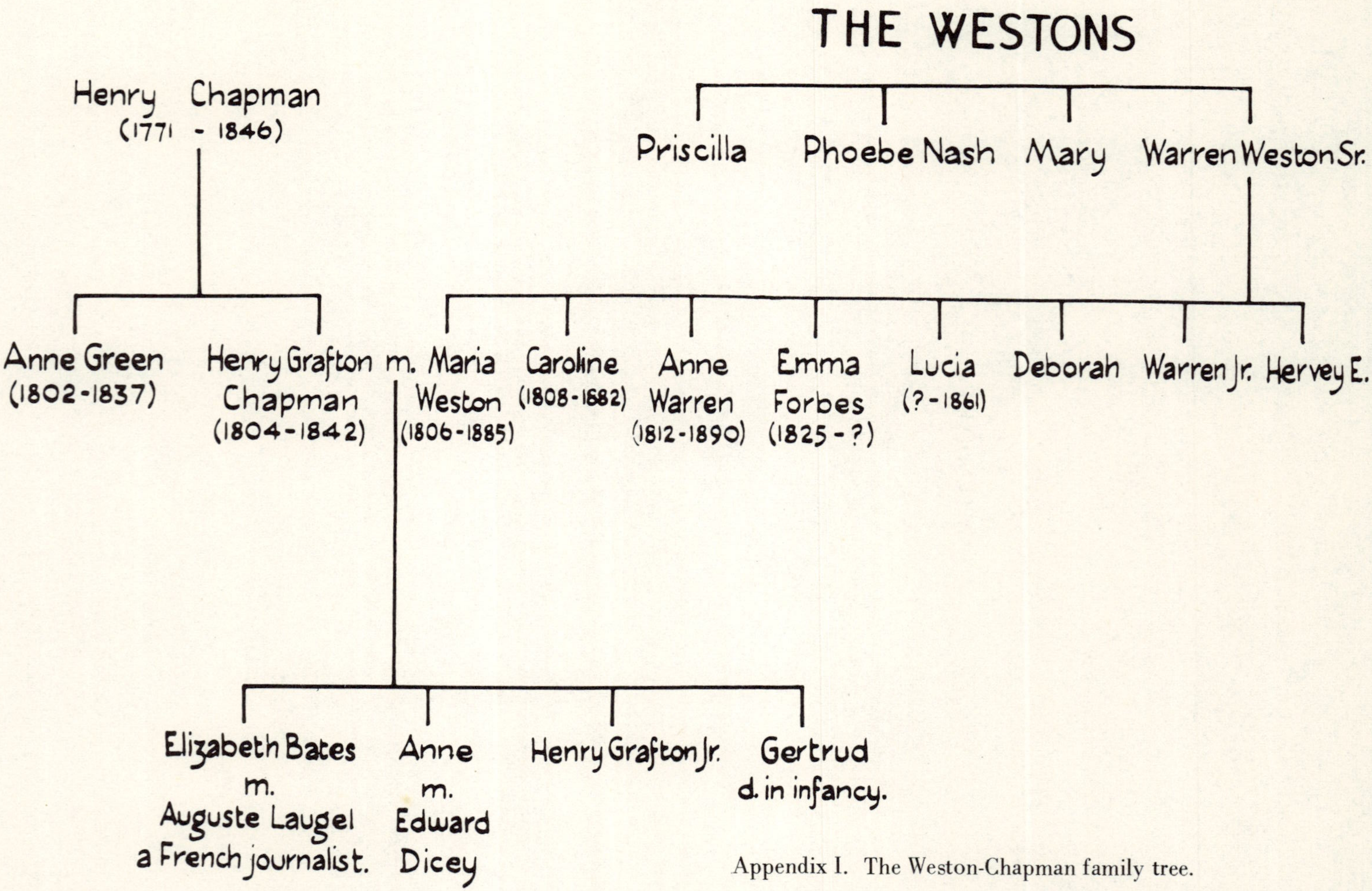

Appendix I. The Weston-Chapman family tree.

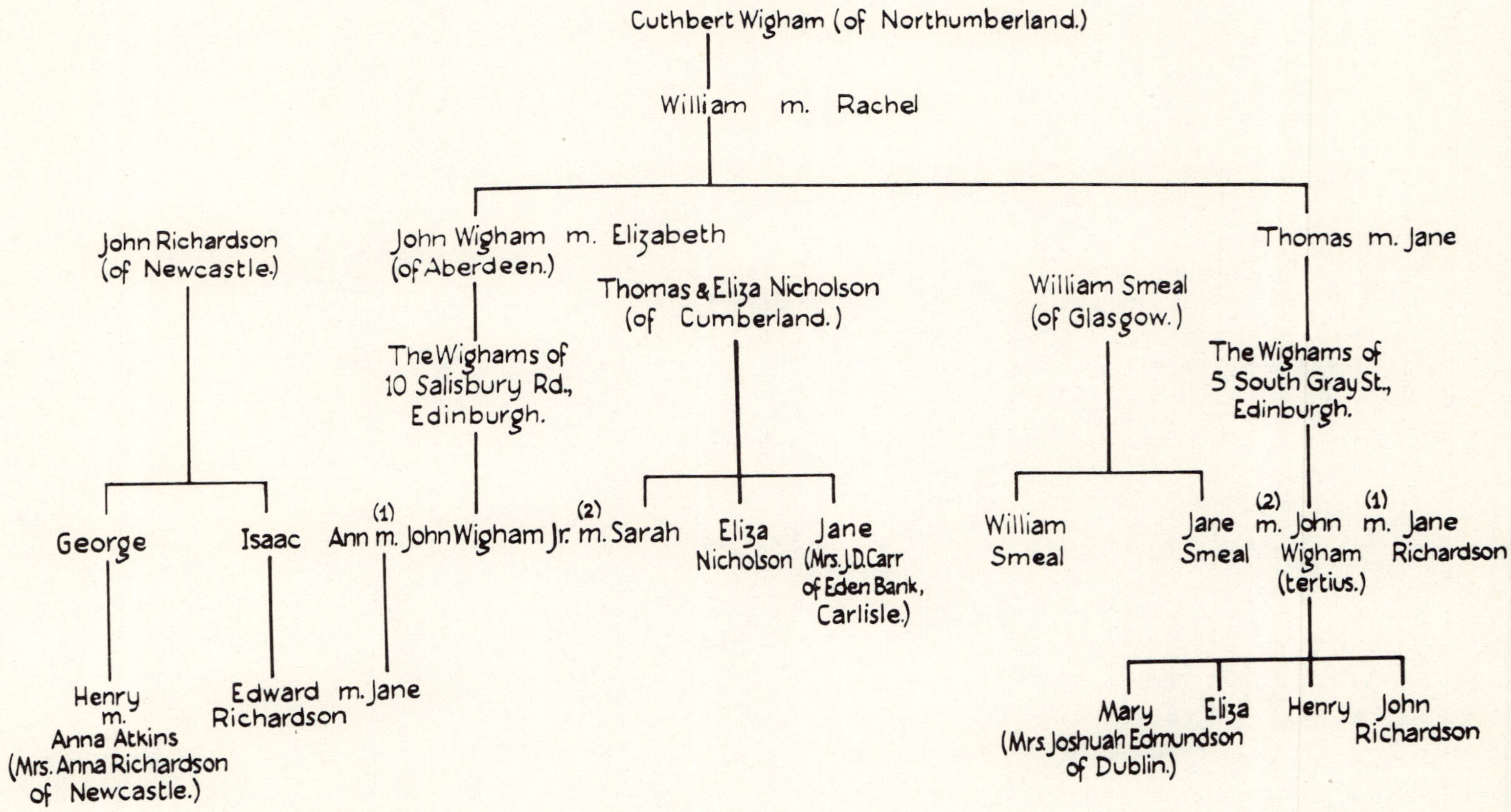

Appendix II. Simplified family tree of the Wighams and their anti-slavery connections.

BIBLIOGRAPHY

The list of writings, pamphlets and Ms. material relating to the Anti-Slavery Movement is almost inexhaustible, and the subject of abolitionism one of the most controversial topics in American History today. This bibliography, therefore, is no more than a selection of some of the main works consulted and found most useful in the present study.

Unpublished manuscript material

The Boston Anti-Slavery Papers are a major collection of abolitionist material, but they are by no means the only Ms. source. A comprehensive guide to the numerous other collections in the United States may be found in the Bibliographical Essay in Louis Filler's *The Crusade Against Slavery*, pp. 282-3 (London, 1960).

British Anti-Slavery Collections are smaller, in part because so many British abolitionists sent their papers to Garrison's sons to help them when writing their father's biography – their donation forms the nucleus of the Boston Anti-Slavery papers. The Estlin Papers in Dr Williams's Library, London, however, are an invaluable small collection, as they contain the Minute Book of the Bristol and Clifton Anti-Slavery Society. (*The Estlin Papers*, eds. Professor George Shepperson and Dr Clare Taylor, has been published by the E. P. Group of Companies, formerly Micro Methods Limited). The Smeal Papers in the Mitchell Library, Glasgow, are another important small collection, and they contain the Minute Book of the Glasgow Emancipation Society. Miss Celia King has edited the material relating to the Birmingham Ladies' Society for the Relief of British Negro Slaves, and the Webb Donation, Trinity College, Dublin, promises to be of major interest. But undoubtedly the most famous British Ms. source is still the collection of The British and Foreign Anti-Slavery Society in Rhodes House, Oxford, which were edited by A. H. Abel and F. J. Klingberg, in *A Side Light on Anglo-American Relations* (Lancaster, Penn., 1927).

Published manuscript material

Many of the Manuscript Sources of Anti-Slavery material have been collected and published. These include:

A. H. Abel & F. J. Klingberg, *A Side Light on Anglo-American Relations.* Lancaster, Penn., 1927.

G. H. Barnes & D. L. Dumond (eds.), *Letters of Theodore Dwight Weld, Angelina Grimkê Weld and Sarah Grimké, 1822-1844*, 2 vols. New York, 1934.

R. A. Billington, *A Free Negro in the Slave Era: The Journal of Charlotte L. Forten.* New York, 1961.
Dwight L. Dumond (ed.), *Letters of James Gillespie Birney.* New York, 1938.
P. S. Foner, *The Life and Writings of Frederick Douglass,* 4 vols. New York, 1950.
Wendell Phillips, *Speeches, Lectures and Letters.* Boston, 1863.
Frederick B. Tolles, *Slavery and the Woman Question, The Diary of Lucretia Mott.* London, 1925.
Theodore Dwight Weld (ed.), *American Slavery as it is: Testimony of a Thousand Witnesses, (1839).* Republished by Frank Cass and Co. Ltd., London, 1968.

Pamphlet literature

The pamphlet literature on Anti-Slavery is too extensive to be quoted. Attention can only be drawn to D. L. Dumond's *Bibliography of the Anti-Slavery Movement* (Ann Arbor, 1961), which lists most of the American Tracts. In itself, the pamphlet literature of anti-slavery is an interesting and little studied field of research.

Nineteenth century works

E. S. Abdy, *Journal of A Residence and Tour in the United States,* 3 vols. London, 1835.
H. Adams, F. W. Chesson & Wilson Armistead, *God's Image in Ebony.* London, 1854.
Wilson Armistead, *Select Miscellanies,* 2 vols. London, 1851.
Hannah Chapman Backhouse, *Extracts from the Journals and Letters of H. C. Backhouse.* London, 1858.
Sir Edward Baines, *The Life of Edward Baines.* London, 1859.
David W. Bartlett, *Modern Agitators.* New York, 1856.
J. H. Bell, *British Folk and British India.* London, 1891.
J. B. Braithwaite, *Memoirs of Joseph John Gurney,* 2 vols. Norwich, 1854.
William Wells Brown, *Narrative of William W. Brown, An American Slave.* London, 1850.
William Wells Brown, *Three Years in Europe.* London, 1852.
William Wells Brown, *The Black Man, His Antecedents, His Genius and His Achievements.* Boston, 1863.
John Candler, *Extracts from the Journal of J. Candler whilst travelling in Jamaica.* London, 1840, '41.
J. Estlin Carpenter, *The Life and Work of May Carpenter.* London, 1879.
Russell Lant Carpenter, *Memoirs of the Life of the Rev. Lant Carpenter, LL.D.* London, 1842.
Maria Weston Chapman, *Right and Wrong in Massachusetts.* Boston, 1840.
J. A. Collins, *Right and Wrong Among the Abolitionists of the United States.* Glasgow, 1841.
William Craft, *Running a Thousand Miles for Freedom.* London, 1860.
James Cropper, *Extracts from the Letters of the Late James Cropper.* Liverpool, 1850.
R. W. Dale (ed.), *The Life and Letters of John Angell James.* London, 1861.
Benjamin Drew, *A Northside View of Slavery.* Boston, 1856.
Frederick Douglass, *Narrative of the Life of Frederick Douglass.* Boston, 1845.
Sarah Hopper Emerson, *Life of Abby Hopper Gibbons, 1801-1893,* 2 vols. London and New York, 1896.

Annie Fields, *Life and Letters of Harriet Beecher Stowe.* London, 1897.
C. G. Finney, *An Autobiography.* London, 1882.
W. P. & F. J. Garrison, *William Lloyd Garrison,* 4 vols. New York, 1885.
William Goodell, *Slavery and Anti-Slavery.* New York, 1852.
Mary Grew, *James Mott, A Bibliographical Sketch.* New York, n.d.
Angelina E. Grimkē, *Slavery in America.* Edinburgh, 1837.
Archibald H. Grimkē, *W. L. Garrison.* New York, 1891.
R. R. Gurley, *Mission to England.* Washington, 1841.
Anna Davis Hallowell, *James and Lucretia Mott.* Boston, 1884.
Robert Henderson, *A Memoir of the late Rev. George Armstrong.* London, 1859.
Josiah Henson, *Uncle Tom's Story of His Life.* London, 1887.
Rev. William James, *Memoir of John Bishop Estlin.* London, 1855.
Oliver Johnson, *William Lloyd Garrison and His Times.* Boston, 1881.
Harriet Martineau, *Retrospect of Western Travel.* New York, 1838.
Harriet Martineau, *The Martyr Age of the United States of America.* 1840.
Harriet Martineau, *Autobiography – With Memorial by M. W. Chapman,* 3 vols. London, 1877.
Samuel J. May, *Some Recollections of our Anti-Slavery Conflict.* Boston, 1869.
Thomas J. Mumford, *Memoir of Samuel J. May.* Boston, 1874.
Parker Pillsbury, *Acts of the Anti-Slavery Apostles.* Boston, 1884.
Henry Richard, *Memoirs of Joseph Sturge.* London, 1864.
Peter Sibree, *Memorial of Joseph Sturge.* Birmingham, 1862.
Wilbur H. Siebert, *The Underground Railroad, from Slavery to Freedom.* New York, 1898.
Goldwin Smith, *William Lloyd Garrison.* Toronto, 1892.
T. C. Smith, *The Liberty and Free Soil Parties in the North West.* New York, 1897.
Elizabeth Cady Stanton, *Eighty Years and More.* London, 1898.
Henry B. Stanton, *Random Recollections.* New York, 1887.
Henry B. Stanton, *Sketches of Reforms and Reformers of Great Britain and Ireland.* New York, 1849.
Henry B. Stanton & T. Nelson, *Reforms and Reformers of England.* London, 1853.
Sir George Stephen, *Anti-Slavery Recollections.* London, 1854.
Anna M. Stoddart, *Elizabeth Pease Nichol.* London, 1899.
Harriet Beecher Stowe, *Uncle Tom's Cabin.* London, 1852.
Harriet Beecher Stowe, *Sunny Memories of Foreign Lands.* London, 1854.
Joseph Sturge, *A Visit to the United States in 1841.* London, 1842.
Lewis Tappan, *The Life of Arthur Tappan.* London, 1870.
Samuel Ringgold Ward, *Autobiography of a Fugitive Negro.* London, 1855.
R. D. Webb, *The Life and Letters of Capt. John Brown.* London, 1861.
Eliza Wigham, *The Anti-Slavery Cause in America and Its Martyrs.* London, 1863.
Anon., *A Brief Memorial to Eliza Wigham,* (n.d.).
Hannah Maria Wigham, *A Christian Philanthropist of Dublin – Richard Allen.* London, 1886.
Henry Wilson, *History of the Anti-Slavery Measures of the 37th and 38th United States Congresses, 1861-64.* Boston, 1864.

But the biographies and histories of more recent times have in most cases superseded these earlier works:

Alice Dana Adams, *The Neglected Period of Anti-Slavery in America, 1808-1831.* Boston, 1908.

Herbert Aptheker, *The Negro in the Abolitionist Movement.* New York, 1943.
Herbert Aptheker, *American Negro Slave Revolts.* New York, 1963.
Frederic Bancroft, *Slave Trading in the Old South.* Baltimore 1931.
Richard Bardolph, *The Negro Vanguard.* New York: Vintage Books, 1959.
G. H. Barnes, *The Anti-Slavery Impulse 1830-1844.* New York, 1933.
Irving Bartlett, *Wendell Phillips – Brahmin Radical.* Boston, 1961.
Gustave de Beaumont, *Marie, or Slavery in the U.S.* Stanford: Stanford University Press, 1958.
Ray Billington, *The Protestant Crusade.* New York, 1952.
Christine Bolt, *The Anti-Slavery Movement and Reconstruction. A Study of Anglo-American Co-operation, 1833-1877.* IRR, Oxford, 1969.
Christine Bolt, *Victorian Attitudes to Race.* London, 1971.
Sarah Bradford, *Harriet Tubman, The Moses of Her People.* New York, 1961.
Jacobus Ten Brock, *Equal Under Law.* New York and London: Collier Books, 1965.
F. K. Brown, *Fathers of the Victorians.* Cambridge, 1961.
C. Buxton, *Memoirs of Sir Thomas Fowell Buxton.* London, 1925.
W. J. Cash, *The Mind of the South.* New York, 1941.
John Jay Chapman, *William Lloyd Garrison.* New York, 1913.
Alfred H. Conrad & J. R. Meyers, *The Economics of Slavery and Other Studies in Economic History,* Chicago, 1964.
Reginald Coupland, *Wilberforce, A Narrative.* London, 1945.
David B. Davis, *The Problem of Slavery in Western Culture.* Ithaca, 1966.
Merton L. Dillon, *Elijah P. Lovejoy, Abolitionist Editor.* Urbana and London: University of Illinois Press, 1961.
Merton L. Dillon, *Benjamin Lundy and the Struggle for Negro Freedom.* Urbana and London: University of Illinois Press, 1966.
Frederick Douglass (ed. B. Quarles), *A Narrative of the Life of Frederick Douglass.* Boston, 1945.
Thomas E. Drake, *Quakers and Slavery in America.* New Haven, Conn., 1950.
M. Duberman (ed.), *The Anti-Slavery Vanguard.* Princeton University Press, 1965.
Dwight L. Dumond, *Anti-Slavery: The Crusade for Freedom in America.* Ann Arbor, Michigan, 1961.
Dwight L. Dumond, *Anti-Slavery Origins of the Civil War in the U.S.* Ann Arbor: University of Michigan Press, 1959.
Clement Eaton, *The Growth of Southern Civilization, 1790-1860.* New York, 1963.
David P. Edgell, *William Ellery Channing, An Intellectual Portrait.* Boston, 1955.
Stanley M. Elkins, *Slavery: A Problem in American Institutional and Intellectual Life.* Chicago, 1959.
Louis Filler, *The Crusade Against Slavery.* London, 1960.
L. Fischel & B. Quarles, *Negro America, A Documentary History.* Illinois: Scott, Foresman and Co., 1967.
B. Fladeland, *James Gillespie Birney.* New York, 1955.
Philip S. Foner, *Business and Slavery.* Chapel Hill: University of North Carolina Press, 1941.
Early Lee Fox, *The American Colonization Society, 1817-1840.* Baltimore, 1919.
John Hope Franklin, *From Slavery to Freedom, A History of American Negroes.* New York, 1947.

John Hope Franklin, *The Militant South.* Cambridge, Mass., 1956.
John Hope Franklin, *The Emancipation Proclamation.* Edinburgh: Edinburgh University Press, 1963.
E. Franklin Frazier, *The Negro in the United States.* New York, 1957.
E. Franklin Frazier, *The Negro Church in America.* Liverpool University Press, 1964.
Roger Fulford, *Votes for Women.* London, 1957.
J. C. Furnas, *Goodbye to Uncle Tom.* London, 1956.
J. C. Furnas, *The Road to Harper's Ferry.* New York, 1959.
Larry Gara, *The Liberty Line, The Legend of The Underground Railroad.* Lexington: University of Kentucky Press, 1961.
Richard Garnett & Edward Garnett, *The Life of William Fox.* London, 1909.
W. P. Garrison, *Letters and Memorials.* Cambridge, Mass., 1908.
Eugene D. Genovese, *The Political Economy of Slavery, Studies in the Economy and Society of the Slave South.* New York, 1965.
Earl L. Griggs, *Thomas Clarkson, The Friend of the Slaves.* London, 1936.
D. K. Gwynne, *Daniel O'Connell, The Irish Liberator.* London, 1930.
Ralph V. Harlow, *Gerritt Smith, Philanthropist and Reformer.* New York, 1939.
Albert Bushnell Hart, *Slavery and Abolition.* New York, 1906.
T. W. Higginson, *Cheerful Yesterdays.* London: Frank Cass and Co. Ltd., 1968.
Richard J. Hinton, *John Brown and His Men.* London: Frank Cass and Co. Ltd., 1968.
Stephen Hobhouse, *Joseph Sturge, His Life and Work.* London, 1919.
Barnett Hollander, *Slavery in America: Its Legal History.* London, 1962.
Walter E. Houghton, *The Victorian Frame of Mind, 1830-1870.* New Haven, 1957.
Warren S. Howard, *American Slavers and the Federal Law, 1837-1862.* University of California Press, 1963.
William Sumner Jenkins, *Pro-Slavery Thought in the Old South.* Gloucester, Mass., 1960.
Samuel A. Johnson, *The Battle Cry of Freedom.* Lawrence: University of Kansas Press, 1954.
Herbert S. Klein, *Slavery in the Americas.* Oxford University Press, 1967.
F. J. Klingberg, *The Anti-Slavery Movement in England.* New Haven, 1926.
Ralph Korngold, *Two Friends of Man.* Boston, 1950.
Aileen S. Kraditor, *Means and Ends in American Abolitionism.* New York, 1969.
Lawrence Lader, *The Bold Brahmins.* New York, 1961.
Amice Lee, *Laurels and Rosemary, The Life of William and Mary Howitt.* Oxford, 1955.
Leon F. Litwack, *North of Slavery, The Negro in the Free States, 1790-1860.* Chicago, 1965.
Arthur Young Lloyd, *The Slavery Controversy, 1831-1860.* Chapel Hill, 1939.
S. C. McCulloch (ed.), *British Humanitarianism: Essays Honouring F.J. Klingberg.* Philadelphia, 1950.
Eric L. McKitrick (ed.), *Slavery Defended: The Views of the Old South.* New Jersey: Prentice-Hall, 1963.
James M. McPherson, *The Struggle for Equality.* Princeton, N.J., 1964.

Carleton Mabee, *Black Freedom, The Nonviolent Abolitionists from 1830 Through the Civil War.* London, 1970.

Jesse Macy, *The Anti-Slavery Crusade.* New Haven, 1919.

Donald G. Mathews, *Slavery and Methodism, A Chapter in American Morality, 1780-1845.* Princeton: Princeton University Press, 1965.

W. L. Mathieson, *British Slavery and its Abolition.* London, 1926.

W. L. Mathieson, *British Slave Emancipation, 1838-1849.* London, 1929.

W. L. Mathieson, *Great Britain and the Slave Trade, 1839-1865.* London, 1929.

Thomas Matthews, *Channing, A Study.* Marseilles, 1929.

W. M. Merrill, *Against Wind and Tide: A Biography of William Lloyd Garrison.* Boston, 1963.

Herman R. Meulder, *Fighters for Freedom.* New York: Columbia University Press, 1959.

R. H. Mottram, *Buxton the Liberator.* London, 1946.

Ruth Anna Nuermberger, *Charles Osborn in the Anti-Slavery Movement.* Columbus, Ohio, 1937.

Ruth Anna Nuermberger, *The Free Produce Movement.* Durham, N.C., 1942.

Russell B. Nye, *Fettered Freedom: Civil Liberties and the Secession Crisis of 1860-1861.* East Lansing, 1949.

F. L. Olmsted (ed. Arthur M. Schlesinger), *The Cotton Kingdom.* New York, 1953.

U. B. Phillips, *American Negro Slavery.* New York, 1936.

U. B. Phillips, *Life and Labor in the Old South.* Boston, 1949.

Kate E. R. Pickard, *The Kidnapped and the Ransomed.* Negro Publication Society of America, Inc., 1941.

James Pope-Hennessy, *Sins of the Fathers.* London, 1967.

Benjamin Quarles, *Frederick Douglass.* Washington, 1948.

Benjamin Quarles, *Black Abolitionists.* New York: Oxford University Press, 1969.

William Lee Rose, *Rehearsal for Reconstruction: The Poet Royal Experiment.* Indianapolis, 1964.

Arthur Rowntree, *Whittier, Crusader and Prophet.* London, 1946.

Redding J. Saunders, *They Came in Chains.* Philadelphia, 1950.

Samuel Sillen, *Women Against Slavery.* New York, 1955.

Elbert B. Smith, *The Death of Slavery, the U.S. 1837-1865.* University of Chicago Press, 1967.

H. G. Soulsby, *The Right of Search and the Slave Trade in Anglo-American Relations, 1848-1862.* Baltimore, 1933.

Kenneth M. Stampp, *The Peculiar Institution.* New York, 1956.

William Stanton, *The Leopard's Spots, Scientific Attitudes Toward Race in America, 1815-1859.* University of Chicago Press, 1966.

Philip J. Staudenraus, *The African Colonization Movement, 1816-1865.* New York, 1961.

Frank Tannenbaum, *Slave and Citizen: The Negro in the Americas.* New York, 1946.

Howard Temperley, *British Anti-Slavery 1833-1870.* Longman, 1972.

Frank Thistlethwaite, *The Anglo-American Connection in the Early Nineteenth Century.* Philadelphia, 1959.

Benjamin P. Thomas, *Theodore Weld, Crusader for Freedom.* New Brunswick, New York, 1950.

John L. Thomas, *The Liberator: A Biography of William Lloyd Garrison.* Boston, 1963.

John L. Thomas, *Slavery Attacked: the Abolitionist Crusade.* New Jersey: Prentice-Hall, 1965.

Oswald Garrison Villard, *John Brown, A Biography, Fifty Years After.* Boston and New York, 1960.
Richard C. Wade, *Slavery in the Cities: The South, 1820-1860.* Oxford University Press, 1964.
Graham Wallas, *William Johnson Fox.* London, 1924.
Howard S. Warren, *American Slavers and the Federal Law, 1837-1862.* Berkeley, California, 1963.
R. K. Webb, *Harriet Martineau – A Radical Victorian.* London, 1960.
Allen Weinstein & Frank Otto Gatell (eds.), *American Negro Slavery.* Oxford University Press, 1968.
Vera Wheatley, *The Life and Work of Harriet Martingau.* London, 1957.
Eric Williams, *Capitalism and Slavery.* University of North Carolina Press, 1944.
Forest Wilson, *Crusader in Crinoline.* New York, 1942.
Harvey Wish (ed.), *Slavery in the South.* New York, 1964.
Bertram Wyatt-Brown, *Lewis Tappan and the Evangelical War Against Slavery.* Case Western Reserve, 1969.
C. G. Woodson & Charles H. Wesley, *The Negro in Our History.* Washington D.C., 1962.
C. G. Woodson, *The Education of the Negro Prior to 1861.* London: Frank Cass and Co. Ltd., 1968.
Arthur Zilversmit, *The First Emancipation: The Abolition of Slavery in the North.* University of Chicago Press, 1967.

Periodical literature

W. G. Addington, Slave Insurrections in Texas. *Journal of Negro History,* XXXV, Oct. 1950.
H. Aptheker, The Quakers and Negro History. *J.N.H.*, XXV, 1940.
H. Aptheker, Militant abolitionism. *J.N.H.*, XXVI, 1941.
Eugene C. Barker, The Influence of Slavery in the Colonization of Texas. *Mississippi Valley Historical Review,* XI, June 1924.
Max Berger, American Slavery as seen by British visitors, 1836-1860. *J.N.H.*, XXX, no. 2, Apr. 1945.
Channcey S. Boucher, In Re that Aggressive Slaveocracy. *M.V.H.R.*, VIII, Sept. 1921.
W. M. Brewer, Henry Highland Garnet. *J.N.H.*, XIII, 1928.
E. Brooks, The Massachusetts Anti Slavery Society. *J.N.H.*, XXX, 1945.
Bertram Wyatt Brown, The Abolitionists Postal Campaign of 1835. *J.N.H.*, L, no. 4, Oct. 1965.
E. M. Coleman, William Wells Brown as a Historian, *J.N.H.*, XXI, 1946.
Richard O. Currie, The Abolitionists and Reconstruction, A Critical Appraisal. *Journal of Southern History*, XXXIV, no. 4, Nov. 1968.
M. E. Curti, Pacifist Propaganda and the Treaty of Guadeloupe Hidalgo. *American Historical Review*, XXXIII (3), 1928.
David B. Davis, The Emergence of Immediatism in British and American Anti-Slavery Thought. *M.V.H.R.*, XLIX, Sept. 1962.
David B. Davis, James Cropper and the British Anti-Slavery Movement, 1821-23. *J.N.H.*, XLV, no. 4, Oct. 1960.
David B. Davis, The Abolitionists and the Freemen. An Essay Review. *J.S.H.*, XXXI, no. 2, May 1965.
Merton Lynn Dillon, The Abolitionists on Slavery: The Critique behind the Social Movement. *J.S.H.*, XXXIII, no. 2, May 1967.
Merton Lynn Dillon, The Abolitionists: A Decade of Historiography, 1959-1969. *J.S.H.*, XXXI, no. 4, Nov. 1969.
Merton Lynn Dillon, The Failure of the American Abolitionists. *J.S.H.*, XXV, May 1969.

Martin B. Duberman, The Abolitionists and Psychology. *J.N.H.*, XLVII, no. 3, July 1962.
Clement Eaton, Slave Hiring in the Upper South: A Step Towards Freedom. *M.V.H.R.*, XLVI, Mar. 1960.
Arvel B. Erickson, Empire or Anarchy: The Jamaica Rebellion of 1865. *J.H.N.*, XLIV, no. 2, Apr. 1959.
D. E. Everett, Free Persons of Color in New Orleans, 1803-1815. *J.N.H.*, XXXVII, Oct. 1953.
Betty Fladeland, Who were the Abolitionists? *J.N.H.*, XLIX, no. 2, Apr. 1964.
Eric Foner, Politics and Prejudices: The Free Soil Party and the Negro, 1849-1852. *J.N.H.*, L, no. 4, Oct. 1865.
Gordon E. Finnie, The Anti-Slavery Movement in the Upper South before 1840. *J.S.H.*, XXXV, no. 3, Aug. 1969.
Serge Garronsky, American Slavery and the French Liberals. *J.N.H.*, LI, no. 1, Jan. 1966.
A. Cameron Grant, George Combe and American Slavery. *J.N.H.*, XLVI, no. 4, Oct. 1960.
R. Greenleaf, British Labor Against American Slavery. *Science and Society*, XVII, 1955.
Clifford S. Griffin, Religious Benevolence as Social Control, 1815-1860. *M.V.H.R.*, XLIV, Dec. 1957.
Clifford S. Griffin, The Abolitionists and the Benevolent Societies, 1831-1861. *J.N.H.*, XLIV, no. 1, Jan. 1959.
Royden Harrison, British Labor and the Confederacy. *International Review of Social History*, II (1), 1957.
W. O. Henderson, The Cotton Famine in Scotland. *Scottish Historical Review*, XXX, 1957.
E. J. Hobsbawm, Methodism and the Threat of Popular Revolution. *History Today*, Feb. 1957.
Richard Hofstadter, U. B. Phillips and the Plantation Legend. *J.N.H.*, XXIX, Apr. 1944.
Winthrop D. Jordan, Modern Tensions and the Origins of American Slavery. *J.S.H.*, XXVIII, Feb. 1962.
F. J. Klingberg, Harriet Beecher Stowe and Social Reform in England. *A.H.R.*, XLIII, 1938.
Gerda Lerner, The Grimké Sisters and the Struggle Against Race Prejudice. *J.N.H.*, XLVIII, no. 4, Oct. 1963.
Robert T. Lewit, Indian Missions and Anti-Slavery Sentiment: A Conflict of Evangelical and Humanitarian Ideals. *M.V.H.R.*, June 1963, Mar. 1964.
Fabian Linden, Economic Democracy in the Slave South. An Appraisal of Some Recent Views. *J.N.H.*, XXXI, Apr. 1946.
Leon F. Litwack, The Federal Government and the Free Negro, 1790-1860. *J.N.H.*, XLIII, no. 4, Oct. 1958.
Williston H. Lofton, Abolition and Labor. *J.N.H.*, XXXIII, 1948.
Anne C. Loveland, Evangelicalism and Immediate Emancipation in American Anti-Slavery Thought. *J.S.H.*, XXXII, 1966.
Staughton Lynd, On Turner, Beard and Slavery. *J.N.H.*, XLVIII, no. 4, Oct. 1963.
Johnston R. Mackay, An American Evangelist in Great Britain. *Bulletin of the Association for American Studies*, VI, Feb. 1958.
Roland C. McConnell, From the Preliminary to Final Emancipation. The First Hundred Days. *J.N.H.*, XLVIII, no. 4, Oct. 1963.
James McPherson, Abolitionists and the Civil Rights Act of 1875. *Journal of American History*, Dec. 1965.

Donald G. Mathews, The Methodist Mission to the Slaves, 1929-1944. *M.V.H.R.*, LI, June 1964 – Mar. 1965.
Donald G. Mathews, The Abolitionists on Slavery: The Critique Behind the Social Movement. *J.S.H.*, XXXIII, no. 2, May 1967.
Peter Mathias, The Brewing Industry, Temperance and Politics. *The Historical Journal of Cambridge*, (2), 1958.
Douglas H. Maynard, The World's Anti-Slavery Convention of 1840. *M.V.H.R.*, XLVII, June 1960 – Mar. 1961.
Richard B. Morris, The Measure of Bondage in the Slave States. *M.V.H.R.*, XLI, Sept. 1954.
Margaret Munsterburg The Weston Sisters and the 'Boston Mob'. *The Boston Library Quarterly*, Oct. 1957.
Margaret Munsterburg, The Weston Sisters and the 'Boston Controversy'. *The Boston Library Quarterly*, Jan. 1958.
John L. Myers, American Anti-Slavery Society Agents and the Free Negro, 1833-1839. *J.N.H.*, LII, no. 3, July 1967.
Ellen Oldham, Irish Support of the Abolitionist Movement. *The Boston Public Library Quarterly*, Oct. 1958.
D. B. Porter, Sarah Parker Remond, Abolitionist and Physician, *J.N.H.*, XX, 1935.
B. Quarles, The Breach Between Douglass and the Women's Rights Movement. *J.N.H.*, XXV, 1940.
B. Quarles, Letters from Negro Leaders to Gerrit Smith. *J.N.H.*, XXVII, 1942.
B. Quarles, Ministers without Portfolio. *J.N.H.*, XXXIX, 1954.
James A. Rawley, Joseph John Gurney's Mission to America, 1837-1840. *M.V.H.R.*, XLIX, June 1962 – Mar. 1963.
Richard W. Resh, Alexis de Tocqueville and the Negro: Democracy in America Reconsidered. *J.N.H.*, XLVIII, no. 4, Oct. 1963.
George I. Rockwood, George B. Cheever, Protagonist of Abolition. *Proceedings of the American Antiquarian Society*, XLVI, N.S., Apr. 1936.
S. D. St. Clair, Slavery as a Diplomatic Factor in Anglo-American Relations During the Civil War. *J.N.H.*, XXX, 1945.
Kempes Schnell, Anti-Slavery Influences and the Status of Slaves in a Free State. *J.N.H.*, L, no. 4, Oct. 1965.
Robert K. Shaw, Elihu Burritt, Friend of Mankind. *Proceedings of the American Antiquarian Society*, XXXVI, 1926.
Caroline L. Shanks, The Biblical Anti-Slavery Argument of the Decade, 1830-40. *J.N.H.*, XVI, no. 2, Apr. 1931.
George Shepperson, Thomas Chalmers, the Free Church of Scotland and the South. *J.S.H.*, XVII (4), Nov. 1951.
George Shepperson, Harriet Beecher Stowe and Scotland. *S.H.R.*, 1953.
George Shepperson, Frederick Douglass and Scotland. *J.N.H.*, XXXVIII, 1953.
George Shepperson, Writings on Scottish American History, A Brief Survey. *William and Mary Quarterly*, 1954.
Samuel Shapiro, The Rendition of Anthony Burns. *J.N.H.*, XLIV, no. 1, Jan. 1959.
Robert Worthington Smith, The Legal Status of Jamaican Slaves Before the Anti-Slavery Movement. *J.N.H.*, XXX, no. 3, July 1945.
Eugene Portlette Southall, Arthur Tappan and the Anti-Slavery Movement. *J.N.H.*, XV, no. 2, Apr. 1930.
K. M. Stampp, The Historian and Southern Negro Slavery, *American Historical Review*, LVII, 1952.

Moorfield Storey, Jr., The May Papers. *More Books, The Bulletin of the Boston Public Library*, XIX, 1944.

Howard Temperley, The O'Connell-Stevenson Contretemps: A Reflection of the Anglo-American Slavery Issue. *J.N.H.*, XLVII, no. 3, July 1962.

Henry Y. Warnock, Southern Methodists, the Negro and Unification: The First Phase. *J.N.H.*, no. 4, Oct. 1967.

C. H. Wesley, The Participation of Negroes in Anti-Slavery Political Battles. *J.N.H.*, XXIX, 1944.

Janet Wilson, The Early Anti-Slavery Propaganda. *More Books*, XIX, 1944, XX, 1945.

Harvey Wish, American Slave Insurrections before 1861. *J.N.H.*, XXII, July 1937.

Harold D. Woodman, The Profitability of Slavery, A Historical Perennial. *J.S.H.*, XXIX, Aug. 1963.

Robert M. Yorke, George B. Cheever: Religious and Social Reformer. *University of Maine Bulletin*, LVI, Apr. 1955.

Roman J. Zorn, The New England Anti-Slavery Society, Pioneer Abolition Organization. *J.N.H.*, XLII, 1957.

INDEX OF LETTERS

INDEX OF NAMES